Sixth Edition

INDUSTRIAL PSYCHOLOGY

Ernest J. McCormick
Professor of Psychology
Purdue University

Joseph Tiffin
Emeritus Professor of Industrial Psychology
Purdue University

PRENTICE-HALL, INC., ENGLEWOOD CLIFFS, NEW JERSEY

Library of Congress Cataloging in Publication Data

McCormick, Ernest James.
 Industrial psychology.

 (Prentice-Hall psychology series)
 Authors' names in reverse order in previous editions.
 Includes bibliographical references.
 1.–Psychology, Industrial. I.–Tiffin, Joseph, joint author.
HF5548.8.M18   158.7   73–9733
ISBN 0–13–463125–0

PRINTED IN THE UNITED STATES OF AMERICA

10   9   8   7   6   5   4   3   2   1

PRENTICE-HALL INTERNATIONAL, INC., London
PRENTICE-HALL OF AUSTRALIA, PTY., LTD., Sydney
PRENTICE-HALL OF CANADA, LTD., Toronto
PRENTICE-HALL OF INDIA PRIVATE LIMITED, New Delhi
PRENTICE-HALL OF JAPAN, INC., Tokyo

INDUSTRIAL PSYCHOLOGY

CONTENTS

PART III

The Organizational and Social Context of Human Work, 221

PREFACE

The field of industrial psychology addresses itself to the wide spectrum of human problems that arise in the production, distribution, and consumption of the goods and services of the economy. The dynamic nature of the technology involved in these processes and of the cultural and economic environment in which they take place has tended to bring about changes in the nature, importance, and priorities of the human problems associated with these processes, and in turn, in chain-reaction manner, has stimulated changes in the field of industrial psychology. These shifts in industrial psychology have been reflected in a broadening of the entire field, changing emphasis on certain areas, the development of new methods and techniques for the measurement and analysis of relevant variables, and increased attention to the development of theories that might serve as generalized bases for "explaining" human behavior in the industrial context.

To reflect the changes in industrial psychology over the recent years, this, the sixth edition of *Industrial Psychology,* has been written. The basic structure of the text essentially parallels that of the previous edition, but this edition incorporates a substantial amount of material from the more current research in the field, with increasing attention to the area of organizational psychology, more extensive treatment of some of the relevant developing theories, and coverage of certain new methods, techniques, and procedures that relate to industrial psychology. At the same time, it has been the intent to provide something of a bridge between the "science" of industrial psychology (rooted in research) and the "practice" or "profession" of industrial psychology (the application of the knowledge, insight, and methods of psychology to the practical human problems in industry). Thus, efforts have been made in part to select and present material to illustrate or demonstrate the practical, applied aspects of psychology, as related to the human problems in industry.

The body of research data that comprises substantial portions of this book reflects the efforts (including some blood, sweat, and tears) of many researchers in universities, industry, and in other organizations. We take this opportunity to express our appreciation to them collectively. Acknowledgment of these individual contributors is given in the body of the text. We also want to thank Mrs. Pat Craycraft and Mrs. Wanda Newmyer for their talents in converting many pages of scrawly handwriting into neat and legible typewritten copy.

ERNEST J. McCORMICK
JOSEPH TIFFIN
West Lafayette, Indiana

INDUSTRIAL PSYCHOLOGY

Courtesy Eli Lilly and Company, Lafayette, Ind.

PART I

Introduction

Psychology is the study of human behavior and, in general, can be considered as embracing two major facets. In the first place, psychology is concerned with the discovery of information relating to human behavior. This involves research and can be considered as the scientific aspects of the field of psychology. The other phase is concerned with the application of information about human behavior to the various practical problems of human life. This facet can be thought of as the professional aspect of psychology, in much the same way that physicians, engineers, and others are concerned with the application of knowledge about some field to the practical problems of the real world.

The field of industrial psychology includes both of these facets. Its scientific aspect is rooted in research that provides the knowledge that is, of course, a prerequisite for any practical applications. The "knowledge" so generated can be in the form of theories or in the form of empirically determined relationships. In either case, such knowledge frequently can be applied by organizations in an effort to minimize some of the human problems that inevitably arise in the operations of all kinds of organizations.

chapter one

Introduction

Each of us plays some role in the processes of the production, distribution, and use of the goods and services of our civilization. The role of those in the labor force is, of course, that of producing and distributing such goods and services; as consumers, we all have a stake in the "outputs" of industry to the extent that such goods and services fulfill our needs. Industrial psychology addresses itself to the study of human behavior in these industrially related aspects of life, and to the application of knowledge about human behavior to the solution of human problems in this context.

The term "industry" normally conveys a rather restrictive connotation. For our purposes, however, let us use this term in a very broad sense, as embracing the production and distribution of all types of goods and services of the economy. Within this broad frame of reference, we will be interested in human behavior in the two types of roles people can have in their involvement with industry. The first of these relates to human work in the production and distribution of goods and services as carried out by various types of organizations; this role will be the primary focus of this book. The second relates to the use of such goods and services, the area that is the subject matter of the subdiscipline sometimes referred to as consumer psychology; this role will be dealt with particularly in the last chapter.

INDUSTRIAL PSYCHOLOGY: ITS PREMISES

The field of industrial psychology is predicated on certain premises, the first three of which may be viewed as desirable objectives of industry:[1]

1. That industry should produce those goods and services that fulfill the reasonable needs of people, considering both the physical welfare and the personal values of people.
2. That it is a desirable objective to enhance the effectiveness of human involvement in the production and distribution of such goods and services. It is virtually an article of faith that reasonable efficiency in such production of human talent in this process is therefore desirable.
3. That in this process it is a desirable objective to maintain or enhance certain human values (health, safety, job satisfaction, etc.). In this regard it is becoming an article of faith that the processes of producing such goods and services should be carried out in such a manner as to avoid any physical impairment of those involved and, if possible, to contribute positively to the personal satisfactions of those so involved.

In a sense, these three objectives can be viewed as being directed toward maximizing the sum of the satisfactions of both the producers and the consumers of goods and services. The final two premises relate to the origin of the problems with which industrial psychology deals and with their resolution:

4. That marked disparities between the above objectives and their reasonable fulfillment are the sources of most of the human problems in industry.
5. That knowledge and insight of human behavior gained through psychological research and through experience can contribute to the minimization of such problems.

In sum, then, the *raison d'être* of industrial psychology is the existence of human problems in organizations, and its objective is to somehow provide the basis for resolving these problems or, more realistically, for minimizing them.

THE SETTING OF INDUSTRIAL PSYCHOLOGY

The technological developments of the past hundred or hundred and fifty years have brought about major changes in the nature and organization of human work. Some of the functions formerly carried out with the use of hand tools have become mechanized, thereby creating jobs involved in the

[1] These are slightly modified restatements from: McCormick, E. J. *Human factors engineering.* (3rd ed.) New York: McGraw-Hill, 1970.

operation and maintenance of machines. And the ongoing trend toward automation is altering further the nature of many jobs. These technological developments and the accompanying changes in the nature of human work have been accompanied not only by certain human benefits (such as the reduction of human labor, improvement in working conditions, and higher income), but also by certain costs (such as the routinization of some work processes, the sense of "meaninglessness" involved in some work, the sense of being "lost" in large organizations, labor-management conflict, and technological unemployment).

Of course, the effects of technological change have been felt outside the workplace itself. The entire economy of the United States and certain other countries has been altered from that of an essentially agrarian and handcraft stage to a highly industrialized one, with corresponding changes in the overall pattern of life for the bulk of the population.

The Development of Industrial Psychology

The field of industrial psychology grew to its present maturity against the backdrop of these major changes in our economy. This field of psychology has developed largely since the turn of the century. One of the first major books in the area was Hugo Münsterberg's *Psychology of Industrial Efficiency*.[2] The early industrial psychologists were concerned particularly with problems of personnel selection, but their interests also embraced other applied areas, such as advertising and selling, accidents, and employee rating processes.

A very significant early step in the application of psychological techniques to personnel problems was the use of personnel tests by the Army during World War I. In particular, tests were developed and used by the Army for the classification and assignment of Army personnel. In Great Britain the Industrial Fatigue Research Board (later called the Industrial Health Research Board) was organized at this time to investigate problems associated with fatigue, hours of work, conditions of work, and related matters. (During and since World War II these and other activities have been carried out by the Applied Psychology Research Unit of the Medical Research Council of Great Britain.)

For several years after the war, the interest in psychology as applied to the human problems of industry was relatively sporadic, but by the 1930s the field of industrial psychology had been established as a reasonably distinct phase of psychology. Its major development and expansion, however, have occurred since then. In the intervening years the field has developed in countries all over the world, with the primary development being in certain countries in Western Europe and in the United States.

[2] Münsterberg, H. *The psychology of industrial efficiency*. Boston: Houghton Mifflin, 1913.

Changes in Emphasis in Industrial Psychology

The last four decades have seen various changes in emphasis with regard to the kinds of problems with which industrial psychologists have been concerned. Probably the dominant emphasis during the early years, and continuing through the 1930s and 1940s, was on personnel selection and placement. This has continued to be an important facet of industrial psychology, and probably will continue to be so in the years to come. But recent years have brought about a critical reevaluation of the use of tests for such purposes in the United States in line with the policies of the Equal Employment Opportunity Commission[3] and various court decisions relating to alleged discriminatory practices in the use of personnel tests. (The main thrust of the federal regulations in this area requires that employers demonstrate the "job-relatedness" of such tests.)

During the 1940s and 1950s considerable interest was generated in the human relations aspects of personnel management, with particular concern for group interaction, supervision and leadership processes, communications, and job satisfaction. This increased emphasis on human relations in industry led to greater attention to human-relations training of supervisory and management personnel and to management development programs generally. What is more, interest in the social aspects of human work has led logically to the crystallization of what is now referred to as organizational psychology; in this new discipline the dominant focus is on human motivation and efforts are made to understand the effects of the organizational setting on motivation, job satisfaction, and work effectiveness. The development of organizational psychology has entailed a growing interest in leadership styles, management philosophies, organizational policies and structures, incentive systems, and other aspects of organizations as they relate to both human satisfactions and organizational effectiveness.

Paralleling these developments during the past three decades or so has been the development of the field of human factors engineering (or *ergonomics,* as it is called in most countries abroad). The objective of this field is to design physical equipment and facilities tailored to human abilities and limitations. Although this field is an interdisciplinary one, psychologists have played an important role in it over the years; the segment of this domain in which psychologists have made inputs is sometimes called *engineering psychology.*

Looking Ahead

To date, the efforts of industrial psychologists have been directed largely toward the study of the independent relationships between specific variables

---

[3] Anderson, B. R., & Rogers, M. P. *Personnel testing and equal employment opportunity.* Washington, D.C.: Equal Employment Opportunity Commission, December 1970.

on the one hand, and various aspects of work-related behavior on the other. Thus, there have been scads of investigations dealing independently with such specific variables as individual differences, organizational character-istics, incentives, group structure, equipment design, and working conditions. But those dealing with *combinations* of these and other variables are rela-tively few and far between, as was pointed out by Uhlaner.[4] According to Uhlaner, effective behavior and work performance are not always the *addi-tive* effects of whatever variables may be involved, for the different variables *interact* in this process and may be complicated further with different types of jobs. Thus, for example, one type of incentive might be appropriate for some kinds of people and jobs but not for others. The burden of Uhlaner's argument is that more behavioral research relating to human work should be carried out in the framework of its total context in order to explore the possible interactions. His own generalized conceptualization of the various possible interactions is illustrated graphically in Figure 1.1, where he depicts the various sets of variables that may interact to contribute to effective work and work performance. It seems reasonable to expect that the same illustra-tion can be applied to criteria of various human values (such as health, safety, satisfactions) as well as to criteria of effective work and work per-

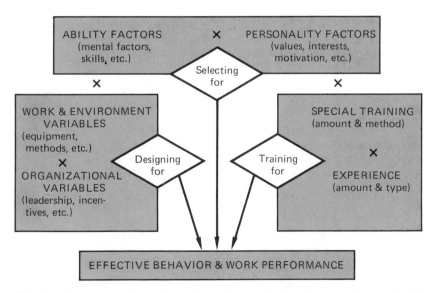

FIG. 1.1 Conceptualization of interactions of human factor system variables as related to human performance effectiveness. These kinds of data provide a "measurement bed" for analyzing interactions of variables as related to effective behavior and work performance. (*Adapted from Uhlaner, 1970, op. cit., Schema I.*)

[4] Uhlaner, J. E. *Human performance, jobs, and systems psychology: The systems measurement bed.* U.S. Army, Behavior and Systems Research Laboratory, Technical Report S–2 (AD 716 346), October 1970.

formance. For this reason one should not view system "design," personnel selection, and training as separate, isolated facets of work-related functions, but rather as an integrated package. Related research should be approached accordingly.

The systems concept. Although, as Uhlaner implies, this multifaceted, interactive approach is not in common use, it has not been entirely neglected. In fact, paralleling the development of human factors engineering has been the development of the *systems concept*. In this specific frame of reference, the intent is to develop a "system" that provides an optimum blend of people, equipment, procedures, and operations in order to capitalize on the relative capabilities of human beings and of physical equipment in performing different functions. Although the systems concept is most obviously applicable to circumstances where human beings are to interact with items of physical equipment, it is also applicable to processes or operations in which little physical equipment is used, such as office operations, service and distribution processes, and communication processes. Even a complete organization can be viewed as a system.

In the past, most of the behavioral research related to systems has been carried out in connection with military man-machine operations, as discussed by Parsons.[5] Some of this work has employed the type of integrated framework discussed above, and some of it has been carried out in laboratory settings, in some instances involving very elaborate experimental facilities and procedures.

Discussion. We have no source of instant insight regarding the future direction of industrial psychology, but we agree with Uhlaner[6] that industrial psychology needs to shift somewhat from the investigation of individual variables and factors relating to human behavior to the study of behavior within various industrial contexts, including whatever interactions there may be in such contexts. It is to be hoped that research in this direction will be rewarding in terms of the greater understanding of and insight into human behavior that might accrue.

THE MODUS OPERANDI OF INDUSTRIAL PSYCHOLOGY

As stated earlier in this chapter, the objective of industrial psychology is to provide the basis for minimizing some of the human problems that arise in industry. The *modus operandi* of industrial psychology in this process comprises a sequence of four phases or stages, as follows: (1) the identification of the problems to be dealt with; (2) the use of various methods of

[5] Parsons, H. M. *Man-machine systems experiments*. Baltimore: The Johns Hopkins Press, 1972.
[6] Uhlaner, *op. cit.*

collection and analysis of relevant data; (3) the findings resulting from these methods and associated analyses; and (4) the application of such findings to the problems at hand.

Identification of the Problems

The problems relevant to industrial psychology are manifest in various ways and at various levels of abstraction—most of them being manifestations of one sort or another of the disparities between the objectives referred to above and the reasonable fulfillment of these in practice. An illustrative inventory of these problems might include the following: indications of organizational ineffectiveness and of inadequate job performance of people: high personnel turnover rates; injuries; poor employee morale; dissatisfaction; controversy and occasional conflict; and failure to fulfill the reasonable needs of consumers.

In connection with the reasonable fulfillment of the goals of the people involved, we need to recognize that there are different groups of participants in this total process, such as owners or stockholders, managers, supervisors, employees, unions, consumers, the government, and the public generally. The opposing interests of some of these groups frequently (and in certain circumstances almost inevitably) lead to controversy and conflict. Thus we must recognize that—almost by definition—the interests of some of the participants cannot be entirely fulfilled.

The realities of life characteristically impose constraints on the achievement of the legitimate objectives of industry discussed earlier. Thus some tradeoffs are required, such as settling for something less than topnotch efficiency in order to reduce accident liability or imposing restrictions on earnings in the interest of maintaining a competitive position (and thus enhance future security). In the best of all possible worlds the potentially conflicting facets would be dealt with in such a manner as to achieve reasonable balance.

Methods

The primary role of industrial psychologists in dealing with human problems in the industrial arena is to bring to bear knowledge and insight that can be used to resolve these problems. Because this is essentially a research function, the methods used in this process are central to the development of such knowledge and insight. A number of the methods used will be described or illustrated throughout this book in connection with the specific topics for which they are relevant, so that for the moment we will limit ourselves to mentioning only a few of them. By and large, they fall into three classes: (1) experimental design (methods of investigation); (2) data collection (the use of such methods as tests, questionnaires, ratings, performance appraisal, observation, and job analysis); and (3) statistical analysis methods.

Findings

The results generated by the use of statistical methods comprise the basis of the "findings" of psychological research. More will be said about this later; here we will observe only that they tend to fall into at least two predominant categories: (1) theories or generalizations (such as the usefulness of feedback in learning); and (2) empirically derived research findings (findings that are specific to certain situations, such as the times required to learn a job by different training methods).

Application of Findings

The "application" of research findings implies the adoption of certain practices, procedures, policies, or actions that are predicated on the findings in question. Examples of such practical steps include: the use of certain tests or other predictors as the basis for personnel selection; the development of training programs that incorporate certain learning principles; the training of supervisors and managers in personnel relations practices; the establishment of financial and other incentives that are compatible with human needs; the creation of physical working conditions that are satisfactory in terms of appropriate health and safety standards; and the design of consumer products that effectively serve their purposes.

The application of the findings of psychological research can be (and often is) carried out by people other than psychologists, such as personnel managers, supervisors, managers, and advertising personnel. In some cases, however, the application of research findings needs to be carried out by, or under the supervision of, professional psychologists who serve in a consulting or advising capacity. In this role a psychologist serves essentially as a professional practitioner.

It should be added that sometimes the area of "application" is by no means manifest at the time the "problem" is identified. A single type of problem (such as poor performance) conceivably could be the consequence of any of several precipitating factors, such as improper personnel selections, inadequate training, improper incentives, poor working conditions, or poorly designed equipment. In fact, one of the primary purposes of this problem-methods-findings-applications sequence is to trace down these sometimes elusive relationships.

INDUSTRIAL PSYCHOLOGY AS A SCIENCE

The solution to most of the human problems in industry requires the application of knowledge of human behavior. Such knowledge can be derived in part through experience, and it would be a poor observer of human behavior who did not, through his own observation and experience, develop some useful insights. The insight into human behavior that is derived from "experience," however, has its limitations. Hence the value of research, for it can provide the basis for developing information about many aspects of human behavior that cannot be inferred from experience.

All scientific endeavor is predicated upon the assumption that events and phenomena are the consequences of precipitating factors. As applied to the study of human behavior in industry or elsewhere, this means that we must assume that behavior is based on complex assortments of variables, both individual and situational. It is the intent of psychological research to identify the variables associated with different aspects of behavior, such as the relationship between aptitudes and job performance or between illumination and the ability of people to make visual discriminations.

Beyond the objective of identifying such relationships, some psychological research is aimed at determining the underlying reasons for the behavior of people—at "explaining" such behavior on the basis of theories. Such research typically is initiated following the development of speculations about the cause of some aspect of behavior, leading to the formulation of a theory. Ultimately the accumulation of research evidence may tend to support the theory in question. Of course, in a sense one can never statistically "prove" a theory, or a cause-and-effect relationship, or "why" people behave in a given manner. But, it is sometimes possible to build up such a persuasive body of evidence that one is willing to accept a theory as being "true," or to conclude that a cause-and-effect relationship does in fact exist.

The Scientific Method

Although we commonly refer to the "scientific method," there actually are many different methods used in research. The method used in any given situation should, of course, be the one that is considered most appropriate to the research problem in question. Many such methods are used in industrial psychology. There are, however, certain basic features that are common to most research, two of which will be discussed here. First there is the requirement for the identification (classification) or measurement of pertinent variables; and second, in the case of certain types of studies (particularly "experimental" studies) it is necessary to control the variables that the investigator is interested in studying.

Independent and dependent variables in research. In research there are two primary types of variables, namely, *independent variables* and *dependent variables* (dependent variables usually are referred to as *criteria*). The independent variable is the factor that is varied, frequently being controlled in some way by the investigator, such as level of illumination on a work task, the method of training, or size of letters in a reading experiment. The dependent variable (or criterion) is the measure of the effects of the independent variable, such as work production, learning time, or words read correctly per minute. More will be said in the next chapter about both types of variables as related to research in the area of industrial psychology.

In the case of both types of variables, the experimenter must measure or identify (or classify) the variables in question. For example, in an illumination study, the illumination level of the experimental conditions must be accurately measured (and, incidentally, "controlled") ; in addition, the dependent variable or criterion (such as units of production per unit of time) also must be measured. In certain instances a variable does not lend itself to measurement as such. For example, an investigator might experiment with two or more methods of performing a particular job. In such a case, the investigator would have to be sure to observe that each repetition of a given method actually corresponds with the method prescribed (this is essentially a classification process). An example of a dependent variable that would be "identified" or "classified" (rather than measured) is the "behaviors" of subjects under experimental conditions of stress. Such behaviors might be classified by observers into one of two or more categories, such as "maintains self-control," "freezes," or "loses self-control." Such classifications must be made in a reasonably reliable manner, meaning that the same behavior usually would be classified by different observers in the same category.

Control of experimental variables. In some types of studies it is necessary to plan on the "control" of the experimental (or independent) variables in question. Such control can be exercised in various ways. In the first place, variables can be manipulated by the experimenter, as in illumination studies in which the level of illumination is physically controlled. In the second place, control can be by selection. For example, if the experimenter is interested in the relationship between age and manipulative skill, he could select subjects of each of various age groups. In the third place, control can be exercised through the use of appropriate statistical analysis. This might be done by taking subjects regardless of age and later ascertaining by statistical analysis the relationship between age and the dependent variable (say, manipulative skill). Other methods of control also can be used.

In addition to controlling the variables in which an experimenter is specifically interested, it is necessary to control other, possibly extraneous, variables in order that the results will not be contaminated by them. For example, in comparing two training methods, it would be important to insure that factors other than the training method do not significantly influence the results. Among such possible contaminating factors might be education, mental ability, age, and experience of subjects. Although, as in this case, the experimenter can readily identify some of the extraneous variables that might influence the results, sometimes certain extraneous variables cannot be foreseen. If they have some contaminating effect upon the results, they can lead to incorrect conclusions. Where extraneous variables can be anticipated, they can be controlled by one of the methods mentioned above, or by other schemes, such as entirely random assignment of subjects to different experimental conditions.

Controlled Experiments vs. Real-Life Research

It should be pointed out that human research can be carried out under either of two types of circumstances. The first involves carrying out what is called a *controlled experiment,* such as in a laboratory or work situation, in which the independent variable is specifically under the control of the experimenter. For example, an experimenter might have subjects perform a task under two or more conditions of noise, or under two or more types of incentives. He then can measure task performance under the different experimental conditions and compare the results.

The other type of circumstance entails studying human behavior in the real-life setting. This approach requires the collection of data under circumstances that make possible an analysis of the variables of concern. Thus, if one could identify equivalent groups of workers on the same task who are working under different noise levels, it would be possible to compare their job performance under the two or more noise levels. Or, to take another example, the experimenter might collect test data and job performance data on a group of employees on a given job, and then make an analysis of the relationship between test scores and job performance.

In some such cases, the "control" of the experimental variables (the independent variables) is by appropriate selection of the specific groups (or individuals) to be studied, rather than by manipulation of the variables in question by the experimenter. In a study on the effects of noise, for example, the experimenter would have to select, say, two "equivalent" groups of people working on the same job but under different noise levels. However, the selection of "equivalent" groups poses a bit of a problem for he must take all reasonable steps to assure that they are generally equivalent in terms of aptitudes, age, sex, length of experience, and possibly other factors.

"Survey" research is characteristically carried out in real-life situations. As the name implies, this type of research involves surveys of some type, such as attitude and opinion research and much of the research in the consumer area.

There are both advantages and disadvantages to controlled experiments and to research in real-life situations. In this connection, the nature of the problem frequently will dictate which approach is the more appropriate for the purpose.

The Conduct of Research

The design and conduct of research investigations is beyond the intended scope of this book. In various chapters of this text, however, examples will be presented which will indicate how at least some investigations have been carried out.

Statistical analysis in research. The typical end result of the experimental phase of a study is the accumulation of raw data, usually in quantitative form. Such data are then summarized and usually subjected to statistical analysis.[7] Certain basic methods and techniques that will be referred to in this text are presented in Appendix A. (It is suggested that the reader who is not already familiar with these methods review that appendix.) The methods discussed in the appendix relate to *descriptive* statistics rather than to *inferential* statistics. As implied by the term, descriptive statistics are concerned with describing people, events, phenomena, and so forth in statistical terms. Inferential statistics are concerned with drawing inference from, or extrapolating from, statistical data about an available sample to the population from which the sample came.

It is essential that the student dealing with statistical material be familiar with the concept of *statistical significance*. This can be illustrated with an example. Let us use as a hypothetical illustration a study of the effects of two methods of training employees on a particular job. The independent variable is the training method. Let us call the two variations methods I and II. Let us assume that the dependent variable (what we will call the criterion) is the production of employees during a specified week (say, the eighth week of training). We might obtain results shown in Example A of Figure 1.2. The difference between these two methods is very clear; assuming a reasonable number of subjects in each group, such differences undoubtedly should be statistically significant. Although the formula for determining the level of statistical significance cannot be discussed here, it is sufficient for our purposes to know that it depends upon the *number* of cases, the statistical *variability* of the cases, and the *numerical values* in question (in this case the difference between the means of methods I and II). Typically, the level of statistical significance is expressed in such terms as the ".01" or ".05" level (or whatever the actual value turns out to be). The statement that a finding "is significant at the .01 level" would be interpreted as follows: the obtained difference (in this case the difference between the

---

[7] For a discussion of various statistical methods, and the analysis of data from experiments, the reader is referred to appropriate statistical texts such as the following: Downie, N. M., & Heath, R. W. *Basic statistical methods.* (3rd ed.) New York: Harper & Row, 1970; Edwards, A. L. *Experimental design in psychological research.* (4th ed.) New York: Holt, Rinehart & Winston, 1972; and Winer, B. J. *Statistical principles in experimental design.* (2nd ed.) New York: McGraw-Hill, 1971.

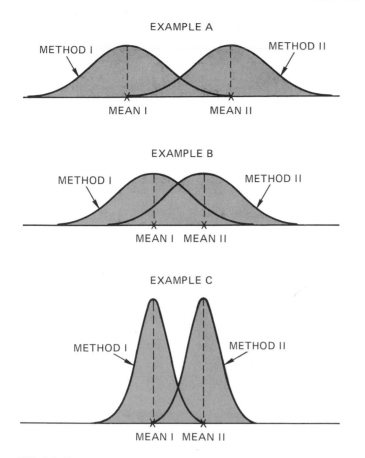

FIG. 1.2 Hypothetical distributions of production records of employees trained by method I and by method II. Assuming a reasonable number of cases, the difference shown in Example A probably would be statistically significant (meaning that the difference could not reasonably be attributed to chance). The difference in Example B (being small) more likely could be a "chance" difference, and would have a lower level of statistical significance; if there were large numbers of cases involved, however, the difference shown in Example B might be highly significant since (with a large number of cases) it would not likely occur by chance. Example C (which has the same means as Example B) would be statistically significant with a smaller number of cases, since there is less variability in the two distributions (and less "overlap" between the two).

means) is of such a magnitude that it would occur *by chance* in only one case out of a hundred replications of such an experiment *if there were no true difference in the methods.* (In the case of the .05 level, such a difference would be expected to occur by chance in five out of a hundred similar experiments.) When we refer to statistically significant relationships, then, we are referring to the "odds." If a relationship is found to be significant at a sufficiently low level (say at the .01 level), we infer that the relationship is not likely to be attributable to chance. (Note that we never can *prove* a relationship; we can only say that the likelihood of the relationship's being due to chance is extremely small.)

In the case of Example B from Figure 1.2, there is a difference between the methods I and II, but this difference is not great and there is considerable overlap in the production records of the two groups. With a small number of cases this difference probably would not be statistically significant; with a large number of cases, it could be. In Example C, the means for the two methods are the same as in Example B, but there is less variability in the performance of the individuals in the two groups—there is less "overlap" between them. This difference could be statistically significant with a smaller number of cases than would be required for statistical significance in Example B.

Statistical significance should not be confused with practical significance. When we say that a relationship is statistically significant we claim merely that the relationship cannot reasonably be attributed to chance. However, the relationship may well be trivial and unimportant, of little or no consequence. On the other hand, practical significance refers to the extent to which (statistically significant) results have possible practical utility, taking into account whatever practical considerations are pertinent, such as cost, amount of possible benefit, and so forth. The possible advantage of method II over method I in Example A (Fig. 1.2) would be much greater than in Example B or C. (In Example B or C, assuming that the differences were statistically significant, there might be some question as to whether it would be worthwhile, in practical terms, to adopt method II rather than I, especially if method II were more costly.)

Discussion

Industrial psychologists become involved in a variety of activities, but in a sense their roles can be viewed as relating either to the *science* of psychology (with an emphasis on research) or to the *profession* of psychology (with an emphasis on the application of knowledge and insight to practical problems). In this regard it should be emphasized that the profession of psychology needs to be rooted in psychological research; indeed, in many instances the practitioner himself carries out research relating to the problems with which he is dealing, such as analyzing the factors that are associated with accidents, conducting an attitude survey, or studying the buying habits of consumers. Thus even psychologists who are serving primarily in a professional role usually need to be well versed in research methodology.

INDUSTRIAL PSYCHOLOGY AS
A PROFESSION

Psychology as a profession is concerned with the "application" of knowledge to some practical problem. Thus industrial psychologists who perform such functions are serving as professional practitioners—they are practicing the profession. In industry this can include consulting, program development, and individual evaluation. Typically, a psychologist engaged in consulting activities advises in some area of his expertise, such as management development, equipment design, or consumer behavior. A psychologist in program development would be responsible for developing and installing some program, such as a training program or a personnel selection program. In the field of individual evaluation, the psychologist functions much like a clinician in assessing the potentialities of individuals for specific positions, promotions, and so forth, or in counseling the individual himself. In this capacity he typically uses interviewing techniques, tests, and related techniques as the basis for his evaluation. Note that it is only in the field of individual evaluation that the psychologist in industry uses his psychological background extensively in dealing with individuals as individuals. In his other functions he deals with human behavior in conceptual terms rather than on an individual basis.

THEORETICAL VERSUS EMPIRICAL BASES
OF APPLICATIONS

As indicated earlier, the primary findings of behavioral research are of two general types. One of these consists of theories or generalizations (such as a theory of motivation). The other consists of emprically determined relationships (such as the relationships between training methods and learning). Of course, there are differences of opinion regarding the appropriateness or utility of these two types of research bases in the the practice of the profession of psychology. For example, some people take it for granted that "applications" of research must of necessity follow the acceptance of some theory. Snijders[8] accurately characterizes this assumption as the belief that "pure or fundamental research must firstly lay the theoretical foundations, on which secondly a technology is erected; only after that can a start be made with applications to practical problems." But Snijders hastens to point out that the facts of contemporary psychology refute the idea that such

[8] Snijders, J. T. Interaction of theory and practice. *Revue Internationale de Psychologie Appliquée,* April 1969, **18**(1), 13–19.

a logical and temporal relationship between theory and application must universally apply. To support his point he states that there can be "practice without a theory" (such as the widescale use of mental tests) and also "theory without practice" (such as the extensive research relating to learning theory that to date has been "applied" very nominally if at all). In connection with the relationship between theory and applications, Chapanis[9] expresses the belief that the best basic work in psychology starts not with psychological theory, but with attempts to solve questions posed by the world around us.

Certainly in the field of industrial psychology much of the research has been directed toward solving practical problems, and thus has been of an applied, empirical nature unaccompanied by much in the way of related theory. Although empirically determined relationships do not explain *why* people behave in some given manner, such relationships nonetheless can serve as the basis for achieving certain practical objectives. For example, we might find, in general, that employees with a given constellation of personal background experiences (i.e., hobbies, family relationships, education, and so forth) tend to remain longer on jobs in an organization than do other employees. Although we may not know why this is so, this information can be useful in the selection of personnel.

The fact that applied, empirical research can serve useful purposes in practice should not lead us to neglect the sorts of understanding that can be gained through theory formulation. But such objectives should not become a fetish that blinds us to the potential practical usefulness of empirical research. We agree with Viteles:[10]

> I have become increasingly concerned about a growing tendency on the part of applied psychologists to subordinate empiricism, in the form of attachment to facts, to a concept of science that gives the latter, especially as represented by its theories, an aura of inner and transcendental perfection—a quality of the *précieux* that sometimes achieves the quality of the absurd.

When the results of psychological research are to be "applied," it is manifest that the objective is some form of control of behavior of the people in question. This control, of course, can range from forms widely held to be desirable (such as vocational counseling, training, education, and the like) to forms that are at odds with commonly accepted values, such as brainwashing. The types of control that are implicit in psychological research essentially are ethically oriented toward the objectives of basic human welfare.

9 Chapanis, A. Prelude to 2001: Exploration in human communication. *American Psychologist,* 1971, 26(11), 949–961.
10 Viteles, M. S. The two faces of applied psychology. *Revue Internationale de Psychologie Appliquée,* April 1969, 18(1), 5–10.

TREATMENT OF INDUSTRIAL PSYCHOLOGY
IN THIS BOOK

This book is intended to be a survey of the field of industrial psychology. As such, it will be concerned with the spectrum of the problems involved, the methods used in investigating these problems, and illustrative findings from such research. Because of the extensive material available, the content of this book must be selective and illustrative rather than inclusive. In the selection of the problems, methods, and findings, however, it has been our intent to include as illustrations at least some of the more important examples.

Aside from the introductory chapters, the book is organized in terms of certain of the major "content" areas of industrial psychology, which generally are the primary areas of application:

Personnel selection and appraisal
The social and organizational context of work
The job and work situation
Human error and accidents
Psychological aspects of consumer behavior

Inasmuch as industrial psychology is directed toward the resolution of practical problems, this organization was suggested in large part because it reflects the primary areas of practice in this field. We should keep continuously in mind, however, the fact that the various areas do not exist in isolation from each other, but are indeed interrelated—so much so that, as noted before, any given "problem" might lead one into any of the several areas of application.

A special comment should be made about the discussion of methods. Some of the methods of collection and analysis of data are relevant to various content areas. In the book they generally will be brought up in the first context in which they are relevant, even though their potential use may well extend to other areas.

chapter two

Individual
and Situational
Differences
in Behavior

In the preceding chapter we expressed the idea that the production, distribution, and use of the goods and services of industry should be focused toward two objectives: (1) the enhancement of the effectiveness of these processes as such; and (2) the enhancement of certain desirable human values (e.g., health, safety, and satisfactions) in the process.

The production and distribution of goods and services in our economy are of course carried out by organizations—private and public—and this text deals largely with the human aspects of the operation of such organizations. The extent to which the twofold objectives of industry are or are not fulfilled in the operation of such organizations is reflected by such factors as: the overall economy of operations; the quality of products or services; the job performance of individuals; turnover and absence rates; labor-management relations; attitudes and job satisfaction of personnel; and the health and safety of personnel. The goods and services of the economy, of course, are "used" by consumers, and from their point of view the extent to which the objectives of industry are fulfilled is reflected by such factors as: the effective use of products and services; the ease of use of products and services; consumer satisfaction; and the health and safety of consumers.

If, in the normal course of events, the production, distribution, and use of goods and services left nothing to be desired, and if relevant human values were fulfilled, there would be no need for industrial psychology—or for this book. But we all know perfectly well that these objectives are not entirely fulfilled—that there are human problems, some of major proportions, associated with their fulfillment. It is these human problems that delineate the arena of the industrial psychologist. In dealing with problems that have human twists, knowledge and understanding are convenient commodities to have on hand to "apply" as needed in order to minimize the problem. Such knowledge and understanding can in part be generated through psychological research.

As we reflect about the human problems in industry, it becomes obvious that they are really manifestations of certain "undesirable" forms of behavior, such as poor quality of work, high turnover, low morale, or whatnot. The key word here is *behavior,* a term which in our usage embraces not only "overt" actions or activities, such as how well a person does on a job, but also "covert" aspects such as attitudes.

FACTORS ASSOCIATED WITH DIFFERENCES IN BEHAVIOR

We can envision any given kind or form of behavior as varying along some scale. Thus, for a sample of people in any given context or in different contexts, we can envision differences varying in such behaviors as: job performance (quantity, quality, accuracy, and so forth); tenure on a job; absenteeism; attitudes (toward the job, company, union, or other aspect of a work situation); ability to make visual or auditory discriminations; heart rate; energy expenditure; time required to complete a particular task; acceptability by subordinates or co-workers; satisfaction (or dissatisfaction) with a product one has bought; and expressed preferences for products. The scales for most such aspects of behavior range along a continuum from undesirable to desirable in terms of some set of values, such as units of production or scores on an attitude questionnaire.

Causation in Human Behavior

The variability in any given form of behavior should not be assumed to be a fortuity, but rather should be assumed to be the consequence of some combination of factors. To illustrate this point, let us take the hypothetical case of employees on a particular type of job and concern ourselves with the differences in performance of the individual employees. Job performance almost inevitably varies among employees (and, to some extent, even from

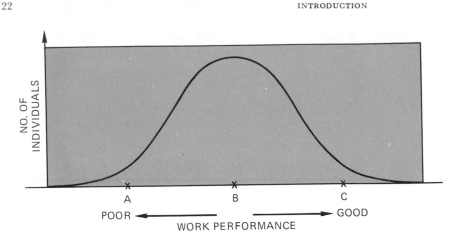

FIG. 2.1 Distribution of differences in work performance of a hypothetical group of workers in a job. Positions A, B, and C represent three hypothetical individuals within the distribution, these being generally below average (A), average (B), and above average (C).

time to time for the same employee). The differences in performance frequently (but not invariably) form a distribution something like a normal distribution, as illustrated in Figure 2.1. Assuming some criterion (such as productivity in units per day or sales in dollars), one would find that individuals fall at different points (A, B, and C) along the performance continuum. If our assumption of multiple causation is valid, then we must infer that individuals A, B, and C fall at their respective positions of below average, average, and above average for some combination of reasons.

If we were to speculate about some of the factors that might be associated with the relative performances of these three individuals, there are certain kinds of factors that almost inevitably would be suggested. Such a list would include a variety of *individual variables,* such as aptitudes, personality characteristics, physical characteristics, interests and motivation, age and sex, education, experience, and other personal variables. In addition, such a list would also include a number of *situational variables,* such as methods of work, design and condition of work equipment, work space and arrangement, physical environment (illumination, noise, and so on), the character of the organization, type of training and supervision received, types of incentives, and the "social" environment. The situational variables, in turn, fall generally into two classes—namely, those we might call *physical and job variables* and those we might call *organizational and social variables.* Some of these variables are represented graphically in Figure 2.2. Each of the categories shown is itself a class of variables. Within each one there might be several more specific variables, such as specific aptitudes, specific physical characteristics, specific aspects of the physical work environment, and specific aspects of the social environment, etc.

Figure 2.2 is a generalized one. Theoretically, one could construct such

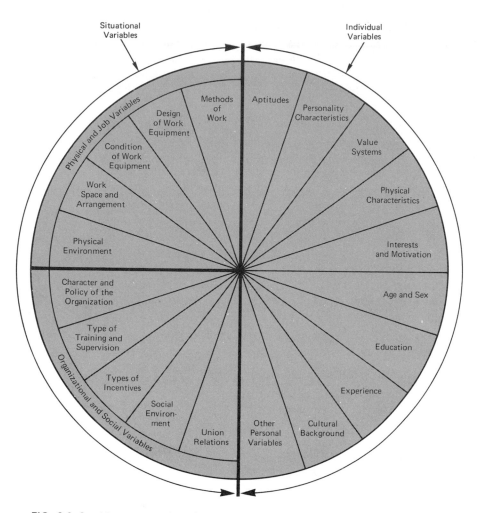

FIG. 2.2 Graphic representation of some of the individual and situational variables that may be associated with job performance. This is a generalized representation. The representation for any given job might include only some of these variables, and their relative importance as influencing factors might be unique to the job in question.

a chart for every type of job. The chart for any given type of job could differ from others in two ways. In the first place, it could be different in terms of the *combination* of specific variables, and in the second place, it could be different in terms of the relative *importance* of the variables. It can be seen that for some types of jobs certain variables simply might not be pertinent to performance on the job; for example, eye-hand coordination presumably would have no bearing on the performance of executives.

The generalized picture presented in Figure 2.2 is applicable to any given type of job on something of an across-the-board basis—wherever the job exists. It should be pointed out, however, that in any *specific* situation such as a given job in a given department of a company, there may be no variability on some of the *situational* variables. For example, if all employees on the job are subject to the same physical working conditions (say illumination), in *that situation* working conditions usually would not operate *differentially* to cause some people to perform better than others. Conversely, if the same job were performed under *other* illumination conditions, as might happen in another department or in another company, one might find a difference in the performance level of employees in the two departments or plants that would be associated with the different illumination.

Although Figures 2.1 and 2.2 are presented as illustrations of variables that might affect performance on a job, the same general model also could be applied to other aspects of behavior of people. This would mean, first, relabeling the criterion in Figure 2.1 to reflect the type of behavior in mind (such as differences in attitudes, reading speed, or time spent looking at a particular magazine advertisement). Second, it might involve categories and groupings somewhat different (in some cases entirely different) from those illustrated in Figure 2.1. (For example, in advertising research, the "situational" variables might include type of advertising medium, such as magazines, newspapers, or television).

Combining Variables Related to Behavior

In general, then, we can postulate the notion that behavior of whatever form (job performance, attitudes, automobile driving, and so forth) is the consequence of the total effects of several variables—individual and situational. If one can somehow measure both the behavior and the specific variables that might be related to it, then it would be possible, at least in theory, to quantify the effects of the several variables as related to the behavior in question, and to express this in terms of an equation. Performance could be measured in terms of units of production, the individual variables might include such variables as test scores and years of education, and the situational variables might include such values as footcandles of illumination and number of people in the work group. Assuming we could obtain a "value" on each pertinent variable for each individual in such a case, the equation to predict behavior (in this case job performance) might look like this:

$$B = (w_a \times v_a) + (w_b \times v_b) + (w_c \times v_c) + \ldots (w_n \times v_n) + k$$

in which

B = the behavior (in quantitative terms such as production units)
a, b, c, ... n = variables

$w_a, w_b, w_c, \ldots w_n$ = weights of variables (determined satistically)

$v_a, v_b, v_c, \ldots v_n$ = "values" for an individual on each variable (such as score on an aptitude test, or quantitative value on some situational variable such as, say, illumination level)

k = a constant

Given quantitative measures of the behavior B in a sample of people, as well as measures of each of the variables for each person, it is possible to determine statistically the weights (w) of the variables and the constant (k). Of course, there may be interactions that enter into the equation. An interaction is an effect that is not strictly "additive" in an equation. For example, in analyzing variables associated with performance on a given job, it may be found that aptitudes add significantly to performance in the case of persons with limited experience, whereas they do not add in comparable proportion in the case of persons with longer experience.

Although it is not possible to predict behavior perfectly in this manner, nonetheless there have been many situations in which behavior (such as job performance) has been predicted to a practically useful degree by such a scheme.

Discussion

The difference between a primary focus on individual variables as opposed to situational variables will become more apparent in later chapters of this text, where each of these types of variables will be examined. Before leaving this point for the moment, however, let us emphasize that this is a very basic distinction that needs to be recognized clearly. Aside from the possibility of interactions, the situational variables (such as equipment, environment, social work groups, procedures, roads, and advertising media) may be viewed as aspects of the "system," if you will, within which individuals function. If there is evidence that situational factors may influence behavior (such as job performance or driving behaviors), it *may* be possible to modify these factors in order to create a situation (a "system") that is reasonably conducive to more acceptable behavior. But let us keep in mind that, in one sense, we are not here looking strictly at human performance as such, but rather at "system" performance. As Taylor[1] pointed out in his discussion of physical equipment, one system (A) might have greater output than another (B), even though system B might make greater demands on human performance than system A. On the other hand, the *individual,* as opposed to *situational,* variables take on importance *within* any given system

---

[1] Taylor, F. V. Psychology and the design of machines. *American Psychologist,* 1957, 15, 249–258.

or situation, such as in the context of a given job, a given highway system, or a consumer service organization.

RESEARCH APPROACHES RELATING TO DIFFERENCES IN BEHAVIOR

For practical purposes we can say that psychological research is directed toward tracing down the relationships between independent variables (usually individual characteristics or situational factors or their combination) and dependent variables or criteria (usually some type of behavior). If one can determine such relationships, one then can use this knowledge in predicting the dependent variable from the independent variable, as is done in predicting job performance of people from scores on aptitude tests, predicting accident frequency of people working day shift versus those working night shift, or predicting what types of women will buy a new variety of floor wax. We should hasten to note that there are circumstances, like the chicken-and-egg conundrum, in which one variable can be used either as the independent or as the dependent variable; for example, job satisfaction may be used to predict job performance or job performance to predict job satisfaction. Thus we should *not* assume that the dependent variable (despite its name) is necessarily brought about by, or caused by, the independent variable.

Research Methods

In carrying out research, there are two different types of research strategies—the correlational method and the experimental method.

Correlational method of research. In the correlational method, data are obtained on the independent and dependent variables for each "case" in the sample, without any experimental manipulation or control. Most typically, this strategy is used in the investigation of the individual variables as predictors of behavior, but occasionally it is also used in the investigation of situational variables. This approach is used when the researcher's intent is to determine the relationship between the dependent and independent variables, this relationship usually being measured by the use of a *coefficient of correlation*. (The reader who is not familiar with this term is referred to Appendix A. Briefly, a coefficient of correlation is a statistical index of the degree of relationship between two variables. It ranges from $+1.00$—a perfect positive relationship—through intermediate positive values down to 0.00—the absence of any relationship—through intermediate negative values to -1.00—a perfect negative relationship. Figure 2.3 illustrates the concept of correlations, showing different *scattergrams* that reflect varying degrees of relationship.)

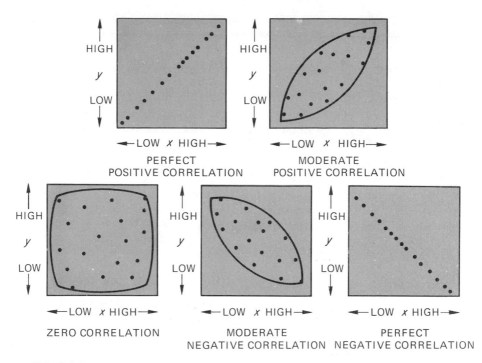

FIG. 2.3 Illustration of scattergrams of several hypothetical correlations between two variables, ranging from a perfect positive correlation (r = +1.00) through a zero correlation (r = 0.00) to a perfect negative correlation (r = −1.00). Lines around dots depict the scatter or concentration of cases.

Thus, with the correlational approach one can determine the relationship between reaction time and number of accidents, between attitudes toward one's supervisor and productivity, or between educational level and television viewing preferences. The research data for the correlational approach can be obtained at places of work (as in the case of employees of an organization), from available records (as in the case of automobile drivers), by the use of surveys (as in market research and public opinion polling), or in other appropriate ways.

Experimental method of research. The experimental strategy of research typically involves some manipulation, control, or "selection" of the independent variables. Thus it is most suitable for research relating to the effects of situational variables such as the illumination level, the size of the work group, the method of training, the media used in advertising research, or the design of road signs. By means of this approach one can see whatever differences exist, if any do, in the mean values of the criterion of behavior associated with different values of the independent variable in question. Although actual manipulation of independent variables sometimes can be done in real-life situations, this usually is difficult to arrange. Such "control" generally can be exercised more readily in a laboratory. In some research undertakings, however, data obtained in different real-life circumstances are specifically selected to represent variations in the independent variable being investigated, as when one purposefully varies the sizes of work groups.

Discussion. Each research method lends itself best to certain research objectives and each should be used when it is most appropriate. There is, however, one point of difference that should be noted. The correlational approach typically does not lend itself to supporting very strong inferences about cause-and-effect relationships, for in any given circumstance a correlation between two variables might be brought about by the relationship of the two variables to a third variable. Although the experimental approach cannot really "prove" any cause-and-effect relationship, it does lend itself to somewhat more confident inferences of this type, for (at least under ideal conditions) the effects of "other" variables can be minimized or eliminated by appropriate "control" of such variables.

INDIVIDUAL DIFFERENCES
IN PERSONAL CHARACTERISTICS

Our interest in individual differences relates primarily to their potential relationship with some type of relevant dependent variable (or criterion), such as job performance, buying behavior, or driving. The spectrum of types of personal characteristics is illustrated very grossly in Figure 2.2, and it should be remembered that there are many specific dimensions of individual differences contained within each of the categories presented there. Although this is not the place to provide a compendium of data on individual differences, a few examples of such data—especially illustrations that might have some relevance to job performance—will be tossed in.

Individual Differences in Job Potential

The purpose of personnel selection and placement is to identify those individuals who have the characteristics that indicate they are optimum prospects for becoming satisfactory (and, it is to be hoped, satisfied) employees. Potentially relevant information about job candidates is available from application forms, personnel tests, employment records, ratings, and other sources. The examples of individual differences given here as illustrations are based on test scores.

One such example, given in Figure 2.4, shows the distribution of scores on the Otis Self-Administering Test of Mental Ability[2] for a group of 112

---

[2] This test and most of the others mentioned in this text are listed in Appendix D, along with the test distributors.

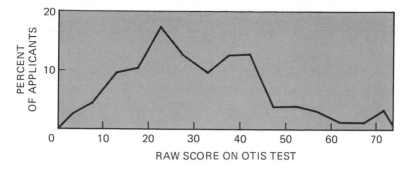

FIG. 2.4 Distribution of scores on Otis Self-Administering Test of Mental Ability (Higher Exam, Form A) of 112 applicants for machine shop apprenticeships.

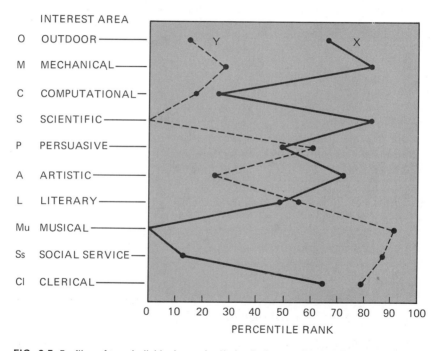

FIG. 2.5 Profiles of two individuals on the Kuder Preference Record. The percentile rank for each interest area is the per cent of persons whose scores are exceeded by the individual in question.

applicants for machine shop apprentice training. The height of the curve at any given score level shows the percentage of individuals at that level. An illustration of a different nature is given in Figure 2.5, which shows the profiles of two individuals (X and Y) on the Kuder Preference Record, a test of interests. The form of the test on which these profiles are based provides for several subscores as shown. Granting that there are marked differences among individuals in terms of various characteristics, in our present discussion the central question about such differences can be phrased as follows: what are the human characteristics or attributes (if any) that differentiate individuals in terms of some relevant criterion such as job performance and thus could be used to predict that criterion? The procedures for making such predictions will be discussed in later chapters, especially in regard to personnel selection and placement.

The Basis of Individual Differences

Psychologists have long been interested in determining the ultimate cause of individual differences among people. Usually they have divided the major causes into the two general categories of heredity and environment. Those who emphasize the importance of one of these factors often minimize or even completely ignore the possible influence of the other. It seems probable that both factors are usually operative but that their relative importance differs markedly in the determination of different personal characteristics. Heredity seems to be of most importance in determining such physical traits as height, weight, and strength, although it is clear that environment also has some effect upon these factors. On the other hand, environmental factors generally have a more dominant influence on personality traits and interests. With respect to mental abilities, there is reason to believe that hereditary factors determine the potential level of development that an individual optimally would achieve. Within this potential limit, however, environmental factors have an important influence on the level of development that actually occurs. Although knowledge and skill factors are, of course, the consequence of experience, education, and training (environmental factors), it is probable that hereditary variables interact with the environmental variables by imposing relevant "ceilings" on the level of knowledge or skill that can be achieved.

IMPORTANCE OF
INDIVIDUAL DIFFERENCES IN JOBS

The infinite variations in human beings that cause each person to be different from every other give rise to the variations in the performance of people in their jobs. Personnel selection and placement is predicated upon this basic fact.

Considerations Relating to Job Performance Differences

Placing individuals in jobs which they can perform at a satisfactory level is important for at least four different sorts of reasons—economic, legal and contractual, personal, and social.

Economic considerations. The economic considerations under which most organizations operate place a premium on the efficient use of all their resources, including human resources. The existence of differences in the abilities of different people to perform effectively on any given job argues for the selection and placement on jobs of individuals who stand a good chance of being able to perform effectively. Although this is especially important in the case of employees on jobs that are paid on the basis of time (by the hour, week, or month), it is also important in the case of piece-rate employees because of such factors as overhead costs, material waste, repairs, and possible customer ill will.

An additional economic consideration relates to costs associated with turnover. High turnover requires additional recruiting, interviewing, testing, medical examinations, and training and indoctrination. Gaudet[3] has provided some rather startling estimates in connection with some of these costs, as the following list shows:

Recruiting: journeyman machinists (newspaper advertising), $800; shipping room packers, $12; experienced electronics engineers, $2,300; engineering graduates (campus recruiting), $1,400 to $2,800.

Letters of application: technicians, $18; engineers, $52.

Interviewing: unskilled workers, $3 to $5; sales engineers, $125.

Physical examinations: unskilled workers, $7; engineers, $150.

Testing: $2 to $200.

Indoctrination and training: orientation briefings, $10 to $50; skill training, from $100 to several thousand dollars.

These estimates take into account all types of costs, prorated. The costs obviously range over a wide gamut depending on the nature of the position. As Gaudet observes, any company that embarks on a systematic study of its turnover costs is likely to be appalled when the figures are added up.

Legal and contractual considerations. Certain legal and contractual considerations place a premium on the employment of persons who will be expected to become satisfactory employees. One of these is concerned with the provision of unemployment compensation laws. In some states, a company with a high rate of employee separations has to pay higher premiums into the unemployment compensation fund than a company that has a better unemployment experience record. Another type of consideration is that associated with the seniority provisions of union contracts. Most contracts provide that individuals who are employed and retained for some specified period of time (frequently ninety days) cannot be separated after that period except for cause. This provision argues powerfully for the initial selection of applicants who can be expected to become satisfactory employees.

[3] Gaudet, F. J. Calculating the cost of labor turnover. *Personnel,* September-October 1958, **35**(2), 31–37.

Personal considerations. As far as the individual employee is concerned, it is, of course, important to him to work on a job that he can perform (or learn to perform) satisfactorily. Human satisfactions in work are directly related to the ability to perform the job in question. Although ability to perform a job is not necessarily a *sufficient* basis for job satisfaction, it is virtually a *necessary* basis. Associated with the possible satisfactions from work are the opportunities for merit increases in pay, promotions to positions of higher skill or responsibility, and considerations of security.

Social considerations. Considering both society as a whole and the objectives of mankind generally to improve his lot in life, a premium is placed on the optimum use of human talent. If people generally can find their way into work activities for which they are qualified, the use of human talent generally will tend to be maximized in terms of society generally. Current efforts to provide higher educational opportunities for all students who are potentially capable of benefiting from such education are, of course, a major step in the direction of more effective use of human potentials. Vocational counseling is a related function focused in this same direction, and the efforts of industry to place people on jobs for which they have potentialities also generally operate toward achievement of this objective.

Individual Differences in Job Performance

The evidence regarding individual differences in job performance is abundant and pervasive. In many circumstances the differences are of appreciable magnitude and of considerable practical importance in terms of productive efficiency, earnings of individuals, and other considerations.

Figure 2.6 shows the performance of employees on three jobs—cablers, mechanical assemblers, and unit wirers—in a company engaged in the manufacture of electronic equipment. The first two jobs are concerned with preparing parts for the wiring operation. The wirer then assembles a component of the finished product. His task includes soldering of the connections and he may take several hours on a difficult component. Production on all of these jobs is expressed in terms of an "efficiency index," as follows:

$$\text{Efficiency} = \frac{\text{Standard production time}}{\text{Actual production time}} \times 100$$

In analyzing the variability in performance of employees on various jobs, it is sometimes the practice to express such differences as a ratio of the productivity of the least productive employee to that of the most productive. In the case of these three jobs, these ratios, based on the efficiency indexes, range from about 1:2.7 to 1:3. In the case of 99 employees on the job of looping in a hosiery mill, the productivity of employees ranged from about 2.5 dozen hose per hour to about 7 dozen pair, a ratio of almost 1:3. Such ratios frequently are about 1:2 and on some jobs may be as much as 1:5 or more.

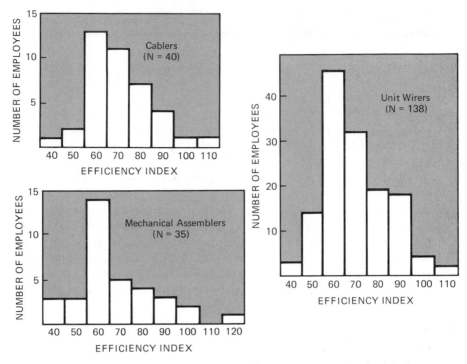

FIG. 2.6 Distribution of efficiency indexes of employees on three production jobs in an electronics company. (*Courtesy Tetronix, Inc., and Dr. Guyot Frazier.*)

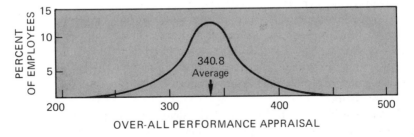

FIG. 2.7 Distribution of over-all performance appraisal ratings of 710 men from one department of a steel mill.

Aside from differences in job productivity as such, differences in the suitability of individuals for various jobs are reflected in other ways, such as in the quality of work, piece-rate earnings, job tenure, accidents, and performance appraisals. A distribution of performance appraisals for 710 men from one department of a steel mill is shown in Figure 2.7. Many cautions should be observed in interpreting the significance of these values inasmuch as they reflect subjective judgments, but it is safe to conclude that the spread from 240 to 450 points suggests definite differences in the quantity and quality of service rendered by the different employees.

TYPES OF CRITERIA

As indicated earlier, any investigation of human behavior involves the use of some appropriate dependent variable, usually referred to as a *criterion*. Whether a criterion is used in connection with the analysis of individual variables or of situational variables, criterion measures usually are obtained for individuals. When the purpose is analysis of individual variables (such as in personnel selection), the criterion measures for individuals (such as a measure of job performance) are related to individual characteristics (such as test scores). When the purpose is analysis of situational variables, the criterion measures for individuals (which might also be a measure of job performance) usually are "averaged" for all individuals in a given situation (such as for each noise level) in order to compare the "effects" of the situational variables (such as noise) on, say, performance. The same type of criterion might well be used in either case.

Basic Types of Criteria

There are, of course, many specific kinds of criteria that can be used in different circumstances in the general domain of industrial psychology. Five of the more important ones are discussed here.

Behavioral and performance criteria. These criteria reflect some aspect of overt behavior or performance, such as job performance, visual discrimination, reaction time, actual purchase of consumer products, or speed in automobile driving. In the optimum form, behavioral and performance criteria are based on some objective measures. Some types of ratings intended to reflect some aspect of behavior or performance are really subjective criteria (see below).

Subjective criteria. Subjective criteria deal with responses that reflect subjective reactions of people, such as their attitudes, opinions, judgments, and preferences. These usually are obtained by the use of interviews, questionnaires, and rating forms. Some examples include employee attitude surveys, ratings of employees by their supervisors, market surveys of consumers, and ratings of consumer products.

Status criteria. On occasions the "status" of individuals with respect to some factor is used as a criterion. This "status" may be some indication of group "membership," such as the occupation or position of individuals, his educational level, or even something as simple as ownership of color television. In other instances the "status" may consist of relevant recorded information about individuals, such as number of promotions received, duration of job tenure, or number of traffic citations.

Physiological criteria. Physiological criteria include such measures as heart rate, blood pressure, electrical resistance of the skin, and oxygen consumption. Such criteria typically are used in studying the effects of environmental variables, physical work load, work periods, methods of work, and so forth.

Accidents and injuries. These criteria are used where the purpose of the inquiry in question is concerned with matters of safety, such as in industry or in driving. Such criteria can be useful either in analyzing the relative safety of two or more circumstances (such as different designs of equipment) or in analyzing the personal variables that are related to accident or injury occurrence.

Job-Related Criteria

Because much of the research in industrial psychology deals with people in work situations, particular reference will be made to job-related criteria. Such criteria can be of any of the basic types mentioned above. We will review here a few of the more specific types of criteria that are used rather frequently.

Job performance criteria. Some of the types of criteria that deal directly or indirectly with job performance are listed below:

> Quantity of work (units produced, sales, piece-rate earnings, commissions, etc.)
> Quality of work (number of acceptable units, rejects, amount of scrap or waste, etc.)
> Job sample (performance on some part of a job, usually under "test" conditions)
> Learning criteria (time to achieve a given level of learning, learning cost, etc.)
> Supervisors' ratings (regular performance appraisals or special ratings)
> Peer ratings
> Promotions (including changes in job status)

Job-attendance criteria. At least three kinds of criteria can be lumped together under the heading of job-attendance criteria inasmuch as they all relate to some aspect of the tendency of employees to "attend" to their jobs. These are: (1) job tenure (how long people remain on their jobs), (2) absenteeism (usually based on the number of days an employee is absent from his job without good cause), and (3) tardiness.

Uses of job-related criteria. Of the various types of criteria used in personnel research it is probable that, for better or worse, supervisory ratings are used most frequently. For example, an analysis by Lent et al.[4] of 406

[4] Lent, R. H., Aurbach, H. H., & Levin, L. S. Predictors, criteria, and significant results. *Personnel Psychology,* 1971, **24,** 519–533.

studies published in *Personnel Psychology* indicates that 897 of 1506 criteria used in those studies were supervisors' evaluations.

Although here we are interested in job-related criteria particularly in the context of research, it should be noted that such measures (such as regular personnel appraisals, piece-rate earnings, production records, and absenteeism records) also may serve very practical administrative purpose.

Dynamic Nature of Criteria

We cannot end our discussion of the criteria of job performance without remarking on the existence of evidence that, at least in some circumstances, some criteria are "dynamic" in nature.[5] This means that the dimensions of job performance may change as a result of the experience of the individuals in question. Ghiselli and Haire[6] report, for example, that with a group of investment salesmen, performance was continuing to change (generally to improve) ten years after initial employment. During that period, average production in sales increased 650 percent and there was still no evidence of leveling off. In numerous studies it has been found that although most individuals generally show continuous improvement, they change somewhat in terms of their relative performance. In this connection it has been proposed that *rate* of change in performance possibly can serve as a criterion. This criterion generally was considered more appropriate for a group of taxicab drivers, for example, than was "productivity" during any given period of the first eighteen weeks of employment.[7]

The fact that job performance levels of individuals change over time implies is that the criterion measures obtained at one time will not necessarily be highly related to those obtained at some other time in the job career of the individuals in question. Therefore, criterion information obtained about employees early in their employment on a given job will not necessarily be indicative of later criterion information.

SELECTION OF CRITERIA

The selection and development of a criterion are critical phases of any research program. In this connection, three basic considerations need to be taken into account—*relevance, freedom from contamination,* and *reliability.*

[5] Ghiselli, E. E. Dimensional problems of criteria. *Journal of Applied Psychology,* 1956, **40**, 1–4; Ghiselli, E. E., & Haire, M. The validation of selection tests in the light of the dynamic character of criteria. *Personnel Psychology,* 1960, **13**, 225–231; Bass, B. M. Further evidence on the dynamic character of criteria. *Personnel Psychology,* 1962, **12**, 93–97.

[6] Ghiselli and Haire, *op. cit.*

[7] *Ibid.*

For illustrative purposes we will frame our discussion of these factors primarily in terms of criteria of job performance, although essentially the same considerations apply to the use of criteria in other contexts, such as consumer research or driving behavior.

Relevance of Criteria

The relevance of a criterion refers to the extent to which criterion measures of different individuals are meaningful in terms of the objectives for which such measures are derived. Every job exists for some purpose, or complex of purposes, whether formally stated or not. Relevance, then, relates to the adequacy of criterion measures as indices of the relative abilities of individuals in fulfilling such purposes. Because most jobs have various objectives (rather than one), there is an issue as to whether it is best to use a single overall criterion, or to use separate criteria (subcriteria) for the individual objectives. This question will be discussed later.

It has been postulated that there is, theoretically, an ultimate criterion that would serve as the basis for characterizing performance of individuals along a "true" scale.[8] Typically, this "ultimate" criterion has been viewed in the context of long-range overall performance, as, for example, "the total worth of a man to a company—in the final analysis," as suggested by Guion.[9] If there were some yardstick by which ultimate performance could be measured, it would be possible to use it to characterize the position along such a scale where each individual on any given job would fall. Although such a yardstick of the ultimate criterion is more theoretical than actual in nature, the more nearly any actual criterion approximates this theoretical ultimate standard, the more *relevant* it is.

In practical situations, it usually is necessary to select or develop a criterion that is in some respects shy of this goal. Such criteria are sometimes referred to as intermediate and immediate criteria, depending upon how close they come (even in point of time) to approximating the ultimate criterion.[10] To illustrate, let us take the case of individuals selected for apprentice training in some craft. The ultimate criterion of performance of a craftsman might be based on long-range considerations of the extent to which he fulfills the variety of work activities expected of craftsmen, including considerations of how well he performs each type of activity, how much work he accomplishes, how well he is able to plan and organize his work, how well he adapts to changing requirements of the work to be done, and how dependable he is. A criterion of such a nature would be hard to come

[8] Thorndike, R. L. *Personnel selection.* New York: John Wiley, 1949.

[9] Guion, R. M. Criterion measurement and personnel judgments. *Personnel Psychology,* 1961, **14**, 141–149.

[10] Thorndike, *op. cit.*

by, but an intermediate criterion might consist of ratings by craft supervisors of the performance of craftsmen. In turn, an immediate criterion might consist of grades in apprentice training courses.

Freedom from Contamination

As indicated earlier, the job performance of individuals is a function of both individual and situational variables. Where one is primarily concerned with criteria that reflect *individual* differences, any influence of differences in *situational* variables can serve to "contaminate" criterion measures for individuals. A couple of examples will illustrate the point. Let us suppose that we have two employees operating looms for weaving textiles, but that each has a different type of loom. The production records of such employees probably would *not* serve as an appropriate index of their *relative* abilities, for each individual's production is in part influenced by the productive capabilities of his own loom. Similarly, criterion contamination can occur in the case of salesmen assigned to sales territories that differ in sales potential. In using production indices as criteria, one has to be wary of the possibility that the production of individuals might have been differentially affected by factors that are not under the control of the individuals, such as variation in the quality of the material handled, the working conditions, or the conditions of machines and equipment used.

The ever-present possibility of many forms of criterion contamination should not cause us to throw up our hands in despair, for there are ways of minimizing if not eliminating their influence. One such approach is that of selecting those individuals for whom the contaminating variables are equal or nearly so. Another method consists of making statistical adjustments for the influence of the contaminating variables.

Reliability of the Criterion

The reliability of a criterion refers to its stability or consistency as an index of that which it measures. In the case of job performance, for example, reliability refers to the extent to which individuals tend to maintain a certain level of performance over time. Sometimes such a time-related measure of reliability is determined by comparing the criterion values for individuals for two periods of time, as illustrated in Figure 2.8, which shows the consistency (in other words, the reliability) of production records of 79 unit wirers for two five-week time periods. The correlation between these two sets of data is .87, which reflects a fairly high degree of stability. The figure shows along the base line the efficiency index of the wirers during the five even-numbered weeks of the ten-week period (i.e., weeks 2, 4, 6, 8, and 10), and on the vertical axis the index for the odd-numbered weeks (1, 3, 5, 7,

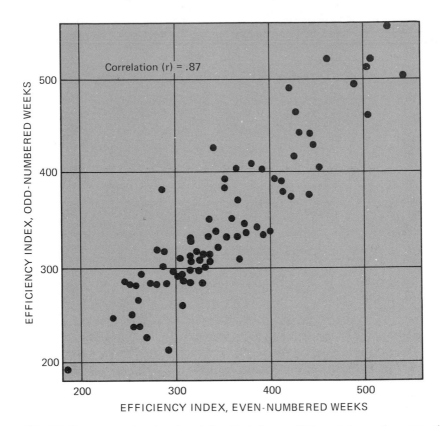

FIG. 2.8 Scattergram showing the relationship between efficiency indexes of a group of 79 unit wirers for two 5-week periods (five even-numbered weeks and five odd-numbered, weeks). (*Courtesy Tetronix, Inc., and Dr. Guyot Frazier.*)

and 9). Each point represents the two values for a given individual—i.e., the index for the even- and for the odd-numbered weeks. The similarity between these is quite apparent.

The reliability of ratings for a group of employees could be determined by correlating two sets of ratings made by a single rater at different times or by correlating two sets of ratings of the same employees made by two different raters. Similarly, one can determine the reliability of consumers' expressions of preference for various products, the heart rate of individuals, or the reaction time of people to given stimuli. Most commonly, reliability is expressed in terms of a statistical measure known as a *correlation coefficient*. Generally speaking, a reliability coefficient of .90 or higher would be considered exceptionally good, and those between .80 and .90 normally would be very acceptable.

Stability of job performance. In connection with the reliability of criteria of various aspects of job performance, we should raise the question as to the stability of such differences in actual practice. In other words, to what extent do people actually tend to maintain consistently their own "levels" of performance over time? A categorical response to this question is not in the cards. Although there are circumstances in which individuals tend to maintain over time an approximately stable level of performance, as illustrated in Figure 2.8, there are some job situations in which there is considerable variability in the performance of individuals. This was found to be the case, for example, in a series of studies of Rothe and by Rothe and Nye. In one such study, for example, Rothe and Nye[11] analyzed the output rates by week of employees operating machine tools. The correlations of output rates between weeks ranged from .48 to .54, indicating considerable variation in relative outputs of individuals from time to time.

Such instability of performance level can occur in part as a consequence of various situational contingencies in jobs that influence the performance of individuals at different times. But further, it has been suggested by Ronan[12] that there are individual differences in "performance stability" itself—in other words, that some people tend to remain on an even keel in terms of job performance whereas others tend generally to wobble around, sometimes performing well and at other times performing poorly. An analysis by Klemmer and Lockhead[13] lends some support to this contention. In analyzing about a billion responses by more than a thousand card punch and bank proof machine operators, Klemmer and Lockhead found that errors made by such operators varied from day to day to a much greater extent for some operators than for others.

In circumstances in which it is meaningful to be concerned about individual differences in job behavior (as in some research projects), one should indeed go out of his way to determine the pattern of stability (or instability) of performance of the individuals in question.

CRITERION DIMENSIONS

In many contexts in which criteria are to be used, there may be no single criterion that is manifestly the one and only one to use. Rather, two or more possible criteria might be relevant in some respects. In the case of human work, for example, most jobs have various facets that typically give rise to what one might call criterion dimensions.[14] Where this is the case, an

11 Rothe, H. F., & Nye, C. T. Output rates among machine operators: III. A non-incentive situation in two levels of business activity. *Journal of Applied Psychology*, 1961, **45**, 50–54.
12 Ronan, W. W. Personal communication to the authors, April 26, 1971.
13 Klemmer, E. J., & Lockhead, G. R. Productivity and errors in two keying tasks: A field study. *Journal of Applied Psychology*, 1962, **46**(6), 401–408.
14 Ghiselli, *op. cit.*

individual might do well in one aspect of a job (such as producing a large quantity of items) but less well on another aspect (such as the quality of the items produced).

Examples of Multiple Dimensions of Criteria

To illustrate the multidimensional nature of criteria, a couple of examples will be given. One example comes from a study by Seashore, Indik, and Georgopoulos[15] of 975 delivery men for whom several different criteria were available, including productivity (based on established time standards), effectiveness (ratings on overall quality of performance), accidents, absences, and errors (based on "nondeliveries" of packages). The correlations among these five criteria are given in Table 2.1. The generally low correlations indicate that these five aspects of job performance are relatively independent; the highest correlations (.28, .26, and .32) are among the variables of productivity, effectiveness, and errors. These and other results were interpreted by the investigators as contradicting the validity of "overall job performance" as a unidimensional construct, and as a refutation of the practice of combining job performance variables into a single measure having general validity.

TABLE 2.1 INTERCORRELATIONS AMONG FIVE CRITERION VARIABLES FOR 975 DELIVERY MEN

	Effectiveness	Accidents	Absences	Errors
Productivity	+.28	−.12	+.01	+.26
Effectiveness		+.02	+.08	+.32
Accidents			+.03	−.18
Absences				+.15
Errors				

Source: Adapted from S. E. Seashore, B. P. Indik, and B. S. Georgopoulos, "Relationship Among Criteria of Job Performance," *Journal of Applied Psychology,* **44** (1960), 195–202. The signs of certain correlations (+ or −) have been changed so that a + sign indicates a positive correlation between "desirable" values of the two variables, and a − sign indicates a negative correlation between the "desirable" values. Copyright 1960 by the American Psychological Association, and adapted with permission.

The second illustration comes from a study by Peres,[16] who developed a checklist of 303 statements of supervisory behavior such as "disciplines when necessary," "doesn't make promises he can't keep," and "keeps abreast of policy changes." Three hundred seventy-two supervisors used this checklist

[15] Seashore, S. E., Indik, B. P., & Georgopoulos, B. S. Relationships among criteria of job performance. *Journal of Applied Psychology,* 1960, **44**, 195–202.

[16] Peres, S. H. Performance dimensions of supervisory positions. *Personnel Psychology,* 1962, **15**, 405–410.

to describe the best and the worst supervisor they knew, indicating by means of a five-point scale the extent to which each statement applied to the individual being rated. A statistical analysis of data based on these ratings (a procedure called factor analysis) indicated that the 303 statements actually tended to form six relatively separate groupings, each of which could be considered as a relatively basic dimension of supervisory behavior. Thus, instead of there being 303 different facets of supervisory behavior, there were six primary dimensions.

Possible Treatment of Multidimensional Job Criteria

From these and other studies, it is evident that in many circumstances (such as in job situations) various criterion dimensions can be used (such as job performance criteria). When such criteria are highly intercorrelated, there is no particular problem involved in the selection of which criterion to use; in such a circumstance any given criterion, or an "overall" criterion, could be used for the purpose at hand inasmuch as the other criteria are highly related to it. The snag comes when the two or more criteria are not highly correlated. In such instances the investigator is faced with various alternatives, such as:

1. To select one of the criteria and use it;
2. To use each criterion independently;
3. To combine the various criterion dimensions into a single "composite" criterion, using some weighting scheme;
4. To develop an "overall" criterion, usually ratings (such as supervisors' ratings of overall job performance).

Since this question has generated quite a bit of controversy,[17] we should explore at least certain aspects of the issues involved in the use either of separate (independent) criterion dimensions or of some composite or overall criterion.

Arguments for multiple criteria. On the one hand, Guion[18] expresses the opinion that where various criteria are clearly independent, they should be used independently and should not be combined. (Where they are shown to be related, however, he suggests that there may be some point in combining them into a composite.) Dunnette[19] also argues for the use of criterion

---

[17] Dunnette, M. D. A note on *the* criterion. *Journal of Applied Psychology,* 1963, **47,** 251–254; Ghiselli, *op. cit.;* Guion, R. M. Criterion measurement and personnel judgment. *Personnel Psychology,* 1961, **14,** 141–149; Schmidt, F. L., & Kaplan, L. B. Composite vs. multiple criteria: A review and resolution of the controversy. *Personnel Psychology,* 1971, **24**(3), 419–434; and Seashore, Indik, & Georgopoulos, *op. cit.*

[18] Guion, *op. cit.*

[19] Dunnette, *op. cit.*

dimensions and suggests that we "cease searching for single or composite measures of job success and proceed to undertake research which accepts the world of success dimensionality as it really exists." On the basis of a study of criteria of performance of skilled tradesmen, Ronan[20] takes the position that a criterion of overall job performance, or any other single criterion, is of limited usefulness in evaluating the performance of such personnel.

The advocates of multiple job criteria view such criteria as what Schmidt and Kaplan[21] call "*behavioral* constructs," for they reflect essentially different facets of job behavior. They point out that the personal characteristics of individuals who perform well on one criterion may be very different from the characteristics of those who perform well on another criterion; for this reason the use of separate criteria contributes to the understanding and to the prediction of the different aspects of job performance. In turn, they argue that the use of a single composite or overall criterion muddies the waters inasmuch as any given value on a composite or overall criterion scale can be brought about by different *combinations* of performance. Thus, two or more individuals might have equal criterion values on a composite or overall criterion, but they could have those same values for different reasons. For example, one person could be high on a quantity criterion dimension and low on a quality criterion dimension, a second person could have the reverse pattern, and a third person might be intermediate on both. Continuing with this line of argument, one could not reasonably expect to identify a common set of personal factors that would aid in identifying (predicting) individuals who might have the same composite criterion level but who achieve it by highly varied job behavior patterns. Rather, one might reasonably expect to identify one combination of factors associated with one subcriterion (say, quantity), and another combination associated with another subcriterion (say, quality).

Arguments for composite or overall criteria. The basic contention of the advocates of a composite or overall criterion of job performance is that such a criterion should provide a measure of the individual's overall "success" or "value-to-the-organization."[22] Insofar as this is the case, such a criterion is more of an *economic* construct than a behavioral construct. In this connection, a significant concept was proposed by Brogden and Taylor.[23] Where one is interested in criteria for individuals within an organization, they suggest that the criterion should measure the contribution of the individual to the overall efficiency of the organization. Toward this end, they propose the

[20] Ronan, W. W. A factor analysis of eleven job performance measures. *Personnel Psychology,* 1963, **16**, 255–267.

[21] Schmidt and Kaplan, *op. cit.*

[22] Schmidt and Kaplan, *op. cit.*

[23] Brogden, H. E., & Taylor, E. K. The dollar criterion—Applying the cost accounting concept to criterion construction. *Personnel Psychology,* 1950, **3**, 133–154.

construction of criterion measures in cost-accounting terms—the "dollar criterion." This proposal is predicated on the proposition that (where possible) the dollar provides a common denominator or a common metric for combining quite different subcriterion measures. To illustrate the concept, they refer to a situation mentioned by Otis[24] in which it was found that in a key-punching operation thirteen cards could be key-punched in the same time required to correct one error. Therefore, one could say that the personnel costs of correcting one error are the same as for punching thirteen cards. Thus, in the case of those jobs for which performance on different subcriteria can be expressed in terms of dollar costs, it would be possible to add the dollar cost values of subcriteria together for each individual, thus providing an economic index of the relative value of different individuals.

Although very few composite or overall criteria actually are expressed in "dollar" terms, most criteria of a composite or overall nature probably do have implications in terms of some concept of total worth or contribution to the organization. The conventional "supervisory rating" probably reflects some such frame of reference.

Discussion. Criteria of job behavior may be used for research purposes or as the basis for making personnel decisions such as selection, placement, or promotion. Certainly some research objectives can be entirely fulfilled by the use of separate criterion dimensions (such as the psychological understanding of the relationship between possible predictors or independent variables and specific dimensions). However, most practical purposes (such as personnel decisions) require the combining of various criterion dimensions into a single composite index of overall worth. This "combining" could be performed in different ways, depending on whether one initially uses multiple criterion dimensions or a single composite or overall criterion.

Let us consider the initial use of multiple criterion dimensions, such as in a validation study directed toward the establishment of a set of personnel specifications for a given job. Although we might be able to determine the personal characteristics that contribute to performance on each criterion dimension, if we want to be able to apply the results of such a study we would have to weight the different dimensions and add these weighted values together to arrive at some relative index of "overall" potentialities of each candidate. Such a weighting might be done subjectively or on other bases (to be discussed later), but no matter how it is done, one cannot avoid some consolidation of criterion dimensions in such a situation.

In the initial use of an overall criterion such as supervisory ratings, the combining (and the associated weighting) of different dimensions of performance usually is done "intuitively" by the rater as he rates the various

[24] Otis, J. (Chapter V, The criterion, in W. H. Stead and C. L. Shartle (Eds.), *Occupational counseling techniques.* New York: American Book Company, 1940.

individuals. Often the rater may not be aware that he is in fact weighing the different aspects of performance, thus creating a composite criterion, which is a consolidation of several separate criterion dimensions that of necessity have to be given some individual weights.

The resolution to the dilemma of using multiple versus single criteria in part is implied by the objectives at hand. To reiterate a point made above, psychological understanding of predictor-criterion relationships is best achieved by the use of individual criterion dimensions, as pointed out by Schmidt and Kaplan.[25] For the practical goals of prediction (as in making personnel decisions about individuals), Schmidt and Kaplan suggest that the ideal approach involves weighting the several criterion dimensions and adding the weighted values together to derive a composite value representing the "economic" or practical construct of overall worth. But in the same breath they urge the simultaneous analysis of predictors and criterion dimensions in order to achieve understanding of these relationships. This approach is one that offers a fairly reasonable resolution to this otherwise controversial issue. With respect to their proposal, it should be pointed out that the fact that equal composite criterion values can arise from various combinations of the separate dimensions does not in fact constrain the identification of relevant predictors of personal characteristics. The prediction of such a composite criterion can be dealt with statistically.[26]

Weighting of Multiple Criteria

When two or more criterion dimensions are to be consolidated into a single composite criterion, some weighting of the separate dimensions or subcriteria is necessary. The weighting system should be such that the resulting composite criterion values will represent relatively valid positions along the scale of overall worth. The weighting can be done either on the basis of judgment by knowledgeable persons or on the basis of some statistical procedure. Probably the most valid basis is a statistical procedure (specifically, regression analysis) that results in the statistical determination of optimum weights as related to some "overall" criterion. This procedure requires that a sample of individuals be "ordered" along a predetermined overall criterion scale, that values on the various specific subcriteria or criterion dimensions be derived for each individual, and that a statistical operation be performed to determine the appropriate weights for each of the subcriteria.

Criteria in Evaluating Situational Variables

So far, our discussion of the use of separate criterion dimensions versus composite or overall criteria has been in the framework of understanding and

[25] Schmidt and Kaplan, *op. cit.*
[26] Brogden and Taylor, *op. cit.*

predicting the relationship between individual characteristics and the criteria. When using criteria as the basis for evaluating situational variables (such as working conditions or equipment design), somewhat the same considerations are pertinent. Here again, however, one can make a strong case for using all relevant criteria (as well as composite or overall criteria) in order to gain as much knowledge as possible about the interrelationships among the variables in question. It is sometimes the case, however, that certain independent criteria are incompatible with each other. For example, in the design of a machine, it might be that a design that is conducive to a high rate of productivity on the part of the employees might also be conducive to high incidence of accidents. In such cases some tradeoff must be made—that is, some degree of one advantage must be given up for the other. In such a case, one would try to develop a design that would be most nearly optimum in terms of the two or more criteria in question. Such an optimum, of course, involves a weighting of the relative importance of the separate criteria in terms of the overall objectives.

DISCUSSION

In large part, research in the field of industrial psychology is directed toward exploring—and understanding—the "sources" of variation in human behavior in the processes of the production, distribution, and utilization of the goods and services of the economy. These possible "sources" include both individual variables and situational variables. Research directed toward such ends, then, critically depends upon the development and use of appropriate criteria of such behavior.

chapter three

Jobs and
Their Requirements

Many facets of industrial psychology have their roots in the jobs people perform in earning their daily bread. Before we take up some of these facets in more detail, let us reflect about the more general aspects of what are essentially two sides of the same coin—namely, the job and the job incumbent. In this chapter we shall deal particularly with jobs and their requirements.

TERMINOLOGY

Although terminology dealing with jobs is fairly loosely used in practice, it may be in order here to set forth certain definitions of terms as defined by Shartle.[1]

[1] Shartle, C. L. *Occupational information.* (3rd ed.) Englewood Cliffs, N.J.: Prentice-Hall, Inc., 1959.

Position. A position is a group of tasks performed by one person. There are as many positions as there are workers in the organization.

Job. A job is a group of similar positions in a single plant, business establishment, educational institution, or other organization. There may be one or many persons employed in the same job.

Occupation. An occupation is a group of similar jobs found in several establishments.

Career. A career covers a sequence of positions, jobs, or occupations that one person engages in during his working life.

JOB DETERMINANTS

As we look at the job side of the coin, we might ask ourselves two questions: (1) How do jobs come into being? (2) What factors cause jobs to be what they are (in terms of content or other characteristics)? The basic answer to the first question relates to the objectives of the organization; presumably any job is created in order to fulfill certain functions that are considered necessary to achieve the objectives of the organization.

Although a job derives its reason for being and its primary characteristics from the role it is to play in the organizational goals, there seem to be two basic types of factors that determine the nature of individual jobs. In the first place, there are those factors that, in effect, are fixed as far as the incumbent is concerned, these being "givens" to him. These include one or more of the following factors: the design of any physical equipment used; the physical arrangement; specified procedures, methods, and job standards; division of labor; traditional practices; organizational structure and policy; legal requirements; and work environment. At least some of these factors, however, may be within the control of the organization and so need not remain unchanged forever.

In the second place, both experience and experimental evidence indicate that, in *some* positions, the incumbent himself can have some influence—moderate or major—on the activities that make up the position and on the way in which they are performed. Thus, some jobs are more "structured" than others in the degree of latitude for variation they permit the incumbent.

In sum, various factors can be considered as "determinants" of the work activities of jobs. The combination of the actual work activities that comprise a job, the physical and social environment, and perhaps other job-related factors collectively predetermine the nature of "job requirements"—that is, the demands that are imposed upon the incumbent. These requirements, of course, have implications both for the personal characteristics that presumably contribute to successful job performance and for the training that should be provided. For example, the use of color-coded electrical wires in a job implies that the worker needs to have adequate color discrimination ability, and needs to be taught the coding system.

USES OF JOB INFORMATION

In the many phases of operating an organization there is no substitute for having relevant information available to contribute to the processes of decision making. Thus it is inevitable that, in the various circumstances in which some decisions are to be made that have to do with jobs on the one hand, and with applicants or workers on the other, relevant information about the jobs and individuals in question usually can increase the odds of making good decisions. Although much information about jobs resides in the memories of people, documented information usually can be obtained through some form of job analysis. Job analysis can be considered as embracing the collection and analysis of any type of job-related information, by any method, for any purpose. Perhaps it can be defined more generally as the study of human work. The information obtained by job analysis can serve a variety of purposes, including certain personnel decision-making purposes, such as those shown in Figure 3.1.

USES OF JOB ANALYSIS			
Personnel Administration	Work and Equipment Design	Administrative Control	Other Uses
Personnel recruitment, selection, and placement Training and personnel development Performance measurement and rating Wage and salary administration Labor relations	Engineering design Methods design Job design	Organizational planning Manpower planning and control	Planning educational curricula Vocational counseling Job classification systems

FIG. 3.1 Some of the uses of information obtained through job analysis.

JOB ANALYSIS

McCormick[2] has proposed that we can study human work from at least four different angles, depending upon (1) the type(s) of information to be obtained; (2) the form in which the information is obtained and/or presented (referring particularly to the extent to which it is qualitative versus quantitative); (3) the method of analysis; and (4) the agent (usually the individual who makes the analysis, such as a job analyst, but in isolated instances a device such as a camera).

Types of Job Analysis Information

Among the types of information sometimes obtained by job analysis are the following: job-oriented work activities (descriptions of work in "job" terms, such as galvanizing, weaving, cleaning); worker-oriented work activities (human behaviors, such as sensing, decision making, performing physical actions, communicating); machines, tools, work aids, etc.; materials processed; knowledge dealt with; working conditions; and personnel requirements.

Form of Job Analysis Information

The form of job analysis information refers essentially to the distinction between qualitative and quantitative features. Qualitative information is typically descriptive (such as narrative descriptions of work or general statements about working conditions, social context, personnel requirements, and so forth), whereas quantitative information is typically characterized by the use of "units" of job information expressed in numerical terms (such as ratings of job characteristics, time required, or oxygen consumption).

Methods of Collecting Job Information

Job information can be obtained by various methods such as: observation of a worker by a job analyst; interview of a worker by a job analyst; technical conferences employing several "experts" in the job; structured questionnaires consisting of lists of job activities and other aspects of jobs to be used in checking or rating each item as it applies to a job; work diaries that workers use in recording what they do during a work day; records (such as maintenance records); mechanical recordings (such as of heart rate); films; and analysis of blueprints of equipment to be used for inferring what workers will have to do in operating the equipment.

2 McCormick, E. J. Job analysis: An overview. *Indian Journal of Industrial Relations,* 1970, **6**(1), 5–14.

Agent Used in Collecting Job Information

Typically, job analysts are the "agents" used in the collection of job information, but sometimes a supervisor or the incumbent himself may serve this function, and in special circumstances some device, such as a camera or automatic recording mechanism, may serve to "collect" job-related data.

Discussion of Job Analysis Procedures

Job analysis has been characterized as "a sort of handmaiden serving in various ways a variety of needs and all the while floundering in a morass of semantic confusion."[3] This castigation, which applies primarily to conventional essay types of job descriptions, is probably fairly well deserved. We should hasten to point out, however, that well-written job descriptions can, and do, serve certain useful purposes, especially in providing personnel people, applicants, and counselees with an organized overview of individual jobs or positions.

However, if one is to deal with job-related information more systematically, a more quantitative approach must be followed. This means that one must identify, and where pertinent measure, relevant aspects or characteristics of jobs. Thus, we have to think in terms of "units" of work (or of other job features) that can be reliably identified, measured, or rated. We could, for example, measure the physiological cost of operating a punch press or the time spent by an automobile mechanic in removing a carburetor. We also could ask job incumbents or their supervisors to give estimates of the time spent or of the importance of various job activities, such as preparing balance sheets, performing laboratory blood tests, or telephoning prospective customers; although such estimates would be somewhat subjective, the use of rating scales in giving such estimates would make it possible to "quantify" the job information derived from them.

STRUCTURED JOB ANALYSIS
QUESTIONNAIRES

For at least certain purposes the structured job analysis questionaire has been demonstrated to be the most useful instrument for shifting job analysis processes in the direction of quantification. Such questionnaires consist of a listing of job activities or other characteristics (such as working conditions), with provision either for *checking* an item if it applies to a given job, or for *rating* an item, using an appropriate rating scale, in terms of its relevance to the job. The structured questionnaire approach lends itself to

[3] Kershner, A. M. *A report on job analysis.* Washington, D. C.: Office of Naval Research, 1955.

the collection of various types of job-related information. Certain examples will be discussed briefly.

Task Inventories

Task inventories (also referred to as job inventories) typically consist of lists of the tasks that are pertinent to some occupational area. In completing an inventory for any given position within the occupational area, each task is either checked or rated as it applies to the position. The rating may be in terms of any of several possible rating factors, such as the *frequency* with which a task is performed, the *time* spent on the task, its judged *importance* or *significance,* its judged *difficulty,* the degree of *delegation* to others, or the estimated *time to learn.*

Task inventories have been used extensively by the U.S. Air Force, as described by Morsh.[4] The Air Force method typically involves having the

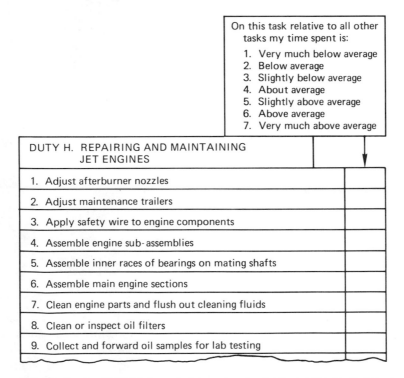

On this task relative to all other tasks my time spent is:
1. Very much below average
2. Below average
3. Slightly below average
4. About average
5. Slightly above average
6. Above average
7. Very much above average

DUTY H. REPAIRING AND MAINTAINING JET ENGINES

1. Adjust afterburner nozzles
2. Adjust maintenance trailers
3. Apply safety wire to engine components
4. Assemble engine sub-assemblies
5. Assemble inner races of bearings on mating shafts
6. Assemble main engine sections
7. Clean engine parts and flush out cleaning fluids
8. Clean or inspect oil filters
9. Collect and forward oil samples for lab testing

FIG. 3.2 Portion of USAF airman task inventory for Jet Engine Mechanic. Basic inventory developed for the USAF by Lifson, Wilson, Ferguson and Winick, Dallas, Texas, and modified and used by the Occupational Research Center, Purdue University in connection with Contract No. AF 41(609)-3162; 30 June 1967.

[4] Morsh, J. E. Job analysis in the United States Air Force. *Personnel Psychology,* 1962, **37,** 7–17.

inventories completed by the incumbents themselves, either airmen or officers. A part of one inventory is shown in Figure 3.2 to illustrate the nature of the tasks, a typical format, and one type of rating scale. Descriptions of jobs based on task inventories can be dealt with statistically—for example, by summarizing the number of people in the occupation who perform each task—or by grouping positions together that involve the same basic combinations of tasks—for example, grouping hospital attendants into groups that are largely involved in patient care tasks and groups that are largely involved in housekeeping tasks.

Position Analysis Questionnaire (PAQ)

A task inventory contains essentially "job-oriented" tasks, and thus its use is restricted to positions that fall within the occupational area for which it was developed. In contrast, a questionnaire that consists more of "worker-oriented" job elements can be used more broadly, inasmuch as it tends to deal with more generalized worker behaviors. One such questionnaire is the Position Analysis Questionnaire (PAQ), developed by McCormick, Jeanneret, and Mecham.[5] The PAQ consists of 194 job elements that fall into the following divisions:

Division	No. of Job Elements
1. Information input (Where and how does the worker get the information he uses in his job?)	35
2. Mental processes (What reasoning, decision making, planning, etc., are involved in the job?)	14
3. Work output (What physical activities does the worker perform and what tools or devices does he use?)	49
4. Relationships with other persons (What relationships with other people are required in the job?)	36
5. Job context (In what physical and social contexts is the work performed?)	19
6. Other job characteristics	41

The first three divisions of the PAQ parallel a conventional model of behavior in which behavior is viewed as consisting of a stimulus (S) acting upon an organism (O) to bring about a response (R). Human work is one manifestation of this model, but might be expressed in different terms, as follows:

[5] The Position Analysis Questionnaire (PAQ) (Form B) is available from the University Bookstore, West Lafayette, Indiana 47906.

Information input $\longrightarrow$ Information processing $\longrightarrow$ Action or response
and decision

The individual job elements within each of the six classes provide either for checking the element if it applies or for rating it on an appropriate rating scale (such as importance, time, or difficulty). Although some of the job elements are not, strictly speaking, behavioral items, it is nonetheless believed that these elements have strong implications in terms of human behaviors. In practice the PAQ can be used in analyzing jobs by job analysts, by supervisors, and in some instances by the incumbents themselves. (Some applications of data based on the PAQ will be discussed later.)

JOB DIMENSIONS

Even though we can describe a job in terms of the dozens or hundreds of tasks or job elements contained in a structured questionnaire, such an ensemble of bits and pieces of job information can be rather uninformative. Therefore it would be handy if we could somehow boil down and consolidate such a welter of information into several more basic job features. Fortunately, in the world of work certain job activities or other characteristics in fact do tend to go together or to coexist in jobs. In a statistical sense they are correlated, which means that certain statistical procedures, such as factor and cluster analysis, can be used to identify the combinations that they form. Such combinations, or groups, or clusters, or bundles of interrelated job elements can be thought of as *job dimensions*. What is more, by subsequent statistical manipulations we can, for any given job, add together (with appropriate statistical weights) the data on the individual job elements that characterize each job dimension in such a manner that we have, for that job, a job dimension score for each of the several dimensions. Thus, we now have a more comprehensible description of each job in terms of a more basic profile—namely, a set of job dimension scores.

One example of the process of identifying job dimensions involves the use of the Position Analysis Questionnaire described above. As one phase of a study reported by McCormick, Jeanneret, and Mecham,[6] 536 jobs of varied types were analyzed with the PAQ, which were then subjected to a factor analysis (technically a principal components analysis). This analysis resulted in the identification of five overall dimensions as follows:

1. Having decision making/communication/social responsibilities. (This dimension reflects activities involving considerable amounts of communication and

---

[6] McCormick, E. J., Jeanneret, P. R., & Mecham, R. C. A study of job characteristics and job dimensions as based on the Position Analysis Questionnaire (PAQ). *Journal of Applied Psychology,* 1972, 56(4), 347–368.

interaction with people, as well as responsibilities associated with decision-making and planning functions, such as might be the case with a general foreman).

2. Performing skilled activities. (This dimension is characterized by activities of a skilled nature in which technical devices or tools tend to be used, and in which there is an emphasis on precision, recognizing differences, and manual control, such as in the case of tool and die makers.)

3. Being physically active/related environmental conditions. (This dimension is characterized by activities involving considerable movement of the entire body or major parts of it, along with such environments as those of factories, shops, etc.)

4. Operating vehicles/equipment. (This dimension is characterized by some aspect of the operation or use of vehicles or equipment, typically involving sensory and perceptual processes and physical functions.)

5. Processing information. (This dimension is characterized by a wide range of information-processing activities such as in the case of budget officers or editors, in some instances accompanied by the use of machines such as office machines.)

Similar analyses of the job elements of each of the six divisions of the PAQ resulted in twenty-seven more specific job dimensions.

Although in some instances the nature of job dimensions identified by statistical analyses may seem simply to confirm "common sense" impressions of the dominant features of jobs, a couple of points should be made. First, because "common sense" is not necessarily valid, statistical confirmation is certainly comforting. And second (and more important), by using statistically identified job dimensions it is possible to convert job information into quantitative terms, such as job dimension scores. Such quantification not only facilitates the evaluation and interpretation of job information, but also makes it possible to engage in further statistical manipulations and analyses, some of which will be illustrated later on.

JOB REQUIREMENTS

If you are sawing a board on a power saw, you have to have the visual acuity to see the saw and the board as well as the hand steadiness to control the movement of the board. From such an example we can see a rather direct relationship between the job activity on the one hand and the job requirements on the other. Job requirements (sometimes called worker requirements) in effect are the characteristics that the worker should have in order to perform the job in question.

Although this example tends to make the question of job requirements seem relatively simple, we should be aware that there is some fuzziness on both sides of the relationship. For example, we might raise a question about how straight and smooth the cut of the board is (as related to any desired standard), or about the time actually taken. On the other hand, we might ask how *much* visual acuity and hand steadiness are "required" for, say, fine cabinet work as opposed to rough carpentry. If we consider the jobs of medical technician, computer programmer, or design engineer, we can see that the fuzziness on both sides can become quite marked.

In a sense, then, job requirements are not absolute and inviolate; rather, they "depend." They depend, for example, upon value judgments about acceptable standards of performance and the extent to which certain values can be sacrificed for others. Granting this, however, the realities of personnel administration processes make it necessary to have some sort of guidelines or standards for use in the placement of individuals on specific jobs. These standards are referred to by different terms, including *personnel specifications* or *job specifications*. Frequently these standards are set forth in formal, written form, to be used in personnel placement operations. Sometimes they exist partly or entirely in the minds of those responsible for such operations.

The Nature of Personnel Specifications

Whether formalized or not, personnel specifications tend to fall into two classes.

Specifications for trained personnel. In the first place, if trained or experienced individuals are sought for placement, the focus of the specifications will be primarily on the nature, length, and quality of any relevant training, education, or experience required for the job. Defining such specifications is essentially the result of a logical process coupled with experience in personnel selection and tempered by value considerations, including, in some cases, compromises that may be indicated by the practical realities of the labor market.

Specifications for untrained personnel. In the second place, if untrained individuals are being sought for the job (usually for training on the job), the focus will be primarily on those qualities which are presumed to reflect the potentialities of individuals for the job. Such qualities might include various specific aptitudes, sensory skills, physical characteristics, personality, and interests, as illustrated in Figure 2.2 (in Chapter 2). In such instances the personnel specifications typically are a step removed from the more basic requirements. For example, the physical activities of a job might require the handling of heavy loads for extended periods of time. It is probable, however, that the personnel specifications relating to this activity would be expressed in terms from which one could *infer* the ability to do this work, such as height and weight, a minimum score on some physical strength test, or previous work experience that involved heavy physical activity, albeit of a different sort. In like manner, specifications expressed in terms of test scores, vision tests, age, general education, and so forth are not statements of "intrinsic" job requirement; rather, they *imply* the potentialities to perform (or to learn to perform) the job activity in question.

Methods of Establishing Personnel Specifications

As suggested above, it is usually not very difficult to determine the personnel specifications for placing already trained individuals on a job. (After all, if you need a pretzel twister and an experienced pretzel twister walks into your employment office, your problem is probably solved.) The stickier problem is that of determining what it takes for individuals to be able to perform effectively on a job after training. Thus, we need to specify qualities that imply *potentialities* for such performance. This brings us to the concept of *validity*. In this context a specification would be valid (i.e., it would have validity) to the extent that those individuals who meet that· specification have a significantly better chance of· performing effectively than those who do not. Referring back to an example above, if individuals who *meet* some height and weight minimum specifications are generally better in performing the physical activities of the job than those who *do not meet* those standards, it could be said that these specifications are valid.

The objective in setting up personnel specifications, then, is to state those personnel characteristics that are valid for the purpose of selecting individuals for the job in question. Actually, the personnel selection and placement process essentially involves the making of predictions of job success on the basis of information about the personal characteristics of candidates. Later chapters will deal more extensively with the prediction of job success, with some of the specific techniques of establishing personnel specifications, and with some of the methods for identifying and quantifying relevant information about individuals in order to determine whether they do or do not meet the stated specifications. At this juncture, however, it would be in order to discuss briefly the relative validity of the basic methods for establishing personnel specifications. In general terms, personnel specifications are established on the basis either of judgments or of statistical analysis.

Personnel Specifications Set by Judgment

The specifications for some jobs are determined on the basis of the judgments of people, such as those of employment-office personnel, job analysts, and supervisors. These specifications may or may not be formally stated in writing. Needless to say, the validity of such judgments can vary a great deal from situation to situation, depending upon the individual making the judgment, the method used in making it, and the specific type of human characteristic in question. In this context, Barrett[7] differentiates between what he calls the "patent medicine" approach to personnel selection and the "man-position matching" approach. To the extent that personnel specifications are virtually pulled out of the hat or based on off-the-cuff guesses, they reflect the patent medicine approach. Such guesswork does not necessarily mean that the "judgments" are invalid, but one simply does not know whether they are valid or not. At the least, this approach raises questions about the validity of any resulting specifications, and also can bring in the matter of professional ethics.

However, judgments regarding personnel specifications need not be of a willy-nilly nature; they can be rooted in knowledge and understanding of the job activities. In effect, as Trattner, Fine, and Kubis[8] have pointed out, judgments of this latter sort are inferences from such knowledge as one has about the human characteristics required for effective performance. Establishing personnel specifications in this manner implies the use of what Barrett[9] refers to as the man-machine matching approach. As he points out, however, this approach receives mixed blessings from the psychological fraternity, in part because there are so many variations on this theme, and in part because of the varied backgrounds of the practitioners of this art. In the hands of a pro who is well fortified with information about a given job, however, the method frequently generates a set of personnel specifications in which one can place reasonable confidence.

Methods of obtaining judgments. Various procedures have been used for obtaining judgments of the specifications of jobs, ranging from completely unsystematic schemes to those that involve standardized systematic procedures. One such procedure is used by the United States Training and Employment Service for setting forth the worker trait requirements of jobs as given in the Dictionary of Occupational Titles.[10] For the various jobs in the Dictionary, ratings are made by job analysts on each of the following worker traits: G (Intelligence); V (Verbal); N (Numerical); S (Spatial); P (Form perception); Q (Clerical perception); K (Motor coordination); F (Finger dexterity); M (Manual dexterity); E (Eye-hand-foot coordination); and C (Color discrimination). The ratings are made on the basis of a rating scale which expresses the amount of each trait possessed by various segments of the working population, as follows:

7 Barrett, R. S. Guide to using personnel tests. *Harvard Business Review,* September-October 1963, **41**(45), 138–146.

8 Trattner, M. H., Fine, S. A., & Kubis, J. F. A comparison of worker requirement ratings made by reading job descriptions and by direct job observation. *Personnel Psychology,* 1955, **8**, 183–194.

9 Barrett, *op. cit.*

10 United States Training and Employment Service. *Dictionary of occupational titles.* (3rd ed.) Washington, D.C.: Superintendent of Documents, Government Printing Office, 1965.

1. The top 10 percent of the population.
2. The highest third exclusive of the top 10 percent of the population.
3. The middle third of the population.
4. The lowest third exclusive of the bottom 10 percent of the population.
5. The lowest 10 percent of the population.

Reliability of judgments. Some indication of the reliability of ratings of jobs in terms of aptitudes comes from a study by Trattner, Fine, and Kubis[11] in which they had ten jobs rated on ten different aptitudes by two groups of job analysts. One group of eight analysts rated the ten jobs on the basis of their job descriptions, and the other group rated corresponding jobs by direct observation. In each instance the analysts estimated the degree of the aptitude required by the job. The reliability coefficients of the ratings (as based on all eight raters) were very respectable, especially for the "mental" aptitudes (intelligence, verbal, and numerical) and the "perceptual" aptitudes (spatial, form perception, and clerical perception), the coefficients ranging from .87 to .96. In the case of the "physical" aptitudes (eye-hand coordination, motor coordination, finger dexterity, and manual dexterity), the reliability coefficients were generally lower ranging from .08 to .87 (with most of them from .57 to .87).

In turn, Marquardt and McCormick,[12] present data on the "attribute ratings" by psychologists of the job elements of the PAQ. Ratings were obtained for seventy-six attributes, there being anywhere from eight to eighteen raters per attribute. The median rating was .90, with only ten being below .80.

Thus, we see that the reliability of judgments about job requirements made by trained raters is reasonably high, although some attributes can be rated more reliably than others. However, inter-rater reliability, by itself, is not necessarily an indication of the validity of such judgments.

Validity of judgments. Even though personnel specifications have been established on the basis of judgments in virtually millions of situations, there is actually little quantitative evidence available regarding the validity of such judgments. Some data relating to the validity of such judgments comes from the study by Trattner, Fine, and Kubis.[13] They had available test data for about sixty workers on each of the ten jobs; the data included a test score for each person on a test of each of the ten aptitudes. For those workers on each job the mean test score was computed for each of the ten aptitude tests. In turn, the mean aptitude rating was computed for each aptitude from the

---

[11] Trattner, Fine, & Kubis, *op. cit.*

[12] Marquardt, L. D., & McCormick, E. J. Attribute ratings and profiles of the job elements of the Position Analysis Questionnaire (PAQ). Department of Psychological Sciences, Purdue University, June 1972. ONR Contract NR 151–231.

[13] Trattner, Fine, & Kubis, *op. cit.*

ratings given by the eight analysts in each of the two groups. Through a procedure that need not be described here, correlations were computed for the two "groups" of aptitudes, as follows:

	Based on Job Description	Based on Observation
Mental and perceptual aptitudes	.60	.71
Physical aptitudes	.01	.27

The results of this rather modest study need to be accepted with some caution, but they tend to indicate that judgments about the mental and perceptual aptitude requirements of jobs may be better (i.e., more valid) than judgments about physical aptitudes. This same indication can be found in the results of a study by Frank[14] in which vocational counselors were asked to judge the minimum aptitude requirements for twenty-five occupations in terms of nine of the same ten aptitudes, following a somewhat parallel type of analysis.

Personnel Specifications Set by Statistical Analysis

The second basic method for establishing personnel specifications involves the use of statistical analysis. Basically, such analysis is directed toward the determination of the relationship between some indication of differences in some human characteristic (usually called a *predictor*) and some indication of job effectiveness (usually called a *criterion*). This is an oversimplification, as we shall see later, but for the moment let us look at this process in this oversimplified manner. (Let us also keep this reservation in mind in connection with later illustrations.) The predictors used can be indications of individual differences of virtually any human characteristic or attribute that might be related to job effectiveness. In practice such indications include biographical data (age, marital status, education, work experience, etc.), test scores, ratings (such as by interviewers), and other types of data. The indications of job effectiveness can consist of any relevant criterion, such as those discussed in Chapter 2. The methods for analyzing the data on the interrelationships between the predictor and the criterion will be elaborated later; they can range from very simple summarization and presentation of data to very sophisticated statistical analyses.

Such an analysis typically is carried out for a sample of people on a

14 Frank, Ellen J. A study of the reliability and validity of counselors' judgment of occupational aptitude requirements. Unpublished M.S. Thesis, Purdue University, January 1972.

particular job in order to determine what predictors are significantly related to the criterion in that sample. In turn, such predictors are then used, in the case of candidates for the job, as the basis for predicting the criterion values for the candidates.

Example of statistical analysis. One fairly straightforward example of a statistical approach to the establishment of personnel specifications was reported by Fleishman and Berniger.[15] They used a sample of 120 women office employees who had been employed over a two-year period. This sample was divided into a long-tenure group who stayed on the job for two years or longer and a short-tenure group who stayed less than two years. A comparison was then made between these two groups for each of certain items of personal data; some of these comparisons are given in Table 3.1. The magnitude of the differences in the percentages of long-tenure versus short-tenure personnel for individual items of data served as the basis for deriving a weighting system, with the weights ranging from $+3$ to -3. Note that age did differentiate, but that previous salary did not. The "corrected" weights shown were derived by the authors of this text in order to illustrate how negative values can be avoided. Specifically, we have added a constant of 3 to each category, and have shown the weight that results. Although this procedure increases the ultimate numerical values of all weighted scores (by 30), it has no effect on the form of the distribution of scores.

The investigators then took another sample of 100 cases hired during the same period. This sample served as a so-called "holdout" sample for "cross-validation" purposes. Each individual in the second sample was scored using the weighted scoring scheme given. This holdout group was also divided into a "short-tenure" and a "long-tenure" group, and the weighted scores were then related to tenure, as shown in Figure 3.3. This shows for both the short-tenure group and the long-tenure group the percentage who had weighted scores below 34 (based on the "corrected" scoring procedure). It can be seen that the scores tend to differentiate reasonably well between the two tenure groups. Thus, this combination of "personnel specifications" could be ex-

PERCENT WITH SCORE
OF 34 AND ABOVE

Short Tenure   22%

Long Tenure   68%

FIG. 3.3 Relationship between weighted scores based on several items of personal data and tenure of a sample of female office employees. One of the items that was scored was age, the "scores" for age being shown in Table 3.1 (*Adapted from Fleishman and Berniger, op. cit.*)

[15] Fleishman, E. A., & Berniger, J. One way to reduce turnover. *Personnel,* May-June 1960, 37(3), 63–69.

TABLE 3.1 EXAMPLE OF ANALYSIS OF TWO ITEMS OF PERSONAL DATA OF FEMALE CLERICAL EMPLOYEES AS RELATED TO JOB TENURE

| | Criterion Groups* | | Weight Assigned to Category | |
	Short Tenure Percent	Long Tenure Percent	"Original"	"Corrected"
Age				
Under 20	35	8	−3	0
21–25	38	32	−1	2
26–30	8	2	−1	2
31–35	7	10	0	3
35+	11	48	+3	6
Previous salary				
Under $2,000	31	30	0	0
$2,000–$3,000	41	38	0	0
$3,000–$4,000	13	12	0	0
Over $4,000	4	4	0	0

Source: Fleishman and Berniger, *op. cit.*
*Some percents do not add to 100 because of omissions, rounding, etc.

pected to be of considerable use in the selection of individuals who might be expected to become long-tenure employees.

More will be said later about cross-validation in such instances as this. In general terms, it is a procedure that involves the use of two groups of subjects in order to be doubly sure that the relationships of predictors to the criterion are stable.

Discussion. The use of statistical analysis generally is the most defensible method available for the development of personnel specifications. Where it is necessary to rely entirely or in part upon judgments in setting the specifications, one should proceed in an orderly way to make these judgments as sound as possible, preferably by the collective decision of various people who have intimate knowledge of the job in question. To be sure, the specifications for jobs sometimes have to incorporate specific standards that may have little bearing on job performance, but rather stem from separately established policies or regulations. State and federal laws, for example, limit the employment of women and minors, and general company policy, whether well-founded or not, sometimes adds further employment restrictions, such as lower or upper age limits, education, and the like.

Bases of Personnel Specifications

In the development and use of personnel specifications one needs to keep in mind that the standards established for the placement of individuals on a particular job should not be used *indiscriminately* in other circumstances.

In this connection, we would like to offer a distinction that may be relevant —albeit a distinction based more on logic than on empirical evidence. We would like to suggest that the specific requirements set forth in personnel specifications tend to fall into two classes.

The first class consists of those specifications that are reasonably *intrinsic* to the job and are required for effective performance as such (for example, the visual acuity and hand steadiness in sawing lumber, as mentioned above). These intrinsic requirements generally include aptitudes and sensory and physical abilities. Such requirements presume reasonable similarity of job content and of acceptable standards of performance.

The second class consists of other specific requirements associated with *labor market conditions;* the implications of this class of specifications manifest themselves in terms of the types of candidates who make themselves available for work. Thus—to illustrate with an actual example—in the case of long distance telephone operators, it was found that married women remained on the job longer than single women in one town, whereas in a town in an adjoining state the reverse was found to be the case.

To the extent that labor market conditions change, the kinds of people available as job candidates also may be expected to change, thus suggesting the need to modify the personnel specifications accordingly, as far as the aspects related to the "labor market" are concerned. Some further distinctions can be made along these lines, especially with regard to personal background data, but we will defer further discussion of the matter until later.

DISCUSSION

In this chapter we have looked primarily at the job side of the coin, with particular reference to job requirements and related personnel specifications. In order to match of people and jobs, one needs to obtain relevant information about the individuals in question, using such means as interviews, application forms, and tests. This process will be covered in the following chapters, along with certain strategies that can be used in the matching process.

A typical employment interview

PART II

Personnel
Selection
and
Evaluation

One of the important aspects of industrial psychology relates to the selection and placement of individuals in various kinds of work and the evaluation of their performance in this work. Historically, industrial psychology over the years has placed a major emphasis on systematic research regarding human characteristics associated with successful performance on various kinds of jobs. The field of personnel testing probably has had more attention from industrial psychologists than any other area. Personnel evaluation follows very logically from personnel selection and placement, for it is concerned with the evaluation of the performance of people in the jobs on which they are working. Various types of procedures have been adapted for use in personnel evaluation. This section examines some of the methods involved in the development of personnel specifications and in personnel evaluation; it also includes illustrations of these methods in actual use.

chapter four

The Interview
and
Related
Personnel Methods

In the administration of a personnel program, an important function is the matching of individuals to jobs for which they are qualified. Getting individuals aligned with appropriate jobs, at the time of employment, is undeniably important, but so is being able to promote or transfer employees to jobs compatible with their potentialities. Thus, even though the discussion in this and the following chapters will be focused primarily on the processes of employment of new personnel, much of what will be said also will be applicable to considerations of promotion or transfer of personnel already employed. It is important that one be aware of the differences in these two functions as well as of their similarities. In the case of individuals who are being considered for employment, the organization that is considering them has to depend fairly heavily upon what "outside" information it can obtain —such as previous employment record and information on the application form. In the case of individuals who are already employed by the organization, but who are being considered for some other positions, the organization has had some exposure to the individuals and should be able to utilize that experience in making a decision about their placement in other jobs.

PERSONNEL SPECIFICATIONS AND
QUALIFICATIONS

When someone makes a decision to place another individual on a job, he is making a prediction. Specifically, he is predicting that the individual will perform effectively on the new job. We all know that predictions made by human beings (including ourselves) are far from perfect. Whatever one is predicting, however—the weather, the stock market, the horses, or anything else—his predictions become more accurate as he has more and more factual, pertinent information to use in making them.

Similarly, in predicting the job performance of applicants, an employment man is able to make *better, more accurate* predictions if he is fortified with appropriate information. In particular, he needs information about *what* human characteristics are related to *success* on the job in question, and information about *which* applicants *possess* such characteristics.

As indicated in Chapter 3, the characteristics or qualifications desired in candidates for a particular job constitute the *personnel specifications*. Assuming that these specifications are reasonably valid, the person involved in making personnel decisions must obtain information about the candidates that is relevant to the job specifications, must compare such information with the specifications, and then must make a prediction about the likelihood of job success of each candidate. The adequacy of the information about candidates is, of course, a critical aspect of this process, and a major emphasis in any successful employment office is placed on obtaining such information.

SOURCES OF INFORMATION ABOUT
JOB CANDIDATES

There are several possible sources of information about candidates for jobs. These sources include the interview, the application form, references, ratings, tests and questionnaires, and perhaps other miscellaneous sources such as records of medical examinations (which are particularly important in some jobs) and the results of credit investigations.

Two Uses of Information About Job Candidates

Before proceeding too far, let us clarify a point that may otherwise serve as a source of confusion. Personnel information obtained from the sources just mentioned can serve two different purposes. In the first place, as we saw in Chapter 3, such information can be used as *group* data in setting up personnel specifications. For this purpose, data are used for samples of people who either are employed on the job at the time or ultimately will be placed on the job. In such a case, the purpose is to ascertain, by statistical analysis, the characteristics that should be included in the personnel specifications. This approach was illustrated in the study by Fleishman and Berniger[1] cited in Chapter 3. Where such statistical analyses of personnel information are carried out, the personnel specifications then are expressed in terms of the personal characteristics in question, such as age, education, marital status, test scores, ratings by interviewers, or work experience. The second use of personnel data is on an *individual* basis in considering various possible candidates for a job. For this purpose, of course, one is interested in obtaining appropriate information about *each candidate* in order to compare his qualifications against the stated personnel specifications.

This and the next few chapters will deal with both of these uses of personnel information in the processes of personnel selection and placement.

PERSONAL DATA

In making personnel selection and placement decisions interviewers and others who make such decisions need to exercise their best judgment, utilizing whatever information they can in the process. Such decisions in part must be made on the basis of subjective impressions and evaluations. However, these decisions sometimes can be improved if the decision maker is provided with reasonably objective data, such as the relationship between personal data concerning individuals (e.g., personal background) and subsequent job behavior. Our purpose here will be to emphasize the statistical analysis of such data as they relate to relevant criteria.

Nature and Sources of Personal Data

What we will here refer to as *personal data* are also referred to by other terms such as biographical data (or bio-data for short), biographical information blank (BIB) data, life history information, personal history data, and application form data. The most typical types of personal data regarding job candidates are, of course, those which are provided for in application forms. Such forms usually cover such items as age, sex, marital status, dependents, education, place of birth, residence, military experience, work experience, height, weight, and hobbies. In addition to conventional application form information, special questionnaires are used on some occasions to obtain additional information. Some of the items included in such question-

[1] Fleishman, E. A., & Berniger, J. One way to reduce turnover. *Personnel,* May-June 1960, **37**(3), 63–69.

naires cover rather strictly factual information, such as participation in high school athletics, number of brothers and sisters, age at time of first job, and number of different places of residence while growing up. Other items (such as favorite high school subject) may tend to allow for somewhat more subjective responses.

The most comprehensive assortment of "items" of personal data has been compiled by a committee under the auspices of the Division of Industrial and Organizational Psychology of the American Psychological Association.[2] The purpose of this compilation is, in part, to provide standard formats of items that can be used by different organizations. Ultimately, a substantial body of data can be built up on the basis of such items so that comparisons can be made across jobs and across companies.

Examples of Personal Data Analysis

In the typical analysis and use of personal data for personnel selection and for placement purposes, two phases need to be differentiated. First, it is necessary to identify what specific "responses" to an item differentiate between or among individuals of different criterion categories (such as above and below average in job performance, or long-tenure versus short-tenure). This analysis typically is done with individuals who presently are, or have been, on the job in question. (An example was given in Table 3.1 in preceding chapter.) Second, some scoring procedure needs to be developed and, if possible, tested with another sample of people. Such scores usually are based on statistical weights assigned to individual responses. A few examples will illustrate further the typical analysis of personal data.

Life insurance agents. Over a period of years, the Life Insurance Agency Management Association has sponsored extensive cooperative research with its member life insurance companies in various aspects of personnel research, including research relating to the selection of life insurance agents. In particular it has developed an *Aptitude Index Battery* (AIB), a major part of which is a section of personal data items. (The other three parts are tests of various types.) In our present context, the personal history part is of particular interest. This application form (actually, several versions have been prepared over the years) has been developed largely on the basis of research focused on identifying, by statistical analysis, those items of personal data that are significantly related to tenure and success in life insurance selling. The items that discriminate on these criteria serve as the basis for

[2] A catalog of life history items. Prepared by Scientific Affairs Committee, Division of Industrial and Organizational Psychology (Division 14), American Psychological Association. Greensboro, N.C.: Creativity Research Institute, The Richardson Foundation, June 1966.

a special scoring key by means of which the scored items, along with scores on the tests that form the complete AIB, are converted into a total rating.

Some of the results obtained with the AIB are shown in Figure 4.1. In

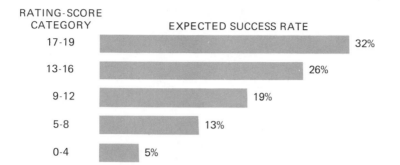

RATING-SCORE
CATEGORY   EXPECTED SUCCESS RATE

17-19   32%

13-16   26%

9-12   19%

5-8   13%

0-4   5%

FIG. 4.1 The "success rate" of life insurance agents in relationship to rating scores on the Aptitude Index Battery (AIB); the "success" rates represent the proportions of agents who survived for 12 months, and who produced above the median volume of life insurance of those who did survive for 12 months. (*Courtesy of Dr. Paul W. Thayer and the Life Insurance Agency Management Association. From Research Report 1969-5, LIAMA, 1969.*)

particular, this figure shows, for various AIB rating-score categories, the "success rate" of the individuals with AIB scores in the various categories. The success rate represents a combination of tenure (twelve months) and success in life insurance selling. The effectiveness of the index as a selection device is clearly demonstrated by the figure, and similar validity patterns have been shown in studies, dating back over a third of a century, with earlier versions of the AIB.

Service station dealers. Another example of this procedure concerns the selection of retail-outlet dealers by an industrial concern.[3] A statistical analysis was made of various items of personal data of sixty dealers, in relationship to ratings made by two regional management officials. The ratings were based on such factors as profitability, cleanliness, and efficiency of the retail outlets; the dealers were then divided into "high" and "low" rated groups. The type of statistical analysis is illustrated below. In order not to divulge the confidential scoring key, the items are not specifically identified.

The weighting system illustrated above is based on a procedure described elsewhere.[4] The weight for any given response is based on the magnitude and direction of the difference in percentages of the two criterion groups.

Using this approach, nine items were identified that differentiated signifi-

[3] The company wishes to remain anonymous.
[4] England, G. W. Development and use of weighted application blanks. Minneapolis: Industrial Relations Center, University of Minnesota, Bulletin 55, 1971.

Item and Response	Percent of "High" Group	Percent of "Low" Group	Difference (Percent)	Weight
Item X				
Response a	15	37	−22	0
Response b	33	11	+22	2
Response c	36	41	− 5	1
Response d	15	7	+ 8	2
Response e	0	3	− 3	0

cantly in terms of the criterion groups. These items were then used as the basis for a scoring procedure that was cross-validated with another sample of fifty-five dealers. The results, shown in Figure 4.2, indicate quite clearly that

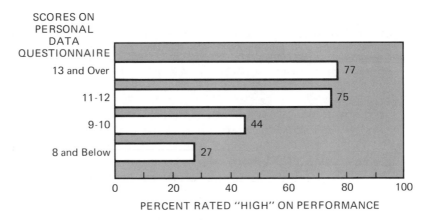

FIG. 4.2 Relationship between total scores based on nine items of personal data and successful performance of retail outlet dealers. (*Reproduced with permission of the company.*)

the "scores" derived by this process could be used very effectively in the selection of potentially successful dealers. The "odds" of success for those with low scores (especially 8 and below) are quite limited. (Cross-validation is important in analyses of this type inasmuch as some personal data items might be found to be related to a criterion simply by chance, and thus will not really be differentially discriminating in terms of the criterion. In other words, cross-validation provides something like a double-check on the stability of the relationships.)

Unskilled employees. Scott and Johnson[5] analyzed the responses to nine-

5 Scott, R. D., & Johnson, R. W. Use of the weighted application blank in selecting unskilled employees. *Journal of Applied Psychology,* 1967, **51**(5), 393–395.

teen items on an application blank in relationship to later job tenure of unskilled employees in a company. The analyses followed the procedures described by England[6] and resulted in the use of weights for twelve of the nineteen items as the basis for scoring individuals. When these weights were applied to the individuals in a separate "holdout" sample for cross-validation purposes, 72 percent of the sample were correctly classified as long-tenure or short-tenure. The mean score for the individuals in the long-tenure group was 13.9, compared to 9.3 for those in the short-tenure group. The results of such an analysis make it possible for management to select job candidates who are more likely to stay on the job longer. Management thus is able to save on hiring, training, and other related costs.

Stability of Personal Data as Predictors

Items of personal data generally have been suspected of being fairly unstable bases for predicting personnel criteria. And there is some evidence to support this suspicion.[7] Because of this, it is important in the analysis and use of personal data items to identify by statistical analysis the wheat from the chaff—those that *are* stable predictors from those that may bear only chance relationship to the criteria. The use of large samples and of cross-validation procedures can be helpful in such analyses.

Personal Data as Predictors: Unique or General?

Although, as we have just observed, there is evidence that the relationship between some items of personal data and criteria is not very stable, it is nevertheless clear that personal data items—*if properly validated*—can serve very effectively as a partial basis for personnel selection and placement on some jobs. Despite the fact that some of the relationships between personal data and criteria appear to be strictly situational—that is, they are applicable to a specific job in a specific organization—there is a growing body of evidence to indicate that some personal data items may have general validity across related jobs or across organizations. These cues come primarily from certain factor analyses of personal data that suggest that *groups of interrelated* items may tend to reflect relatively basic patterns of previous experience that may, in turn, have some general validity as predictors of job behavior. A couple of examples may illustrate this approach.

Research scientists. In one example of this research approach, Morrison,

6 England, *op. cit.*
7 See Schuh, A. J. Application blank items and intelligence as predictors of turnover. *Personnel Psychology,* 1967, **20**(1), 59–63.

Owens, Glennon, and Albright[8] conducted a study in which the subjects consisted of 418 petroleum research scientists employed by a large oil company. These men completed a questionnaire that included 484 personal data items. The responses to the questionnaires were subjected to a factor analysis that revealed the groupings or clusters of items that typically occur in combination—that have high intercorrelations. Five different factors emerged: (1) favorable self-perception; (2) inquisitive, professional orientation; (3) utilitarian drive; (4) tolerance for ambiguity; and (5) general adjustment. Each factor can be characterized in terms of the personal data items that "hang together" to form it. For example, individuals who obtain high scores on the factor "utilitarian drive" characterize themselves generally as follows in their responses to pertinent items: desire extrinsic rewards (i.e., from business and society); prefer urban dwelling; started dating prior to age twenty; feel free to express their views and perceive themselves as influencing others in group and individual situations; do not want to work autono-

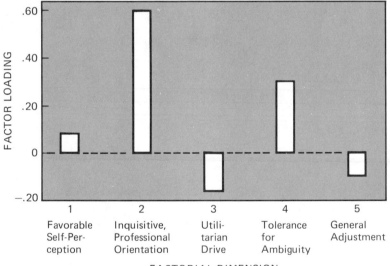

FACTORIAL DIMENSION

FIG. 4.3 "Factor loadings" of patent disclosures on five "dimensions" of personal history information for 418 research scientists. The factor loading indicates the relative relationship between number of patents and the dimension in question. (*Adapted from Morrison, Ownes, Glennon, and Albright,* op. cit. *Copyright 1962 by the American Psychological Association, and adapted by permission.*)

[8] Morrison, R. F., Owens, W. A., Glennon, J. R., & Albright, L. E. Factored life history antecedents of industrial research performance. *Journal of Applied Psychology,* 1962, **46**, 281–284.

mously; want to choose their own method, but not necessarily the goal toward which they are working.

As another aspect of this study, information was obtained on the number of patents (patent disclosures) that had been submitted during the previous five years. It was then possible to determine the relationship of numbers of patents to each of the five factors. These relationships are shown in Figure 4.3. The individual values in this figure are "factor loadings" of the number of patents on the several factors. The most meaningful implications from this figure can be obtained by looking at the overall profile. By and large, the most creative individuals (as reflected by number of patents) tend to be high in "inquisitive, professional orientation" and "tolerance for ambiguity," and to be low on "favorable self-perception," "utilitarian drive," and "general adjustment." Thus, an impression is given of the various dimensions that characterize creative research scientists.

In a subsequent study by Buel, Albright, and Glennon,[9] a scoring key consisting of thirty-three of the personal data items that had been validated on the petroleum research scientists mentioned above was applied to 132 research personnel in a pharmaceutical laboratory. The resulting scores were then correlated with four criteria for these personnel, with the following results:

Criterion	Correlation
Rank on "creativity" (rated by superiors)	.52
Number of patents	.22
Number of publications	.32
Performance ratings	.33

Thus, we find that the same items of personal data that tended to differentiate relative performance of research scientists in a petroleum company also tend to do so with research scientists in a pharmaceutical company.

Salesmen and sales managers. Another example comes from a pair of studies by Baehr and Williams.[10] In the first, they administered a personal history index[11] to a heterogeneous sample of 680 men and then subjected

[9] Buel, W. D., Albright, L. E., & Glennon, J. R. A note on the generality and cross-validity of personal history for identifying creative research scientists. *Journal of Applied Psychology,* 1966, 50(3), 217–219.

[10] Baehr, Melany E., & Williams, G. B. Underlying dimensions of personal background data and their relationship to occupational classification. *Journal of Applied Psychology,* 1967, 51(6), 481–490; and Baehr, Melany E., & Williams, G. B. Prediction of sales success from factorially determined dimensions of personal background data. *Journal of Applied Psychology,* 1968, 52(2), 98–103.

[11] Baehr, Melany E., Burns, R. K., & McMurry, R. N. Personal history index. (Rev. ed.) Chicago: Industrial Relations Center, University of Chicago, 1965.

the responses to a factor analysis. This resulted in the identification of fifteen "first order" factors.[12] In the second study the personal history index was administered to 210 food products salesmen. A factor score was then derived for each man for each of the fifteen factors (by a statistical combination of responses to the personal history items), and these scores were then correlated with criterion measures obtained for each man. By the use of multiple regression analysis it was possible to identify the combination of factor scores which gave the highest (multiple) correlation with each criterion, with the following results:

Criterion	Factors Used in Correlation	Multiple Correlation
Performance rating	No. 1, 4, 5, 6, 7, 13	.42
Mean sales volume	No. 1, 2, 5, 8, 15	.50
Maximum sales volume	No. 5, 6, 7, 8	.36

In predicting each of these criteria, the scores of individuals on the factors listed were statistically combined in order to derive a single composite score for each person. These composite scores were then correlated with the criterion values (such as performance ratings) of the 210 salesmen.

Other examples. Still other examples could be cited, such as a study by Cassens[13] of 561 executives from a large international petrochemical corporation. The subjects were divided into three groups, Americans in the United States, Americans working in Latin America, and Latin Americans working in their native country. Separate factor analyses of sixty-two items of personal data revealed substantially similar factors for the different cultural groups. In more general terms, Owens and Henry[14] summarize the results of other studies that also indicate that there is substantial "structure" in the personal backgrounds of people—in other words, that certain types of personal background variables tend to exist in combination in the personal histories of people, thus reflecting different "dimensions" of life style. These

12 These were labeled as follows: (1) School achievement; (2) Higher educational achievement; (3) Drive; (4) Leadership and group participation; (5) Financial responsibility; (6) Early family responsibility; (7) Parental family adjustment; (8) Situational stability; (9) School activities; (10) Professional-successful parents; (11) Educational-vocational consistency; (12) Vocational decisiveness; (13) Vocational satisfaction; (14) Selling experience; and (15) General health

13 Cassens, F. P. Cross cultural dimensions of executive life history antecedents. Greensboro, N.C.: Creativity Research Institute, Richardson Foundation. Inc., February 1966.

14 Owens, W. A., & Henry, E. R. Biographical data in industrial psychology: A review and evaluation. Greensboro, N.C.: The Creativity Research Institute, Richardson Foundation, February 1966.

dimensions (or factors) have been identified by statistical analysis, but also can be formulated on theoretical grounds; they generally seem to reflect the personal interests and motivation of people.

Discussion. There is quite a bit of apparently conflicting evidence as to whether the relationships between personal data items and criteria of job performance are *situational* (applying only to the specific job in the specific organization) or *general* (applying across related jobs and organizations). After reflecting on this question, we believe that the apparently conflicting evidence can be explained by suggesting that personal data items fall into two general classes.

In the first group are those items that have some stable implications (direct or indirect) in terms of the human qualities that are required for successful performance on a job or group of jobs. The results of factor analysis studies tend to substantiate the notion that there are "dimensions" of personal background and experience that reflect relatively stable personal behavioral syndromes that in turn contribute to success (or failure) in certain classes of job activities. If this be the case, such *personal* dimensions would tend to predict job performance wherever performance on the given *job* dimensions is predicated on the human qualities implied by the personal dimensions in question. In this regard, Owens and Henry[15] express the firm conviction that personal data potentially comprise the most valid measure of personality, broadly conceived, which we possess. For this reason, they propose the replacement of personality inventories by such data for the purpose of prediction.

In the second group of personal data items are those that are more reflective of labor market conditions and the effects thereof on the kinds of people who present themselves as job candidates. (For example, in some communities more married women are available as job applicants than in other communities.) Labor market conditions are of course transitory, and as they change they can cause changes in the kinds of people who are available for work. In this regard, it is interesting to note that most analyses of personal data have been found to be more predictive of *tenure* criteria than of *job performance* criteria. (Some of the exceptions to this generalization were reported above for research scientists and salesmen, but in these cases predictions generally were based on personal background *factors* rather than individual *items*.) In turn, it is reasonable to expect that job tenure will be influenced by labor market conditions inasmuch as such conditions might well influence not only those who make themselves available as job candidates but also how long people stay on jobs. Thus, personal background items of candidates that are essentially a function of the labor market can be expected to be less stable, and to vary more with the shifting winds of

[15] *Ibid.*

the labor market, than the basic "personal dimensions" that are associated more with job performance than with tenure.

We have no substantive evidence to support this distinction. (Indeed, even if such a distinction does in fact exist, it would not consist of a neat dichotomy.) We have elaborated on this theme, however, in the hope that it may have some validity, or at least that it could lead to some further clarification of the sources of apparent inconsistency and ambiguity in dealing with personal data.

Even though we have been discussing various types of information with regard to use as predictors of job performance, it should not be forgotten that some of these same types of information also can be useful as predictors of other aspects of human behavior such as driving, buying and "consuming" goods and services, or repayment of financial obligations. In other words, many of the techniques and approaches to the study of job behavior (which is of primary concern in this book) also have potential applications to other practical aspects of human life.

REFERENCES

References are sometimes used in personnel selection, especially in the case of higher-level positions. However, many people view references with some skepticism, and probably with at least moderate justification. For references to be useful for this purpose, at least four conditions must be fulfilled on the part of the person serving as a reference: (1) he must have had adequate opportunity to observe the individual in situations that are relevant (such as on the job); (2) he must himself be competent to make the kinds of assessments and evaluations that are relevant; (3) he must be willing to give his frank opinions; and (4) he must be able to express them in such a manner that the recipient interprets them in the manner that was intended. All of these factors can serve as stumbling blocks to the use of references in personnel selection, but the willingness to convey one's real opinions is probably the most serious. There is abundant evidence that many people do not like to say negative things about others, and tend rather to mention only their good sides.

To overcome some of these deficiencies, the use of questionnaires offers some advantages over conventional letters of recommendation, inasmuch as questionnaires provide the opportunity to solicit more specific information about candidates, in a more standardized (and therefore interpretable) form. Even such questionnaires, however, frequently fail to provide information that would be useful in predicting future job performance, as reported by Mosel and Goheen[16] in a study in which they analyzed data based

---

[16] Mosel, J. N., & Goheen, H. W. The validity of the employment recommendation in personnel selection: I. Skilled trades. *Personnel Psychology,* 1958, **11**, 481–490.

on the Employment Recommendation Questionnaire (ERQ). The ERQ provides for an evaluator to rate a job candidate on five factors, including occupational ability, character, and reputation. A statistical comparison was made between these ratings (obtained from former employers), and the performance of 1,117 employees in twelve skilled trades, as rated by supervisors some time after the men were employed on a new job. Correlations were computed between the mean ratings of individuals on the five factors and the ratings on occupational ability, character, and reputation. The ranges and medians for the twelve trades are given below:

Rating Factor	Range of Correlations	Median Correlation
Occupational ability	+.03 to +.21	+.10
Character and reputation	+.03 to +.33	+.23
Mean (of 5 factors)	−.10 to +.29	+.10

Although significant positive correlations were derived for certain jobs, the general implication is that such questionnaires *do not necessarily* provide information that is useful in predicting future job success of candidates.

Browning[17] reports equally discouraging correlations between pre-employment ratings of 508 candidates for teaching positions in a public school system and evaluations of teaching performance made after a year of teaching in the system. The overall correlation was +.13.

Although letters of reference and reference questionnaires do have obvious limitations in personnel selection, it is probable that references are used most commonly in a negative fashion; that is, unfavorable information tends to be used to reject candidates. When some of the conditions mentioned above are fulfilled, however—especially when the information is received from persons who are known to the prospective employer—references can be used in a positive fashion, as the basis for affirmative decisions about candidates.

THE INTERVIEW

The interview, as a communication process, is used for various purposes in industry, such as in employment operations, in employee counseling, in attitude and opinion surveys, and in market and consumer surveys. In our present context, our interests are focused primarily on the employment interview for personnel selection and placement, although certain phases of our discussion may also be relevant in other contexts. In the employment process the interview can serve what we may think of as three interrelated purposes.

[17] Browning, R. C. Validity of reference ratings from previous employers. *Personnel Psychology,* 1968, 21(3), 389–393.

In the first place, it frequently is used as the basis of obtaining some factual information about candidates. In the second place, the interchange can serve as the basis for the interviewer's forming certain kinds of judgments or evaluations about certain characteristics of interviewees. And in the third place, interviewers may participate in the process of making selection or placement decisions—in some cases by actually making such decisions and in others by making overall evaluations or recommendations that contribute to such decisions.

As an almost universal ingredient in the employment process, however, the interview has been raked over the coals by many knowledgeable people (especially research workers), and in turn praised to the heavens by others (usually personnel people). In this connection Webster[18] states that reviews of the literature pertaining to the interview have stressed four principal points:

1. Judgments made by two or more interviewers examining the same applicants tend to differ markedly from one interviewer to another.
2. The validity of predictions tends to differ markedly from one interviewer to another.
3. Predictions made by clinicians tend to be no better than those made by actuarial methods (i.e., those based on statistical data).
4. The interview is an important technique because of its widespread use. Compared to test procedures, the interview is simpler, more flexible, and evokes a greater degree of confidence in judgments.

Why Use the Interview?

In the light of quite widespread criticism about the interview, one might wonder why it is used so extensively. Why not do away with it? There are, perhaps, certain replies that can be made to this proposition. In the first place, it is probable that the employment interview would not be used as widely as it is unless it were viewed as having more values on the positive side of the ledger than on the negative side. Although this is not an entirely rational argument, it must be inferred that at least it is generally *perceived* as having useful positive values. In the second place, some of the aspects of the interview that have been criticized are not necessarily beyond redemption. Just because the bathwater is a bit dirty, one does not necessarily throw the baby out with it .

Perhaps the staunchest answer to questions about the usefulness of the interview comes from Dr. Walter V. Bingham.[19] He points out that skilled interviewers will always be at a premium in every well-run business. Even

18 Webster, E. C. *Decision making in the employment interview.* Montreal: Industrial Relations Centre, McGill University, 1964.
19 Bingham, W. V. Today and yesterday. *Personnel Psychology,* 1949, **2**, 267–275.

with the trend toward the use of computers in personnel decision making, Bingham suggests that there are four duties of the employment interviewer that will never be delegated to a computer:

1. He must answer fully and frankly the applicant's questions about your business, the job and the working conditions.
2. He must convince the man he is interviewing that the organization is a good firm to work for since it furnishes such and such opportunities for growth (if it does). In other words he must be skillful in selling the firm to the applicant.
3. He must steer the applicant toward a job for which he is better suited, if there is one somewhere, lest he later discover that job and shift to it only after the firm has spent a few hundred dollars in training him.
4. Finally, the interviewer should leave the prospect, in any case, with the feeling that he has made a personal friend.

Because the interview appears to be a fixture in personnel selection, it behooves us to do whatever can be done to make it as effective an instrument for the purpose as possible. Toward this end, it may be useful to survey briefly some of the studies relating to the interview that have been carried out, and to examine some of the possible methods of improvement.

Accuracy of Information Obtained from Interviewees

As indicated above, one of the uses of the employment interview is to obtain information from the interviewees—i.e., the job candidates. It is therefore reasonable to be curious about the reliability and accuracy of the information so obtained. Although actual data about this are hard to come by, Kahn and Cannell[20] suggest that there are persistent and important differences between interview data and data obtained from other sources. Some support for this pessimistic view is provided by the results of studies by Weiss and Dawis,[21] and Weiss, Dawis, England, and Lofquist.[22] The second of these studies dealt with information about the work histories of 325 physically handicapped individuals who were interviewed at their homes, following a structured interview procedure. For each job reported by each individual, a questionnaire was sent to the employer asking for information on job title, job duties, starting and ending dates, hours, pay rates, type and length of training, promotions, and reason for separation. Replies were

[20] Kahn, R. L., & Cannell, C. F. *The dynamics of interviewing.* New York: John Wiley, 1957, p. 179.

[21] Weiss, D. J., & Dawis, R. V. An objective validation of factual interview data. *Journal of Applied Psychology,* 1960, **40,** 381–385.

[22] Weiss, D. J., Dawis, R. V., England, G. W., & Lofquist, L. H. Validity of work histories obtained by interview. Minnesota Studies in Vocational Rehability: No. 12. Minneapolis: University of Minnesota, September 1961.

received from 92 percent of the former employers to whom questionnaires were sent, covering 607 jobs.

These reports from former employers then made it possible to check the accuracy of the information given by the individuals. The results of some of the comparisons are summarized in Table 4.1. In deciding whether the information reported was or was not valid, a standard basis of comparison was used for each different item. In the case of quantitative data, for example, the information was considered valid if it was within 10 percent of the value given by the employer. It can be noted that the percentages of

TABLE 4.1 VALIDITY OF WORK HISTORY INFORMATION OBTAINED DURING INTERVIEW AS COMPARED WITH DATA FURNISHED BY FORMER EMPLOYERS

Item and Basis for Accepting as Valid	Index of Validity Percent	Correlation
1. Reason for separation (3 categories)	83	
2. Hours worked ($\pm 10\%$)	78	.60
3. Starting date ($\pm$ one month)	71	
4. Promotion (4 categories)	70	
5. Training (3 categories)	69	
6. Title and duties*	67	
7. Ending date ($\pm$ one month)	66	
8. Final pay ($\pm 10\%$)	60	.82
9. Length of job ($\pm 10\%$)	60	.92
10. Starting pay ($\pm 10\%$)	55	.78
11. Pay increases ($\pm 10\%$)	38	.81

Source: Adapted from Weiss, Dawis, England, and Lofquist, *op. cit.*

* Job titles were considered the same if they were within the same first three digits of the *Dictionary of Occupational Titles.*

agreement range from 83 to 38. The lower percentages indicate considerable inaccuracy in interview reports of some types of work history data. It should be noted, however, that although the *percentages* of inaccuracy of some items are low (such as final pay, length of job, starting pay, and pay increases) the *correlations* between interview and employer data are fairly high. These differences are largely attributable to the distinct tendency of individuals to report "upgraded" or "inflated" information about themselves. To the extent that this is a general tendency, it is possible for the percentage of accuracy to be low but for the correlation to be high. In an earlier study of 236 cases by Keating, Paterson, and Stone,[23] a comparison was made of certain work history information obtained during employment interviews with information obtained later from former employers. The researchers reported a remarkably close agreement between these two sources

[23] Keating, E., Paterson, D. G., & Stone, H. C. Validity of work histories obtained by interview. *Journal of Applied Psychology,* 1950, **34**, 6–11.

relating to wages, duration of job, and duties of job, as indicated in the following summary:

Item	Type	Index of Agreement Men	Women
Wages	Correlation	.90	.93
Duration of employment	Correlation	.98	.98
Duties of job	Per cent	96%	96%

In this study, there was no appreciable upgrading in reporting either wages or duration of employment; the average values of the interview data were very nearly the same as those reported by the employers. In this respect, the results of this survey differed from those reported by Weiss et al.,[24] who reached the dreary conclusion that: "The use of interview-obtained work history without further verification is unwarranted, certainly for research purposes, and for applied, that is practitioners' purposes as well."

The apparent differences between the results of this survey and that of Keating *et al.* cause one to wonder just how much confidence can be placed in work history information obtained by interview. Our own reflections lead us to the following conclusions: that at least some types of data are reported with sufficient reliability and validity—although usually somewhat upgraded —to make them of use for typical employment functions; that one needs to be wary of placing substantial confidence in certain types of data reported (such as pay increases and starting pay as listed in Table 4.1) ; and that if positive confirmation of such information is required for some purpose, a check with previous employers would be in order.

Judgments about Interviewee Characteristics

In the interview exchange the interviewer obtains certain impressions of the interviewee (and vice versa!) that are the basis for his judgments of the interviewee. In some circumstances these evaluations are made a matter of record (as on a rating form), and it is only when they are so recorded that anyone else can use them either in making employment decisions or in research relating to the interview. When dealing with such evaluations, of course we like to have some feel for their *reliability* and *validity*. (Reliability is the degree of consistency or agreement between two or more judges, or between judgments made by the same person on two or more occasions. Validity is the degree to which the judgments are accurate or correct or true. Usually this can be determined by a comparison of the judgments against separate relevant criteria.)

[24] Weiss, Dawis, England, and Lofquist, *op. cit.*

On the basis of a very thorough survey of interview or interview-like evaluations, Wagner[25] summarized information on the judgments that have been reported for ninety-six human traits or characteristics. For each trait or characteristic, he reported the number of studies in which it had been investigated and, where originally given, the reliability and/or the validity of the judgments. Note that the validity in this context refers to the accuracy of the judgment as far as characterizing that trait or characteristic itself is concerned—not the validity of predicting some separate, independent criterion such as job performance.

Some of the results of this survey are presented in Table 4.2, which shows

TABLE 4.2 RELIABILITY AND VALIDITY OF JUDGMENTS OF SELECTED HUMAN TRAITS AND CHARACTERISTICS IN INTERVIEW-LIKE SITUATIONS

Trait or Characteristic	Reliability			Validity		
Ability to present ideas	.42					
Alertness	.36					
Background, family and socio-economic				.20		
Energy	.64					
Initiative	.57					
Intelligence or mental ability	.96	.87	.77	.58	.82	.45
	.62	.90		.94	.51	.70
Personality				.21		
Self-confidence	.77					
Sociability	.87	.72		.37		
Social adjustment				.22		
Tact	.26					
Over-all ability	.71	.48	.24	.27	.21	.16
	−.20	.26	.43	.87	.23	
	.68	.61	.85			
	.55					

Source: Wagner, *op. cit.*

the reliabilities or validities of each of twelve of the ninety-six characteristics investigated. Because this information comes from a wide variety of situations, it must be accepted with reservations, but nonetheless we can see that there are marked differences in the reliabilities and validities of the various traits and characteristics. For example, the reliability of ratings on "Alertness" was .36, whereas for "Sociability" the reliabilities (in two situations) were .87 and .72. The validities ranged from .20 for "Background," to those in the .80s and .90s for "Intelligence or mental ability." We also can see, however, that for a given characteristic, such as "Overall ability," the range of validities and reliabilities varied a great deal. The validity coefficients for

25 Wagner, R. The employment interview: A critical summary. *Personnel Psychology,* 1949, **2,** 17–46.

this characteristic ranged from .16 to .87, and the reliability coefficients ranged from $-.20$ to .85.

Such studies, as well as experience with the interview, suggest that interviewers can make better judgments about some characteristics or traits than about others. In general terms, it is probably reasonable to expect that interviewers can form opinions about those characteristics or traits that are overtly manifest in the behavior of the interviewee during the interview, or that can be inferred from his behavior. On the other hand, interviewers should not be expected to be able to form opinions about those traits or characteristics that typically would become manifest only over a period of time, and perhaps only during the "normal" behavior of the individual but not during an interview situation. Thus, interviewers probably could not adequately form judgments about such characteristics as creativity, dependability, industriousness, honesty, originality, or punctuality. Neither can interviewers generally be expected to judge some of the acquired skills and abilities of interviewees, such as ability to diagnose mechanical disorders, add columns of numbers, spell words correctly, or assemble small parts. (Note, however, that inferences about some such abilities can be made from information about work experience.)

Methods of Studying the Interview

Two of the principal approaches to the investigation of the interview have been referred to as the *microanalytic* and the *macroanalytic* approaches.[26] In the microanalytic approach, of which Mayfield and Mayfield and Carlson[27] are the primary proponents, the interview is "dissected" into units for intensive probing and analysis in order to study interviewer bias, the structuring of questions, and other aspects of the interview process. On the other hand, the macroanalytical approach, which deals with the interview more as a complete entity, lends itself more to the study of the validity of the interview for personnel selection and placement purposes.

Factors that Influence Interviewers' Decisions

Despite the murkiness of interview decision processes, research is beginning to add a bit of understanding to these processes. We are now aware of the dependence of interviewers upon stereotypes, the types of information

---

[26] See Mayfield, E. C. The selection interview: A re-evaluation of published research. *Personnel Psychology,* 1964, **17**(3), 239–260; and Wright, O. R., Jr. Summary of research on the selection interview since 1964. *Personnel Psychology,* 1969, **22**(4), 391–413.

[27] Mayfield, *op. cit.;* Mayfield, E. C., & Carlson, R. E. Selection interview decisions: First results of a long-term research project. *Personnel Psychology,* 1966, **19**(1), 41–53.

used in making evaluations, the time used in making decisions, interview set, and the structure of the interview. Each of these will be discussed below.

Interviewer Stereotypes. One aspect of the decision process about which we seem to have fairly well confirmed information concerns the stereotypes of "ideal" candidates that interviewers use as their "standard" in assessing actual candidates. One phase of a major research program sponsored by the Life Insurance Agency Management Association[28] dealt with this aspect; but before reporting the results let us describe the procedures used in this project, as an illustration of the microanalytic research approach.

To begin with, a number of life insurance managers were asked to list the types of information about applicants that they the managers considered important in reaching a hiring decision. Using these sources a list of 250 such items was developed and classified in three groups:

1. *Factual items* which might have been obtained from application blanks or from interviews, such as: "The applicant is twenty-four years old," or "The applicant has a net worth of $5,000." In constructing items of this type, a number of different items in each area were included, such as those indicating different ages or different levels of net worth.
2. *Statements* which an applicant might make during an interview, such as: "I will go out to be the best insurance agent in this area," or "I like work which requires considerable attention to detail."
3. *Descriptions of mannerism and appearance,* such as: "The applicant likes to walk around the room while talking."

Next, a number of life insurance managers were asked to rate each item on how favorable or unfavorable it would be if it were true of an applicant, these ratings being on a seven-point scale from "extremely favorable" to "extremely unfavorable," plus an eighth category "I would no longer consider this man." Each item was rated by over one hundred managers. As one would expect, these ratings showed very high agreement on some items, such as "earned all of his college expenses" (which was consistently rated as favorable) and "The applicant is separated from his wife" (which was consistently rated as unfavorable). But more surprising was the fact that the ratings on some items showed marked disagreement, such as "The applicant says he feels he's gotten nowhere for the last five years and it's change jobs now or never."

In the next phase of the research, seven "hypothetical" applicants were constructed, each consisting of six items of information. The items used were those on which there had been substantial disagreement regarding their favorability and unfavorability. An example of such an hypothetical applicant follows:

[28] Mayfield and Carlson, *op. cit.*

Has a net worth of $3,000.

Received a C average in college.

Is more satisfied than dissatisfied with his present job.

Owns $8,000 of life insurance (face value).

Has seven close friends in the community.

His favorite hobby is listening to music.

Sixty-nine managers then ranked these "applicants" in order of their suitability for the job of a life insurance agent, with the result that *each* applicant was ranked *best* by one or more managers, and *worst* by one or more, and at *each intervening rank* by one or more! Following are three examples:

Applicant No.	Number of Raters Ranking Applicant as:						
	Best	2nd	3rd	4th	5th	6th	Worst
1	10	5	12	8	8	13	13
4	16	17	12	7	9	7	1
7	8	6	10	9	10	12	14

With these differences in rankings of applicants by different raters, we can readily see how an applicant would fare if interviewed by different interviewers. For example, applicant number 1 probably would be accepted by the 10 interviewers who rated him "best," and rejected by the 13 interviewers who rated him "worst."

In marked contrast with these rating divergencies, Rowe[29] reports a much higher level of interviewer consistency. In her study the hypothetical "applicants" (applicants for the Canadian Army) were described by items that had been more reliably rated as clearly favorable or unfavorable. She inferred that the interviewers who made the evaluations had a common stereotype of a "good soldier" that they used as a standard against which to judge each hypothetical applicant. In reflecting about the results of their study, Mayfield and Carlson[30] also speak of stereotypes, but their use of admittedly inconsistent ratings provides evidence that the stereotypes in question consist of two parts. The first part is the common stereotype of the ideal applicant which most interviewers share; this part is analogous to Rowe's "good soldier" stereotype. The other part consists of a "specific" stereotype which is different for different interviewers; the specific stereotypes of different individuals consist of those items on which interviewers disagree as to favorability.

[29] Rowe, Patricia M. Individual differences in selection decisions. *Journal of Applied Psychology*, 1963, **47**, 304–307.

[30] Mayfield and Carlson, *op. cit.*

Types of information used in making evaluations. In trying to gain insight into the interview process, it would be useful to have some actual data (rather than opinions) about the types of information interviewers take into account in making their evaluations of candidates. Some inklings about this come from a study by Hakel, Dobmeyer, and Dunnette[31] in which twenty-two experienced interviewers and twenty students evaluated sets of twenty-four resumés of hypothetical college seniors for accounting positions. (Although no actual interviews were involved, of course, the evaluation of resumés usually is an aspect of interviewing activities.) The details of the experiment need not concern us; the important point is that the "applicants" varied in terms of three "types" or "dimensions" of information—namely, scholastic standing, business experience, and interests and activities. In part the results indicated that each of the three dimensions contributed significantly to evaluations of overall suitability, but that the interviewers depended overwhelmingly on information about scholastic standing.

In another study, Carlson[32] found that life insurance agency managers, in making final ratings of hypothetical candidates as life insurance agents, placed much more weight upon the factual information about the candidates than on their appearance as presented by photographs.

In reflecting about the results of such studies, one should be wary, of course, about extrapolation to other types of jobs. For example, scholastic standing obviously would be beside the point in selecting trapeze artists, lumberjacks, or roulette croupiers; and appearance, which is given only nominal weight in selecting life insurance agents, would of course be high in the list for choosing models for a model agency. The important point is that, for any *given* type of occupation, there may be some dimension of information that is *dominant* in the evaluations of candidates by interviewers.

Time used in making decisions. It has been found that interviewers typically make some tentative decision about candidates early during the interview. In a study by Springbett[33] (which was one of the several studies sponsored by Webster[34] at McGill University), it was found that interviewers tended to make such decisions within the first four minutes of the typical fifteen-minute interview. This pattern of decision making is reasonably com-

---

31 Hakel, M. D., Dobmeyer, T. W., & Dunnette, M. D. Relative importance of three content dimensions in overall suitability ratings of job applicants' ratings. *Journal of Applied Psychology,* 1970, 54(1), 65–71.

32 Carlson, R. E. Selection interview decisions: The relative influence of appearance and factual written information on an interviewer's final rating. *Journal of Applied Psychology,* 1967, 51(6), 461–468.

33 Springbett, B. M. Factors affecting the final decision in the employment interview. *Canadian Journal of Psychology,* 1958, 12, 13–22.

34 Webster, *op. cit.*

patible with Bruner's[35] concept of the "gating" phenomenon—a term which refers to the process of selective attention in which the perceiver tends to attend to an increasingly narrower range of stimuli as the sequence of perceptual activities proceeds from initial to final stages. Webster suggests that, as applied to the interview, the gating or selective attention phenomenon suggests that the effect of a particular item of information on a decision will depend on the time of the item's occurrence in the decision sequence. Thus, if "unfavorable" information bobs up early in the interview it might lead to an early negative decision, and vice versa. In other words, the "first impression" may tend to persist, even to the extent of causing a later disregard of conflicting information.

Interview "set." The tendency of first impressions to affect decision making led to further investigation by Springbett[36] in which he varied the "order" in which interviewers received three "types" of information—an application form, a physically present applicant, and a personal history interview. In part this was done with actual industrial applicants, with an active interviewer and a passive interviewer (observer), and in part it was done with descriptions of hypothetical army applicants. Without going into the specific procedures used, we may note that the interviewers rated each applicant (whether real or hypothetical) on the basis of the three types of information (the application form, appearance, and the total interview).

An analysis of the ratings thus produced led Springbett and Webster to suggest that the interviewer approaches applicant appraisal with a "set" of caution that can be described as essentially a search for *negative evidence*. In this search, however, the interviewer is influenced by the confidence he can place in the information at hand, for there is a tendency to place more confidence in application form information (which is relatively objective and unambiguous) and less confidence in appearance or the personal history interview (which is more ambiguous). Thus, when application forms are presented and rated first, the ratings based on such information (whether favorable or unfavorable) are reflected quite consistently in the final ratings. When appearance or personal history interview are rated first, however, the effect depends more on whether the rating is favorable or unfavorable: if favorable, it tends to intensify the set of caution in the interviewer's search for negative evidence; if unfavorable, it tends to confirm the set of the interviewer to reject.

Thus, in general, the review of an application form before or during the early part of the interview in itself tends to generate a distinct frame of

---

[35] Bruner, J. S. On perceptual readiness. *Psychological Review,* 1957, **64,** 123–152.

[36] Springbett, *op. cit.*; also reported by Webster, *op. cit.*

reference toward acceptance or rejection of an applicant. The tendency of interviewers to seek negative evidence has been generally confirmed in various studies, such as by Miller and Rowe,[37] who found that when information contains both favorable and unfavorable evidence, the evaluation will be influenced more by the unfavorable evidence than by the favorable.

Interview structure. Interviews vary a great deal in terms of their degree of structure; some wander all over the map while others follow a fairly standardized pattern.

In a structured interview the conversation is guided adroitly by the interviewer in order to cover a specified assortment of topics, but the interviewee is encouraged to speak freely about the topics that are considered relevant. As pointed out by Fear,[38] the control of the interview is maintained so that all important areas of the candidate's background can be covered systematically, but the information is obtained in an *indirect* manner. Although such an interview follows a logical pattern, its content is not automatic or stereotyped.

Usually a form is used, with provision for making notes and comments and for rating the candidate on each of several qualities. One such interview procedure, presented by Fear, is referred to as *The Interview Guide*.[39] This particular interview procedure provides for covering four background areas; work history; education and training; early home background; and present social adjustment. In addition, provision is made for rating the applicant on various qualities of personality, motivation, and character. For each area the interviewer rates the candidate on a scale from above average to below average. He also provides an overall rating.

An example of part of the form used in another structured interview procedure is given in Figure 4.4. One feature of the typical structured interview is the provision for systematic rating of the candidate on various factors.

It is commonly believed that structured or patterned interviews generally are superior to less structured ones. Although there are bits and pieces of evidence that tend to confirm this assumption, on the whole the evidence is somewhat equivocal. As pointed out by Mayfield,[40] there have been no rigorously controlled studies focused on this question. Recently, one study has been directed to this problem.[41] In this investigation, eighteen experienced interviewers interviewed the same five girls who were "applicants"

[37] Miller, J., & Rowe, P. M. Influence of favorable and unfavorable information upon assessment decisions. *Journal of Applied Psychology,* 1967, **51**(5), 432–435.

[38] Fear, R. A. *The evaluation interview: Predictions of job performance.* New York: McGraw-Hill, 1958.

[39] Copyright 1943, The Psychological Corporation, New York, N.Y.

[40] Mayfield, *op. cit.*

[41] Schwab, D. P., & Heneman, H. G., III. Relationship between interview structure and interviewer reliability in an employment situation. *Journal of Applied Psychology,* 1969, **53**(3), 214–217.

SUMMARY OF APPLICANT'S QUALIFICATIONS

Use the following questions to help you analyze the various qualifications of your applicant. Determine, through unbiased consideration, whether or not you should employ. Don't jump to conclusions. Heed all "danger signals."

| DOES THE APPLICANT QUALIFY FOR THE JOB? | 1. Do the applicant's appearance and manner fit him for the work? | Yes __ No __ Maybe __ |
| | 2. Does this applicant present himself well? (expression-voice-self-confidence) | Yes __ No __ Maybe __ |

| IS HIS RECORD CLEAN OF UNFAVORABLE FACTORS? | 1. Is applicant's work record satisfactory? | Yes __ No __ Maybe __ |
| | 2. Do reasons for leaving former jobs appear logical? | Yes __ No __ Maybe __ |

| WILL HE ADVANCE WITH McKESSON? | 1. Does he have capacity for growth and advancement? | Yes __ No __ Maybe __ |
| | 2. Do his stated business interests and ambitions seem to be in line with company possibilities? | Yes __ No __ Maybe __ |

| | 7. Will he have the stamina for the job? | Yes __ No __ Maybe __ |

CONCLUSION

You have now reached the point where it is necessary to decide whether or not the applicant should be employed. This can be done only through the exercise of judgment. You must recognize that no one is perfect. So, while you must compromise, be thorough. Weigh the answers you gave on each of the 20 questions in the above summary one against another for the solution.

1. Have you devoted sufficient time to arrive at conclusion?

Length of interview _____ Length of 2nd interview _____
               Minutes   Minutes

2. What over-all rating do you give this applicant? Rating Scale | Outstanding | Excellent | Good | Fair | Poor |

3. Do you recommend his employment (Remember you should always replace one man with another as strong or stronger) Yes _____ No _____

4. For what position _____ Starting Rate _____

1st Interviewer's Signature _____ 2nd Interviewer's Signature _____

Comments:

FIG. 4.4 Two sections of an interview guide used by one company. The first section provides for the interviewer to rate the applicant in response to a number of questions, but only a few illustrative questions are shown here. (*Courtesy of McKesson and Robbins, Inc., New York.*)

for the job of clerk-stenographer. A hypothetical description, which included a completed application form, was prepared for each girl, and each girl was instructed to play her hypothetical role and to provide consistent answers to similar questions when being interviewed by different interviewers.

In turn, the interviewers were divided into three groups, one using structured interviews, one using semi-structured interviews, and the third using unstructured interviews. Each interviewer subsequently ranked the five girls as potential clerk-stenographers, and the consistency of their ratings was analyzed by the use of a coefficient of concordance. The coefficients are given below:

Interview Method	Coefficient
Structured	.79
Semistructured	.43
Unstructured	.36

This study, of course, is not completely conclusive, in part because it was carried out in a simulated context, but it at least lends strong support to the notion that more structured interviews tend to result in higher interviewer reliability in terms of the consistency of the evaluations of applicants.

The Reliability of Selection and Placement Decisions

It generally has been assumed that the reliability of evaluations of candidates in terms of their overall suitability for various jobs has been relatively low. Wagner,[42] for example, reported that the median reliability of such evaluations is quite dismal—about .48. Of course, there are exceptions, such as a coefficient of .68 reported by Hakel, Dobmeyer, and Dunnette.[43]

The Validity of Selection and Placement Decisions

In our discussion of the interview so far, we have alluded only indirectly to the validity of the decisions relative to the selection or placement of candidates. Although such decisions have been made millions of times by interviewers and placement officers, there is an abysmal absence of hard data about their validity as related to criteria of subsequent job performance of candidates actually selected on the basis of such decisions. In fact, Ulrich and Trumbo[44] make the bleak statement that, with the evidence at hand, it simply is not possible to determine the utility of the interview—in essence, its validity as a predictive procedure.

However, the evidence is perhaps not as systematically negative as it is inconclusive. In fact, there are some hints that the interview does have value as a predictive procedure. For example, Sydiaha[45] compared the effect of two methods of arriving at selection decisions. One of these was a "clinical" method in which scores were assigned to candidates by interviewers on the basis of an interview. The other was an "actuarial" method in which the candidates received scores based on a statistical combination of personal data and test data. An analysis of the selection decisions that would have been made by these two methods indicated that the clinical approach presumably involved the use of more information than is contained in actuarial biographical and test data. Perhaps the interview, with its "clinical" approach, does add something new, supplying a dimension over and above that provided by actuarial data.

42 Wagner, *op. cit.*

43 Hakel, Dobmeyer, & Dunnette, *op. cit.*

44 Ulrich, L., & Trumbo, D. The selection interview since 1949. *Psychological Bulletin,* 1965, **63**(2), 100–116.

45 Sydiaha, D. The relation between actuarial and descriptive methods in personnel appraisal. Unpublished Ph.D. Dissertation, McGill University, 1958; reported in Webster, *op. cit.*

Another moderately encouraging note is added from occasional isolated studies, such as the one by Hovland and Wonderlic.[46] In this study, which dates from the 1930s, the researchers used a patterned interview procedure that provided for ratings that were converted to an interview score. They obtained interview scores of about three hundred individuals who had been hired by one company. At a later date a follow-up survey was made to find out what happened to these employees. The original group was divided into three groups—those who were still on the job, those who had resigned, and those who had been dismissed. Comparisons for these three groups were then made against their original interview scores. Figure 4.5 rather clearly shows that more persons with high scores remained on the job than did those with

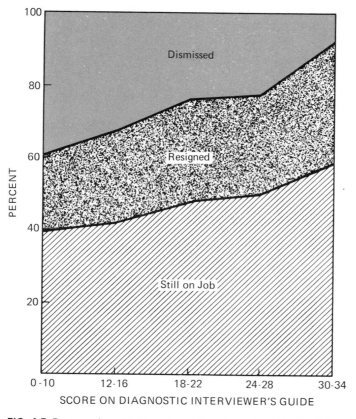

FIG. 4.5 Percent of employees still on job, resigned, and dismissed, in relation to scores on Diagnostic Interviewer's Guide. (*Adapted from Hovland and Wonderlic,* op. cit.)

[46] Hovland, C. I., & Wonderlic, E. F. Prediction of success from a standardized interview. *Journal of Applied Psychology,* 1939, **23,** 537–546.

low scores, and that the percent who had to be dismissed was much lower among those with high scores.

In turn, McMurry[47] summarizes the results obtained with a patterned interview in several companies. For example, a study at the Link-Belt Company in Chicago showed that interviewers' ratings of 587 men based on patterned interviews were significantly related to tenure of the employees on the job. A further study of 407 men who remained on the job in this company showed a significant relation between interviewers' ratings and subsequent success on the job. Similar results were obtained in studies conducted with truck drivers employed by the White Motor Company and operators employed by the York Knitting Mills.

Discussion. The interview is an almost universal step in the process of personnel selection, and its usefulness as a means of information exchange and as a public relations measure undoubtedly justifies its survival. A more definitive evaluation of the interview in terms of its validity for purposes of selection and placement, however, will have to be postponed until more substantive research is available. Such research could provide further cues as to the specific ways in which the interview can contribute to prediction of the job performance of candidates.

Present Guidelines

Pending the millenium, when such answers might become available, it behooves us to do the best we can on the basis of what is now known. A number of source books include suggested interviewing techniques,[48] but in using them we should be mindful of Webster's[49] observations that they typically have not taken into account some of the research findings that actually are available. For this reason, he suggests that the philosophies expressed in these source books and the suggestions they contain are more likely to be profitable if the structure of the interview is organized somewhat as follows:

1. Someone other than the person conducting the evaluation interview should do all of the preliminary screening. (This would minimize the possibility of "early" information about the applicant predisposing the evaluation interviewer to make a premature decision.)

[47] McMurry, R. N. Validating the patterned interview. *Personnel,* 1947, **23,** 263–272.

[48] For more extensive discussion of interview techniques, the reader is referred to such sources as: Bingham, W. V. D., Moore, B. V., & Gustad, J. W. *How to interview.* (4th ed.) New York: Harper & Row, 1959; Cash, H. C., & Crissy, W. J. E. *Tools of personnel selection.* Flushing, N.Y.: Personnel Development Associates, 1963; Fear, *op. cit.* Kahn, R. L., & Cannell, C. F. *The dynamics of interviewing.* New York: John Wiley, 1957; McMurry, R. N. *Tested techniques of personnel selection.* Chicago: Dartnell Corporation, 1955; and U.S. Civil Service Commission. *Employment interviewing.* Personnel Methods Series No. 5. Washington, D.C.: Superintendent of Documents, 1955.

[49] Webster, *op. cit.*

2. This situation should be explained to the applicant.

3. The interview should commence by asking the applicant to talk about his early life.

4. Permit the examinee to bring his story up to date, including his reasons for wanting to change jobs.

5. The interview should become more systematic and probing.

6. Review the application form with the applicant.

7. Time should be taken following the interview to clarify impressions and to formulate a judgment.

8. Other information should be examined.

A Look Ahead

Of course, the decision processes in personnel selection and placement are not based exclusively on information and impressions derived from the interview as such. Typically, they also take into account other information, such as from the application form, test scores, and other sources. Combining the many "units" of information about a single candidate and making a corresponding prediction of success is indeed a complex process. In the case of one employment situation described by Smith,[50] the combinations of the many different units of information (such as individual test scores) were computed to be in the order of 10^{76}—nearly the estimated number of atoms in the known universe! Smith proposes that the complex thought processes required for dealing with such a magnitude of information can be simulated reasonably well by computers. He reports the results of one test of this notion in which twenty-four female applicants were evaluated by both human and machine methods. The procedures will not be described except to say that the experience of the decision maker was organized into graphic representations of thought processes and subsequently transformed into a form of heuristic simulation of those processes. (A heuristic approach is one in which general decision rules or "rules of thumb" make it possible to limit the area of "search," thus limiting the number of possibilities to consider so that they are within the boundaries of reasonable human and machine capabilities.) Smith found that such a computerized simulation resulted in the same "decisions" as those reached by human decision makers in the case of twenty-two of the twenty-four candidates. (The four decision categories were to hire, reject, hire as a fair risk, or check background further.)

Such a computerized approach to personnel decision making will not be in widespread use tomorrow, but it is not outside the bounds of possibility to think in terms—years away—of a synthesis of the decision maker's thought processes and the decision rules used by a computer as it grinds out "decisions" about candidates.

---

[50] Smith, R. D. Heuristic simulation of psychological decision processes. *Journal of Applied Psychology*, 1968, 52(4), 325–330.

chapter five

General Principles
of
Personnel Testing

Personnel tests have been used as an integral part of personnel management in many organizations. Their primary use has been for personnel selection and placement purposes, but they also have been used for certain other purposes, such as effecting personnel transfers from one job to another, influencing the promotion of employees, determining areas in which training is needed, and evaluating the effectiveness of training programs. Although tests are used for various purposes other than personnel selection and placement, the primary emphasis in this and the next couple of chapters will be on their use for selection and placement. (Of course, much of what will be said about tests in this context is also applicable to the other purposes mentioned above.)

A central point we would like to make here about the use of tests, for whatever purpose, is that they should be used only when there is reasonable evidence that they can be expected to serve their purpose—that is, when they have reasonable *validity* for the purpose. (In the use of tests for personnel selection and placement, for example, this means that job candidates who score well on a test would be expected to have a higher probability of performing effectively on the job than those who perform less well on the test.) The validation of tests will be discussed later in this chapter. Unfortunately, many organizations have been using (and may still be using) tests for which there is no such validity evidence. One of the authors of this text, for example, conducted a survey in 1968 dealing with the use of personnel tests among 175 companies that were members of a trade association. Of these, 158 were using personnel tests but only a small proportion had any solid validation data to justify their use of the tests.

In recent years the use of tests for personnel selection and placement has been subjected to considerable public scrutiny on various grounds, especially on the grounds of possible discrimination against minority groups in employment and upgrading in accordance with Title VII of the Civil Rights Act of 1964. To enforce the Civil Rights Act, two United States government agencies were established—the Equal Employment Opportunity Commission (EEOC) and the Office of Federal Contract Compliance (OFCC). These two federal agencies, in turn, have issued guidelines relating to employee selection procedures.[1] More will be said later in the chapter about the use of tests in light of these guidelines, but the essential point of the guidelines is that employment tests should be used only when there is demonstrated evidence of their validity for the purpose, and that tests must not discriminate unfairly against minority groups. These are principles which we believe are quite proper. They are, in a sense, the principles which many industrial psychologists have been promoting for many years.

GENERAL CONSIDERATIONS
IN USING TESTS

In using tests for most purposes, it generally is desirable to employ them in combination with other sources of information about the individuals in question. In employment office operations, for example, tests preferably should be used in combination with information obtained by interview, from application forms, and from other sources.

Selection or Placement as the Function of Tests

Personnel tests often are considered primarily as devices to aid in the selection of employees. From this it follows that (1) when tests are used systematically, many applicants will be rejected—that is, not employed at

[1] The EEOC guidelines were published in the Federal Register, Vol. 35, No. 149, August 1, 1970. The OFCC guidelines were published in the Federal Register, Vol. 36, No. 77, April 21, 1971.

all—and that (2) unless there are significantly more applicants than there are jobs to be filled, the testing program loses its effectiveness.

It is generally true that at times when there is considerable unemployment a company will have greater choice in the *selection* of applicants than at times when there are few people seeking employment. Nevertheless, a personnel testing program can still be a very useful one—for *placement* purposes—even when a shortage of applicants requires the employment of virtually all available applicants. Under such circumstances, provided there is more than one kind of job open, the testing program enables an organization to place the applicant in that job for which he appears to be most suited.

Psychological Tests Are Not Infallible

The advocate of testing procedures should never allow himself to forget that psychological tests are not infallible, for they sometimes give results that are not a true indication of the potential job success of the applicant. Any new procedure, whether in employment, production, advertising, or whatever, should be evaluated not in terms of whether it achieves perfection but in terms of whether it results in some useful degree of improvement over methods that have preceded it. For example, let us take a company that has been selecting candidates for a particular job and finds that only 60 percent of those selected turn out to be successful on the job. If the company finds that by using tests, 70 percent of the applicants hired are successful, it might consider the use of the test to be worthwhile in spite of the fact that 30 percent of the applicants hired do not turn out to be successful on the job.

Types of Tests

Tests that have been and are being used for employee selection and/or placement may be classified in several different ways. They may be *group* or *individual* tests. The group variety may be given to almost any number of persons simultaneously, the only limitation being on the number that can be seated and provided with writing facilities and an adequate opportunity to hear the instructions given by the group examiner before the test is begun.[2]

Individual tests, on the other hand, are given to one person at a time and usually call for the undivided, or nearly undivided, attention of the examiner while the test is being administered. The phrase "nearly undivided attention" is used because in certain cases, as with the Purdue Pegboard Test of Manual Dexterity, it is possible for an attentive examiner to test several persons simultaneously if the necessary sets of equipment are available.

2 A list of some commonly used tests is given in Appendix D.

In terms of their content, most of the tests used in industry are of three types. The first includes tests of basic human abilities, such as mental abilities and psychomotor skills. These tests generally are used as *aptitude* tests in the sense that they are used to determine whether individuals have the capacity or latent ability to learn a given job if they are given adequate training. The second type of test includes those that measure job-specific abilities, such as typing skill and knowledge of machine-shop practices. Some such tests are referred to as *achievement* tests because they measure the level of achievement in some job-related area. Typically, they are used for such purposes as in the employment of experienced workers and in evaluating learning acquired during training. In some instances such tests also are used for the employment of inexperienced job candidates, but in these cases they are used more as aptitude tests inasmuch as their purpose is to predict future performance. The third class of tests consists of measures of personality and interest; these are usually referred to as *personality and interest inventories*. Personality and interest tests (or inventories) are intended to measure personality characteristics or patterns of interests of individuals, on the assumption that such characteristics or interests may be related to performance on various kinds of jobs. When such tests are used as employment tests, they typically are used to predict job performance in essentially the same manner as aptitude tests. There are certain serious limitations to the usefulness for employment purposes of presently available personality and interest tests; these limitations will be discussed in a later chapter.

RELIABILITY

For a test to be potentially useful, it must provide the basis for *consistency* of measurement—that is, it must measure *reliably* whatever it does measure. Reliability—specifically, the reliability of criterion values—was discussed in Chapter 2, but the same basic concept applies to tests of all kinds.

Methods of Determining Test Reliability

There are different methods of determining test reliability, each resulting in a different type of reliability measure.

Test-retest method. The test-retest method of measuring reliability consists of administering the test to the subjects at two different times and determining the correlation between the test and the retest scores. This method results in what is called a *coefficient of stability*. However, this method involves several assumptions which are not always justified. One assumption is that memory or practice on the basis of the first test administration will not significantly affect scores made on a second administration. For this reason, this method is not suitable with tests where memory or practice on the test can influence the scores made at a later time. A second assumption is that the items in the test adequately sample the universe of items that might have been used. Ordinarily, there is no reason to believe that one set of, say, fifty items is superior (or inferior) to another comparable (equivalent) set of fifty items. Thus it is desirable to determine not only the degree of response variation by the subject from one time to another, but also the extent of the sampling fluctuation involved in using a given set of fifty items.

Alternate form method. Both of these objectives may be accomplished by correlating scores on one set of, say, fifty items with scores made by the same subject on an independent but similar set of fifty items in an "alternate form" of the test. This method cannot be used, however, unless two strictly comparable forms of the test are available. The two forms must be equivalent in terms of difficulty, average scores, variability (or variance) of scores, as well as in type of content covered. Many, if not most, commercially available tests are available in two or more such equivalent forms. When this is the case, the correlation between scores made on two equivalent forms is a very good way to estimate the reliability of the test. Obviously, the higher the obtained correlation, the more consistently the test is measuring whatever is being measured—i.e., the higher is the test's reliability. This method results in what is called the *coefficient of equivalence.*

Split-halves method. When there are not two equivalent forms of the test available, a method often used in estimating test reliability is known as the *split-halves method.* With this method, the test is administered in the standard manner. When it is scored, however, two keys are used, each covering only half of the items. The two halves may be chosen randomly or they may consist of alternate items, with one scoring key used on all the even numbered items and the other used on all the odd numbered items. The correlation between scores made on the two halves is then computed. This provides a reliability measure of a test half as long as the original test. By using a commonly accepted statistical procedure, the correlation is corrected by the Spearman-Brown prophecy formula[3] to determine the reliability of the entire test. The split-halves method should never be used in the case of speed tests—i.e., tests which most subjects do not finish in the time allowed. If this method of reliability is used with speed tests, a spuriously high estimate of reliability is obtained. When used properly, the split-halves method of estimating test reliability results in what is called the *coefficient of internal consistency.*

Discussion. There are ways of determining or inferring test reliability

---

[3] Guilford, J. P. *Fundamental statistics in psychology and education.* (3rd ed.) New York: McGraw-Hill, 1956.

other than those discussed here, but these are the ones most commonly used. It should be noted that there is no such thing as *the* reliability of a test; rather, reliability is in part a function of the group of individuals tested. In the use of personnel tests, it is desirable to determine the reliability with individuals similar to those on whom the tests are validated. This is not usually done, however. Rather, a person using a test will rely on reliability information based on previous groups of subjects, as reported by the test publisher.

Of what importance is test reliability? This question can be answered by saying that if a test is highly reliable, it is possible to put greater reliance on the scores that individuals receive on the test than if the test is not very reliable. Because, in most employment situations, one has only a single score on a given test for each applicant, it is useful to know how reliable the test is in order to know how stable such scores are. Generally speaking, the reliability of most tests is considered to be satisfactory if the coefficients of reliability are in the .80s or .90s. There are some circumstances, however, in which tests with lower reliabilities might still be acceptable.

VALIDITY OF TESTS

In a very broad sense, the *validity* of a test refers to the degree to which the test is capable of achieving the aims or purposes it is intended to serve. The nature of the "evidence" about the validity of a test depends very much upon the particular circumstance.

Types of Validity

Our current interest in tests is related primarily to their use for personnel selection and placement. However, it is helpful to be aware of the various specific *types* of test validity that are appropriate in the use of tests in various situations, such as education, vocational counseling, and clinical practice, as well as in personnel work. There are basically three types of validity, which are related to the different aims or purposes of testing.[4]

1. Content validity. Content validity is evaluated by showing how well the *content* of a test samples the subject matter or kinds of situations that the test is intended to measure. It applies particularly to achievement tests. Generally speaking, the determination of content validity needs to be made on the basis of the *judgments* of "experts" with regard to the *appropriate-*

---

[4] A thorough discussion of the concepts of validity and reliability of tests is included in *Standards for educational and psychological tests and manuals,* available from the American Psychological Association, 1200 Seventeenth St. N.W., Washington D.C. 20036.

ness of the questions or problems (the "content" of the test) as measures of whatever the test is supposed to measure.

2. Criterion-related validity. This is determined by comparing test scores with one or more independent criteria. In personnel selection and placement, the criterion usually is a measure of job performance of individuals, but it also may consist of "membership" in different groups, such as occupational groups. There are two kinds of criterion-related validity—concurrent validity and predictive validity.

Concurrent validity is established by relating test scores with the criterion values or categories that are available at the same time. Usually this involves the correlation of test scores with currently available criteria of job performance of the individuals in question. (The procedures used in this process are covered a bit later in the discussion of the present-employee method of test validation.)

As related to the use of personnel tests, *predictive validity* is determined by relating test scores obtained at one time (such as at the time of employment) with criterion measures (such as job performance) obtained at a later time. (The procedures used in determining predictive validity are covered later in the discussion of the follow-up method of test validation.)

3. Construct validity. Construct validity is evaluated by determining what psychological *quality* a test measures, such as "introversion" or "intelligence." Such validity frequently is determined by correlating one test with another that previously has been found to measure the quality in question, or by using a statistical process called "factor analysis" to identify the extent to which various tests measure the same human quality.

As indicated above, the present treatment of personnel tests in industry typically involves the concepts of criterion-related validity, which covers both predictive validity and concurrent validity.

Methods of Test Validation

It is of utmost importance that tests never be used for any purpose unless there is reasonable evidence that they are valid for that purpose. This means that there must be some sort of evidence that scores on the test for some sample(s) of individuals have been found to discriminate among those in the sample(s) in terms of a suitable criterion of job performance. Among the methods for obtaining such evidence in relation to personnel tests are the following (along with the type or types of validity involved):

Method	*Type of validity*
Present-employee	Concurrent
Follow-up	Predictive
Job-status	Usually concurrent; could be predictive
Job component	Depends on procedures used

Of these, the first two require the use of individual criterion measures (such as job performance criteria) of all of the individuals in the sample(s) used. The last two more typically involve the use of a criterion of membership in some group (e.g., working on a particular job or occupation). Of these, the present-employee and follow-up methods are the most commonly used in industry and are sometimes referred to as "testing the test."

Present-employee method of test validation. This method of test validation involves the use of a sample of present employees on the job in question. The procedure is as follows:

1. Select battery of experimental tests. An early step in a test validation project is the selection of a battery of tests to be tried out. These tests should be chosen in terms of the extent to which they are considered to measure attributes that are judged to be important to job success. This selection preferably should be made on the basis of information obtained from a job analysis.

2. Administer tests to present employees. The tests selected are then given to employees presently on the job. When an organization plans to carry out a test validation research project that will involve the experimental testing of present employees, the organization should make such participation voluntary and should give full assurance that the tests are being given *strictly* for experimental purposes and that the results will not in any way affect the employees' relationships with the organization. It is usually desirable to distribute among the employees a sheet such as this:

> The Personnel Department is conducting a series of experiments. You have our assurance that this testing is being done to "test the tests" and that the results will *not* be used, now or later, in any way that will affect your standing with the company.

3. Select appropriate criteria. At some early phase of a test validation project it is necessary to determine what criterion of job performance to use. Criteria were discussed in Chapter 2, so we need not repeat that discussion here; we will only remind you that the criterion or criteria used in any test validation study should be *relevant,* meaning that it should reflect the standards by which the performance of employees should be evaluated in terms of management's objectives.

4. Obtain criterion information on present employees. After determining what criterion or criteria to use, it is then in order to obtain criterion information on the individual employees now on the job. Depending on the criterion in question, this may involve the accumulation of available records (such as production records, sales volume, and the like), or it may consist of obtaining ratings from supervisors on job performance of the employees, or other appropriate processes.

Depending on the manner in which the results are to be analyzed, the criterion information may be used to divide the total employee group into two groups such as "high" (or above average) and "low" (or below average), or it may be expressed in quantitative terms such as units of production or numerical ratings.

5. Analyze results. After the test scores and criterion information have been obtained, the results may be analyzed in several different ways. One method consists essentially of three steps. First, the total group of employees is divided into a "high" criterion group and a "low" criterion group, as mentioned above. Next, the employees are divided on the basis of test scores into two test score groups, those scoring in the top half on the test and those scoring in the lower half. Then the percentage of "high" criterion employees in each test score group is determined. If there is a higher percentage of high criterion employees among the employees in the top half on the test than there is among those in the lower half on the test, the difference is subjected to a statistical check to determine whether it is "significant." (This check is a common procedure in statistics and shows the probability that the obtained difference could have occurred by chance.[5] If the analysis shows that the difference could have occurred by chance only one time in one hundred, the difference is said to be significant at the .01 confidence level. If the difference could have occurred by chance five times in one hundred, it is said to be significant at the .05 confidence level. It is standard practice in the field not to use tests when the confidence level is not at least at the .05 level.)

When a test has been found to be acceptable on this basis, employees are then split into smaller groups by test score, such as fifths—i.e., the highest fifth on the test, the second fifth, the third fifth, the fourth fifth, and the lowest fifth. The percentage of "high" criterion employees is then computed for each of these test score groups and the resulting data are then plotted in an expectancy chart such as the one shown in Figure 5.1.[6] The chart shows the "odds" of being a superior employee for employees in each test score bracket.

An even more effective method of determining the relationship between test results and job performance is to compute a coefficient of correlation between the test scores of the employees and their criterion values. This has certain advantages over the expectancy chart method mentioned above. In the first place, it gives a more accurate indication of the *amount* of the relationship between test scores and job performance. In the second place, it enables the employment manager more effectively to take advantage of the all-important selection ratio (see p. 111) in using the test. In the third

[5] For a brief discussion of the concept of statistical significance, see above, p. 14 ; for fuller discussion, see Guilford, *op. cit.*

[6] The procedure for constructing a five bar expectancy chart such as the one shown in Figure 5.1 is given in detail in Lawshe, C. H., & Balma, M. J., *Principles of personnel testing.* New York: McGraw-Hill, 1966.

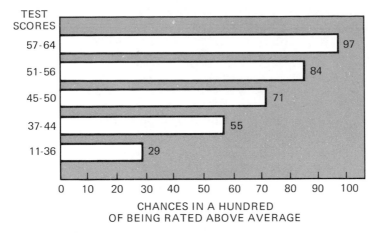

FIG. 5.1 Expectancy chart showing the relation between scores made on the Minnesota Paper Form Board and rated success of junior draftsmen in a steel company.

place, it makes possible the computation of the relative importance of several tests in an employment battery so that the tests may be "weighted" according to their importance. Finally, the use of the correlational method makes it possible to offset, statistically, whatever influence such factors as experience on the job or age may have had both on the test scores and on job performance of the employees. Further mention will be made later of these possible influences.

Although the correlational approach has certain advantages over the expectancy chart method, these are largely statistical advantages. In terms of understanding by nonstatisticians, the expectancy chart method probably cannot be excelled.

Follow-up method of test validation. As indicated earlier, this method consists of administering tests to individuals at the time they are candidates for the job in question. The tests, however, are *not* used as the basis for selection. Rather, the individuals are selected just as they normally would have been selected if the test had not been administered, and the test scores are later related to whatever criterion is appropriate. The steps involved in this method are described below.

1. Select battery of experimental tests. This step is essentially the same as with the present-employee method.

2. Administer tests to applicants. The tests are administered to applicants who are to be employed for the job in question, but the applicants should not know at the time that a decision has been made to employ them. The test results are then filed until a later date.

3. Select appropriate criterion. This determination is made in the same way as with the present-employee method.

4. Obtain criterion information on the new employees. The criterion information on the new employees should not be obtained until after sufficient time has elapsed for them to demonstrate their actual abilities on the job. Usually this would be after completion of training, or at least after the completion of most of the training.

5. Analyze results. This step is carried out in the same manner as with the present-employee method.

Comparison of present-employee and follow-up methods. Each of these methods of test validation has certain advantages and disadvantages. In the validation of aptitude tests with the present-employee method, it is possible that a test may in part be measuring some ability that is improved significantly by experience on the job. In other words, it may be measuring achievement more than aptitude. In validating aptitude tests by this method, then, it is necessary to be sure that the tests, besides differentiating between employees in terms of a criterion of actual job performance, do *not* show a significant correlation with length of experience on the job, for an aptitude test should be one on which the employees who score high on the test do not score high simply because they have had the opportunity—on the job— to develop the ability which the test measures. If test scores *do* show some correlation with length of experience, the net relationship between test scores and job performance, after the effect of experience has been eliminated, can be determined by partial correlation. The procedure for computing partial correlations may be found in any standard textbook of statistics.

Although the influence of experience on test scores in such a situation can be eliminated by the use of partial correlations, a more straightforward manner of getting around such a problem is through the use of the follow-up method. In this case the test scores are obtained *prior* to any experience on the job, and therefore cannot be influenced by job experience.

The present-employee method has certain other possible disadvantages. In some instances, the *present* employees on a job may represent a highly select group, inasmuch as most of those who were *not* satisfactory either were dismissed or left of their own accord. In such a case, the correlation between test scores and criterion values would *not* represent the relationship that one would expect with the follow-up method.

Further, the "mental set" of present employees toward taking tests on a voluntary "experimental" basis may be different from the "mental set" of applicants. This difference in set can influence performance on some types of tests, especially personality and interest tests. Where this influence is of some consequence, it would be preferable to validate the test by the follow-up method. If this is done, the test is then validated in the same type of situation as the one in which it will later be used.

Another disadvantage of the present-employee method is that the arrangements for testing present employees sometimes are difficult to work out, especially because it is necessary to take people away from their jobs in order to test them.

The follow-up method is clearly the preferable method for validating tests, except for the possible disadvantage of the time required. Fortunately, it is possible in some cases to use the present-employee method for developing a battery of tests for immediate use, and still plan on later "follow-up" of those selected. Although the range of test scores (and of criterion values) for those so selected usually would be restricted (thus bringing about a low correlation), it sometimes is possible to adjust for this restricted range statistically. Such an adjustment makes it possible to obtain an estimate of what the follow-up validity coefficient *would* have been had the tests *not* been used for initial selection. This adjustment procedure would not be appropriate, however, if some nontest basis (e.g., membership in a minority group) has been used for excluding some applicants.

Job status method of test validation. In this method the "criterion" categories consist of those individuals who are in specific jobs or occupations. When this method is used, the test scores of employees on each of two or several jobs are compared to ascertain whether there are significant differences. In one company the Bennett Test of Mechanical Comprehension was administered to employees on each of several jobs. Following are the mean test scores for those on certain jobs.

Job	Mean Test Score
Insulators	30.9
Pipefitters	33.8
Electricians	36.4
Welders	39.7
Instrument mechanics	42.4

The use of this method is predicated on the assumption that by "natural selection" people in an organization tend to "gravitate" into the kinds of jobs that are reasonably in line with their abilities. If it can be assumed that, in general, most persons on a job are achieving a reasonable degree of success on that job, it is then possible to *compare* the employees on various jobs in order to ascertain what *differences* there are from job to job, as in the above example. It is then possible to select for initial placement, or for promotion, those individuals whose test scores most nearly correspond with the test scores of individuals now on the job.

Job Component Validity

The conventional validation methods are the present-employee and follow-up methods previously described. But in some cases—e.g., jobs with small numbers of employees—such empirical, situational validation procedures simply may not be possible, or may be too time consuming and costly. Thus one would wish for a generalized, simplified, and yet valid method that bypasses conventional test validation procedures for ascertaining what tests to use for selection of personnel for a given job.

In this regard, one could hypothesize that those jobs that have in common the same basic kind of human behavior or job characteristic or job component would require the same human attributes. In turn, it would seem that the same test(s) should be valid for personnel selection purposes for all such jobs. Thus, if one could by some method identify a test that is valid for the selection of individuals for a sample of jobs with a given human behavior or job characteristic in common, it would be reasonable to expect the test to be valid for all jobs with that *same* behavior characteristic. These hypotheses give rise to the concept of job component validity. This concept generally has been referred to as "synthetic validity," a term coined by Lawshe,[7] but because we feel that the term *job component validity* is somewhat more descriptive, this term will be used in this text.

Job component validity for clerical jobs. A few isolated studies have been made in which this concept has been tested in the case of specific jobs, with generally confirming results. These include one study by Lawshe and Steinberg[8] dealing with clerical jobs. They used the *Job Description Check List of Clerical Operations*[9] to identify the work operations of 262 positions in twelve companies. The people in these positions were given the *Purdue Clerical Adaptability Test,* which results in several subscores. By a procedure that need not be discussed here, various operations had been determined to have "critical" requirements on each of the several subscores on this test, such as "spelling." In general, it was found that the larger the number of "critical" work operations in a job, the higher the scores of individuals on such jobs, as shown in Figure 5.2.

A generalized basis for job component validity. A basic prerequisite for determining job component validity is a systematic scheme for identifying or measuring the job characteristics that might serve as the common denominators for comparing, or contrasting, jobs. Probably the most generalized such basis consists of the use of the Position Analysis Questionnaire (PAQ),[10] which was described in Chapter 3. (It will be recalled that the

7 Lawshe, C. H. Employee selection. *Personnel Psychology,* 1952, 5, 31–34.

8 Lawshe, C. H., & Steinberg, M. D. Studies in synthetic validity. I: An exploratory investigation of clerical jobs. *Personnel Psychology,* 1955, 8, 291–301.

9 Available from Village Book Cellar, 308 West State Street, West Lafayette, Indiana 47906.

10 Copyright © 1969, Purdue Research Foundation. Available through the University Bookstore, West Lafayette, Indiana 47906. See McCormick, E. J., Jeanneret, P. R., & Mecham, R. C. A study of job characteristics and job dimensions as based on the Position Analysis Questionnaire (PAQ). *Journal of Applied Psychology,* 1972, 56(4), 347–368.

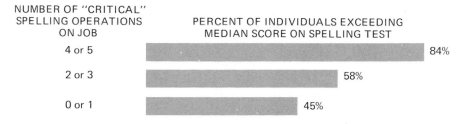

NUMBER OF "CRITICAL"
SPELLING OPERATIONS   PERCENT OF INDIVIDUALS EXCEEDING
        ON JOB   MEDIAN SCORE ON SPELLING TEST

        4 or 5   84%

        2 or 3   58%

        0 or 1   45%

FIG. 5.2 Percent of individuals exceeding median score on spelling subtest by number of "critical" spelling operations in their jobs. (*Adapted from Lawshe and Steinberg,* op. cit.)

PAQ includes job elements that characterize the "human behaviors" in jobs).

As a prelude to the use of the PAQ in the job component validity context, PAQ data for 536 jobs were subjected to a factor analysis as reported by McCormick, Jeanneret, and Mecham.[11] This analysis resulted in the identification of twenty-seven factors referred to as *job dimensions*. For any given job, scores on these job dimensions serve as measures of job characteristics for use in the job component validity context.

In exploring the possible use of the PAQ as the basis for job component validity of tests, data for 179 positions were used; these positions correspond to ninety jobs for which the United States Training and Employment Service had published test data for job incumbents. The test data for each job included the mean test score of the incumbents on each of the nine tests of the General Aptitude Test Battery (GATB).[12] These mean test scores were used as an indication, or criterion, of the relative "importance" of the attribute measured by each test to the jobs in question. The use of such a criterion is predicated on the assumption that people tend to "gravitate" into those jobs which are reasonably commensurate with their own levels of abilities. Thus, for any given test, jobs on which the incumbents have "high" mean test scores presumably require more of the attribute measured than do jobs on which the incumbents have "low" mean test scores.

A "regression analysis" was then carried out with the 179 positions using their job dimension scores as predictors of the criterion values of mean test scores. This procedure made it possible, in this situation, to identify the particular combination of job dimension scores, with their statistically derived weights, that best predicted the mean test scores of incumbents on each of the nine tests. The correlations (actually multiple correlations) of the weighted combinations of job dimension scores with the mean test scores ranged from .59 to .80 for the nine tests, with a median of .71. Thus, it appears reasonable to believe that statistically derived data from a structured

[11] McCormick, Jeanneret, & Mecham, *op. cit.*
[12] These tests are as follows: G (intelligence); V (verbal); N (numerical); S (spatial); P (form perception); Q (clerical); K (motor coordination); F (finger dexterity); and M (manual dexterity).

job analysis questionnaire such as the PAQ can be used—at least in some circumstances—as the direct basis for establishing test batteries. When this is the case, it obviates the need for conventional test validation procedures.

FACTORS DETERMINING THE FUNCTIONAL VALUE OF PERSONNEL TESTS

There are several factors of both a practical and a theoretical nature that determine the functional utility of personnel tests. These include the *reliability* and *validity* of the tests used, the *selection ratio,* and the *percentage of present employees who are "satisfactory" on the job.*

Reliability

As stated earlier, a test must have an acceptable level of reliability if it is to be useful. The fact that a test has high reliability, however, provides no assurance of its criterion-related validity. Thus, a test might have *high reliability* but *low validity,* or even no validity at all. The converse is not true, for if a test has *low reliability* it cannot be expected to have any appreciable degree of validity as related to a criterion. (This is not only a rational conclusion but is also based on the principles of statistical theory. The coefficient of reliability of a test imposes a theoretical maximum on its possible coefficient of validity.)

Validity

Recognizing the potential "ceiling" of validity imposed on a test by its reliability, it is logical for us to ask: How high must the concurrent or predictive validity coefficient of a test be for the test to be worthwhile in actual use?

The answer to this question depends upon the use that is being made of the test. The user of tests is nearly always interested in one of two objectives, but is seldom interested in both at the same time. Either he is interested in making a careful and accurate aptitude analysis of *each person tested,* which is to be used for individual prediction or vocational guidance, or he is interested in selecting from a large group of individuals a smaller group that, *on the average,* will surpass the larger group in some particular respect. In individual counseling work, which deals with vocational aptitude and guidance, the psychologist is interested in the former objective. His work will stand or fall on the accuracy of his predictions for individual clients. He therefore has little use for aptitude tests that do not have a validity sufficiently high to justify their use in individual prediction. The exact value of the validity coefficient that meets this requirement is not completely agreed upon by all students of the subject, but it is uniformly agreed that the higher the validity of the test the better and that *there is no substitute for validity for individual prediction.*

On the other hand, one may be interested in segregating from a large group of persons tested a smaller group that, on the average, will surpass the larger group in whatever trait is being tested. This is, in fact, the situation that confronts the employment manager. He is willing to accept, on the basis of tests, a few individuals who will fail on a given job, and to reject (or place upon some other job) a few who, had they been placed upon that job, would have succeeded, *if on the whole his percentage of successful placements is higher with the tests than it is without them.* In other words, although the employment manager would like to have every swing result in a home run, he usually recognizes that under normal circumstances this is not practical, and is therefore satisfied if he can improve his batting average. Under these circumstances the acceptable validity of the tests can be much lower. But one may still ask: How low can it be? A categorical answer to this question can be given, but the full significance of the answer will be clear only after a thorough study of the next section, which deals with the *selection ratio.* The answer is that a test probably will be valuable, no matter how low the coefficient of validity, if it indicates a *statistically significant* relationship between test scores and the criterion. Often this rule will admit tests whose validity is as low as .30 or even lower. The use of tests with such low validity is sufficiently contrary to much current thought among psychologists to warrant a fairly detailed justification for this conclusion.

The Selection Ratio

Given a personnel test that has a validity coefficient indicating *some* relationship with the criterion, and given more candidates than can be placed on the job in question, the functional value of the test depends upon the ratio of those placed to those tested who are available for placement. This has been referred to as the "selection ratio."[13] An example will clarify the operation of this principle.

If a certain test is given to a large number of employees for whom a criterion of successfulness as employees is available, and if the scattergram of test scores against the criterion is plotted, the points ordinarily will fall into an oval-shaped area somewhat similar to the oval in Figure 5.3. The higher the coefficient of validity, the narrower will be the oval; and the lower the

13 Taylor, H. C., & Russell, J. T. The relationship of validity coefficients to the practical effectiveness of tests in selection: Discussion and tables. *Journal of Applied Psychology,* 1939, **22,** 565–578.

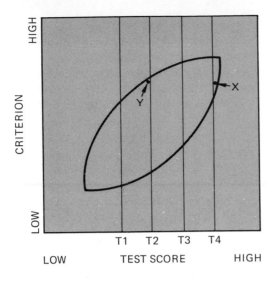

FIG. 5.3 Effect of shifting the critical score required of applicants on average criterion score of employees hired.

validity, the more nearly the oval will approach a circle. A validity coefficient of approximately .60 will result in a scattering of scores approximately covering the oval area shown in Figure 5.3. Now, if candidates are placed without regard to test scores, their criterion scores usually will be the average of all individuals falling within the oval. If only those are placed upon this job who have test scores as high as or higher than T_1, those not placed on the job will clearly have, on the average, lower criterion scores than the group as a whole, and those placed will accordingly be higher in their criterion scores, on the average, than the group as a whole. A still higher average criterion score for the group placed can be achieved by setting the critical test score at T_2. By moving the critical score to T_3, T_4, or even higher, still more favorable placements, according to average criterion score, can be made.

If a given number of persons, say sixty, are to be placed, any one of the conditions mentioned above may exist; which one exists will depend upon the selection ratio that is utilized: that is, the ratio of the number placed to the number tested. Suppose we work with a ratio of 1.00—that is, all those tested are placed. In this case, the distribution of test scores will be over the whole range of possible test scores; the criterion scores will be over the whole range of possible criterion scores; and the test will contribute nothing whatever to the efficiency of the placement procedure. Now suppose that we test eighty individuals and place the sixty who score highest on the test, either not hiring the twenty who score lowest or placing them on some other job. We thus reduce those placed to 75 percent of those tested, or reduce the selection ratio to .75. Under these conditions, we will place on this job only individuals who test at least as high as T_1, and the average criterion scores of those so placed will clearly be higher than the average of the group as a whole. By testing 120 persons and placing the sixty who score highest on the test, the selection ratio will be reduced to .50 and only individuals to the right of T_2 will be placed. The average criterion score of this group not only will be higher than that of the whole group, but also will be higher than that of the group placed when the critical test score was at T_1. Thus, by increasing the number tested before the sixty to be placed are identified, the selection ratio will be decreased with a continuous increase in the average criterion score for the group of sixty finally placed. If, for example, the organization is expanding so greatly that six hundred new employees can be tested before sixty are selected for this particular job (or if the labor market were such that six hundred applicants were tested before sixty were hired for this job), the selection ratio would be decreased to .10, only those testing at least as high as T_4 would be placed on the job, and the average criterion score of the group of sixty placed under these circumstances would be much higher than the score of sixty placed under any larger selection ratio.

The foregoing discussion is of course based on the assumption that the placement of employees is successful in proportion to the average success of the employees placed. Anyone can readily see that even working with a selection ratio of .10, some individuals (like X in Figure 5.3) will be placed who will be poorer according to the criterion than a few other individuals (like Y in Figure 5.3) who have not been allocated to this job. But if one is willing to measure the success of the testing program by average results rather than by individual cases, the results will be more and more favorable as the selection ratio is decreased.

The main burden of the present discussion is that—in *group* testing—one can effectively use a test with a relatively low (statistically significant) validity coefficient by sufficiently reducing the selection ratio. In other words, in group testing, *a reduction in the selection ratio is a substitute for high validity.* This principle applies as well when only a few candidates are to be selected as when many are to be selected. (A selection ratio of .50 applies equally well when selecting five out of ten candidates as when selecting fifty out of one hundred.) And the principle also applies under conditions of a tight labor market when virtually every applicant is to be employed, so long as the people employed are to be placed on two or more different jobs. In this regard, a *reduction* in the selection ratio can be utilized *whenever two or more candidates* are to be placed on *two or more different jobs,* if tests of some validity are available for each of the jobs.

Percentage of Present Employees Considered Satisfactory

A further factor that affects the efficiency of a personnel test in a given employment situation is the percentage of present employees who are considered satisfactory. This factor may be made clear by reference to Figure 5.4. Suppose we are working with a test having a validity coefficient such

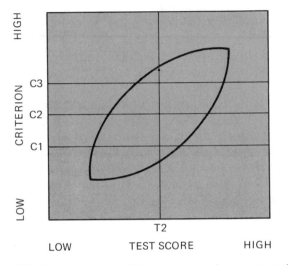

FIG. 5.4 Variation of efficiency of an employment test with differences in percentage of present employees who are considered satisfactory.

that the employees tested fall into the oval-shaped area. Suppose, further, that we are working with a selection ratio of .50—that is, only persons falling in the oval-shaped area to the right of T_2 will be placed on the job. If 50 percent of the present employees are satisfactory, any increase over this amount in the percentage of satisfactory employees placed that can be achieved by using the test is a gain. Under these conditions, the ratio of satisfactory employees among those placed to the total of those placed would be the ratio of the number of individuals falling to the right of line T_2 and above C_2 to all persons falling to the right of line T_2. This ratio would clearly be higher than .50, and the amount by which it exceeds .50 would be indicative of the functional value of the test under the conditions discussed.

If all conditions named above remain the same except that previous employment methods have resulted in 75 percent satisfactory employees, then the criterion separation line of the successful and unsuccessful employees would be C_1 and the percentage of satisfactory employees placed by means of the test would be the ratio of the individuals to the right of line T_2 and above C_1 to all persons to the right of line T_2. In the latter case, a larger percentage of employees hired will be satisfactory than in the former case, even though the test, selection ratio, and other controlling factors remain the same. In other words, if everything else is equal, the smaller the percentage of present employees who have been placed satisfactorily without tests, the larger will be the percentage increase of satisfactory employees when employees are placed by means of test results. This may be illustrated by an example. Suppose we have available a test with a validity coefficient of .50 and are using a selection ratio of .50. Table 5.1 shows the increase, due to using the test, over the percentage of satisfactory employees prior to the use of the test. The values in Table 5.1 were obtained from the Taylor-Russell tables[14] reproduced in Appendix B. If only 5 percent of employees placed by traditional means are successful, then the expected increase to 9 percent represents an 80 percent increase in the number of satisfactory employees placed by the test, under the specified conditions of test validity and selection ratio. If larger percentages of satisfactory employees have been achieved without the test, the percentage of increase achieved by using the test will become increasingly smaller. If 90 percent of employees placed by traditional means have been successful, the increase of this percentage to 97 percent by the test, used under the specified conditions, results in an improvement of only 8 percent in the number of employees satisfactorily placed.

TABLE 5.1 INCREASES IN PERCENTAGE OF SATISFACTORY EMPLOYEES PLACED ON A JOB OVER VARIOUS ORIGINAL PERCENTAGES OF SATISFACTORY EMPLOYEES WHEN A TEST WITH A VALIDITY COEFFICIENT OF .50 IS USED WITH A SELECTION RATIO OF .50

A *Percentage of Satisfactory Employees Placed on the Job without the Test*	B *Percentage of Satisfactory Employees Placed on the Job with the Test*	*Difference in Percentage Between Columns A and B*	*Percentage of Increase of Values in(B) over Values in (A)*
5	9	4	80
10	17	7	70
20	31	11	55
30	44	14	47
40	56	16	40
50	67	17	34
60	76	16	27
70	84	14	20
80	91	11	14
90	97	7	8

[14] *Ibid.*

The general conclusion is that, other things being equal, the more diffi-cult it has been to find and place satisfactory employees without using test procedures, the greater the gain one may expect from a suitable testing program.

Use of Taylor-Russell Tables

The purpose of the foregoing discussion is to point out that the four factors mentioned earlier—reliability, validity, percentage of present em-ployees who are considered to be satisfactory, and selection ratio—operate to determine the functional value of a personnel selection test. Assuming that the reliability of a test is reasonably satisfactory, and knowing the values of the other three factors, we can predict the improvement in personnel placement that would result from the use of the test. What is more, we also can estimate the further improvement that would result from the reduction of the selection ratio.

Figure 5.5 reproduces a chart that shows how the percentage of em-

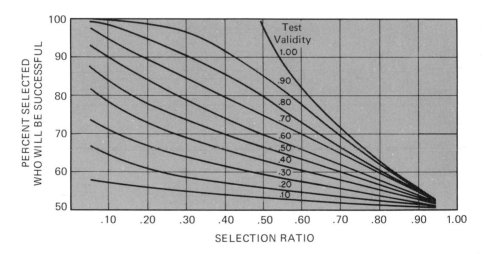

FIG. 5.5 Effect of test validity and the selection ratio upon the working efficiency of an employee selection test.

ployees selected who will be successful is determined by the validity of the test and the selection ratio. This chart deals with an employment situation in which 50 percent of present employees are considered satisfactory. The base line in this figure gives the selection ratio, and each of the curves plotted indicates a different test validity. It will be seen that, by using a test with a validity of .90 and by reducing the selection ratio to .60, the percentage of satisfactory employees placed will be raised from 50 percent to 77 percent. It also will be noted that a corresponding increase to 77 percent in the number of satisfactory employees will be achieved by a test with a validity of only .50 if the selection ratio is decreased to .20.

The Taylor-Russell tables, reproduced in Appendix B, make it possible to determine what percentage of employees hired will be satisfactory under different combinations of test validity, selection ratio, and percentage of present employees considered satisfactory.

The use of these tables may be made clear by an example. Suppose an employment manager has a test with a validity coefficient of .40, has twice as many applicants available as there are jobs to be filled, and is placing in a department where 30 percent of the present employees are considered satisfactory. Looking in the upper half of the table on p. 597 (entitled "Proportion of present employees considered satisfactory = .30"), we find in the row representing a validity coefficient of .40 and in the column representing a selection ratio of .50, the value .41 where the indicated row and column cross. This means that under the conditions specified, 41 percent of the employees placed will be satisfactory instead of the 30 percent attained without the test. If conditions are such that the selection ratio may be still further reduced, the same test will place a still higher percentage of successful employees. For example, if only the highest 10 percent of the persons tested are placed on the job, the percentage of satisfactory employees will be raised to 58 percent, or nearly double the percentage of satisfactory employees placed without the test.

The "Direct Method" of Estimating Test Effectiveness

In the foregoing discussion, the use of the selection ratio requires that test validity be expressed in terms of a coefficient of correlation. McCollom and Savard[15] have shown that a simple and direct method can be used to obtain essentially the same results. With this method, which they call the Direct Method, the following steps are taken:

1. Select a cutting point on the test.
2. Select a cutting point on the criterion.
3. Count the number of cases falling above both cutting points: test and criterion.
4. Compare the number of cases found in step 3 with the number that would have been secured by random selection.

If 50 percent of the entire group of employees are satisfactory, and if the test has no validity at all, 50 percent of the employees above *any* so-called critical test score will be satisfactory. But if the test has *any* validity,

15 McCollom, I. N., & Savard, D. A. A simplified method of computing the effectiveness of tests in selection. *Journal of Applied Psychology,* 1957, **41,** 243–246.

more than 50 percent of employees above a critical test score will be satisfactory. The extent to which the satisfactory percentage of those above the critical test score exceeds the satisfactory percentage without regard to the test score indicates the validity of the test in the particular situation.

McCollom and Savard make several empirical comparisons between this Direct Method and results obtained with the Taylor-Russell tables, which, of course, require the use of coefficients of correlation. Three such comparisons are summarized in Table 5.2, which is based on a table from McCollom and Savard's article. They divided the data from each study into a "tryout" group and a "followup" group. They then computed the validity coefficient for each tryout group and determined from the Taylor-Russell tables what percentage of satisfactory employees would be expected among subsequent groups of employees. The tryout groups were then subjected to the Direct Method analysis, and the expected percentages in this analysis were obtained.

Using selection ratios of .30, .40, .50, and .60 and proportions of satisfactory employees of .50, .60, .70, and .80, the average percentage error for all three studies was 6.6 when the Taylor-Russell tables were used on the follow-up groups. The corresponding average error for the Direct Method was 5.6. These results strongly suggest that one can make effective use of the selection ratio concept without computing a coefficient of correlation.

Possible Limitations of Taylor-Russell Tables

Several cautions concerning the use of the Taylor-Russell tables have been given by Smith.[16] He points out that the tabled values do not apply to triangular distributions of test scores plotted against a criterion. Figures 5.3 and 5.4, which were used to explain the operation of the Taylor-Russell tables, assume that every increase in average test score is associated with an increase in average criterion measure. The tables further assume that the criterion measure in relation to test score is a linear function. Under certain conditions, however, neither of these assumptions is fulfilled. For example, it is sometimes found that success on a job increases with test scores up to a certain point, but that above this point, further increases in test scores bear no relation or even (in rare cases) a negative relation to job success. Guilford[17] states that an inspection of the scattergram between test scores and criterion is usually sufficient to determine whether the relation is essentially linear, but several methods are available if it seems desirable to test the linearity of the plot. If it is decided that the scattergram represents a definitely nonlinear function, the Taylor-Russell tables should not be used

---

[16] Smith, M. Cautions concerning the use of the Taylor-Russell tables in employee selection. *Journal of Applied Psychology*, 1948, **32**, 595–600.

[17] Guilford, *op. cit.*, p. 149.

to predict the proportion of successful employees that will be obtained by using the test.[18]

TABLE 5.2 COMPARISON OF AVERAGE ERROR (IN PERCENTAGES) OF PREDICTION FOR TAYLOR-RUSSELL METHOD AND DIRECT METHOD FOR THREE JOBS

Job and Data Source	Test	r	Average Error in Prediction	
			Taylor-Russell	Direct Method
Aircraft workers (50) (Aircraft Co.)	Wonderlic Personnel Test	.59	3.8	5.7
Clerical workers (60) (Bellows)	Clerical Aptitude Test	.57	9.0	2.2
Machine operators (46) (Tiffin)	Bennett Test of Mechanical Comprehension	.36	7.5	9.1
Averages of all three groups			6.6	5.6

Source: McCollom and Savard, *op. cit.* Copyright 1957 by the American Psychological Association, and reproduced by permission.

Although there is a definite theoretical point to the above caution advanced by Smith, some work by Tiffin and Vincent[19] suggests that one usually can safely assume that the relationship shown by a correlation coefficient is sufficiently linear to justify the use of the Taylor-Russell tables. Using fifteen independent sets of predictor-criterion data, the theoretical expectancies obtained from modified Taylor-Russell tables (which are known as the Lawshe Expectancy Tables[20] see Appendix B)—were compared with the empirical expectancies determined directly from the raw data. The data of each sample were split into fifths on the test score continuum, and the percentage of satisfactory employees in each test score category was computed directly. These percentages were then compared with the theoretical percentages predicted from the Lawshe tables. In no one of the fifteen sets of data did the empirical percentages differ from the tabled percentages more than could be accounted for by chance, and in the majority of cases there was rather remarkable agreement between the empirical and the theoretical expectancies. Figure 5.6 (a) gives an example

[18] *Ibid.,* p. 294.

[19] Tiffin, J., & Vincent, N. L. Comparisons of empirical and theoretical expectancies. *Personnel Psychology,* 1960, **13**, 59–64.

[20] Modified by Lawshe, C. H., Bolda, R. A., Brune, R. L., & Auclair, G. Expectancy charts. II: Theoretical development. *Personal Psychology,* 1958, **11**, 545–559.

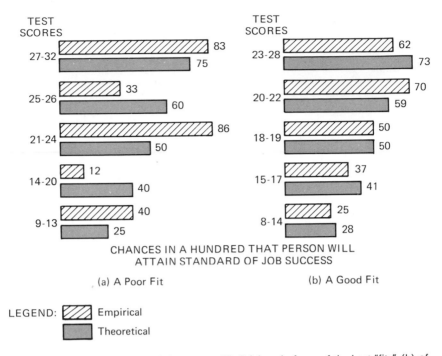

TEST
SCORES

27-32	83 / 75
25-26	33 / 60
21-24	86 / 50
14-20	12 / 40
9-13	40 / 25

TEST
SCORES

23-28	62 / 73
20-22	70 / 59
18-19	50 / 50
15-17	37 / 41
8-14	25 / 28

CHANCES IN A HUNDRED THAT PERSON WILL
ATTAIN STANDARD OF JOB SUCCESS

(a) A Poor Fit   (b) A Good Fit

LEGEND: ▨ Empirical
         ▓ Theoretical

FIG. 5.6 An example of one of the poorest "fits" (a) and of one of the best "fits" (b) of empirical to theoretical expectancies. (*From Tiffin and Vincent,* op. cit.)

of one of the worst fits from the fifteen studies, and Figure 5.6 (b) gives an example of one of the better fits. On the basis of these results, the authors concluded that in the majority of instances it is advisable to use theoretical instead of empirical expectancies in constructing expectancy charts.

A second caution advanced by Smith concerns the source of the validity coefficient used with the Taylor-Russell tables. When, as is often the case, the validity coefficient of a test is based upon the present-employee method of test validation, the validity coefficient obtained usually will be lower than what one would have obtained if the follow-up method had been used with a group of new employees. The reason for this difference is that many unsatisfactory employees have terminated their employment and only those doing at least well enough to remain on the job are available for the determination of the validity coefficient of the test. This reduction in the range of the criterion measures reduces the validity coefficient. The difference between the available and the true validity coefficients tends to result in underestimating the increase in satisfactory employees that would be obtained by using the test as a part of employment procedures.

An example of the application of the Taylor-Russell tables to a set of data is shown in Figure 5.7. The validity coefficient of a battery of three dexterity tests (treated finally as a single measuring instrument, as discussed later on page 125) was found by Surgent[21] to be .76. A tryout of this battery on a "holdout" group of employees, who had not been used in determining the validity coefficient, gave the results that have been plotted in Figure 5.7. Interpolation from the Taylor-Russell tables gave expected theoretical percentages that also have been plotted in Figure 5.7. The two curves

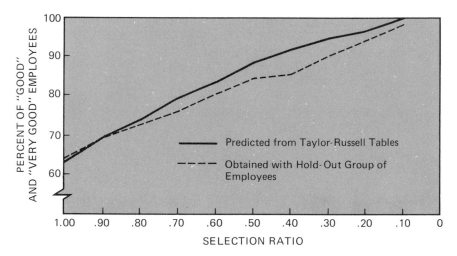

FIG. 5.7 Curves showing the percents of high criterion employees predicted from the Taylor-Russell tables and the empirical results obtained with a "hold out" group of employees not used in determining the validity of the tests.

plotted do not differ significantly. It is therefore advisable, whenever possible, to make this kind of empirical check on the application of the Taylor-Russell tables to personnel test data.

INDIVIDUAL VERSUS INSTITUTIONAL
EXPECTANCY CHARTS

The use of expectancy charts to show graphically the validity of a test was discussed on page 104 and illustrated in Figure 5.1. There are two types of such charts—the individual and the institutional. The individual chart (which was illustrated in Figure 5.1) shows what percentage of employees in *each test score bracket* will be superior on the job. Who is considered a "superior" employee (i.e., the criterion) must, of course, be

[21] Surgent, L. V. The use of aptitude tests in the selection of radio tube mounters. *Psychological Monographs,* 1947, **61**(2), 1–40.

decided before the analysis can be made. Another example of an individual expectancy chart is shown in Figure 5.8(a). The employees tested in this study were maintenance men in an artificial ice plant. Each man was rated on a five-point scale by the supervisor, and men receiving a rating of 4 or 5 were considered "superior." As Figure 5.8(a) shows, if a man makes a test score between 103 and 120, there are ninety-four chances in one hundred that he will be given a rating that would classify him as superior. On the other hand, if he makes a test score between 60 and 86, he has only twenty-five chances in one hundred of being rated superior. The individual expectancy chart thus permits individual prediction—i.e., the employing official can say what *each applicant's* chances are of being superior once he knows the applicant's test score on the test involved.

However, the primary task of the employment official is to be sure that, on the *average,* he is hiring men who will be most satisfactory on the job. He therefore ordinarily will be more concerned with the *institutional expectancy chart* than with the *individual expectancy chart.* The institutional chart shows the percentage of superior employees that will be obtained *if all applicants above a certain score are employed.* An example of an institutional chart constructed from the same data used in Figure 5.8(a) is shown in Figure 5.8(b).

If the labor market will permit doing so, only men scoring 103 or above on the test should be employed. In this case, it can be expected that ninety-four out of every hundred men employed, or 94 percent, will be superior. If it is impossible to get enough men who make a score of 103, the hiring standard will need to be reduced. If it is necessary to employ men who

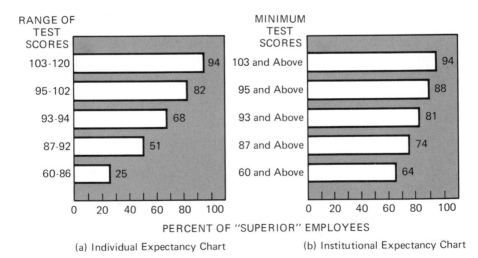

(a) Individual Expectancy Chart   (b) Institutional Expectancy Chart

FIG. 5.8 Illustration of (a) an individual expectancy chart, and (b) an institutional expectancy chart as a function of scores on the Purdue Mechanical Adaptability Test for the same sample of job incumbents.

score lower on the test, say down to 95, then only 88 percent of those employed will be "superior." With an institutional expectancy chart available to him, the employment man can be constantly aware of the chances he is taking as he reduces the hiring score when he is faced with a tight labor market.[22]

HOW TO USE TESTS FOR EMPLOYMENT

When a test has been found to be valid for a certain job, the next question to be answered is how the test should be used in the employment situation. What critical score (cutoff score) on the test should be required? Is it necessary, or desirable, to change the critical score from time to time? The answer to all these questions is that the critical score should be as high as the labor market will permit. Because labor markets vary from one time to another, the critical score on the test likewise should vary.

Specifically, the critical score to be used at any given time depends upon the use of test norms and the selection ratio under which the hiring is being done. An example in which both of these data were used will clarify this point. First, the validity of the Adaptability Test for first-line supervisors was determined. This investigation resulted in the institutional expectancy chart shown in Figure 5.9. It is clear from Figure 5.9 that there were

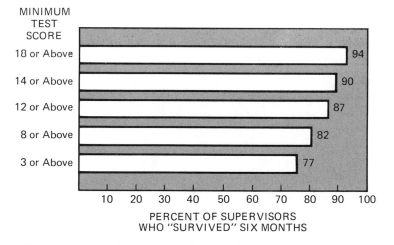

FIG. 5.9 Institutional expectancy chart showing the percent of new supervisors who "survived" six months as a function of minimum score on the adaptability test.

[22] An excellent discussion of *individual* and *institutional* expectancy charts will be found in Albright, L. E., Glennon, J. R., & Smith, W. J. *The use of psychological tests in business and industry.* Cleveland: Howard Allen, Inc., 1963.

ninety-four chances in one hundred that men making scores of 18 or higher would survive as supervisors for a period of six months. Figure 5.9 also shows the percentages surviving among men making successively lower critical scores. Obviously, in placing men in the supervisory job, the higher the Adaptability Test score, the greater the chances that men will be selected who will be able to handle the new assignment. However, to decide without regard to the pool of eligible men that only men making a score of 18 or higher will be placed on the job is quite unrealistic. At this point, therefore, we should look at norms on the test derived from the eligible men. These norms are shown in Table 5.3. They show the percentile ranks (see Appendix A, p. 584) equivalent to various raw scores for the group of men with whom we are concerned. As Table 5.3 shows, 100 percent of the men made scores of 27 or below, 95 percent made scores of 26 or below, 90 percent made scores of 21 or below, 80 percent made scores of 17 or below, and so on down the table. In other words, with 80 percent of the men making scores of 17 or below, only 20·percent made scores of 18 or above. This means that to find twenty men scoring 18 or above, we would need a pool of one hundred men from which to select and we would therefore need to use a selection ratio of .20. Because a pool of one hundred men might not be available, we would have to reduce our critical score in order to fill the vacancies. If we needed twenty men and there were only fifty to choose among, we would be operating with a selection ratio of 20:50 or .40, which means that we would have to reduce the critical score to 13. The reason for this change in the critical score is that, as Table 5.3 shows, a score of 12 is at the 60th percentile, which means that 60 percent of the group made a score of 12 or below, with only 40 percent of the men scoring 13 or higher. Referring again to the expectancy chart shown in Figure 5.9, it will be seen that we will not have as high a percentage of men sur-

TABLE 5.3 PERCENTILE NORMS ON THE ADAPTABILITY TEST FOR FOREMEN IN ONE PLANT

Percentile Rank	Score on Test
100	27
95	26
90	21
80	17
70	15
60	12
50	11
40	10
30	9
20	7
10	5
5	4
1	3

viving on the supervisor's job for six months when we use the critical score of 13 as we had when the critical score of 18 was used.

The point is that the critical (cutoff) score on a test must be varied with the tightness or looseness of the labor market. The tighter the market, the lower the critical score. The looser the market, the higher the critical score can be.

COMBINING TESTS INTO A BATTERY

No single test will measure all of the capacities or abilities required on any job. Even the simplest of jobs is complex if one considers the combination of capacities or abilities required of a person who is to remain on the job and to do it well. The aptitude for any job consists of a syndrome of abilities, and one needs all of these to be successful. This fact makes it desirable, and in some cases necessary, to use a battery of tests rather than a single test. There are two basic methods of using tests in a battery—the *multiple cutoff* method and the *multiple correlation* method. With both methods, it is assumed that the validity of each test in the battery has been established for the job in question.

The multiple cutoff method[23] involves the application of the tests one at a time and the elimination of applicants who do not score at a satisfactory level with each test. After the first test has been administered, certain low-scoring applicants are eliminated, and no further tests are administered to this group. In a similar way more applicants will be eliminated after the second test has been administered. This process is continued with all tests in the battery. After this has been completed, the only applicants remaining will be those who have made an acceptable minimum score on every test in the battery. Sometimes this method is used in such a way that applicants (or candidates for promotion) are required to make a certain score on a stated number of tests in the battery but do not have to "pass" all of the tests. In one investigation of this sort,[24] in which IBM proof machine operators were being hired, it was required that two of three tests be passed at the median score of the entire group tested. The battery used in this way had a very good selective efficiency and resulted in a 13 percent increase in production.

The other method of combining tests into a battery involves the adding of the scores (with or without differentially weighting them) to give a

---

[23] Grimsley, G. A comparative study of the Wherry-Doolittle and a multiple cutting score method. *Psychological Monographs,* 1949, **63**(2), 1–24.

[24] Harker, J. B. Cross-validation of an IBM proof machine battery. *Journal of Applied Psychology,* 1960, **44**, 237–240.

single composite test score predictor.[25] A great deal of sophisticated work on the weighting of test scores has been published during the past twenty or thirty years. Theoretically, it seems that appropriate weighting would result in a more efficient (valid) predictor than simply adding the raw scores made on the tests that are to be combined. The logic in favor of differentially weighting the scores seems unassailable, and therefore the method has been widely used for many years. However, some fairly recent empirical research on the topic has been conducted by Lawshe[26] and some of his students which makes it quite clear that the differential weighting of test scores seldom results in a higher validity coefficient than the simple adding of raw scores.

An example of the combination of test scores into a single composite score may be found in a set of tests worked out for placing menders in a hosiery mill. A number of tests were given to one hundred employees on this job. For each employee, data were obtained on age and experience as well as on average hourly earnings for the twelve-week period preceding the administration of the tests. The correlations between several of the tests and the earnings criterion are given below:

Test	Correlation
Purdue Hand Precision Test	.27
Finger Dexterity Test (Error Score)	.18
Hayes Pegboard	.16
Composite Score of Three Above Tests	.35

It will be noted that the maximum correlation of any individual test with earnings was .27, but that a battery made up of all three correlated at the .35 level with the same criterion. In obtaining the composite score the following formula was used: Composite Test Score = 12 (Hayes Pegboard) − 4 (Purdue Hand Precision Test) − 2 (Finger Dexterity Error Score). The constants by which the raw test scores are multiplied in this formula result in the theoretically best combination of the tests to make a prediction of job success from a combination of test scores. The usefulness of a test battery that correlates at the .35 level with a criterion may be inferred from Figure 5.10, which shows the percentage of employees placed by this battery who will be above the average of present employees when different selection ratios are used in hiring or placement. For example, if the selection ratio could be reduced to .10, approximately 74 percent of the em-

25 The procedure for making such a combination is beyond the scope of this book. It is thoroughly covered in Guilford, *op. cit.*

26 These studies are summarized by Lawshe, C. H., Statistical theory and practice in applied psychology. *Personnel Psychology*, 1959, **22**, 117–124.

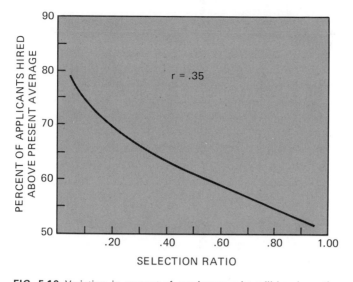

FIG. 5.10 Variation in percent of employees who will be above the present average of employees when different selection ratios are used with a test having a validity coefficient of .35.

ployees placed would be above the present average. The value of the testing procedure in this case is enhanced by the use of several tests in combination, inasmuch as no single test, of those tried, gave as high a validity coefficient as did the battery as a whole.

In some cases the form of a scattergram of test scores and criterion values will itself indicate that a single test covers only one phase of the job requirements. This is especially indicated when a scattergram shows that persons scoring high on a test may be either high or low on the criterion, whereas virtually all of those testing low on the test are low on the criterion. An example of this is shown in Table 5.4. The scattergram in this table shows, for employees on a job in a hosiery mill, the relationship between scores on the Purdue Grooved Pegboard Dexterity Test and a criterion of learning cost. (In this particular case the learning cost criterion was the amount the company had to "make up" between the actual piece-rate earnings and the legal minimum wage.)

The triangular form of the scattergram shown in Table 5.4 indicates that some of the employees who had high test scores actually turned out to be slow learners—that is, they were in the high learning cost criterion groups— but that none of those with poor test scores turned out to be rapid learners. The significance of this finding is that the test in question apparently is measuring one essential requirement of a rapid learner but only one. An employee who lacks this requirement is practically certain to be a slow

TABLE 5.4 SCATTERGRAM SHOWING RELATION BETWEEN LEARNING COST TO COMPANY OF 35 LOOPERS IN A HOSIERY MILL AND SCORES AT TIME OF EMPLOYMENT ON THE PURDUE GROOVED PEGBOARD DEXTERITY TEST

Learning Cost to Company	Score on Grooved Pegboard Dexterity Test				
	60 Seconds or over	55–59	50–54	45–49	40–44
$15–$24			2	2	5
$25–$34		1	3	3	
$35–$44			2		3
$45–$59	1			3	
$60 or over	2	3	3	1	1

learner, but an employee who tests high—that is, who has an abundance of this requirement—may still be a slow learner if he lacks certain other basic requirements for the job. The triangular shape of the scattergram thus indicates the existence of a hierarchy or syndrome of capacities required for this job.

For the reasons discussed on page 118, the Taylor-Russell table predictions are not applicable to data of the type shown in Table 5.4. Although reducing the selection ratio in this situation will increase the proportion of rapid learners, the tabled expectancies will not be correct because the scattergram is triangular.

Analyses of combinations of tests in predicting job performance criteria have led to some interesting implications regarding interactions among tests. In this connection, Ghiselli[27] presents some evidence that indicates that the performance of *some* individuals can be predicted from tests more accurately than the performance of *others*. But beyond this, he has found, in the case of certain jobs, that it is possible to use *one* test to identify those individuals for whom *another* test (or tests) *could* be used to predict their job performance. As he puts it,[28] in certain cases it seems possible that one can predict predictability! In a study of executives, for example, Ghiselli[29] reports that one test (referred to as a "moderator" variable or moderator test) was used to differentiate those individuals whose job performance could be adequately predicted by another test (a "predictor" test). For the entire group, the validity coefficient of the predictor test was .41. For the 21 percent with lowest scores on the moderator test, however, the validity

27 Ghiselli, E. E. Differentiation of individuals in terms of their predictability. *Journal of Applied Psychology*, 1956, **40**, 374–377.

28 Ghiselli, E. E. The prediction of predictability. *Educational and Psychological Measurement*, 1960, **20**(1), 1–8.

29 Ghiselli, E. E. Moderating effects and differential reliability and validity. *Journal of Applied Psychology*, 1963, **47**, 81–86.

of the predictor test was only .10, whereas for the 26 percent with highest scores on the moderator test, the validity of the predictor test was .68.

It should be noted, however, that the identification of the moderator and the predictor tests presumably needs to be done through research in the specific situation. Even though this interaction seems to be fairly situational, it suggests directions of research that may lead to improved prediction of job performance.

TEST ADMINISTRATION AND CONFIDENTIALITY

The use of personnel tests should be mutually advantageous both to the organization and to the individuals in question. Toward this end, the tests should be administered under conditions that help to place the individual at ease, for some people tend to become nervous and apprehensive at the prospect of being tested. Success in this area depends in large part on the test administrator and his manner in administering tests to job candidates. In order further to ensure reasonably adequate test results, the following guidelines should be followed:

1. The test room should be light, roomy, and quiet.
2. Each person should have a comfortable chair and table or desk.
3. The test administrator should follow whatever instructions there are for administering the test, including adherence to any specified time limits.

Once tests have been administered to individuals, they should be used in a professionally ethical manner, which in part means that test scores of individuals should be available only to those persons who have a legitimate use for them and that the scores and tests should be considered entirely confidential by those persons who do have access to them. The fact that they will be kept in confidence should be stated by the test administrator before the tests are given to the candidates. This helps to allay their apprehensions.

Questions have been raised about the possible invasion of privacy involved in asking people to take tests (especially personality and interest inventories) or in obtaining certain types of personal data about job candidates. We will not elaborate on this issue here further than to note that persons involved in the selection, administration, and use of tests should be aware of this matter and should ensure that the tests and other types of personnel information do not violate reasonable bounds.

ETHNIC FACTORS IN PERSONNEL TESTING

Recent years have witnessed an increasing concern in the United States about the appropriateness of personnel tests (especially aptitude tests) as the basis for the selection of individuals of different ethnic backgrounds and cultures. As indicated earlier, the possibility of discrimination on the basis of race has led to the passage of legislation such as the Civil Rights Act of 1964, the establishment of guidelines by the Equal Employment Opportunity Commission (EEOC) and the Office of Federal Contract Compliance (OFCC), as well as various court decisions. The primary thrust of such legislation and policies is the insistence that there must be reasonable evidence of the validity of personnel tests and that such tests must not discriminate unfairly against members of any particular group (such as minority groups).

One of the most important court cases in this area was *Griggs et al. v. Duke Power Company,* which was heard in the U.S. District Court in North Carolina. The decision in this case, handed down in 1968, pointed out that inasmuch as the tests being used by the company had no demonstrated relation to job success, the company could no longer use them as a basis for employment. This decision was appealed by the company and the case finally ended in the United States Supreme Court. In 1971 the Supreme Court reversed the 1968 decision. A part of the Supreme Court decision read as follows:

> Nothing in the Act precludes the use of testing or measuring procedures; obviously they are useful. What Congress has forbidden is giving these devices and mechanisms controlling force unless they are demonstrably a reasonable measure of job performance. Congress has not commanded that the less qualified be preferred over the better qualified simply because of minority origins. Far from disparaging job qualifications as such, Congress has made such qualifications the controlling factor, so that race, religion, nationality, and sex become irrelevant. What Congress has commanded is that any tests used must measure the person for the job and not the person in the abstract.

In view of the laws and legal decisions cited above, at least some of the companies that have been using personnel tests are now making a serious effort to be sure that the use of the tests is in conformance with the legal requirements.

The Issue of Fairness

A central issue in the problem of testing and discrimination relates to the *fairness* of tests and other predictors as the basis for personnel selection.

In this regard, Guion[30] points out that discrimination *per se* is not unfair if the people who are less likely to do well on a job are less likely to be hired; discrimination is unfair only "when persons with equal probabilities of success on the job have unequal probabilities of being hired for the job." As Kirkpatrick *et al.*[31] put it, a test may be considered to be unfairly discriminatory against members of a minority group if: (1) the minority group members obtain significantly lower test scores than nonminority applicants; *and* (2) the minority applicants would in fact be as successful on the job as the nonminority applicants. In other words, unfair discrimination occurs only if the *predicted* criterion scores of one ethnic group are lower than their *actual* criterion scores would be. Of course, this basic concept of "unfair" discrimination is predicated on the assumption that the criterion measures of job success are not biased in the same direction as the effects of ethnic background on test performance. And it is probable that there have been some circumstances in which this assumption has not been fulfilled, such as when a supervisor permits his criterion ratings to be biased by ethnic factors.

Test-criterion relationships. The implications of this concept of fairness are depicted, albeit in an overly simplified form, in the positions of the outlines of hypothetical scattergrams in Figure 5.11. Each of the three parts of this figure represents a different possible relationship of the scattergrams of two groups (such as different ethnic groups), A and B; these relationships are described below the figure in terms of whether the test scores and/or criteria are the same or different. Of these, part 3 represents the circumstance in which the use of the test would be unfair. In this case, the test scores of group B are clearly below those of group A, but their criterion performance is equal. Using such a test without some type of correction for the difference clearly would discriminate unfairly against individuals in group B inasmuch as they would tend to be rejected for the job even though they would be equally able to perform well at it.

Comparative Validity of Tests for Different Groups

A number of studies have been made in which the validity of individual aptitude tests has been determined separately for different ethnic groups, such as blacks and whites. In this regard, Boehm[32] makes a distinction be-

[30] Guion, R. M. Employment tests and discriminatory hiring. *Industrial Relations,* 1966, **5**, 20–37.

[31] Kirkpatrick, J. J., Ewen, R. B., Barrett, R. S., & Katzell, R. A. *Testing and fair employment.* New York: New York University Press, 1968.

[32] Boehm, V. R. Negro-white differences in validity of employment and training selection procedures. *Journal of Applied Psychology,* 1972, **56**(1), 33–39.

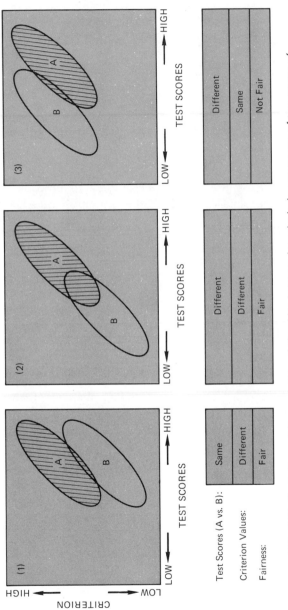

FIG. 5.11 Illustrations of three possible relationships between hypothetical scattergrams of two groups of people (such as different ethnic groups). Of these (3) represents a relationship that would be unfair in the selection of people of group B.

tween *differential validity* (in which there is a statistically significant difference in the validity coefficients for two groups) and *single-group validity* (in which a test has a statistically significant validity for one group but not the other). A couple of studies relating to this distinction will be discussed.

One such study, reported by Gael and Grant,[33] dealt with telephone service representatives; the sample used consisted of 107 black males and 193 white males. It was found that a battery of tests predicted the job performance of employees of both groups with "relatively the same degree of accuracy." In another study, Grant and Bray[34] found that the same combination of test scores was about equally predictive for performance of blacks and whites in a training program for telephone installation and repair occupations. The relationship for the two groups between composite test

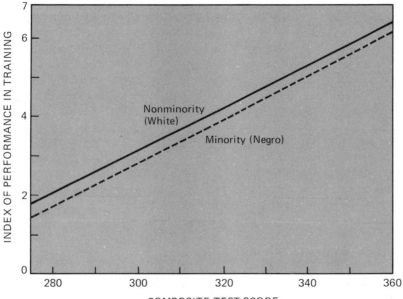

FIG. 5.12 Comparison of relationship for minority and non-minority groups between composite test scores on two tests and an index of performance in a training program for telephone installation and repair. The two lines (actually regression lines) were so nearly the same in this case that it was concluded that the same weighted combination of tests could be used for both groups without any unfair discrimination. (*Adapted from Grant and Bray,* op. cit., *Fig. 1, p. 13.*)

[33] Gael, S. & Grant, D. L. Employment test validation for minority and non-minority telephone company service representatives. *Journal of Applied Psychology,* 1972, **56**, 135–139.

[34] Grant, D. L., & Bray, D. W. Validation of employment tests for telephone company installation and repair occupations. *Journal of Applied Psychology,* 1970, **54**(1), 7–14.

scores and an index of performance in training is shown in Figure 5.12. The difference was so negligible that it was concluded that the same combination and weighting of tests could be used for both ethnic groups.

Two summaries of various studies of the comparative validity of tests for blacks and whites have been reported. One of these, by Ruch,[35] covered twenty studies in which separate analyses for blacks and whites were made. Ruch concluded that these studies showed no systematic evidence of differential validity for the two groups. In the survey by Boehm[36] of sixty comparative cases, there were only seven in which differential validity occurred. Although there were a number of instances of single-group validity (twenty for whites and thirteen for blacks), these were attributed largely to small sample sizes and to certain methodological aspects. The prevailing impression from these surveys, as well as from the results of other studies, is that differential validity (which would have the most serious implications in terms of fairness) may not be as widespread as generally has been presumed to be the case.

Comparative Test Performance

The question of possible differential validity of tests is related, of course, to the test performance of different groups, such as blacks and whites. In this regard, there is fairly substantial evidence of differences between blacks and whites in performance on mental ability tests, as discussed by Tyler,[37] although there are still ongoing arguments regarding the basis for such differences—whether genetic, nutritional, cultural, educational, or otherwise. Comparative test performance, especially with cognitive tests, has been presented in conjunction with several personnel test validity studies. In most instances, significant differences have been reported.[38]

Although it has commonly been thought that such group differences were primarily associated with mental ability tests, Ruda and Albright[39] report differences in spatial ability tests as well. For this reason they caution against the use of "nonverbal" tests as a means of avoiding the "verbal" emphasis of typical mental ability tests. There are also some reports of ethnic differences in scores on other types of tests, such as mechanical tests and various verbal tests.

[35] Ruch, W. W. A re-analysis of published differential validity studies. Paper read at the American Psychological Association, Honolulu, September 6, 1972.

[36] Boehm, op. cit.

[37] Tyler, L. E. The psychology of human differences. (3rd ed.) New York: Appleton-Century-Crofts, 1965.

[38] Boehm, op. cit.; Ruda, E., & Albright, L. E. Racial differences on selection instruments related to subsequent job performance. Personnel Psychology, 1968, 21(1), 31–41; and Moore, C. L., Jr., MacNaughton, J. F., & Osburn, H. G. Ethnic differences within an industrial selection battery. Personnel Psychology, 1969, 22(4), 473–482.

[39] Ruda & Albright, op. cit.

Resolution of Ethnic Group Differences

Although there are, as we have seen, some indications that different ethnic groups manifest differences in performance on some tests, this fact does not necessarily imply that the use of such tests would result in unfair discrimination. The critical issue concerns the relationship between test scores and criterion values of the groups in question—in other words, the validity of the test for the groups.

In discussing the use of selection tests, Krug[40] reminds us that treating people *equally,* in the sense of providing equal opportunity for employment, does not mean treating them *identically.* After expressing his uneasiness about the term "double standards" because of its unpleasant associations, he raises the question: "Double standards on what? Predictor or criterion?" In answering his own question, he rejects the possibility of applying a double standard to the criterion, for it is asking much of industry to expect it deliberately to hire people who will not perform up to standard. But if the double standard applies to the predictor—that is, the test—who cares? If by some means one can identify *one* set of predictors for one group of people and *another* set for another group that predict the performance criterion values equally well, why not use them differentially? Such a notion applies equally well to whatever groups one may have in mind—male versus female, blacks versus whites, rural versus city dwellers, college graduates versus non-college graduates, or tall versus short—as long as such procedures aid in the prediction of the criterion and as long as there are some individuals within both groups who can perform the job at a satisfactory level.

Basically, then, we have arrived at the principle that a test validation sample should not be comprised of people of different groups if there is any reason to suspect that differences between groups could result in inequitable treatment of some individuals who actually have potentialities for the job—and thus muddy the validation waters. In effect, this means that in the validation process separate validation analyses should be made for those groups for which there is any reason to suspect that differences in prediction *might* exist. If separate validation studies *do* reflect differences in test scores and/or criterion values, and if these differences could result in unfair discrimination, separate selection standards should be established, as urged by Enneis, Krug, and others.[41] If, on the other hand, the same set of predictors is found to be equally predictive for the two groups, then of course that single set can be used with confidence for both groups.

---

[40] Krug, R. E. Some suggested approaches for test development and measurement. *Personnel Psychology,* 1966, **19**(1), 24–35.

[41] Enneis, W. H. The black man in the world of work. *Professional Psychology,* 1970, **5**(1), 435–439.; Krug, *op. cit.*

chapter six

Human Abilities
and
Their
Measurement

The spectrum of human abilities demonstrated in the ongoing scene of human life is a source of amazement, as reflected by the performance of the sleight-of-hand entertainers, glib auctioneers, engravers, and astronauts. As we consider the range of human abilities, however, we can view them as forming two somewhat separate bundles. In the first group are those that we will refer to as basic human abilities, those general classes of human abilities that most of us have in common—but in varying quantity—such as various types of mental abilities and psychomotor skills. In the second group are those that we will refer to as job-specific abilities—those that are rather unique to individuals who have learned to perform a particular activity, such as playing an oboe or programming a computer. In this chapter we will discuss both of these types of abilities and their measurement as well as their relevance to the personnel field.

THE NATURE OF BASIC HUMAN ABILITIES

We recognize full well that people differ in their capacities to be able to acquire specific skills and knowledges such as those needed for certain jobs and other activities. Such capacities conventionally are referred to as *aptitudes*. These aptitudes (or capacities) actually are basic human abilities, there being marked individual differences on each such ability. Measurements of these human abilities frequently are used in the prediction of job performance and other criteria.

The concept of basic human abilities is rather elusive. We all would agree that the ability to perform a heavy handling activity is different from the ability to add and subtract numbers. But is being able to remember numbers (such as telephone numbers) the same as being able to remember words (such as names or a set of directions)? Although there are arguments regarding the intrinsic nature of what we here refer to as basic human abilities, for our present purposes a suitable operational definition was provided by Fleishman[1] when he defined a basic human ability as ". . .a more general trait of the individual which has been inferred from certain response consistencies (e.g., correlations) on certain kinds of tasks."

Farina[2] points out that these basic abilities are fairly enduring traits which have both learning and genetic components underlying their development, and that they derive their "conceptual existence"—that is, our concepts of them—from the prior existence of a *factor* as identified by factor analysis.

As used in this context, factor analysis involves the following processes: (1) administering a variety of tests to a sample of people; (2) correlating each test with every other test; (3) identifying the various factors by means of statistical manipulations (essentially, this step is based on the identification of the several tests that tend to form individual "groups" or "clusters" on the basis of their correlations with each other); and (4) naming each factor on the basis of subjective judgment regarding the "common denominator" that characterizes those tests which have high statistical "loadings" on each factor. Although some human abilities actually are quite separate and independent from others (in the sense of having virtually no correlation with them), most abilities tend to have some correlation with one or more other abilities. In a fairly major effort aimed at the identification of the spectrum of human abilities viewed in this way, Fleishman and his

[1] Fleishman, E. A. Performance assessment based on an empirically derived task taxonomy. *Human Factors,* 1967, **9**, 349–366.

[2] Farina, A. J., Jr. *Development of a taxonomy of human performance: A review of descriptive schemes for human task behavior.* Silver Spring, Maryland: American Institutes for Research, Technical Report 2(R69–8), January 1969.

coworkers[3] have crystallized an assortment of thirty-seven abilities, some of which will be mentioned later.

The basis for any classification of human abilities is a bit arbitrary, but for purposes of this discussion the following categories will be used: (1) mental abilities; (2) mechanical and related abilities; (3) psychomotor abilities; and (4) visual skills.

MENTAL ABILITIES

Interest in human mental—that is, cognitive or intellectual—abilities goes way back to some of the research of Sir Francis Galton[4] and the development of the early tests by Binet,[5] specifically those for identifying mentally deficient children in schools. After years of discourse about the nature of intelligence, Spearman[6] came forth with a postulated concept of a "g" (or "general") factor of *mental energy* available to an individual, plus a variety of "s" (or specific) factors. The next major stage in the analysis of the nature of intellectual abilities consisted of the monumental work of Thurstone,[7] who by factor analysis sorted out seven primary mental abilities, as follows:

S—Spatial visualization
P—Perceptual speed
N—Number facility
V—Verbal comprehension
W—Word fluency
M—Memory
I—Inductive reasoning

The next major development was that of Guilford,[8] who, on the basis of a series of studies, formulated the concept of the "three faces of intellect,"

3 Theologus, G. C., Romashko, T., & Fleishman, E. A. *Development of a taxonomy of human performance: A feasibility study of ability dimensions for classifying tasks.* Silver Spring, Maryland: American Institutes for Research, Technical Report 5 (R70–1), January 1970.

4 Galton, F. *Inquiries into human faculty and its development.* London: Macmillan, 1883.

5 Binet, A., & Henri, V. La psychologie individuelle. *Année psychologie,* 1895, **2,** 411–465.

6 Spearman, C. E. *The abilities of man.* New York: MacMillan, 1927.

7 Thurstone, L. L. *Primary mental abilities.* Chicago: Psychometric Laboratory, University of Chicago, Report No. 50, 1948.

8 Guilford, J. P. Three faces of intellect. *American Psychologist,* 1959, **14,** 469–479; *The nature of human intelligence.* New York: McGraw-Hill, 1967; and Thurstone's primary mental abilities and structure-of-intellect abilities. *Psychological Bulletin,* 1972, **77**(2), 129–143.

or what is called the structure of intellect (SI). Guilford's model provides for three main ways of classifying mental abilities, with various specific breakdowns of each, as follows:

> *Operations:* C—cognition (rediscovery or recognition); M—memory (remembering what is cognized); D—divergent production (searching for different ideas or solutions to problems); N—convergent production (processing information to arrive at correct answer or solution); E—evaluation (judging adequacy of one's thinking).
>
> *Content:* F—figural (size, form, color, etc.); S—symbolic (letters, digits, etc.); M—semantic (verbal meanings and ideas); B—behavioral (dealing with social situations).
>
> *Products* (the nature of the responses of people): U—units; C—classes; R—relations; S—systems; T—transformations; I—implications.

These three aspects—operations, content, and products—are represented in Figure 6.1 as a cube. The combinations of the subcategories of the three aspects add up to 120 different facets of intellect. Each such ability is designated by a trigram in the form of a letter identification, such as CMU

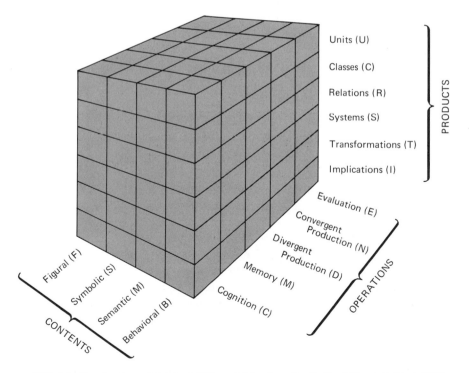

FIG. 6.1 The structure-of-intellect (SI) model developed by Guilford (*From Guilford, 1967, op. cit., Fig. 3.9, p. 63.*)

(standing for *C*ognition of *S*emantic *U*nits). Guilford[9] points out that, although there are similarities between certain of Thurstone's primary mental abilities and certain of the categories in his own structure-of-intellect model, there also are differences, the primary difference being that certain of Thurstone's factors are equivalent to "bundles" of facets in Guilford's si model. (It should be noted, also, that the cognitive abilities set forth in Fleishman's[10] taxonomy stem in part from Guilford's si model, but include only those few specific categories that have been rather widely dealt with.)

Tests of Mental Abilities

Many standardized tests of mental abilities are available. Most such tests (along with many other types of tests) are listed and described in the *Seventh Mental Measurements Yearbook* by Buros,[11] which also gives information on the source of the test, references to research with the test, and in most cases some evaluation of the test and data on validity and reliability. (Appendix D of this book lists certain tests that are used widely in industry, along with their publishers.)

Tests differ in various respects, such as mode of administration (group versus individual) and level (for children, teenagers, adults, and so forth). They also differ in their content—that is, in the aspect of mental ability covered. Some such tests are intended to measure specific facets of mental abilities, whereas others are broader or more heterogeneous in content in that they cover a variety of aspects. (Some of the tests of mental abilities used in industry are listed in Appendix D.)

Examples of Mental Ability Tests in Use

Mental ability tests have been used as the basis for the selection of personnel for quite a wide variety of jobs, especially for those that involve substantial decision making, reasoning, or other cognitive activities. For purposes of illustration, a couple of examples of test validation studies with such tests will be given.

Clerical jobs. Shore[12] conducted one such study dealing with the job of bank teller. Among several tests given to seventy-seven employed tellers was the Thurstone Test of Mental Alertness (Form A). The scores were correlated with a criterion of supervisory ratings and the resulting correlation was .63. Figure 6.2 is an expectancy chart based on such a correlation.

In another study by one of the present authors, the Adaptability Test

9 Guilford, 1972, *op. cit.*
10 Theologus, Romashko, & Fleishman, *op. cit.*
11 Buros, O. K. (Ed.) *The seventh mental measurements yearbook.* (Vols. I and II.) Highland Park, N.J.: The Gryphon Press, 1972.
12 Shore, R. P. Validity information exchange, No. 11–23. *Personnel Psychology,* 1958, **11**, 437.

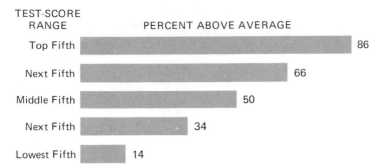

TEST-SCORE
RANGE   PERCENT ABOVE AVERAGE

FIG. 6.2 Individual expectancy chart for the Thurstone Test of Mental Alertness as a predictor of job success for the job of bank teller. This chart is based on a correlation of .63 between the test and supervisors' ratings. (*Adapted from Shore,* op. cit.)

was administered to clerical employees in several departments of a paper company. The correlation of this test with supervisors' ratings ranged from .40 to .65 for the employees in the various departments. In one department where only 57 percent of the current employees were rated as "satisfactory," it was found that among those scoring 25 or above on the test, 86 percent were "satisfactory."

Supervisors. Mental ability tests frequently have been found to have substantial validity as the basis for the selection of supervisors. This was illustrated, for example, by the results of a study of seventy employees of a rubber company who had been promoted to supervisory jobs. During the first session of a training program for these men, they were administered the Adaptability Test. The test results were filed for six months, at which time a follow-up analysis was made in relation to a criterion of being "still on the job." Approximately one-fourth of the men had not "survived" as supervisors for that period; they had either quit voluntarily, or had been

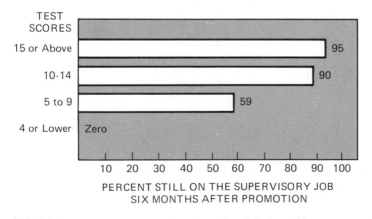

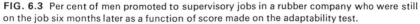

FIG. 6.3 Per cent of men promoted to supervisory jobs in a rubber company who were still on the job six months later as a function of score made on the adaptability test.

demoted, transferred, or dismissed. Figure 6.3 shows the percentage of men still on the job after these six months in relation to their test scores. It is interesting to note that not a single man with a score of 4 or below was still on the job, and that of those with scores between 5 and 9 only 59 percent had survived (as contrasted with 90 percent or more in the case of those with higher scores).

Other types of jobs. Another illustration of a job in which a mental ability test has been found to be valid is that of teletype operators. A total of 219 trainees for this job were given the Adaptability Test after their selection for training. The test scores were later analyzed in relation to their success in passing the training course and the results are summarized below:

Score on Adaptability Test	Percent Passing Training Course
22 or above	96
16–21	94
10–15	89
9 or below	61

In this instance it seems to be appropriate to select individuals with scores of 10 or above, for the test apparently measures some quality that is required in the training course. The percentage of those with scores lower than 10 who succeeded in the training course was noticeably lower than the percentage of those with scores of 10 or above who passed. (In this case, we should note, the cost of the training program argued strongly for more careful screening of applicants.)

Discussion. The examples discussed above are clearly instances in which mental ability tests have been found to be related to relevant criteria. There are, of course, many other types of jobs for which such tests also have been found to be valid predictors of job success. But it should be clearly understood that there are many other types of jobs for which such tests have little or no validity. Further reference to the level of validity of mental ability tests for various types of jobs will be made later in this chapter.

MECHANICAL ABILITY

The wide range of "mechanical" jobs that have been spawned by the mechanisms of our present-day world has increased the importance of mechanical ability as a human quality involved in jobs.

The Nature of Mechanical Ability

Although most "mechanical" jobs involve physical activities, *mechanical ability* deals essentially with the mental or cognitive aspects of such jobs as contrasted with the physical or motor aspects. Actually, as Tyler[13] points out, there are two classes of such ability, which she calls "mechanical aptitude." One of these involves the comprehension of mechanical relations, the recognition of tools used for various purposes, and related cognitive abilities. This syndrome seems to jibe quite well with a statistically derived factor called *mechanical experience* that resulted from factor analyses by Friedman and Ivens[14] and Friedman and Detter.[15] This factor appears to represent knowledge gained from experience with mechanical apparatus and tools. For convenience of terminology, it can be called *general mechanical aptitude*.

The other class of mechanical ability discussed by Tyler involves the perception and manipulation of spatial relations—that is, the ability to visualize how parts or components fit together as a whole. This was also identified as a factor by Friedman and Ivens and Friedman and Detter and corresponds with the visualization ability of Fleishman's[16] formulation and the spatial visualization factor reported by Thurstone in his studies of primary mental abilities. The potential relevance of this factor to performance on various mechanical jobs is obvious in jobs that require the visualization of physical relationships between objects, such as in putting your carburetor back together.

Tests of Mechanical Ability

A few of the most commonly used tests of mechanical ability are listed in Appendix D. Examples of certain of these, or items from them, are shown in Figures 6.4, 6.5, and 6.6. In addition, particular mention will be made of the Purdue Mechanical Adaptability Test, to illustrate the processes involved in developing standardized tests of this type.

The Purdue Mechanical Adaptability Test was developed to aid in identifying men or boys who are mechanically inclined, and who, therefore, are most likely to succeed on jobs or in training programs calling for mechanical abilities and interests. The test measures one's experiential background in mechanical, electrical, and related activities. The test was constructed to measure experiential background because there was reason to believe from a previous study that, other things being equal, those persons who have most profited in knowledge from previous mechanical experiences may do better

[13] Tyler, L. E. *The psychology of individual differences.* New York: Meredith Publishing Company, 1965, pp. 144–145.

[14] Friedman, G., & Ivens, F. C. Factor analysis of the airman classification battery AC–1B; the USES General Aptitude Test Battery, experimental visualization and spatial tests, and psychomotor tests. *Research bulletin,* AFPTRC–TR–54–67, Air Force Personnel and Training Research Center, Lackland Air Force Base, San Antonio, Texas.

[15] Friedman, G., & Detter, H. M. Factor analysis of airman classification battery and selected air force and civilian tests. *Research bulletin,* AFPTRC–TR–54–75.

[16] Theologus, Romashko, & Fleishman, *op. cit.*

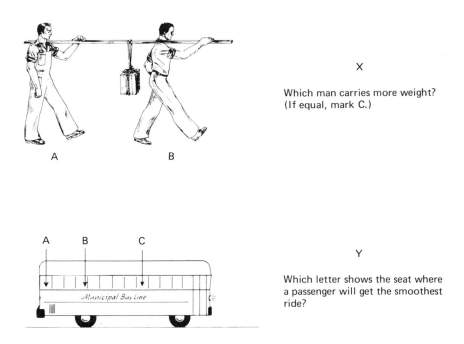

X

Which man carries more weight?
(If equal, mark C.)

Y

Which letter shows the seat where
a passenger will get the smoothest
ride?

FIG. 6.4 Two items from Forms S and T of the Bennett Test of Mechanical Comprehension *(Reproduced by permission. Copyright 1940, renewed 1967; 1941, renewed 1969; 1942, renewed 1969; © 1967, 1968 by The Psychological Corporation, New York, N. Y. All rights reserved.)*

on mechanical jobs than those persons who have not so profited. The test is one of general mechanical aptitude.

The questions comprising Form A of the Purdue Mechanical Adaptability Test were selected by statistical methods designed to achieve maximum reliability of the final test and as low a correlation as possible with general intelligence. The effort to develop a mechanical ability test which would not depend very much upon the general intelligence of the persons being tested payed off quite well, for the correlations of scores on this test with scores on various mental ability tests are generally rather low.

General mechanical ability and spatial visualization ability frequently have been found to be requirements for jobs such as craftsmen, mechanics and repairmen, draftsmen, and engineers. Figures 6.7 and 6.8 are expectancy charts based on validation studies with the Purdue Mechanical Adaptability Test for railroad trade apprentices and for airplane engine mechanic trainees. In both instances the criterion used consisted of instructor ratings. These two figures illustrate the relevance of mechanical ability tests to successful performance in job activities of the types represented.

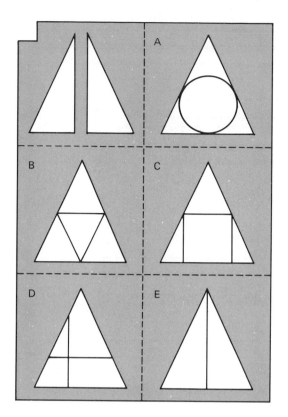

FIG. 6.5 An item from the Minnesota Paper Form Board Test. The person tested is asked to select the set of lettered parts (A, B, C, D, or E) which may be formed by the parts shown in the upper-left square.

Hub Assemblies 1–6.   Hub Assemblies 7 and 8.

FIG. 6.6 Parts of the Purdue Mechanical Assembly Test. These are the hub assembly parts of the test.

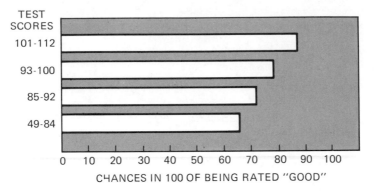

FIG. 6.7 Expectancy chart showing relation between Purdue Mechanical Adaptability Test Scores and rated success of railroad trade apprentices.

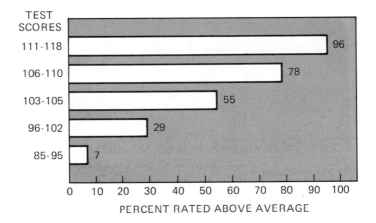

FIG. 6.8 Relation between scores on the Purdue Mechanical Adaptability Test and ratings of 34 airplane engine mechanic trainees.

The use of mechanical ability tests in the case of professional jobs is illustrated by the investigation of engineers conducted by Spencer and Reynolds,[17] who gave the Minnesota Engineering Analogies Test (MEAT) to twenty-eight recent bachelor's degree mechanical and electrical engineering graduates who had been employed by a manufacturer of business machines. Scores on this test were correlated with the three criteria listed below:

Criterion	Correlation
1. Training program class standing (at 6 mo.)	.40
2. Job performance ratings (at 6 mo.)	.58
3. Job performance ratings (at 18 mo.)	.64

17 Spencer, G. M., & Reynolds, H. J. Validity information exchange, No. 14–04. *Personnel Psychology,* 1961, **14,** 456–458.

It is interesting to note that the validity of the test was higher at the end of eighteen months of employment than at the end of the first six months.

PSYCHOMOTOR ABILITIES

Psychomotor abilities cover the range of abilities that we commonly call dexterity, manipulative ability, motor ability, eye-hand coordination, and other aspects of relatively skilled muscular performance, frequently involving some degree of visual control.

The Nature of Psychomotor Abilities

Substantial evidence indicates that there are various *kinds* of psychomotor abilities. Probably the currently most adequate representation of these was presented by Theologus, Romashko, and Fleishman,[18] who extracted their account of psychomotor abilities from their more comprehensive taxonomy of human abilities. The following list of psychomotor activities is based in large part on several previous factor analyses by Fleishman and his associates.

> *Choice reaction time.* This is the ability to select and initiate a response when the response is selected from two or more alternatives relative to two or more stimuli.
> *Reaction time.* This is the speed with which a single motor response can be initiated relative to a single stimulus.
> *Speed of limb movement.* This ability involves the speed with which discrete movements of the arm or leg can be made.
> *Wrist-finger speed.* This ability is concerned with the speed with which discrete movements of the fingers, hands, and wrists can be made.
> *Finger dexterity.* This is the ability to make skillful, coordinated movements of the fingers where manipulation of objects may or may not be involved.
> *Manual dexterity.* This is the ability to make skillful, coordinated movements of the hand, or of a hand together with its arm.
> *Rate control.* This is the ability to make timed, anticipatory motor adjustments relative to changes in the speed and/or direction of a continuously moving object.
> *Control precision.* This is the ability to make controlled muscular movements necessary to adjust or position a machine or equipment control mechanism.

Relationships Between Psychomotor Abilities

Although in general psychomotor abilities can be considered to be relatively separate types of abilities, there is still some question as to how accurate it would be to regard them as *completely* independent. In discussing

18 Theologus, Romashko, & Fleishman, *op. cit.*

this question, Vernon[19] points out that in several studies with psychomotor tests, it has been found that such tests typically have some relationships with each other, although the average intercorrelations among groups of them are quite low—for example, .25, .27, .30, and .13. In other circumstances even lower correlations have been reported. Although some psychomotor tests tend to be correlated with each other, the correlations usually are so low that the various psychomotor abilities must be considered as predomi-

FIG. 6.9 Bennett Hand-Tool Dexterity Test. (*Photograph courtesy of The Psychological Corporation.*)

FIG. 6.10 Purdue Pegboard.

[19] Vernon, P. E. *The structure of human abilities.* London: Methuen & Co.; New York: John Wiley, 1950.

FIG. 6.11 Stromberg Dexterity Test. (*Photograph courtesy The Psychological Corporation.*)

nantly specific. This implies that it is *particularly* important when using tests of such abilities to be sure that the test or tests used in a given situation are thoroughly validated for the job in question before they are used. A few typical psychomotor tests are listed in Appendix. D. Illustrations of some of these are shown in Figures 6.9, 6.10, and 6.11.

Examples of Psychomotor Tests in Use

A typical job for which psychomotor abilities are of considerable importance is that of packer. In a test validation study of packers in a handcraft company, Wolins and MacKinney[20] gave the Purdue Pegboard and the Minnesota Rate of Manipulation Test to twenty-seven employees. The job involves packing handcraft kits in boxes or envelopes. The packers were rated by their supervisor, who classified each in one of five rating categories. The correlations of the various parts of the two tests with these ratings are given below:

Test	*Correlation**
Purdue Pegboard	
Right Hand	.19
Left Hand	.32
Both Hands	.19
Right + Left + Both	.27
Assembly	.47
Minnesota Rate of Manipulation Test	
Placing	.21
Turning	.40
Displacing	.16
1 hand turn and place	.26
2 hand turn and place	.27

* The correlations for the Minnesota test were actually negative inasmuch as this test is a work-limit test with scores being based on the *time* taken to complete it. Because good performance on the test (low time scores) is related to good job performance (and vice versa), the correlations are shown here as positive.

[20] Wolins, L., & MacKinney, A. C. Validity information exchange, No. 15–04. *Personnel Psychology,* 1961, 15, 227–229.

It can be seen from these data that all parts of both tests were correlated with the ratings, although certain parts had noticeably higher correlations than the others, especially the Assembly Part of the Purdue test and the Turning Part of the Minnesota test.

Job-component dexterity tests. Previous mention has been made of the concept of job-component (or synthetic) validity. In line with this concept, Drews[21] developed an assortment of manipulative test materials (especially pegboard components) that could be used in various ways. After an analysis of the elemental motions of each of several jobs, he developed (using the test materials) a test for each job that approximated the combination of elemental motions in the job. These specially designed tests generally were found to be more valid for prediction of job success than standardized tests that were used.

VISUAL SKILLS

Most jobs involve the use of vision, but of course there are some jobs in which various types of visual skills are especially important to successful job performance, such as in some inspection operations, the operation of some machines, most office jobs, and the operation of vehicles.

The Nature of Visual Skills

Some of the more important visual skills are described below, along with some observations regarding tests for measuring each.

Visual acuity. Visual acuity is the ability to discriminate black and white detail, usually measured in terms of the minimum separable areas that can be distinguished. The ability to make such discriminations at near distances is relatively independent of the ability to do so at far distances. Therefore, tests should be given both for far visual acuity and for near visual acuity if both are relevant to job performance.

Depth perception (stereopsis). This function is an important phase of correct perception of spatial relationships. Of several cues for judging relative distances of objects, the most important for persons with normal vision, and the one that can be controlled and measured most reliably, depends on the slight difference in the position of the two eyes. The two eyes perform a geometric triangulation upon a distant object, and the distance of that object is perceived through an integration of the minute differences in appearance of the object to the two eyes. Other cues for perceiving distance in the

21 Drewes, D. W. Development and validation of synthetic dexterity tests based on elemental motion analysis. *Journal of Applied Psychology,* 1961, **45,** 179–185.

third dimension may augment but cannot adequately substitute for this cue from two-eye functioning.

Color discrimination. Although absolute color blindness is relatively rare, certain aspects of color deficiency are somewhat more common, such as the inability to discriminate between the reds and greens or between the blues and yellows. Even those who do not have distinct color deficiencies differ in the degree to which they can discriminate between and among various hues, shades, and tints of colors.

Postural characteristics of the eyes (phorias). Under normal seeing conditions the two eyes must move in relation to each other so that both converge symmetrically upon the object. It is this convergence that gives us a clear, single image of the object when it is viewed binocularly. Under certain testing conditions which eliminate the necessity for such convergence of the eyes on a single point, the eyes assume a posture that may converge or diverge from that required in normal seeing at the test distance. Such postures, called "phorias" in clinical terminology, are measured in terms of angular deviation from the posture normally required for that distance. The deviation may be lateral or vertical and is measured separately in each direction. In addition, such deviations should be measured at the optical equivalent of both near and far vision. Many individuals have "learned" to overcome phoria conditions by controlling the muscles that direct both eyes to the point of visual regard, but in so doing they may have to maintain the eyes in a "strained" posture, thereby running the risk of muscular fatigue if the postures have to be retained for some time.

Examples of Vision Tests

Probably the most commonly used vision test is the Snellen letter chart that is a familiar sight on the walls of physicians' offices. The test consists of several rows of block letters of decreasing size, usually placed at a distance of twenty feet from the subject. A typical Snellen chart is shown in Figure 6.12. The test is administered by determining, separately for each eye, the smallest letters that the subject can read. The smaller the letters the subject can read, the greater the visual acuity. The Snellen notation of acuity scores is in the form of a fraction—the smaller the fraction, the poorer the vision. In this fraction the numerator is constant and represents the distance of the test. Thus, visual acuity scored 20/20 is standard. A score of 20/40 means that the subject can read at twenty feet only a letter twice as large as standard, a letter that the "standard eye" can read at forty feet.

In order to simplify interpretation of visual acuity scores and to set up an equitable scale for awarding compensation in proportion to actual incapacity due to eye injury, the American Medical Association has adopted

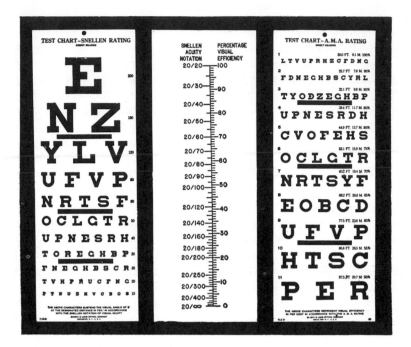

FIG. 6.12 Snellen and "A.M.A." test charts with scale for converting Snellen scores to per cent of visual efficiency.

and recommended for use in industry a percentage system of acuity notation, with the distinguishing title of "Visual Efficiency." Where the Snellen test measures acuity from the angles subtended by the letters, the American Medical Association notation interprets these angles in terms of percentage of visual efficiency. The difference between this percentage and 100 percent is the percentage "loss of vision." A conversion scale for translating acuity scores into the percentage notation is shown in Figure 6.12. Also shown is the first half of a letter chart that measures visual angles in steps directly equivalent to intervals of 5 percent on the American Medical Association scale.

This American Medical Association percentage notation is ordinarily not carried above 100 percent or below 20 percent, and for compensation purposes in industry no extension of this range is necessary. However, the Snellen and American Medical Association tests do not provide sufficient differentiation of visual acuity for satisfactory placement of people on at least some types of jobs. Neither do they measure visual skills other than acuity. Therefore, certain other vision testing devices have been developed for specific use in personnel selection and placement procedures. Such devices measure various visual skills in addition to visual acuity, and also provide for the testing of people at the optical equivalent of both near and far distances. Four such instruments are the Ortho-Rater, the Sight-Screener, the Telebinocular, and the Vision Tester.[22]

The Bausch & Lomb Visual Classification and Placement Tests for Industry[23] were the first battery of vision tests to be constructed on the basis of specifications derived from extensive investigations among industrial employees in industrial situations. These tests cover the visual functions described previously and, for maximum speed and convenience in testing, are incorporated in a single instrument, shown in Figure 6.13. This instrument, called the Ortho-Rater, is a precision stereoscope of relatively long focal length that permits adequate and separate control of test stimuli for each eye. Tests are given at optical equivalents of twenty-six feet and thirteen inches. Stereoscopic methods of vision testing have been used since the late nineteenth century and were early described by Wells.[24] The early statistical

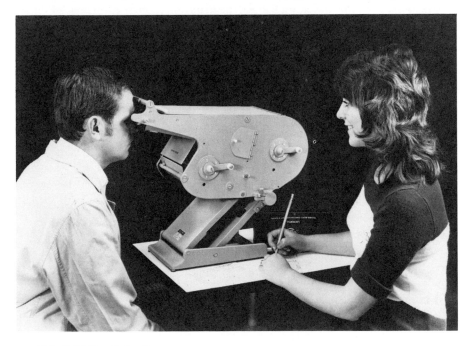

FIG. 6.13 The Ortho-Rater.

[22] The Ortho-Rater is manufactured by Bausch & Lomb Optical Company, Rochester, New York; the Sight-Screener by American Optical Company, Southbridge, Massachusetts; the Telebinocular by Keystone View Company, Meadville, Pennsylvania; and the Vision Tester by the Titmus Optical Co., Petersburg, Virginia.

[23] The Bausch & Lomb Optical Company, Rochester, New York.

[24] Wells, D. *The stereoscope in ophthalmology.* (2nd ed.) Boston: Globe Optical Company, 1918.

data upon which these tests are based have been published in technical and professional journals.[25]

The Ortho-Rater includes the following twelve tests: far-distance tests of vertical phoria, lateral phoria, acuity both eyes, acuity left eye, acuity right eye, depth perception, and color discrimination; near-distance tests of vertical phoria, lateral phoria, acuity both eyes, acuity left eye, and acuity right eye.

Examples of Vision Tests in Use

Extensive research carried out over a period of years at the Occupational Research Center of Purdue University, and elsewhere, has demonstrated conclusively that jobs differ in the visual demands they make upon the worker. These variations are both qualitative and quantitative. Some jobs, for example, require the ability to see at a distance, such as in operating a crane or driving a truck; and others require the ability to see close at hand, such as in watchmaking or fine assembly work. These are qualitative differences, inasmuch as they are predicated on different visual skills. In addition, jobs vary in the amount of a given skill that is required; some jobs, for example, require greater color discrimination than others.

It should be added here that the correlations among visual skills are not particularly high. It is therefore not possible to predict one visual skill from a knowledge of a person's score on a different type of vision test. Being able to read the chart across the doctor's room gives no assurance of being able to read the fine print on the insurance policy.

In the industrial vision research conducted at the Occupational Research Center, it was found that vision tests could be more effectively used if visual standards for jobs were set up in the form of "visual profiles," each profile specifying the minimum acceptable scores on the various Ortho-Rater tests. If a person had scores above the specified minimums, he "passed" the profile, and if he had one or more scores below any specified minimum, he "failed" the profile. Profiles for individual jobs were developed, using various criteria such as quantity of work, quality of work, ratings, and accidents.

The Ortho-Rater is also used in some states in connection with drivers' tests.

25 Giese, W. J. The interrelationship of visual acuity at different distances. *Journal of Applied Psychology,* 1946, **30,** 91–106; Jobe, F. W. Instrumentation for the Bausch & Lomb Industrial Vision Service. *Bausch & Lomb Magazine,* 1944, **20**(2), 3–5, 19–21; Tiffin J., & Kuhn, H. S. Color discrimination in industry. *Archives of Ophthalmology,* 1942, **28,** 851–859; Tiffin, J., & Wirt, S. E. Near vs. distance visual acuity in relation to success on close industrial jobs. *Supplement to Transactions of the American Academy of Ophthalmology and Otolaryngology* June 1944, 9–16; and Wirt, S. E. The validity of lateral phoria measurements in the Ortho-Rater. *Journal of Applied Psychology,* 1943, **27,** 217–232.

Visual job families. Over a period of years, data were collected on vision test scores and criteria of job success for individuals on several thousand jobs. A careful analysis of the relationships between vision test scores and job success as they have been revealed in these many different job situations has shown that certain jobs in industry are similar to each other in terms of visual requirements. Jobs thus can be grouped in terms of their visual requirements, and the requirements of each group vary from those of the next group. Thus we have a series of job groupings, each representing a different pattern of visual requirements. This has led to the concept of "visual job families." A visual job family is composed of a group of jobs whose visual requirements are similar. Six such visual job families have been identified, as follows: clerical and administrative; machine operator; inspection; laborer; vehicle operator; and mechanic. Research has shown that the vast majority of jobs fall into one or the other of these families. Examples of the visual performance profiles of a couple of these groups are given in Figure 6.14.

In order to investigate the relationship between visual skill test score requirements as represented by these six visual standards and success on industrial jobs, the method of cross-validation was used. A random sample of forty-three individual job studies was selected, representing 2420 individuals. These jobs were categorized by job family, and the individuals on each job were divided into those whose visual skills "passed" or "failed" the visual performance profile for their job family. Because job performance criteria also were available for each individual, it was possible to determine the percentage of "high criterion" employees on the jobs among both those who had "adequate" and those who had "inadequate" vision, as measured by whether they passed or failed the vision profile standards. These results are summarized below:

| | Percent of "High Criterion" Employees among Those with: | |
| | Adequate | Inadequate |
Visual Job Family	Vision	Vision
1. Clerical and administrative	71	37
2. Inspection and close work	62	50
3. Vehicle operator	59	45
4. Machine operator	63	45
5. Laborer	67	34
6. Mechanic and skilled tradesman	69	57
Total	65	46

It is obvious that there is generally a higher percentage of high criterion employees among those whose vision met the specified profiles than among

INSPECTION

Visual Performance Profile

FAR

Phoria	Vertical	1	x	1	2	3	4	5	6	7	8					9	
	Lateral	2	x	1	2	3	4	5	6	7	8	9	10	11	12	13	14 15
Acuity	Both	3	0	1	2	3	4	5	6	7	8	9	10	11	12	13	14 15
	Right	4	0	1	2	3	4	5	6	7	8	9	10	11	12	13	14 15
	Left	5	0	1	2	3	4	5	6	7	8	9	10	11	12	13	14 15
	Unaided																
Depth		6	0	1	2	3	4	5	6	7	8	9	10	11	12		
Color		7	0	1	2	3	4	5	6	7	8	9	10	11	12	13	14 15

NEAR

Acuity	Both	1	0	1	2	3	4	5	6	7	8	9	10	11	12	13	14 15
	Right	2	0	1	2	3	4	5	6	7	8	9	10	11	12	13	14 15
	Left	3	0	1	2	3	4	5	6	7	8	9	10	11	12	13	14 15
	Unaided																
Phoria	Vertical	4	x	1	2	3	4	5	6	7	8					9	
	Lateral	5	x	1	2	3	4	5	6	7	8	9	10	11	12	13	14 15

VEHICLE OPERATOR

Visual Performance Profile

FAR

Phoria	Vertical	1	x	1	2	3	4	5	6	7	8					9	
	Lateral	2	x	1	2	3	4	5	6	7	8	9	10	11	12	13	14 15
Acuity	Both	3	0	1	2	3	4	5	6	7	8	9	10	11	12	13	14 15
	Right	4	0	1	2	3	4	5	6	7	8	9	10	11	12	13	14 15
	Left	5	0	1	2	3	4	5	6	7	8	9	10	11	12	13	14 15
	Unaided																
Depth		6	0	1	2	3	4	5	6	7	8	9	10	11	12		
Color		7	0	1	2	3	4	5	6	7	8	9	10	11	12	13	14 15

NEAR

Acuity	Both	1	0	1	2	3	4	5	6	7	8	9	10	11	12	13	14 15
	Right	2	0	1	2	3	4	5	6	7	8	9	10	11	12	13	14 15
	Left	3	0	1	2	3	4	5	6	7	8	9	10	11	12	13	14 15
	Unaided																
Phoria	Vertical	4	x	1	2	3	4	5	6	7	8					9	
	Lateral	5	x	1	2	3	4	5	6	7	8	9	10	11	12	13	14 15

FIG. 6.14 Visual performance profiles for two illustrative job families as based on the use of the Ortho-Rater. An individual "passes" the visual requirements of a given profile if all his scores fall in the shaded areas. He "fails" if one or more of his scores fall in a unshaded area.

those whose vision did not meet the profile standards, although this differs for the various job families. These differences occur in part because of the relative importance of different visual skills for the jobs in question. In the case of jobs where adequate vision is highly correlated with criterion success, the selection of candidates with adequate vision for the job undoubtedly would result in obtaining workers who are more likely to perform their jobs satisfactorily.

COMBINATIONS OF APTITUDE TESTS

The aptitude test validity studies given as examples earlier in this chapter dealt with individual tests. In practice, however, combinations of tests are often used. As discussed in Chapter 5, two or more tests can be used as a battery in various ways. One of these methods consists of the use of a composite score derived by "adding together" scores on two or more individual tests, usually with statistically derived weights based on regression analysis to give the optimum degree of prediction.

An example of the use of such a composite score is given by Sparks[26] in the case of the job of maintenance mechanic in a petroleum refinery. The criterion used in the study consisted of the combined ratings of a training instructor, a mechanical supervisor, and a unit supervisor. The following three tests were administered to the men in the sample: Learning Ability; Shop Arithmetic; and Mechanical Comprehension. A composite score (called a "battery score") was derived by combining the scores on all three tests in such a way as to give them statistically equal weights. In turn, these scores were related to the criterion values for the men in such a manner as to show the percentage of men at or above any score who were above average on the criterion ratings. This relationship is shown in Figure 6.15, which clearly shows the potential utility of the tests for future personnel selection. Incidentally, these three tests had a multiple correlation of .45 with the criterion.

A special note should be added about this particular test validation study. It frequently happens that, because of the use of tests for actual selection or because of subsequent personnel attrition, the personnel on a job may represent a "restricted range" either on the tests, the criterion, or both. Such was the case in this study. As one aspect of this study, however, a statistical correction was made for this restriction and the results given in Figure 6.15 incorporate this correction. (By contrast, the "uncorrected" multiple correlation was .27 instead of .45.)

[26] Sparks, C. P. Validity of personnel tests. *Personnel Psychology,* 1970, **23**(1), 39–46.

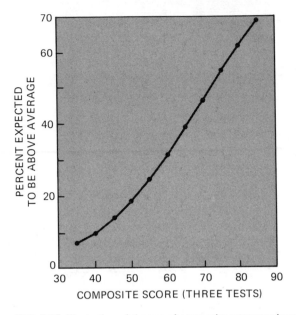

FIG. 6.15 Illustration of the use of composite scores to show the percent of new personnel at or above various scores who would be expected to be above average on criterion ratings. This particular example is for the job of maintenance mechanic in a petroleum refinery. The multiple correlation (R) of three tests with criterion ratings was .45. (*Adapted from Sparks, op. cit.*)

VALIDITY OF APTITUDE TESTS FOR VARIOUS OCCUPATIONS

In the preceding sections of this chapter various studies have been mentioned that deal with the validity of aptitude tests for specific jobs. It may now be in order to present an overview of the validity of different kinds of aptitude tests for the selection of people for various occupations and occupational groups. In this regard, the field of industrial psychology owes a debt of gratitude to Ghiselli[27] for his major effort in assembling and organizing most of the published data on the validity of personnel tests. The data from any given validity study were classified in terms of type of test used; the major categories in this classification were as follows:

Intellectual abilities
Spatial and mechanical abilities
Perceptual accuracy

[27] Ghiselli, E. E. *The validity of occupational aptitude tests.* New York: John Wiley, 1966.

Motor abilities

Personality traits

In turn, each job represented was classified in an occupational category on the basis of two classification systems—(1) a General Occupational Classification system (GOC) with twenty-one categories developed for this purpose; and (2) certain categories of the classification system of the Dictionary of Occupational Titles (DOT) of the United States Training and Employment Service. A further distinction was made as to whether the criterion used in the validation study in question was a training criterion or a performance criterion.

Variability of Validity Coefficients

Some indication of the variability of the validity coefficients is given in Figure 6.16, which shows distributions of the coefficients for certain tests for particular job categories. The type of criterion is indicated in each case. In discussing these coefficients, Ghiselli[28] suggests that the variation may result from any of a number of factors such as: sampling differences; differences in the nature of the jobs within each group; the range of scores of the people on each job; and the conditions under which the tests were administered. Whatever the reasons, the fact of the variation is obvious and it should be noted that some of the coefficients hovered around zero and a few were even negative.

Mean Validity Coefficients

An impression of the average validity coefficients for the five classes of tests and for various occupation categories is given in Figure 6.17. The coefficients for training criteria are shown as part (a) and the coefficients for proficiency criteria as part (b). A scanning of this figure gives rise to the following conclusions: the validity coefficients of each class of test vary across the occupation categories (but for certain classes of tests the differences are greater than for other classes of tests); training criteria generally are predicted better than proficiency criteria; prediction for certain occupation categories is somewhat better than for others; the mean validity coefficients for the different classes of tests are rather different for certain occupation categories but quite similar for others; and the general level of the coefficients is not particularly high, with most of the coefficients falling in the range from about .15 to .35 or .40. This last point implies that a very great amount of variability in the criteria is not accounted for by the tests.

[28] *Ibid.*, p. 28.

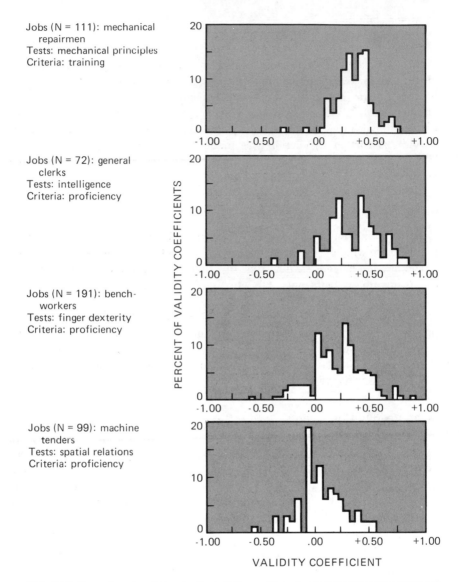

Jobs (N = 111): mechanical repairmen
Tests: mechanical principles
Criteria: training

Jobs (N = 72): general clerks
Tests: intelligence
Criteria: proficiency

Jobs (N = 191): bench-workers
Tests: finger dexterity
Criteria: proficiency

Jobs (N = 99): machine tenders
Tests: spatial relations
Criteria: proficiency

FIG. 6.16 Examples of variation in the validity coefficients of given tests for certain job categories. (*From Ghiselli,* op. cit., *Fig. 2-4, p. 29.*)

Coefficients for Training and Proficiency Criteria

Figure 6.17 shows that validity coefficients tend to be somewhat higher when training criteria are used in validation studies than when proficiency criteria are used. The differences between results obtained with these two types of criteria are illustrated more clearly in Figure 6.18, which is based

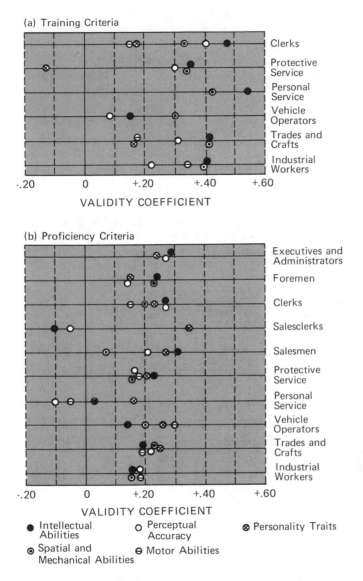

(a) Training Criteria

VALIDITY COEFFICIENT

(b) Proficiency Criteria

VALIDITY COEFFICIENT

- ● Intellectual Abilities
- ○ Perceptual Accuracy
- ⊗ Personality Traits
- ◉ Spatial and Mechanical Abilities
- ⊖ Motor Abilities

FIG. 6.17 Mean validity coefficients for five classes of personnel tests for jobs in various occupation categories. Part (a) shows validity coefficients for training criteria, and part (b) for proficiency criteria. This figure represents hundreds of validity coefficients covering thousands of individuals. (*Adapted from Ghiselli,* op. cit., *pp. 68 and 69.*)

on data for 107 jobs for which both types of criteria were used. If such differences are considered in terms of the type of test used, it is apparent that intellectual as well as spatial and mechanical abilities are more important in determining success in training than in determining success on the

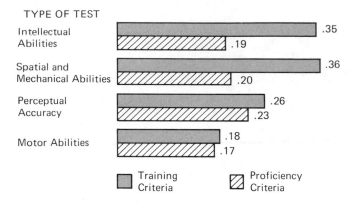

TYPE OF TEST

FIG. 6.18 Comparison of mean validity coefficients for training and proficiency criteria by type of test, for 105 jobs for which both criteria were available. (*Adapted from Ghiselli, op. cit., Table 6-2, p. 116.*)

job, whereas perceptual accuracy and motor abilities are equally important to both. Ghiselli suggests that it might be inferred from these findings that business and industrial training programs give stress to the "academic" or "intellectual" abilities in much the same way as does education in formal school situations.

Bemis[29] reports at least partially confirming evidence from an examination of 424 validity studies using the General Aptitude Test Battery of the United States Training and Employment Service. He found that tests of "cognitive" aptitudes (general intelligence, verbal, numerical, and spatial) typically were correlated to a higher degree with training criteria than with job proficiency criteria. In moderate contrast with Ghiselli's findings of no appreciable difference between the two types of criteria with regard to motor abilities, Bemis found that manipulative tests (coordination and finger and manual dexterity) tended to have slightly higher correlations with proficiency criteria than with training criteria.

Discussion

From the data summarized by Ghiselli[30] and shown in Figures 6.16, 6.17, and 6.18, it is obvious that the validity of individual aptitude tests in general is fairly moderate. However, some additional predictability in the use of such tests frequently is possible if such tests are combined into batteries. This increase in predictability is reflected, for example, by some pieces of data from Bemis.[31] The data in question are the median validity coefficients

29 Bemis, S. E. Occupational validity of the General Aptitude Test Battery. *Journal of Applied Psychology,* 1968, 52(3), 240–244.
30 Ghiselli, *op. cit.*
31 Bemis, *op. cit.*

of all tests for all 424 jobs, as compared with median coefficients (actually *phi* coefficients) for jobs for which *batteries* of tests were available. Each *phi* coefficient was based on the fourfold combination of "pass" or "fail" on all tests in the battery and "high" or "low" on the criterion. These results are summarized below, for both types of criteria used:

	Type of Criterion	
	Training	*Proficiency*
Median validity of individual tests	.22	.22
Median validity of test batteries	.42	.40

It thus appears that the combining of tests into batteries—in these instances from two to four tests—typically raises the prediction ante by a substantial amount. Although coefficients of the order of .40 still leave a substantial amount of job performance variability unaccounted for, we need to remind ourselves that there are numerous other possible sources of such variability—both individual and situational—as pointed out in Chapter 2.

In discussing the combining of tests into batteries, we should recall our earlier discussion of the two methods for doing this. One method consists of the use of composite scores in which the scores of individuals on two or more tests are added together, usually with statistically derived weights. The second method consists of using multiple cutoffs, with a minimum cutoff score on each of the two or more tests. There are pros and cons to both methods, but in general, the multiple cutoff method should be used if the relationship between scores on a test and the criterion is nonlinear—that is, if criterion values do not increase in direct proportion to test scores, but rather have some other form. In some such cases, for example, the criterion values increase rather sharply relative to test scores up to some approximate score, and then tend to level off. Such a relationship implies a "lower bound" on the test (which is sometimes used as the "cutoff" score), such that persons with scores *below* the cutoff have quite limited probabilities of successful job performance. Conversely, persons with scores *above* the cutoff have a reasonable probability of successful performance, but those with very high scores do not have much more chance of successful performance than those whose scores are only moderately above the cut off score.

JOB-SPECIFIC ABILITIES

As indicated earlier, job-specific abilities are those that have some unique relevance to particular jobs; such abilities typically are learned through experience, training, or education. The most common uses of tests of such abilities are for personnel selection and placement and for measuring performance in a training program, but they also are used for certain other purposes; for example, they may serve as the basis for maintaining and up-dating performance levels (as with an airplane pilot) or as the basis for licensing and certification procedures (as with drivers' licenses and licenses to practice various occupations). The validity of job-specific tests frequently is of the *content* validity variety in which the appropriateness of the content (performance tests, questions, and so forth) is determined by expert judg-ment. When an achievement test is to be used rather widely, however, as might be the case with a standardized test for commercial distribution, it is better to validate the test with an appropriate criterion. Typically, this is done by using two or more job groups—such as a group of journeymen in a trade and a separate group of nonjourneymen (possibly apprentices)—as the criterion groups.

Types of Job-Specific Tests

Many types of job-specific tests have been developed, some of which are very elaborate. For our purposes we will illustrate only a few examples.

Work sample tests. The work sample test (also called a job sample test) is a test that provides for having the individual perform specific operations of the job in a controlled testing situation. Some job sample tests involve the use of actual equipment used on the job, but if such equipment is hazardous or excessively costly, simulated equipment may be used. A scoring procedure is developed, and norms of experienced and inexperienced work-ers usually are obtained in the test situation as a basis for evaluating the scores of persons taking the test.

An example of this approach is the miniature punch press illustrated in Figure 6.19, which is a replica in all essential features of a small industrial punch press. It differs from a real press in that the punch is located in a vertical bearing and is held down only by a spring. This feature prevents the punch itself from descending when an obstacle is encountered. When this occurs, the punch remains stationary while a mechanical counter records an error or mispunch. The test is administered by having an individual put through the press two hundred prepunched pieces of galvanized sheet iron. The time required to feed these pieces is recorded by means of a stopwatch. During the test period the mechanical counter records the number of errors or mispunches. The test thus results in simultaneous time and error scores. The validity of this test was determined by comparing the average perform-ance of punch press operators with the average of a group of students and a group of insulation stripping machine operators; the punch press opera-tors demonstrated clearly superior performance.

A very different type of work sample test has been developed by the Philadelphia Quartermaster Depot for fork-lift operators.[32] A fork-lift truck

---

[32] This test was prepared by the U.S. War Department, Office Quartermaster General, Philadelphia Quartermaster Depot, Testing Section.

FIG. 6.19 Applicant being given the Miniature Punch Press Test.

is used for moving materials in a warehouse or around an industrial plant. The test consists of driving a loaded fork-lift truck around a standard driving course as shown in Figure 6.20. The "walls" and the obstacles are constructed from pallets 32 by 40 inches, painted yellow to contrast with the floor. Without going into detail, it should be pointed out that the equipment used and instructions should be standardized. The person giving the test has a check sheet on which he records his observations. This checklist includes a listing of forty-two poor operating techniques such as "Did not start in low gear," "Started jerkily," "Scraped side walls of tires," "Lowered load too quickly," and "Number of pallets displaced." Scoring is based on the number of errors made, as recorded on the checklist.

Although it might appear that many jobs would not lend themselves to work sample tests, it can be seen from an example such as this that the use of imagination and inventiveness can result in the development of tests that can be objectively scored for a wide variety of jobs.

Another area in which the work sample method of testing has resulted in very satisfactory results is the selection of employees for stenographic, clerical, and secretarial positions. Among the most commonly used work sample

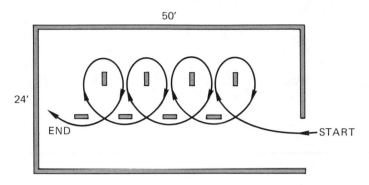

FIG. 6.20 Standard driving course diagram for performance test for fork-life operator. (*Test prepared by U.S. War Dept., Office of Quartermaster General, Philadelphia Quartermaster Depot, Testing Station.*)

tests for office jobs are typing tests, such as the Typing Test for Business, the SRA Typing Skills Test, and the Thurstone Examination in Typing. Some of these tests provide for typing from straight copy while others, such as the Thurstone Examination in Typing, also provide for typing from corrected copy, as shown in Figure 6.21. Stenographic tests typically consist of recordings on tape or record from which the subject is to transcribe and then type. The Seashore-Bennett Stenographic Proficiency Test, for example, consists of five letters, dictated by a typical business voice and varying in length and speed of dictation.

Written achievement tests. Most written achievement tests are "tailor made" for the particular situation, such as a specific training program. In such contexts, they should be developed with acceptable test development practices in mind. In addition to such tailor-made tests, however, there are a few standardized achievement tests that have been developed for more general use.

For example, the Purdue Vocational Tests include tests for certain trade areas such as machine shop practice, welding, sheet metal work, and carpentry. The following item from one of the tests in this series, the Trade

The typical business man is an optimist. For him, the future is full of possibilities that have never been realized in the past. He is not, however, a dreamer, but one whose imagination is used in setting up purposes which lead to immediate action. His power of execution and planning often surpass that of his imagination, and he is often surprised to have realized his vision in less time than he had even dared hope.

FIG 6.21 Part of the Thurstone Typing Test (which is a portion of the Thurstone Employment Tests). The person tested is required to copy this material, making the indicated corrections.

Information Test in Engine Lathe Operation, is reprinted, along with the introductory instructions, in order to illustrate the nature of such tests.

> *Instructions.* In each of the multiple-choice statements to be listed below, there are four possible answers, but only one is correct. Read each statement carefully before making your choice of answers:
> When grinding a tool bit:
>> (A) It should be moved back and forth across the face of the tool
>> (B) It should be held on the wheel until the tool is blue
>> (C) It should be ground the same shape to cut all metals
>> (D) A tool rest should never be used

Oral achievement tests. Oral achievement tests usually consist of true-false or completion types of questions much like these found in some written tests; the respondent usually gives a short answer which can be scored on the spot by the person administering the test. Such tests are not in very common use, however. The most extensive research with this type of test was carried out some years ago by the United States Training and Employment Service[33] for use in the public employment offices as the basis for rough screening of applicants for jobs in various trades.

Validation of oral trade questions. The general procedure used by the United States Training and Employment Service in validating these tests consisted of comparing the responses to the items by successful journeymen with those of apprentices and helpers in the trade as well as of individuals in related occupations. The intent was to identify items which were answered correctly by most journeymen, by a smaller percentage of apprentices, and by a still smaller percentage of persons in related occupations. The differentiation obtained by a set of fifteen such items for asbestos workers is shown in Figure 6.22. The expert asbestos workers scored over a range from 7 to 15, with most scoring 12 or more. The other groups scored systematically lower, thus reflecting substantial concurrent validity of the test.

Although oral achievement tests have not been adopted very widely by industry, this technique seems to offer reasonable promise for obtaining at least a rough estimate of the level of achievement of individuals in various occupations. In addition to differentiating different *job* groups (such as journeymen and apprentices), such tests also can differentiate rather well different levels of ability *within* a job. This was indicated, for example, in a study by McCormick and Winstanley[34] of machinists in a shipyard. Ninety-eight machinists took a twenty-one-item oral test that included ques-

[33] Stead, W. H., Shartle, C .L., *et al. Occupational counseling techniques.* New York: American Book Company, 1940.

[34] McCormick, E. J., & Winstanley, N. B. A fifteen-minute oral trade test. *Personnel,* September 1950.

Score	Expert Asbestos Workers (50 subjects)	Apprentices and Helpers (25 subjects)	Related Workers (25 subjects)
15	xxxxxxxx		
14	xxxxxxxxxxxxxxxxx*		
13	xxxxxxxxxxxx		
12	xxxxxx	xx	
11	xx		
10	x	x	
9	x		
8	xx	xx	
7	x	x	
6		xxxxxxxx*	
5		xxx	xxxx
4		xxxx	xx
3		xx	xxx
2		x	xx
1		x	xxxx*
0			xxxxxxxxxx

*Median Score

FIG. 6.22 Distributions of scores for expert asbestos workers, apprentices and helpers, and related workers on a 15-question oral trade test.

tions such as those shown in Table 6.1. The twenty-one items in this test had been identified from an original test of ninety-five items as being the ones that were most discriminative. The machinists were divided into three approximately equal groups (A, B, and C) on the basis of ratings by their supervisors on "overall" job performance. Figure 6.23 summarizes the results, by indicating the percentage of workers in each criterion group (A, B, and C) whose scores were 13 and above: It shows that the test differentiates quite clearly among the three criterion groups. It was suggested that such a test might well be used for determining an individual's need for training, for upgrading, for placement or transfer, for selection, for measuring level of ability, and for use in handling grievances that deal with questions of promotions.

In-basket test. As indicated before, certain tests—such as work samples, discussed earlier in this chapter—are, in effect, simulations of a job or of a

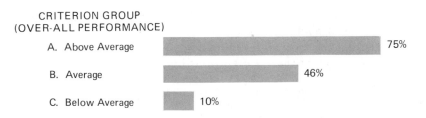

CRITERION GROUP
(OVER-ALL PERFORMANCE)

A. Above Average   75%

B. Average   46%

C. Below Average   10%

FIG. 6.23 Per cent of machinists in each of three criterion groups scoring at or above critical score of 13 on oral trade test. (*Adapted from McCormick and Winstanley,* op. cit.)

TABLE 6.1 TYPES OF QUESTIONS INCLUDED IN ORAL TRADE TEST FOR SHIPYARD MACHINISTS

---

1. *Q*. What material is used in the manufacture of lapping plates?
   A. Cast iron.
2. *Q*. How many turns of a handle are required to make a half turn of the most common index head?
   A. 20.
3. *Q*. What is the meaning of the Brinnel test?
   A. A method of determining the hardness of metal.
4. *Q*. For what purpose would you use transfer calipers?
   A. Used to determine size of recesses and places where the legs of the calipers must be moved to get them out.

Source: McCormick and Winstanley, *op. cit.*

part of a job. A type of simulation applicable to management performance that has received a fair amount of attention in recent years is the in-basket test. This has been used particularly in management training, but it also can be used as a selection technique. The name derives from the fact that the test consists of an assortment of items such as a manager might find in his in-basket—letters, reports, memoranda, notes, and related materials. Each subject taking such a test is confronted with these, and must "do" something with each of the items or note down what action he would take about them if he were in a manager's job. For example, he may "answer" a letter; in some instances he is also asked to indicate the reason for his "action." A procedure is provided for scoring such tests. Examples of items of an in-basket test described by Meyer[35] are shown in Figure 6.24. In scoring this test, three different approaches were used:

1. The *content* of the behavior (such as "referred it to a subordinate," or "decided to change the production schedule").
2. The *style* of behavior (such as "involves subordinates" or "makes a concluding decision").
3. Rating on *overall performance* by the scorer.

In this particular study, scores were given on twenty-seven specific categories. The split-half reliability of these scores ranged from .50 to .95. For a sample of forty-five managers there was a correlation of .31 between a composite score (based on certain in-basket test items) and criterion ratings made by their superiors on "planning-administrative" performance.

Although in-basket tests probably have been used more as training exercises than for management selection,[36] Meyer[37] suggests on the basis of his

[35] Meyer, H. H. The validity of the in-basket test as a measure of managerial performance. *Personnel Psychology,* 1970, **23**(3), 297–307.
[36] See Lopez, F. M., Jr. *Evaluating executive decision making: The in-basket technique.* New York: American Management Association, 1966.
[37] Meyer, *op. cit.*

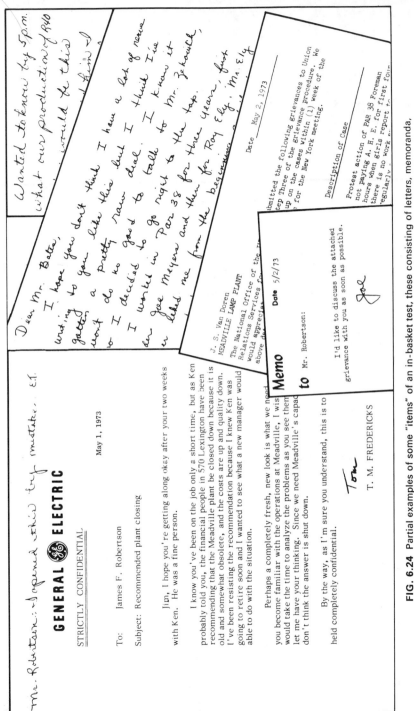

FIG. 6.24 Partial examples of some "items" of an in-basket test, these consisting of letters, memoranda, etc. that an individual is to deal with. (*Courtesy H.H. Meyer and General Electric Company.*)

study that such tests might well be used as a partial basis for management selection.

Job-Specific Tests in Employment of Experienced Workers

One of the traditional uses of job-specific tests is in the selection of candidates for jobs for which experienced or trained personnel are sought. Such tests have been used especially in the selection of candidates for certain types of office jobs (e.g., typing, stenography) and of craftsmen. An example of the validation of a test for craftsmen involved the use of the Purdue Trade Information Test for Engine Lathe Operation with a group of thirty journeymen machinists and a group of thirty high school students who had had at least one year of vocational shop instruction. Figure 6.25, which shows the results of this comparison, reveals a very sharp differentiation between those two groups. Such results indicate that the test could be used as the basis for the selection of candidates for machine jobs with considerable assurance of identifying those who would be qualified for the work.

Job-Specific Tests Used in Training

Typically, job-specific tests are used in a training context in order to measure achievement in training. An interesting variation in the use of achievement tests in training is described by Taylor[38] in connection with an automotive mechanics course at an Army Ordnance School. The course

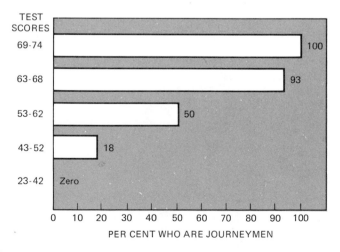

FIG. 6.25 Percent of men who were journeymen machinists as a function of score made on the Purdue Trade Information Test in Lathe Operation.

[38] Taylor, C. W. Pre-testing saves training costs. *Personnel Psychology,* 1952, 5, 213–239.

consisted of three four-week phases adding to a total of twelve weeks. A combination of five written and work sample tests were used to determine the level of proficiency of the incoming students with the objective of having the most highly qualified students begin the course with the second four-week session. From a total of 807 incoming trainees, the 178 with the highest scores were selected for "skipping" the first session. At the end of their training (eight weeks) their performance was compared with that of the 629 who had gone through the full twelve weeks, with the results as shown in Figure 6.26. This shows very clearly that those who skipped the first four weeks were, as a group, superior to the others at the end of training, despite the fact that they had had only eight weeks of training. For this group of 178 men, 4,272 actual days of training were saved as a result of eliminating their first four weeks of training. The practical implication of these findings is that a test such as the one in question could be used as the basis for starting trainees in a training program at that point in training that represents their own level of achievement. This would, of course, save training costs and also preclude trainees from having to go through training content with which they are already familiar.

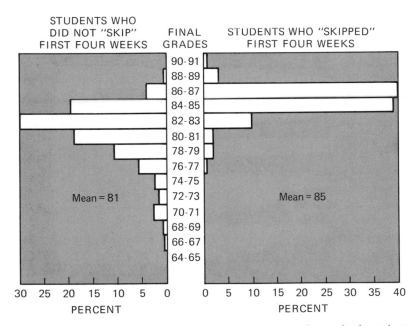

FiG. 6.26 Distributions of final average scores for automotive mechanic students who "skipped" the first four weeks of training and for those who did not. Those who "skipped" were individuals who scored highest on five achievement tests taken at the beginning of training. (*From Taylor,* op. cit.)

New Directions in the Use of Job-Specific Tests

Over the years there have been occasional circumstances in which job-specific tests have been used as the basis for the selection of job candidates, such as in the selection of individuals for apprentice training. In such instances, the tests really are being used as aptitude tests. In recent years, however, increased interest has been generated in the expanded use of job-specific tests in personnel selection and placement. These stirrings of interest arise in part from the fact that typical predictions of job success with conventional aptitude tests is relatively modest. And in part this interest has been stimulated by the concern for ensuring equal employment opportunities for persons of various ethnic groups. There are indications that conventional aptitude tests may in some circumstances result in unfair discrimination, and because of court rulings and governmental equal opportunity policies that require evidence that tests used for personnel selection are "job-related," personnel people are increasingly turning to job-specific tests, which are more likely to fulfill the legal and policy requirements for such evidence.

In general, then, the current trend toward reexamination of the approaches to personnel selection appears to be stimulating an increased use of job-specific tests for this purpose.

The concept of behavioral consistency. One example of this search for new approaches appears in the work of Werniment and Campbell,[39] who suggest the notion of *behavioral consistency* as a frame of reference. By consistency of behavior they mean little more than the familiar bit of conventional wisdom, "the best indicator of future performance is past performance." They propose that one should rely less on "signs" of future job performance than on "samples" of relevant behavior. "Signs" refer to the relatively conventional predictors such as aptitude tests and biographical data. They argue for the use of "samples" of behavior—that is, behaviors similar to the actual behaviors to be performed on the job.

Such an approach requires a systematic study of the job. The first step in this process is the identification of the critical dimensions of job performance. This is followed by a thorough search of each applicant's previous work experience and educational background to determine if any behaviors (e.g., "samples") relevant to these dimensions have been required of him or have been exhibited by him in the past. The adequacy of such "behaviors" then could be used as the basis for predicting performance in corresponding aspects of the job. If the person's past repertoire has not included such behaviors, one might then obtain a measure of such behaviors by the use of work sample or simulation exercises.

[39] Werniment, P. F., & Campbell, J. P. Signs, samples and criteria. *Journal of Applied Psychology,* 1968, 52(5), 372–376.

An example of work sampling for personnel selection. A tryout of this approach was carried out by Campion[40] with a sample of thirty-four maintenance mechanics. On the basis of an analysis of the job, a work sample of four tasks was developed, as follows: installing pulleys and belts; disassembling and repairing a gearbox; installing and aligning a motor; and pressing a bushing into a sprocket and reaming to fit a shaft. These tests and a battery of paper and pencil tests were administered to the men, and paired comparison criterion ratings were obtained from the foremen of the men. Scores on the work sample test had a correlation of .46 with the criterion, but none of the five paper and pencil tests had a significant correlation. Although one would feel more comfortable had the study been carried out on a follow-up (i.e., predictive validity) basis rather than on a present employee (i.e., concurrent validity) basis, the findings nevertheless suggest that the behavioral consistency approach may offer reasonable promise in the personnel selection arena.

40 Campion, J. E. Work sampling for personnel selection. *Journal of Applied Psychology,* 1972, **56**(1), 40–44.

chapter seven

Personality
and
Interest Factors

It is almost an article of faith that some people are better "suited" for some kinds of jobs than for others, by reason of their personalities and interests. Thus we may refer to someone as a "born salesman" and to someone else as the "executive" type. There is little question but that the personalities and interests of people in at least some jobs can affect their job performance, for better or worse. Most generally, this effect takes place via an individual's motivation toward the job in question. In other words, a person's motivation is very much rooted in what are conventionally referred to as personality and interest, and in turn a person's motivation toward a job can affect his performance in the job. Thus, for example, an outgoing, energetic, always-on-the-move individual might start to climb the walls if he were on a job in which he would be working alone on a very detailed, demanding office job. In this situation, it is reasonable to assume that his job performance might be adversely affected.

Obviously, any worker has to have the ability to perform a job, including the relevant basic abilities and the training and/or experience to develop the requisite skills and knowledge. But although such ability is a *necessary* condition for satisfactory job performance, it is not a *sufficient* condition. In many jobs the motivation of individuals (as predicated on personality and interest variables) comprises the "sufficient" condition.

Besides having implications relating to motivation as such, personality and interest variables can have a more direct effect on job performance in certain types of jobs. For example, the success of some salesmen, interviewers, supervisors, and even politicians can be attributed to how well they "go over" with the people with whom they have contact.

THE STRUCTURE OF PERSONALITY AND INTERESTS

The various dimensions of personality and interests (if in fact there are reasonably distinct dimensions) are at present fairly vague and ill-defined, as was pointed out by Guion.[1] It is indeed common practice to describe people in terms of various personal qualities or traits, such as introversion-extroversion, sociability, dominance, or impulsiveness. However, it is not yet possible to say that these and other qualities are in fact distinct dimensions of personality, for they may merely represent behavioral syndromes that we can use in characterizing the outward behavior of people and that reflect our "conception" of basic personality dimensions.

Be that as it may, the conventional personality and interest tests typically result in measures of such constructs, and it must be said that such measurements have been found to have practical utility for some purposes.

TYPES OF PERSONALITY TESTS

Personality tests generally fall into two categories—*projective techniques* and *questionnaire inventories*.

Projective Techniques

Examples of projective techniques are the Rorschach Ink Blot Test and the Thematic Apperception Test (TAT). In using these tests, the subject is presented with an intentionally ambiguous stimulus (such as an ink blot or picture) and is asked to tell what he "sees" in it. In other words, he "projects" himself into the stimulus. A trained administrator interprets the individual responses and patterns of responses and makes an assessment of the individual. Such tests are not used very commonly in industry, although

---

[1] Guion, R. M. *Personnel testing.* New York: McGraw-Hill, 1965, p. 306.

they are used more in the selection of executives than of other types of personnel. They are used rather widely in clinical practice.

Personality Inventories

The second class of personality tests consists of paper and pencil questionnaires. Although such questionnaires are commonly referred to as tests, they are in a sense not really "tests" inasmuch as there are no right or wrong answers; the term *inventory* is more accurate.

Conventional format and scoring of inventories. Conventional personality inventories typically contain statements or questions relating to behavior, attitudes, feelings, or beliefs. The subject is asked to respond to these as they apply to him. An example of such an item is given below:

I feel uncomfortable with other people
   (a) Yes
   (b) Don't know
   (c) No

The responses to individual items usually are "scored" on one of several personality attributes or traits, such as dominance, sociability, or impulsiveness. Responses are scored for a particular attribute or trait after they have been identified—either by statistical analysis or on rational grounds—as the responses characteristic of individuals who possess that attribute or trait.

Forced-choice personality inventories. Because of the possibility of what is referred to as "faking" with conventional personality inventories, some inventories are based on the use of the forced-choice technique. In the final form, such inventories include blocks of two or more statements from which the subject is asked to select the one that is "most" or "least" like himself. The items within any given block have been combined into that block because they are about equal on their "favorability." (This is based on a *favorability* index or *preference* index derived from the responses of a sample of subjects who were asked to make such judgments about the various items.) Of those with equal favorability within a block, however, one will have been selected because it has been found to discriminate statistically between a couple of criterion groups (e.g., between introverts and extroverts). Because the individual presumably cannot select the "best" response (all responses being "equal" in favorability), he presumably would tend to select the one that really is most like himself. Such a response "adds" to the person's score on the dimension on which the item has been found to discriminate. (In some variants of the forced-choice technique there are both favorable and unfavorable items. In such cases the favorable ones are equally favorable, and the unfavorable ones are equally unfavorable, and the respondent is asked to select the response that is "most" applicable to him and the one that is "least" applicable.)

EXAMPLES OF PERSONALITY AND INTEREST INVENTORIES

Examples are given below of a few personality and interest inventories that are used in personnel selection and placement.

Personality Inventories

A number of the personality inventories used for personnel selection and placement are listed in Appendix D. Two of these will be described briefly here.

California psychological inventory (CPI). This inventory is essentially a spinoff of the Minnesota Multiphasic Personality Inventory (MMPI), except that where the MMPI was designed for use with "abnormal people," the CPI was developed for use with "normal individuals." It provides scores on eighteen components in four classes, as follows:

Class I. Measures of poise, ascendancy, and self-assurance.
   Components: 1. Dominance; 2. Capacity for status; 3. Sociability; 4. Social presence; 5. Self-acceptance; 6. Sense of well-being.
Class II. Measures of socialization, maturity, and responsibility.
   Components: 7. Responsibility; 8. Socialization; 9. Self-control; 10. Tolerance; 11. Good impression; 12. Communality.
Class III. Measures of achievement potential and intellectual efficiency.
   Components: 13. Achievement via conformance; 14. Achievement via independence; 15. Intellectual efficiency.
Class IV. Measures of intellectual and interest modes.
   Components: 16. Psychological-mindedness; 17. Flexibility; and 18. Femininity.

Gordon personal inventory. This inventory is based on the use of the forced-choice technique discussed earlier in this chapter. The items consist of four descriptions of personal characteristics. The individual is asked to indicate that statement which is *most* like himself and the one which is *least* like himself. Two of the statements are generally "favorable" (but about equally so) and the other two are generally unfavorable (but also equally so). Here is a sample set:

Prefers to get up early in the morning
Doesn't care for popular music

Has an excellent command of English

Obtains a poorly balanced diet

This inventory results in scores on the following four personality components:

Cautiousness (C)—reluctance to take chances

Original thinking (T)—enjoyment of creative or intellectual activity, curiosity

Personal Relations (P)—patience, understanding tolerance

Vigor (V)—ability to work rapidly and energetically

Interest Inventories

Interest inventories typically require the person being tested to indicate the strength of his interests in such things as hobbies, recreation, leisure-time activities, jobs, and other activities. Sometimes this is done by presenting groups of activities and asking the individual to indicate which one he likes most and which least, or by indicating for each stated activity how much he likes it. Brief descriptions of three interest inventories are given below.

Strong vocational interest blank (SVIB). This inventory has been developed primarily for use in vocational guidance counseling. It determines whether the subject's pattern of interests agrees with the interest pattern of men in each of a number of professions and occupations. Other things being equal, a person choosing a profession or occupation is more likely to be happy and successful if his basic interests are similar to the interests of men actually in that field. The scoring of the SVIB results in a standard score for each of a number of occupations, with corresponding letter grades of A, B+, B, B−, and C. The higher the score for any "occupation," the more nearly the person's pattern of interests jibes with that of successful people in that occupation. Part of a record form for the SVIB is shown in Figure 7.1, which illustrates the scores of one individual for a few of the many occupations. This example is based on the form for men. There is a separate form for women.

Kuder interest inventories. The items in the Kuder interest inventories consist of triads of activities, from each of which the individual chooses the most preferred and the least preferred. There are different forms of these inventories, the primary one being the Kuder Preference Record (KPR)— Vocational (Form C). This form assesses interests associated with ten broad occupational areas: mechanical, outdoor, computational, scientific, persuasive, artistic, literary, musical, social service, and clerical. The Kuder Occupational Interest Survey (KOIS) (Form DD) provides for scoring on the basis of the interest patterns of people in various occupations who are satisfied

PROFILE — STRONG VOCATIONAL INTEREST BLANK — FOR MEN

	Occupation	Std. Score	C	B-	B	B+	A
I	Dentist	31					
	Osteopath	31					
	Veterinarian	32					
	Physician	42					
	Psychiatrist	30					
	Psychologist	32					
	Biologist	40					
II	Architect	32					
	Mathematician	29					
	Physicist	32					
	Chemist	44					
	Engineer	37					

20   30   40   50   60

FIG. 7.1 Part of the report form for the Strong Vocational Interest Blank for Men, showing the scores of one individual for a few of the occupation scales. The white area for any occupation represents the range of scores of the middle third of a sample of men-in-general. (*Reprinted with permission of the publishers, Stanford University Press.*)

with their work choices; in this respect it is much like the Strong Vocational Interest Blank (SVIB). Indeed, when Zytowski[2] compared the scores on these two inventories for 332 individuals across fifty-two pairs of "identical" or "similarly named" occupational scales (e.g., banker was correlated with banker, purchasing agent with buyer), he found that the median of the 332 correlations was .57. This is a fairly respectable general level of relationship. Although the correlations for some individuals were much lower than this, the reason for'those lower correlations could not be ascertained.

Vocational preference inventory (Holland). A more recent interest inventory, Holland's Vocational Preference Inventory (vpi),[3] provides for scoring of interests for the following six categories: (R) Realistic; (I) Intellectual; (A) Artistic; (S) Social; (E) Enterprising; and (C) Conventional. An interesting elaboration is possible with this inventory by using these categories as the basis for assigning occupations to different classifications consisting of "combinations" of the above categories; for example,

2 Zytowski, D. G. Equivalence of the Kuder Occupational Interest Survey and the Strong Vocational Interest Blank revisited. *Journal of Applied Psychology*, 1972, 56(2), 184–185.

3 Holland, J. L. A psychological classification scheme for occupations and major fields. *Journal of Counseling Psychology*, 1966, **13**, 278–288.

advertising agents and salesmen are located in a category designated ESC (Enterprising, Social, Conventional).

LIMITATIONS OF PERSONALITY AND
INTEREST INVENTORIES

As one might imagine, personality and interest inventories have rather serious limitations for personnel selection purposes, of which the most critical is the possibility of what is called faking on the part of the individual taking the test.

Faking of Personality and Interest Inventories

A person taking a personality or interest inventory for personal counseling or for vocational guidance purposes usually will be motivated to give relatively truthful answers for it is to his interest to find out all he can about himself. If he is applying for a job, however, his motivation to get the job might consciously or unconsciously induce him to give responses that he *thinks* will make him appear to be the kind of person for which the employer is looking.

Ability to fake inventories. Evidence of the ability of people to fake such inventories is available from various studies. One such study, for example, was carried out using the Humm-Wadsworth Temperament Scale with sixty-five college students.[4] Each student was given the scale twice: first, in a "clinical" situation, with instructions to be as frank as possible, and second, in an "employment" situation in which each student was to assume that he was in an employment office after a job and had been asked to take the test as a part of the employment procedure. Table 7.1 shows the mean scores for the seven components obtained under these two conditions.

It is apparent from Table 7.1 that the "employment" situation, when compared with the "clinical," shows a higher average value for the normal component and lower values for all except the epileptoid of the remaining six components. In other words, when the students assumed an attitude of "applying for a job," they were able to change their test profiles toward more of the normal and less of the undesirable traits.

Because the forced-choice technique is designed specifically to minimize faking, it is reasonable to wonder whether in fact people can fake such inventories if they want to do so. Some evidence indicates that at least certain inventories of this type are not immune to this possibility. For example,

---

[4] This study was conducted by W. J. Giese and F. C. Christy at Purdue University.

TABLE 7.1 MEAN SCORES ON HUMM-WADSWORTH TEMPERAMENT SCALE OBTAINED IN A CLINICAL AND AN EMPLOYMENT SITUATION BY 65 COLLEGE STUDENTS*

Component	Clinical Mean	Employment Mean	Shift from Clinical to Employment
Normal	981	1023	+ 42
Hysteroid	1023	980	− 63
Manic	1035	937	− 98
Depressive	1061	913	−148
Autistic	1024	938	− 86
Paranoid	970	955	− 15
Epileptoid	983	1002	+ 19

* All scores were computed by the log method, with correction for no-count, as described in the manual of directions.

Rusmore[5] administered the Gordon Personal Profile to eighty-one college students in a simulated "industrial" situation (in which they were to act as though they were applying for a job) and also in a simulated "guidance" situation. The first two columns of Table 7.2 show the results. They indicate that there were significant differences on the *Responsibility* component and on *Total* scores, although these differences were only about 8 and 9 percent, respectively. Dicken[6] also found that scores on three of four scales of the Edwards Personal Preference Schedule differed significantly when a group of college students took the inventory under "standard" instructions and when they took it with instructions to make the best impression they could on a specific trait that was described to them. (Each of four sub-

TABLE 7.2 MEAN SCORES ON THE GORDON PERSONAL PROFILE TAKEN TWICE UNDER SPECIFIED TEST CONDITIONS

Test Component	Group and Condition			
	College Students (81)		H. S. Students (121)	
	Simulated "Guidance"	Simulated "Industrial"	Guidance	Employment
Ascendancy	3.7	4.4	2.9	3.2
Responsibility	7.4	8.9†	4.3	6.8†
Emotional Stability	7.3	8.0	5.3	6.8†
Sociability	4.4	4.8	4.8	4.5
Total	23.0	26.1*	17.2	21.3†

* Difference between the "Guidance" and "Industrial" mean scores significant at the 5% level of confidence.
† Difference between the two means significant at the 1% level of confidence.
Source: Adapted from articles by Rusmore and by Gordon and Stapleton, *op. cit.*

5 Rusmore, J. T. Fakability of the Gordon Personal Profile. *Journal of Applied Psychology,* 1956, **40,** 175–177.
6 Dicken, C. F. Simulated patterns on the Edwards Personal Preference Schedule. *Journal of Applied Psychology,* 1959, **43,** 372–378.

groups was instructed to consider a different trait on the second administration.)

Faking in real situations. The studies just cited as well as others using simulated conditions indicate that people can distort their responses to personality inventories if they wish to do so—even in the case of forced-choice inventories. But in actual circumstances do they do so? And to what extent do they do so? Hard evidence regarding these questions is sparse, but there are a few straws-in-the-wind. Unfortunately, these straws are a bit mixed. Gordon and Stapleton[7] compared the scores on the Gordon Personal Profile of 121 high school students who first took that inventory in connection with their regular guidance program, and who later took the inventory when applying for outside summer employment. The results, shown in the last two columns of Table 7.2, reveal significant differences on the components of *Responsibility* and *Emotional stability* as well as on *Total* scores.

In another circumstance Kirchner *et al.*[8] found that the scores on the Edwards Personal Preference Schedule for a group of 362 male applicants for sales positions differed significantly from those of a college male "norm" group on nearly all of the fifteen scales covered by the test. This comparison does not provide strongly convincing evidence of faking, however, for it is highly possible that the sales applicants really *were* different from a general population of college males.

There are at least a couple of indications that the degree of faking in actual selection conditions may not be as marked as has been assumed. For instance, Orpen[9] extracted thirty randomly selected questions from the Edwards Personal Preference Schedule and used them with the following groups:

College students
    1st administration: standard instructions
    2nd administration: "simulated" employment
Clerical applicants (insurance company)
    1st administration: actual employment
    2nd administration (2 weeks later): part of research project (anonymous)

The mean scores of the students for the *thirty* items were derived for both administrations and the rank order of these was correlated. The result was a correlation (*rho*) of .17, indicating marked juggling of the rank

[7] Gordon, L. V., & Stapleton, E. S. Fakability of a forced-choice personality test under realistic high school employment conditions. *Journal of Applied Psychology,* 1956, **40,** 258–262.

[8] Kirchner, W. K., Dunnette, M. D., & Mousky, N. Use of the Edwards Personal Preference Schedule in the selection of salesmen. *Personnel Psychology,* 1960, **13,** 421–424.

[9] Orpen, C. The fakability of the Edwards Personal Preference Schedule in Personnel Selection. *Personnel Psychology,* 1971, **24**(1), 1–4.

orders. The corresponding correlation for the applicants was .74, indicating much less alteration in the mean values between the two administrations. Further, a mean "consistency" score reflected much less consistency for the students than for the applicants, which indicates *less* difference between the two administrations for the applicants (who took the inventory under *actual* conditions) than for the students (who took it under simulated employment conditions).

Another somewhat confirming study is reported by Abrahams *et al.*[10] with the Strong Vocational Interest Blank (svib). The subjects used were applicants for Navy scholarships and the inventory was given in a real-life situation. Scores obtained during this actual situation were compared with those taken under routine testing programs for two groups: (1) those who had previously taken the svib when in high school, and (2) those who took the svib when in college—a year after applying for the scholarship. The mean scores (on a special scoring key) for these groups are given below:

Test Condition	Group 1	Group 2
Routine test administration (mean)	102.7	98.9
Applying for scholarship (mean)	103.5	102.3
Correlation	.79	.71

The means reflect virtually no difference between the two test conditions for either group, and the correlations are reasonably acceptable. Further, the two profiles for the fifty-five occupational scales of the svib were virtually the same both for group 1 (a correlation of .95) and for group 2 (a correlation of .98).

Discussion. In reflecting about the faking problem, it may be said with reasonable confidence that people *can* distort responses somewhat if they set their mind to it, or if they are "coached" to do so by someone else. But it is *not* as evident that there is a *generalized*, pervasive tendency for people actually to distort their responses in real-life situations in which they have (or think they have) something to gain by so doing. This is not to say that some individuals would not fake, nor that in certain circumstances faking would not occur more generally. But it does suggest that faking may not be as major a factor in the use of personality and interest inventories as has generally been suspected.

Methods of Minimizing Effects of Faking

The potential utility of personality and interest inventories is reduced by the extent—whatever it is—to which people distort their responses. However, there are ways and means of minimizing such effects.

10 Abrahams, N. M., Neumann, I., & Gilthens, W. H. Faking vocational interests: Simulated versus real life motivation. *Personnel Psychology,* 1971, 24(1), 5–12.

Forced-choice technique. Even though it has been shown that some forced-choice inventories are vulnerable to faking, it probably is not possible to indicate the extent of this vulnerability in real-life situations. But even granting the possibility of some unspecified amount of faking, it still seems that such inventories are somewhat preferable to conventional inventories that do not use this method.

In the development of forced-choice inventories it is possible that rigorous analysis of the social desirability of items could result in the selection of those which are least transparent, thus reducing the possibility of faking. However, as Guion[11] points out, this might result in reduced reliability (for reasons related to the "response set" which need not be explained); if this were the case, it could possibly reduce the validity of the inventories. But one should not rule out the possibility of future improvements in the forced-choice technique.

Identification of fakers. Some inventories have special scoring procedures for identifying individuals who tend to give faked responses. These scores are based on the responses to items which are seldom chosen by persons responding honestly, but which are chosen frequently by those who deliberately try to fake the inventory. Such scores are provided for in such tests as the Minnesota Multiphasic Personality Inventory, the California Psychological Inventory, and the Kuder Preference Record. In fact, such scores by themselves sometimes are predictive. For example, Ruch and Ruch[12] found that such a score on the Minnesota Multiphasic Personality Inventory (the K score) had a correlation of .39 with rated performance of 182 sales representatives. The correlations of scores on the five scales of the inventory ranged from $-.10$ to $-.41$. Thus the K score was more predictive than all but one of the regular scores. Ruch and Ruch hypothesized that the good salesman is more likely than the poor salesman to have a clear conception of what demands the selling job puts on him in terms of personality and thus is better able to put his best foot forward. This insight may then also carry over to the responses the salesman gives on the inventory, thus producing a higher K score. They refer to the hypothetical construct responsible for such behavior as "job-image discrepancy" (JID).

Use of special scoring keys. Another scheme that can help to minimize the effects of faking involves the development of a special scoring key for use in each circumstance, using the follow-up (i.e., predictive) validation procedure. The steps involved are:

1. Administer a personality or interest inventory to a group of applicants for a particular type of job.
2. Select candidates in the usual way (*without* reference to the inventory).

---

[11] Guion, *op. cit.,* p. 358.
[12] Ruch, F. L., & Ruch. W. W. The K factor as a (validity) suppressor variable in predicting success in selling. *Journal of Applied Psychology,* 1967, **51**(3), 201–204.

3. Later obtain relevant criterion data for the personnel selected (such as measures of job performance, tenure, etc.).

4. Item-analyze the responses to the inventory against the criterion in order to identify those responses which differentiate in terms of the criterion.

5. Incorporate these into a special scoring key.

In this procedure the responses that were given by individuals when they were candidates would have been influenced by whatever mental set the candidates had at the time. If some such responses—whether honestly given or not—do differentiate, they of course could be used in an empirically based scoring procedure.

A study by Tiffin and Phelan[13] illustrates this approach. A metal parts factory had been giving the Kuder Preference Record (Vocational Form C-H) to applicants for hourly-paid jobs for a period of fourteen months. The inventories, however, had not been used in the employment process. In the follow-up analysis a criterion of job tenure was used. Of the original subjects, 1,109 were still on the job and 684 had left, 450 of them "voluntarily." The inventories of the 1,109 present employees and the 450 "voluntary" quits were randomly assigned to two groups. Two-thirds were used to form a "primary" group for item and subscore analysis; the remaining third were set aside as a "holdout" group for later cross-validation. From the primary group two "extreme" criterion groups were selected; 250 present employees with 11–14 months' tenure formed a "long-tenure" group, and 200 voluntary quits, who had worked for three months or less, formed a "short-tenure" group.

Two analyses were made for these two criterion groups. The first consisted of an item analysis, as a result of which seventy-six items having a difference between the two groups of 10 percent or more were retained to form a new scoring key. The second analysis was made on the basis of the correlations of scores on the several subtest components with the tenure criterion groups. Four of the scales gave evidence of a significant relationship with tenure. These scales were incorporated in a composite score formula with appropriate statistically determined weights. Both the special scoring key and the composite scores (based on subtests) were then tried out with the holdout group to see to what extent they would differentiate that group on the basis of tenure. For this purpose the holdout group was divided into a "long-tenure" group (those who stayed more than three months) and a "short-tenure" group (those who stayed three months or less). The relationships are shown in Figure 7.2.

With this type of cross-validated evidence, an organization could use the inventory in question with considerable confidence that it really would be

13 Tiffin, J., & Phelan, R. F. Use of the Kuder Preference Record to predict turnover in an industrial plant. *Personnel Psychology*, 1953, 6, 195–204.

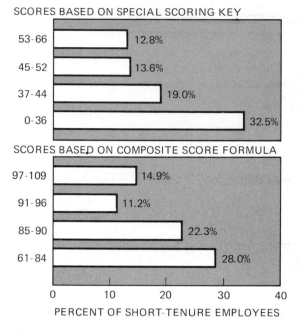

FIG. 7.2 Per cent of short tenure employees by test-score categories based on special scoring key and on composite score formula as used with Kuder Preference Record. (*Adapted from Tiffin and Phelan,* op. cit.)

useful in screening out before employment many persons who were likely to be short-tenure employees.

PERSONALITY AND INTEREST INVENTORIES IN USE

The hypothesis underlying the use of personality and interest inventories in personnel selection and placement is that those individuals whose personality and interest patterns tend to jibe with those of workers who are already successful in a given type of work will stand a better chance of adjusting to the job and working efficiently at it than individuals with quite different personality and interest patterns. The validation of personality and interest inventories, then, is directed toward identifying the personality and interest patterns that characterize successful workers in the job in question.

Keeping in mind some of the reservations implied above regarding personality and interest inventories, let us examine a few validation studies. Some of the studies to be illustrated here employed a correlational approach in validation by correlating inventory scores with a criterion (such as ratings) for the individuals in the sample. Others employed the "job status" criterion method by comparing the scores of individuals in a given occupation with the scores of other individuals.

Examples of Personality Inventories in Use

Newspaper writers and advertising space salesmen. In one study, Maher[14] used the Study of Values test with samples of forty-five newspaper writers and forty-four advertising space salesmen. This test is intended to reflect the level of a person's personal value system in each of six areas—theoretical, economics, aesthetic, social, political, and religious. Significant correlations with criterion ratings were found in the following cases:

Newspaper writers:
    religious (r = −.33)
Advertising space salesmen:
    aesthetic (r = .42)
    political (r = .45)
    religious (r = .31)

Architects. A rather interesting use of personality and interest inventories was made by Hall and MacKinnon[15] with architects. Hall and MacKinnon were especially interested in finding out what personality correlates there might be with a criterion of creativity. A nationwide sample of 124 architects was selected, and these men took several inventories. Their creativity was rated by over a hundred architects and architectural experts across the country; these ratings had a very commendable level of reliability, for the mean intercorrelation was .84. In the analysis of data, the scores on the components of the various inventories were correlated with the criterion ratings for sixty-two of the men, and the three most predictive scores were identified. Statistically determined weights for these were used for deriving composite scores for the remaining sixty-two men in a cross-validation procedure. These composite scores were then correlated with the criterion rankings. The cross-validated correlations for two inventories are given below, along with an indication of the inventory components used in the composite scores (the weights, with signs, are in parentheses):

Inventory and Components	Correlation
California Personality Inventory: Social presence (+.547); Achievement via conformity (−1.015); Femininity (.990)	.47
Strong Vocational Interest Blank (SVIB): Office man (−.543); Banker (−.503); President—manufacturing concern (−.258)	.55

14 Maher, H. Validity information exchange, 16–01, 16–02. *Personnel Psychology,* 1963, **16**, 71–77.
15 Hall, W. B., & MacKinnon, D. W. Personality inventory correlates of creativity among architects. *Journal of Applied Psychology,* 1969, **53**(4), 322–326.

Examples of Interest Inventories in Use

The study of architects just mentioned also involved the use of an interest inventory (the SVIB), which, incidentally, had a slightly higher correlation with rated creativity than the California Personality Inventory. Certain other validation studies with personality inventories are summarized below.

Computer programmers. The Strong Vocational Interest Blank (SVIB) usually is used by comparing the score of an individual on each of the many "occupation" scales (e.g., optometrist, dentist, farmer) in order to identify the scores that differ noticeably from those of "men-in-general" and that are very distinctly akin to those of people in specific occupations. When there is no scale or scoring key for a particular occupation, however, special scoring keys sometimes can be developed on the basis of statistical analysis. This was done, for example, with computer programmers by Perry and Cannon.[16] In fact, they developed four such experimental keys using a sample of five hundred programmers and then cross-validated them on a second sample of five hundred. Figure 7.3 shows the percentage of computer programmers and of "men-in-general" receiving "grades" of A, B, and C on one of these computer programmer scoring keys. The differentiation is very clear.

Engineers. Although engineers generally tend to have patterns of interests different from nonengineers, there are also some differences between and among engineers. This was reflected, for example, by the results of a study by Dunnette *et al.*[17] in which the Strong Vocational Interest Blank as well as other tests were administered to various groups of engineers. With certain groups the researchers used four special scoring keys that previously

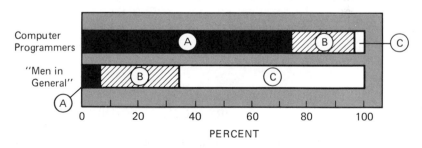

FIG. 7.3 Percentages of computer programmers and of "men-in-general" receiving "grades" of A, B, and C on a special computer programmer scoring key of the Strong Vocational Interest Blank (SVIB). (*Based on data from Perry and Cannon, op. cit., Table 4.*)

16 Perry, D. K., & Cannon, W. M. Vocational interests of computer programmers. *Journal of Applied Psychology,* 1967, **51**(1), 28–34.

17 Dunnette, M. D., Wernimont, P., & Abrahams, N. Further research on vocational interest differences among several types of engineers. *Personnel and Guidance Journal,* January 1964, **42**(5), 484–493.

had been developed for use with engineers: R—Research; D—Development; P—Production; and S—Sales. They found that, with groups of engineers of these four types, the scoring keys generally differentiated among them, as indicated below:

Group of Engineers	Mean Scores on Four Scoring Keys			
	R	**D**	**P**	**S**
Research	**.59**	.54	.36	.41
Development	.54	**.57**	.44	.48
Production	.48	.51	**.53**	.53
Sales	.46	.47	.52	**.60**

Each group scored highest on the scoring key that was relevant to the group. On the basis of these and other data, these investigators point out that the interest patterns of different types of engineers are somewhat different. Information about the unique interest patterns of individuals thus would be useful in mapping their occupational careers.

General Predictiveness of Inventories

In Chapter 6 reference was made to a summarization by Ghiselli[18] of the validity of various kinds of tests for many different jobs. Although that summary dealt primarily with aptitude tests, it also covered personality and interest inventories. Figure 6.17 in Chapter 6 shows the mean validity coefficients for jobs in various categories. In that figure the mean validity coefficients (as measured against proficiency criteria) were highest for sales-clerks and salesmen, with those for executives and administrators, clerks, vehicle operators, and tradesmen and craftsmen being of intermediate value. The predictiveness for sales occupations is shown in greater detail in Figure 7.4, which gives the mean validity coefficients of personality and interest inventories for each of six more specific occupations.

THE USE OF PROJECTIVE TECHNIQUES

The dreary history of the use of projective techniques in personnel selection (as summarized by Kinslinger[19]) probably justifies their restricted use in industry. In recent years, however, their use in assessment centers seems to

18 Ghiselli, E. E. *The validity of occupational aptitude tests.* New York: John Wiley, 1966.

19 Kinslinger, H. S. Application of projective techniques in personnel psychology since 1940. *Psychological Bulletin,* 1966, **66,** 134–149.

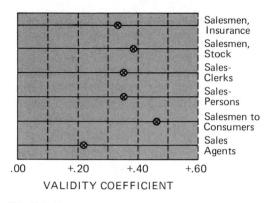

FIG. 7.4 Mean validity coefficients of personality and interest inventories for several sales jobs in each of certain sales occupation categories. (*Adapted from Ghiselli,* op. cit., *Fig. 4-4, p. 79.*)

offer some hint of increased utility, at in least certain circumstances. A number of organizations have developed assessment centers for the evaluation of management potential—primarily for present managers, but to some extent also for initial selection. (These centers will be discussed further in Chapter 8.) In general, individuals in these centers undergo a series of tests, interviews, management games, and other activities for two, three, or more days. One common feature of these centers is the clinical assessment of candidates by psychologists on the basis of observation of the candidates and the data obtained from them.

As a part of an assessment center program, Grant *et al.*[20] administered three projective tests to 201 management personnel. These tests, one aspect of which was the rating of each candidate on nine variables (e.g., achievement motivation, self-confidence), were used as the basis for clinical assessments of the men. Without going into details, these ratings, based on the test protocols, were correlated with a subsequent criterion of progress (as reflected by later salary increases), and it was found that ratings on several of the variables had significant (although moderate) correlations with the criterion. The correlations for these variables were somewhat higher than those of certain paper-and-pencil personality inventories. In brief, the results of this study indicate that there may be certain specific circumstances (such as in assessment centers) in which projective tests have predictive potential, even though they have not been found to be generally useful in personnel selection. When they are used, however, they must be used in the hands of experienced psychologists.

[20] Grant, D. L., Katkovsky, W., & Bray, D. W. Contributions of projective techniques to assessment of management potential. *Journal of Applied Psychology,* 1967, 51(3), 226–232.

DISCUSSION

Personality and interest variables can be relevant to work-related behavior in one or both of two ways: (1) as the basis for motivation, such as to perform effectively or to remain on the job; and (2) in the case of *certain* jobs, as the direct basis for effective job performance when job performance depends in part on "personality" (as in some sales positions). Despite the fact that these variables bear an obvious relation to work-related behavior, however, the use of measures of such variables is fraught with problems that might preclude these measures from having any practical utility. In view of this, the most defensible use of such tests is under circumstances in which they have been validated with the follow-up method (i.e., on the basis of predictive validity).

chapter eight

Performance
Evaluation

The informal evaluation of subordinates by their superiors (and vice versa) has always been a part of superior-subordinate relationships. More formal, systematic procedures for making such evaluations, however, are of somewhat recent origin. In this regard, various labels have been applied to the formal processes of evaluation, such as *merit rating, employee appraisal, employee evaluation, personnel rating, performance rating, performance appraisal,* and *performance review.* Lopez[1] makes a logical case for the term *performance evaluation,* which is the term we will use here. We should hasten to reinforce the distinction that he makes between employee *performance evaluation* (i.e., the evaluation of the actual behavior of people in a "system" such as an organization) and *employee assessment* (i.e., the assessment of an employee's strengths and weaknesses in specific areas for development purposes). This distinction is indeed a real one and will be discussed later. For semantic convenience, however, we generally will use

[1] Lopez, F. M. *Evaluating employee performance.* Chicago: Public Personnel Association, 1968.

the terms *performance evaluation* or simply *rating* except when discussing what Lopez refers to as "assessment."

PURPOSES OF PERFORMANCE EVALUATION

In general, the purposes of performance evaluation fall into two major categories: administrative and performance improvement. In its administrative use, such evaluations may serve as the basis for granting wage or salary increases, for determining training needs (either for individuals or for groups), or for personnel actions such as promotions, transfers, and discharges. In addition, evaluations also may serve as criteria in personnel research (as discussed in Chapter 2).

For a personnel evaluation system to serve the purposes of performance improvement, it is necessary for each individual to know how he is doing in his work to understand what he needs to do in order to improve himself. This purpose can best be served by formal or informal discussions between a supervisor and the individual himself.

PERFORMANCE EVALUATION SYSTEMS

The individual performance evaluation plans of specific organizations vary a great deal, but they usually fall into one or another of certain basic types. Some plans embody certain aspects of two or more methods. The most important basic systems are:

1. Rating scales
2. Personnel comparison systems
   a. Rank-order system
   b. Paired comparison system
   c. Forced distribution system
3. Behavioral checklists and scales
   a. Weighted checklist
   b. Forced-choice checklist
   c. Scaled expectancy rating scale
4. Critical incident technique
5. Other methods

These five categories are all based on essentially different rating procedures. Because each of the various methods has certain inherent advantages and disadvantages, there is no single "best" method; rather, one method may best serve one purpose, and another method may best serve a different purpose.

Rating Scales

Rating scales are the most widely used type of performance evaluation system. The basic principle of this method provides for the rating of employees on each of a number of different traits or factors. There are two primary variations in the manner in which the ratings may be made. In the *graphic* rating scale, a line represents the range of the factor and the rater places a check mark at the position along this line that he considers to represent the degree of the factor possessed by the employee being rated. The *multiple-step* rating scale provides for rating on each factor in terms of any one of a number of "degree" categories, usually from five to nine. Some examples of typical rating scales are shown in Figure 8.1 for a few different rating factors.

Rating factors. The rating scales used by different organizations differ widely in the number of traits or factors to be rated and the particular factors used. Among the more commonly used factors are: quantity, quality, judgment, dependability, initiative, cooperation, leadership, and job knowledge. It should be noted, however, that some of the traits or factors used in rating scales do not really represent different dimensions of behavior. In a study by Ewart, Seashore, and Tiffin,[2] for example, the ratings of a random sample of 1,100 employees out of a work force of 9,000 were analyzed. The ratings for each employee were made on twelve separate traits. The ratings on each of these twelve traits were correlated with those on every other trait, and were then subjected to factor analysis. As discussed earlier, factor analysis is a statistical technique that reduces a set of measurements (such as test scores or ratings) to the minimum number of basic variables or factors that will account for the variations in the original data. The factor analysis of the ratings revealed that for practical purposes there were only two basic factors—ability to do the present job (a very general factor) and quality of performance.

Personnel Comparison Systems

Where the rating scales provide for rating against some defined standard, the use of personnel comparison systems allows individuals to be rated in comparison with each other. With conventional rating scales there is a tendency for the raters to pile up the ratings at one end of the scale, frequently at the higher end. To the extent that this occurs, the results are of limited value, for they do not differentiate adequately among the individuals. Personnel comparison systems avoid this problem completely, for individuals are rated relative to each other. There are three principal variations in the methods of comparing people with each other.

[2] Ewart, E., Seashore, S. E., & Tiffin, J. A factor analysis of an industrial merit rating scale. *Journal of Applied Psychology,* 1941, 25, 481–486.

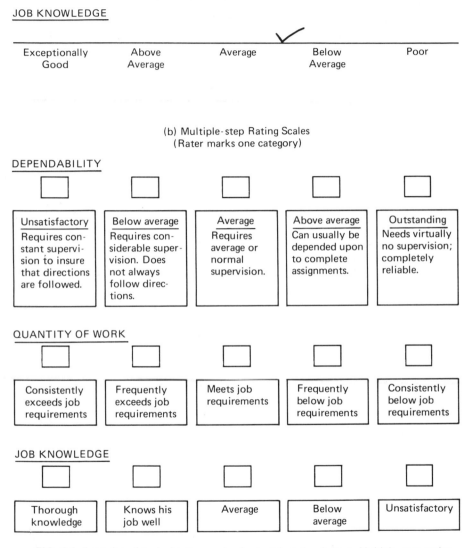

FIG. 8.1 Examples of typical rating scales for certain rating factors. Multiple-step scales usually have anywhere from five to nine categories.

Rank-order system. With this method the rater simply ranks the individuals. Each person's rating is then determined by his position in rank. If a system involving several traits is used, the rankings should be made separately for each trait.

Paired comparison system. Some work on the application of a standard psychological method, paired comparisons, to the problem of performance evaluation has shown very favorable results.[3] This method ordinarily involves rating individuals on only a single general trait—overall ability to do their present job—but it can be applied separately to more traits or characteristics if it is desirable to do so. Cards or slips of paper are prepared so that each contains the names of two of the persons who are to be rated. In this manner, each ratee is paired with every other one. The rater then simply checks the name of the person who is considered better on the characteristic on which they are being compared. The number of pairs of names involved when this system is used in the form described is given by the equation:

$$\text{No. of Pairs} = \frac{N(N-1)}{2}$$

where N is the number of individuals to be rated. If 20 ratees are involved, the number of pairs is thus $20(20-1)/2$, or 190. But if 100 ratees are involved, the number of pairs, $100(100-1)/2$, or 4,950, is obviously far too great to permit expedient use of the system. Two solutions have been proposed to the problem that arises when the number of pairs becomes too unwieldy to handle. One method is to divide the original group into a number of smaller groups and set up the pairs for the smaller groups.[4] Scales have been developed so that ratings of those in several subgroups, which may not be equal in size, can be converted to a common base.

A second procedure that may be used if division into smaller groups is not practicable, and if there is good reason to believe that the rater is sufficiently familiar with the work of each ratee on the job so that the rating will be reasonably valid, is to extract from the table of all possible pairs of ratees a patterned sample of pairs. It has been shown that the ratings obtained from such a patterned sample correlate approximately .93 with ratings obtained from the complete matrix of pairs.[5]

Forced distribution system. This method is particularly useful when a large number of individuals is to be evaluated by the same rater. Most typically, this scheme is used in rating overall job performance, but it lends itself equally well to rating specific factors or traits. In either case the rater

[3] Lawshe, C. H., Jr., Kephart, N. C., & McCormick, E. J. The paired comparison technique for rating performance of industrial employees. *Journal of Applied Psychology*, 1949, **33**, 69–77.

[4] *Ibid.*

[5] McCormick, E. J., & Bachus, J. A. Paired comparison ratings: I. The effect on ratings of reductions in the number of pairs. *Journal of Applied Psychology*, 1952, **36**, 123–127.

is asked to distribute the individuals into a limited number of categories (usually five) according to a predetermined and specified percentage distribution, such as the following:

Lowest 10%	Next 20%	Middle 40%	Next 20%	Highest 10%
☐	☐	☐	☐	☐

Such a procedure reduces the tendency to concentrate the ratings in one or a limited number of rating categories. In some situations the percentages are used more as guideposts than as rigid requirements.

Behavioral Checklists and Scales

Another basic method of performance evaluation embodies the use of some type of behavioral checklist or rating scale. The rater is provided with descriptive statements of job-related "behavior," and he is asked to indicate, in one way or another, those statements which are (or might be expected to be) descriptive of the individual in question. Thus, the rater tends to be more of a *reporter* of the *work behavior* of individuals than an evaluator of their performance or of their personal characteristics.

Because these methods are difficult and time-consuming to develop, they usually can be justified only if they are to be used on a wide basis. They offer some advantages, however, that warrant their serious consideration for circumstances where they would be widely used.

Weighted checklist. This type of rating system incorporates a listing of statements of work behavior such as those shown in Table 8.1. This partic-

TABLE 8.1   EXAMPLES OF ITEMS FROM WEIGHTED CHECK LIST PERFORMANCE RATING FOR BAKE SHOP MANAGER

Item	*Scale Value*
His window display always has customer appeal.	8.5
He encourages his employees to show initiative.	8.1
He seldom forgets what he has once been told.	7.6
His sales per customer are relatively high.	7.4
He has originated one or more workable new formulas.	6.4
He belongs to a local merchants' association.	4.9
His weekly and monthly reports are sometimes inaccurate.	4.2
He does not anticipate probable emergencies.	2.4
He is slow to discipline his employees even when he should.	1.9
He rarely figures the costs of his products.	1.0
He often has vermin and insects in his shop.	0.8

Source: Adapted from Knauft, *op. cit.* Copyright 1948 by the American Psychological Association, and adapted by permission.

ular checklist, reported by Knauft,[6] has been prepared for rating bake shop managers. In rating an employee, the rater simply checks each statement he considers to be descriptive of the work behavior of the individual. (The scale values shown are *not* on the rating form, but are used later in deriving the person's rating.)

A brief description will be given of the procedures used in developing such a checklist. First, a large number of statements are written that describe, in relatively objective terms, various aspects of work behavior, ranging from those that are desirable to those that are undesirable. Next, these statements are "judged" by a number of "experts" on the *degree* to which they are considered to indicate favorable or unfavorable behavior. This is done by the method of "equal-appearing intervals" (originally described by Thurstone[7]), in which the judges classify the statements in categories ranging from those they consider to be extremely favorable to those they consider to be extremely unfavorable.

These judgments are then summarized and analyzed in order to identify the statements that are most reliably judged. Table 8.2 illustrates three hypothetical examples as "judged" by ten judges. Statement A was placed in the same category (number 4) by all ten judges and is therefore a highly stable item. Statement B, for which the judgments are scattered a great deal, is a very unstable item. Statement C has moderate stability.

The scale value assigned to an item usually is the mean or median of the categories in which the statement has been classified by the several judges. A possible fallacy in the use of the median for this purpose has been pointed out by Jurgensen.[8] The fallacy depends upon the fact that for some employees many more items are checked by the rater in the top half of the

TABLE 8.2 HYPOTHETICAL EXAMPLES OF JUDGMENTS BY TEN JUDGES ON THREE CHECK-LIST RATING STATEMENTS*

| | | | | *Rating category* | | | | | |
| | *Unfavorable* | | | | | | *Favorable* | | |
Statement	*1*	*2*	*3*	*4*	*5*	*6*	*7*	*8*	*9*
A				10					
B		1	2	1	3	2	1		
C	2	5	3						

* The number entered under each category is the number of judges who placed the statement in that category.

[6] Knauft, E. B. Construction and use of weighted checklist rating scales for two industrial situations. *Journal of Applied Psychology*, 1948, **32**, 63–70.

[7] This method is described in Edwards, A. L. *Techniques of Attitude scale construction*, New York: Appleton-Century-Crofts, 1957, Chapter 4.

[8] Jurgensen, C. E. A fallacy in the use of median scale values in employee checklists. *Journal of Applied Psychology*, 1949, **33**, 56–58.

scale than in the lower half. Therefore, Jurgensen proposes that median values be replaced by positive and negative values obtained by subtracting the mid-value of the scale (4, 5, or 6 depending on whether there are 7, 9, or 11 categories in the scale) from each median. The rating score for each individual then would be the algebraic sum of these revised weights for the items checked by the rater.

This type of scale also can be used as the basis for a more generally applicable rating procedure, as illustrated by the results of a study by Uhrbrock[9] in which 724 behavioral statements were scaled in this manner. A few examples are given in Table 8.3, along with their scale values based on the judgments of twenty foremen. The "variability" column consists of an index of the variability of the judgments (the smaller this value, the greater the degree of consistency in the judgments).

Forced-choice checklist. The forced-choice technique was described briefly in Chapter 7 in the discussion of personality tests. Originally used in employee rating, this method subsequently was extended in its applications to personality tests. In forced-choice rating systems, two or more statements (typically statements of behavior) are grouped together in blocks and the rater is asked to indicate which statement is most descriptive of the person being rated (and in some cases which is least descriptive). In practice there are a number of variations in the method, such as differences in the num-

TABLE 8.3 SCALE VALUES OF SELECTED CHECKLIST RATING SCALE STATEMENTS AS DERIVED FROM JUDGMENTS OF TWENTY FOREMEN

Statement	Scale[*] Value	Variability[†]
6. Makes the same mistakes over and over.	14	33
34. Is a clock-watcher	22	179
83. Can't seem to get the hang of things.	29	79
171. Conduct borders on insubordination.	36	535
238. Can do good work if he (she) tries.	49	79
257. Never quits ahead of time.	64	124
277. Is orderly in work habits.	69	219
377. Gets production out in less than average time.	79	109
498. Can concentrate under difficult conditions.	90	190
539. Merits the very highest recommendation.	107	51

* Scale values have been multiplied by 10 to avoid decimal values.

† The "variability" is the square of the standard deviation of the placements multiplied by 100. It can be interpreted as a relative index of the consistency of judgments.

Source: Uhrbrock, *op. cit.*

9 Uhrbrock, R. S. Standardization of 724 rating scale statements. *Personnel Psychology,* 1950, **3,** 285–316.

ber of statements in a block and in the number and type of response required. Some variations studied by Berkshire and Highland[10] included blocks
with two, three, four, and five statements, with certain groups including
only favorable or unfavorable statements, but not both. The example of a
block of forced-choice statements given below was drawn from a rating
form used for rating Air Force instructors; all of these statements are
"favorable."

    a. Patient with slow learners.
    b. Lectures with confidence.
    c. Keeps interest and attention of class.
    d. Acquaints classes with objective for each class in advance.

The selection of the statements for each block is based on extensive preliminary research to determine the *degree* to which each statement is considered by raters generally to be "favorable" or "unfavorable" (favorability
index) and the extent to which the statement, when used in a rating situation, tends to *discriminate* between above-average and below-average individuals (discrimination index). The statements are then grouped together
on the basis of relatively comparable favorability indexes; the statements
above, for example, have been placed in the same block because they have
approximately *equal favorability* indexes. The items placed in a block, however, *differ* in their *discrimination* indexes. Usually only one item in a block
is a discriminative item.

A major advantage of this method is that a rater, who may attempt (consciously or unconsciously) to rate a man higher or lower than the man's
true worth, has no way of knowing which of the statements to check to raise
(or lower) the man's rating from what it should be. There are, however,
certain disadvantages to the method. In the first place, because the rater
does not (and should not) know how the final rating values are derived, he
may resent the system as a whole, and may therefore not give it his whole-
hearted support. In addition, the method does not lend itself readily to
counseling with the employee.

Of the various versions of this method, Berkshire and Highland[11] found
that the form with four favorable statements from which the rater was to
select the two most like the ratee had advantages over other forms. It was
the most resistant to bias, it yielded consistently high validities under various
conditions, it had adequate reliability, and it was one of the two forms
preferred by the raters.

   10 Berkshire, J. R., & Highland, R. W. Forced-choice performance rating—A
methodological study. *Personnel Psychology*, 1953, **6**, 355–378.
   11 *Ibid.*

In some situations, the forced-choice method is used in combination with other rating procedures. This has the advantage of making the combined rating procedures useful for more purposes.

Scaled expectancy rating scale. Another variation of behaviorally based rating procedures is one in which each scale consists of a series of "scaled expectancies" such as the one presented by Campbell, Dunnette, Lawler, and Weick[12] and reproduced in Table 8.4. With such a scale, the rater is asked to indicate the behavior that the person being rated could be "expected" to demonstrate in his work; this "expectation," of course, is an inference from the past behaviors of the individual in question. Such scales have been developed for rating personnel in particular occupations. The example given here is for department store managers. The original scales of this type were developed by Smith and Kendall[13] for use with nurses.

TABLE 8.4   SCALED EXPECTANCY RATING SCALE, FOR USE WITH DEPARTMENT STORE MANAGERS ON DIMENSION OF "MEETING DAY-TO-DAY DEADLINES"

Meeting Day-to-day Deadlines

Instructions to rater: In his job as department manager how well does this man meet his day-to-day deadlines? Consider not only his *typical* job behavior but also how he does when at his *best*. Write BEST on the scale opposite the action that seems to fit him most closely when he's doing his best in meeting day-to-day deadlines. Write TYPICAL opposite that action that seems to fit him most closely when he is doing his usual or typical job in meeting day-to-day deadlines.

9. Could be expected *never* to be late in meeting deadlines, no matter how unusual the circumstances.

8. Could be expected to meet deadlines comfortably by delegating the writing of an unusually high number of orders to two highly rated selling associates.

7. Could be expected always to get his associates' work schedules made out on time.

6. Could be expected to meet seasonal ordering deadlines within a reasonable length of time.

5. Could be expected to offer to do the orders at home after failing to get them out on the deadline day.

4. Could be expected to fail to schedule additional help to complete orders on time.

3. Could be expected to be late all the time on weekly buys for his department.

2. Could be expected to disregard due dates in ordering and run out of a major line in his department.

1. Could be expected to leave order forms in his desk drawer for several weeks even when they had been given to him by the buyer after calling his attention to short supplies and due dates for orders.

Source: Adapted from Dunette, M.D., Campbell, J.P., and Hellervic, L.W. Job behavior scales for Penney Company Department Managers, Figure 5.2. Minneapolis: Personnel Decisions, 1968.

12 Campbell, J. P., Dunnette, M. D., Lawler, E. F., & Weick, K. E. *Managerial behavior, performance and effectiveness.* New York: McGraw-Hill, 1970.

13 Smith, P. C., & Kendall, L. M. Retranslation of expectations: An approach to the construction of unambiguous anchors for rating scales. *Journal of Applied Psychology,* 1963, 47(2), 149–155.

The first step in the development of such scales is the determination of the job dimensions to be used. Typically, this is done on the basis of group consensus of experienced personnel. For each such dimension examples of "behaviors," ranging from desirable to undesirable, are obtained; these usually are specific behaviors that actually have been observed by supervisors. Such behaviors are somewhat akin to those mentioned in the "critical incident" technique discussed below. However, they are here described in terms of the behaviors that one might "expect" a person to engage in, rather than what the person has in fact demonstrated. The statements are then "scaled" in the same way as those used in the weighted checklist rating method already described. The examples shown in Table 8.4 are arranged in order of their scaled values (from high to low). In rating an individual with such a scale, the rater indicates, for each separate dimension, the behavior that he would "expect" of the person being rated. In this particular example, the rater marks not only the statement that would be most *typical* of the person but also the one that would fit him most closely when he is doing his *best*.

Critical Incident Technique

This method of performance evaluation, developed by Flanagan and Burns,[14] provides for the recording, by supervisors, of critical "behaviors" on the part of employees. Whenever an employee does something that is especially noteworthy or especially undesirable ("critical" to either good or poor performance), a notation is made in the employee's record. These "critical behaviors" usually are classified into certain categories, such as judgment and comprehension; productivity; dependability; and initiative. A tally can be made of the number of positive and negative incidents recorded in each category.

The use of the critical incident method in the evaluation of salesmen has been discussed by Kirchner and Dunnette.[15] Each of eighty-five sales managers was asked to report as many critical incidents as possible illustrating both effective and noneffective behavior among his group of salesmen. Sixty-one usable instances were obtained. Using these instances, a rating form was prepared which the authors feel to be a very promising instrument.

Another use of critical incidents, this time in the training of salesmen, has been reported by Bridgman et al.[16] In this investigation, critical incidents

[14] Flanagan, J. C., & Burns, R. K. The employee performance record: A new appraisal and development tool. *Harvard Business Review,* 1955, 33(5), 95–102.

[15] Kirchner, W. K., & Dunnette, M. D. Identifying the critical factors in successful salesmanship. *Personnel,* 1957, 34(2), 54–59.

[16] Bridgman, C. S., Spaeth, J., Driscoll, P., & Fanning, J. Salesmen helped by bringing out jobs' critical incidents. *Personnel Journal,* 1958, 36, 411–414.

of effective and ineffective behavior among salesmen were utilized with good results in a training program for new salesmen in the field.

Although the critical incident method does not readily lend itself to objective quantification, it offers a strong advantage for purposes of employee counseling because it provides the supervisor with a record of "specifics" to discuss with the employee.

Other Evaluation Methods

Other methods of performance evaluation are sometimes used.[17] One of these is a group evaluation plan reported by Rowland,[18] in which each person is evaluated by a group of supervisors during a conference. In certain situations a "free written" rating procedure is used; in this procedure the evaluator (usually a supervisor) "describes" the person in question by writing a "word picture" of him. In still other circumstances those being evaluated participate in some type of group problem, discussion, or "game," and the evaluation is made by observers. Other methods include the use of peer ratings, individual tests, and individual or group interviews.

Discussion

The selection of a performance evaluation scheme for a particular purpose is a complex business, as Barrett[19] points out. Each type of rating system has certain features that lend itself to certain uses. A partial summary of

TABLE 8.5 SUGGESTED USES OF CERTAIN TYPES OF PERFORMANCE APPRAISAL SYSTEMS

Type of System	Rating Scale	Personnel Comparison Systems	Weighted Check List	Forced Choice Check List	Critical Incident
Wage and salary administration	Yes	No	Yes	No	No
Personnel promotion	Yes	Yes	Yes	No	No
Personnel transfer	Yes	No	Yes	Yes	No
Personnel layoff	Yes	Yes	No	No	No
Discharge or demotion	Yes	No	No	No	No
Administrative control	Yes	Yes	No	No	Yes
Personnel development	Yes	No	Yes	No	Yes
Research	Yes	Yes	Yes	Yes	Yes

Source: Barrett, *op. cit.,* Table 5, p. 61.

17 For a discussion of some methods see: Whistler, T. H., & Harper, S. H. (Eds.) *Performance appraisal.* New York: Holt, Rinehart, & Winston, 1962.

18 Rowland, V. K. The mechanics of group appraisal. *Personnel,* 1958, **34**(6), 36–43.

19 Barrett, R. S. *Performance rating.* Chicago: Science Research Associates, Inc., 1966.

the judged appropriateness of various types of rating systems is given in Table 8.5, which has been adapted from Barrett. A few of his more general comments about appraisal systems are given below:

Rating scales:	Most generally useful
Personnel comparison:	Limited because only order of merit is known
Weighted checklist:	Establishing appropriate weights and interpreting results are difficult
Forced-choice:	Useful only when desirable to hide quality of rating from rater
Critical incident:	Too burdensome for routine use

ASSESSMENT CENTERS

In recent years there has been quite a flurry of interest in the use of assessment centers in the assessment of individual characteristics and potential, especially of management personnel. In the operation of typical assessment centers, a small group of managerial personnel is brought together for a few days during which the members of this *ad hoc* group engage in a variety of individual and group activities under the observation of an assessment center staff. Typical activities include: group problem-solving and management games, oral presentations, group discussions, individual tests, interviews, self-ratings, and peer ratings. The ultimate assessments by the staff are based on the "data" resulting from these activities (test scores, self-ratings, peer ratings, and so forth) and on the observations of the participants by the staff. In arriving at their judgments the staff can employ a variety of specific assessment methods. The staff typically prepares a report on each individual; this report is then made available to certain managerial personnel as input into the processes of personnel development and promotion.

The Bell System Assessment Centers

The first such program to be created, and undoubtedly the most extensive one in operation today, is that of the Bell Telephone System. As reported by Bray and Grant[20] this particular program includes the following methods for collecting information on the participants:

Interview
In-basket test

20 Bray, D. W., & Grant, D. L. The assessment centers in the measurement of potential for business management. *Psychological Monographs: General and Applied.* Whole No. 625, 1966, 80(17), 1–27. See also Moses, J. L. Assessment center performance and management progress. Paper given at meetings of American Psychological Association, Washington, D. C., September 1971.

Manufacturing problem (a management game in which the participants assume the roles of partners in an enterprise)

Group discussion (a leaderless group situation focused around a management personnel function)

Projective tests

Paper-and-pencil tests and questionnaires

Miscellaneous (including a personal history questionnaire and a short autobiographical essay)

In this particular program the performance of the participants on the manufacturing problem and on the group discussion was rated by the individuals themselves, by their peers, and by observers. The projective tests were evaluated by a clinical psychologist.

RELIABILITY AND VALIDITY OF PERFORMANCE EVALUATIONS

The concepts of *reliability* and *validity,* previously discussed in connection with tests, have corresponding meanings in relationship to performance evaluations.

Reliability of Ratings

The reliability of ratings is the consistency with which they are made, either by different raters or by the same rater at different times. The reliability is to some degree a function of the rating method used. For example, the reliability of rating scales is typically somewhat lower than that of the employee comparison systems. Coefficients of the reliability of ratings on the twelve factors of a conventional rating scale, for example, ranged from .35 to .55. (These coefficients were based on the ratings of pairs of raters.) On the other hand, the reliability coefficients of rank order ratings reported by Taylor[21] ranged from .85 to .95. And in one study involving the paired comparison ratings of three groups of employees by two raters, the correlations between the various pairs of raters ranged from .81 to .86, with an average of .83.[22]

The reliability of forced-choice ratings is also quite respectable, as reflected by the results of the study by Berkshire and Highland.[23] The split-

[21] Taylor, H. C. Upjohn Foundation for Community Research. Personal communication.

[22] Lawshe, C. H. Kephart, N. C., & McCormick, E. J. The paired comparison technique for rating performance of industrial employees. *Journal of Applied Psychology,* 1949, **33,** 69–77.

[23] Berkshire & Highland, *op cit.*

half and test-retest reliability coefficients for different variations of numbers and types of item within the "blocks" were:

Split-half (6 variations): .74; .82; .85; .90; .95; .96
Test-retest (4 variations): .59; .72; .72; .74

To the extent that ratings are unreliable, one cannot regard small differences (such as for the same person at different times, or for different persons) as reflections of "real" differences in the attribute being rated. By a simple statistical procedure it is possible to compute the standard error of measurement of a set of ratings. Unless two ratings differ by more than three standard errors of measurement, it is unsafe to assume that they reflect true differences.

Validity of Ratings

The validity of ratings is associated with the extent to which they reflect the "true" variable being evaluated—such as a human attribute, some aspect of behavior, or job performance. Quantitative evidence about such validity, however, depends upon the availability of a relevant separate criterion. In the few reported studies in which ratings have been correlated with some type of separate criterion, the resulting correlations have tended to be of only moderate magnitude, as reported by Barrett.[24] Although such results are not very encouraging, it should be noted that the evidence here is quite sparse. It must be frankly acknowledged that not much is known about the validity of ratings. In the absence of evidence to the contrary, one may have to assume that, if there is a high degree of consistency between and among raters in rating the same employees, the ratings have reasonable validity. One should never forget, however, that this is not always a correct assumption.

Validity of assessment center assessments. The assessments resulting from assessment center programs typically are used as the basis for subsequent administrative actions, such as promotions. The validity of such assessments therefore depends upon the extent to which they in fact predict relevant future criteria. Such validity, then, is a predictive form of criterion-related validity. Although the collective evidence regarding the validity of the assessments made by assessment center staffs is fairly sparse and sketchy, the results of the most comprehensive such analysis are generally positive. This analysis, as reported by Moses,[25] was based on data for 5,943 men who were evaluated at Bell System assessment centers from 1961 to 1968. In one

[24] Barrett, *op. cit.*, pp. 68–72.
[25] Moses, J. L. Assessment center performance and management progress. Paper given at meetings of American Psychological Association, Washington, D.C., September 1971.

phase of this study, the criterion measure was "management level" as of December 1970. Upon completion of the assessment center activities, the participants had been given a composite rating by the staff in terms of management potential. For each of the rating categories—more than acceptable, acceptable, questionable, and not acceptable—the percentage who received two or more promotions after their assessment center participation was determined, as shown in Figure 8.2. It is clear from this figure that, in this situation, the assessment center ratings were appreciably related to subsequent managerial performance as reflected by the "two-promotion" criterion.

Some more general hints about the effectiveness of assessment centers are reported by Byham,[26] who summarized the results of several studies (some unpublished) about assessment centers. In six studies, assessment center evaluations of managerial personnel were correlated with subsequent performance as rated by superiors. These correlations ranged from .27 to .64. And in twenty-three studies, Byham was able to compare assessment center evaluations with other methods (including conventional personnel tests) in terms of their effectiveness for spotting potentially superior personnel. In these studies various criteria were used, such as performance ratings, subsequent advancements, and salary. A recap of these studies shows how the assessment center evaluations stacked up against other methods:

	No. of Studies
Assessment center *more* effective	22
Assessment center *equally* effective	1
Assessment center *less* effective	0

These results are very encouraging, but let us not be overly hasty and jump to the conclusions that assessment centers are just what the doctor

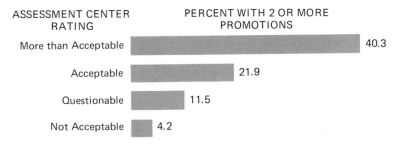

FIG. 8.2 Percent of managerial personnel in various rating categories (as based on assessment center results) who subsequently received two or more promotions. (*Adapted from Moses*, op. cit., *1971, Table 2.*)

26 Byham, W. C. Assessment centers for spotting future managers. *Harvard Business Review*, July-August 1970, **48**(4), 150–167.

ordered to achieve instant organizational success. In the first place, one needs to be a bit circumspect in accepting such findings at face value. The validation of assessment center operations is a long, arduous process, fraught with stumbling blocks such as the possibility that—at least in some instances —the assessments have influenced (and thus have contaminated) the subsequent measures of performance. Further, the evaluations of some programs do not have as positive a tone as some of the findings mentioned above.

In reflecting about assessment centers and their potential utility for assessing the potentialities of personnel, it is our belief that the indications of such utility are on the positive side of this ledger, but we must record our qualms about such matters as: the possibility of criterion contamination; the feeling that there has not yet been a long enough time or enough experience to be able to effectively evaluate such programs on a broad scale; and the nagging suspicion that some of the current euphoria about assessment centers may in part be the result of a bandwagon effect. Let us hope that time will allay these modest qualms.

SOURCES OF POSSIBLE DISTORTIONS
IN EVALUATIONS

In our previous discussion of performance evaluation there have been some suggestions of undesirable distortions in the evaluations. These possible distortions can arise from various sources, including certain raters' tendencies, contamination from extraneous sources, and inappropriate weighting of factors.

Raters' Tendencies

Some of the distortions in personnel evaluation arise from rather common tendencies on the part of raters, in particular the halo effect and the constant error.

The halo effect. More than fifty years ago Thorndike[27] pointed out on the basis of experimental evidence that some raters have a tendency to rate an individual either high or low on many factors because the rater knows (or thinks) the individual to be high or low on some specific factor. Thorndike called this tendency the "halo" effect. Applied to the industrial situation, this means that if a supervisor regards an employee as very satisfactory in terms of one factor (such as general personality or tact), he is likely to rate the employee high also on other factors (such as productivity, ingenuity, inventiveness, and adaptability). In general, the result of the halo effect is

[27] Thorndike, E. L. A constant error in psychological ratings. *Journal of Applied Psychology*, 1920, **4**, 25–29.

that ratings on various factors tend to have higher correlations with each other than would otherwise be the case.

Constant error. The constant error is a tendency to concentrate the ratings in one section of the rating scale, such as toward the upper end of the scale (sometimes referred to as the *leniency tendency*), in the center of the scale (the *error of central tendency*), or toward the lower end of the scale. These tendencies all were reflected in the ratings obtained from different raters in one company in which the ratings made by one supervisor averaged 405 points out of a possible 600, whereas those of another supervisor averaged 295 points. When such disparities occur, the numerical ratings obviously cannot be compared unless they are somehow converted to a common base.

Contamination of Ratings

It sometimes happens that raters are influenced—perhaps unknowingly—by various factors that are extraneous to whatever is being rated. Among such extraneous factors are the organizational unit, the job of the ratee, and the sex, age, and length of experience of the ratee. These and other factors can serve as sources of contamination of ratings.

Organizational unit. Frequently the ratings reported from one organizational unit (such as a department) are different from those from other units. Although such differences may be due in part to "true" differences in the performance of individuals in the various units, it is also possible that they may result from differences in the standards or rating "policies" of raters in the different units. Illustrations of the actual differences in ratings of three departments in one company are shown in Figure 8.3. From this we can see that a rating of 350 would be very low for a man in the engineering department, approximately average for a man in the maintenance department, and very high for a man in the plant-protection department.

Job differences. Somewhat similar differences sometimes occur in the ratings of people on various jobs. In a steel mill, for example, the average ratings of people on various jobs ranged from about 385 for tinners to about 275 for openers and examiners. The same tendency was reported by Klores[28] for professional personnel in various job levels, as the following Figures show:

Job level:	A (low)	B	C	D	E	F (high)
Mean rating (1 = high; 5 = low):	4.0	3.6	3.4	2.3	2.3	2.5

28 Klores, M. S. Rater bias in forced-distribution performance ratings. *Personnel Psychology*, 1966, **4**, 411–421.

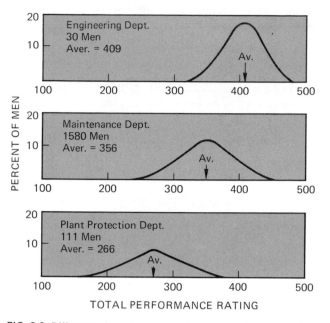

FIG. 8.3 Differences in performance ratings among departments in a steel mill.

Discussion. Data could be given to illustrate the relationship between ratings and various other factors. For example, a summarization of the ratings of the nine thousand personnel in the steel mill mentioned before showed the following relationships with certain personal factors:

Age: personnel between the ages of thirty and thirty-five had higher average ratings than those who were younger or older.

Years on present job: the average ratings decreased from those with less than five years of service to those with twenty-five years or more.

The existence of differences in ratings between groups does not necessarily imply contamination of the ratings. In part such diffferences may be valid. For example, it is possible that the higher average ratings mentioned above for personnel between thirty and thirty-five years of age could be valid, perhaps because younger workers are less experienced and older members are "slowing down." Thus, such differences need to be interpreted with caution.

Some of the relationships mentioned in our illustrations, it should be noted, will not necessarily be found in other organizations. Indeed, obverse relationships might be found in other organizations. The point to keep in mind is that the organization should know what these relationships are and should endeavor to figure out the basis for them in order to make some judgment as to whether they reflect "true" differences or whether they represent some form of contamination.

Inappropriate Weighting of Factors

In the use of conventional rating scales for performance evaluation, it is common practice to rate personnel on each of two or more factors and then to sum the ratings on the several factors. The several factors may be assigned *equal* weights or *differential* weights. Where differential weights are used, the scales for the different factors typically have different ranges; for example, one factor may have possible ratings from 1 to 10 while another factor has a range from 1 to 20.

The assignment of inappropriate weights to different factors is a possible source of distortion in ratings. Ideally, the weighting of different factors should be based on the relevance of the individual factors to individual jobs. For example, competence in interpersonal relations obviously is more important in the job of supervisor than in the job of file clerk. Differential weights assigned to different factors usually are based on the judgment of those responsible for the performance evaluation program, but there are methods available by means of which weightings can be based on statistical analyses. (One such procedure involves a large number of cases, the availability of a very good "overall" criterion, and the use of regression analysis procedures.)

Even if the *intended* set of factor weights, whether based on judgment or on statistical analysis, is appropriate, however, the *actual* weights of the various factors can differ from the intended weights. This effect arises from the fact that, when one combines scores, the scores weight themselves *automatically* in proportion to their *respective variability*—that is, to put it in statistical terms, the scores weight themselves in proportion to their respective standard deviations. Therefore, if the variability of all employees on one rating item—say, judgment—is twice as large as the corresponding variability of all employees on some other item—say, initiative—a direct combination of ratings for any employee on these two factors results in the actual weighting of the "judgment" ratings twice as heavily as the "initiative" ratings. Thus if a different weighting of these two factors is intended, some adjustment must be made.

Although the statistical explanation of this effect is discussed in Appendix A, an example here may further clarify the principle. Suppose one thousand men have been rated on two factors—judgment and initiative—using in each case a fifty-point scale. Suppose, for the present illustration, that all of the men have received ratings on initiative of between 30 and 35 points. Suppose, further, that the judgment ratings vary from 25 to 45. If we now combine for each man his rating on initiative and his rating on judgment we will obtain a combination rating. It has often been assumed in such instances that the two factors would be weighted equally because both factors originally were rated on the same scale. Under these circumstances, however, the factors are not weighted equally at all. The judgment ratings, which vary over a range of twenty points—from 25 to 45—will have approximately four times as much effect on the combined ratings as the ratings on initiative, which vary over a range of only five points—from 30 to 35.

The simple adding of ratings for several factors not only can fail to weight the factors equally (if equal weights are intended) but also can fail to give them any preassigned weights. Suppose, for example, that management has decided that accuracy is twice as important as production and therefore has adopted a rating system in which accuracy is rated on a forty-point scale and production on a twenty-point scale. This arrangement will not necessarily result in accuracy being weighted twice as heavily as production, for the relative weights of the factors are determined by the *variability* or *spread* of the actual ratings on each, and *not* by the maximum values or by the range of values assigned to each.

Adjusting Ratings for Raters' Tendencies or Distortion

When there is evidence, or even strong suspicion, that performance evaluations have been distorted by raters' tendencies or by contamination, the ratings cannot be accepted as actual reflections of "true" evaluations of the individuals in question. When this is the case, a question is raised about how one can use these ratings, or indeed whether one can use them at all. Of course, the distortions are not of major consequence *if* there is reasonable validity among the ratings, and *if* the ratings are to be used *entirely within the context of the group*. But if the ratings are to be compared *between or among* groups of ratees, however, they should *not* be used *unless* they are adjusted for whatever distortions may be present. There are at least two ways of doing this.

Adjusting for differences in means. Let us use, an an example, the situation in which the ratings given by different raters differ significantly. In such a case, one solution is to determine the average of the ratings given by each rater, and compute the difference between *each rater's* average, and the average of *all raters*. This difference can then be added to or subtracted from the ratings given by a particular rater, in order to bring his ratings into alignment with those of other raters. This simple adjustment is satisfactory if the *variabilities* of the ratings given by the different raters are about the same.[29]

Adjusting for differences by standard scores. A more systematic method of adjusting for such differences consists of converting all ratings to a common numerical scale. Some type of *standard score* (comparable score) may be used for this purpose. There are various types of standard scores, such as

[29] The variabilities in the ratings can be compared by comparing their *standard deviations*. See Appendix A, pp. 571–94.

z-scores. Standard scores, including *z*-scores, indicate the *relative* position of individual cases in a distribution. Such scores are based on deviations of individual cases from the mean and are expressed in *standard deviation units*. A "standard deviation" is a statistical index of the degree of variability of the cases within a distribution.[30] It is expressed in terms of the numerical values of the original distribution. In a relatively normal distribution, two-thirds of the cases fall within one standard deviation above and below the mean, about 95 percent are within two standard deviations above and below the mean, and about 99 percent fall within three standard deviations. Thus, regardless of what the mean of a distribution is, or what the magnitude of its standard deviation, it is possible to express the deviation of any given numerical value in terms of the number of standard deviation units it is above or below the mean. A *z*-score is simply the deviation of a given raw score from the mean expressed in terms of standard deviation units.

Let us now see how this helps us in comparing the ratings produced by a "tough" rater with those produced by a "lenient" rater. Let us suppose that the distributions A and B of Figure 8.4 represent, respectively, the total ratings given to their respective groups by rater A and rater B. We can see clearly that a rating of 110 by itself is meaningless unless we relate it to the distribution of which it is a part. (It means a very high rating by rater A, and a very low rating by rater B.) These two distributions, however, can both be converted to *z*-scores, as illustrated at certain points on the distributions by the broken lines and dotted lines from the merit rating scale to the *z*-score scale below it. We can now see that a rating of 110 by rater A would mean a *z*-score of *plus* 2, but by rater B would mean a *z*-score of *minus* 2, and that a rating of 100 from rater A would correspond to a rating of 125

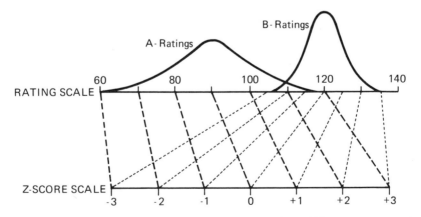

FIG. 8.4 Illustration of conversion of two sets of ratings (A and B) to a common scale of z-scores.

[30] *Ibid.*

from rater B, since both convert to *z*-scores of plus 1. Similar conversions can be made with other groups of ratees for which some form of contamination is apparent, such as for employees on different jobs or in different departments.

Adjusting for Unintended Factor Weights

We have seen that the actual or effective weights of different factors will be different from the intended weights if the *variabilities* of the ratings for the various factors are markedly different. When this is the case, one basic solution to the problem caused by such differential variabilities consists of the conversion of the ratings on the different factors to standard scores (such as *z*-scores), the multiplication of these by their desired weights, and the summation or averaging of these weighted values.

IMPROVING PERFORMANCE EVALUATIONS

The quality of performance evaluations and assessments of personnel basically depends upon the abilities of the raters to make the kinds of judgments that are called for. This implies: (1) that—where possible—those who would be most competent should be selected as raters; and (2) that the raters be given adequate training. This training should cover such subjects as the sources of distortion of ratings, the desirability of focusing on the observable behaviors of ratees (as contrasted with their personal traits), and the desirability of spreading the ratings over the whole range of possible ratings (but doing so discriminantly). With reference to the training of raters, Driver[31] reports that a seven-hour training program in rating methods had the effect of reducing the halo effect, as measured by subsequent reductions in the intercorrelations among the rating factors.

Developing Rating Forms and Instructions

The forms and instructions developed should be those that will help the rater make and record the kinds of judgments he is being asked to make. In this regard, there has developed a fair amount of lore about conventional rating scales, and especially about those scale features that purport to reduce the influence of the halo effect and of constant errors. Particular emphasis has been placed on the practice of alternating the "good" and "bad" ends of scales, and of rating all individuals on the same attribute at the same time. In addition, there have been proponents of graphic rating scales, on which rating variables are represented by continuous lines, and proponents of categorical scales, which use several—usually from five to nine—distinct rating categories. Data to support or reject these and other practices

[31] Driver, R. S. Unpublished study. Philadelphia: Atlantic Refining Co.

are fairly skimpy, but a study by Blumberg, DeSoto, and Kuethe[32] suggests that such variations in format have no appreciable effect on ratings.

Correction for Distortion

When there is evidence of some form of distortion, one should either correct for the distortion if it is feasible to do so or use the ratings in an extremely guarded manner that takes fully into consideration the nature of the distortion.

Pooling of Ratings from Different Raters

Sometimes ratings for the same individuals are obtained from two or more raters and then pooled. There is evidence from a study by Bayroff, Haggerty, and Rundquist[33] to support the contention that pooled ratings *by competent raters* generally are better than single ratings. However, it is frequently the case that the most *competent* raters available are the supervisors of the individuals being rated. This was reflected, for example, in the results of a study by Whitla and Tirrell[34] which indicated that the raters closest to the ratees (in terms of organizational level) were able to rate the ratees better than raters who were at higher levels of the organization. These findings suggest that the ratings of competent raters can be safely combined, but that one should avoid the pooling of ratings of poor raters with those of competent raters.

FEEDBACK OF EVALUATIONS

If a performance evaluation program is intended to facilitate performance improvement on the part of personnel, it is of course necessary that there be provision for feedback to them of the results of such evaluation. Sound psychological principles of learning indicate that knowledge about one's previous performance is essential if improvement (learning) is to take place.

The Role of Supervisors in Feedback

It is logical to view supervisors as the individuals who should assume the role not only of evaluating their subordinates but also of providing feedback to them of the results thereof. However, qualms have been expressed con-

32 Blumberg, H. H., DeSoto, C. B., & Kuethe, J. L. Evaluation of rating scale formats. *Personnel Psychology,* 1966, **19**(3), 243–259.
33 Bayroff, A. G., Haggerty, H. R., & Rundquist, E. A. Validity of ratings as related to rating techniques and conditions. *Personnel Psychology,* 1954, **7**, 93–113.
34 Whitla, D. K., & Tirrell, J. E. The validity of ratings of several levels of supervisors. *Personnel Psychology,* 1954, **6**, 461–466.

cerning the role of supervisors in this regard. McGregor,[35] for example, expresses the opinion that conventional evaluation places the supervisor in the untenable position of judging the subordinate and then acting on this judgment. It is probably true that many supervisors do not feel comfortable in performing these functions and, indeed, are not very adept at it; this is especially true of the feedback role. At the same time, displacing responsibility for the evaluation of subordinates and the subsequent feedback of information to them would seem to constitute an abrogation of supervisory responsibilities. Perhaps the primary focus in this matter should be on trying to provide guidance (including training) for supervisors relating to the most effective approaches in the counseling of subordinates.

The Evaluation Interview

In this regard, it is the practice of some organizations to have supervisors arrange for scheduled evaluation interviews with their subordinates once a year or at some other stated interval. In reflecting on the evaluation interview, Burke and Wilcox[36] suggest that three outcomes appear to be important—(1) the satisfaction of the subordinate with the interview; (2) the motivation of the subordinate to improve job performance; and (3) subsequent actual improvement on job performance. In the case of 323 female telephone operators, it was found (through responses to anonymous questionnaires) that these three outcomes were in fact correlated as follows:

Variables	Correlation
Satisfaction and desire to improve	.43
Satisfaction and actual improvement	.32
Desire to improve and actual improvement	.57

Although we cannot positively attribute these correlations to a cause-and-effect relationship, they at least suggest the possibility that the desire to improve oneself and actual improvement may in part be a function of how satisfying the interview process is to the individual.

It is obvious from this and other studies that the reactions of individuals to evaluation interviews comprise a mixed bag. Thus one would wish to have some clues as to the characteristics of interviews that are associated with more positive outcomes. Some inklings about this come from a series of studies in a plant of the General Electric Company. These studies by Meyer and his associates[37] probably comprise the most comprehensive studies of the evaluation interview.

[35] McGregor, D. An uneasy look at performance appraisal. *Harvard Business Review,* 1957, **35,** 89–94.

[36] Burke, R. J., & Wilcox, D. S. Characteristics of effective performance review and development interviews. *Personnel Psychology,* 1969, **22**(3), 291–305.

[37] French, J. R. P., Jr., Kay, E., & Meyer, H. H. Participation and the appraisal system. *Human Relations,* 1966, **19,** 3–20; Kay, E., French, J. R. P., Jr., & Meyer,

In one of these studies,[38] ninety-two salaried employees were interviewed by research personnel; they also completed questionnaires before and after their regular salary action interview with their supervisory managers and were interviewed again after a delayed second discussion with their managers dealing with subsequent performance improvement. Half of the managers were instructed to use a *high participation* approach during the salary action interview, in which the manager asked his subordinate to prepare a set of goals for improved job performance and to submit them for the manager's review and approval. The other managers were instructed to use a more traditional *low participation* approach in which the manager formulated a set of goals for the subordinate; these goals were later reviewed in the performance improvement session. In general, those subordinates in the high participation group reacted more favorably to their interviews and to the appraisal system than did those in the low participation group. What is more, they achieved a somewhat higher percentage of their predetermined "improvement goals."

As another facet of the General Electric Company studies, Kay, Meyer, and French[39] investigated the relationship between "threats" during the appraisal interview and subsequent goal achievement. The "threats" during the interview were statements made by the managers about the subordinate which were interpreted by trained observers to be of a critical nature and to represent threats to the subordinate's self-esteem. (The subordinates in all cases had agreed to the presence of an outside observer.) The relationship between the number of threats (categorized as above or below average) and later estimates of goal achievement is shown in Figure 8.5. This figure also differentiates between those who had been characterized, on the basis of a questionnaire, as having high or low "occupational self-esteem." It can be seen that the number of "threats" during the interviews had no appreciable effect in the case of those subordinates who were high on occupational self-esteem. But in the case of those who were low on occupational self-esteem, a high level of threat can have a distinctly dampening effect. These and other results led the investigators to conclude that:

1. Comprehensive annual performance appraisals are of questionable value.
2. Coaching should be a day-to-day, not a once-a-year activity.
3. Goal setting, not criticism, should be used to improve performance.
4. Separate appraisals should be held for different purposes.

H. H. *A study of the performance appraisal interview.* Behavioral Research Service Report No. EBR–11, General Electric Company, 1962; Kay, E., Meyer, H. H., & French, J. R. P., Jr. Effects of threat in a performance appraisal interview. *Journal of Applied Psychology,* 1965, **49**(5), 311–317; Meyer, H. H., & Kay, E. *A comparison of a work planning program with the annual performance appraisal interview approach.* Behavioral Research Service Report No. ESR–17, General Electric Company, 1964; and Meyer, H. H., Kay, E., & French, J. R. P., Jr. Split roles in performance appraisal. *Harvard Business Review,* 1965, **43**, 123–129.

[38] Meyer, Kay, & French, *Ibid.*
[39] Kay, Meyer, & French, *op. cit.*

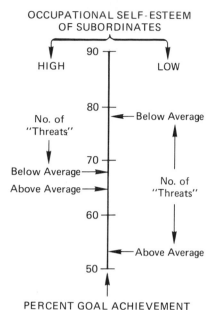

FIG. 8.5 Relationship between number of "threats" during evaluation interviews and subsequent estimated goal achievement for subordinates with high and low occupational self esteem. (*Adapted from Kay, Meyer, and French, 1965, op. cit., Table 2.*)

The upshot of all this was that the company developed a new appraisal program, the work-planning-and-review method, the basic features of which departed from the more traditional evaluation programs in that: (1) there are more frequent discussions of performance; (2) no summary judgments or ratings are made; (3) salary action discussions are held separately; and (4) emphasis is on mutual goal planning and problem solving.

Discussion

The General Electric Company studies do not necessarily imply that all organizations should cast evaluation interviews to the four winds—especially inasmuch as such interviews have been well received by some employees. For example, Mayfield[40] reports that in one company 90 percent of the employees expressed satisfaction with the evaluation interviews. But the experience of the General Electric Company at least suggests that in some situations a more "continuous," day-to-day practice of feedback to, and counseling of, subordinates may be appropriate.

In any event—whether such supervisor-subordinate interchange is "scheduled" (as in the annual evaluation interview) or is on a day-to-day basis— it appears that there are certain ingredients that enhance the odds of bringing about desirable outputs, such as training the supervisors, conducting the interchange in a nonthreatening manner, and focusing on mutual goal setting for the subordinate.

[40] Mayfield, H. In defense of performance appraisal. *Harvard Business Review,* March-April 1960, **38**(2), 81–87.

Joseph R. Garber, AT&T

PART III

The Organizational
and Social Context
of Human Work

A person's working relationships comprise a major aspect of his total life. His involvement in and commitment to his work, and the satisfactions derived from it, are (or should be) the mutual concern of the organization and the individual himself. Thus, the interaction of motivation factors, value systems, attitudes, and the like with the various aspects of the working situation is an integral component in the study of human behavior in industry. The working situation is composed in part of the organizational and social environment, and the individual is subject to whatever features this environment may have. Some of the aspects of the environment are planned and organized; some are the consequence of fortuitous events and circumstances. Included in this organizational and social context is whatever training is provided by the organization to persons who work within it. In addition, the organizational context is characterized by the structure of the organization, the type of supervision, the policies and managerial practices that are used, the social environment (including inter-action with fellow workers), the communications, the financial compensation policies, and many other factors. This section deals with some of the dimensions of the interaction between people and the organizations in which they work. Consideration also is given to human motivation and the implications of various aspects of the organizational and social context of work in relation to human behavior and job satisfaction.

chapter nine

Learning:
The Basis
of
Personnel Training

Let us reflect for a moment about this question: What causes people to behave the way they do—in their personal and family lives or in their jobs? Within certain constraints imposed by hereditary factors, the basic answer to this question is simple: They have *learned* to behave as they do.

As an individual becomes an employee within an organization or begins a new job, he brings with him his own unique assortment of previously learned "behaviors," including his physical skills, the knowledge he has acquired, his language skills, his temperament and interests, his motivation, his attitudes, his habits, and his idiosyncrasies, as well as other "types" of behavior. The additional learning that people acquire after they become employees or undertake a new type of work can take place in either of two ways: through everyday work experience, or as the consequence of systematic training.

Day-to-day work experience probably is the most effective means of developing expertise in some jobs, or at least in some aspects of them. In fact, the "school of hard knocks" has a way of driving home some lessons that might otherwise not be learned. On the other hand, it is manifest that for many jobs (or aspects thereof), some form of well planned and well executed training program provides the best bet for people to develop relevant job expertise—that is, relevant "learning."

Depending upon the job and the purpose of the training program, the training may be directed toward: (1) the development of actual job knowledge and skills; (2) the transmission of information, as in orientation training; or (3) the modification of attitudes—for example, increasing the sensitivities of supervisors and management personnel to the feelings and reactions of others, or influencing employee attitudes toward the organization.

Whatever its purposes, however, a training program should be established on sound principles and practices that are conducive to human learning. Although many training programs have been established on such principles, some have been ill conceived and have failed to meet real needs.

THE NATURE OF LEARNING

Inasmuch as training is essentially the management of learning, in this chapter we will consider the nature of learning and will explore some of the factors associated with the learning process. The next chapter will deal with training needs, methods, and evaluation.

Learning has been defined by McGehee and Thayer[1] as a term used to describe the process by means of which behavioral changes result from experience. It is impossible to observe directly the process that we call learning. The fact that learning has occurred can only be inferred from a comparison of an individual's behavior prior to and subsequent to experiences of specific kinds. This is not to say that there has been no "learning" if there is no overt behavioral change, but this cannot be *known* unless there *is* a behavioral change.

The Instigation of Behavior

Behavior of whatever form (starting a motor, dispatching a taxi, calling a meeting, or kicking the cat) is instigated; it is not fortuitous, even though it sometimes looks like it is. In characterizing human behavior it is conventional to talk in terms of a stimulus (S) acting upon an organism (O) to bring about a response (R). The stimuli frequently are external to the individual (such as a part coming down a conveyor belt, the change in a traffic light, or instructions from a supervisor); but they may be internal (such as the completion of one operation that triggers another, as in a

---

[1] McGehee, W., & Thayer, P. W. *Training in business and industry.* New York: John Wiley, 1961, p. 132.

sequence of bookkeeping operations). Some external stimuli are very definite, such as a traffic light; others are very subtle and might be picked up only by those who are especially attuned to them—for example, the tone of a supervisor's voice, or slight differences in the appearance of tobacco leaves as perceived by a tobacco buyer.

In the job context there usually is, for each stimulus or syndrome of stimuli, some behavior or range of behaviors (i.e., responses) that would be optimal (i.e.. most appropriate) in terms of the objectives at hand. The purpose of training generally is to "establish the connection" between given stimuli and their optimum responses. This is a fairly straightforward proposition in the case of, say, routine assembly work, but it is a very complex affair in the case of jobs that involve complex decision making.

In many jobs, as well as in many circumstances in personal life, the "stimuli" are not identifiable individual stimuli; rather, they may consist of combinations of individual stimuli such as one finds in complex traffic conditions. In this regard, Cunningham and Duncan[2] cite certain industrial jobs in which the "cue" for a task was not a single environmental event, but rather several, each in itself not constituting an adequate cue for the action in question. In some circumstances the environmental events may consist of personal contacts, problems to be resolved, or other complex "events."

In turn, the response does not always consist of a single discrete act, but may be composed of many separate acts, in some instances forming a pre-determined routine, and in other instances consisting only of behaviors generated on the spot.

The Learning Process

To say that training generally is directed toward establishing stimulus-response connections, however, tells us nothing about what goes on in this process. "What goes on" can be discussed either at a descriptive level or at a more theoretical level.

Types of learning. At the descriptive level, Gagné[3] postulates different types of learning that he refers to as a *cumulative learning sequence*. He postulates further that any given level in this sequence depends on all the lower levels, as shown in Figure 9.1. The lowest level consists of simple stimulus-response connections that are virtually conditioned, such as picking up the telephone when it rings. The higher sequences include chains of

[2] Cunningham, D. J., & Duncan, K. D. Describing non-repetitive tasks for training purposes. *Occupational Psychology,* 1967, **41**, 203–210.

[3] Gagné, R. M. *The conditions of learning.* New York: Holt, Rinehart & Winston, 1965; and Gagné, R. M. Contributions of learning to human development. *Psychological Review,* 1968, **75**, 177–191.

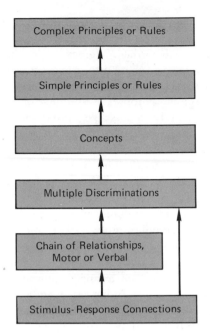

FIG. 9.1 A generalized illustration of the cumulative learning sequence proposed by Gagné. In this model the learning at any given level depends on relevant learning at the lower levels. (*From* The conditions of learning *by Robert M. Gagné, p. 182. Copyright © 1965 by Holt, Rinehart and Winston, Inc. Reprinted by permission of Holt, Rinehart and Winston, Inc.*)

relationships in which each act triggers the next, multiple discriminations in which the appropriate response must be made to each of various possible stimuli, the learning of concepts, and the application of simple and complex principles. A question has been raised by Annett and Duncan,[4] however, as to whether this sequence of categories represents a true hierarchy in the sense that the learning at any one level depends upon learning at the subordinate levels. In fact, they cite an example that is at odds with Gagné's hierarchical model. Aside from this question, however, Gagné's formulation provides at least a tentative frame of reference for categorizing learning tasks.

In terms of the problem of training—that is, "making the connection" between stimuli and responses—the implication of Gagné's formulation is that training methods must be different for the different categories of this learning sequence. These differences would range from virtual conditioning in the case of the stimulus-response connections to more subtle training methods for the learning of concepts, principles, and approaches to problem solving. In general, the shift from strictly sensory stimuli and physical responses to the more vague domain of concept learning increases the problem of setting forth training requirements.

We might back up a moment to make a distinction between two types

[4] Annett, J., & Duncan, K. D. Task analysis and training design. *Occupational Psychology,* 1967, **41,** 211–221.

of conditioning. *Classical* conditioning consists of the process of causing a *new* stimulus to bring about a natural or unconditioned response, as in Pavlov's early studies of conditioning a dog to salivate to a bell, by simultaneously presenting the dog with two stimuli—the bell and food. On the other hand, *operant* conditioning consists of somehow getting people or animals to make a response that is not in their "natural" repertoire of unconditioned responses, as when they operate the keyboard of a calculating machine while reading the numbers on a price list. When such responses are "reinforced" by some reward, the responses tend to be repeated later when the same stimuli are presented. When conditioning is dominant in learning job activities, it is typically operant conditioning.

One of the most important types of learning involves learning from verbal presentations, both oral and written. Carroll[5] makes the point that learning "by being told" is not simply the learning of responses, but does in fact involve a process of acquiring knowledge through experience—although this experience is vicarious. This is sometimes called *cognitive* learning as contrasted with response learning. Verbal messages may or may not be of such a nature as to require an overt response. It still remains true, however, that the *fact* of actual learning from verbal messages can only be known when a response is made.

Learning theories. Various theories have been put forward to "explain" the learning process. A theory has been described as a "way of binding together a multitude of facts so that one may comprehend them all at once."[6] Thus, a learning theory is one that is intended to explain in conceptual terms what takes place when learning occurs, how the learning takes place, and what variables facilitate the learning process. To be valid, such a theory must account for all of the types of human learning behavior that occur, whether in raising children, in school, in learning to play golf, or in learning a job in industry. As of this date, however, no single theory has been generally accepted as completely adequate in these terms.

It is not within the province of this book to describe and evaluate the various learning theories.[7] It may be useful, however, to examine briefly those aspects of learning theories that have implications for industrial training. On the basis of a synthesis of various theories, McGehee[8] points out that certain generalizations seem to be common to different theories

[5] Carroll, J. B. On learning from being told. *Educational Psychologist* (Newsletter of Division 15, American Psychological Association), March 1968, 5(2), 1 & 5–10.

[6] Kelley, G. A. *The psychology of personal constructs.* Vol. I. New York: Norton, 1955.

[7] For a discussion of learning theories the reader is referred to such sources as Hilgard, E. R., & Bower, G. H. *Theories of learning.* (3rd ed.) New York: Appleton-Century-Crofts, 1966.

[8] McGehee, W. Are we using what we know about training?—Learning theory and training. *Personnel Psychology,* 1958, **11**, 1–12.

(though presumably to varying degrees). These generalizations may be considered as statements of "what happens" when an individual learns. Thus, they can serve as guideposts for ordering the experiences one intends to use for the purpose of modifying behavior—i.e., training the individual. These generalizations include the following: the goals of training must be those which are meaningful to the learner (although these are amenable to modification); the learner must be provided with the opportunity to make appropriate responses (to "do" something, to take an active rather than a passive part); the responses required must be within the capabilities of the learner; and there must be assurance that the learner has learned the desired behaviors (which implies continual evaluation of the training).

Learning Curves

As indicated above, learning cannot be observed directly. Rather, one can observe, or measure, only the behavioral changes that occur as the consequence of learning. Learning curves typically show the cumulative changes in an appropriate criterion that occur during the learning period. Such curves may represent either individuals or groups. The criteria used, of course, will depend upon the circumstances; they may be measures of productivity, performance on tests, or other factors.

The form and length of learning curves varies considerably from one situation to another. The total period of training on some jobs, for example, may be months or even years, whereas on other jobs it may be only days or weeks. Further, the shape of the curve may vary. Figure 9.2 illustrates several generalized forms of learning curves. Most of these curves represent the curves of actual jobs, but the natures of the specific jobs are

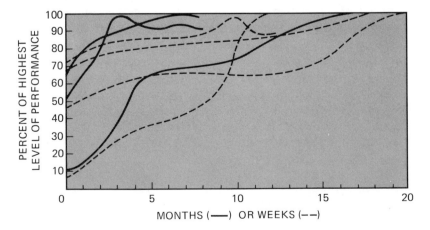

FIG. 9.2 Illustrations of generalized learning curves for several different jobs. While the original curves were somewhat irregular, for illustrative purposes they have been smoothed.

not particularly pertinent to the central point, which is to illustrate the differences in the curves from one job to another. These curves are averages for groups of employees, and the criterion scales for all of them have been converted to a common, arbitrary base.

The curve for any single individual can be similarly drawn. In fact, a very practical use for learning curves is to allow us to compare the curve for an individual with that for a group. For such purposes, however, it is preferable to include curves that also show the ranges of performance for some segment of the total illustrative group, such as the 25*th* and 75*th* percentiles.

With reference to learning and learning curves, it is generally the case that the *relative* degree of improvement in learning is greater in the case of more difficult jobs than in the case of easier jobs. This is illustrated by the comparisons shown in Figure 9.3. Each part of this figure shows the production throughout training of employees on two pairs of related jobs in the manufacture of oscilloscope accessories; in each pair, one job had been judged by management representatives as "most difficult" and the other as "least difficult." The greater relative improvement in the case of the most difficult job is evident in each pair. This difference generally can be attributed to the fact that an "easy" job is one for which most people already have the basic acquired skills and knowledges in ready-to-use form requiring little adaptation; thus they start out closer to their ultimate ceiling. In the case of more difficult jobs, initial performance is much lower relative to final performance, which leaves more "room" for improvement.

The plateau. In learning any complex task it often happens that after a certain level of efficiency has been attained, a period of time passes in which little or no improvement takes place. This period is followed by a later increase in skill. The period during which no apparent improvement occurs is known as a *plateau*. Examples of plateaus in learning are shown in a couple of the curves of Figure 9.2. Although the cause of plateaus is not clear, it is important for the trainer to be aware of their existence so that he can give assurance to the trainees when they reach a plateau that this is "par for the course," and that they can expect later additional progress. Such information can aid in preventing the trainees from becoming discouraged with the apparent leveling in their progress. By analyzing the activities and training procedures it may be possible for the trainer to diagnose the reasons for a plateau, and possibly to modify the training so as to minimize it.

Retention of Learning

For better or for worse, we humans do not store permanently all the information we "learn." This is especially true with information that we do not "use." How much falls by the wayside through disuse depends pretty

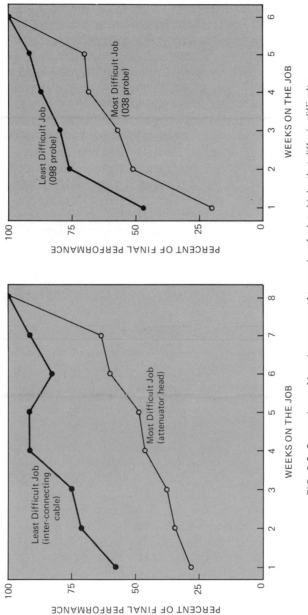

FIG. 9.3 Comparison of learning curves of two pairs of related jobs that differ in difficulty level. In each case productivity is shown relative to the productivity during the last week (which is equated to 100 percent). Note that the *relative* improvement is greater for the more difficult jobs (and, in fact, on those jobs was continuing to rise at the end of the period shown). (*Courtesy of Tetronix, Inc., and Dr. Guyot Frazier.*)

much on the type of information and the individual; age also takes its toll of our ability to hang onto what we have learned. For what consolation it might be, it can be said that generally the relearning of material takes less time than the original learning; perhaps this is a bit like clearing away the underbrush from an old path through the forest as compared with blazing a completely new trail.

In connection with the learning of perceptual-motor skills, there is some fairly current evidence to suggest that retention of proficiency over time may be fairly high. This inference comes from a study by Fleishman and Parker.[9] In this experiment the subjects were trained on a tracking device, and were then brought back in groups of about ten for retraining at varying time intervals after original training. These time intervals ranged between one, five, nine, fourteen, and twenty-four months. The results are summarized in Figure 9.4, which shows the learning during the original learning period and also the average level of performance during the later relearning sessions. The two curves represent different learning groups—those who were given formal guidance versus those who learned "on their own." In the case of both groups, the performance during the relearning

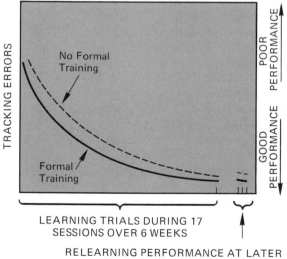

LEARNING TRIALS DURING 17
SESSIONS OVER 6 WEEKS

RELEARNING PERFORMANCE AT LATER
DATE (1, 5, 9, 14, or 17 MONTHS)

FIG. 9.4 Comparison of performance on a perceptual-motor task during original learning period and during a relearning period at a later time. Note that the performance during the relearning period was about the same as at the end of the original learning period. (*Adapted from Fleishman and Parker*, op. cit. *Copyright 1962 by the American Psychological Association, and adapted by permission.*)

[9] Fleishman, E. A., & Parker, J. F., Jr. Factors in the retention of and relearning of perceptual-motor skill. *Journal of Experimental Psychology*, 1962, **64**, 215–226.

period was virtually the same as at the end of the original learning period. There were virtually no differences in performance between those whose time span since original learning was short (one, five, or nine months) and those whose time span was long (fourteen or twenty-four months).

CONDITIONS OF LEARNING

There is much still to be learned about learning, and unequivocal pronouncements about it are hard to come by. Experience and research, however, have contributed to the evolution of some generalizations relating to the conditions that are conducive to learning. A few of these will be discussed below,[10] but in doing so we should be mindful of Gagné's[11] admonition that the generality of some of these theories is still suspect.

Knowledge of Results

There is quite wide acceptance of the usefulness of feedback—that is, knowledge of results of one's behavior—in learning. Actually, there are two ways in which knowledge of results can have an effect upon learning. In the first place, it can provide the basis for correcting one's errors. There are some kinds of tasks in which such information is virtually mandatory for learning. A crane operator, for example, would have trouble learning to manipulate the controls of a crane appropriately unless he knew how the crane responded to his control actions. The second way in which knowledge of results can have a facilitating effect is by making the task more interesting to the learner—that is, it can have a motivational effect.

The effects upon learning of knowledge of results have been confirmed in a number of studies. One such study dealt with rifle practice.[12] The situation was one in which men fired rifles at moving targets in a simulated rifle range on each of ten days. Where "knowledge of results" was to be furnished to the subjects, an electronically activated "check" informed them when they had made a hit. The subjects were divided into two equivalent groups, one group receiving knowledge of results, the other not, for the four hundred "runs." After that, the knowledge of results was removed from the group that previously had received such feedback. The results,

10 For a review and summary of factors associated with learning see Gagné, R. M., & Bolles, R. C. A review of factors in learning efficiency. In E. Galanter (Ed.), *Automatic Teaching*. New York: John Wiley, 1959.

11 Gagné, R. M. Military training and principles of learning. *American Psychologist,* February 1962, 17(2), 83–91.

12 Stockbridge, H. C. W., & Chambers, B. Aiming, transfer of training, and knowledge of results. *Journal of Applied Psychology,* 1958, 42, 148–153.

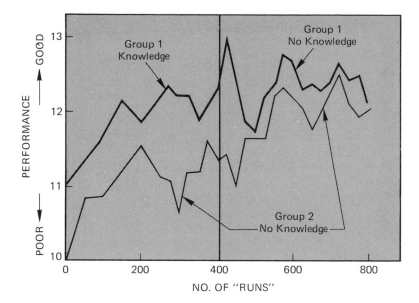

FIG. 9.5 Illustration of effects of knowledge of results in a learning task. This particular task was rifle practice. Note the leveling off of learning on the part of group 1 after knowledge of results was removed. (*Adapted from Stockbridge and Chambers, op. cit. Copyright 1958 by the American Psychological Association and adapted by permission.*)

shown in Figure 9.5, indicate a distinct difference between these groups during the first four hundred trials. After that, however, the first group leveled off in its performance (aside from a brief spurt) while the second group (with no knowledge at any time) continued to improve, and finally caught up with the first group; but it took nearly twice as long to reach the same level of performance.

Another example of the effects of knowledge of results comes from a study by Alexander, Kepner, and Tregoe.[13] They had four thirteen-man crews of operators of a military information-processing system perform simulated military tasks twice a day, five days a week, for two months. Two crews were provided knowledge of results and a debriefing session after each exercise. The other two groups received no such feedback. Pretests and post-tests were used to provide thirteen different measures of performance. The average performance gains over all these functions are given below:

Groups with feedback:	A: 35.1%
	C: 49.6%
Groups without feedback:	B: 0.1%
	D: 4.6%

[13] Alexander, L. T., Kepner, C. H., & Tregoe, B. B. The effectiveness of knowledge of results in a military system-training program. *Journal of Applied Psychology,* 1962, **46**(2), 202–211.

Figure 9.6 shows the performance of the four groups on a "unique problem," given after the two-month study. Performance is shown as a percentage on each of three groups of functions. The difference between the feedback and no-feedback crews drives home the importance of feedback in such a task.

But it is not enough simply to say that feedback is a fine thing. In the actual training situation it is necessary to spell out what kind of feedback is to be provided to trainees, and when. Clearly, any feedback needs to be relevant to the task, and the more relevant and specific, the better.

Types of feedback. In considering feedback we should differentiate between different species. One basic distinction can be made between intrinsic and extrinsic feedback, and in the case of extrinsic feedback we can differentiate between direct (or primary) and indirect (or secondary). Some examples are given below.

Intrinsic feedback (based on internal cues)
    Examples: body balance in walking; sensing by touch; hearing own speech; feel of steering wheel

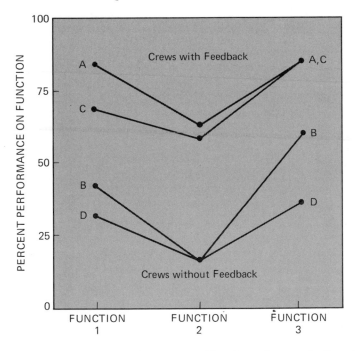

FIG. 9.6 Performance on three groups of functions of crews of military information-processing system on "unique problem" at end of two-month training program. Two crews (A and C) had been given knowledge of results and debriefings throughout the two months. The others (B and D) had no such feedback. (*Adapted from Alexander, Kepner, & Tregoe, ibid.*)

Extrinsic (stimuli external to individual)
  Direct (or primary)
    Examples: observing meter on gauge when controlling gasoline pump; clarity of sound when tuning radio; observing typed page while typing letter
  Indirect (or secondary)
    Examples: commendation from supervisor; rejection of product by inspector

Role of trainer in providing feedback. The trainer has no direct opportunity to influence intrinsic feedback. However, as Holding[14] points out, there are some tasks in which intrinsic feedback does *not necessarily* provide cues as to whether what the trainee does is correct (such as in pronouncing a foreign word). In such cases the trainer should inject appropriate extrinsic feedback in order to aid the trainee in recognizing and acting upon his intrinsic cues.

The trainer may or may not have the opportunity to influence the nature of any direct intrinsic feedback; this will depend upon the nature of the task. When the direct intrinsic feedback is inadequate for the trainee, the trainer should go out of his way to provide indirect feedback.

Motivation

As indicated above, feedback can be a source of motivation as well as a means of providing knowledge about performance on the activity itself. Although there are still some theoretical questions about the importance of motivation in learning, there is general agreement that motivated learners learn better than those who are unmotivated or insufficiently motivated. We will discuss motivation further in Chapter 12, but we should like to point out here that motives generally can be characterized as *intrinsic* or *extrinsic* —which is essentially the same distinction as the one made above regarding feedback. Although human motives and task feedback are different entities, we can see that, to some extent, one hand can wash the other.

Intrinsic motivation is related to the task itself; there is some direct relationship between the task and the goal of the learner, such as in the case of a mechanic who achieves satisfaction from a job well done. Extrinsic motivation is independent of the task—i.e., the task is viewed as a possible means to some other end, such as for the income the job might ultimately bring to the learner. Intrinsic motivation, of course, has an advantage over extrinsic motivation, for it can provide the trainee with a continuing job interest even after completion of training. But in the case of new employees on many jobs in industry, there may be no initial basis for intrinsic motivation on the part of the trainees. Where this is the case,

[14] Holding, D. H. *Principles of training.* Oxford: Pergamon Press, 1965, p. 23.

it is up to the trainer to do what he can to generate the basis for the ultimate development of intrinsic motivation, and also to provide incentives that can stimulate external motivation. Some such incentives have been suggested by McGehee and Thayer.[15] These include: praise (sincerely put and from a valued person); good working conditions; pleasant relations with peers, supervisors, and subordinates; and status within the work group and community. Other incentives include earnings (or the prospects thereof), the recognition of the need for training, respect for the trainer, and job security.

Reward versus Punishment

With reference to motivation, a question might be raised as to the relative effectiveness of positive rewards (for desirable behavior) versus negative punishment (for undesirable behavior) in learning. Although we cannot examine the supporting evidence here it has been concluded that, in general, punishment is less effective in learning than is reward. Bass and Vaughan[16] set forth the following arguments against the use of punishment: (1) the results of punishment are not as predictable as those of reward, for punishment means *Stop it: you have made the wrong response,* but does not indicate what the correct action is; (2) the effects of punishment are less permanent than those of reward; (3) it tends to fixate behavior, rather than to eliminate it; and (4) it is sometimes accompanied by unfortunate by-products, such as negative attitudes. On the other hand, it has been pointed out that mild punishment can be reasonably effective under some circumstances, if it is administered immediately following the incorrect response, and if it is informative.[17]

Scheduling of Training Periods

In the terminology of experimental psychologists, the scheduling of learning sessions can be either "massed" or "distributed." In general it is believed that, for any given training situation, there is some "optimum" schedule that contributes most effectively to learning. The fact of different schedules having differential effects has been documented time and again, as in a study by Mahler and Monroe.[18] The training in question was job instruction training to supervisors, designed to qualify the super-

[15] McGehee & Thayer, *op. cit.*

[16] Bass, B. M., & Vaughan, J. A. *Training in industry: The management of learning.* Belmont, California: Wadsworth Publishing Company, 1966.

[17] McGehee & Thayer, *op. cit.,* p. 160.

[18] Mahler, W. R., & Monroe, W. H. *How industry determines the need for and effectiveness of training.* Personnel Research Section, Department of the Army, PRS Report No. 929, March 15, 1952.

visors to be more effective in giving job training to new employees. One group of three hundred supervisors received six hours of training spread over a two-week period. Another group received the six hours in three two-hour sessions on successive days. In a later follow-up it was found that the first group, for which the training had been spaced over two weeks, made fewer mistakes in the training of new workers than did those in the second group, for which training had been concentrated in three days.

The problem for any specific trainer, however, is that of figuring out what duration and spacing would be optimum for the particular training he is planning. This has been determined experimentally in some circumstances, but we would hope there would be some general guidelines to follow in scheduling reasonably optimum training sessions for any given job. Unfortunately, one would be hard pressed to tease out of the available evidence any really solid, universal "truths" to provide such guidance. However, Bass and Vaughan[19] do offer the following suggestions: distribution of learning has been more consistently beneficial to the learning of motor skills than to verbal learning and other complex forms of learning; the less meaningful the material to be learned and the greater its difficulty and amount, the more distributed practice will be superior to massed practice; and material learned by distributed practice will tend to be retained longer than material learned in concentrated doses. In addition, two or three other points might be made. In the first place, it seems desirable to have each training period cover some cohesive segment of training content. Secondly, one should avoid the onset of excessive boredom or inattention by interspersing breaks in the training sessions now and then. (Most trainers can get some cues about lag of attention by observing their captive audience.) Thirdly, it has been found that even short breaks frequently facilitate the learning process.

Part versus Whole Learning

We have seen in many areas of human behavior (including the area of learning) that research frequently results in a great deal of apparently ambiguous, if not conflicting, results or implications. This has been the case with regard to the question of training by "parts" or by the "whole" —in other words, training on each of the separate components of the total material, or training on the entire content as a complete entity. But sometimes a careful analysis of research results in an area will reveal a pattern that previously was elusive. This has been the case in this area, for Naylor[20]

---

[19] Bass & Vaughan, *op. cit.*, p. 48.

[20] Naylor, J. C. *Parameters affecting the relative efficiency of part and whole practice methods: A review of the literature.* United States Naval Training Devices Center, Technical Report No. 950–1, February 1962.

has teased out some organization and system from an otherwise apparently confusing array of evidence. In briefly summarizing his analysis, let us first clarify a distinction he makes between *task complexity* and *task organization*. Most activities (which we might call composite tasks) consist of component tasks. *Task complexity* refers to the relative difficulty of the separate component tasks viewed individually; and *task organization* refers to the extent to which the component tasks are interrelated (i.e., are dependent upon each other).

By analyzing relevant studies in terms of the levels of task complexity and task organization of the activities investigated, it was possible to present data on the superiority of whole versus part learning for various combinations of complexity and organization. The results are shown graphically in Figure 9.7. From such relationships Naylor suggested a couple of training principles.

The first of these principles relates to tasks of relatively *high organization;*

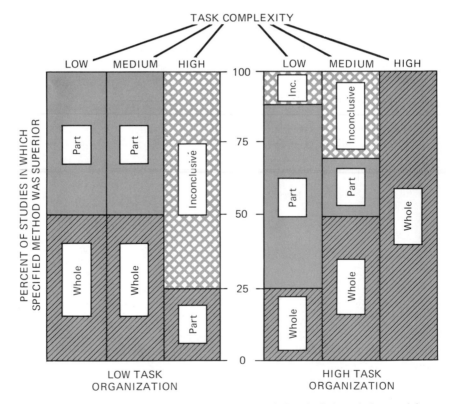

FIG. 9.7 Percent of studies which demonstrated superiority of whole and of part training, as a function of task complexity and organization. The "inconclusive" studies were those in which neither method was demonstrably superior. (*Adapted from Naylor, op. cit.*)

as *task complexity* is increased, *whole* task training should become relatively more efficient than part task training. The second relates to tasks of relatively *low organization;* as *task complexity* is increased, *part* task training should become relatively more efficient than whole task training. However, the high proportion of "inconclusive" findings in the studies of low-organization high-complexity tasks may suggest that in such instances the effect of method becomes indifferent.

Even within the framework of these principles, however, as Hilgard[21] suggests, the effects of part versus whole learning can be influenced by other factors, such as the intelligence of the subject (the more intelligent the subject, the more likely the whole method will prove advantageous) and the effects of practice (the advantage of the whole method increases with practice in using it).

Generalizations about Human Learning

The hassles among the theorists make it virtually impossible to set forth any set of generalizations about human learning on which there would be universal concurrence. However, Silverman[22] formulated nine principles, as "useful generalizations" which he felt would be acceptable to spokesmen for most theories. These are given below, with occasional explanations added:

1. The learner learns what he does.
2. Learning proceeds most effectively when the learner's correct responses are immediately reinforced.
3. The frequency with which a response is reinforced will determine how well the response will be learned. (Practice does not itself make perfect, but reinforced practice helps in that direction.)
4. Practice in a variety of settings will increase the range of situations in which the learning can be applied.
5. Motivational conditions influence the effectiveness of rewards and play a key role in determining the performance of learned behavior. (The motivated learner is more likely to learn and to use what he learns than is his unmotivated partner.)
6. Meaningful learning, that is, learning with understanding, is more permanent and more transferable than rote learning or learning by some memorized formula. (The learner should be encouraged or helped to find summarizing or governing principles to enable him to organize what he is learning.)
7. The learner's perception of what he is learning determines how well and how quickly he will learn. (The learner should thus be assisted to learn to dis-

---

[21] Hilgard, E. R. *Introduction to psychology.* (3rd ed.) New York: Harcourt, Brace, Jovanovich, 1962, p. 314.

[22] Silverman, R. E. Learning theory applied to training. In C. P. Otto & O. Glaser (Eds.), *The management of training.* Reading, Mass.: Addison-Wesley Publishing Company, 1970, chapter 8.

criminate the important stimuli in each situation, so they can be associated with appropriate responses.)

8. People learn more effectively when they learn at their own pace.
9. There are different kinds of learning and they may require different training processes.

Discussion

Some questions have been raised by Gagné[23] regarding the relative utility of some of the commonly accepted principles of learning as applied to the practical problems of job training. He cites chapter and verse to illustrate that such "principles" as distribution of practice, reinforcement, and response familiarity have not been found to be effective in certain job training situations. He indicates, rather, that the more effective principles (in at least the cases cited) were those of a very different nature, as follows:

1. Any human task may be analyzed into a set of component tasks which are quite distinct from each other in terms of the experimental operations needed to produce them.
2. These task components are mediators of the final task performance. That is, their presence insures positive transfer to a final performance, and their absence reduces such transfer to near zero.
3. The basic principles of training design consist of: (a) identifying the component tasks of a final performance; (b) insuring that each of these component tasks is fully achieved; and (c) arranging the total learning situation in a sequence which will insure optimal mediational effects from one component to another.

Gagné points out, however, that such "principles" as task analysis, intratask transfer, component task achievement, and sequencing do not impugn the *relevance* of the traditional principles of learning, but rather raise questions about their *relative importance*. Although these newly proposed principles are not yet supported by any well organized body of experimental evidence, it seems that their implied focus of attention on the job tasks and operations to be performed contributes to the pinpointing of training toward specific, meaningful job objectives.

TRANSFER OF LEARNING

The circus tight-rope walker probably has a better chance of getting safely to the other end of an I-beam on a new skyscraper than you or I. And a pretzel twister probably could do a better job of tying bows on

---

[23] Gagné, (1962), *op. cit.*

Christmas packages than the typical man on the street. One could cite other instances of transfer of learning—that is, the carrying over to one situation of something that has been learned in another situation. This is essentially what most industrial training is all about. Much of the training in industry is, of course, carried out in an artificial or simulated situation, with the expectation that it will, in effect, transfer to the "real job" as such. In addition to its relevance for the training situation, the question of possible transfer of learning also comes up when an individual changes from one job to another, especially if there is some kind of similarity between the two jobs.

Psychologists have given a great deal of attention to the study of transfer of learning, beginning with the very early work of Thorndike and Woodworth.[24] Thorndike[25] long ago concluded that transfer in a general way does not occur at all and that what is often regarded as transfer is simply the result of *identical elements* that are common to the two activities. The identical elements might be overt activities as such (e.g., the operation of a spray painter, whether in painting automobile bodies or railroad cars), or methods or approaches (e.g., the procedures used in balancing accounts, whether the accounts deal with girdles or dog whistles). In connection with this explanation of transfer of learning, however, some nagging questions have led to other possible explanations, some of which are predicated on the assumption of much more generalization than Thorndike implied.

Osgood's Transfer Surface

Among the various formulations relating to transfer of learning are those of Gagné *et al.*[26] and Osgood.[27] These explanations, as well as others, tend to be somewhat more analytical than Thorndike's, for they are concerned in particular with the "degree" of similarity of the stimuli and the responses between the training situation and the actual real-life situation. Osgood has developed a "transfer surface" to characterize the relationships that he has postulated. This is shown in Figure 9.8. For any given combination of stimulus similarity (between the training and real situation) and of response similarity, the amount (and direction) of transfer is indicated by the vertical scale. Transfer would be greatest where the stimulus and

[24] Thorndike, E. L., & Woodworth, R. S. The influence of improvement in one mental function upon efficiency of other functions. *Psychological Review*, 1901, 8, 247–261, 384–385, 553–564.

[25] Thorndike, E. L. Mental discipline in high school studies. *Journal of Educational Psychology*, 1924, 15, 1–22, 83–98.

[26] Gagné, R. M., Baker, K. E., & Foster, H. *On the relationship between similarity and transfer of training in the learning of discriminative motor tasks*, United States Naval Special Devices Center, Technical Report SDC 316–1–5, 1949.

[27] Osgood, C. E. The similarity paradox in human learning: A resolution. *Psychological Review*, 1949, 56, 132–143.

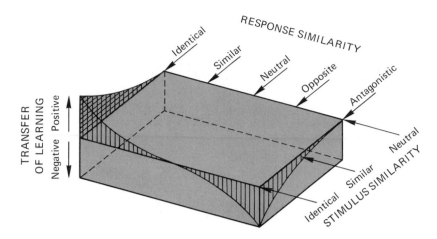

FIG. 9.8 The "transfer surface" suggested by Osgood, *op. cit.,* to demonstrate the relationship between degree of stimulus similarity, response similarity, and transfer of learning (amount and direction). (*Copyright 1949 by the American Psychological Association, and reproduced by permission.*)

the response during training are identical with those of the job. Where both are unrelated (neutral), no transfer would be expected. Where the stimulus is identical but the response is antagonistic, the transfer would be expected to be negative. This frame of reference, then, leads one to think not in terms of identical elements but rather in terms of degree of similarity. It also leads one to look at the training situation in terms of both the stimuli and the responses involved—and their degree of relationship with their counterparts in the job itself.

To be sure, questions have been raised regarding certain aspects of Osgood's formulation. For example, Gagné and Bolles[28] question the implied requirement of response similarity and express the opinion that response similarity is a factor concerning which we know very little. It should also be noted that Osgood's model is not quantitative in nature; how does one "measure" the degree of similarity, say, of stimuli? Thus Ellis,[29] for example, points out that the training surface model is not applicable to learning situations in which the tasks cannot be analyzed into distinct stimulus and response components; he adds the further comment that Osgood's formulation is not as much a theory of transfer as a set of empirical generalizations. Granting some of these constraints, however, the Osgood approach does seem to crystallize a frame of reference for considering transfer of learning in at least some contexts.

[28] Gagné & Bolles, *op. cit.*
[29] Ellis, H. *The transfer of learning.* New York: Macmillan, 1965.

Fidelity in Simulation

The persisting ambiguity about the factors associated with transfer of learning raises questions about the degree of fidelity of the "simulation" provided during training. Although this question applies to virtually every facet of training, it is particularly relevant to the development of various types of training devices, equipment, and other physical facilities used in some training programs. In this connection, one needs to distinguish between the degree of *physical* fidelity and that of *psychological* fidelity. Psychological fidelity refers to the degree of similarity of the human operations and activities involved. It is the psychological fidelity that is critical in the transfer-of-learning context. Although in most cases the psychological fidelity would be optimum when there is also a high degree of physical fidelity of the training situation, a high degree of physical fidelity is by no means a universal requirement for psychological fidelity. To cite a hypothetical (and somewhat obvious) example, if one were using a mock-up of the control room of a refinery as a training device, it probably would not matter a whit that the mock-up was of wood and the "real thing" of metal; but the operational aspects of the mock-up presumably should be comparable to those of a real control room.

chapter ten

Personnel Training

Having completed our overview of learning in Chapter 9, let us now shift to the consideration of personnel training. Training generally is intended to provide learning experiences that will help people to perform more effectively in their present or future jobs; education, in contrast, generally is directed toward broader objectives. Training programs in organizations take on many forms, but in broad terms they fall into the following classes:

> *Orientation training.* Typically used for orienting new employees to an organization by providing information about the organization, its history, products, policies, and so forth.
>
> *On-the-job training.* Used in helping personnel to learn new jobs; may be on an organized, systematic basis, or on a catch-as-catch-can basis.
>
> *Off-the-job training.* Covers a wide range of training activities given by an organization, such as vestibule training (training for specific jobs), supervisory and management training and development, some apprentice training, and job-improvement training. May be combined with on-the-job training, as in the case of apprentice training programs.

Outside training. Training that is arranged with outside organizations, such as universities or trade and professional associations.

TRAINING NEEDS

The training needs of people in organizations tend to fall into two groups which more or less blend into each other. In the first place, there is the need to provide specific job training, especially for new employees and sometimes for present employees who are deficient in job performance. In the second place, there is the need in most organizations to provide training of a personal development nature that will contribute to the longer-range effectiveness of the individuals in question.

Training Needs: Job Training

Where inexperienced personnel are to be trained for new jobs, the training "needs" are fairly obvious—namely, the need to help individuals acquire the knowledge, skills, and attitudes required in the performance of the jobs in question. Such training content, then, must be rooted in a detailed study of the job itself. Most typically, this involves some method of identifying the tasks to be performed in the job.

Task description. The description of a task involves a statement (or statements) of what Miller[1] refers to as the *requirements* of the task in question. In other words, the description usually describes the overt, observable activities involved in the task—the things a person "does." Where a task involves some fairly standard cycle of activities, Miller suggests that task activity statements specify the *indication* or *cue* which calls for a response, the *object* to be used (such as a control device that is to be activated), the *activation* or *manipulation* to be made, and the *indication of response adequacy* or feedback. Thus, such a task description would specify *when* the individual is to do something, *what* he is to do it with, what *action* he is to take, and what *feedback* will indicate that the action has been performed adequately. As a simple illustration let us take the task of opening an automatic door at a garage. An analysis of this task in the above terms might be something like the following:

> *Task:* opening automatic garage door
>   *Indication or cue (when):* sound of automobile horn
>   *Object (what):* push-button control
>   *Activation or manipulation (action):* press push-button
>   *Indication of response adequacy (feedback):* observe door raised to overhead
>   position and hear motor stop.

---

[1] Miller, R. B. Task description and analysis. In R. M. Gagné (Ed.), *Psychological principles in system development.* New York: Holt, Rinehart, & Winston, 1962.

Miller's approach to task description reminds us of our earlier discussion of stimulus, response, and feedback. But although this approach can comprehend most simple, structured tasks (such as opening the garage door), the process can break down if the activity is nonstructured and complex, as was pointed out by Cunningham and Duncan,[2] and Annett and Duncan.[3]

A somewhat different approach to the description of tasks for the purpose of specifying training course content was proposed by Rundquist.[4] His basic scheme is predicated on a logical analytical process of identifying tasks at different and descending levels of scope. This produces a pyramidal hierarchy of task components in which a major task is subdivided into more specific tasks down to as many as six or seven levels. In an analysis of the job of commanding officers of naval amphibious ships, Rundquist, West, and Zipse[5] have demonstrated that the technique lends itself to use with complex jobs as well as with structured jobs.

A task description of the job to be learned specifies what a person must learn to do; these specifications in turn are based on specifications of the skills and knowledge that the learner must acquire. In effect, this process is one of building a bridge between tasks and their skill and knowledge requirements in order to provide a basis for the development of training course content.[6] This is, in effect, the objective of the scheme proposed by Rundquist.[7]

Methods of determining job-related training needs. In the case of present employees whose job performance leaves something to be desired, it may be that some type of additional training can help to bring them up to par. Such training needs may be associated with individual employees (as in the case of a department store complaint clerk who always ruffles the feathers of the customers) or with *groups* of employees (as in the case of a pickle sorter who can't tell the difference between good pickles and bad pickles). In the case of an individual who needs additional training, it is necessary to determine what training he needs. This is what McGehee

---

[2] Cunningham, J. D., & Duncan, K. D. Describing non-repetitive tasks for training purposes. *Occupational Psychology,* 1967, **41,** 203–210.

[3] Annett, J., & Duncan, K. D. Task analysis and training design. *Occupational Psychology,* 1967, **41,** 211–221.

[4] Rundquist, E. A. *Job training course design and improvement.* (2nd ed.) San Diego: Naval Personnel and Training Research Laboratory, Research Report SRR 71–4, September 1970.

[5] Rundquist, E. A., West, C. M., & Zipse, R. L. *Development of a job task inventory for commanding officers of amphibious ships.* San Diego: Naval Personnel and Training Research Laboratory, Research Report SRR 72–2, August 1971.

[6] See Crawford, M. P. Concepts of training. In R. M. Gagné (Ed.), *Psychological principles in system development.* New York: Holt, Rinehart, & Winston, 1962; Miller, *op cit.;* and Altman, J. A. Methods for establishing training requirements. In United States Air Force, *Uses of task analysis in deriving training and training equipment requirements.* WADD Technical Report 60–593, December 1960.

[7] Rundquist, *op. cit.*

and Thayer[8] refer to as *man analysis*. Regular personnel appraisals may provide the basis for pinpointing the training needs of individuals. But when there are indications of training deficiencies with groups of employees, a general approach to the determination of their training needs may be in order, looking toward the development of a training program to improve their job performance.

There are many variants to the processes of determining such training needs. Johnson,[9] for example, describes thirty-four specific procedures. Aside from those which derive from job analysis, however, most are predicated on the judgments and observations of people—the incumbents themselves, supervisors, managers, personnel officers, and so forth. Although we are sometimes inclined to view human judgments and observations with a jaundiced eye (frequently with good cause), it should be kept in mind that sometimes the *method* of obtaining judgments or observations can have a beneficial effect on their validity. For example, there have been at least a few training circumstances in which some interesting techniques have developed for eliciting judgments and observations. Although we cannot elaborate here on methods of determining training needs, two or three examples will be given as illustrations.

One such method is the use of a checklist. An example of a checklist is given in Table 10.1. This particular example, presented by Fryer, Feinberg, and Zalkind,[10] employs training department officers to record "obser-

TABLE 10.1 SAMPLE CHECK LIST FOR SUPERVISORS

Items Recorded by Training Specialist	Checked for Adequate Performance		Possible Training Need
	YES	NO	
Keeps inventory of tools	x		
Prepares training outline for apprentices		x	x
Takes unsafe machinery out of service	x		
Checks all repairs	x		
Maintains "hours of work" record	x		
Inspects regularly for quality of product		x	x
Informs on elimination of waste		x	x
Plans workspace layout		x	x
Instructs on cost of materials		x	x
Explains company policy to workers		x	x

Source: Fryer, Feinberg, and Zalkind, *op. cit.*

[8] McGehee, W., Thayer, P. W. *Training in business and industry.* New York: John Wiley, 1961.

[9] Johnson, R. B. Determining training needs. In R. L. Craig and L. R. Bittel (Eds.), *Training and development handbook.* New York: McGraw-Hill, 1967.

[10] Fryer, D. H., Feinberg, M. R., & Zalkind, S. S. *Developing people in industry.* New York: Harper & Row, 1956.

vations" related to the behavior of supervisors. Those items that are checked "no" suggest possible training needs for the individual under observation.

Another procedure utilizes the critical incident technique. This method was used in a program reported by Folley[11] for determining the training needs of department store sales personnel. The "critical incidents" were actually based on reports by regular customers who volunteered to prepare statements about the sales personnel who had served them in three department stores in a large city. The written statements by customers were analyzed in order to identify the critical incidents which differentiated both very effective and very ineffective performance. The two thousand resulting incidents were then categorized by content analysis into twenty-five categories of effective behavior and eleven of ineffective. These were then grouped into seven and six broader categories respectively. Figure 10.1 shows the percentage of incidents in these categories. Although these percentages do not necessarily represent the relative importance of the categories, they do provide the trainer with some basis, during training, for ensuring that the sales personnel know the implications of these behaviors from the customers' point of view, and that they know how to avoid the undesirable behaviors.

Training Needs: Personal Development

Training for personal development is generally directed toward providing learning experiences that will be useful to people in enhancing their long-range effectiveness in their organizations, thus serving useful objectives both for themselves and for their organizations. Although personal development training programs generally have been limited to executives, the changing times are emphasizing the desirability of such training for other groups, in order to combat occupational obsolesence of professional and scientific personnel, to help disadvantaged groups adapt to the occupational world, and to help older people retain or enhance their capacities to function effectively in the labor market. For illustrative purposes we will touch briefly on the training needs of certain such groups.

Managerial and supervisory training. The training needs of managerial and supervisory personnel usually have been studied within the confines of individual organizations. Occasionally, however, general surveys across industries have been carried out. Dubin, Alderman, and Marlow,[12] for example, carried out a statewide survey of managerial and supervisory training needs in Pennsylvania. Perhaps it would be more appropriate to

11 Folley, J. D., Jr. Determining training needs of department store sales personnel. *Training and Development Journal,* July 1969, **23**(7), 24–26.

12 Dubin, S. S., Alderman, E., & Marlow, H. L. *Managerial and supervisory educational needs of business and industry in Pennsylvania.* University Park: The Pennsylvania State University, 1967.

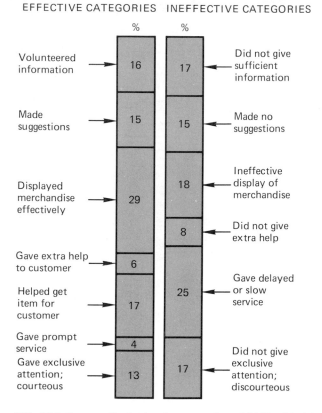

FIG. 10.1 Percent distribution by categories of 2000 critical incidents regarding sales personnel as reported by customers. The critical incidents were divided into those that represented effective performance, and ineffective performance. (*Adapted from Folley,* op. cit.)

describe this study in terms of educational needs for their intention was to adapt the "continuing education" program to the needs revealed by the study. We will illustrate the methodology and the results. Different questionnaires were sent to top management personnel, middle management, and first-line supervisors. For top and middle management personnel, the respondents were to report, for each of many topics, the following perceptions:

Your own training needs. Should have; could use; or don't really need.
Training needs of those you supervise. Should have.

The resulting tables and figures could fill the rest of this book, but we will confine ourselves to the example given in Figure 10.2.

Occupational obsolescence. One of the prices we pay for a fast-moving

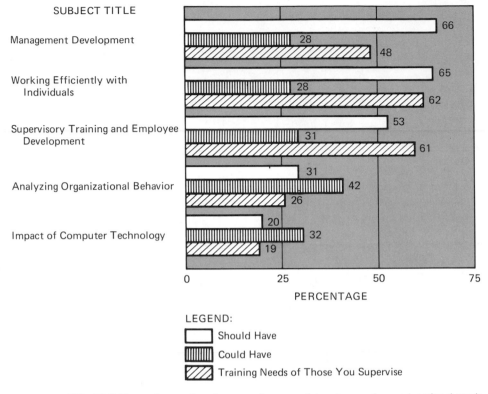

SUBJECT TITLE

Management Development

Working Efficiently with Individuals

Supervisory Training and Employee Development

Analyzing Organizational Behavior

Impact of Computer Technology

PERCENTAGE

LEGEND:
Should Have
Could Have
Training Needs of Those You Supervise

FIG. 10.2 Illustrative results of survey of managerial and supervisory educational needs resulting from survey by Pennsylvania State University. This particular figure shows those relating to "general management," as reported by 1093 top managers. (*From Dubin, Alderman, and Marlow, op. cit., Figure XI.*)

technology is an increase in obsolescence in certain occupations, especially those of a scientific and professional nature. There are different manifestations of this phenomenon. One such indication is reported by Zelikoff[13] on the basis of an examination of the content of engineering curricula in five engineering institutions for five engineering specializations. The curricula were examined for the changes in pedagogical material as reflected by course offerings dropped and added from 1935 to 1965. The results for civil engineering are shown in Figure 10.3. The figure shows the "erosion curves" for selected graduation classes and demonstrates rather dramatically the decline of courses dealing in "applied" knowledge from 1935 to 1965. The implications of these and other cues about the extent of occupational obsolescence drive home the point that, in certain occupations, training is a never-ending process during a career. The training

13 Zelikoff, S. B. On the obsolescence and retraining of engineering personnel. *Training and Development Journal*, May 1969, **23**(5), 3–14.

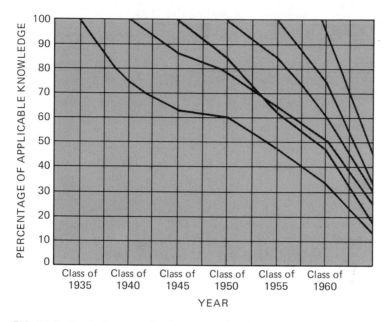

FIG. 10.3 "Erosion" curves showing occupational obsolescence in the field of chemical engineering as reflected by an analysis of curriculum content of five engineering universities for selected graduating classes since 1935. (*From Zelikoff,* op. cit.)

director is, of course, the person who needs to coordinate this ongoing process for personnel in his organization.

Disadvantaged persons. The problems associated with various disadvantaged groups (such as the hard-core unemployed, certain minorities, and the uneducated) have many dimensions—social, personal, economic and so forth. These problems have important implications for training, inasmuch as opportunities for gainful employment are predicated on the development of relevant job skills. Actual training is in part offered by various governmental agencies and school systems, and in part by employing organizations. In either case, the training of such groups usually needs to embrace a scope of content that heretofore generally has been outside the baliwick of typical training activities. Byars and Schwefel,[14] for example, refer to the need to teach such prospective employees to be reliable, neat, and punctual, and in some instances to provide basic education in reading, arithmetic, and sometimes in the moral obligations of citizenship. The actual training in these and other areas should be grounded in sound learning principles, as pointed out by Hallstein.[15] In particular

[14] Byars, L. L., & Schwefel, L. Training the hard-core unemployed. *Training and Development Journal,* July 1969, **23**(7), 48–51.

[15] Hallstein, R. W. We know where to start. *Training and Development Journal,* July 1969, **23**(7), 32–33.

he emphasizes the principles that learning must satisfy a need, should be active, should be arranged in a logical sequence, should be broken down into small steps, should provide repetition, and should provide feedback. But the special demands made on the application of these principles to the training of the disadvantaged may require, in turn, specially trained instructors, as pointed out by Byars and Schwefel.[16]

This road is not an easy one, as some organizations have found out. But there have been some encouraging successes, such as those of Lockheed, some of the automobile manufacturers, Southern Bell Telephone and Telegraph Company, and International Harvester (mentioned by Byars and Schwefel), and the program of the Humble Oil and Refining Company (reported by Mahoney[17]).

As an indication of the efforts being made by some organizations, Hansknecht[18] reports the results of a survey by the Detroit chapter of the American Society for Training and Development among seventy-nine Detroit firms regarding special training programs for hard-core unemployed and minority groups. Of these companies about two-thirds were already involved to some extent in recruiting and hiring such groups, and about half had some special training program for such groups, in particular for entry-level jobs. About 20 percent had programs for upgrading or preparing such personnel for technical, professional, or managerial positions.

Older workers. Another group that may have special training needs is that of older workers. This is not the place to elaborate on changes that occur through age and their implications for personnel selection and training, but we should at least draw attention to certain types of difficulties that some older people experience in learning new tricks. Belbin[19] points out that learning difficulties increase with age: (1) when tasks involve the need for memorizing; (2) when there is interference from other activities; (3) when there is need to "unlearn" something; (4) when there is need to translate information from one medium to another; (5) when tasks are paced; (6) as tasks become more complex; (7) when the trainee lacks confidence; and (8) when learning becomes mentally passive. To be sure, some people do experience such difficulties with increasing age. Belbin points out that special approaches to training can overcome some such difficulties and offers some specific suggestions for so doing. Further, he cites numerous encouraging instances in which the training of older workers has resulted in job performance levels that equal or approximate those of younger workers. Perhaps age forty is then not the beginning of the end!

[16] Byars & Schwefel, *op. cit.*

[17] Mahoney, F. X. New approaches for new employees. *Training and Development Journal,* January 1969, **23**(1), 22–28.

[18] Hansknecht, J. L., Jr. Hard core and minority group training activities surveyed in Detroit. *Training and Development Journal,* November 1969, **23**(11), 50–51.

[19] Belbin, R. M. *Training methods for older workers.* Paris: Organization for Economic Cooperation and Development, 1965.

TRAINING METHODS AND TECHNIQUES

A wide spectrum of training methods and techniques, each with its own unique uses and constraints, is available for the various types of training programs sponsored by training organizations. Some of these are: lecture; audio-visual aids; simulators and training aids; conference methods; human relations laboratory training; case method; role playing; management games; and programmed instruction (PI), and computer-assisted instruction (CAI).

It is not appropriate here to attempt an exhaustive analysis of the various methods and techniques and their relevant uses.[20] Instead, we will describe a few of them briefly and a few of them more extensively.

Lecture

The lecture has been severely criticized as a method of training, primarily on the grounds that it normally does not provide for active participation on the part of the trainees; this lack of participation, in turn, precludes any feedback to them. Although such criticisms argue against its indiscriminate use, there are various circumstances in which it is an appropriate method of training. It has been proposed for use, for example, under the following circumstances:[21] when presenting completely new material to a group; when working with a large group; when introducing another instruction method; when classroom time is limited; and when summarizing material developed by another instruction method. It also can be useful in reducing anxiety about upcoming training programs, job changes, and other changes.

Audio-Visual Aids

Technology has made possible the use in training of a variety of audio-visual aids such as motion pictures, slides, filmstrips, overhead and opaque projectors, and television.[22] The equipment that is available makes possible the presentation of a wide range of subject matter in audio and/or visual form. The basic question relating to the use of these techniques is that of their effectiveness in helping people to learn; Hollywood-type presentations may be very impressive but are not necessarily instructive. In this

[20] The interested reader is referred to such sources as: Craig, R. L., & Bittel, L. R. *Training and development handbook.* New York: McGraw-Hill, 1967.
[21] Proctor, J. H., & Thornton, W. M. *Training: A handbook for line managers.* New York: American Management Association, 1961.
[22] For an excellent discussion of the equipment available and the techniques involved in the use of audio-visual aids, the reader is referred to Otto, C. P., & Glaser, O. (Eds.). *The management of training.* Reading, Mass.: Addison-Wesley Publishing Company, 1970.

regard, three points will be made with respect to these techniques as they relate to the learning process.

In the first place, there are certain kinds of presentations that can be made more effectively by such methods than by any other. Cameras, for example, can sometimes be placed where a learner cannot be—as, for example, in demonstrating surgical techniques or certain mechanical operations. In addition, these techniques facilitate demonstrations (such as by animation) that otherwise might not be feasible. In the second place, there is no substantial evidence to suggest that such methods are *generally* more effective in presenting regular course material than other methods, but in some *individual* circumstances they have been found to be more effective. This was found to be the case, for example, in a study reported by Fryer[23] on three methods of training Air Force personnel in code learning. Four groups of men, equivalent in initial ability, were covered by the study. The training for the four groups was as follows: (1) lecture (oral instruction with slides); (2) manual (students read illustrated manual); (3) film (fifteen-minute animated film); and (4) no training. The content of the three training methods was the same. Immediately after training, and again after two months, an objective twenty-five-item test was given to the groups: the mean test scores are given below:

Method	Mean Test Scores Following Training	After Two Months
Film	17.9	16.3
Manual	15.4	13.0
Lecture	15.2	13.0
No training	5.4	7.0

In this particular instance the film was the most effective method.

In the third place, a possible disadvantage of these methods is the characteristic lack of opportunity for participation by the learners. Participation sometimes can be provided for afterward, however, in such ways as by having discussion groups.

Simulators and Training Aids

Simulators and training devices are used to provide trainees with physical equipment that resembles to some degree the equipment that is to be used on the job. Usually such devices are used when it is impractical for some reason (such as possible injury to the trainees or others), to use the actual equipment or when the cost of the actual equipment is excessive.

23 Fryer, D. H. Training with special reference to its evaluation. *Personnel Psychology*, 1951, **4**, 19–37.

Such devices range from simple mock-ups, models, and prototypes, to extremely complex simulators such as those used by the military services for training aircraft pilots.

As indicated earlier in the discussion of transfer of training, the potential utility of such devices depends more on the psychological fidelity than on the degree of physical fidelity. In terms of their utility in training, it is critical that they reproduce with reasonable accuracy the aspects of the real job that are central to the process of transfer of training. In other words, the various stimuli and responses, and the intervening mental operations and decisions that are involved in the training situation, should correspond reasonably well with those of the job itself.

It is generally accepted that training aids add to the effectiveness of training, and there is experimental evidence to lend support to this belief. There is, however, also a danger in the use of training aids, for the instructor may become "training-aid happy," relying on them to the detriment of the effectiveness of the training. In other words, they should be used judiciously, and, where used, they should be appropriate to the purpose.

Conference Methods

In the training context the conference method provides the opportunity for the participants to pool ideas, to discuss ideas and facts, to test assumptions, and to draw inferences and conclusions. This method, which is intended to improve job performance and personnel development, is most appropriate for such purposes as: (1) developing the problem-solving and decision-making faculties of personnel; (2) presenting new and sometimes complicated material; and (3) modifying attitudes.

The particular purpose of a conference will determine the manner in which it is carried out. If the purpose is that of developing the problem-solving and decision-making skills of the participants, the conference leader must adroitly facilitate the participation of the individuals, but at the same time prevent the conference from straying too far from the objective. When the conference is directed more toward modification of attitudes, its "direction" may be extremely limited.

Probably the most important psychological principle involved is the active participation of those taking part in the conference. In addition, however, the conference provides the opportunity for "reinforcement" of such participation by the trainer, as pointed out by McGehee and Thayer.[24] However, the reinforcement should be for the participation as such, and should not consist of verbal rewards or punishments for the *nature* of the

[24] McGehee & Thayer, *op. cit.*

participation; otherwise the conference leader loses his neutrality and is taking sides.

Human Relations Laboratory Training

In recent years there has been quite a flurry of interest in what is sometimes referred to as human relations laboratory training. Central to such training are the variations of techniques known by such names as *sensitivity training, T-group training* ("t" standing for "training"), and *laboratory training*. In their most common applications, these techniques are used as a form of supervisory and managerial development. Sessions typically are scheduled for a week or two or three in a residential facility away from the place of employment of the participants. In such a setting, a small group and a trainer interact in a very unstructured situation, in which, as Bradford and Mial[25] express it, normal "givens" (such as stated agenda, established membership and leadership roles, and norms) are absent, thus creating an environment in which anxieties and tensions almost inevitably arise. Within this ambiguous and tension-generating environment, the interaction among the participants is intended to bring about greater self-awareness by the sensitivity to and understanding of others, and thus to improve their facility in interpersonal relationships. As Lewin,[26] the ancestral progenitor of laboratory training, observed, the process of learning and changing can be characterized as an unfreezing-moving-refreezing cycle. In this cycle the first purpose of training is to help the trainee "unfreeze" his current behavior pattern, the second is to help him move to a more effective level of behavior, and third to "re-freeze" his behavior at that level in order to avoid regression.

The interchange among participants is intended to help the participant learn about himself, frequently a painful therapeutic process. Bradford and Mial[27] point out that the T-group and training laboratory are designed to facilitate such learning by providing the following conditions of learning: (1) exposure of one's own behavior to others; (2) feedback from others about one's own behavior; (3) a "supportive" climate or atmosphere (which reduces defensiveness); (4) knowledge as a "map" (to provide for growth and change); (5) experimentation and practice; (6) application (how to maintain changed behavior back on the job); and (7) learning how to learn.

It should be noted that the experience of undergoing T-group and

25 Bradford, L. P., & Mial, D. J. Human relations laboratory training. In Craig & Bittel, *op. cit.,* Chapter 13.

26 Lewin, K. Frontiers in group dynamics: Concept, method, and reality in social science; social equilibria and social change. *Human Relations,* 1947, 1(1), 5–41.

27 Bradford & Mial, *op. cit.*

laboratory training is indeed a traumatic one for some individuals. There have been instances of breakdowns following such training, for example. And in some instances the leaders or members have failed to protect some individuals from aggressive members of the group.

Evaluation of laboratory training. The problem of evaluating the effectiveness of laboratory training is, to use a British phrase, a sticky wicket. One can get testimonials from the participants as well as other measures linked directly to the content and processes of the training (such as measures of attitude change and performance in simulated problem-solving situations). These are what Campbell and Dunnette[28] refer to as internal criteria. But any such changes are not in themselves indicative of actual behavioral changes on the job. In one sense, the proof of the pudding should be in terms of changes in job behavior; such changes, which Campbell and Dunnette refer to as external criteria, can be reflected by ratings from superiors, subordinates, or peers, by changes in production or other aspects of job performance, by turnover, or by other indices.

One evaluation study in which an external criterion was used was based on an analysis of a laboratory training program carried out by a large petroleum refining company.[29] The participants were formed into groups of eight for a period of three days. At the beginning and end the participants completed a "perceptionnaire" in which they in effect rated themselves on each of several behavior areas, including the following:

Behavior Area	Mean Self-rating	
	Before	After
Problem solving	5.9	6.4
Problem diagnosis	5.7	6.2
Consideration	6.6	6.8

As an additional indication of their reactions, eighty-six of the participants were brought together six months later and were asked to give their opinions about their experiences in the training program. These were in the form of ratings of the impact of the training in terms of three questions; the results are given in Figure 10.4. The somewhat higher mean values for the first and second questions suggest that the participants felt that the training had helped *them* more than it had helped the *organization*. In both of these sets of data, the responses indicate somewhat favorable reactions to sensitivity training on the part of the participants. Although these opinions suggest benefits derived from the program, they need to be

---

[28] Campbell, J. P., & Dunnette, M. D. Effectiveness of T-group experiences in managerial training and development. *Psychological Bulletin,* 1968, **70**(2), 73–104.

[29] *An action research program for organization improvement.* Ann Arbor: The Foundation for Research on Human Behavior, 1960.

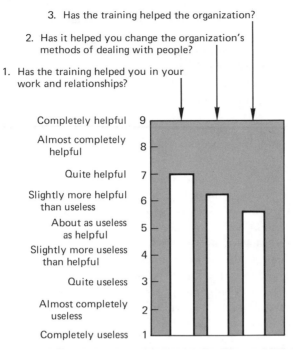

3. Has the training helped the organization?

2. Has it helped you change the organization's methods of dealing with people?

1. Has the training helped you in your work and relationships?

Completely helpful	9
Almost completely helpful	8
Quite helpful	7
Slightly more helpful than useless	6
About as useless as helpful	5
Slightly more useless than helpful	4
Quite useless	3
Almost completely useless	2
Completely useless	1

FIG. 10.4 Mean ratings of answers to three questions regarding the impact of sensitivity training. These ratings were obtained from 86 men who had been through such training six months before. (*From* An Action Research Program for Organization Improvement, op cit., *p. 31*.)

accepted with some reservations, for they may have been influenced in part by a tendency (perhaps entirely unintentional) to report what is "expected."

On the basis of a thoroughgoing review of thirty-seven studies that dealt in part with the evaluation of T-group training, Campbell and Dunnette[30] offer a couple of observations. With respect to internal criteria, they indicate that the results of available research are not conclusive—that it cannot be said with certainty whether T-groups lead to greater or lesser changes in self-perception than other types of group experiences, or even the simple passage of time. With respect to external criteria, they indicate that the evidence is reasonably convincing that such training does induce some form of behavioral changes "back home." However, these implications must be accepted with some serious qualifications; for example, there are indications that many of the "changes" are unique to the individual, and that the measures used to record "perceived change" usually have not related observed behavior changes to actual job effectiveness.

[30] Campbell & Dunnette, *op. cit.*

In adding up the black and red sides of the ledger regarding laboratory training, let us paraphrase the observations of Campbell and Dunnette: the assumption that such training has positive utility for organizations must necessarily rest on shaky ground, for it has been neither confirmed nor disconfirmed; on the other hand, it should be emphasized that utility for an organization is not necessarily the same as utility for the individual.

In connection with the individuals who have undergone such training, it is undoubtedly true that many people have gained useful personal insight and understanding about themselves as a result of such programs. But it should be added that such training programs have been criticized on the grounds that some participants may feel pressured into participating when in fact they would rather not, and on the grounds that their personal privacy may be invaded either during the training or in subsequent feedback that they may be asked to give. Further, the traumatic aftermath of such training in the case of some individuals must be considered as one of the liabilities of this method.

Case Method

The case method is one in which an actual or hypothetical problem is presented to a training group—usually consisting of supervisors or management personnel—for discussion and solution.[31] The cases typically involve some human relations problem, and may be presented in writing, "live" (with individuals playing different roles), on film, or by recordings. There are a number of variations in the techniques and procedures, but they typically have the same constituent elements, including a case report (in some form), a case discussion (of some sort), case analysis (systematic or otherwise), and the current situation (the interaction of the group members and course director in learning to work together).[32] The case method is intended to help the participants to analyze problems and to discover underlying principles. Because most of the cases do not have any "single" answers, as is the case with most problems in the real world, the method helps to bring out the fact that many problems have multiple causes and effects, thus aiding the participant to recognize that simple answers are few and far between.

It has been proposed[33] that the case study method is especially appropriate under the following circumstances: when employees need to be

[31] For further discussion of the case method the reader is referred to: Pigors, P. Case method. In Craig & Bittel, *op. cit.,* Chapter 10; and Pigors, P., & Pigors, F. *Case method in human relations: The incident process.* New York: McGraw-Hill, 1961. For a bibliography of cases the reader is referred to Lindfors, G. V. *Intercollegiate bibliography: Cases in business administration.* Boston: Intercollegiate Case Clearing House, April 1963.

[32] See Pigors, *op .cit.*

[33] Proctor & Thornton, *op. cit.,* p. 81.

trained to identify and analyze complex problems and to frame their own decisions; when employees need to be exposed to a variety of approaches, interpretations, and personalities (to be shown, in short, that there are very few pat answers to business problems); when the personnel are sufficiently sophisticated to draw principles from actual cases and to formulate solutions to problems themselves; and when a challenge is needed for overconfident individuals. On the other hand, the procedure should be avoided with "beginners" or persons who lack maturity, or when internal jealousies and tensions make people reluctant to air their opinions and ideas freely.

Role Playing

Role playing has been defined[34] as "a method of human interaction that involves realistic behavior in imaginary situations." In role playing, each participant plays the "part" (role) of someone in a simulated situation. As pointed out by Shaw,[35] there are many variations of role playing, but generally they are either preplanned or spontaneous. In the preplanned format the (hypothetical) situation is structured by setting forth the "facts" of the situation, such as the job situation in question, the events that led up to the "present" situation, and other relevant information. It is in these respects much like the case method. In role playing, however, individuals are designated to play the roles of the persons in the "case." The cases used can be built up around many different kinds of problems that can generate conflicting interests, such as unscheduled coffee breaks, work assignments, or vacation schedules. Once the case has been stated and the individuals assigned to their roles, they "play" those roles as though the situation were real. Thus, a supervisor might play the role of a subordinate, a salesman the role of a customer, and a nurse's aide the role of a hospital patient. Having to put one's self in someone else's place and play the part of that person generally increases one's empathy for the other person and one's understanding of his behavior.

In the spontaneous form of role playing, the participants play the roles of different individuals in the discussion of some problem without the backdrop of a prepared script.

Shaw[36] suggests that role playing can be used in any training situation involving interaction between two or more people, such as in counseling, interviewing, performance review, supervision, job instruction, or selling. In whatever context it is used, the intent of role playing is to teach

[34] Corsini, R., Shaw, M. E., & Blake, R. *Roleplaying in business and industry.* New York: The Free Press, 1961.
[35] Shaw, M. E. Role playing. In Craig & Bittel, *op. cit.,* Chapter 11.
[36] *Ibid.*

principles or skills or to provide a tool for changing attitudes and behavior in interpersonal relationships.

Management Games

A management game has been described[37] as a dynamic training exercise utilizing a model of a business situation. In these games, the trainees (who are often executives) make the same kinds of operating and policy decisions as are required in real life. Usually several participants comprise a "team," with various teams being placed in competition with each other. Typically each team represents a "company" and is presented with a statement of the problem about which the game revolves. Some typical problems, presented by Greene and Sisson,[38] are: materials inventory; personnel assignment; retailing operations; production scheduling; industrial sales; top management decisions; and market negotiation. Whatever the problem, the team is provided with appropriate information. Depending on the problem, this information can cover such factors as assets, inventories, labor costs, storage costs, demand curves (the demand for a product as it varies with price), and interest charges. The team then organizes itself (perhaps by selecting a president and other officials) and proceeds to make decisions about its policies and operations. The effects of these decisions typically can be computed in quantitative terms, such as profits; this may be done either by computers or by hand. At the end it is possible to determine which team "won." Whether the game takes hours, days, or even months, it actually represents a longer time span, for the theoretical total time is compressed into the time spent on the game itself. The game is then followed by a critique in which the actions of the teams are analyzed.

This method of training provides active participation in a somewhat lifelike situation, with the opportunity for feedback of the consequences of one's (actually the team's) decisions. It has been suggested that a player might benefit in some of the following ways from participation in such a game:[39] the player should learn which key factors to observe in the actual on-the-job situation; his attention is focused on established policies or strategies and on longer-range planning, rather than on "putting out fires"; he learns to make better use of decision-assisting tools such as financial statements and statistical inventory control; the game illustrates the value of analytic techniques such as the use of mathematical models to

[37] Kibbee, J. M., Craft, C. I., & Nanus, B. *Management games: A new technique for executive development.* New York: Reinhold Publishing Corp., 1961, p. 3.

[38] Greene, J. R., & Sisson, R. L. *Dynamic management decision games.* New York: John Wiley, 1959.

[39] Adapted from *ibid.*, pp. 3–4.

arrive at "optimum" solutions; and feedback allows for actions taken in one "period" to affect future conditions and results.

There is as yet little factual evidence of the long-range effects of management games as a training procedure. Subjective evaluations of participants and observers, however, generally are very favorable. Perhaps more significant, however, is the rational argument based on transfer-of-learning concepts. To the extent that the games do parallel the problems and situations of the real world, it would be expected that some of the "learning" would rub off on the participants and would therefore have a carryover effect to their jobs.

Programmed Instruction (PI)

In programmed instruction (frequently referred to as PI), the material to be learned is presented in a series of steps or units that generally progress from simple to complex. At each step the learner makes a response and receives feedback in some way so that he knows whether his response was correct or not. If the response was incorrect the trainee backs up and is guided in some way to learn the correct response (and why it is correct) so that he can proceed further in the program. The features of this method are rooted in certain psychological principles of learning, which Hawley[40] gives as follows:

Features: What the learner does	*Principles: The effect on the learner*
1. Works way through material by series of small steps.	1. Minimizes risk of error. Errors are believed to interfere with learning.
2. Active response by answering questions, solving problems, etc.	2. People learn best by doing.
3. Confirms correctness, or is provided with additional information to correct response.	3. Immediate reinforcement.
4. Proceeds at own pace.	4. Because of individual difference, people learn best at their own rate.

Of particular importance in programmed instruction is the principle of reinforcement.

Background. The forerunner of programmed instruction was a simple mechanical device developed by Pressey[41] in 1926 for use in testing stu-

---

[40] Hawley, W. E. Programmed instruction. In Craig and Bittel, *op. cit.,* Chapter 12.

[41] Pressey, S. L. A simple apparatus which tests and scores—and teaches. *School and Society,* March 20, 1926, **23**(586), 373–376.

dents. It contained a window through which a multiple-choice test item was presented, and a keyboard with four keys corresponding to the four possible responses. Only when the key of the correct answer was pressed did the next question appear. Thus, feedback was made available immediately.

Although Pressey laid the groundwork for programmed instruction, it was the later research of Skinner[42] relating to operant conditioning that probably sparked the recent flurry of interest in this technique.

Variations in programmed instruction methods. Most of the essential features of programmed instruction can be embodied in any of a number of different methods of presentation.[43] These include elaborate teaching machines (some of which are tied in with computers) that present material visually, on films, or on sound tapes; more simple machines (still involving electronic or mechanical features); simple devices that hold the paper on which the "program" is printed (some with a manual procedure for uncovering the "frames" successively); programmed books; and, at the simplest level, illustrations, diagrams, and other printed material.[44]

Whatever method of presentation is used—elaborate or simple as the case may be—it performs at least three functions: (1) it presents information and/or questions or problems to the learner; (2) it provides an opportunity for him to respond; and (3) it provides feedback as to whether the response is right or wrong.

The mechanics of performing these three functions are in one sense incidental; they are means to an end. The critical feature of programmed instruction is the programming itself. It should be noted, however, that computer-based instructional systems and certain other types of teaching machines make possible the programming of material that otherwise might not be possible.

Programming. The typical instructional program used in programmed instruction consists of a series of "frames" (also referred to as "images," "items," or "pages"). Each frame deals with a small segment of informa-

---

[42] Skinner, B. F. The science of learning and the art of teaching. *Harvard Educational Review*, 1954, **24**, 86–97.

[43] The reader interested in further material relating to programmed instruction is referred to such sources as: Hughes, J. L. *Programmed instruction for schools and industry.* Chicago: Science Research Associates, 1962; Lumsdaine, A. A., & Glaser, R. *Teaching machines and programmed learning: A source book.* Washington, D.C.: National Education Association of the United States, 1960; Margulies, S., & Eigen, L. D. (Eds.) *Applied programmed instruction.* New York: John Wiley, 1962; and Ofiesh, G. D. *Programmed instruction: A guide for management.* New York: American Management Association, 1965.

[44] Various types of devices are discussed or illustrated in the following: Margulies & Eigen, *op. cit.;* and Ross, W. L., Jr., *et al. Teaching machines: Industry survey and buyers guide.* New York: The Center for Programmed Instruction, Inc., 1962.

tion that is intended to provide for some sort of response on the part of the learner. The nature of the frames varies from one program to another; examples are given in Figure 10.5.[45] The frames are ordered in sequence, and typically one frame builds upon the preceding frame. As the learner progresses from frame to frame (receiving feedback in each case), he then builds up, bit by bit, the total subject matter of the program.

Certain variations in approaches to programming should be noted. In the first place, the responses can be "constructed" or "multiple-choice" in nature. A constructed response is one in which the learner actually writes in his response; it requires recall, or the formation of an answer based on what he has learned. A multiple-choice response is one in which the learner selects one of several possible responses; this requires recognition rather than recall. The evidence regarding the pros and cons of these two approaches generally has shown no systematic superiority of one over the other. Another distinction is that between "linear" and "branching" programs. With linear programs, each subject goes through all frames in sequence, and he must master each one in turn. This is the form proposed by Skinner.[46] A "branching" program is one that makes it more possible to adapt to the level of achievement of the learner. This is done by providing, at specific frames in the program, "branches" to be followed by those who have not adequately mastered the material to the point in question. This is the practice followed by Crowder.[47] The branching technique is used in various "scrambled texts," which are books that have been developed on

---

S. The + sign stands for addition; the ÷ sign stands for d _____ n.

R. division

S. A proper <u>noun</u> names a <u>particular</u> person, place or thing. John, Austria, Rochester, Genesee River are all proper nouns. New York is a _____ noun because it is the name of a _____ state.

R. proper
   particular

FIG. 10.5 Illustrative programmed instruction frames from various programs. Only one or two frames are shown from each program; thus, these examples do not illustrate the sequence of frames within a single program. The correct response (shown as R) is not in view of the respondent until he has entered his response. (*From Lysaught and Williams,* ibid.)

[45] Lysaught, J. P., & Williams, C. M. *A guide to programmed instruction.* New York: John Wiley, 1963.

[46] Skinner, B. F. Teaching machines. *Science,* 1958, **128**, 969–977.

[47] Crowder, N. A. Automatic tutoring by means of intrinsic programming. In Galanter, E. (ed.). *Automatic teaching: the state of the art.* New York: John Wiley, 1959.

programmed instruction principles. If, on the basis of a learner's response, he is to take one of the "branches" of the program, he will be instructed to refer to the appropriate page.

Programming is a time-consuming process, that requires well qualified individuals to carry it out. In developing an industrial program, for example, it was estimated that it took between thirty and sixty minutes to develop each frame.[48] When one considers that a program can take hundreds or thousands of frames, one can recognize that programs are not simply pulled out of a hat; they require time and effort.

Uses in industrial training. Although programmed instruction was initially used in education, it has been picked up by a number of industries as a method of training. In evaluating programmed instruction as used in industry, let us first summarize the experience of an insurance company as reported by Hedberg, Steffen, and Baxter.[49] Using this procedure with new life insurance agents in instruction in insurance knowledge, they were able to compare the effects of their program with those of a conven-

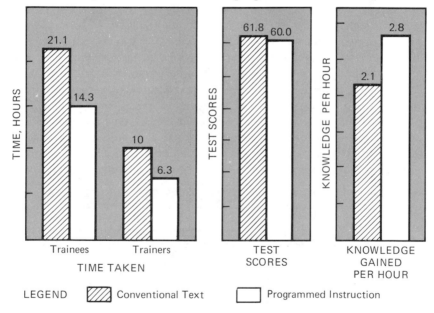

FIG. 10.6 Comparison of effects of conventional text and programmed instruction as used by new life insurance agents. Comparisons are in terms of time required (of both trainees and trainers), test scores (one month later), and "knowledge" gained (based on test scores) per hour of time. (*Adapted from Hedberg, Steffen, and Baxter,* op. cit.)

[48] Lysaught, J. P. Programmed learning and teaching machines in industrial training. In Margulies & Eigen, *op. cit.*

[49] Hedberg, R., Steffen, H., & Baxter, B. Insurance fundamentals—a programmed text versus a conventional text. *Personnel Psychology,* 1965, **18**(2), 165–171.

tional text in terms of time and amount learned (as measured by a test). Some of these comparisons are shown in Figure 10.6. There was no appreciable difference in the test scores of trainees a month later, but the programmed instruction procedures took less time and thus resulted in more "knowledge" (as measured by test scores) per unit of time.

The experiences of different companies using programmed instruction procedures and the evaluations of the effectiveness of programmed instruction by different people have been somewhat mixed. In an effort to provide the basis for some general evaluation of its practical effectiveness, Nash, Muczyk, & Vettori[50] analyzed the results of over a hundred empirical studies in which programmed instruction had been used either in academic or industrial circumstances. In about half of these, programmed instruction was reported to be of "practical effectiveness" (meaning that the differences in results between it and conventional instruction were statistically significant and exceeded 10 percent of the criterion values in question). However, the evidence indicates some interesting differences in terms of the kinds of criteria used, specifically training time, immediate learning, and retention over a period of time. Figure 10.7 shows a comparison among these in the case of several studies in industry. This comparison and other data show that the use of programmed instruction almost always reduces training time to a significant extent; the average saving in time is about one third. However, such a procedure usually does not improve training performance in terms of immediate learning or retention, for the studies show no significant difference in favor of either method. Thus, the primary advantage of programmed instruction seems to be in terms of training time. This suggests that economic considerations are important in considering programmed instruction, specifically a comparison between the

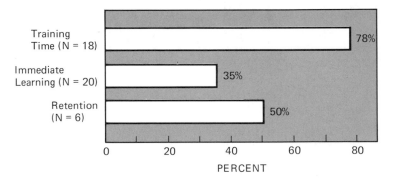

FIG. 10.7 Percent of settings in industry in which programmed instruction (PI) was "practically superior" to conventional training methods for three types of criteria. (*Adapted from Nash* et al., *1971,* op. cit., *Table 3.*)

[50] Nash, A. N., Muczyk, J. P., & Vettori, F. L. The relative practical effectiveness of programmed instruction. *Personnel Psychology,* 1971, **24**, 397–418.

savings in instruction costs and time of the trainees and the cost of developing programmed instruction materials (which can run into many thousands of dollars).

There are those who view programmed instruction as the wave of the future. These people tend to believe that it might become the dominant mode of instruction, virtually replacing other forms. In contrast, Pressey[51] takes a dim view of the "boom" trend in the use of teaching machines and programmed instruction generally; he argues for viewing such instruction as "adjunct autoinstruction" which can aid in the use, and increase the value, of other instructional methods and materials.

Although we acknowledge that the use of programmed instruction undoubtedly will increase, we are inclined toward Pressey's point of view and feel that it should be considered more of an adjunct to other methods than as a wholesale replacement of them. Its potential utility in given circumstances, it is reasonable to assume, will depend upon the training content in question. For example, it obviously is more suitable for transmitting factual material than for use in skill training.

Even when, because of their high cost, complete programs are not economically feasible, it is still possible on a limited basis to apply some of the principles of programmed instruction to those segments of training programs for which they seem especially appropriate, such as in the preparation of manuals and related materials.

The point we are leading up to is that its primary advantage seems more to be in terms of its *efficiency* in training. This is essentially a time advantage; in other words a theme that seems to pervade at least some of the studies is that people may take less time to learn a given amount than by some other methods.

Whatever learning advantage programmed instruction does offer (such as savings in time and in some instances perhaps increased learning or improved performance), however, needs to be weighed in relation to cost considerations, which can be fairly formidable. The cost of program development (which can run into thousands of dollars) plus any additional costs for the purchase of equipment may give programmed instruction an edge only if the costs can be spread over a substantial number of personnel. In this connection, some programs have been developed for industry-wide use, usually sponsored by trade associations.

But, while complete programs may not be economically feasible in specific situations, it is still possible on a limited basis to apply some of the principles of programmed instruction to those segments of training programs for which they seem especially appropriate, such as in the preparation of manuals and related materials.

---

[51] Pressey, S. L. Teaching machine (and learning theory) crisis. *Journal of Applied Psychology*, 1963, **47**, 1–6.

Computer Assisted Instruction (CAI)

Computer assisted instruction (CAI) is essentially a sophisticated descendent of programmed instruction. A major advantage of computers lies in their memory and storage capabilities which make possible various types of interaction with the learner that are not possible with programmed instruction procedures. These capabilities permit drill and practice, problem solving, simulation, and gaming forms of instruction, and certain very sophisticated forms of individualized tutorial instruction. To date computer assisted instruction procedures have been used primarily in educational institutions. Although it has substantial potential use in personnel training, its limited use for this purpose to date probably is in large part a function of costs. Although long-range future developments (especially in the form of reduced costs) may cause computer assisted instruction to blossom and bloom as a training procedure in industry, its use within the reasonably forseeable future would probably be limited to special circumstances in which computer facilities are available and in which costs can be spread over many trainees.

Discussion

The field of training is still rather boggy, lacking definitive guidelines. This is especially the case when it comes to the matter of translating learning theory into practical procedures. In this connection, Bass and Vaughan[52] have set forth their assessments of the use, by various methods of training, of at least a few "principles of learning," and also have indicated the typical uses of the various methods. These assessments and judgments are shown in part in Figure 10.8.

THE EVALUATION OF TRAINING

It is probable that most organizations assume that their training programs are achieving their intended objectives. Such faith, however, may sometimes be unwarranted. If an organization really wants to know whether its training program is accomplishing its purposes, it must go through a systematic evaluation process. There usually are few shortcuts in this. In general, such evaluation is directed toward determining how effective the training program is in helping *groups* of employees acquire the desired skills, knowledges, and attitudes. Although a trainer needs to be perceptive of the progress of individuals during training, the program as such should be evaluated in terms of the progress of the group generally.

Even though training usually is evaluated in terms of "training" versus

52 Bass, B. M. & Vaughan, J. A. *Training in industry: The management of learning.* Belmont, California: Wadsworth Publishing Company, 1966.

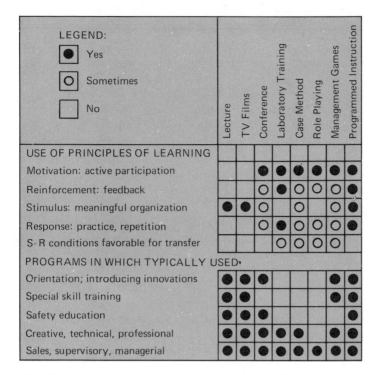

	Lecture	TV Films	Conference	Laboratory Training	Case Method	Role Playing	Management Games	Programmed Instruction
LEGEND: ● Yes ○ Sometimes ☐ No								
USE OF PRINCIPLES OF LEARNING								
Motivation: active participation			●	●	●	●	●	●
Reinforcement: feedback			○	●	○	○	○	●
Stimulus: meaningful organization	●	●	○		○		○	●
Response: practice, repetition			○	●	○	○	○	●
S-R conditions favorable for transfer				○	○	○	○	
PROGRAMS IN WHICH TYPICALLY USED								
Orientation; introducing innovations	●	●	●				●	●
Special skill training	●	●					●	●
Safety education	●	●	●					●
Creative, technical, professional	●	●	●	●	●		●	●
Sales, supervisory, managerial	●	●	●	●	●	●	●	●

FIG. 10.8 Extent to which selected training methods utilize certain principles of learning and indications of typical use of training methods. (*Adapted from Training in industry: The management of learning by Bernard M. Bass and James A. Vaughan, Tables 7-3 and 7-4. Copyright 1966 by Wadsworth Publishing Company, Inc. Adapted by permission of the publisher, Brooks/Cole Publishing Company, Monterey, Cal.*)

"not training," it is also appropriate to evaluate the relative effectiveness of different methods of training.

Basis of Evaluation of Training

The evaluation of training involves the use of an appropriate criterion. In the selection of the criterion, the same considerations should be used that are pertinent to the selection of criteria for other purposes. As discussed in Chapter 2, these considerations include *relevance, reliability,* and *freedom from contamination.* In their discussion of training evaluation, Catalanello and Kirkpatrick[53] refer to four steps involved in such evaluation:

1. *Reaction.* How well did the trainees like the program?
2. *Learning.* To what extent did the trainees learn the facts, principles, and approaches that were included in the training?

[53] Catalanello, R. E., & Kirkpatrick, D. L. Evaluating training programs—The state of the art. *Training and Development Journal,* May 1968, **22**(5), 2–9.

3. *Behavior.* To what extent did their job behavior change because of the program?

4. *Results.* What final results were achieved (reduction in cost, reduction in turnover, improvement in production, etc.)?

In a sense these items can be viewed as four different types of criteria, but with the distinct implication that "results" are clearly the most appropriate criterion in most circumstances. (In the case of jobs in which objective measures of results are available, the criteria might consist of measures of quantity, quality, time required to achieve some level of performance, and so forth.)

Basic Methods of Evaluation of Training

In discussing various approaches to the evaluation of training, Mac-Kinney[54] makes the point that the only procedure that provides a solid basis for evaluation is "controlled experimentation" in which two groups of subjects are used—a training group and a control group. Both "before" and "after" criteria should be obtained—in the case of the training group before and after training, and in the case of the control group before and after a corresponding work period. The evaluation would be inconclusive if a control group is lacking or if "before" criterion values are not obtained.

Although practical considerations sometimes make it difficult to pursue the controlled experimentation procedure, this procedure demonstrates the principle of applying scientific, experimental methods to the personnel problems of industrial organizations. One also can apply similarly rigorous methods to the comparison of the effectiveness of two or more methods of training.

A Survey of Evaluation Practices

Some reflection of the actual practices of companies in the evaluation of training programs comes from a survey by Catalanello and Kirkpatrick.[55] They queried 110 organizations that were known to be concerned with human relations training about their training evaluation practices. Of these, about 78 percent reported that they attempted to measure trainee *reactions,* and about half said they attempted evaluation in terms of *learning, behavior,* and/or *results.* More detailed questionnaires were sent subsequently to the "half" just referred to, with forty-seven companies re-

[54] MacKinney, A. C. Progressive levels in the evaluation of training programs. *Personnel,* November-December 1957, **34**(3), 72–78.

[55] Catalanello & Kirkpatrick, *op. cit.*

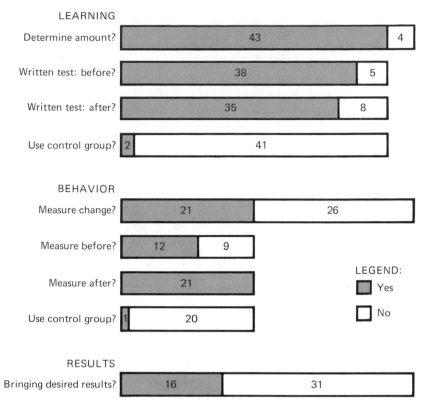

FIG. 10.9 Responses of 47 selected companies to questionnaire regarding their practices in measuring learning, behavior, and results in relation to human relations training programs. (*Adapted from Catalanello and Kirkpatrick,* op. cit.)

sponding. Replies to certain questions are summarized in Figure 10.9. We can see that a large portion did attempt to measure learning both before and after the training programs, but that less than half attempted to measure changes in behavior as such, and about a third attempted to measure results. Those that did measure results reported that they did so on the basis of observation, interviews, analysis of production reports, turnover figures, and other indices. It might be noted that the number using control groups was virtually negligible; collectively, then, the companies would not stack up very well on the basis of MacKinney's plea for "controlled experimentation!"

EXAMPLES OF TRAINING

The general benefits of training have been illustrated in some of the studies discussed above, but a few other examples will be cited here.

Skill Training

A comparison of the learning curves of employees in a cotton weaving mill is shown in Figure 10.10.[56] Both of these curves are expressed in terms of wages earned (which was directly related to productivity on the job), but one shows the average earnings during a period in which there was no organized training whereas the other shows earnings for those who went through a specialized training program. It can be observed that those who received the specialized training reached the "shed average" within about twenty-six weeks, as opposed to the previous full year required to reach par.

Anxiety-Reduction Training

A rather unusual approach to operator training was taken at Texas Instruments Incorporated, as reported by Gomersall and Myers.[57] On the

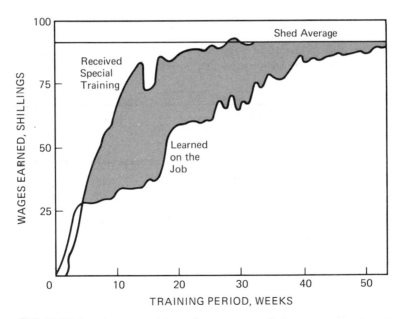

FIG. 10.10 Learning curves (shown in wages earned) for two groups of employees in a cotton weaving mill. One group simply learned "on the job" without any organized training effort; the other group went through a specialized training program. (*Originally published by Fielden House Productivity Centre Ltd., as presented by Singer and Ramsden, Fig. 3.2.*)

[56] This study carried out by Cotton Board Productivity Centre was reported by Singer, E. J., & Ramsden, J. in The practical approach to skills analysis. London: McGraw-Hill, 1969. (Published and distributed in the United States by Daniel Davey & Co., Inc., Hartford, Connecticut.)

[57] Gomersall, E. A., & Myers, M. S. Breakthrough in on-the-job training. *Harvard Business Review*, July-August 1966, 44(4), 62–72.

basis of interviews with over four hundred operators, it was suspected that a major impediment to learning during training arose from the anxieties of the trainees. So, in addition to the regular orientation training for the various groups of operators, a special one-day program was worked up specifically to help the trainees overcome the anxieties that were not sloughed off during the regular training. This orientation emphasized the following four points: (1) Your opportunity to succeed is very good; (2) Disregard "hall talk" (i.e., the hazing typically practiced by older employees on new employees by exaggerating allegations about work rules, work standards, discipline, and so forth); (3) Take the initiative in communication; and (4) Get to know your supervisor.

The "before" and "after" results of this training are shown in Figure 10.11 in the form of learning curves for one of the experimental groups and a control group. The improvement in performance, converted into dollars and cents, was almost 50 percent. For one hundred new hires in the department, the gain was equivalent to a first-year saving of at least $50,000; and additional savings in reduced turnover, absenteeism, and other factors would result in additional savings of $35,000.

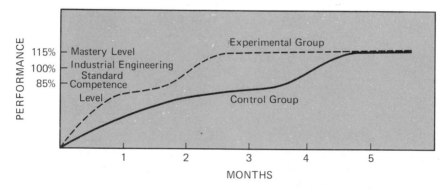

FIG. 10.11 Performance during training period of a control group of assemblers (who received conventional job training) and of an experimental group (who in addition received a day of "anxiety-reduction" training). The performance scale shows a "competence" level, the industrial engineering standard, and a "mastery" level. (*From Gomersall and Myers,* op. cit.)

chapter eleven

The Measurement
of Attitudes
and Opinions

As indicated earlier, one of the objectives of an organization is to create an environment in which the personnel are reasonably motivated to perform their job-related activities effectively, and in which they have a reasonable opportunity to fulfill some of their own objectives. This gets us into the realm of human motivation and the related reactions of people to their work situation, including their attitudes and their sense of job satisfaction. Employees bring with them to their jobs their own built-in sets of values and motivations, including desires for security, dignity, income, self-expression, achievement, social interchange, and many other factors. If the work situation fulfills the desires of employees, it is to be expected that the attitudes of the employees will tend to be favorable. In turn, frustration of such desires tends to produce unfavorable attitudes and possibly, by a sort of chain reaction, hostility, poor job performance, attendance problems, high labor turnover, and other undesirable side effects.

For this reason, management should keep its antennae tuned in to the prevailing feelings and attitudes of the employees, in order to be able to make policy decisions and to take actions that will help to create a working environment that will be conducive to effective job performance and to the reasonable fulfillment of the goals of the employees. Thus, the sensing of employee attitudes should be an ongoing, built-in facet of management, and in some circumstances efforts should be made to measure such reactions systematically. In this chapter we will be concerned primarily with the measurement of attitudes and related factors.

THE NATURE OF ATTITUDES AND RELATED VARIABLES

Part and parcel of human life consists of various types of subjective reactions toward, or about, the many aspects of our environment. Such reactions may be kept entirely within the individual, or they may be reflected in speech (either overtly or covertly) or in other forms of behavior.

The Meaning of Terms

There is a spate of confusion in the use of terms relating to the reactions of people, so let us first clarify a few of them.

Attitudes. Attitudes are described by Fishbein[1] as learned dispositions to respond to an object (or concept), or to a class of objects (or concepts), in a favorable or unfavorable way. An elaboration of the same theme has been set forth by Shaw and Wright,[2] who refer to an attitude as a relatively enduring system of affective, evaluative reactions based upon and reflecting the evaluative concepts or beliefs which have been learned about the characteristics of a "social object" or class of social objects, including of course the people with whom the individual is associated.

Various people, including Fishbein[3] and Shaw and Wright,[4] differentiate among three separate, albeit related components of "attitude": the affective (or evaluative) component; the cognitive (or conceptual) component; and the action (or conative) component. In their view, only the affective (evaluative) component should be labeled attitude, and we will consider attitudes in this light.

Job satisfaction. Job satisfaction (and its obverse, job dissatisfaction) has been characterized by Smith et al.[5] as the feeling or affective response

---

[1] Fishbein, M. (Ed.) *Readings in attitude theory and measurement.* New York: John Wiley, 1967, p. 257.

[2] Shaw, M. E., & Wright, J. M. *Scales for the measurement of attitudes.* New York: McGraw-Hill, 1967.

[3] Fishbein, *op. cit.,* p. 479.

[4] Shaw & Wright, *op. cit.,* p. 11.

[5] Smith, P. C., Kendall, L. M., & Hulin, C. L. *The measurement of satisfaction in work and retirement.* Chicago: Rand McNally, 1969.

of a worker about his job or facets thereof. In this sense, then, job satisfaction is an attitude, in particular an attitude toward one's job.

Opinions. Years ago Thurstone[6] defined opinions as expressions of attitudes. They are essentially what Fishbein[7] refers to as beliefs. He defines beliefs as hypotheses concerning the nature of objects or concepts, or, more particularly, concerning one's judgment of the *probability* regarding their nature. (In this sense a belief is the "cognitive" component mentioned above in our discussion of attitudes.) Although attitudes tend to be generalized predispositions to react in some way toward objects or concepts, opinions tend to be focused on more specific aspects of the object or concept. Thus, if a foreman calls the attention of his work group to the fact that some of the safety rules have been violated, one person (who has an "unfavorable" attitude toward the foreman) might later express the opinion to one of his buddies that the foreman is "just picking on us"; another person (who has a "favorable" attitude toward the foreman) might later express the opinion that the foreman is simply "trying to keep us from getting our fingers cut off."

Actually, the measurement of attitudes generally is based on the expressions of opinions (what Fishbein refers to as beliefs). But, as we shall see shortly, we should distinguish between *attitude scales,* which like a thermometer or barometer, reflect the generalized "level" of individuals' attitudes toward some object or concept, and *opinion surveys,* which typically are used to elicit the "opinions" of people toward specific aspects of, for example, their work situation.

Morale. The term morale has the Alice-in-Wonderland quality of meaning what the user of the term wants it to mean. Guion,[8] after considering several definitions, defines morale as *"the extent to which an individual's needs are satisfied and the extent to which the individual perceives that satisfaction as stemming from his total job situation."* For some people, however, the term refers more to the interacting reaction of a group of people, such as the *esprit de corps* or team spirit of a football team, military unit, or work group. Although we are inclined to use it in the group sense, it is fairly common practice to use it in the individual sense expressed by Guion. In any event, anyone using the term should make its intended meaning clear.

The Formation of Attitudes and Related Variables

Peoples' basic attitudes toward objects and concepts are formed through experience, which means that they are learned. Once a person has developed

---

[6] Thurstone, L. L. Attitudes can be measured. *American Journal of Sociology,* 1928, **33,** 529–554.

[7] Fishbein, *op. cit.,* pp. 257–260.

[8] Guion, R. M. Some definitions of morale. *Personnel Psychology,* 1958, **11,** 59–61.

a particular attitude, it may be difficult for him to determine how he acquired it. In fact, an individual may not be consciously aware of his own fundamental attitudes. Whether a person's attitudes are based on rational considerations and factual information, or whether they have a strong emotional bias, has little bearing on the *effect* of the attitudes on the person's thinking or behavior. In either case, the factor that affects behavior is the *attitude, not* the consideration of whether it is or is not a rational attitude. In turn, an individual's "learned" attitudes tend to color his reactions to many specific aspects of his environment.

Although the attitudes of people tend to be relatively stable, they can be modified, at least to some degree. Such modification, of course, is essentially a relearning process; as such, it must be based on experiences that both dislodge existing attitudes and provide for the formation of modified attitudes.

ATTITUDE MEASUREMENT

Attitudes, of course, are subjective attributes of people. They can be regarded as "constructs" in the sense that they are "conceptualizations" of human qualities that are formed on the basis of either rational considerations or statistical evidence. Thus, we might conceive of people varying along each of a number of attitudinal dimensions, such as attitudes toward religion, political systems, women drivers, or people who let their dogs run loose.

Attitude measurement, which was developed largely by social psychologists and has been carried over into the field of industrial psychology, is concerned with efforts to tap these attitudes as they are characteristic of individuals. In measuring attitudes one hopes to be able to assign numbers to the measurements in such a way that the numbers (really scores) are reasonably approximate indices of the prevailing attitudes of the different individuals toward whatever the attitude object may be. Of course, the attitudes of people are not directly observable. Thus their "measurement" needs to be based on inferences from more overt manifestations. In pulling together numerous studies dealing with attitude measurement, Summers[9] uses the following organization which, in effect, is a classification of methods of attitude measurement: (1) self-reports (usually elicited with questionnaires dealing with beliefs, feelings, and behaviors); (2) indirect tests and objective tests (such as projective techniques and "disguised" approaches); (3) direct observation techniques; and (4) physiological reaction techniques. Attitude measurement of employees in organizations is most commonly carried out with self-report questionnaires.

[9] Summers, G. F. *Attitude measurement.* Chicago: Rand McNally, 1970, pp. 4–11.

The attitude questionnaires with which we shall be concerned in this context typically provide for deriving an index of each respondent's attitudes toward the organization or some facet thereof. Typically, an "attitude score" for any given individual is based on the summation of responses to individual questionnaire items. In turn, it is common practice to average all the individual attitude scores of the members of a group, such as a job group, department, or company. Various types of scales are used for this purpose; a few of these will be discussed below.

Thurstone Type of Scale

The Thurstone type of attitude scale goes back to the early work of Thurstone and Chave.[10] An example of such a scale, developed by Uhrbrock,[11] is given in Table 11.1. This particular scale is intended to measure the attitudes of employees toward the companies in which they worked. Table 11.1 gives the scale values of the items, but these are not shown on the questionnaires that are filled out by the employees.

Development of Thurstone scale. The development of the Thurstone type of scale is essentially the same as the development of the weighted check test type of performance appraisal system illustrated in Chapter 8. In this process the first step is to write out a large number of statements, perhaps a hundred or more, each of which, if endorsed by a respondent as reflecting his attitude, would imply a viewpoint—favorable or unfavorable —toward the attitude "object" (e.g., the organization or some aspect of it). An effort should be made to have these statements express all possible viewpoints from extremely favorable to extremely unfavorable. Each of these statements is typed on a separate slip of paper and a judge is asked to place each statement in one of several piles (usually seven, nine, or eleven), ranging from statements judged to express the *least* favorable viewpoints (placed in pile 1), to statements judged to express the *most* favorable viewpoints (placed in the top pile, 7, 9, or 11). Statements judged to express varying degrees of favorableness between these extremes are placed in the piles that characterize their judged degrees of relative favorableness. Usually many judges are used in this process.

The objective here is to identify a limited number of statements to use in a final scale. This selection is made on the basis of two primary considerations. The first is the consistency of the judgments about each statement; those statements that tend to be concentrated by the judges in one or a limited number of categories reflect greater agreement than those that are

[10] Thurstone, L. L., & Chave, E. J. *The measurement of attitude.* Chicago: University of Chicago Press, 1929.
[11] Uhrbrock, R. S. Attitudes of 4,430 employees. *Journal of Social Psychology,* 1934, 5, 365–377.

TABLE 11.1 STATEMENTS USED IN UHRBROCK'S SCALE FOR MEASURING ATTITUDE OF EMPLOYEES TOWARD THEIR COMPANY

Statement	Scale Value
I think this company treats its employees better than any other company does	10.4
If I had to do it over again I'd still work for this company	9.5
They don't play favorites in this company	9.3
A man can get ahead in this company if he tries	8.9
The company is sincere in wanting to know what its employees think about it	8.5
On the whole the company treats us about as well as we deserve	7.4
The workers put as much over on the company as the company puts over on them	5.1
The company does too much welfare work	4.4
I do not think applicants for employment are treated courteously	3.6
I believe many good suggestions are killed by the bosses	3.2
My boss gives all the breaks to his lodge and church friends	2.9
You've got to have "pull" with certain people around here to get ahead	2.1
In the long run this company will "put it over" on you	1.5
An honest man fails in this company	0.8

Source: Uhrbrock, *op. cit.* Copyright 1934 by the American Psychological Association, and reproduced by permission.

spread across several categories. From those that have been judged with reasonable agreement, several statements are then selected to represent varying positions along the scale. For each statement that is kept for the final scale, a scale value is computed; usually this is the mean or median of the numerical identifications of the categories in which the statement was placed by several judges. An example of such a scale is shown in Table 11.1, along with the scale values of the statements that represent various positions along the scale.

The question has been raised as to whether, in the judging of the scale items, the attitudes of the judges toward the stimulus object or concept bias the scale values assigned to the items. After examining the pieces of evidence about this, Shaw and Wright[12] conclude that this is not the case, although there are still some dangling questions in this area.

Scoring of Thurstone scale. As indicated above, the scale, as it is presented to respondents, does not include the scale values. Further, the items are presented in jumbled order. Each respondent checks those statements with which he agrees. His "attitude score" is then based either on the average or the median scale value of the statements that he checked. Mention was made in Chapter 9 of a possible fallacy in the use of the median value as related to the use of the Thurstone type of scale in a weighted checklist appraisal system. The same fallacy also can occur in attitude measurement. The solution to this problem was discussed in Chapter 8.

[12] Shaw & Wright, *op. cit.,* p. 561.

Likert Type of Attitude Scale

Soon after Thurstone brought out his scale, Likert[13] experimented with certain other varieties of attitude scales and ended up proposing the use of a scale that is illustrated below:

My supervisor is consistently fair in dealing with his subordinates.

> 5 Strongly agree
> 4 Agree
> 3 Undecided (neither agree nor disagree)
> 2 Disagree
> 1 Strongly disagree

The numbers (which may or may not be included in the questionnaire) are the numerical values used in scoring. An individual's score is derived by a simple addition of the numerical values of the responses he selects for the several items.

Comparison of Likert and Thurstone Scales

There has been a bit of controversy over the relative virtues of the Likert and Thurstone scales. In this regard, Seiler and Hough,[14] in recapping several studies, refer specifically to Likert's hypothesis that the Likert scale was (1) equally or more reliable than the Thurstone, (2) faster, and (3) equally or more valid. They state that two of these issues seem to have been resolved. In the first place, comparisons of the reliability coefficients, which usually are derived by the alternate forms or split-halves methods, tend to give Likert the edge; of several such coefficients—for various scales dealing with different attitude objects—the median coefficients for the Likert scales was around .90 and for the Thurstone scales in the lower .80s. And in the second place, in terms of time required, it appears that a Likert scale of twenty to twenty-five items is usually enough to produce a reliability coefficient of .90 or more, whereas it would take a scale consisting of about fifty items in a Thurstone scale (and presumably proportionately more time) to achieve comparable reliability. The third issue, relating to relative validity, still remains something of an open question.

It should be noted in passing that the Likert type of scale has what is

13 Likert, R. A technique for the measurement of attitudes. *Archives of Psychology,* 1932, No. 140.

14 Seiler, L. H., & Hough, R. L. Empirical comparisons of the Thurstone and Likert techniques. In G. F. Summers (Ed.), *Attitude measurement.* Chicago: Rand McNally, 1970, Chapter 8.

sometimes considered an advantage over the Thurstone scale in that it does not require the use of any unfavorable statements about the attitude object (e.g., the company). There is sometimes a reluctance on the part of sponsors of attitude surveys to include overtly unfavorable statements in questionnaires. Although the statements in the Likert type of scale are expressed in positive terms, it is of course possible to express unfavorable attitudes by "disagreeing" with the statements.

The Semantic Differential

The semantic differential is an attitude scaling technique that lends itself to various applications; it was developed by Osgood, Suci, and Tannenbaum.[15] For any given purpose it consists of several or many pairs of opposite adjectives or phrases, with scale values in between. The following examples are items that might be used in a scale for eliciting attitudes toward management:

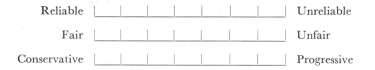

In using this scale, the respondent marks the position along each scale that reflects his attitude toward the attitude object or concept. Scale values (often ranging from 1 to 7) are associated with the different responses and individual's attitude score usually is the sum of these.

Other Attitude Scales

There are a few other attitude scaling techniques that have not found their way into very common usage in business and industrial organizations. Some of these are discussed or illustrated by Shaw and Wright[16] and by Summers.[17] These include the Guttman (or Cornell) technique,[18] the error-choice method developed by Hammond,[19] and the sentence completion technique.

[15] Osgood, C. E., Suci, G. J., & Tannenbaum, P. H. *The measurement of meaning.* Champaign: The University of Illinois Press, 1957.
    [16] Shaw & Wright, *op. cit.*
    [17] Summers, *op. cit.*
    [18] Guttman, L. The Cornell technique for scale and intensity analysis. *Educational and Psychological Measurement,* 1947, **7**, 247–280.
    [19] Hammond, K. R. Measuring attitudes by error-choice: An indirect method. *Journal of Abnormal and Social Psychology,* 1948, **43**, 34–48.

MEASUREMENT OF JOB SATISFACTION

Attitudes toward one's job (i.e., job satisfaction or dissatisfaction) represent a special facet of attitudes that has been worked over rather thoroughly. Various forms of attitude scales have been used in this regard. A couple of examples will be illustrated.

Job Description Index (JDI)

One such scale is the Job Description Index (JDI),[20] developed by Smith and some of her associates over the years and reported by Smith et al.[21] In earlier versions of the scale, individuals were asked to describe the job they would most like to have (their "best" job) and the one they would least like to have (their "worst" job). Responses thus elicited were used in an item analysis in order to identify those items which tended to be most discriminating; such items were then included in the final scale. In its final form the scale provides for measurement of attitudes in five areas: work; supervision; pay; promotions; and coworkers. The scale consists of a series of adjectives or statements for each of these categories, and the individual is asked to mark each one as yes (Y), no (N), or cannot decide (?) as it relates to his job. A few examples are given below:

Work
_____Fascinating
_____Routine
_____Frustrating

Supervision
_____Hard to please
_____Praises good work
_____Stubborn

Pay
_____Adequate for normal expenses
_____Less than I deserve

Promotions
_____Promotion on ability
_____Dead-end job

Co-workers
_____Stimulating
_____Talk too much

Although the scale actually provides for "describing" one's job, the "description" implies the individual's evaluation of it. Scores based on this scale have been found to be related to other measures of job satisfaction.

The reliability of the JDI, derived by correlating scores of random split-halves of the items for eighty men, ranged from .80 to .88 for the five separate scales.[22] And the intercorrelations of the five scales for a sample

[20] The Job Description Index is copyrighted (1962) by Dr. Patricia C. Smith, Bowling Green State University. Inquiries about it should be addressed to her at Bowling Green State University, Bowling Green, Ohio 43403.
[21] Smith et al., op. cit.
[22] Ibid., p. 74.

of 980 men ranged from .28 to .42. These intercorrelations reflect only moderate relationships, thus implying that the five scales are tapping somewhat separate facets of job satisfaction.

"Faces" Job Satisfaction Scale

A rather unique scheme for obtaining measures of job satisfaction was developed by Kunin.[23] This consists of a series of drawings of people's faces with varying expressions, including variations in the curvature of the mouth ranging from a broad smile to a deep frown, as illustrated in Figure 11.1. The respondent simply marks that face which best expresses how he feels about his "job in general."

Put a check under the face that expresses how you feel about your job in general, including the work, the pay, the supervision, the opportunities for promotion and the people you work with.

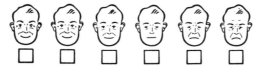

FIG. 11.1 Illustration of the "Faces" scale for measuring job satisfaction. (*From Kunin* op. cit.)

OPINION SURVEYS

Attitude scales such as those mentioned above typically are used to derive an attitude index for each individual (usually anonymously), which in turn can be averaged for individuals within a unit, department, or organization. In contrast, opinion surveys typically provide for eliciting opinions about specific matters such as working conditions, fringe benefits, and communications. An example of part of such a questionnaire is shown in Figure 11.2. The usual practice in opinion questionnaires is to obtain a single response to each item or question which will indicate the degree of satisfaction with, or an opinion about, some specific aspect of the total work situation.

COMBINATION QUESTIONNAIRES

Aside from the types of questionnaires mentioned above for measuring attitudes, job satisfaction, opinions, and so forth, there are also certain

[23] Kunin, T. The construction of a new type of attitude measure. *Personnel Psychology,* 1955, **8**, 65–78.

EMPLOYEE SURVEY QUESTIONNAIRE

4. Do you feel you would rather be doing some other type of work? Yes ☐   No ☐
   If yes, have you discussed it with the Personnel Office? Yes ☐   No ☐
6. Does your foreman "know his stuff"? Yes ☐   No ☐
7. Does your foreman play favorites? Yes ☐   No ☐
9. Does your foreman keep his promises? Yes ☐   No ☐
22. Do you feel that you are receiving considerate treatment here? Yes ☐   No ☐
   If not, why? _____

---

23. Do you feel top management is interested in the employees? Yes ☐   No ☐
26. Are you interested in Company athletic activities? Yes ☐   No ☐
28. Do you feel you have a good future with this Company? Yes ☐   No ☐
32. Are you getting the kind of information about the Company that you want? Yes ☐   No ☐
33. What do you think of working conditions here as compared with other plants?
   Above average ☐   Average ☐   Below average ☐
34. How do you think your average weekly earnings (gross earnings before deductions) compare with that paid in other companies for the same type of work?
   Better here ☐   About the same ☐   Lower here ☐

FIG. 11.2 Selected items from a questionnaire used in an employee survey conducted by the Victor Adding Machine Co. (*Courtesy Victor Adding Machine Co., Chicago, Ill.*)

other varieties of questionnaires that can serve these and related purposes, including some that might be called combination questionnaires—that is, questionnaires that tap a couple of different facets.

Rating of Job Satisfaction and Importance

One such variant is reported by Youngberg, Hedburg, and Baxter.[24] In their job satisfaction questionnaire they provided for the employees (life insurance agents) to respond to items dealing with each of various "aspects" of their jobs, such as benefit plans and quality of supervision. For each such aspect, however, the agent was asked to give two responses, as follows:

24 Youngberg, C. F. X., Hedburg, R., & Baxter, B. Management action recommendations based on one versus two dimensions of a job satisfaction questionnaire. *Personnel Psychology*, 1962, **15**, 145–150.

Satisfaction	Importance
_____Satisfied	_____Great importance
_____Neutral	_____Some importance
_____Dissatisfied	_____Little importance

Two scoring schemes were used, one based only on the "satisfaction" responses and the other also taking into account the "importance" of the various aspects. Although the correlation between these two sets of scores was .71, there were some rather noticeable differences in the "problem areas" identified by the two methods. Of the top six problem areas identified, only one was common to both methods, a fact which emphasizes the point that the "importance" to employees of various aspects of their jobs might well be taken into account in such surveys.

Modified Attitude Questionnaire

As another variation of attitude measurement scales, Rosen and Rosen[25] propose a questionnaire in which the respondent gives three responses to essentially the same "topic"; these responses deal with *standards, perceptions,* and *evaluations*. An example of each taken from a questionnaire relating to attitudes toward the union's role in various union activities, is given below:

Standard (what should be done):
a. In collective bargaining the union *ought* to emphasize wage increases.
   ____always____usually____sometimes____seldom____never
Perception (what was seen as being done):
b. In collective bargaining the union *actually does* emphasize wage increases.
   ____never____seldom____sometimes____usually____always____don't know
Evaluation (the feeling about what was seen as being done):
c. I *approve* of the emphasis the union puts on wage increases in collective bargaining.
   ____strongly agree____agree____undecided____disagree____strongly disagree

Rosen and Rosen present some fairly persuasive evidence to indicate that the responses to these different ways of posing questions can be rather different. Over a range of twenty-eight questions, for example, the responses of members of one union were noticeably more positive to the "standards" question (a) than to the "evaluation" question (c). In correlating the mean responses to the twenty-eight questions, they found that "evaluation" questions had a correlation of .13 with "standards" questions and a correlation of .78 with "perceptions" questions. Although the correlation of evaluations

[25] Rosen, R. A. H., & Rosen, H. A suggested modification in job satisfaction surveys. *Personnel Psychology,* 1955, **8**, 303–314.

with perceptions was reasonably high, the two sets of questions cannot be viewed as interchangeable. Rather, in interpreting the results the investigators point out that satisfaction with union activities tended to result when their desires were perceived as being fulfilled, and dissatisfaction tended to occur when their desires were perceived as not being fulfilled.

In addition, Rosen and Rosen make the point that the particular frame of reference in responding to attitude survey questions affects the responses to the questions. For this reason it is sometimes useful to elicit different responses in order to provide further insight into the attitudes of the subjects.

Opinion and Attitude Questionnaire

As still another example of a combination questionnaire, Misa[26] developed what is basically an opinion survey questionnaire for which frequencies of responses of the employees were tabulated in the manner illustrated below (for two of the nineteen questions):

How do you feel toward your immediate supervisor?

Friendly	82% checked this response
No feeling	13% ″ ″ ″
Unfriendly	3% ″ ″ ″
Don't know	1% ″ ″ ″
Left blank	1% left this question blank

Considering the difference between your job and hourly paid jobs in the plant, do you feel that your take-home pay is:

About right	12% checked this response
Too low	74% ″ ″ ″
Can't compare	8% ″ ″ ″
Don't know	5% ″ ″ ″
Left blank	1% left this question blank

In addition to this conventional presentation of opinion survey results, a further analysis was made of the data. In particular, for each question a "high morale" response was identified. (In the above examples the first response was the "high morale" response.) In turn, the average number of "high morale" responses given by each employee was used as an attitude index for each employee; this was done separately for the questions within each of three blocks–attitude toward supervisor, the company, and income. And as still another variation, provision was made for write-in comments generally relating to things the employees did not like or that were sources of dissatisfaction. Some examples of the 220 unfavorable write-in comments provided by employees in one department are given below:

[26] Misa, K. F. Relationship between three blocks of attitude questions. Unpublished M.S. Thesis, Purdue University, 1963.

Steady work but no advances.
Lack of coordination in the organization.
Some supervisors do not really know the people under them.
I see little opportunity for advancement in my department.
Our supervisor doesn't care about anything.

The number of such comments was tallied for each person. Thus, for each person there was an attitude index for each of the three blocks of questions plus the number of write-ins. These were then averaged for each of fifteen departments, and then these mean scores were correlated by rank-order correlation. The results are shown below:

	Company Block	Income Block	Written Comments
Supervisor block	.69	.62	.71
Company block		.71	.80
Income block			.75

It can be seen that the number of write-in comments was a reasonably good index of the attitude indexes for the three blocks of items for the various departments. Although the correlations among the three blocks are fairly substantial (.69, .62, and .71), the employees presumably were making some discriminations among them in their responses, which suggests that these are three somewhat different dimensions of attitudes

As an example of the further analysis of the write-in comments, the comments were classified by a content analysis process (to be discussed later) into a number of different categories. The frequencies of mention

TABLE 11.2 SUMMARY OF TOPICS MENTIONED UNFAVORABLY TEN OR MORE TIMES IN OPINION SURVEY

	No. of Mentions
Cafeteria food poor and/or expensive	46
Merit increases too slow or inconsistent	13
Hourly wages out of line with salaries	85
Too much hiring from outside	25
Work space crowded, noisy, hot, etc.	15
Poor cooperation between departments or divisions	13
Classification should be reviewed	22
Poor communication of policy and plans	72
Organization of department poor	36
Supervision poor	61
Coffee break needed	11
Better equipment needed	12
Sick leave and vacation should be cumulative	13
Foremen should have more authority	10
Management should take a firmer stand with union	10

of some of these categories are given in Table 11.2. This tally can provide some cues about actual or developing sore spots in the organization.

CONTENT ANALYSIS

Content analysis is a technique for the systematic determination of the content of written material. In its simple form it can consist of the rather straightforward classification into certain categories of write-in comments entered on various types of questionnaires or of written statements made in other sources. In its more elaborate forms it can consist of the intensive analysis of documents relating to international relations, as illustrated by North et al.[27]

Most of the applications of content analysis in the field of industrial psychology probably have consisted of the classification of the content of statements made by employees (as in questionnaires) that reflect their attitudes and opinions about some features of their work-related situation. In this process the following steps typically are carried out:

1. A review of a sample of statements or comments in order to identify the "content" that is covered; a tentative listing is made during this process.
2. The development of a final list of categories from this tentative list.
3. A review of all statements or comments and the categorization of each one into a specific category.
4. A tally of the frequency of mention of the statements or comments in each category (as illustrated in Table 11.2).

In this process, a question arises about reliability of the categorization. In very general terms it can be said that, in different contexts, the inter-rater reliability is quite respectable.

This technique probably is not widely used in industry, and in fact there is only one reported major study that has involved this scheme, although its incidental use (as illustrated in Table 11.2) is perhaps somewhat more common. The one major study was an analysis by Evans and Laseau[28] of a program sponsored by the General Motors Company some years ago. This study was based on 174,854 letters entered in the General Motors My Job and Why I Like It Contest. Letters were entered by 58.8 percent of all eligible employees. The letters which were evaluated for the purpose of awarding prizes, proved to be a source of valuable information

[27] North, R. C., Hosti, O. R., Zaninovich, M. G., & Zinnes, D. A. *Content analysis.* Evanston, Ill.: Northwestern University Press, 1963.
[28] Evans, C. E., & Laseau, L. N. *My Job Contest.* Personnel Psychology Monograph No. 1, 1950.

regarding opinions of employees in the various divisions. To "mine" this source of information, the letters were subjected to content analysis—which Evans and Laseau refer to as "theme analysis." In an initial review of a sample of letters, fifty-eight themes were identified. Some examples are: supervision, wages, pride in product, security, employee relations, and pension plans.

After identification of the themes, each letter was analyzed in order to determine what theme or themes it mentioned. An example will illustrate how this was done. Below are excerpts from one letter, with the corresponding theme for each of three portions of the letter.

Excerpts from letter	Theme
My job with General Motors has given me what every man wants—*security for his family*	*Security theme*
In less than a month I was getting top rate	*Success theme*
Knowing that a *chance for advancement is possible...*	*Opportunity for advancement theme*

Although the participants would be expected to mention only the *positive* factors of their jobs, it was believed that their *lack of mention* of certain factors might be meaningful. Among the various analyses that were made, one consisted of a rank order of the frequency of mention of themes in the letters from the various divisions. A comparison was then made of the rank order of frequency of themes mentioned in *each* division with the rank order for *all* divisions. A comparison of the rank orders of a few themes for one division (Division 48) with those for all divisions is given below:

	Rank Order	
Theme Name	All Divisions	Division 48
Supervision	1	1
Associates	2	2
Benefits from wages	9	13
Training, education, experience	13	7
Opportunity for advancement	14	8
Medical Facilities	15	23

Although certain themes were ranked the same, there were some obvious disparities, suggesting that the factors associated with certain themes in Division 48 were more favorable than for the Corporation as a whole in certain instances and less favorable in others.

PERSONAL CONTACT AND INTERVIEWS

It would be an ineffective supervisor or manager who would not be able to pick up some inklings about the attitudes and reactions of his subordinates in regular day-to-day contacts. Such cues can indeed be very useful, although it is manifest that indications of this nature tend to be fairly spotty and not systematic or thorough.

Systematic interviewing of employees occasionally has been carried out for purposes of attitude or opinion research, but this is not a very common practice. Somewhat more prevalent is the practice of exit interviewing. When exit interviews are conducted, it is in part the objective of the interviewer to encourage the departing employees to let their hair down and to express their real feelings about the organization. It is then typically the practice to categorize the responses from the individual in order to determine the frequency with which different reactions, including reasons for leaving, are expressed. (Incidentally, the categorization of such responses is a form of content analysis.)

In the summarization of such data it generally is presumed that the complaints or reasons for leaving that are reported most frequently must have their roots in some unsatisfactory condition or circumstance within the organization (such as insensitive supervisors or favoritism in promotions). Although exit interviews can be somewhat useful in focusing attention on some of the sore spots within an organization, there are some serious questions about the degree of dependence that can be placed on such cues as the dominant basis for feeling the pulse of the organization.

DISCUSSION

As indicated earlier, an organization somehow should be attuned to the feelings of its personnel. In some circumstances it may be appropriate to use some systematic procedure to do this, such as by the use of attitude, opinion, and job satisfaction questionnaires. When such an approach is used, the questionnaires need to fulfill the requirements of sound measurement methodology, in the same sense that an aptitude test needs to be based on sound methodology. The appropriate application of such methodology provides reasonable assurance that one will be able to obtain quantitative data about employee attitudes, opinions, job satisfaction, and so forth. This chapter has dealt largely with some of the methods that can be used for such purposes, although we have not dealt with some aspects of this methodology in detail.

The insight gained from the data resulting from an attitude or opinion survey among personnel in an organization can provide the basis for establishing policies or taking other actions that seem to be appropriate. Thus, the results of such surveys might lead to the establishment of training programs for supervisors, or to steps being taken to reduce accident hazards, revise incentive plans, reschedule work shifts, improve physical working conditions, restructure jobs, or any of a number of other actions. In fact, it is suggested that an organization should embark on such surveys only if it is committed to taking whatever reasonable action seems to be indicated by the results of the survey. It also should be committed to providing feedback to the employees of the results of any such survey and—where feasible—some indication of what the company proposes to do about some of the matters raised by the survey findings.

chapter twelve

Motivation
and
Job Satisfaction

We all have heard, or even ourselves have made, such comments about other people as: "Bill must be *crazy* to do that!" "Someone ought to set a fire under Pete." "George is going to kill himself working as hard as he does." "You never *can* tell what Elmer is going to do next!"

Such observations reflect in common our incredulity in realizing that other people do not behave the way we think they should. In the words of a common adage, "One man's meat is another man's poison." Clearly the diversity of human motivation and its manifestations in human behavior are central to one of the most enigmatic aspects of the management of organizations. The manifestations of the apparent vagaries of human motivation are reflected, on the one hand, by such circumstances as low production, wildcat strikes, personal conflicts between supervisors and subordinates, restriction of output, absenteeism, and high turnover, and, on the other hand, by such circumstances as individual creativity, outstanding organizational achievements, high *esprit de corps,* and the strong personal commitment of individuals to their organization that generates work effort above and beyond the call of duty.

SOME RELEVANT DISTINCTIONS

Terminology relating to motivations, satisfaction, and so forth is distressingly confused. Before proceeding further, however, some general clarification of certain concepts should be made.

Motivation

The assembler who slows down when he has reached some unofficial group-determined "quota" is doing so in order to fulfill some perhaps vaguely perceived need, such as the need to be accepted as one of the bunch. Likewise, the eager-beaver salesman who drums up a lot of sales is doing so to fulfill some need—perhaps to receive the approbation of the sales manager, or perhaps to increase his commission, or perhaps for a combination of these and other reasons. The way a person behaves is in large part a function of his motivation—that is, his desire to fulfill certain needs. Thus, the work behavior of people—be it good, bad, or indifferent—must be viewed in part as the consequence of the motivation of the individuals in question. In discussing human motivation as related to work, it should be made clear that there now are no clear-cut, unambiguous, sure-cure guidelines or practices for "motivating" people. To complicate things, any "understanding" of human motivation usually needs to be qualified by platitudinous statements such as that motivation is complex and highly individual. The complexities, however, should not preclude us from trying to gain some understanding of human motivation—even though it can be at best incomplete. In fact, some modest beginnings have been made toward such understanding. The beginnings include certain theories we shall be examining in this chapter.

Needs and Incentives

In seeking some such understanding, let us first differentiate between *needs* and *incentives*. *Needs* are the internal, felt wants of individuals. They are also referred to as *drives* or *desires*. *Incentives* (also referred to as *goals*) are external factors which the individual perceives (rightly or wrongly) as possible satisfiers of his felt needs. Thus, *thirst* is a *need* and *water* is an *incentive*. Water (the incentive) satisfies thirst (the need). Incentives can be either positive or negative. A positive incentive is one that attracts a person like a magnet—for example, the prospect of a promotion. On the other hand, there are some consequences or events that people seek to avoid; these are negative incentives. Thus, an employee continues to work at a job that he does not like because of the loss of pay he would experience if he did not go to work.

Given a particular need, there typically is a certain incentive that most logically fulfills that need. When it is not possible to achieve that particular incentive, or its costs in terms of other satisfactions are excessive, a person might view some other goal as a *substitute incentive.* A man might have his heart set on becoming a foreman to fulfill some need for status, but when this goal fails to materialize he may become more active in his lodge and ultimately end up as its president. Further, there are *instrumental incentives,* such as money, that usually do not satisfy needs directly, but rather are "instrumental" in fulfilling other needs.

We will refer later to the postulated *basic* needs of people—such as the physiological, safety, social, ego, and self-fulfillment needs—but for the moment the point to be borne in mind is that the nature and strength of the *specific* needs are highly individualized matters, presumably the consequences of previous experience and learning.

Because the specific needs of people are highly individualized, it is of course reasonable to expect that the specific incentives to which people respond would also be individualized. And thus we start to see the fallacy of trying to develop some single type of "incentive" that would be equally effective with all people. You may see in overtime pay the opportunity to buy shoes for one of the kids, a golf set, or a gold-plated back-scratcher. Your friend, however, may place a higher premium on using the time himself instead of working for the overtime pay.

Frustration

In discussing the instigation of behavior we should make a distinction between that which results from positive motivation as such, and that which is induced by frustration. Frustration occurs when some obstacle is placed in the direct path of an individual's movement toward a goal (incentive). As defined by Costello and Zalkind,[1] *frustration* refers to the event rather than to the internal feeling state.

Positive and negative reactions to frustration. Frustration in some circumstances leads to positive, constructive resolution of the circumstances that block the achievement of the goal. This effect presumably occurs because increased energy is then directed toward problem solving—in particular, trying to get around the barrier that prevented the achievement of the original goal. It is probable that many of the scientific, technological, and cultural developments of history, as well as many less spectacular developments, have been stimulated by frustrating events in the lives of the individuals. In other situations the frustration may cause the individual

[1] Costello, T. W., & Zalkind, S. S. *Psychology in administration.* Englewood Cliffs, N.J.: Prentice-Hall, Inc., 1963, p. 131.

to divert his energies into an entirely different type of activity, but one that is also constructive in its nature.

On the other hand, frustration can generate various forms of nonconstructive behavior such as aggression, regression, fixation, resignation, negativism, repression, and withdrawal.

Discussion. There are numerous other reactions to frustration, such as fantasy and rationalization. In whatever form, reactions to frustration are efforts on the part of the individual to resolve the frustrating circumstance. This means, in the first place, that the way in which an individual behaves has implications in terms of his own personal adjustment. In some accentuated cases, the maladjustive behavior may be indicative of serious emotional disturbance that requires professional attention. In the second place, it suggests that the behavior of individuals with respect to frustration has implications relating to their job performance. Supervisors, executives, or others can perhaps deal more effectively and constructively with individuals whose job performance under frustration is undesirable if they are able to understand the underlying basis of the behavior.

Cognitive Dissonance

Frustration stems from events in which individuals are prevented from achieving their goals. It is, then, the consequence of a conflict between the individual and his environment—the world about him. On the other hand, there also can be conflicts internal to the individual. These, too, enter into the motivation of people and therefore have implications relating to human behavior. In recent years the concept of *cognitive dissonance* has been applied to such internal conflicts. This concept, crystallized by Festinger,[2] deals with the degree of "consistency" that characterizes an individual's opinions, attitudes, and behavior. In general, an individual strives to maintain reasonable consistency in these matters, for a high degree of inconsistency usually causes a person to feel "uncomfortable."

In his theory Festinger uses the terms *consonance* (instead of *consistency*) and *dissonance* (instead of *inconsistency*). These terms generally refer to the degree of congruence or noncongruence between two aspects of one's psychological environment; these aspects can be attitudes, beliefs, perceptions, opinions, or behaviors. Dissonance exists where for some reason or other, there is a significant disparity between elements of a situation which are in some respect incompatible. For example, if a supervisor believes basically in treating his subordinates courteously, but is expected by his management to rule with an iron hand—and does so—the behavior "forced" upon him by his superiors is at odds with his own personal beliefs and

[2] Festinger, L. *A theory of cognitive dissonance.* New York: Harper & Row, 1957.

convictions. This disparity between his beliefs and his (forced) behavior would be the source of his dissonance.

Variables that influence dissonance. Whether dissonance will occur in a given situation, and its extent, depends upon a number of variables. One of these is the *importance* of the relevant aspects of the situation, as perceived by the individual. Another factor is the *extent of choice* that is available. Where there is only one course of action available to an individual (even a course that is intrinsically distasteful to him), dissonance usually would be less than if two or more equally distasteful courses were available to him. In addition, the *magnitude of the reward*—the potential gains to the individual—enters into the equation. Where, for example, the rewards of two possible courses of action are both high, the dissonance that might occur typically would be greater after a choice is made than where the gains from the two courses of action are relatively nominal.

Situations in which dissonance occurs. Some of the events and circumstances of everyday life inevitably introduce disparities of one sort or another.[3] Although various types of circumstances are dissonance-producing, only two will be mentioned here. One type relates to disparities between one's personal, private beliefs and attitudes and those which for one reason or another one presents to the public. An employee, for example, may personally approve of some policy of management but "publicly" indicate disapproval because this is the prevailing attitude of his fellow workers.

Another type of circumstance in which dissonance may occur is exemplified when a choice must be made from among two or more alternatives that are about equally desirable (or undesirable). A decision to choose one may later raise questions in one's mind as to whether the choice that was made was really the best one. For example, if an individual has accepted one position instead of another, he may start to compare the pros and cons of the one he chose and the one he rejected.

Reaction to dissonance. When an individual experiences dissonance, he tends to take steps to reduce it in one way or another. The recognition of the disparity may lead to any one of several "solutions" that tend to minimize its magnitude. Depending on the type of circumstance in question, some methods of resolution are: enhancing a chosen action by perceiving it in a more favorable light; depreciating a rejected choice; magnifying the rewards associated with a chosen action; adopting an attitude of apathy; tolerating the disparity; seeking additional information to bring to bear on the matter; and questioning the "facts" that are at odds with one's opinions or behavior. This last method of reducing the dissonance is illustrated by the results of a survey of opinions about the linkage between cigarette smoking and lung cancer. The results of this survey are given in Table 12.1. This shows that, in general, heavy and moderate smokers were

[3] *Ibid.*

more likely to be of the opinion that the linkage had not been proved than were nonsmokers or light smokers.

Discussion. Festinger[4] has argued that cognitive dissonance is an important determinant of human behavior. In particular, he hypothesizes that the existence of dissonance is comparable to any other need state in that it gives rise to behavior that is directed toward eliminating it. Successful reduction is rewarding in the same sense that eating when one is hungry is rewarding.

In the industrial setting, discrepancies inevitably arise, such as in labor-management relations, in policy-determination, and in personal relations. Such conflicts can serve as externally frustrating events, but they also can generate internal dissonance within individuals. Thus, a supervisor who is asked to place into effect a policy or procedure of which he does not approve may feel a dissonance between his own attitude toward the policy in question and the implied requirement for him to do what his supervisors expect.

An understanding of the influence of cognitive dissonance in the behavior of others is helpful in dealing with the consequences of it. There are, of course, many different ways in which dissonance can influence the behavior of individuals. In some cases, dissonance may even force persons to look

TABLE 12.1 OPINIONS OF RESPONDENTS CONCERNING THE LINKAGE BETWEEN CIGARETTE SMOKING AND LUNG CANCER: AN EXAMPLE OF COGNITIVE DISSONANCE*

| | Per cent who thought linkage was | | |
	Proved	Not proved	No opinion
Nonsmokers (n = 348)	29	55	16
Light smokers (n = 59)	20	68	12
Moderate smokers (n = 105)	16	75	9
Heavy smokers (n = 41)	7	86	7

* From *Minneapolis Sunday Tribune,* March 21, 1954. Courtesy of the *Minnesota Poll* and the *Minneapolis Sunday Tribune.*

more favorably on their activities and thus to be more productive in their accomplishment. Weick,[5] for example, has demonstrated that persons who strongly dislike their supervisor but agree to perform a task which he assigns are significantly more productive than persons who comply with a more neutral task-setter. This is assumed to occur because the person justifies his compliance by enhancing the value of the task.

Dissonance can lead either to constructive actions or to actions that are

[4] Festinger, L. The motivating effect of cognitive dissonance. In G. Lindzey (Ed.), *Assessment of human motives.* New York: Holt, Rinehart & Winston, 1958, pp. 65–86.

[5] Weick, K. E. Reduction of cognitive dissonance through task enhancement and effort expenditure. *Journal of Abnormal and Social Psychology,* 1964, **68**, 533–539.

undesirable in terms of the organization. On the positive side of the ledger, for example, it can lead to rational analysis of choices, or to the collection of more information for use in making decisions. On the other hand, it can generate apathy, it can lead to the avoidance of making any decision, it can cause people to be less critical in analyzing problems, or it can contribute to political maneuvering toward the end of gaining support for one's point of view.

Although it is not realistic to hope to create situations in which dissonance would not develop, it is desirable to take whatever steps are feasible to minimize it and that reduce its undesirable consequences. Some of the actions discussed in the next chapter have the effect of creating situations conducive to these ends.

Job Involvement

Job involvement has been characterized by Lodahl and Kejner[6] as the degree of psychological identification with one's work. This construct was confirmed as a relatively distinct factor as the result of a study by Lawler and Hall.[7] This study consisted in part of a factor analysis of responses of 291 scientists in several research laboratories to a specially designed questionnaire. This factor analysis resulted in the identification of three previously hypothesized factors, one of which is called job involvement. This factor in a sense reflects the extent to which a person perceives his job as being one that itself fulfills his needs. The questionnaire used in the survey by Lawler and Hall incorporated certain items previously developed by Lodahl and Kejner,[8] including such statements as: "The most important things that happen to me involve my job," and "I live, eat, and breathe my job." Varying levels of involvement are reflected by the degree of agreement or disagreement with such statements.

Job Satisfaction

Satisfaction with one's job, in turn, is a function of the degree of need satisfaction derived from, or experienced in, the job. In the study by Lawler and Hall,[9] satisfaction also emerged as a distinct factor. Its nature is reflected by questionnaire items such as "The feeling of self-fulfillment a person gets from being in my position" and "The feeling of worthwhile

6 Lodahl, T. M., & Kejner, M. The definition and measurement of job involvement. *Journal of Applied Psychology,* 1965, **49,** 24–33.

7 Lawler, E. E., III, & Hall, D. T. Relationship of job characteristics to job involvement, satisfaction, and intrinsic motivation. *Journal of Applied Psychology,* 1970, **54**(4), 305–312.

8 Lodahl & Kejner, *op. cit.*

9 Lawler & Hall, *op. cit.*

accomplishment in my position," where varying levels of job satisfaction were reflected by the varying values placed upon these items.

THEORIES OF MOTIVATION AND JOB SATISFACTION

As implied earlier, the study of human behavior is carried out at two levels. One of these is descriptive (or empirical), in the sense of characterizing or demonstrating the existence of certain relationships or phenomena (such as demonstrating that feedback contributes to learning). The other is explanatory (or theoretical), in the sense of offering possible explanations or theories relating to the "why" of such relationships or phenomena. Of course, we would like to have instant and unequivocal insight into the "whys" of human motivation as related to behavior in industry; but such neatly confirmed explanations must await another (probably far-off) day. However, certain theories have been postulated, some of which are alternatives to each other and some of which are complementary. Here we will discuss some of these, realizing that support, denial, or modification of any of them must await further evidence. But as one reflects about theories of motivation *per se,* it becomes difficult to consider motivation as separate and apart from personal or job satisfaction. In this connection Wernimont, Toren, and Kapell[10] point out that analyses of the procedures used in studies of work motivation are remarkably similar to those used in studies of job satisfaction. They note, however, that there are both practical and theoretical differences between these two concepts. Because these two areas are related, however, we shall touch on theories of both domains.

Hierarchy of Needs

Perhaps the most widely discussed theory of motivation is that of Maslow.[11] He proposes that sound motivational theory should assume that people typically are continuously in a motivational state, but the nature of the motivation is fluctuating and complex; further, human beings rarely reach a state of complete satisfaction except for a short time. As one desire becomes satisfied, another arises to take its place, and as this desire becomes satisfied, another replaces it. This never-ending sequence gives rise to Maslow's theory of motivation in which a hierarchy of needs is postulated. This theory has as its central feature the concept of human

[10] Wernimont, P. F., Toren, P., & Kapell, H. Comparison of sources of personal satisfaction and of work motivation. *Journal of Applied Psychology,* 1970, 54(1), 95–102.

[11] Maslow, A. H. *Motivation and personality.* (2 ed.) New York: Harper & Row, 1970.

needs being generally ordered in terms of their relative potency as human motivators. Some modifications of Maslow's original categories (especially in terms of labels) have been made by McGregor.[12] These are described and discussed briefly.

The physiological needs. The physiological needs are taken as the starting point and are conceived to be the most prepotent of all. To the person in a state of virtual starvation or water deprivation, matters other than food or water are of little concern. In some countries of the world, food deprivation is indeed a dominant motivator. In other countries, however, there is little actual starvation, and for most people the basic physiological needs are fulfilled. Even when we say we are hungry, we are not really seriously deprived of food. Frequently this "need" becomes intertwined with other nonphysiological needs, such as those associated with comfort or dependence. The expressed "need" for a sandwich or cup of coffee may really be based more on a desire to avoid continuing with one's job or a desire to have a chat with a buddy.

The safety needs. Once the physiological needs are relatively well met, there emerges a new set of needs which are categorized generally as safety needs. These generally are concerned with protection against danger, threat, and deprivation. Protection against physical dangers are of less consequence now, in our civilization, than was the case in the past. On the other hand, in an industrial society the safety needs may take on considerable importance in the context of the dependent relationship of employees to employers. As pointed out by McGregor, the safety needs may serve as motivators in such circumstances as arbitrary management actions, behavior which arouses uncertainty with respect to continued employment, and unpredictable administration of policy.

Social needs. Once the physiological and safety needs are reasonably well fulfilled, the social needs become important motivators of behavior— needs for belonging, for association, for love, for acceptance by one's fellows, and for giving and receiving friendship.

The ego needs. Next in the hierarchy are the ego needs. McGregor distinguishes two kinds: (1) those needs that relate to one's self-esteem— needs for self-confidence, for achievement, for competence, for knowledge; and (2) those that relate to one's reputation—needs for status, for recognition, for appreciation, for the deserved respect of one's fellows. In contrast with the lower needs, the ego needs are rarely fully satisfied. These needs, however, usually do not become dominant until the lower needs have been reasonably fulfilled.

Self-fulfillment needs. Highest on the postulated totem pole of needs

[12] McGregor, D. M. The human side of enterprise. *Management Review,* November 1957, 46(11), 22–29, 88–92.

is that of self-fulfillment—the need for realizing one's own potentialities, for continual self-development.

Discussion. Keeping constantly in mind that the above hierarchy represents the *general* order of relative potency of the various needs and does not apply invariably to all *individuals,* Maslow[13] points out that the hierarchy is characterized by some supporting aspects or features, a few of which are given below:

1. The higher needs are a later evolutionary development.
2. The higher the need, and the less imperative it is for sheer survival, the longer gratification can be postponed, and the easier it is for the need to disappear permanently.
3. Living at the higher need level means greater biological efficiency, greater longevity, less disease, better sleep, appetite, etc.
4. Higher needs are less urgent, subjectively.
5. Higher need gratifications produce more desirable subjective results, i.e., more profound happiness, serenity, and richness of the inner life.
6. Pursuit and gratification of higher needs represent a general healthward trend.
7. Higher needs require better outside conditions (economic, educational etc.) to make them possible.
8. Satisfaction of higher needs is closer to self-actualization than is lower-need satisfaction.

Maslow suggests that the various levels are interdependent and overlapping, each higher-level need emerging before the lower-level need has been completely satisfied. In addition, he points out that individuals may jumble the "order" and importance around.

It should be noted here that even though there is reasonable support for the hypothesis that to some extent human needs do have some hierarchical order, questions have been raised regarding the generality of Maslow's formulation. Herzberg, Mausner, and Snyderman,[14] for example, seriously question the theory that motivation in human work is primarily predicated on a hierarchy of needs.

Vroom's Theory of Work Motivation

Certain theories of work motivation have been proposed in recent years that are sometimes referred to as valence-instrumentality-expectancy (VIE) theories, or expectancy theories, or instrumentality theories. As discussed by Miner and Dachler,[15] these theories have as their central theme the assump-

---

[13] Maslow, *op. cit.,* Chapter 7.

[14] Herzberg, F., Mausner, B., & Snyderman, B. B. *The motivation to work.* New York: John Wiley, 1959.

[15] Miner, J. B., and Dachler, H. P. Personnel attitudes and motivation. *Annual Review of Psychology,* 1973, **24**, 379–402.

tion that behavior in organizations is viewed as a function of the interaction of personality (e.g., ability, values, needs, expectancies, instrumentalities, and role demands) and the general environment (e.g., organizational contingencies, environmental constraints, supervision, and available alternatives.) One example of a VIE theory was proposed by Vroom.[16] Three concepts are basic to his formulation—*valence, expectancy,* and *force.*

Valence. In the first place, Vroom places heavy emphasis on Lewin's concept of valences,[17] which refers to an individual's "affective" orientations toward particular outcomes of possible alternative courses of action— or, to put it another way, the strength of a person's desire for, or attraction toward, the outcomes of alternative courses of action. The valence for given outcomes might be positive, negative, or zero and, at least theoretically, may vary over a wide range of both positive and negative values. In his formulation, however, Vroom makes the point that many outcomes which are positively or negatively valent to persons may not *in themselves* be anticipated as being satisfying or dissatisfying. Rather, in such instances a person's desire or aversion for them is based *not* on their intrinsic properties but on the anticipated satisfaction or dissatisfaction associated with other outcomes to which they are expected to lead. For example, a person may desire to perform his job effectively because of the possible outcome of so doing—namely, that this may lead to a promotion. Thus, given actions may acquire valence as a consequence of the extent to which they are "instrumental" in achieving related ends (outcomes). This leads to one of Vroom's two propositions, as follows:

Proposition 1. The valence of an outcome to a person is a monotonically increasing function of (i.e., is directly related to) the algebraic sum of the products of the valences of all other outcomes and his conception of its instrumentality for the attainment of these other outcomes.

Expectancy. The second concept is that of expectancy, which is defined as the momentary belief concerning the likelihood that a particular act will be followed by a particular outcome. Expectancy is a person's subjective estimate of the probability, or of the "odds," of the outcome, and can range from $+1.00$ to $.00$ to -1.00.

Force. In Vroom's formulation *force* refers to the combining of the valences of various possible outcomes and their expectancies (or probabilities). As incorporated into the theory, this leads to the second proposition:

[16] Vroom, V. H. *Work and motivation.* New York: John Wiley, 1964.
[17] Lewin, K. The conceptual representation and the measurement of psychological forces. *Contributions to psychological theory.* Durham, N.C.: Duke University Press, 1938, **1**, No. 4.

Proposition 2. The force on a person to perform an act is a monotonically increasing function of the algebraic sum of the products of the valences of all outcomes and the strength of his expectancies that the act will be followed by the attainment of these outcomes.

Discussion. The first proposition provides the basis for predicting the valences of possible outcomes, and the second for predicting the actions a person will take (as influenced by the expectancies of the possible outcomes). In the work situation this theory would then predict that the behaviors of people, insofar as they reflect their motivation, will depend upon how they "add up" the pros and cons of various possible outcomes as "weighted" by their subjective estimates of the probabilities of the outcomes occuring. For example, in deciding to quit a particular job, an individual presumably would take into account his valences for the various features of his present job and their "expectancies" — some of which would be virtually +1.00 inasmuch as he already can predict them with great certainty—along with the valences for other possible jobs and his estimates of their expectancies.

Although valence-instrumentality-expectancy theories such as Vroom's have received considerable attention, there still are some nagging questions about them, as pointed out by Miner and Dachler,[18] and some suggested modifications. For example, Graen[19] proposes the addition of a concept of "boundary conditions." In particular, he makes the point that such a theory can help to make work behavior understandable only if the organization "behaves" in a manner that is understandable and predictable to the employees. If the employees perceive the organization's behavior toward them as being puzzling and unpredictable, their own motivation likewise will be puzzling and unpredictable. This phenomenon relates to the "expectancies" of people, for Graen's point is that if people have no basis for "figuring the odds," they are placed in a quandary and their own behavior therefore becomes unpredictable.

Herzberg's Two-Factor Theory of Job Satisfaction

Among theories relating directly to job satisfaction, the one proposed by Herzberg[20] has received the greatest amount of attention in recent years and has generated the greatest amount of controversy. Postponing discussion of the controversial aspects until later, let us first summarize the basic study from which the theory arose.

[18] Miner & Dachler, *op. cit.*

[19] Graen, G. Instrumentality theory of work motivation: Some experimental results and suggested modifications. *Journal of Applied Psychology Monograph*, April 1969, 53 (No. 2, Part 2), 1–25.

[20] Herzberg *et al., op. cit.;* and Herzberg, F. *Work and the nature of man.* Cleveland: World Publishing Company, 1966.

Nature of the study. The study consisted of an intensive analysis of the experiences and feelings of two hundred engineers and accountants in nine different companies. During structured interviews they were asked to describe a few previous job experiences in which they felt "exceptionally good" or "exceptionally bad" about their jobs. They also were asked to rate the degree to which their feelings had been influenced—for better or worse—by each experience which they described.

Analysis of interview data. The recorded interview data were broken down into "thought units," each of which related to a single event or condition that led to a feeling, a single characterization of a feeling, or a description of a single event. A few examples are given below:[21]

1. The way it was given to me showed that the supervisor had confidence in my work.
2. Feel fresh and eager, ready to come to work.
3. Gave me an attitude of indifference toward my job, didn't care whether it got done or not.
4. Wasted time doing unnecessary tasks. After the job, I knew it wouldn't work, just sat there until he came back for it.
5. I like to know there's a reason for doing the job.

Five thousand such statements were classified by content analysis into categories such as those given in Figure 12.1. Within each such category there were subcategories that provided for various specific kinds and degrees of responses, both positive and negative.

A major phase of the analysis consisted of comparisons between the "high" and "low" job attitude events (those in which respondents reported that they felt "good" or "bad" about their jobs). It should be noted that the mention by the respondents of any given factor typically was in *favorable* terms in connection with the "high" job attitude events and in *unfavorable* terms in connection with the "low" job attitude events.

Results of analysis. Some of the most significant results are shown in Figure 12.1. This shows, for the high and for the low job attitude events, the percentage of respondents who made statements that were classified by the researchers in the individual categories on the basis of the content of the statements. The major inferences of these and other data from the study relate to the distinction between what are variously referred to as *motivator* (or satisfier) factors on the one hand, and *hygiene* (or dissatisfier or maintenance) factors on the other hand. The categories that are primarily associated with high job attitudes generally are linked directly or indirectly with the *job activities* as such; these categories are achievement, recognition, the work itself, responsibilities, and advancement. Such factors

---

[21] Herzberg *et al., op. cit.,* p. 38.

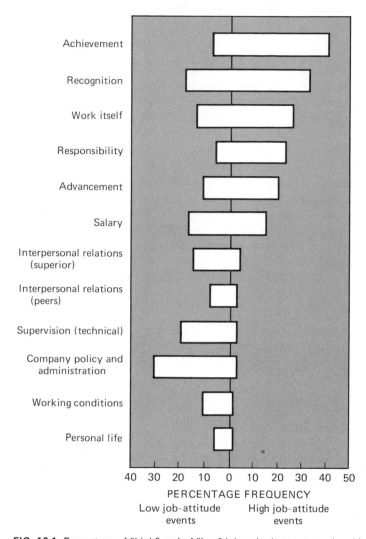

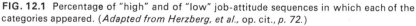

FIG. 12.1 Percentage of "high" and of "low" job-attitude sequences in which each of the categories appeared. (*Adapted from Herzberg, et al.,* op. cit., *p. 72.*)

are thus essentially related to *job content,* which means that they are *intrinsic* to the job itself. Because positive expressions relating to these factors generally are associated with high job attitude situations, they are referred to as *motivators.* On the other hand, the factor categories that were dominantly associated with low job attitude situations are those that are *extrinsic* to the work itself and that are associated primarily with the *job context* rather than with the job activities. The more important of these are company policy and administration, technical supervision, inter-personal relations (supervision), and working conditions. Because these deal essentially with the environment or work situation they are called *hygiene* factors.

Such results have led Herzberg to conclude that only the fulfillment of the motivator factors can lead to positive satisfaction on the job, and that the fulfillment of the hygiene factors can prevent dissatisfaction but cannot contribute to positive satisfaction. In other words, in Herzberg's view, job satisfaction and dissatisfaction should not be considered as opposite ends of the same continuum, but rather as different factors. Thus, in the words of Whitsett and Winslow,[22] the opposite of satisfaction is *no satisfaction,* whereas the opposite of dissatisfaction is *no dissatisfaction.*

Related to Herzberg's theory is the distinction between two sets of human needs. One set stems from man's animal nature and his need to avoid "pain"; this set consists of the needs for which the hygiene factors are relevant. Because these factors serve only to reduce pain, they cannot contribute to positive satisfaction but only to the avoidance of dissatis-faction. The second set of needs within this framework relates to the human drive toward self-realization—that is, essentially the self-fulfillment need as postulated by Maslow.[23] According to the theory, self-realization can be achieved only through the fulfillment of factors which are intrinsic to the work itself—in other words, the motivator factors. Such factors can-not satisfy the avoidance needs, just as the hygiene factors cannot fulfill the need for self-fulfillment.

Supporting studies. A number of studies have been viewed as generally supporting Herzberg's two-factor theory, and several of these are sum-marized by Herzberg[24] and Whitsett and Winslow.[25] One such study, carried out at Texas Instruments, is reported by Myers.[26] The procedures followed those used by Herzberg with intensive interviewing of 282 subjects (in-cluding fifty-two females) in various occupation groups. Although the results generally were in line with what would be predicted from Herz-berg's theory, there were some differences in the specific motivator and hygiene factors that were dominant in the responses of individuals in the different occupational groups.

The company subsequently sought to put into practice some of the implications of the research by directing efforts toward improving various aspects of the organization and its policies that might in turn aid in the

22 Whitsett, D. A., & Winslow, F. K. An analysis of studies critical of the moti-vator-hygiene theory. *Personnel Psychology,* 1967, 20(4), 391–415.

23 Maslow, *op. cit.*

24 Herzberg, *op. cit.*

25 Whitsett & Winslow, *op. cit.*

26 Myers, M. S. Who are your motivated workers? *Harvard Business Review,* January-February 1964, 42, 73–88.

fulfillment of both the maintenance needs and motivational needs of employees. Figure 12.2 depicts these two types of needs in graphic form. In its efforts to deal with the motivation needs, the company focused attention on some of the factors shown in the top half of the figure; and in its approach to the maintenance needs it concentrated on some of the environmental and work-situation factors shown in the bottom half.

THE JOB

GROWTH, ACHIEVEMENT, RESPONSIBILITY, RECOGNITION

delegation, access to information, freedom to act, atmosphere of approval, merit increases, discretionary awards, profit sharing, company growth, promotions, transfers & rotations, education, memberships.

involvement, goal-setting, planning, problem solving, work simplification, performance-appraisal, utilized aptitudes, work itself, inventions, publications.

MOTIVATION NEEDS

PHYSICAL	SOCIAL	ECONOMIC
work layout, job demands, work rules, equipment, location, grounds, parking facilities, aesthetics, lunch facilities, rest rooms, temperature, ventilation, lighting, noise.	work groups, coffee groups, lunch groups, social groups, office parties, ride pools, outings, sports, professional groups, interest groups.	wages & salaries, automatic increases, profit sharing, social security, workmen's compensation, unemployment compensation, retirement, paid leave, insurance, tuition, discounts.
SECURITY	ORIENTATION	STATUS
fairness, consistency, reassurance, friendliness, seniority rights, grievance procedure.	job instruction, work rules, group meetings, shop talk, newspapers, bulletins, handbooks, letters, bulletin boards, grapevine.	job classification, title, furnishings, location, privileges, relationships, company status.

MAINTENANCE NEEDS

FIG. 12.2 Illustration of the motivation and maintenance needs of employees as formulated by one organization. (*Adapted from Myers*, ibid., *Exhibit XIII.*)

Nonsupporting studies. On the other side of the coin, there have been numerous studies that have been interpreted as not supporting the two-factor theory. Some of these studies have been summarized by House and Wigdor.[27] In one of these, one Dunnette, Campbell, and Hakel[28] asked over five hundred people in six occupational groups to describe both a previously satisfying and a previously dissatisfying job situation by choosing from among thirty-six preselected, analyzed, and scaled statements presented to them on cards. Such statements were worded both positively and negatively so that they could be used to describe either a satisfying or a dissatisfying job event. An example of such a pair of statements is:

I felt a great deal of satisfaction because of doing a job well.
I felt a great deal of dissatisfaction because of doing a job poorly.

Responses to these statements were used in deriving "scores" on each of twelve factors that corresponded essentially with those of Herzberg. These scores then reflected the importance of each factor as related to each situation being "described." The investigators reported that certain motivator factors as well as certain hygiene factors were found to characterize both satisfying and dissatisfying situations, as reported by the subjects. This is illustrated in Table 12.2, which shows the factors that were among the six most important factors in both the satisfying and dissatisfying situations for four or more of the six occupation groups.

Thus, some "motivators" (such as achievement, responsibility, recognition, and advancement) frequently were used to characterize dissatisfying situations and certain "hygiene" factors were used to describe satisfying situations. These patterns of response are inconsistent with Herzberg's theory.

Discussion. The two-factor theory has given rise to a controversy of substantial proportions. Among the criticisms of the theory are those expressed by House and Wigdor[29] as follows: (1) the results are method-bound, especially by reason of the dependence upon recounting by the respondent which might capitalize on the tendency of people to attribute the causes of satisfaction to their own achievements but to attribute their dissatisfaction to external factors, namely the job context; (2) the theory is based on faulty research procedures, of which several have been cited, such as dependence on a rater to categorize the subject's responses; and (3)

---

[27] House, R. J., & Wigdor, L. A. Herzberg's dual-factor theory of job satisfaction and motivation: A review of the evidence and a criticism. *Personnel Psychology,* 1967, 20(4), 369–389.

[28] Dunnette, M. D., Campbell, J. P., & Hakel, M. D. Factors contributing to job satisfaction and job dissatisfaction in six occupational groups. *Organizational Behavior and Human Performance,* 1967, 2(2), 143–174.

[29] House & Wigdor, *op. cit.*

TABLE   12.2

Factor	Satisfying Situations	Dissatisfying Situations
"Motivator" Factors		
Achievement	x	x
Responsibility	x	x
Work itself	x	
Recognition	x	x
Advancement		x
"Hygiene" Factors		
Coworkers	x	
Supervision—technical		x
Supervision—human relations	x	x
Company policies and practices		x

Source: Source book of a study of occupational values and the image of the federal service, by Franklin P. Kilpatrick, Milton C. Cummings, Jr., and M. Kent Jennings, chapter 5, copyright © 1964 by the Brookings Institution, Washington, D.C.; and Occupational goals and satisfactions of the American work force, by Leonard Goodwin, Tables 1 and 2, Personnel Psychology, 1969, 22(3), 313–325.

the theory runs into certain inconsistencies with other evidence. These and other considerations lead Dunnette et al.[30] to express the hope that the theory will be laid to rest and buried peaceably.

On the other hand, the defenders at the gates of the theory such as Whitsett and Winslow[31] charge the attackers with such errors as the following: (1) persistent misinterpretation of the theory, such as by the use of measures of overall job satisfaction as the basis for evaluating the two-factor theory when, in fact, the theory explicitly makes a distinction between satisfaction and dissatisfaction; (2) the weakness of the methods of investigation; and (3) misinterpretation of results.

It probably will be some time before the smoke blows away from this emotionally laden controversy, and at this stage it may be premature to predict the final fate of the theory—whether it will be fully supported, subjected to modification, or forced to join the dodo in a state of extinction. If we may indulge in a bit of editorial licence, however, we should like to suggest that there is some logic to, and some support for, the argument of Dunnette et al.[32] to the effect that the two-factor theory is an oversimplified portrayal of the mechanism by which job satisfaction or dissatisfaction comes about. The virtually infinite number of variations in individual differences in value systems seems to render unlikely any explanation of job satisfaction that can be crystallized into two dimensions.

[30] Dunnette, Campbell, & Hakel, op. cit.
[31] Whitset & Winslow, op. cit.
[32] Dunnette, Campbell, & Hakel, op. cit.

However, although we are skeptical about the general applicability of the theory, we would like to offer certain admittedly subjective reflections relating to Herzberg's research. In the first place, it is entirely conceivable that the theory may have reasonable validity in certain situations with certain groups or classes of people, even if it is not universally applicable on an across-the-board basis. Further, the behavioral sciences owe Herzberg a vote of thanks for brashly wading into the boggy marshlands of the field of job satisfaction—which is indeed a problem area of high priority from the point of view both of the personnel who produce the goods and services of the economy and of the organizations of which they are a part. Aside from the question of the validity of the theory, he has stimulated a tremendous amount of interest and research in this area which cannot help but provide in the long run greater insight into human work motivation. And in addition—again aside from the validity of the theory—he crystallized a distinction between the concepts of job content and job context—between the intrinsic and extrinsic aspects of jobs—that may be relevant to a large number of research undertakings. In this regard, Burke,[33] while expressing the conviction that the two factors are neither unidimensional nor independent, points out that the distinction between opportunities for self-actualization (job content factors) and the social and technical environment of the job (job context factors) is an important one. This is a point with which we strongly agree. In this regard, Hulin and Waters[34] present some data that indicate that intrinsic (i.e., job content) variables are generally more potent and account for more of the statistical "variance" in workers' overall attitudinal responses to their jobs than extrinsic variables.

Need Gratification Theory

The questions left dangling after the controversy over Herzberg's two-factor theory press for some sort of resolution. One such possible resolution is offered by Wolf[35] in the form of his need gratification theory. Referring to this controversy, he starts with the thesis that there are elements of truth and error in both the two-factor theory and the more traditional theory which is predicated on the assumption of some overall (one-factor) concept of job satisfaction. In somewhat abbreviated form, the hypotheses underlying Wolf's theory include the following:

[33] Burke, R. J. Are Herzberg's motivators and hygienes unidimensional? *Journal of Applied Psychology,* 1966, 50(4), 317–321.

[34] Hulin, C. L., & Waters, L. K. Regression analysis of three variations of the two-factor theory of job satisfaction. *Journal of Applied Psychology,* 1971, 55(3), 211–217.

[35] Wolf, M. G. Need gratification theory: A theoretical reformulation of job satisfaction/dissatisfaction and job motivation. *Journal of Applied Psychology,* 1970, 54(1), 87–94.

1. Persons whose lower-level needs (as postulated by Maslow[36]) are as yet un-gratified derive both their satisfaction and their dissatisfaction from the degree of gratification of their lower-level needs (primarily the job context factors).

2. Persons whose lower-level needs are conditionally gratified receive both their satisfaction and their dissatisfaction from the degree of gratification of their higher-level needs (primarily job content factors), and their dissatisfaction also can come when continued gratification of their lower-level needs is disrupted or threatened.

3. Persons whose lower-level needs are unconditionally gratified obtain both their satisfaction and their dissatisfaction from the degree of gratification of their higher-level needs.

4. Dissatisfaction results from the frustration of the gratification of an *active* need, and from interruption or threatened interruption of a previously gratified (lower-level) need.

5. Satisfaction results from the gratification of any need.

In general, then, Wolf's formulation places particular emphasis on the "level" within Maslow's hierarchy of the individual's needs that are gratified, in effect suggesting that the "active" needs play a particularly dominant role in job satisfaction and job motivation. Thus, job motivation would tend to be stronger when an individual perceives an opportunity to gratify an active need through job-related behaviors.

Achievement Motivation

In their separate studies of one aspect of motivation, McClelland[37] and Atkinson[38] have addressed themselves to achievement-oriented activity. McClelland formulated the concept of the need to achieve (*n* Achievement, sometimes abbreviated *n* Ach), postulating that this seemed to be a relatively stable personality trait rooted in experiences in middle childhood. McClelland's interest in this construct is related especially to entrepreneurial activities in developing countries, as reported, for example, by McClelland and Winter.[39] The possible implications of this construct, however, cover a wide range, embracing the achievement motivation of people in various occupations in industry and business.

Before proceeding, let us first discuss briefly the measurement of *n* Achievement. McClelland and Winter[40] make the point that a "score" on *n* Ach is of an *operant*, not a *respondent*, nature, in that it records *how often* a person spontaneously thinks about improving things, not how inter-

[36] Maslow, *op. cit.*

[37] McClelland, D. C. *The achieving society.* Princeton, N.J.: Van Nostrand, 1961.

[38] Atkinson, J. W. Motivational determinants of risk-taking behavior. *Psychological Review,* 1957, **64,** 359–372.

[39] McClelland, D. C., & Winter, D. C. *Motivating economic achievement.* New York: The Free Press, 1969.

[40] *Ibid.*

ested he *says* he is in so doing. The actual scoring of individuals on *n* Ach is most commonly done by the use of special scoring procedures with various projective tests. Herman[41] lists a number of these, of which the Thematic Apperception Test (TAT) is probably most common. Because of the laborious procedures and technical training necessary for interpreting projective tests to derive *n* Ach scores, however, Herman[42] and Hornaday and Aboud[43] express the need for some objective and structured measuring system. On the basis of one study, Hornaday and Aboud present some evidence that the Gordon Survey of Interpersonal Values and a modified form of the Edwards Personal Preference Schedule offer some promise for this purpose. It must be stated, however, that in general different measures of *n* Ach are not highly correlated.

A theory related to achievement motivation. Given some basis for differentiating people in terms of *n* Ach, the theory related to this measure concerns the prediction of the behavior of those who are high, or low, on this factor. In particular, it has been postulated that those who have high *n* Ach tend to "approach" those tasks for which there is reasonable probability of success and to avoid those tasks which are either too easy (because they are not challenging) or too difficult (because of fear of failure). Thus, the opportunity for success associated with a task can affect the tendency to "approach" it. These relationships have been worked into a theoretical formulation by Atkinson and Feather.[44] Their theory postulates that achievement-oriented activity is undertaken by an individual with the expectation that his performance will be evaluated in terms of some standard of excellence. Further, it is presumed that any situation which presents a challenge to achieve (by arousing an expectation that action will lead to success) also must pose the threat of failure (by arousing an expectancy that action may lead to failure). Thus, achievement-oriented activity is influenced by the resultant of a conflict between two opposing tendencies, the tendency to achieve success and the tendency to avoid failure. Achievement-oriented activities usually are also influenced by other extrinsic *motivational* tendencies. Atkinson and Feather propose, then, that the tendency to approach or continue a task is a simple multiplicative product of the initial level of *n* Ach (or motive to achieve success, M_s), the probability of success of the task (P_s), and the incentive value of the task (which is a simple function of its difficulty, $1 - P_s$). Thus:

$$\text{Tendency to approach} = \text{Motive } (M_s) \times \text{Probability } (P_s) \times \text{Incentive } (1 - P_s)$$

[41] Herman, H. J. M. A questionnaire measure of achievement motivation. *Journal of Applied Psychology,* 1970, 54(4), 353–363.

[42] *Ibid.*

[43] Hornaday, J. A., & Aboud, J. Characteristics of successful entrepreneurs. *Personnel Psychology,* 1971, **24,** 141–153.

[44] Atkinson, J. W., & Feather, N. T. *A theory of achievement motivation.* New York: John Wiley, 1966.

A generalized model of this theory is presented in Figure 12.3. Those with high *n* Ach are shown as having the strongest tendency to "approach" tasks of intermediate difficulty; those with low *n* Ach tend also to approach tasks of intermediate difficulty, but the curve is much flatter. However, those with high fear of failure (the *negative* aspect of *n* Ach) tend to avoid such tasks, preferring the easier tasks in which they are almost certain to succeed or the harder tasks (because failure at such tasks is clearly not their fault).

Discussion. Atkinson and Feather[45] present evidence from a number of studies that tends to support the basic premise of their theory that persons high on *n* Ach tend to be attracted to those activities that offer reasonable likelihood of their achieving success and tend to avoid both the "sure things" or those activities that have very high risks associated with them.

With respect to the underlying construct involved, namely *n* Ach, Mc-Clelland and Winters[46] summarize the results of a number of studies that reflect relationships between *n* Ach and various indices of entrepreneurial

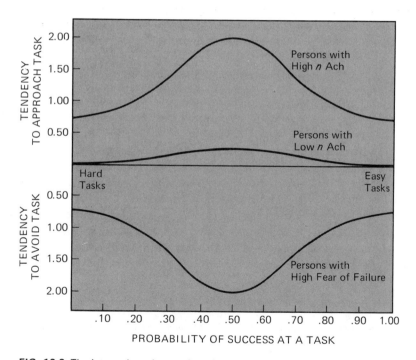

FIG. 12.3 The interaction of type of motive and probability of success in influencing the tendency to approach, or avoid, a task, as based on the theory of Atkinson and Feather, (*op. cit.*). (*Adapted from McClelland and Winter, op. cit., Fig. 1-1, p. 17.*)

[45] *Ibid.*
[46] McClelland & Winters, *op. cit.*

success. For example, Koch[47] reports correlations ranging from .27 to .63 between the *n* Ach scores of executives at fifteen Finnish knitwear factories and several indices of business expansion (such as increase in number of workers and gross investments). Such data tend to suggest that the success of the companies is in part a function of the high achievement motivation of their executives. McClelland and Winters make the additional point that achievement motivation apparently can be "learned" and is not exclusively predetermined by childhood experiences. Such "learning" has been brought about through special training programs and, in some instances, presumably as a result of being placed in a position in which achievement-motivated behavior is in some measure expected and rewarded.

WHAT PEOPLE SEEK IN THEIR JOBS

As we reflect about human motivation as it is related to work, and about related factors such as job satisfaction, we can do so from at least two points of view—that of the workers, with particular reference to their work-related values and attitudes, and that of the organization. In the latter case we will be interested in ascertaining the implications such factors have for relevant criteria such as productivity, turnover, and so forth. Let us consider first the frame of reference of the workers.

Work Values

As implied earlier, the work values of people—that is, those values for which individuals seek fulfillment in their jobs—have their roots in the basic needs of the individuals. In this regard, Porter[48] has used Maslow's hierarchy of needs[49] as a framework in investigating the importance of various needs to people (especially managerial personnel) and the extent to which such needs are perceived as being fulfilled in their jobs. As his basic approach, he used a questionnaire consisting of thirteen items grouped in terms of the following five needs, which correspond generally to Maslow's hierarchy: security needs, social needs, esteem needs, autonomy needs, and self-actualization needs. Responses being on a seven-point scale from 1 (minimum) to 7 (maximum). A sample item is given below:

The opportunity for independent thought and action in my management position:

47 Koch, S. W. Management and motivation. Summary of doctoral thesis presented at the Swedish School of Economics, Helsingfors, Finland, 1965.
48 Porter, L. W. Job attitudes in management: II. Perceived importance of needs as a function of job level. *Journal of Applied Psychology,* 1963, **47**(2), 141–148.
49 Maslow, *op. cit.*

(a) How much is there now?
(b) How much should there be?
(c) How important is this to me?

An analysis of responses of 1,916 managers of various levels revealed that higher-level managers tended to regard certain needs (chiefly autonomy and self-actualization) as more important to them than did lower-level managers. However, all levels of management tended to be similar in the relative (average) ranks they assigned to the five different need areas, with autonomy and self-actualization being generally most important. Going one step further, the responses to question (a) (How much is there now?) can be subtracted from the responses to question (b) (How much should there be?) to provide an index of *deficiencies* in need fulfillment, or *mean dissatisfaction.* This manipulation was carried out by Porter and Mitchell[50] for samples of both military and business managers. The results for three levels of business managers are shown in Figure 12.4. Although, as indicated above, autonomy and self-actualization are generally the most important needs as perceived by managers, we also can see that they are the ones in regard to which there is greatest dissatisfaction or deficiency in need fulfillment. This deficiency is greater for the middle managers than for vice presidents. Only nominal dissatisfaction is expressed with regard to the security and social needs.

Occupational goals of the work force. Although the studies mentioned above deal with the needs of managers, there is every reason to believe that these findings apply to people in general and that we can view the basic needs of all people as the wellsprings from which arise their specific work-related goals. Recognizing the existence of marked individual differences in this regard, Kirkpatrick et al.[51] nevertheless have provided, on the basis of a survey, an overall impression of the occupational goals of the general work force. Each respondent was asked to describe in his own words the attributes of an "ideal" job and of the "worst possible" job. The responses were classified into different categories on the basis of content analysis and the results, as presented by Goodwin,[52] are summarized in the first two columns of Table 12.3. (The last two columns also are based on data from Goodwin and will be referred to later.) The data are presented in two groups—categories 1 to 9 in which the desire for fulfillment of positive

[50] Porter, L. W., & Mitchell, V. F. Comparative study of need satisfactions in military and business hierarchies. *Journal of Applied Psychology,* 1967, 51(2), 139–144.
[51] Kilpatrick, F. P., Cummings, M. D., Jr., & Jennings, M. K. *Source book of a study of occupational values and the image of the Federal service.* Washington: Brookings Institution, 1964.
[52] Goodwin, L. Occupational goals and satisfactions of the American work force. *Personnel Psychology,* 1969, 22(3), 313–325.

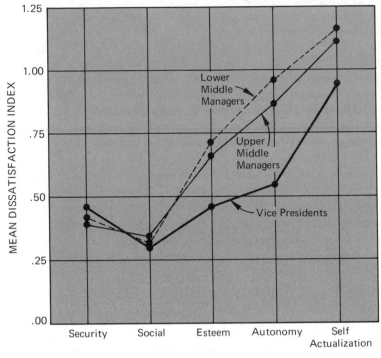

FIG. 12.4 Mean dissatisfaction for five need categories for three levels of business managers. Dissatisfaction was measured by the difference in responses to "how much" (of a need) there *is now* in one's position and how much there *should be.* (*Adapted from Porter and Mitchell,* ibid.)

goals appears to be stronger (in terms of percentages of responses) than the desire for the avoidance of their negative counterparts, and categories 10 to 14 in which the reverse is the case. This division has some obvious parallels with Herzberg's two-factor theory,[53] inasmuch as the first group (with certain exceptions) consists largely of categories that relate to Herzberg's motivator (job content) factors, whereas the second group consists of hygiene (job context) factors. (The primary exceptions to this pattern are categories 2, 3, and 5, Financial rewards, Personal relations, and Security, which Herzberg characterizes more as hygiene or job context factors.)

Although this general pattern of responses does not in any way confirm the two-factor theory, it does suggest that *positive* work goals generally are associated with the work itself and the "intrinsic" rewards thereof,

[53] Herzberg *et al., op. cit.*

TABLE 12.3 PERCENTS OF WORK FORCE EXPRESSING POSITIVE AND NEGATIVE OCCUPA-
TIONAL GOALS AND REPORTING SATISFACTIONS AND DISSATISFACTIONS ON
PRESENT JOBS

	Occupational Goals			
	Ideal	Worst	Satisfaction on	
	Attributes	Attributes	Present Job	
Category (Including	of Job	of Job	Satisfactions	Dissatisfactions
Positive/Negative Aspects)	(N = 1136)	(N = 1135)	(N = 1000)	(N = 1000)
1. Enjoyment of work: like/dislike	72	48	37	10
2. Financial reward: good/inadequate	43	27	33	32
3. Personal relations: good/bad	30	19	21	4
4. Self-determination: present/lack	29	15	15	7
5. Security: present/insufficient	15	9	12	8
6. Work that fits one's capacity: yes/no	14	7	14	2
7. Work that is worthwhile: yes/no	14	1	6	0
8. Leisure, time off: adequate/inadequate	10	4	4	0
9. Opportunity for growth: present/lack	10	3	5	2
10. Working conditions: good/bad	41	48	22	23
11. Routine: absence/too much	10	21	7	4
12. Supervisor: good, fair/bad, unfair	11	18	12	5
13. Workload: not excessive/excessive	0	10	0	7
14. Menial, manual work: no/yes	0	10	0	0

Source: Kilpatrick et al., 1964, *op. cit.,* and Goodwin, 1969, *op. cit.*

whereas the *negative* goals generally reflect the desire to avoid bad working
conditions and other job context variables. Special note should be made,
however, of pay (item 2), which—in this survey but not in a number of
other studies—occupies a very significant place in the hierarchy of values.

Individual and cultural aspects of work values. There are no two people
who have the same set of work values, just as no two people have the
same fingerprints. The work values of individuals take on many hues
from the combination of their individual experiences and their cultural
backgrounds. It follows, then, that an individual's reaction to, and satisfaction from, any job is the consequence of how that job is perceived as

fulfilling the goals of his own unique value system. The all-too-common tendency to attribute all variations in job satisfaction to the job or some aspect of the total job situation overlooks the fairly obvious fact that people bring various work goals with them to the job.

The work value systems of individuals tend to take on the overtones of the culture within which the individual grows up and lives. Some evidence of such culturally related differences in work value systems comes from a study by Blood.[54] In this study the agreement of subjects with the Protestant Ethic was used as the basis for measuring work values. The ideals of the Protestant Ethic, as crystallized by Weber,[55] are reflected by attitudes such as the belief that hard work brings rewards and that occupational achievement brings prestige. Blood used two sets of attitude items, one of which was intended to be in agreement with the Protestant Ethic (pro-Protestant Ethic), and the other of which was not in agreement (non-Protestant Ethic). The 420 subjects were administered these two sets of items plus other questionnaires that provided eight measures of job and life satisfaction. Very briefly, the results tended quite consistently to show that agreement with the Protestant Ethic is directly related to expressed job and life satisfaction, and that agreement with the non-Protestant Ethic items is *inversely* related to satisfaction.

Blood alludes to the effects of differences in value systems on attempts to assimilate some of the hard-core unemployed into the industrial work force. In connection with such programs, it will be useful to determine if work values are changed as a result of such programs and if such changes are accompanied by changes in job satisfaction and performance.

Work values as related to cultural background. There are various clues that part of the variation in work values of individuals is associated with their socioeconomic or occupational group affiliation. This relationship probably is a manifestation of culturally based factors. In this regard Friedlander[56] carried out a study of the work values of 1,468 civilian workers at a United States Government installation in an isolated community to determine what differences there were, if any, in the work values of blue-collar and white-collar personnel. The questionnaire covered fourteen work characteristics that corresponded essentially with the variables used by Herzberg *et al.*[57] These fourteen characteristics previously had been subjected to factor analysis and the three resulting factors were called Social Environment, Task-centered Opportunities for Self-actualization,

[54] Blood, M. R. Work values and job satisfaction. *Journal of Applied Psychology,* 1969, 53(6), 456–459.

[55] Weber, M. *The Protestant ethic and the spirit of capitalism.* (Translated by T. Parsons.) New York: Scribner's, 1958. (Originally published 1904–5).

[56] Friedlander, F. Comparative work value systems. *Personnel Psychology,* 1965, 18(1), 1–20.

[57] Herzberg *et al., op. cit.*

and Recognition through Advancement. Some of the results are summarized in Figure 12.5, which shows the differences in the two groups, as given in response to a question about the *importance* of each characteristic to the individual (1 = extreme importance to 5 = no importance). We can see that the white-collar workers tended to place greater values on those characteristics associated with opportunity for self-actualization, whereas the blue-collar workers tended to place greater store on the social environment factors, especially security and work-group relationships. Although the pattern is not entirely consistent, the fact of generally different patterns implies that people in various socioeconomic groups tend to bring with them to the job different sets of work values. These different values, in turn, may in part be a function of the level of fulfillment of the various needs in Maslow's hierarchy.

Work values of various groups. Over the years, a number of surveys have dealt in one way or another with the work values of people in various groups. By securing rankings by individuals of the importance of various job factors to them, certain of these surveys have provided an opportunity to make some rather guarded comparisons between and among the various groups to which these individuals belonged. The results of a

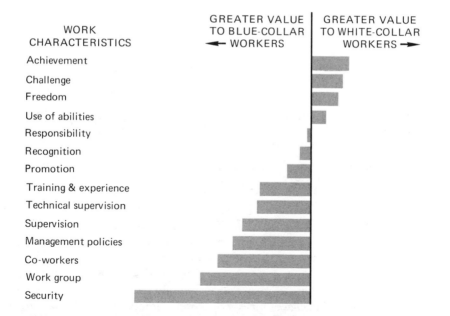

FIG. 12.5 Differences in the mean responses of blue-collar and of white-collar workers to question regarding the importance of 14 job characteristics. (A negative difference, shown by the bars to the left, indicate greater value to blue-collar workers.) The factors with which the characteristics are associated are; I. Social environment; II. Self-actualization; and III. Recognition through advancement. (*Adapted from Friedlander,* ibid., *Table 4.*)

TABLE 12.4 RANK ORDER OF JOB FACTORS AS OBTAINED FROM VARIOUS SURVEYS

Relative Importance of Factors

Source	Chant	Chant	Wyatt et al.	Berdie	Blum and Russ		Jurgensen
Group		Dept.	Women				
	Misc.	Store	Factory	Male H.S.			
	Workers	Workers	Workers	Graduates	Male	Female	Applicants
Number	150	100	325	150	181	105	3345
Opportunity for advancement	1	1	5	2	1	1	2
Job security	2	2	1	1	2	2	1
Opportunity to use ideas	3	3	7	4			
Opportunity to learn a job	4	4	8	7			
Opportunity for public service	5	7		8			
Type of work							3
Supervisor	6	5	4	9	4	3	7
Company							4
Pay	7	6	6	3	3	4	5.5
Co-workers	8	8	3	5			5.5
Working conditions	9	9	2	11			9
Clean work	10	11		10			
Working hours	11	10	9	6	5	5	8
Easy work	12	12	10	12			
Benefits							10

Note: Entries of 5.5 represent ties for fifth and sixth ranks.

S. M. F. Chant, "Measuring the Factors that Make a Job Interesting," *Personnel Journal,* 11 (1932) 1–4.

S. Wyatt, J. N. Langdon, and F. G. L. Stock, "Fatigue and Boredom in Repetitive Work," *Industrial Health Research Board, Report No. 77* (London, 1937).

R. F. Berdie, "Can Factors in Vocational Choice be Weighted?," *Occupations,* 22 (1943), 43–46.

M. L. Blum and J. J. Russ, "A Study of Employee Attitude Toward Various Incentives," *Personnel,* 19 (1942), 438–444.

C. E. Jurgensen, "What Job Applicants Look for in a Company," *Personnel Psychology,* 1 (1948), 443–445.

few such surveys are summarized in Table 12.4. For each group the table shows the average rank order of importance of each of the factors ranked by the individuals in the group. (Some factors were not included in all surveys, and the terms used in some instances were slightly different from those given in the table.) Two words of warning need to be made about such data: in the first place, the *average* rank orders given here can mask over very marked *individual* differences in ranks; and in the second place, economic conditions and social factors at given points in time might influence responses to such surveys and thus make comparisons across time a risky undertaking.

Recognizing these cautions, we can see that there are certain general similarities in rank orders across the several groups, such as the fact that opportunity for advancement and job security tend to be fairly high for most groups, and that pay tends to be generally around the middle. However, there also are noticeable differences among the lists, pointing up the fact that different occupational groups do have different value systems.

JOB SATISFACTION OF WORKERS

The discussion above has dealt with the occupational goals and work values of people. Let us now shift to consideration of the satisfactions experienced by people in their work activities, and to some of the determinants these satisfactions.

Individual Versus Situational Factors

In studies dealing with job satisfaction there has been an implicit assumption that certain characteristics of the job or work situation—what Vroom[58] refers to as the work role—have some causal relation with job satisfaction. Granting that there is at least some modest evidence to support this assumption, we should not expect that variations in job satisfaction among people are exclusively or dominantly the consequence of such situational factors. In part the satisfaction (or dissatisfaction) that people experience in their work is a function of personality variables. As Vroom points out, the explanation of satisfaction requires the use of both work-role and personality variables. Although, in our present discussion, we are more concerned with the situational or work-role aspects, we need constantly to remind ourselves that not all the variation in job satisfaction can be attributed to such aspects. To put the matter in overly simplified terms, we may say that people differ in their propensities to react favorably or unfavorably to given situations.

Job Satisfaction of Work Force

Some indication of the job satisfaction of the general work force is presented in the last two columns of Table 12.3. These data, reported by Goodwin,[59] show the percentage of persons in a general labor force sample who reported satisfactions (positive reactions) and dissatisfactions (negative reactions) related to the fulfillment of the various goals listed. The dominant theme that comes through from these data is that the American

---

[58] Vroom, *op. cit.*
[59] Goodwin, *op. cit.*

work force feels more positive satisfaction than dissatisfaction about the fulfillment of almost all of these goals. The only goal for which there is any appreciable variance from this pattern is number 13, work load. With respect to earnings, the percentages of those expressing satisfaction and dissatisfaction were nearly equal. In general, then, the overall impression is one of substantial goal fulfillment. This is somewhat in line with the analysis made by Blauner.[60] On the basis of many different surveys, he reports that, in general, about 13 percent of the employees covered indicate that they are "dissatisfied" with their work. From these data he concludes that even under existing conditions, which are far from satisfactory, most people tend to like their jobs. Even adjusting for some tendency to exaggerate the degree of actual satisfaction, he estimates that over 80 percent indicate general job satisfaction.

Occupational differences in job satisfaction. Although these general findings indicate a reasonably high level of job satisfaction generally, there are noticeable differences in the level of job satisfaction among people in various occupational groups, just as there are differences in job values. This was initially pointed out by Hoppock[61] in his classic survey carried out with 309 people in one community. These people completed a questionnaire dealing with certain aspects of job satisfaction. As an example, one of the questions is shown below, along with the percentage of people giving each response.

If you could have your choice of all the jobs in the world, which would you choose?

Your present job	48%
Another job in the same occupation	16%
A job in another occupation	36%

Differences in the level of job satisfaction for people in different occupational groups are given below:

Occupational group	Mean job satisfaction index
Unskilled manual	401
Semiskilled	483
Skilled manual; white collar	510
Subprofessional; business; minor supervision	548
Professional; managerial; executive	560

---

[60] Blauner, R. Extent of satisfaction: A review of general research. In Costello & Zalkind, *op. cit.,* Chapter 6.

[61] Hoppock, R. *Job satisfaction.* New York: Harper & Row, 1935.

Such occupational group differences are rather characteristic of the results of job satisfaction surveys and have led England and Stein[62] to argue for the use of separate occupational norms when analyzing job attitude data.

Factors associated with occupational differences. The factors that account for the occupational differences we have been observing in job satisfaction are not readily identifiable, but Blauner[63] has suggested four which may be of use in explaining at least some gross differences. These are: (1) occupational prestige; (2) control; (3) integrated work groups; and (4) occupational communities.

Of these, differences in occupational prestige seem to be particularly important, as reflected by the fact that the rank order of job satisfaction of various occupational groups corresponds generally with the rank order of prestige of the groups. The control factor deals with the relative amount of "control" the employee exercises over his own work and the work of others. Satisfaction generally is higher in the case of people whose jobs involve control over their own work and that of others, and is lowest for those people who are in jobs that are at the lower end of the organizational hierarchy, for whom there is little opportunity for such control. The third factor, degree of integration of work groups, usually is a function of the nature of the work and the requirement it places upon people to work together as a team. In general, the higher the degree of integration of work groups, the higher the level of job satisfaction. The fourth factor, occupational communities, refers to the nature of the association among workers off-the-job. One type of association cited by Blauner consists of isolated communities of people who generally are engaged in the same work; an example is that of mining, which typically requires that people live together in a community made up largely of fellow workers. On the other hand, he points out that there is relatively little such off-the-job socialization among urban factory workers. One characteristic of an occupational community is that its participants "talk shop" in their off hours. Such communities tend to be little worlds in themselves; the occupational group is a reference group in that its standards and its systems of status and rank guide the conduct of the group, as is the case among railroaders.

Work and Life Satisfaction

Although the relationship between satisfaction in work and in life has not often been investigated, the dominant role of work in human life

[62] England, G. W., & Stein, C. I. The occupational reference group—a neglected concept in employee attitude surveys. *Personnel Psychology,* 1961, **14,** 299–304.
[63] Blauner, *op. cit.*

would suggest that one's work cannot be viewed as being in a neatly isolated corner of one's life. In connection with such a relationship, however, Kornhauser[64] offers two alternative hypotheses. His "spillover" hypothesis implies that one factor affects the other in the same direction, whereas his "compensatory" hypothesis implies that a person compensates for job dissatisfaction by finding more enjoyment in other aspects of life. Kornhauser's own research tends to support the spillover hypothesis. In a related study by Iris and Barrett,[65] the foremen in two departments of a large chemical plant were selected for comparison because the foremen in one department (A) had been identified as a "problem" with low morale; the foremen in another department (B) were not considered to have poor morale. The foremen in the two groups completed a Job Description Index (JDI), which is a job satisfaction questionnaire developed by Smith, Kendall, and Hulin,[66] and a Satisfaction with Life questionnaire designed to measure overall satisfaction with family, leisure, job, and life in general. The mean values of the responses to the Satisfaction with Life questionnaire are shown in Figure 12.6 for the two groups of foremen. Group A

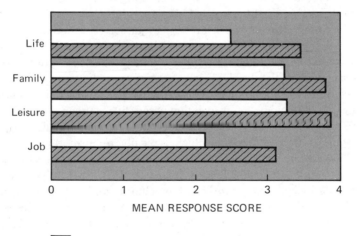

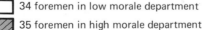 34 foremen in low morale department
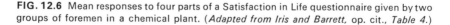 35 foremen in high morale department

FIG. 12.6 Mean responses to four parts of a Satisfaction in Life questionnaire given by two groups of foremen in a chemical plant. (*Adapted from Iris and Barrett, op. cit., Table 4.*)

[64] Kornhauser, A. W. *Mental health of the industrial worker.* New York: John Wiley, 1965.

[65] Iris, B., & Barrett, G. V. *Effect of job attitudes upon satisfaction with life.* Technical Report 38, Management Research Center, The Graduate School of Management, The University of Rochester.

[66] Smith, P. C., Kendall, L. M., & Hulin, C. L. *The measurement of satisfaction in work and retirement.* Chicago: Rand McNally, 1969.

was systematically lower on all four factors. These data, plus generally positive correlations between responses to this questionnaire and the JDI, tend to confirm the spillover hypothesis, and other indications suggested that the spillover effect was *from* the job *to* the life situation.

In a related study, Hulin[67] demonstrated that workers' satisfaction with community characteristics and with job characteristics considered jointly had significant effects on their satisfaction with life in general.

EMPLOYEE ATTITUDES AND
WORK-RELATED BEHAVIOR

As indicated above, some of the variability in job satisfaction and other work-related attitudes can be attributed to the personality proclivities of individuals. Thus as we now turn to the relationship between work-related attitudes and behavior, we will limit our discussion to that "portion" of the variation in attitudes that can be associated with such behavior.

It has long been held as an article of faith that there is some positive relationship between job satisfaction (and other work-related attitudes) on the one hand, and work-related behavior (such as productivity and job tenure) on the other hand. Because of the importance of this question we should examine this assumption. In addition to finding out whether— or under what circumstances—this assumption holds up, we also would like to have some satisfying rationale for any such relationship. We will postpone our discussion of this matter until after we have reviewed the evidence.

Employee Attitudes and Job Attendance

Let us begin by seeing what relationships have been reported between employee attitudes and job tenure (i.e., the tendency of employees to remain on the job), getting to work regularly, and doing so on time. We will refer to these factors collectively as "job attendance" behaviors. Their negative counterparts are referred to as labor turnover, absenteeism, and tardiness.

Fournet *et al.*,[68] on the basis of analysis of a number of relevant studies, conclude that the findings of such studies are generally consistent across a number of different occupations, indicating that job satisfaction is negatively related to turnover. This means that satisfaction tends to be *positively* related to job *tenure*—i.e., the tendency to *remain* on the job. Although a somewhat similar pattern was apparent from studies dealing

[67] Hulin, C. L. Sources of variation in job and life satisfaction: The role of community and job-related variables. *Journal of Applied Psychology*, 1969, 53(4), 279–291.

[68] Fournet, G. P., Distefano, M. K., Jr., & Pryer, M. W. Job satisfaction: Issues and problems. *Personnel Psychology*, 1966, 19(2), 165–183.

with absenteeism, the pattern was not as consistent across the studies surveyed; in one study cited,[69] for example, a negative relationship between satisfaction and absenteeism was found for blue-collar men and white-collar men and women working at low-level skills, but not for white-collar men and women working on higher-level jobs. In a somewhat similar review, Vroom[70] concludes that the research evidence indicates that job satisfaction tends to be negatively related to turnover and (perhaps less consistently so) to absenteeism.

A couple of examples will be summarized to illustrate the studies carried out in this area. As a part of a survey by Van Zelst and Kerr,[71] 340 employees in fourteen companies completed a questionnaire that included their own reports of absenteeism and tardiness. In addition, the question-naire included two questions regarding job satisfaction. Responses to these two questions were combined to give a single index. This job satisfaction index had a correlation with a reported favorable absentee record of .31, and with a reported favorable tardiness record of .26. Both correlations were statistically significant.

In still another absenteeism study, Mann and Baumgartel[72] took a look at various aspects of attitudes and opinions of both white-collar and blue-collar male employees of an electric power company. In one aspect of the study, a measure of "overall satisfaction" of white-collar employees was obtained by the use of a questionnaire. This index was then compared with absenteeism rates for the various work groups (departments, units, and so forth). The results (shown in Figure 12.7) show that, of the employees in groups with absence indices of 4 or more, only 22 percent were "satisfied" with their jobs. By comparison, in groups with absence indices of 1, and of 2 or 3, the percentages of employees who were "satisfied" were 62 and 52, respectively.

GROUP ABSENCE RATES
(EIGHT MONTHS)   PERCENT SATISFIED WITH JOBS

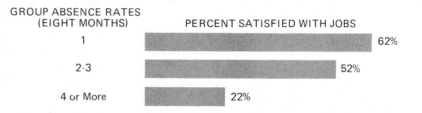

FIG. 12.7 Relationship between over-all satisfaction with company and job, and absence rate, of male white-collar employees. (*Adapted from Mann and Baumgartel, op. cit., p. 22.*)

[69] Metzner, H., & Mann, F. Employee attitudes and absences. *Personnel Psychology*, 1953, **6**, 467–485.

[70] Vroom, *op. cit.*

[71] Van Zelst, R. H., & Kerr, W. A. Workers' attitudes toward merit rating. *Personnel Psychology*, 1953, **6**, 159–172.

[72] Mann, H., & Baumgartel, H. *Absences and employee attitudes in an electric power company.* Survey Research Center, University of Michigan, December 1952.

Granting that the relationship between attitudes and job attendance factors is far from consistent and clear-cut, we nonetheless must conclude that the data do suggest a tendency toward at least a modest relationship.

Employee Attitudes and Job Performance

Somewhat in contrast with the studies relating to job attendance, it appears that there is no *consistent* pattern of relationship between employee attitudes and actual job performance. This was the conclusion reached by Brayfield and Crockett,[73] who analyzed the results of a number of studies dealing with this issue. In a later analysis of twenty-three studies that also dealt with this relationship, Vroom[74] presents the correlation coefficients between satisfaction and performance that were reported for these studies. These ranged from −.31 to .86 with a median of .14. Actually, the correlations for sixteen of the studies fall between .00 and .25, with four being larger (.26, .31, .68, and .86) and three smaller (actually negative).

One example of the types of studies carried out was conducted in a large insurance company and reported by Katz, Maccoby, and Morse.[75] In this study it was possible to identify certain "high-producing" sections and other "low-producing" sections because various sections were doing identical types of office work and records were available of the actual clerical time spent in completing a given amount of work. In one phase of the study four attitudinal variables were developed—(1) pride in work; (2) intrinsic job satisfaction; (3) involvement in the company; and (4) financial and job status. Attitudes on these four variables were obtained by the use of interviews. After deriving attitude scores on these variables from the interview, it was possible to compare the attitudes of employees in the "high" and "low" sections.

The results for two of the attitudinal areas are summarized in Figure 12.8. This gives, for the "high-producing" and the "low-producing" sections, the percentages of employees who had high, medium, and low "morale" in these areas. This figure shows that pride in work was related to production but that intrinsic job satisfaction was not. (Neither were the other two areas, which are not shown in the figure.)

The analyses of surveys by Brayfield and Crockett[76] and by Vroom[77] lead one to agree with Kahn,[78] who asserts that productivity and job

---

[73] Brayfield, A. H., & Crockett, W. H. Employee attitudes and performance. *Psychological Bulletin,* 1955, **52,** 396–428.

[74] Vroom, *op. cit.,* pp. 184, 185.

[75] Katz, D., Maccoby, N., & Morse, N. C. *Productivity, supervision, and morale in an office situation.* Survey Research Center, Institute for Social Research, University of Michigan, 1950.

[76] Brayfield & Crockett, *op. cit.*

[77] Vroom, *op. cit.*

[78] Kahn, R. L. Productivity and satisfaction. *Personnel Psychology,* 1960, **13,** 275–287.

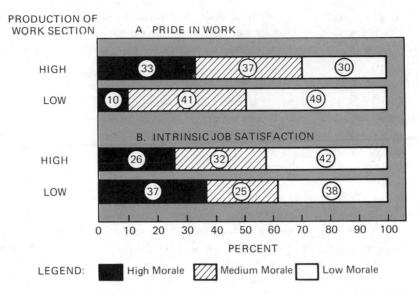

FIG. 12.8 Percent of employees in high and low producing sections who had high, medium, and low "morale" indices for each of four morale areas. The relationship between "morale" and section productivity was significant only for the first morale area, namely, "Pride in Work" groups. (*Adapted from Katz, Maccoby, and Morse, op. cit., Tables 23, 25, 26, and 32.*)

satisfaction do not necessarily go together. Although a number of the correlations reported by Vroom were positive, the fact that they hovered between .00 and .25 suggests that the typical "measured" relationship is indeed very nominal.

Discussion

In discussing job satisfaction and job turnover (or its positive inverse, tenure), Vroom[79] suggests that his motivational theory offers a logical basis for explaining the relationship between these two variables. It follows from his model (discussed earlier) that the outcome of a person's decision to remain in or leave his job depends on the relative strength of the forces to remain and to leave. The more "satisfied" the worker, the stronger the force to remain. In a somewhat similar vein, decisions to go to work (or, conversely, to be absent from work) are dependent on the relative strength of the forces urging the worker to do so.

In discussing job satisfaction and job performance, Vroom[80] emphasizes that there is no simple relationship between these two factors and laments the fact that we do not know the conditions which affect the magnitude

[79] Vroom, *op. cit., p.* 283.
[80] *Ibid.,* p. 186.

and direction of the various relationships that have been reported. Thus, the *generality* of the assumptions of such a relationship must be rejected. In those instances in which such a relationship does in fact exist, the commonly held hypothesis is that employees who experience positive satisfaction in their work are more productive as a result. However, one also can contemplate the reverse explanation—namely, that those employees who are more productive have higher levels of satisfaction because of their superior work performance. In regard to this chicken-and-egg conundrum, Porter and Lawler[81] make a plea to stop putting the satisfaction cart before the performance horse; rather, they express the conviction that job satisfaction should be viewed as something that results *from* performance behavior rather than as the *cause* of good or bad performance. In discussing this postulated cause and effect further, Lawler[82] argues that, in fact, satisfaction (as a "cause" of job performance) should tend to induce a *negative* relationship inasmuch as a satisfied need tends to lose its potency as a motivator; thus, high satisfaction should lead to lower motivation (and hence, presumably, lower performance) rather than to higher motivation (and hence to higher performance). Because of the many other factors usually involved, however, such negative relationships are not often manifest.

In those circumstances in which the performance horse is presumably the energizer of the satisfaction cart, Lawler[83] suggests that it may play this role in one of two ways. In the first place, performance can provide *intrinsic* rewards if in fact the job is one that can provide such satisfaction to the incumbents; there are, however, some jobs that typically would not be expected to provide the opportunity for intrinsic satisfaction. And in the second place, performance can lead to *extrinsic* rewards such as pay and promotion, which in chain-reaction fashion influence satisfaction. But Lawler hastens to point out that if the extrinsic reward system is *not* sensitive to differences in performance—in other words, if good performance is not recognized and rewarded appropriately—there is some reason to expect a zero or negative relationship between performance and satisfaction.

The implication of this argument leads Porter and Lawler[84] to strongly urge organizations to actively and visibly give rewards directly in proportion to the quality of job performance of the employees. An organization which takes this view of job satisfaction would then adopt an approach which is

---

[81] Porter, L. W., & Lawler, E. E., III. What job attitudes tell about motivation. *Harvard Busines Review,* January-February 1968, **46**(1), 118–126.

[82] Lawler, E. E., III. Job attitudes and employee motivation: Theory, research, and practice. *Personnel Psychology,* 1970, **23**(2), 223–237.

[83] *Ibid.*

[84] Porter & Lawler, *op. cit.*

different from the usual one. Its aim would not necessarily be to increase everyone's satisfaction, and thereby to make "everybody happy," but rather to make sure that the best performing employees are the most satisfied employees.

We will defer until the next chapter further discussion of the organizational implications of Porter's and Lawler's hypotheses, except for adding here a comment or two. There does indeed seem to be reasonable support for creating work incentive situations in which people receive rewards in relation to their work performance. This is an objective with which we are in full agreement. But it seems to us that, in addition to making efforts to reward people in relation to their work performance, one should also endeavor to create those conditions that are conducive to at least a reasonable level of job satisfaction on the part of the work force generally.

In this vein we would suggest that, although the "cause-and-effect" relationship between job satisfaction and work-related behavior has by no means been demonstrated (especially as related to criteria of productivity), a work force that experiences at least a reasonable level of job satisfaction may bring some benefits to the organization that are difficult to identify or measure. There may be values *other* than those having a direct influence on employee productivity (or for that matter, absenteeism, tardiness, and tenure). Brayfield and Crockett,[85] for example, suggest that conditions conducive to job satisfaction may have an effect on the quality of the applicants drawn into the organization, on the quality of job performance, and on the harmony of labor-management relations. There may be various types of "hidden" costs in having dissatisfied employees—costs such as having to have more supervision, greater time devoted to handling grievances and complaints, poor community relations, and unmeasurable (but nonetheless real) effects on the total organizational efficiency.

Our discussion of employee attitudes so far has been from the point of view of the employing organization. The point of view of employees themselves also should be considered. The total welfare of individuals, and of society as a whole, depends, in part, on the satisfactions that people experience in the various aspects of their lives, including their employment relationships. In recent years there has been increasing acceptance on the part of industry of "social" obligations to the community and to the nation as a whole.

Thus, in terms both of the immediate interests of industry itself and of long-range human welfare, there seems to be adequate justification for the actions taken by management to create work situations that are conducive to the increase of human satisfactions.

[85] Brayfield & Crockett, *op. cit.*

chapter thirteen

Management Philosophies
and Practices

People and the organizations of which they are a part comprise mutually dependent entities, and the degree of symbiosis achieved by such an entity undoubtedly has a marked effect upon the effectiveness with which the organization functions. What is more, the degree of symbiosis achieved probably is, in turn, partially dependent upon the degree to which the goals of the organization itself and those of the personnel are compatible. In other words, organizational objectives may themselves best be fulfilled if the organization is able to create an environment within which the employees are motivated to exercise their talents in their jobs toward the objective of fulfilling their own legitimate goals.

But you will now ask: How can an organization create such an environment? Or what are some of the types of actions that are within the potential control of management that would contribute toward this end? Or what are the features of organizations that somehow have created such environments? There are no ready-made answers to such questions, but some factors that have a bearing on this matter include: the structure of organizations; management and leadership philosophies and practices; the opportunity for employee participation; work groups; communications; the way in which conflict situations are resolved; and the manner in which organizational change is effected. This chapter will deal largely with some of the general aspects of management and leadership, and the next chapter will follow with a discussion of certain more specific aspects of management-employee relationships.

The possibility of introducing organizational changes to bring about improved employee performance raises justifiable apprehensions about possible manipulation and exploitation, as pointed out by McGregor.[1] In this connection a statement by Worthy[2] is uniquely appropriate:

> I agree...that gimmicks and devices employed for purposes of manipulation will soon lose their effectiveness. The important question is management's motives in employing the results of human relations research. If its motives are those of narrow self interest, of finding subtler and smoother ways of bending workers to its will, the effort will be worse than useless for it will widen further the gap between workers and management. But if management's motives are sincerely those of better understanding the problems of people at work, of finding ways for making work a more rewarding experience, of discovering its own shortcomings and means for improvement, management's efforts to apply the findings of human relations research are likely to create positive benefits for all concerned.

Worthy's statement and similar expressions by others, along with the results of a welter of behavioral research studies, point up the critical role of management in creating the psychological "atmosphere" of an organization—for better or for worse, as the case may be. The influence of the patterns of behavior and attitudes on the part of top management tends to set off something like a chain reaction through the levels of the organization. This was illustrated, for example, by the results of a study by Fleishman[3] that involved leadership training for foremen which was given away from the company. Although there was evidence of change on the part of the foremen by the completion of their training, when they returned to their jobs they tended to adopt the behavior patterns of *their* superiors. If the supervisor of a foreman generally behaved on the basis of different leadership principles than those covered in the training program, the foreman, when back on the job, tended to pattern his behavior more like that of *his* supervisor than that covered by the training itself.

This is explainable on the basis of the motivational effects of the rewards

[1] McGregor, D. *The human side of enterprise.* New York: McGraw-Hill, 1969, p. 12.

[2] Worthy, J. C. Comments on Mr. Wilensky's chapter. In *Research in industrial human relations.* New York: Harper & Row, 1957.

[3] Fleishman, A. F. Leadership climate, human relations training, and supervisory behavior. *Personnel Psychology,* 1953, **6**, 205–222.

and punishments that an individual receives in doing his job. In the above situation, a foreman presumably would be "rewarded" for behavior of which his superior approved and "punished" otherwise; thus, the behavior and attitudes of subordinates tend to be molded somewhat along the lines of the behavior and attitudes of *their* superiors via the powerful forces of reward and punishment.

MANAGEMENT THEORIES AND PHILOSOPHIES

As McGregor[4] pointed out, virtually every act on the part of management and supervisory personnel that involves human beings is predicated upon some assumptions, generalizations, and hypotheses relating to human nature and human behavior—in other words, on some theory of behavior. These assumptions may be neither consciously crystallized nor overtly stated, but they nonetheless serve to influence our predictions about human behavior. Thus, if a subordinate makes a serious error and the supervisor patiently explains again to him the correct procedures to be followed, the latter is operating on the assumption that further information to the subordinate will be more effective in avoiding such future events than a reprimand would have been. This leads us to a consideration of various possible "theories" of human behavior that different people, such as managers and supervisors, might use as the basis of their own behavior in dealing with others.

McGregor's Theory X and Theory Y

McGregor[5] has postulated two opposing theories, which he refers to as Theory X and Theory Y.

Theory X: the traditional view. The traditional view of human behavior that has been accepted by some companies is characterized by certain assumptions, including the following:[6]

1. The average human being has an inherent dislike of work and will avoid it if he can.
2. Because of this, most people must be coerced, controlled, directed, and threatened with punishment to get them to put forth adequate effort toward achievement of the organizational objectives.
3. The average human being prefers to be directed, wishes to avoid responsibility, has relatively little ambition, wants security above all.

[4] McGregor, *op. cit.*, p. 6.
[5] *Ibid.*, Chapters 3 and 4.
[6] *Ibid.*, pp. 3–4.

In accentuated form, this theory of behavior is characteristic of organizations that specify very rigid standards of work behavior and have stringent rules and regulations that are rigorously enforced. In more modified form, some companies have adopted what are purported to be new approaches to human relations, although (as pointed out by McGregor) some of these are simply old wine in new bottles; they are different tactics (programs, procedures, gadgets, and so forth) based on the same, unchanged strategy of theory X.

It should be noted that some human behavior probably can be explained in terms of this theory; the underlying assumptions probably would not have persisted had there not been some confirmation of it in the practical affairs of industry. But on the other hand, there are many aspects of human behavior that are incompatible with such a theory.

Theory Y: the integration of goals. The other theory postulated by McGregor[7] is predicated upon such assumptions as the following:

1. The expenditure of physical and mental effort in work is as natural as play or rest.
2. External control and the threat of punishment are not the only means for bringing about effort toward organizational objectives. Man will exercise self-direction and self-control in the service of objectives to which he is committed.
3. Commitment to objectives is a function of the rewards associated with their achievement.
4. The average human being learns, under proper conditions, not only to accept but to seek responsibility.
5. The capacity to exercise a relatively high degree of imagination, ingenuity, and creativity in the solution of organizational problems is widely, not narrowly, distributed in the population.
6. Under the conditions of modern industrial life, the intellectual potentialities of the average human being are only partially utilized.

The core of this theory is the value placed on the integration of the goals of individuals and of organizations—on creating those conditions in which the members of an organization can best achieve their goals by directing *their* efforts toward achievement of the goals of the organization.

Schein's Alternative Assumptions about Man

In a somewhat similar vein, Schein[8] also sets forth various alternative assumptions about the nature of man that managers, supervisors, and others might accept as the basis for their own behavior in relation to others.

[7] *Ibid.,* pp. 47–48.

[8] Schein, E. H. *Organizational psychology.* (2nd ed.) Foundations of Modern Psychology Series. Englewood Cliffs, N.J.: Prentice-Hall, Inc., 1970.

Schein, however, offers four alternatives, presented roughly in the order of their historical appearance: (1) the rational-economic man theory; (2) the social man theory; (3) the self-actualizing man theory; and (4) the complex man theory.

Rational-economic man. The assumptions which underlie the doctrine of rational-economic man correspond substantially with those of McGregor's Theory X reported above, with further emphasis on such assumptions as these: that man is primarily motivated by economic incentives and will do that which gets him the greatest economic gain; and that man's feelings are essentially irrational, and must therefore be neutralized by the organization.

Schein points out that the best evidence for the existence of such an image of man comes from day-to-day experience and most of the history of industry. In many industries the application of these assumptions, such as in the use of money and other individual incentives, has in fact been found to be effective. However, some reexamination of certain of these assumptions was generated by such factors as recognition of the exploitation of workers and their reaction to it, the increasing complexity of jobs, the greater dependence of organizations upon people, and increased expectations on the part of employees.

Social man. The reaction against the philosophies implicit in the rational-economic man image led Mayo[9] to develop an alternative set of assumptions about the nature of man. These assumptions are expressed by Schein[10] as follows:

1. Man is basically motivated by social needs and obtains his basic sense of identity through relationships with others.
2. As a result of the industrial revolution and the rationalization of work, meaning has gone out of work itself and must therefore be sought in the social relationships on the job.
3. Man is more responsive to the social forces of the peer group than to the incentives and controls of management.
4. Man is responsive to management to the extent that a supervisor can meet a subordinate's social needs and needs for acceptance.

Self-actualizing man. The rationale for accepting this third image of the nature of man arises from the opinion that organizational life tends to remove meaning from life because it fails to satisfy man's inherent need to use his capacities and skills in a mature and productive way—a need which is clearly distinct from man's social needs. The assumptions underlying this image can be summarized as follows:

[9] Mayo, E. *The social problems of an industrial civilization.* Boston: Harvard University Graduate School of Business, 1945.
[10] Schein, *op. cit.*

1. As the lower-level needs are satisfied, they release some of the higher-level motives.
2. Man seeks to be mature on the job and is capable of being so.
3. Man is primarily self-motivated and self-controlled.
4. There is no inherent conflict between self-actualization and more effective organizational performance. If given a chance, man will voluntarily integrate his own goals with those of the organization.

Complex man. The rationale for this fourth concept of the nature of man arises from the impression that other theories tend toward overly simplified and generalized conceptions of man, and that, although empirical evidence provides some support for such explanations, it does so only in part. The assumptions on which the complex man theory are based include the following: human motivations are arranged in something of a hierarchy, but are subject to change; man is capable of learning new motives; man's motives may differ as they are related to different aspects of an organization; man can become productively involved with organizations on the basis of many different motives; and man can respond to many different kinds of managerial strategies, depending on his own motives and abilities and the nature of the task. In other words, there is no one correct managerial strategy that will work for all men at all times.

Discussion

In reviewing these various theories or philosophies of management, one can see some similarities as well as disparities. For example, McGregor's Theory X and Schein's concept of rational-economic man have much in common, as do Theory Y and Schein's and Maslon's concept of self-actualizing man. In reflecting about the divergencies of these philosophies, we should guard against the temptation to assume that any one of them could serve as a completely satisfying frame of reference for management on an across-the-board basis. There is both historical and empirical evidence to suggest that different philosophies have proved to be successful in different circumstances. Likert,[11] for example, reports that some organizations have experienced considerable success, especially those in industries that involve a great deal of repetitive work, by utilizing what he referred to as a job-organization system, which is predicated essentially on McGregor's Theory X. What he referred to as a cooperative-motivation system, predicated essentially on Theory Y, in turn, has been found to be more effective in situations where varied work is more dominant. In such situations there is greater opportunity for the development of enthusiasm regarding the job itself and the achievements of the job. These suggestions that different

[11] Likert, R. *New patterns of management.* New York: McGraw-Hill, 1961.

philosophies (such as Theory X and Theory Y) have been found to be effective in different circumstances tends to add considerable appeal to the relatively flexible, eclectic theme characterized by Schein[12] in his concept of complex man, and to other related philosophies of management.

HOW THEORIES OF MANAGEMENT
ARE IMPLEMENTED

Regardless of whether a "theory" or philosophy of management is recognized as such, virtually every act of management or supervision relating to people is predicated on some assumptions about human behaviors. These underlying assumptions or theories—whether formally recognized or implicit—have their impact on the organization in various ways. Some of the ways in which they can be implemented include: by policies and procedures; by administrative actions relating to organization, personnel, operations, crises and emergencies, training, promotions, rewards and punishments, labor relations, and the host of other matters with which management is concerned; and by comments and expressed attitudes. The policies, actions, and attitudes of top management representatives collectively create the organizational climate—for better or for worse, as the case may be. This climate, in turn, is infused throughout the organization by a process that is somewhat akin to osmosis.

Because some of the management actions that affect people can have something of a chain-reaction effect on the people in the organization, it may be useful to have some inklings about their possible effects. For this reason we will give some specific attention to some of the aspects of organizations over which management does have some control, with the particular purpose of studying the relationship between such organizational characteristics and the behavior of individuals and groups.

THE ROLE OF INCENTIVES

One of the inescapable responsibilities of management is the establishment of incentives for employees. Although pay in some form is an important incentive, there are other forms as well that are operative in the industrial setting. (Let us keep in mind, however, that their relative values for individuals will vary markedly. Financial incentives in particular will be examined in a later chapter.) The incentives can be either formal or informal, either positive or negative. Some examples of these are given below:

[12] Schein, *op. cit.*

Formal incentives
>   Positive: money, bonuses, promotions, awards, formal commendations, special privileges (membership in clubs, officer dining room privilege, special parking location, etc.), choice of work schedule.
>   Negative: reprimands, disciplinary actions, demotions, lay-offs, discharges, withholding or withdrawal of privileges.

Informal incentives
>   Positive: praise, encouragement, friendly attitudes by others, acceptance by group, minimum supervision, respect by management and fellow workers.
>   Negative: disapproval and rejection by others, criticism, assignment to more onerous job, lack of work cooperation by fellows, being "picked on" by supervisors and fellow workers.

The importance of incentives in industry cannot be overemphasized. It is a well substantiated principle that behavior that is "rewarded" will tend to be repeated and that behavior that is unrewarded (or punished) will tend to be eliminated. Thus, the "reward" system—formal or informal —should be so tuned that good work performance is somehow recognized and rewarded. It is in part through the system of rewards and punishment that—intentionally or not—management influences the behavior of people in the organization.

ORGANIZATION STRUCTURE

We often hear individuals express the opinion that people "get lost" in large organizations or that there are too many "layers" in the hierarchy. Such reflections raise the question as to whether the various properties of organization structure do or do not have some bearing upon employee attitudes and job behavior. Porter and Lawler[13] pulled together most of the research relating to this matter with the intent of determining what generalizations might be inferred from the varied investigations—in particular, those that reflect relationships between each of seven different "properties" of organizations on the one hand, and job attitudes and job behavior of people on the other hand. We will make no effort to review the studies covered or to present any of the substantive evidence they dredged up, but rather will recap some of the generalizations they found to be warranted on the basis of the data.

Suborganization properties
>   1. Organizational levels
>   Job attitudes: increasing job and need satisfaction at each higher level.
>   Job behavior: level of job affects amount of information a person receives,

---

13 Porter, L. W., & Lawler, E. E., III. Properties of organization structure in relation to job attitudes and job behavior. *Psychological Bulletin,* 1965, **64**(1), 23–51.

the types of interpersonal relationships in job, and the types and nature of the decisions made.

2. Line and staff hierarchies

   Job attitudes: staff managers (in contrast with line managers) derive less satisfaction from their jobs and feel they have to be more "other-directed" (rather than "inner-directed").

   Job behavior: staff members tend to have higher turnover rates and to be "better informed" about organization activities.

3. Span of control (number of subordinates supervised)

   Job attitudes: available data inconclusive.

   Job behavior: available data inconclusive.

4. Size: subunits (departments and work groups)

   Job attitudes (blue-collar workers): employees in small subunits better satisfied than those in larger subunits.

   Job behavior (blue-collar workers): small subunits are characterized by lower turnover rates, lower absence rates, and fewer labor disputes; no consistent pattern relating subunit size to productivity.

Total-organization properties

5. Size: total organization

   Job attitudes: job satisfaction tends to be lower in larger organizations than in smaller organizations, but data are based on limited number of cases.

   Job behavior: inadequate data available for analysis.

6. Shape: tall (like a pyramid) or flat (with very few "levels" of management)

   Job attitudes (management personnel): with organizations of less than five thousand employees, managerial need satisfaction is greater in flat organizations than in tall organizations; relationships inconclusive in larger organizations.

   Job behavior: insufficient data for analysis.

7. Shape: centralized or decentralized

   Job attitudes: no clear pattern of relationship.

   Job behavior: no clear pattern of relationship.

In sum, it was found that five of the seven properties of organizations did tend to have some kind of significant relationship to job attitudes, job behavior, or both. (The exceptions were span of control and centralization/decentralization). However, the strength and clarity of the relationships that were found varied from one property to another, the strongest relationships being with organization level and subunit size.

MANAGEMENT

The ongoing operations of an organization depend in large measure, of course, upon its management and leadership, ranging from top management to first-line supervision. The distinction between management and leadership is a rather fuzzy one, but in general terms management tends to be concerned more with policies, procedures, organizational structures, and so forth, whereas leadership tends to be concerned more with the inter-personal relationships between superiors and subordinates.

Management Systems

Likert[14] has postulated the notion of "management systems" which, in a sense, can be viewed as the operating procedures and practices in the management of the human component of organizations. Any such "system" in turn is predicated on the theories or philosophies that are assumed by management. In this context Likert differentiates four systems which in effect reflect various positions along a continuum. These are listed below, along with the terms he had earlier used to characterize each:

System 1: Exploitive-authoritative
System 2: Benevolent-authoritative
System 3: Consultative
System 4: Participative group

Characteristics of Likert's systems. The labels above tend to reflect the dominant focus of the four systems characterized by Likert. Particular note will be made here of the following basic features of System 4 as described by Likert:[15]

1. The use by the manager of the principle of supportive relationships. Following this principle, efforts are made to maximize the probability that in all interactions and in all relationships within the organization, each member, in the light of his background, values, desires, and expectations, will view the experience as supportive and one which builds and maintains his sense of personal worth and importance.

2. The use of group decision-making and group methods of supervision. Following this principle, a supervisor is responsible for building his subordinates into a group which makes the best decisions and carries them out well, but in which the supervisor is accountable for the decisions, for their execution, and for the results. Such a principle should *not* be confused with "committee" decisions—frequently of a "wishy-washy" or "common-denominator" nature—that permit the supervisor to abdicate his responsibilities.

3. High performance goals for the organization. The objective of this concept is to provide the basis for setting objectives which represent an optimum integration of the needs and desires of the members of the organization, the shareholders, the customers, and others who have an interest in it. In line with this objective, there should be a mechanism through which employees can help set the high-level goals which the satisfaction of their

14 Likert, R. *The human organization.* New York: McGraw-Hill, 1967.
15 *Ibid.,* pp. 47.

own needs requires. In general terms, Likert suggests that these include stable employment, job security, opportunity for promotion, and satisfactory compensation.

In his research, Likert has developed procedures for "measuring" organizations in order to develop a profile of their characteristics; the profile then depicts an organization in terms of where it falls along the continuum represented by Likert's four systems. This is accomplished with a questionnaire developed by Likert[16] that consists (in its various forms) of a number of "operating characteristics." In one form these are grouped into the following categories:

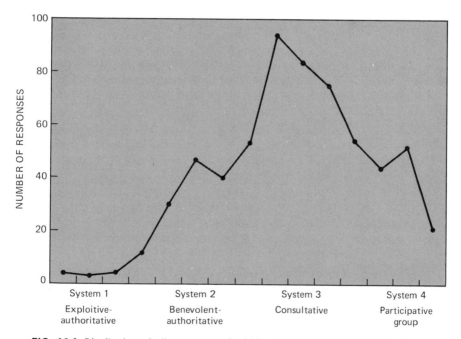

FIG. 13.1 Distribution of all responses of middle- and upper-level managers in several well-managed companies to 43-item questionnaire relating to organizational characteristics. The scale represents the four management systems characterized by Likert. (*Consolidation of data from* The human organization *by Rensis Likert, Fig. 3-2. Copyright © 1967 by McGraw-Hill, Inc. Used with permission of McGraw-Hill Book Company.*)

[16] *Ibid.,* pp. 197–211.

The specific items within each of these categories have response categories that characterize each of the four systems with respect to the particular item in question. A couple of examples relating to decision making are given below, in slightly abbreviated form:

Responses of sample of managers. In practice the questionnaire can be used to elicit responses from managers that reflect their opinions about an organization or that describe the organizational characteristics they would themselves desire. Figure 13.1 shows the distribution of responses of middle- and upper-level managers in several well-managed companies as they described their own companies. This frequency distribution consolidates the responses to forty-three different items in the form of the questionnaire being used, and so it can be considered as reflecting their generalized opinions. A relatively wide range of responses is apparent, although most of them fall under System 2 and System 3.

Discussion. In a sense, the management systems characterized by Likert are the reflections—in terms of operating procedures and policies—of the assumptions that underlie management's actions. Although such differences in operating procedures and policies have been depicted in many different ways on many occasions, Likert has helped to crystallize, and to quantify, these differences.

CHARACTER OF DECISION MAKING PROCESS

	a. At what level in organization are decisions formally made?	b. How adequate and accurate is the information available for decision making?	c. To what extent are decision makers aware of problems, particularly those at lower levels in the organization?
System 1 Exploitive authoritative	Bulk of decisions at top	Partial and often inaccurate information only is available	Often are unaware or only partially aware
System 2 Benevolent authoritative	Policy at top, many decisions within prescribed framework made at lower levels	Moderately adequate and accurate information available	Aware of some, unaware of others
System 3 Consultative	Broad policy and general decisions at top, more specific decisions at lower levels	Reasonably adequate and accurate information available	Moderately aware of problems
System 4 Participative group	Decision making widely done throughout organization	Relatively complete and accurate information available	Generally quite well aware of problems

Source: R. Likert, *The human organization.* New York: McGraw-Hill, 1967, p. 20, Table 3. See also Table 14-1 in R. Likert. *New patterns of management.* New York: McGraw-Hill, 1961.

Management Systems and Their Effects

It is of course reasonable to be curious about the consequences of different management systems, such as those depicted by Likert. This leads to consideration of the possible effects or consequences of such systems. In this regard Likert[17] differentiates among three classes of variables. These are illustrated graphically in Figure 13.2. We can see that, in general, the causal (i.e., independent) variables (over which management has some possible control) can influence the intervening variables (which are essentially attitudinal in nature) and thus influence the end-result (i.e., dependent) variables.

A case history. As one illustration of the effect of management systems on the effectiveness of an organization, Marrow, Bowers, and Seashore[18] report the case history of a shirt manufacturing plant that had been unprofitable for several years before it was taken over and revitalized by another organization. Starting in 1962, a number of changes were introduced by the management, including efforts to shift the management system into a more participative form characterized as System 4. Figure 13.3 shows the profile of the organization both in 1962 and in 1964. These profiles are based on the responses of supervisors to the questionnaire developed by Likert, referred to above. (The figure shows the mean responses of the supervisors for the various items in the categories listed.) A distinct shift

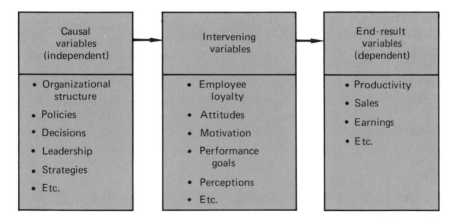

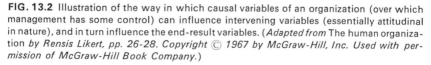

FIG. 13.2 Illustration of the way in which causal variables of an organization (over which management has some control) can influence intervening variables (essentially attitudinal in nature), and in turn influence the end-result variables. (*Adapted from* The human organization *by Rensis Likert, pp. 26-28. Copyright* © *1967 by McGraw-Hill, Inc. Used with permission of McGraw-Hill Book Company.*)

[17] *Ibid.*, p. 26.
[18] Marrow, A. J., Bowers, D. G., & Seashore, S. E. (Eds.), *Strategies of organizational change.* New York: Harper & Row, 1967.

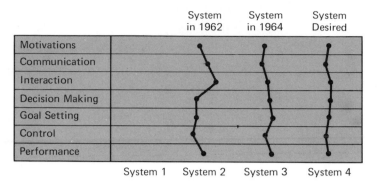

FIG. 13.3 Profile of management systems in a shirt manufacturing plant in 1962 and 1964 as described by supervisors, and the system "desired" by them. These profiles represent means of the responses to the several items within each category. The profiles based on responses of managers, and of assistant supervisors, paralleled these. (*Based on data from Marrow, Bowers, and Seashore, op. cit., as presented in* The human organization *by Rensis Likert, Figs. 3-4, 3-5, and 3-6. Copyright © 1967 by McGraw-Hill, Inc. Used with permission of McGraw-Hill Book Company.*)

from System 2 to System 3 is apparent. The figure also shows the system "desired" by the supervisors in 1964 but not yet achieved; the "desired" system is at the System 4 end of the scale.

Although there was a distinct shift in the management system of the company during the time span of the study, the effect of this shift should be judged in terms of appropriate end-result variables, such as productivity. Such results are shown in Figure 13.4. Actual productivity undoubtedly was affected by changes in technology but this figure, which expresses productivity as based on hourly earnings (actually piece-rate payments), eliminates the effects of such changes. Thus, the change in productivity was undoubtedly due to the changes in the management system.

Other indications about management systems. The case study of the shirt manufacturing plant probably represents an unusually successful change in a company's management system, and in its corresponding productivity. Data from other studies, however, tend to confirm the same general impression that the more productive organizations are those which tend to have management practices toward the System 4 end of the scale. For example, Likert[19] summarizes an exercise in which several hundred managers using his questionnaire were asked to "describe" the highest-producing and lowest-producing departments they knew well. The resulting profiles of the highest-producing departments were quite varied, but tended to fall in the System 3 and System 4 areas of the scale. However, the profiles of the lowest-producing departments almost invariably fell to the left of those of the highest-producing departments.

[19] Likert (1967) *op. cit.,* p. 3.

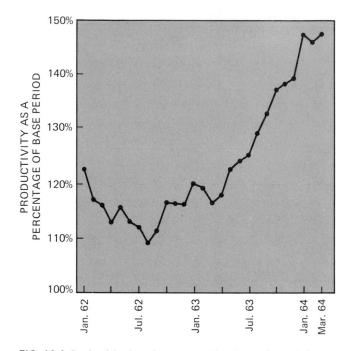

FIG. 13.4 Productivity based on average hourly earnings of piece-rate employees in shirt manufacturing plant over two-year period following management efforts to alter the "management system." See Figure 13.3 for profile of management systems at beginning and end of period. (*Based on date from Marrow, Bowers, and Seashore,* op. cit., *as presented in* The human organization *by Rensis Likert. Copyright* © *1967 by McGraw-Hill, Inc. Used with permission of McGraw-Hill Book Company.*)

There are few generalizations in this life that are universal in their scope, and it is not here proposed that the adoption of a management strategy corresponding to System 4 will necessarily be effective in pulling any given organization up by its own bootstraps. But, even though "causation" evidence about the possible effects of such a management strategy is rather sparse, it does seem that the odds are in favor of such effects.

LEADERSHIP

In discussing leadership, Fiedler[20] asserts: "Except perhaps for the unusual case, it is simply not meaningful to speak of an effective leader or of an ineffective leader; we can only speak of a leader who tends to be effective in one situation and ineffective in another." Thus he would suggest that we forsake all efforts to identify "the" traits or behaviors of

[20] Fiedler, F. E. *A theory of leadership effectiveness*. New York: McGraw-Hill, 1967, p. 261.

"effective leaders" in general, and rather should seek to study leadership behavior in various types of situations.

The Nature of Leadership

The leadership behavior of individuals is an amalgam of many factors and, as in the case of any complex phenomenon, it can be described in various ways and at various levels of abstraction. Various such sets of leadership attributes have been identified through research or postulated on rational grounds. Certain of these will be discussed briefly.

Consideration and structure. As the result of a series of studies carried out at Ohio State University, Fleishman and Harris[21] crystallized the following two primary dimensions of leadership behavior:

> *Consideration* includes behavior indicating mutual trust, respect, and a certain warmth and rapport between the supervisor and his group. This does not mean that this dimension reflects a superficial "pat-on-the-back," "first name calling" kind of human relations behavior. This dimension appears to emphasize a deeper concern for group members' needs and includes such behavior as allowing subordinates more participation in decision-making and encouraging more two-way communication.
> *Structure* includes behavior in which the supervisor organizes and defines group activities and his relation to the group. Thus, he defines the role he expects each member to assume, assigns tasks, plans ahead, establishes ways of getting things done, and pushes for production. This dimension seems to emphasize overt attempts to achieve organizational goals.

These two dimensions were developed on the basis of a previous factor analysis of responses to items in the *Leader Behavior Description Questionnaire,* which is completed by subordinates who "describe" the behavior of their respective superiors. On the basis of responses of subordinates to items on the questionnaire, it is possible to derive separate scores for the supervisors on *consideration* and on *structure*. In general, these two aspects of leadership behavior are not opposite ends of the same continuum. Rather, they are separate, relatively independent dimensions of behavior. Thus, it is not incompatible for a supervisor to be characterized by any combination of these two dimensions, such as being high on both, low on both, or high on one and low on the other. (This study will be referred to again later in this chapter.)

A four-dimension formulation. Bowers and Seashore[22] reviewed a number of factor-analytic studies of leadership behavior, in particular com-

---

[21] Fleishman, E. A., & Harris, E. F. Patterns of leadership behavior related to employee grievances and turnover. *Personnel Psychology,* 1962, **15**, 43–56.

[22] Bowers, D. G., & Seashore, S. E. Predicting organizational effectiveness with a four-factor theory of leadership. *Administrative Science Quarterly,* 1966, **11**(2), 238–263.

paring the dimensions (i.e., the factors) reported for these studies. They discovered a great deal of common conceptual content among these studies, from which emerged four dimensions that comprise, according to Bowers and Seashore, the basic structure of what one may term "leadership." These dimensions are:

1. *Support.* Behavior that enhances someone else's feeling of personal worth and importance.
2. *Interaction facilitation.* Behavior that encourages members of the group to develop close, mutually satisfying relationships.
3. *Goal emphasis.* Behavior that stimulates an enthusiasm for meeting the group's goal or achieving excellent performance.
4. *Work facilitation.* Behavior that helps achieve goal attainment by such activities as scheduling, coordinating, planning, and by providing resources such as tools, materials, and technical knowledge.

It might be noted that one end of these dimensions has a very strong similarity with Likert's[23] management System 4, discussed earlier. In effect, at the level of superior-subordinate relationships the leader in his own behavior virtually "implements" whatever management system is in operation.

The concepts implied by these four dimensions appeared, sometimes separately, sometimes in combination, in all but two of eight investigations analyzed, thus lending substantial confidence to the leadership structure reflected by them. The support dimension corresponds essentially with the consideration dimension reported by Fleishman and Harris,[24] and the work facilitation dimension corresponds with the structure dimension. Such dimensions are not regarded as indivisible, for they are capable of further subdivision in more specific descriptions of leadership behavior.

Leadership style. The dimensions mentioned above generally refer to certain aspects of leadership activities; in effect, any leader could be pegged as falling at some point along each of those dimension scales. Another way of describing leadership behavior is in terms of leadership style. Such styles have been characterized by Lippett[25] as falling into three classes— autocratic, democratic, and laissez-faire. These differ essentially in the location of the power and decision-making functions. In the case of autocratic leadership, power and decision making reside in the *leader* himself, with democratic leadership they tend to reside in the *group,* and with laissez-faire leadership the *individuals* have a dominant role in decision making and the exercise of power.

Fiedler's leadership measures. One of the most sustained research pro-

[23] Likert (1967), *op. cit.,* Chapter 2.
[24] Fleishman & Harris, *op. cit.*
[25] Lippett, G. L. What do we know about leadership? *National Education Association Journal,* December 1955, 44(9), 556–57.

grams relating to leadership was conducted by Fiedler.[26] As a major phase of this program he has developed certain self-description measures of leadership style, in particular the two called "assumed similarity between opposites" (ASO) and "least-preferred coworker" (LPC). The ASO scale is based on the similarity between the leader's reported perception of his *most*-preferred and *least*-preferred coworkers. In turn, the LPC scale is a measure of his perception of his *least*-preferred coworker. Let us first describe briefly the derivation of these measures. They are both derived from the same questionnaires, which are based on the semantic differential of Osgood.[27] A portion of the LPC scale is shown as Figure 13.5; the complete scales include anywhere from sixteen to thirty bipolar adjective scales. The respondent is asked to think of the person with whom he can work *least well,* and then to "describe" that person using the complete scale. In the derivation of the ASO score, the respondent is also asked to describe his *most*-preferred coworker with the same scale; the ASO score is then based on the *difference* between his description of the most-preferred and least-preferred coworkers, as illustrated in Figure 13.5.

Let us now see what scores on these scales reflect about a leader. A leader with a *high* LPC score is saying, in effect, that the person with whom he is *least* able to work on a common task still might be reasonably pleasant, friendly, intelligent, and so forth. In turn, a leader with a *low* LPC score is saying, in effect, that his least-preferred coworker is unpleasant, unfriendly, unintelligent, and so forth. In other words, the high-LPC leader thus tends to separate work performance and personality in evaluating people, whereas the low-LPC leader tends to link an individual's poor performance with undesirable personality characteristics. In effect, then, the ASO score is a measure of the leader's tendency to separate work performance from personality characteristics when describing his most-preferred and least-preferred coworkers. In practice, however, these two scores are highly correlated (about .80 to .90), so for practical purposes they are interchangeable, and as a result the LPC score is most typically used by itself.

Leadership and Employee Attitudes

It is logical to wonder what effect, if any, the different leadership styles and practices have on the attitudes of subordinates. Deferring for the moment the consideration of possible cause-and-effect relationships here, let us turn to the handful of studies that have shown a relationship between certain leadership characteristics and behavior on the one hand and attitudes of subordinates on the other—not only attitudes toward the

[26] Fiedler, *op. cit.*
[27] Osgood, C. E. The nature and measurement of meaning. *Psychological Bulletin,* 1952, **49**, 251–262.

(a) Part of scale for deriving LPC score

Think of the person *with whom you can work least well*. He may be someone you work with now, or he may be someone you knew in the past.

He does not have to be the person you like least well, but should be the person with whom you had the most difficulty in getting a job done. Describe this person as he appears to you.

Pleasant	8 7 6 5 4 3 2 1	Unpleasant
Friendly	8 7 6 5 4 3 2 1	Unfriendly
Rejecting	1 2 3 4 5 6 7 8	Accepting
Helpful	8 7 6 5 4 3 2 1	Frustrating
Unenthusiastic	1 2 3 4 5 6 7 8	Enthusiastic
Tense	1 2 3 4 5 6 7 8	Relaxed

(b) Illustration of computation of LPC and ASo scores (based on responses to 4 items)

Scale Item	Most-Preferred Coworker (MPC)	Least-Preferred Coworker (LPC)	Difference between MPC and LPC	Squared Difference
1 Pleasant-Unpleasant	7	3	4	16
2 Friendly-Unpleasant	4	4	0	0
3 Accepting-Rejecting	8	2	6	36
4 Helpful-Frustrating	6	5	1	1
		LPC = 14		$D^2 = 53$
				ASo $= \sqrt{D^2} = 7.28$

Note: A high ASo score indicates low similarity between opposites

FIG. 13.5 Illustration of part of one of the scales for deriving an LPC (least-preferred coworker) score, and of the method of deriving LPC and ASo (Assumed Similarity between opposites) scores. (*Adapted from* A theory of leadership effectiveness *by F. E. Fiedler, Figs. 3-1 and 3-2. Copyright © 1967 by McGraw-Hill, Inc. Used with permission of McGraw-Hill Book Company.*)

supervisor himself but also toward other features of the work situation. One such study, reported by Bowers and Seashore,[28] was a survey in which 873 life insurance personnel in forty different agencies completed various questionnaires that provided, among other things, for characterizing managers in terms of their four leadership dimensions mentioned above,

[28] Bowers & Seashore, *op. cit.*

and for quantifying the satisfaction of agents in terms of five areas of satisfaction— namely, the company, fellow agents, job, income, and the manager. For our present purposes, the correlations between certain of these will be given, in particular the correlations between the leadership measures of the managers and the satisfactions of agents with their managers and with the company.

Leadership Measure	Satisfaction of Agents with: Manager	Company
Support	.86	.31
Interaction facilitation	.78	.30
Goal emphasis	.31	.11
Work facilitation	.41	.31

It is apparent that the various dimensions of leadership behavior have some "effect" in the satisfaction of agents with their managers; this is especially the case with the dimension of support. And in turn, there seems to be some spillover effect from certain dimensions of leadership behavior to satisfaction with the company and—although this is not shown—to the other areas of satisfaction as well.

As another indication of the relationship between supervisory behavior as perceived by subordinates and the attitudes of the subordinates, Katz[29] surveyed five thousand employees in a large utility company. On the basis of these questionnaires, forty high-morale groups and forty low-morale groups were chosen for intensive study. During the interviews, employees were asked, "In what way does your immediate boss supervise you?" In reply they could indicate which of several behaviors were characteristic of their supervisors. For those in the high- and in the low-morale groups, the percentage of employees who characterized their supervisors in terms of each of the various behaviors was determined. Some of these results are given in Figure 13.6. It will be noted that although there were no appreciable differences in the percentages for the first three behaviors, the percentages for the high-morale groups were higher than for the low-morale groups in all other cases. These data are generally in accord with evidence from some other studies and imply that the reaction of subordinates to their supervisors tends to have a chain-reaction effect upon their attitudes toward other aspects of the work situation—in this case measures of their general morale.

A couple of notes of caution are in order in interpreting and evaluating data from such studies. In the first place, there are individual differences

[29] Katz, D. Morale and motivation in industry. In W. Dennis (Ed.), *Current trends in industrial psychology.* Pittsburgh: University of Pittsburgh, 1949, pp. 145–171.

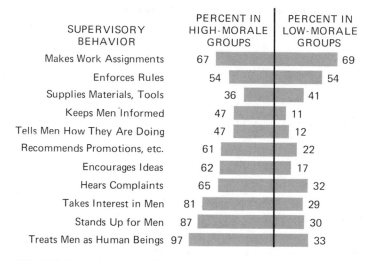

FIG. 13.6 Supervisory behavior as reported by subordinates of 40 high-morale and 40 low-morale groups in a public utility. Each bar represents the percent of individuals who attributed the behavior to their supervisors. (*Adapted from Katz, op. cit., and Likert, 1961, op. cit., p. 17.*)

in expressed attitudes. In the second place, the "situation" can have a significant relationship to the attitudes of groups. This is indicated by the results of a study by Vroom and Mann[30] in which they found significant differences within the same company in the reaction of employees to authoritarian leadership and to "equalitarian" leadership. Employees in small work groups which were characterized by a great deal of interaction among workers had more positive attitudes toward equalitarian leadership than did employees in large work groups in which there was less interaction; the latter were found to have more positive attitudes toward authoritarian leadership. Further, one needs to avoid the temptation to interpret the fact of a relationship as indicating cause and effect. But even though we should be very circumspect in interpreting relationships, the accumulating evidence inclines one a bit toward believing that in some circumstances the behavior of supervisors does influence the attitudes of subordinates.

Leadership and Employee Behavior

The probings of the relationship between leadership and its variations on the one hand, and employee performance and behavior on the other hand, have resulted in at least a moderately mixed bag, albeit the bag

[30] Vroom, V. H., & Mann, F. C. Leader authoritarianism and employee attitudes. *Personnel Psychology*, 1960, **13**, 125–140.

tends to be more loaded with positive indications than with negative. The potpourri of results probably is in part a function of the conviction that leadership is not the same thing in all circumstances; in fact it probably has tended to support this conviction. Although we cannot summarize the many studies of leadership, we will touch on a few such studies as examples. Here again, however, we should caution against uncritical assumptions that a statistically derived relationship implies cause and effect.

Life insurance study. One of the important earlier studies in this area was carried out by Katz, Maccoby, and Morse[31] in a large insurance company. In this study, various sections performing similar work were characterized as "high-producing" or "low-producing" on the basis of available production records. All of the supervisors of both the "high" and "low" sections were interviewed to determine: (1) a description of supervisory behavior, and (2) attitudes toward their own jobs, subordinates, superiors, the company, and company policies. It was then possible to determine what relationship there was, if any, between supervisory practices and attitudes on the one hand and section productivity on the other hand.

On the basis of the interviews the supervisors were classified as "employee centered" or "production centered." To help to characterize this distinction, following are the verbatim answers of two supervisors to a question regarding the most important part of the job:

> Supervisor X: "Well, there are two things—keeping the section running smoothly; keeping the clerks happy; keeping production up; making impartial assignments of work; making the proper decisions on some difficult cases involving some payments and maybe a premium that hadn't been paid before." (This supervisor was classified as "employee centered.")
> Supervisor Y: "Well, the most important part is to get the reports out. The biggest thing is to get the work out." (This supervisor was classified as "production centered.")

In a similar manner the supervisors were classified as "democratic" or "authoritarian," and as having "high or average judgment" or having "poor judgment." The results of comparisons on these classifications for the supervisors of the "high" and "low" sections are shown in Figure 13.7. This shows that the supervisors of the "high" sections tended to be "employee centered," "democratic," and to have "high or average judgment." The supervisors of the "low" sections, in turn, tended more to be "production centered," "authoritarian," and to have "poor judgment."

Manufacturing company. Another study that deals with the possible influence of the supervisor on the performance of the work group was

31 Katz, D., Maccoby, N., & Morse, N. C. *Productivity, supervision, and morale in an office situation.* Survey Research Center, Institute for Social Research, University of Michigan, December 1950.

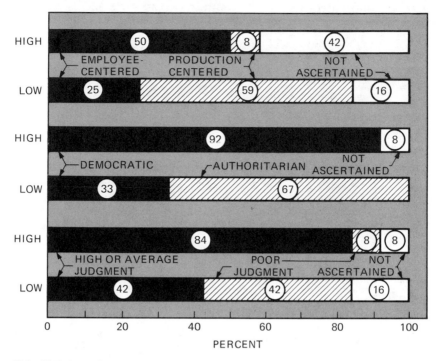

FIG. 13.7 Supervisor characteristics in relation to "high" and "low" producing work sections in insurance company. (*Adapted from Katz, Maccoby, and Morse, op. cit.*)

reported by Lawshe and Nagle.[32] In this survey, 208 employees in fourteen departments of a manufacturing company completed a questionnaire of twenty-one items relating to attitudes toward their immediate supervisor. The mean responses of the employee attitudes toward their supervisors in the fourteen departments were then related to the rated productivity of the departments, the results being shown in Figure 13.8. The correlation between the mean attitude scores and rated productivity of the fourteen departments was .86. If one interprets this as reflecting the relationship between group morale and productivity, one could speculate about what causes what. Does the supervisor influence the morale? And does the level of morale influence the level of productivity? Or does the supervisor's management of his department influence productivity, which in turn influences morale? These and other possible speculations are the kinds of considerations which give one pause in interpreting such relationships.

Consideration and structure in leadership behavior. Previous reference was made to the dimensions of consideration and structure as these were

[32] Lawshe, C. H., & Nagle, B. F. Productivity and attitude toward supervisor. *Journal of Applied Psychology,* 1953, **37,** 159–162.

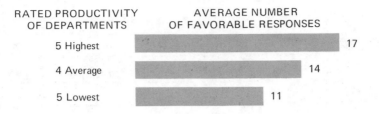

FIG. 13.8 Attitudes toward supervisor (based on responses to attitude questionnaire) of 208 employees in 14 departments of industrial plant in relation to rated productivity of departments. (*Adapted from Lawshe and Nagle,* op. cit.)

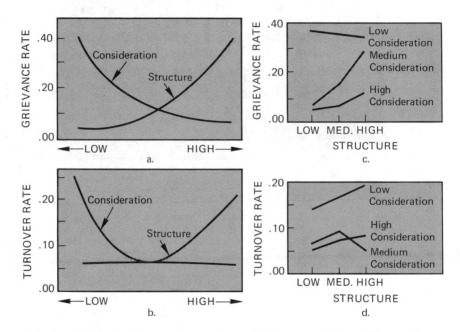

FIG. 13.9 Relationship between degree of *consideration* and *structure* of 57 supervisors and the grievance and turnover rates of their units. (*Adapted from Fleishman and Harris,* op. cit.)

characterized by Fleishman and Harris.[33] They present some data from their original study, in particular data from a motor truck manufacturing plant showing the relationship between the scores of fifty-seven supervisors on these two dimensions as related to grievance and turnover rates in their respective units. Some of the results are shown in Figure 13.9. It will be noticed in parts *a* and *b* that, in general, grievance rate and turnover rate increase with *low consideration* scores and with *high structure* scores. The form of the curves is of interest; in each case there is a range within which differences in consideration or structure make no difference.

[33] Fleishman & Harris, *op. cit.*

At the extremes (low consideration and high structure), however, there is a marked rise in both criteria.

Parts *c* and *d* of Figure 13.9 show the interactions. Note especially that *low consideration* is associated with high grievance and turnover rates regardless of the degree of structure. On the other hand, workers under high-consideration foremen (who establish a climate of mutual respect, rapport, and tolerance) are more likely to accept higher levels of structure. Thus, as implied by this study, consideration seems to be the more dominant factor.

However, a review by Korman[34] of a number of studies dealing with the constructs of consideration and structure casts some pretty cold water on the generality of their relevance to different criteria. This review encompassed studies in which these constructs were correlated with criterion measures of various types. Although some of the correlations were of respectable magnitude and in the predicted directions, many of them were very modest in their magnitude, and some were even in the opposite direction to that predicted. Korman then concluded that little is now known as to how these variables may predict work group performance or about the conditions which affect such predictions. One must concur with Korman in concluding that the overall results of the several studies are not very impressive. But at the same time, one cannot discount the fact that in *some situations* the constructs of consideration and structure are related to organizationally meaningful criteria. The intriguing, still-dangling question relates to the situational variables that may account for the varied patterns of results.

Degree of supervision. One particular aspect of leadership behavior that seems generally to be associated with productivity of work groups is the degree of supervision—that is, the closeness with which people are supervised and the freedom they have in such matters as work pace. In a study reported by Likert,[35] for example, thirty-one departments of a service organization were divided into three groups in terms of the mean degree of "freedom" expressed by the workers. Figure 13.10 shows for these three groups the number of departments that were above and below average in productivity; this figure indicates a distinct relationship, with the departments in which the men felt "most" free generally being above average in productivity. Somewhat similar results were reported on the basis of the studies by Katz, Maccoby, and Morse,[36] and by Katz, Maccoby, Gurin, and Floor.[37]

---

[34] Korman, A. K. "Consideration," "initiating structure," and organizational criteria—a review. *Personnel Psychology,* 1966, **19**(4), 349–361.

[35] Likert (1961), *op. cit.,* p. 20.

[36] Katz, Maccoby, & Morse, *op. cit.*

[37] Katz, D., Maccoby, N., Gurin, G., & Floor, L. *Productivity, supervision, and morale among railroad workers.* Ann Arbor, Michigan: Institute for Social Research, University of Michigan, 1951.

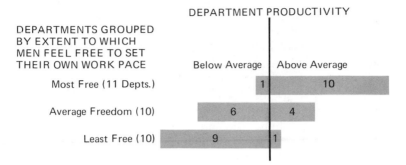

FIG. 13.10 Relationship between freedom service men feel to set own work pace and the productivity of their departments. (*From* New patterns of management *by Rensis Likert, p. 20. Copyright © 1961 by McGraw-Hill, Inc. Used with permission of McGraw-Hill Book Company.*)

Fiedler's contingency model and performance. In his studies of leadership, Fiedler[38] found that his LPC measure of leadership style was sometimes positively correlated with group performance and sometimes negatively. In trying to tease some order out of his mixed results, he found the following interesting relationships based on the combinations of three variables:

1. Leader-member relations (divided between good and moderately poor)
2. Task structure (divided between structured and unstructured)
3. Leader position power (divided between strong and weak).

The combinations of these three variables, each of which was divided into two categories, provide eight combinations that Fiedler referred to as octants. On theoretical grounds these, in turn, were ordered in terms of the degree of favorability or unfavorability for the leader. Then, on the basis of a number of laboratory studies of group performance, he had sixty-three correlations between his LPC measure and group performance. These, in turn, were arrayed in relation to the eight octants to form the pattern shown in Figure 13.11, which shows the correlations for each of the eight octants, with an obviously bow-shaped line through the median correlations.

Let us now try to see what this pattern means. To begin with, positive correlations of LPC with group effectiveness generally indicate the group effectiveness is best with "relationship-oriented" leaders and visa versa. And negative correlations generally indicate that group effectiveness is best with "task-oriented" leaders. The figure then indicates that the appropriateness of the leadership style for maximizing group performance is contingent upon the favorableness of the group-task situation. Fiedler refers to this as a *contingency model* inasmuch as group performance is

[38] Fiedler, *op. cit.,* Chaps. 9 & 10.

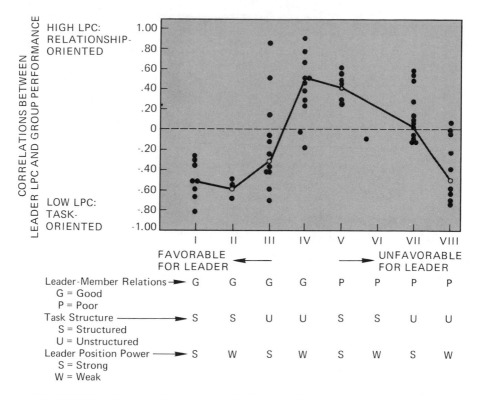

FIG. 13.11 Correlations between leaders' LPC scores (least-preferred co-worker) and group effectiveness for various levels (octaves) of leadership favorableness-to-unfavorableness, as characterized by various combinations of leader-member relations, task structure, and leader position power. (*From* A theory of leadership effectiveness *by F. E. Fiedler, Fig. 9-1. Copyright* © *1967 by McGraw-Hill, Inc. Used with permission of McGraw-Hill Book Company.*)

contingent upon these aspects of the situation. In discussing this model he points out that by and large it fits our everyday experiences. In a very favorable leadership condition in which the leader has power, informal backing, and a relatively well-structured task, the group is ready to be directed and the group members expect to be told what to do. (He cites the case of an airline captain in its final landing approach, in which the crew would not be expected to "discuss" how to land.) In an unfavorable leadership situation, one also would expect a task-oriented leader to be more effective than a relationship-oriented leader; here Fiedler refers to the old army adage that it is better in an emergency that the leader make a wrong decision than no decision at all.

On the other hand, Fielder makes the point that a relationship-oriented attitude seems to be more effective than a task-oriented attitude in situations which are only moderately favorable or moderately unfavorable for the leader (such as when an accepted leader faces an ambiguous, nebulous task, or when the task is structured but the leader is not well accepted). Other combinations of circumstances could likewise be given as illustrations. Fiedler[39] also offers some evidence from certain industrial studies that he interprets as confirming his model. On the basis of his studies, then, Fiedler argues that one can speak of an effective leader only in terms of the particular features of the leadership situation.

His model has a certain intuitive appeal, for it accounts for some of the otherwise apparently conflicting indications from some other studies. However, there have been some rather sharp barbs directed toward the model that should cause one to hang a "tentative" label on it at the present time, rather than accepting it as the gospel truth.

Work-Group Linking Pins

It is an article of faith, supported in part by empirical evidence, that organizational effectiveness depends to some extent on the way in which groups at various levels within the organizational hierarchy are integrated. In this connection, Likert[40] has postulated the *principle of supportive relationships*. This principle implies that an organization will function best when its personnel function as members of highly effective work groups with high performance goals. Starting from this base, Likert proposes that management should deliberately endeavor not only to develop such effective groups, but also to link them into an overall organization by means of people who hold overlapping group membership; the superior of one group is a subordinate in the next group, and so on. This overlapping relationship is illustrated in Figure 13.12; Likert refers to it as a "linking pin" function. Partial support for this type of relationship comes from studies by Pelz[41] in which it was found that subordinates expect their superiors to be able to exercise upward influence when dealing with problems which affect the workers themselves; when the supervisor's influence is perceived as being limited, the subordinates are likely to have unfavorable reactions.

Needless to say, it is not possible to "legislate" through policy pronouncements that a supervisor will have "upward influence," or that a supervisor will become an effective member of both the group he supervises and the one above. But even though those consequences cannot be brought about by management action, it is possible for management to create the kind of situation in which such developments can take place and are encouraged.

---

39 *Ibid.,* Chap. 10.
40 Likert (1961), *op. cit.,* Chap. 8.
41 Pelz, D. C. Influence, a key to effective leadership in the first-line supervisor. *Personnel,* 1952, **11**, 3–11.

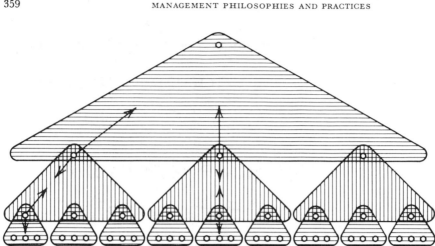

(THE ARROWS INDICATE THE LINKING PIN FUNCTION)

FIG. 13.12 The "linking pin" concept of group organization. The supervisor of one group is also a member of the next higher group, and so on. Communication links are implied within each of the work groups. (*From* New patterns of management *by Rensis Likert, p. 113. Copyright © 1961 by McGraw-Hill, Inc. Used with permission of McGraw-Hill Book Company.*)

This can be accomplished through organization and policy determinations, but perhaps more through the creation of a climate that encourages such developments.

chapter fourteen

Employee-Management
Relationships

The management of an organization can have a dominant influence on the prevailing "tone" of the management-employee relationships, in part by reason of its own prevailing general philosophies and human relations practices. We will now examine a few particular aspects of employee-management relationships, for it is to some extent via the factors we will be considering here that prevailing "philosophies" of management are implemented.

EMPLOYEE PARTICIPATION

In recent years much has been said—pro and con—about the participation of employees in some of the decisions relating to the work situation. Viteles,[1] for example, summarizes the conclusions reported from some of the research on employee participation, as follows: "... major outcome of such

[1] Viteles, M. S. *Motivation and morale in industry.* New York: Norton, 1953, p. 164.

research is the conclusion that *employee participation in decision-making* in a *democratic atmosphere* created by 'permissive' leadership, facilitates the development of 'internalized' motivation, and serves to raise the levels of the employee production and morale."

On the other hand, there are those who raise words of caution about viewing participation as a panacea for all of the ailments of organizations. Lowin,[2] for example, expresses the view that any simplistic hypothesis about participative decision making (PDM) is too gross to be proven or disproven. He therefore urges that future research about this should be focused on the possible mediating conditions that might shape the effects of such participation. Recognizing full well that participation in decision processes in organizations has its limits—although as yet we know not what those limits are—we cannot but be impressed by the fact that some form of participation in some circumstances has resulted in very respectable benefits both to the organizations and to the personnel. Unfortunately, we cannot yet specify those circumstances in which such benefits might be expected to accrue.

Types of Employee Participation

Participation in decision making within an organization can take place in various ways. For example, it can be either formal or informal. Formal participation can be of various types. For example, in some organizations there are formal plans for labor-management cooperation that can provide the mechanism for genuine participation. In the survey of 201 plans reported by Dale,[3] for example, there were twenty-two areas of cooperation. Among the most commonly mentioned areas of cooperative planning were accident prevention, elimination of waste and defective work, furthering labor understanding of policies, attendance, employee insurance plans, quality control, and job evaluation. On the other hand, much employee participation in decision processes occurs in very informal, unstructured ways such as in interpersonal relations between superiors and subordinates, either as individuals or groups.

Further, employee participation in decision making can be a practice that is imbedded in the day-to-day job activities of employees through the process of supervisors encouraging subordinates to take on additional decision-making responsibilities, or it can be practiced through group interaction that is also stimulated by supervisors.

[2] Lowin, A. Participative decision-making: A model, literature critique, and prescription for research. *Organizational Behavior and Human Performance,* 1968, 3(1), 68–106.

[3] Dale, E. *Greater productivity through labor-management cooperation.* New York: American Management Association, Research Report No. 14, 1949.

The Nature of Participation

In discussing employee participation (whether formal or informal, individual or group), we are reminded of the fact that Likert[4] has characterized his System 4 (discussed in Chapter 13) as *participative group*, thus implying that the management strategy appropriate to this system is the most effective. But let us recall the distinction he made between what he refers to as "committee" decisions of the "wishy-washy" or "common-denominator" nature, and the practice implied by his System 4 in which the supervisor is responsible for building his subordinates into a group which makes the best decisions and carries them out well—but in which the supervisor is accountable for these decisions.

This same distinction comes through when Maier,[5] in discussing group decision making, makes the following distinctions between what group decision making is not (or should not be) and what it is (or should be):

Group Decision Is Not	*Group Decision Is*
1. Abandoning control of the situation.	A way of controlling through leadership rather than force.
2. A disregard of discipline.	A way of group discipline through social pressure.
3. A way of giving each individual what he wants.	A way of being fair to the job and all members of a group.
4. A way of manipulating people.	A way of reconciling conflicting attitudes.
5. A way of selling the supervisor's ideas to a group.	Permitting the group to jell on the idea it thinks will best solve a problem.
6. Sugar-coated autocracy.	A way of letting facts and feelings operate.
7. A matter of collecting votes.	Pooled thinking.
8. Consultative supervision in which mere advice is sought.	Cooperative problem-solving.
9. A way of turning the company over to employees.	A way of giving each person a chance to participate in things that concern him in his work situation.
10. Something anyone can do if he wishes.	A method that requires skill and a respect for other people.

As Likert and Maier see it, then, participation in decision making should not degenerate into unstructured general discourses that result in common-denominator "decisions," but rather should consist of the process

---

[4] Likert, R. *The human organization.* New York: McGraw-Hill, 1967.
[5] Maier, N. R. F. *Principles of human relations.* New York: John Wiley, 1952, p. 30.

of capitalizing on the experiences and ideas of others and on the increased motivation that this might bring about.

Possible Advantages of Participation

The primary theme running through discussions of the value of participation in decision making is that of motivation. In normal circumstances people become ego-involved in the decisions they have made as individuals, or in the making of which they have participated in groups. Such increased motivation, it is argued, might in turn lead to other outcomes, such as the following, suggested by Tannenbaum and Massarik;[6] (1) a higher rate of output and increased quality; (2) a reduction in turnover, absenteeism, and tardiness; (3) a reduction in the number of grievances and more peaceful manager-subordinate and manager-union relations; (4) a greater readiness to accept change; (5) a greater ease in the management of subordinates; and (6) the improved quality of managerial decisions. Whether, or to what extent, these possible benefits might accrue presumably depends upon the interaction of a variety of conditions and situational variables.

Conditions for Effective Participation

There is no "formula" for ensuring effective participation and its possible benefits; there are, however, certain conditions that are prerequisites for the process, even though they do not ensure its success. The first such prerequisites include certain psychological conditions associated with the individuals, some of which are set forth by Tannenbaum and Massarik,[7] as follows: (1) the subordinate must be capable of becoming psychologically involved in the participational activities; (2) he must favor the activity; (3) he must see the relevance to his personal life pattern of the thing being considered; and (4) he must be able to express himself to his own satisfaction. The other (nonpersonal) conditions include the following: (1) time availability (if a decision is urgent, time may not permit group decision making); (2) rational economics (the decision must be one that is economically sound); (3) subordinate security (his participation must not adversely affect his status or role); (4) manager-subordinate stability (the process must not threaten to undermine the formal authority of the manager, or lead to doubt about the competence of the manager); (5) provision for communication channels through which employees may take

[6] Tannenbaum, R., & Massarik, F. Participation by subordinates. In R. Tannenbaum, I. R. Weschler, & F. Massarik, *Leadership and organization.* New York: McGraw-Hill, 1961, Chapter 7.

[7] *Ibid.*

part in the process; and (6) education of the participants regarding the function and purpose of the enterprise.

In connection with group participation, Mann, Indik, and Vroom[8] report some data that may have some implications regarding the conditions that are conducive to group participation in problem solving. These data come from an intensive study of 1,158 drivers and 288 sorters employed by a parcel delivery service in twenty-eight different locations. The researchers found that the groups that described their supervisors as higher (as opposed to lower) on "participativeness" both sensed less pressure and tension and had higher levels of work-situation satisfaction.

Examples of Employee Participation

A few studies will be summarized to give some impression of the "effects" of employee participation. Although these reported studies reflect substantial benefits from employee participation programs, it is probably unwise to assume that such benefits invariably would result from such programs.

Garment manufacturing company. One of the classic studies of employee participation was carried out at a pajama manufacturing company, the Harwood Manufacturing Corporation, and reported by Marrow[9] and by Coch and French.[10] Because of changes in style trends, it became necessary to change the design of garments being made; such changes in turn necessitate changes in work assignments and usually result in reduced piece-rate earnings until the operators learn their new tasks. Such disruptions cause the operators to resist changes in work assignments. Because circumstances made job changes necessary, an opportunity existed for an experiment in group participation. In this experiment, four groups of sewing-machine operators were formed, all four groups being matched for the difficulty of the new jobs, for the amount of change in their jobs, and for the level of productivity before the experiment. Three variations in the manner of dealing with these groups were used in the experiment, as follows:

> *Control group.* This group was changed to the new jobs by the normal factory procedure. They were given an explanation of why a change in job methods was necessary, what the new job would be like, and what the new piece rates would be.

8 Mann, F. C., Indik, B. P., & Vroom, V. H. *The productivity of work groups.* Ann Arbor: Survey Research Center, Institute for Social Research, University of Michigan, 1963.

9 Marrow, A. Industrial psychology pays in this plant. *Modern Industry,* July 15, 1948, **16**(1), 67ff.

10 Coch, L., & French, J. R. P., Jr. Overcoming resistance to change. *Human Relations,* 1948, **1**, 512–532.

Experimental group 1. A moderate degree of democratic participation was used with this group. They received more information and explanation about the need for change, and they were provided the opportunity to choose representatives who, in turn, participated in designing the new job, setting the new piece rate, and later in training the remaining members of the group. The feeling of participation on the part of the group was such that they spoke of the new job and piece rates as "our job" and "our piece rates."

Experimental groups 2 and 3. These groups participated directly in designing the job and setting the new piece rates, having a greater degree of participation than did experimental group 1, which "participated" through chosen representatives.

Records of performance of these groups are shown in Figure 14.1. The "units per hour" is an index based on standard units of work determined by time and motion study methods. The results were quite dramatic. It can be seen for the period of time before the change that all groups were approximately equal. After the change the control group dropped to an index of about 50—the usual occurrence after such a change. Many of those in this group quit their jobs. Group 1, which had participation through chosen representatives, dropped to begin with, but consistently recovered over a period of time, ultimately achieving an index of about 65. Groups 2 and 3, which had direct participation, experienced practically

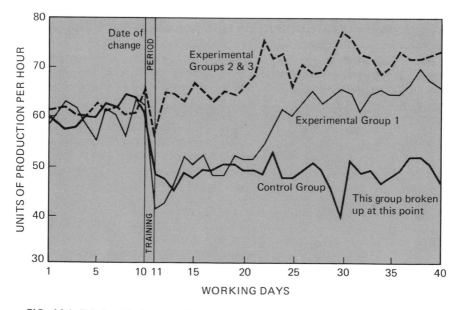

FIG. 14.1 Relationship between degree of participation and work performance of four groups of sewing machine operators. See text for description of participation of groups. (*Adapted from Marrow,* op. cit.)

no drop and continued to increase their performance until they finally levelled off at an index in the low 70s. Not only was the change in productivity after change proportional to the degree of participation of the three groups, but the turnover rates and amount of aggression expressed against management were inversely proportional to the degree of participation.

At a later point in time the company embarked on an extensive modernization program in three of its plants, and in this situation it also encouraged employee participation through group meetings in various aspects of the changes to be effected.[11] A comparison of the before and after productivity is given below for the three plants for "items" A and B (types of garments):

Item	Plant	Average Production Index Base Period	Average Production Index One Year Later
A	1	79	76
A	3	79	80
B	2	67	75
B	3	69	75

The productivity for item A remained about the same, and that for item B increased by about 10 percent. Although these changes are not very impressive, there were other reported benefits, such as reduced overall costs of production, improved quality, reduced grievances, and no increase in turnover (which normally occurs in such circumstances). The collective results were highly gratifying to management.

Telephone repair crew. In connection with situations in which more informal participation has been used, Maier[12] cites the case of a telephone repair crew consisting of twelve men. The number of repair "visits" varies with the types of repairs to be performed, but these differences tend to average out over a period of time. The average for the crew in question for a six-month period had been between eight and nine per day, as compared with the company average of 10.8 visits per day.

In part because of their below-average performance, the foreman held a group meeting to ask his men whether they would care to discuss, as a group, any ideas on how their work could be better coordinated, and any obstacles and difficulties that they thought might be overcome. In their discussions the men made certain suggestions, such as in handling repeat calls (by having the same repairman go back), and in designating each man to be responsible for a particular area (in order to reduce travel time and to reduce "subsequents," which are second or third calls from customers before a repairman arrives).

11 French, J. R. P. Jr., Ross, I. C., Kirby, S., Nelson, J. R., & Smith, P. Employee participation in a program of industrial change. *Personnel* 1958, 35, 16–29.
12 Maier, *op. cit.*, pp. 225–228.

During the next two-and-a-half years the effectiveness of this plan reflected itself in the records of the work group. Some of these records are summarized in Figure 14.2. The increase in the number of calls from 8.5 to 12.5 per day, and the reductions in *repeats* and *subsequents* suggest very strongly the effectiveness of group participation in decision making in this situation.

Participation in pay incentive plans. As another example of employee participation, Lawler and Hackett[13] tell about an interesting experiment carried out with nine groups of part-time employees of a small company that provides building maintenance services on a contract basis. The groups clean the buildings at night, each group being relatively autonomous. The groups had been characterized by high absenteeism and turnover rates. The experiment was concerned with the possible effects on absenteeism of employee participation in developing an incentive plan. In the experiment the work groups were allocated to the following experimental conditions:

1. Participative groups (3). One or both investigators met each group to help the employees develop a proposed incentive plan. As finally instituted, all three plans provided cash bonuses of about $2.50 per week for perfect attendance.

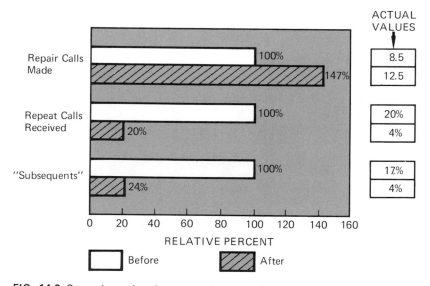

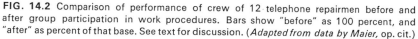

FIG. 14.2 Comparison of performance of crew of 12 telephone repairmen before and after group participation in work procedures. Bars show "before" as 100 percent, and "after" as percent of that base. See text for discussion. (*Adapted from data by Maier,* op. cit.)

[13] Lawler, E. E., III, & Hackman, J. R. Impact of employee participation in the development of pay incentive plans: A field experiment. *Journal of Applied Psychology,* 1969, 55(6), 467–471.

2. Imposed groups. Two of the same plans developed by the participating groups were "imposed" on a sample of other groups.
3. Control groups. In the case of two control groups, the investigators talked to the groups about incentive plans and about the problems of absenteeism and turnover; in the other two groups no "changes" were made and no group meetings held.

A later comparison was made of the attendance of the various groups in terms of percentage of "scheduled" hours actually spent at work. Figure 14.3 shows these data for twelve weeks before, and sixteen weeks after, for the "participation" groups and the "imposed" groups. It can be seen that the attendance record of the participation groups increased during the sixteen weeks after the plan went into effect. No such change occurred with the imposed groups (or in the case of the control groups, for which data are not shown).

Quality of Individual and Group Decisions

"Participation" in the affairs of an organization—especially in the decision-making processes—can be on an "individual" basis (by operationally providing the opportunity for individuals to take on increased responsibilities within the framework of their own jobs), or on the basis of group interaction. Likert's[14] concept of System 4 (Participative group) presumably embraces both of these forms of participation.

In those circumstances in which decisions are to be made or problems solved by a group, it is logical to be curious as to the quality of the decisions or solutions arrived at. In a research approach to the study of the "quality" of the solutions of problems generated by individuals and groups, Taylor, Berry, and Block[15] had ninety-six college students participate in

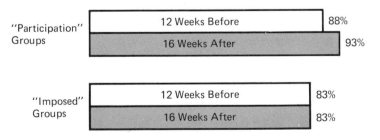

FIG. 14.3 Attendance (as percent of scheduled hours) of groups of building service workers under same pay incentive plan (1) who had participated in development of plan, and (2) on whom the same plan was "imposed." (*Adapted from Lawler and Hackman, op. cit., Figs. 1 and 2.*)

14 Likert, *op. cit.*
15 Taylor, D. W., Berry, P. C., & Block, C. H. Does group participation when brainstorming facilitate or inhibit creative thinking? *Administration Science Quarterly*, 1958, **3**, 23–47.

three problem-solving exercises; in each instance the subjects were asked to come up with as many "solutions" as possible. (In one of the problems, for example, the subjects were asked to suggest what steps could be taken to get more European tourists to come to this country.) Forty-eight of the students were formed into twelve four-man brainstorming groups. The other forty-eight actually worked individually, but were considered to form twelve "nominal" four-man groups for later comparison purposes. Performance was measured in terms of number of suggested solutions. The mean numbers of unique solutions produced by the real groups and the nominal groups are given below:

Groups	Problems A	B	C	Mean of Means
Real	7.5	17.7	7.3	10.8
Nominal (individuals)	13.6	28.1	17.5	19.8

In this experiment the mean number of solutions pooled from four people *working independently* was nearly twice that of four people *working as a group*. In addition, in an additional phase of the analysis, it was found that the "quality" of the solutions of the real groups was significantly less than that of the nominal groups. It was concluded from the study that group participation tends to inhibit creative thinking.

In another investigation, Campbell[16] prevailed upon eighty second- and third-line managers in a public utility organization to participate in a somewhat similar experiment. Here again, subjects working on a particular problem *individually* served as "nominal" groups, and subjects engaging in group problem solving served as "real" groups. The scoring of the solutions was carried out by three individuals (including the investigator). A summary of the mean "scores" is given below:

	Mean Score
Nominal groups	8.1
Real groups	3.9

Although these specific studies imply a superiority for individual solutions, the collective evidence is by no means conclusive. Maier[17] postulates certain assets and liabilities of group problem solving as well as certain forces that can operate either as assets or liabilities, depending on the skills of the members, and especially those of the leader.

[16] Campbell, J. P. Individual versus group problem solving in an industrial sample. *Journal of Applied Psychology,* 1968, **52**(3), 205–210.

[17] Maier, N. R. F. Assets and liabilities in group problem solving: The need for an integrative function. *Psychological Review,* July 1967, **74**(4), 239–249.

Discussion

In considering various forms of participation in the management of organizations, we should keep in mind Wilensky's[18] observation, based on an analysis of a number of studies of employee participation, that "participation" has had both positive and neutral, or negative, effects in workplaces that are both union or nonunion, big and small, prosperous and marginal, and among employees of various social classes.

When contemplating such mixed evidence, however, let us not lose sight of the possible *purposes* of participation by asking ourselves these questions: Is the purpose (in any given situation) that of arriving at the best solution (or decision) ; or is it that of enhancing the motivation of the participants? In terms of the technical quality of solutions and decisions, the evidence is somewhat ambiguous, but probably tends to tilt the scales somewhat in favor of individual decisions, at least under many normal circumstances. This finding tends to argue for "participation" on an individual basis by placing increased responsibility for problem solving and decision making upon *those individuals who have the technical competence to handle these assignments*. On the other hand, if the intent is to enhance the motivation of the individuals implementing the solution, group participation probably has a distinct advantage, as Maier[19] implies. It has been demonstrated time and again that people are more willing to accept decisions (including those that involve change) if they have somehow participated in the decision or problem-solving process. In some such circumstances the "quality" of some of the solutions generated by the group may not be technically as "good" as the quality of solutions that might have been generated individually, but the enhanced motivation of people that results from participation in group decision making might in turn be reflected in terms of such criteria as job performance or reduced turnover.

WORK GROUPS

In various contexts in the previous discussions references have been made to the implications of work groups in industrial and other organizations. The interaction of people within a group can have a powerful influence on the behavior of the individuals within the group.

Differences in Group Behavior

As pointed out by Wilensky[20] and others, the group can influence the behavior of those in the group in various ways, such as by the practice

---

[18] Wilensky, H. Human relations in the workplace: An appraisal of some recent research. In *Research in human relations,* New York: Harper & Row, 1957.

[19] Maier (1967), *op. cit.*

[20] Wilensky, *op. cit.*

of group restriction of work output. In discussing output restrictions, Drucker[21] expresses the opinion that open restrictions on output provided under the provisions of restrictive union rules and "featherbedding" policies are "only the part of the iceberg that is above the water. Much more important are the invisible, unwritten, informal restrictions decreed by the custom and common law of every plant," as reflected in the tacit setting of production quotas by the work group which a worker would be "ill-advised" to exceed.

The more positive effects of work-group unity are revealed by various studies in which it has been demonstrated that there is a relationship between feelings of group cohesiveness and increases in work performance, or other desirable changes in employee behavior, such as reduction of absenteeism. In a study of employees in an insurance company reported by Katz, Maccoby, and Morse,[22] for example, the employees in the high-producing sections were more strongly "identified" with their groups than were employees in the low-producing sections. There was also evidence from the electric power company investigation reported by Mann and

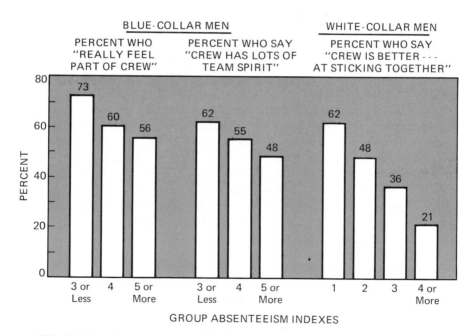

FIG. 14.4 Relationship between absence indexes and attitudes of employees toward their work groups in electric power company. (*Adapted from Mann and Baumgartel,* op. cit.)

[21] Drucker, P. F. *The new society.* New York: Harper & Row, 1950, p. 83.
[22] Katz, D., Maccoby, N., & Morse, N. C. *Productivity, supervision and morale in an office situation.* Ann Arbor: Institute for Social Research, Survey Research Center, University of Michigan, December 1950.

Baumgartel[23] of a distinct relationship between group unity and absenteeism. Some evidence of this type is shown in Figure 14.4. In particular, this shows the percentage of employees who expressed favorable attitudes toward their work groups in relationship to the absenteeism averages of their groups. The patterns of relationship are somewhat similar for both blue-collar and white-collar men; in work groups with high absence rates there were fewer who expressed feelings of "group unity" than in work groups with low absence rates.

Group Cohesion

The cohesiveness of work groups varies greatly from group to group. The factors that contribute to cohesiveness, however, are a bit obscure, as reported by Seashore[24] on the basis of a survey among employees of a machine manufacturing company. No appreciable relationships were found between age, educational level, and "cohesiveness" among the members of work groups, although there were indications that cohesiveness was somewhat higher among smaller groups and among groups with longer length of service shared by the members.

The participation in group activities by individuals is attributed by Stogdill[25] to the "expectancy" of the individuals, which he defines as a "readiness for reinforcement." He suggests, further, that it is a function of the individual's *drive,* of the *desirability* to him of the possible outcome (the "reinforcement") of his participation in the group, and of the *probability* of that outcome. The nature of the expectancy for individuals obviously varies with their individual value systems. One person might be active in a group because it bolsters his sagging ego, another because it offers the opportunity to exert authority, another because he wants to work off his aggressions, another because of the social interchange. It would be expected, Stogdill points out, that individuals tend to seek affiliation with other persons who are perceived to have the same value systems as their own—and who might then "reinforce" their own value systems.

Group Influence upon Individuals

Members of a group are subject to pressures from the group to conform to certain standards, patterns of behavior, or opinions. This pressure

23 Mann, F., & Baumgartel, H. *Absences and employee attitudes in an electric power company.* Ann Arbor: Survey Research Center, University of Michigan. December 1952.

24 Seashore, S. E. *Group cohesiveness in the industrial work group.* Ann Arbor: Institute for Social Research, Survey Research Center, University of Michigan, 1954.

25 Stogdill, R. M. *Individual behavior and group achievement.* New York: Oxford University Press, 1959.

toward conformity has been well documented by various people,[26] and we need not give supporting evidence here. Such pressures apply, however, in varied types of group situations, such as in school, political life, social situations, and work groups. In connection with group pressures, Festinger[27] provides evidence to suggest that the stronger a member's attraction to a group, the greater his tendency to conform to group norms and the greater the pressure that the group can apply to an individual without driving him out of the group. The ways and means of pressuring members of a group to conform to group norms vary in subtlety and degree. These pressures can be positive (rewarding conformity) or negative (punishing deviation). A verbal jibe or a cold shoulder can do much to bring a deviating member of a group back into line. It is a durable individual who can withstand the pressures of a group for which he has a strong affinity.

In an industrial organization the pressures of the various groups upon their members can bring about behaviors that are compatible with the goals of the organization or that are at odds with such goals. These differences in group behavior, then, stem basically from the nature of the group goals. Where group goals tend to correspond with those of the organization, the behavior of those in the group will tend to contribute toward the objectives of the organization, and vice versa.

The effects of group pressures upon work performance of employees are implied in some of the data resulting from the study by Seashore[28] mentioned above, as shown in Figure 14.5. Keeping in mind that the vertical scale reflects *variability* in production, we can see that there is *less* variability *within* the groups that are high in cohesiveness than within those that are low. Seashore suggests that this can be regarded as confirmation of the existence of more effective group standards in the high cohesive groups. But we also see that there is more variability *between* groups (from group to group) among groups that are high in cohesiveness than among those that are low. This pattern suggests that the high cohesive groups differ substantially in their production "norms"; in some instances high cohesiveness may function in a positive direction, and in other instances in a negative direction.

Implications for Management

As indicated above, the potential effectiveness of a group within an organization in influencing the behavior of individuals varies with the degree of cohesiveness of the group. The possibility that group influence

---

[26] *Ibid.*, pp. 291–335.

[27] Festinger ,L. A theory of social comparison processes. *Human Relations,* 1954, **7**, 117–140.

[28] Seashore, *op. cit.*, pp. 67 and 71.

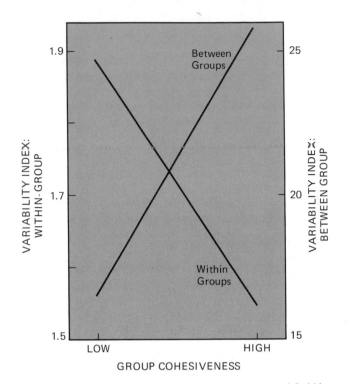

FIG. 14.5 Relationship between group cohesiveness and "within-group" and "between-group" variability in production. The scale reflects relatively the "variability" in production *within* groups and *between* groups. (*Adapted from Seashore,* op. cit., *Fig. 6 and Fig. 8.*)

will be contrary to the interests of management has tended to cause the managements of some concerns to view dimly the development of strong, cohesive groups within the organization. Granting such risks, and recognizing that there may be those who would argue with this point of view, there seems to be adequate justification for proposing that one objective of a human relations program is to develop a situation in which the employees have a strong sense of group unity, and in which they have goals in common with those of the management. In fact, Worthy[29] expresses the opinion that "One of the measures of the effectiveness of an organization is the extent to which the aims of the informal organization correspond with those of the formal." Continuing in this vein he makes the following statement:

> The manager's problem is not that of "bending the informal work group to the purposes of the enterprise." Rather, it is so conducting the enterprise that the

[29] Worthy, J. C. Comments on Mr. Wilensky's chapter. In *Research in industrial human relations, op. cit.,* pp. 52–53.

relationship between its purposes and those of the primary work group are clearly apparent.

To say this is easier than to do it, and there are no cookbook rules that can be followed. The mutual unity-of-purpose of an organization and of the groups within it is typically the end product of many factors, including some of those mentioned above, such as the nature of the leadership, the opportunity for participation, as well as all of the other practices that make up a good personnel program.

Formation of congenial work groups. Although much can be done by a supervisor in building a group spirit with an existing work group, sometimes there is an opportunity to form new work groups of individuals who indicate that they would like to work together.

A case of this type is reported by Van Zelst[30] in connection with a construction job in which rows of identical houses were being built. Groups of carpenters and bricklayers were given the opportunity to develop mutually acceptable work groups. It was possible, then, to compare the labor costs, material costs, and turnover rates on a "before" and "after" basis. These comparisons (given below) all reflect improvements following the formation of the new work groups:

	Before	*After*
Labor cost index	36.7	32.2
Materials cost index	33.0	31.0
Turnover index	3.1	.3

COMMUNICATIONS

The emphasis on "communications" which is so prevalent today almost brings on a sense of ennui. Discounting some of the platitudinous pronouncements about communications, however, we must recognize that the communication function is undoubtedly one of the most important processes of management. Communication has been defined by Brown[31] as the "process of transmitting ideas or thoughts from one person to another . . . for the purpose of creating understanding in the thinking of the person receiving the communication." This emphasis on *understanding* focuses attention on the *effectiveness* of communications rather than simply on the mechanics of transmitting information, for the processes of talking to unwill-

[30] Van Zelst, R. H. Sociometrically selected work teams increase production. *Personnel Psychology,* 1952, 5, 175–185.
[31] Brown, C. A. Communication means understanding. *Personnel Administration,* January-February 1958, 12–16.

ing ears or passing out pieces of paper do not automatically ensure that the "message" gets through to the person or group for whom it is intended.

In discussing the importance of communication in management, Drucker[32] makes the following statement:

> The manager has a specific tool: information. He does not "handle" people; he motivates, guides, organizes people to do their own work. His tool—his only tool—to do all this is the spoken or written word or the language of numbers. No matter whether the manager's job is engineering, accounting, or selling, his effectiveness depends on his ability to listen and to read, on his ability to speak and to write. He needs skill in getting his thinking across to other people as well as skill in finding out what other people are after.

These observations by Brown and Drucker imply two objectives of communications in management. In the first place, communications are needed to convey information necessary for ongoing operations (information about policies, procedures, decisions, work schedules, and so forth). And in the second place, communications can have an effect (for the better, it is to be hoped) on the attitudes of people in the organization.

The Nature of Organizational Communications

Communications within an organization can be characterized in various ways.[33] Some communications are *formal,* in the sense that they are "official," others are *informal.* Further, communications can flow in various directions, such as *downward, upward,* or *horizontally* through the organization. In addition, communications can be either *written* or *oral.* Aside from the nature of the communication as such, the communication process also can be characterized in terms of different features of communication networks, including: the size of the loop (that is, the portion of an organization on the communication circuit); whether there is repetition or "filtered" modification of the circuit (that is, whether a communication is modified at different levels or is transmitted in its original form); the feedback or closure character (that is, whether there is some provision for return feedback from the transmission); the efficiency of communication nets; and the "fit" between the communication circuit and systemic functioning (that is, whether the circuit includes all relevant individuals, but not others).

Obviously, there are many facets of a communications system that can enhance or reduce the effectiveness of the communications in serving their

[32] Drucker, P. F. *The practice of management.* New York: Harper & Row, 1954, p. 346.

[33] Katz, D., & Kahn, R. L. *The social psychology of organizations.* New York: John Wiley, 1966.

intended functions. Because we cannot cover the entire topic here, we will discuss only a few selected aspects of it.

Comparison of Methods in Transmitting Information

Among the different methods of organizational communication, certain methods have rather obvious advantages and disadvantages. Written communications, for example, have the aura of authority, usually are accurate, can be stored permanently, and can be transmitted to all persons for whom they are intended. On the other hand, oral communications tend to be more personal, to permit two-way interchange, and to be flexible; they also can be fairly fast but are subject to inaccuracy. These and other considerations argue for use of one form of communication or another for various specific purposes, but such pros and cons do not necessarily explain whether or not a particular form will be effective in "getting through" to people.

Actually, there is relatively little evidence to go by in making such comparisons, but a study by Dahle[34] sheds some light on this matter. This study involved the "transmission" of information in various departments of an industrial plant by five different methods. Later, tests of information were given to the employees in order to determine how much of it they had learned. The results, given in Table 14.1, show that a combination of oral and written methods was most effective, as indicated by the fact that employees with whom this method had been used had an average test score of 7.70, as contrasted with an average of 6.17 for oral only, and 4.91 for written only. (The written messages were duplicated materials passed out to the employees.) The bulletin board and grapevine methods resulted in average scores of 3.72 and 3.56, respectively.

The attitudes of people sometimes affect what they really "tune-in" on or how they interpret information they receive. *Selective perception* is the

TABLE 14.1 AVERAGE SCORES ON INFORMATION TEST OF EMPLOYEES WITH WHOM VARIOUS INFORMATION METHODS HAD BEEN USED

Method of Communication	No. of Employees	Average Score on Test*
Combined oral and written	102	7.70
Oral only	94	6.17
Written only	109	4.91
Bulletin board	115	3.72
Grapevine only	108	3.56

* All adjacent values in this column differ at the 5% level, except the last two.
Source: Dahle, *op. cit.*

[34] Dahle, T. L. Transmitting information to employees: A study of five methods. *Personnel,* 1954, **31**, 243–246.

tendency to "filter out" information that does not jibe with one's own convictions and beliefs. Further, people sometimes discount information that comes from certain sources (such as from people for whom they have some hostility), and the human inclination toward wishful thinking can result in more favorable interpretations of information than is warranted.

The grapevine. The grapevine is the communication system of the informal organization of a company. As pointed out by Davis,[35] it arises from the social relationships of people. Its speed and effectiveness as a communication system—especially in the case of real "newsy" bits of information—are well known. Although it lends itself to the transmission of unfounded rumor and to the distortion of true information, it has been estimated that in typical business situations between 90 and 95 percent of grapevine information is true.

Despite the fact that the grapevine can have its liabilities in an organization, Davis expresses the opinion that it provides certain benefits such as contributing to the development of group identification and interest in work, and serving as a means of upward communication, especially about how people feel about certain situations. In discussing the grapevine, Davis points out that three facts must be recognized: it is here to stay; it is a normal part of any organization; and it offers certain benefits. He therefore suggests that an organization learn to live with it. To do so, he suggests such steps as the following: to become aware of it and take it into account in decision making; to learn something about it; to "tune in" on it; to take advantage of its upward-communication benefits; to work with its leaders; and to "feed" it useful facts—facts that it can aid in transmitting and interpreting.

Needless to say, such an unorthodox approach would be feasible only under conditions of mutual trust and confidence. Further, such a policy should be carried out in such a manner as not to undercut the authority of line managers and supervisors in their official communication functions. This implies that the types of communications that are "fed" to the grapevine should be the types that subordinates should reasonably expect to receive directly from their supervisors. In addition, such information should be made available in some form through official channels.

Distortion in transmission. In the transmission process some information can be lost or distorted. This is especially the case where the "information" has to be "interpreted" or evaluated—that is, where it is not of a strictly factual nature. Loss or distortion typically is greater with oral than with written material. Brief mention will be made of a few aspects of such loss.

In the first place, as oral information is transmitted from one person to

[35] Davis, K. Making constructive use of the office grapevine. In K. Davis and W. G. Scott (Eds.), *Readings in human relations.* New York: McGraw-Hill, 1959, p. 346.

another, there usually is some loss of detail. In addition, some distortion can occur. This is illustrated by the parlor game in which one person transmits a message by whisper to another, and he to another, and so on. The message that ends up with the last recipient frequently has no relationship to the original message. The same phenomenon can occur in an organization where the information is spread by word of mouth. Even though the distortion may be entirely unintentional or unrelated to the attitudes or values of individuals, it can be influenced by the receiver's frame of reference. Thus, a change in procedures designed to eliminate a bottleneck in an operation may be interpreted as a new policy of "putting the screws" on the employees.

Certain other distorting influences have been discussed by Campbell.[36] Some of these are: loss of information of the "middle" parts of a message (as opposed to the beginning and ending); expectancy (messages that are "expected" are received more reliably than those that are not expected); association with reward and punishment (messages that have reward or punishment implications to the individual usually are assimilated better than "neutral" messages); and relevance to prior input (messages that are relevant to previous messages usually are received more accurately than those that are unrelated to previous messages).

Other influencing factors. Some other factors that influence the effectiveness of communications have been set forth by Scholz.[37] Some of these are given below:

1. The credibility of the communicator and the motives attributed to him have a profound influence on the reception of his messages.
2. The most successful communications are those which reinforce at least some of the audience's beliefs, those which state conclusions as well as premises, and those which call for action.
3. People are interested first in people, then in things, last in ideas. Their attitudes and opinions are strongly influenced by the groups to which they belong or want to belong.
4. It is better to communicate information little by little over a period of time than all at once. Repeating a communication obviously prolongs its influence.
5. Short sentences, familiar words, and active verbs help to make communications both interesting and persuasive.
6. In changing opinion, oral presentation tends to be more effective than the written word.
7. Only rarely is it possible for communication, particularly over the short range, to change deep-seated attitudes or beliefs.
8. Mass communication *alone* is hardly ever an effective agent of change.

[36] Campbell, D. T. Systematic error on the part of human links in communication links. *Information and Control,* 1958, **1**, 334–369.

[37] Scholz, W. *Communication in the business organization.* Englewood Cliffs, N.J.: Prentice-Hall, Inc., 1962.

Readability of Written Communications

The preparation of written communications does not ensure that they can "communicate" with those for whom they are intended; they must be written in such a manner that they are understandable by the readers in question. Various formulations for measuring the readability of written material have been devised, but the best known one is by Flesch.[38] His reading ease index is based on the following formula:

$$RE \text{ (reading ease)} = 206.835 - .846(wl) - 1.015sl$$

where wl (word length) is the average number of syllables per 100 words of the passage being considered, and
sl (sentence length) is the average sentence length in words of the passage.

The index ranges from 0 to 100 for various samples of writing. "Reading ease" scores tend to follow the pattern shown in Table 14.2.

TABLE 14.2   PATTERN OF "READING EASE" SCORES

"Reading Ease Score"	Description of Style	Typical Magazine	Syllables per 100 Words	Average Sentence Length in Words
0 to 30	Very difficult	Scientific	192 or more	29 or more
30 to 50	Difficult	Academic	167	25
50 to 60	Fairly difficult	Quality	155	21
60 to 70	Standard	Digests	147	17
70 to 80	Fairly easy	Slick-fiction	139	14
80 to 90	Easy	Pulp-fiction	131	11
90 to 100	Very easy	Comics	123 or less	8 or less

Source: Flesch, op. cit., Table 5.

A handful of studies have been made of the reading ease level of written communications used in industry, some of which have indicated that the difficulty level of the material is higher than it should be for easy reading, taking into account the educational levels required for reading different levels of material. A case in point is an analysis of the readability of fifty-nine union-management agreements, as reported by Tiffin and Walsh.[39] Figure 14.6 shows the distribution of reading-ease scores of these agreements, along with a comparison of the estimated percentage of adult readers having attained the indicated educational level. This indicates very clearly that 96.6 percent of the agreements were written at levels that required high school graduation or some college education for easy

[38] Flesch, R. A new readability yardstick. *Journal of Applied Psychology,* 1948, **32,** 221–233.
[39] Tiffin, J., & Walsh, F. X. Readability of union-management agreements. *Personnel Psychology,* 1951, **4,** 327–337.

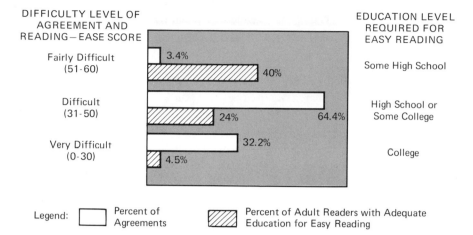

DIFFICULTY LEVEL OF AGREEMENT AND READING—EASE SCORE

Fairly Difficult (51-60) — 3.4% / 40% — Some High School

Difficult (31-50) — 24% / 64.4% — High School or Some College

Very Difficult (0-30) — 32.2% / 4.5% — College

EDUCATION LEVEL REQUIRED FOR EASY READING

Legend: ☐ Percent of Agreements   ▨ Percent of Adult Readers with Adequate Education for Easy Reading

FIG. 14.6 Relationship of reading ease of 59 union-management agreements and percent of adult readers having educational levels required for easy reading. (*Adapted from Tiffin and Walsh,* op. cit.)

understanding, whereas only about 28.5 percent of the potential adult readers would be expected to have such education.

In practical situations these indexes can be used to evaluate the reading ease of written communications. If they are then compared with the reading abilities of those who are to read the communications, it is possible to see whether the communications are within, or above, the reading abilities of the people concerned.

Communication Networks

In an organization of some size, the prospect that each person can "communicate" directly with everyone else in a willy-nilly fashion is of course absurd. Katz and Kahn,[40] citing Thelen,[41] for example, point out that a group of sixty people offers the possibility of 1,770 potential communication channels $(n(n-1)/2)$. But with a network of twelve five-man teams, each person has only ten completely interdependent channels within the group; and in turn each group has sixty-six possible channels with the other groups. The "structures" of organizations (consisting of divisions, departments, groups, units, and so forth) probably have come into being in part to facilitate organizational communications.

Types of group networks. In a sense, each group has some form of communication network through which its functions are performed. This

[40] Katz & Kahn, *op. cit.,* p. 225.
[41] Thelen, H. A. Exploration of a growth model for psychic, biological, and social systems. Mimeographed paper, 1960.

network results either from the formal organization as such or from the effective "practices" employed (such as by a leader). A fair amount of research has been conducted relating to group networks, most of it having been carried out in laboratory settings. Although one needs to be cautious about extrapolating the results of laboratory research such as this to actual work groups, such research may have some ultimate applicability to the real world.

Some of the types of networks used in such research are illustrated in Figure 14.7. In each case the communication relationships are represented by the lines. Certain configurations (as the wheel, "Y," and chain) are centralized in that all communications are forced through a central position so that one member of the group has more channels and more information than the other members. Other networks, such as the all-channel and circle, are decentralized in that there is no central member and all members have equal numbers of channels and the opportunity to share equal amounts of information. An index of "centrality" was proposed by Bavelas;[42] although the formula will not be given, this index is the ratio of the sum of the minimal "distances" of the positions to all others over the sum of the minimal distance of the position in question. Centrality indexes are given for the various positions shown in Figure 14.7.

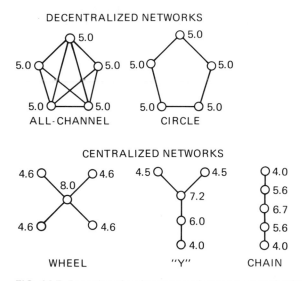

FIG. 14.7 Examples of various types of group communication networks. The lines represent the possible communication channels in a problem-solving task. The numerical values are indexes of "centrality."

[42] Bavelas, A. Communication patterns in task-oriented groups. *Journal of the Acoustical Society of America*, 1950, **22**, 725–730.

Some examples of networks as they might occur in industries and other organizations are shown in Figure 14.8. In each case the L stands for the leader. Network 4 shows the pattern typical of a supervisor who has all of his subordinates report directly to him, and Network 5 shows that of a supervisor who prefers to divide his four staff people into two seniors and two juniors. The decentralized networks (1, 2, and 3) reflect circumstances in which individuals within a group have communication channels with all, or some, of the persons other than those in chain of command. Leavitt[43] makes the point that the *actual* network of a group may be quite different from the *official* network. In addition to the fact that communication networks are a part of continuing, functional groups, they also develop in committees and other ad hoc groups, as a result of the way in which a leader guides the group, the relative "ranks" of the members as perceived by others, and other factors.

Effects of networks. In laboratory experiments with different networks, it is typically the practice to present groups with a problem of some sort to resolve. Leavitt[44] describes a typical problem in which each of the individuals of a group, separated by screens from each other, has a cup with five colored marbles, with one color being common to all of the members of the group. The problem is to find out what the one color in common is. This is done by passing messages (i.e., notes) back and forth through the channels that are available to the individual. The various

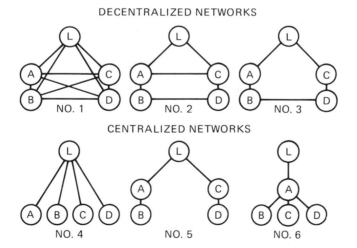

DECENTRALIZED NETWORKS

CENTRALIZED NETWORKS

FIG. 14.8 Examples of networks as they might be established in industrial situations. The leader is designated as L in each case.

[43] Leavitt, H. J. *Managerial psychology.* Chicago: The University of Chicago Press, 1964, p. 235.
[44] Leavitt, *op. cit.,* p. 233.

groups are then compared in terms of two types of criteria—those relating to the efficiency of resolving the problem (such as the number of messages required to solve the problem, the time required, and so forth) and those relating to the subjective reactions of the participants (e.g., their expressed satisfaction). In discussing the research relating to networks, Leavitt points out that centralized networks such as wheel-shaped or Y-shaped systems, generally are more efficient in solving the problems at hand in that they typically result in fewer errors, take less time, and require fewer messages than the decentralized networks. The results of a study by Vermillion[45] are consistent with these generalizations; he reports greater efficiency with centralized networks (a wheel and a chain) than with decentralized networks (all-channel and chain) in solving problems of varying difficulty.

But this is not the complete story. Participants in such experiments typically reflect greater "satisfaction" with the decentralized networks such as the circle or all-channel. Costello and Zalkind[46] express the opinion that this is probably because such networks are more democratic. They also suggest that decentralized networks seem to facilitate the handling of ambiguous and unpredictable situations, and are more likely to be responsive to innovation.

Thus, the question as to what networks are "best" must be answered in terms of the objectives in question. In this regard, Leavitt[47] suggests that for small meetings, conferences, and other situations where everyone's ideas are worth something, the "best" networks are those that have two characteristics: they are equalitarian (in that everyone has access to about the same number of channels), and they provide everyone with at least two direct communication channels. The all-channel, circle, and variations thereof generally meet these criteria; these tend to yield higher morale and greater willingness to work. In terms of "efficiency," however, the centralized networks have the advantages of imposing clear-cut organization on the group, defining each person's job, and leaving little leeway for wandering away from that job.

Communication and Attitudes

There are many indications to the effect that various forms of "communications" can serve to modify attitudes of people within an organization. One such demonstration comes from an attitude survey conducted in two plants by the National Industrial Conference Board and reported by

---

[45] Vermillion, W. H. *Problem solving as a function of group structure and problem complexity.* Unpublished Ph.D. Thesis, Purdue University, 1964.

[46] Costello, T. W., & Zalkind, S. S. *Psychology in administration.* Englewood Cliffs, N.J.: Prentice-Hall, Inc., 1963, p. 457.

[47] Leavitt, *op .cit.,* p. 236.

TABLE 14.3 Responses of Employees in Two Plants to Questions on Attitude Questionnaire

	Per cent Giving Response	
Question and Response	Plant A	Plant B
1. Can you talk things over with your foreman when you want to?		
Yes, I always can	34*	56*
Usually I can	42	27
He is generally too busy	6	4
Usually he doesn't want to be bothered	13	13
I can hardly ever talk with him	5	0
2. Have you been able to get your ideas up to the top men?		
Almost always	21*	49*
Sometimes	31	28
Hardly ever	32	13
Not interested in doing so	16	10
3. Do you feel a part of your company?		
I feel I really belong	29*	62*
I feel I just work here	42	14
Sometimes I feel one way, sometimes the other	29	24

 * This is the most favorable response. A comparison for the two plants on this response points up the differences between them.
 Source: Habbe, *op. cit.*, pp. 36–38.

Habbe.[48] In Plant B, special attention had been paid to communications, including the inauguration of regular work-unit meetings in which each foreman met with his employees and discussed matters of common interest. In plant A no such program had been developed. A comparison of the responses of employees in the two plants to a few of the questions provides some revealing contrasts. Results from a few of the questions are given in Table 14.3. A comparison of the percentages giving the favorable responses (especially the most favorable response—marked with an asterisk) reflects that the employees in Plant B felt much more on the same "wave length" with their supervisors than was true of employees in Plant A, and that they had a greater feeling of "belongingness" to the organization.

INDUSTRIAL CONFLICT

 Conflict in some form and degree is part and parcel of virtually every facet of human life, and one would, therefore, not expect the industrial scene to be free of it. By and large, people tend to view conflict as an undesirable component of human life, which it indeed can be. History and

 [48] Habbe, S. *Communicating with employees.* Studies in Personnel Policy, No. 129, National Industrial Conference Board, 1952.

experience lead one to the conclusion, however, that conflict can lead to changes regarded as desirable in terms of generally acceptable human values. In industry, for example, conflict has undoubtedly brought about improvement in working conditions for employees. The "desirability" of certain changes, however, may be viewed differently by different people. As Stagner[49] points out, one needs to ask, "Bad—from what point of view?" and "Good—from what point of view?" When conflict gets out of hand, however, it tends to become destructive and undesirable for all parties concerned. It has been suggested in a study conducted by the Foundation for Research on Human Behavior[50] that an objective of management is to see that conflicts remain on the creative and useful side of an invisible, but enormously important, barrier that divides "good" conflict from "bad."

Types of Industrial Conflict

The very nature of industrial organizations carries with it built-in sources of potential conflicts between different individuals and groups. Individuals may differ in their opinions about organizational policies or procedures, or may be mutually antagonistic in terms of personality differences. Organizational units that have different functions, such as production, quality control, sales, maintenance, and financial control, may find themselves at odds with each other by reason of their respective functions. Perhaps the dominant source of potential conflict arises from differences between management and employee groups regarding such matters as wages, working conditions, and other related matters.

The Basis for Conflict

Whatever its specific nature, conflict arises basically from motivational factors. Stagner[51] expresses this point when he states that the phenomena of industrial conflict (and its opposite, industrial cooperation) grow out of the needs of individual human beings. In this connection, he points out that motivation is distinctly an *individual* phenomenon and that there is *no group mind*. Groups cannot feel, see, desire, fear, or hate any object. Individuals, however, can be influenced by group pressures, as discussed in an earlier section, and their motivation can thus be changed in group situations, generally in the direction of conformity to the group norms. A group of individuals with reasonably common motivation can, of course, be in conflict with another group.

[49] Stagner, R. *Psychology of industrial conflict.* New York: John Wiley. 1956, p. 13.

[50] *Conflict management in organizations.* Ann Arbor: Foundation for Research on Human Behavior, 1961.

[51] Stagner, *op. cit.,* p. 119.

Somewhat related to the motivational origins of conflict is the role of perception. Human behavior is predicated more on the "perceptions" of people than on objective "facts." The perceptions of people sometimes tend to be distorted, generally in the direction of conformity with the individual's own frame of reference. Selective perception, the tendency toward "perceiving" only those aspects of a situation that are compatible with one's frame of reference, is related to this phenomenon. Thus, if an employee group perceives or interprets a supervisor's discharge of a fellow employee as an act directed toward breaking up the group, the members of the group would tend to react as though this were the supervisor's motive, whether or not this was the case.

The perception of social phenomena is influenced by various factors, including the following:[52] past experience of the individual; the individual's "expectancy" of what might happen; inner needs (the motivational aspect mentioned above); the possible consequences of some action or event; "field structure" (the organized "pattern" of one's perceptions, into which one's perception of individual events or circumstances tends to be "fitted" in order to form a total pattern).

Group and individual behavior. Although group behavior stems basically from the motivation and behavior of individuals, the mere fact of individuals' being members of a group can bring about collective (group) behavior that would not be characteristic of any single individual. Thus, a mob may engage in violence that the individuals in it would not otherwise carry out. The anonymity to the outside world that individuals experience within groups seems to offer some promise of their not being "identified" individually in group activities.

Labor-Management Conflict

It is virtually inevitable that there be some conflict between labor and management, inasmuch as their objectives are often quite different and, in fact, typically are at odds with each other. Because of the importance of this source of conflict in our economy, efforts to minimize it, and to keep it within reasonable bounds, are desirable. Toward this end, further understanding of the nature of the conflict would be useful. Such understanding can come in part through research. Although we cannot cover this topic extensively, a couple of examples of such research may be useful.

Perceptions of labor-management relations. Four groups of people were surveyed by the Opinion Research Corporation[53] regarding their views on wages, unions, and related matters. Some results from this survey are given in Figure 14.9. In particular, this shows the percentage of respondents in

---

[52] *Ibid.*, Chapter 2.
[53] *Public opinion index for industry.* Opinion Research Corporation, May 1964.

FIG. 14.9 Percentages of individuals in various groups giving specified responses in opinion survey. (*Adapted from* Public Opinion Index for Industry, op. cit.)

certain groups who expressed the opinion that "companies have to be forced" to pay higher wages, and that "most companies would like to break the unions." The results show very marked differences among the groups. Note especially the differences between managers and union members. Data such as these point up the gulf between the perceptions of groups in conflict; regardless of who is right and who is wrong as far as "facts" are concerned, such differences in perception are indeed real, and need to be recognized and dealt with.

Opinion Survey of Union Members

In another study, Uphoff and Dunnette[54] surveyed 1,251 members of thirteen unions about their opinions relating to unions. The responses to some of the questions are given in Table 14.4, which shows the percentages of "officers" and of "rank-and-file" members who agreed with each statement. Based on these and other data not given here, the investigators

54 Uphoff, W. H., & Dunnette, M. D. What union members think of unionism. *Personnel,* January 1957, **34,** 347–52.

TABLE 14.4 PER CENT OF UNION OFFICERS AND OF RANK-AND-FILE UNION MEMBERS
WHO AGREED WITH SELECTED QUESTIONNAIRE STATEMENTS

Statement	Union Officers	Rank and File
If it were not for unions, we'd have little protection against favoritism	90	82
Unions should have something to say about the person the employer hires	52	33
Workers should not have to join a union to hold a job	16	38
Fines should be levied for not attending union meetings	57	30
The local union officers are doing a good job	90	73
Our union meetings are run in an efficient manner	77	66

Source: Uphoff and Dunnette, *op. cit.*

came to the following conclusions: union members agree overwhelmingly
that unions protect their rights, and that employees enjoy better wages and
working conditions when all of them belong to the union; agreement is far
from unanimous on seniority, union participation in hiring, and union-
shop provisions; there is need for improved communications within the
unions; for the most part, the members feel their officers are doing a reasonably good job; many members have no opinions about the national unions;
and officers very consistently express more "favorable" opinions than do
rank-and-file members.

Aspects of Union-Management Relationships

In still another example of research relating to labor-management relations, Derber *et al.*[55] carried out a survey of management and union officials
of forty-one establishments, categorizing each one in terms of each of the
following three features of their union-management relationships:

1. Influence (union influence in union-management relationships).
2. Pressure (extent to which settlements were based on use of pressure, such as work stoppages, slowdowns, movement of the plant, etc.).
3. Attitude (a combination of the "ranking" of management attitude to union and of union attitude to management).

For each of these, all establishments were categorized as "high" or "low"
on the variable, with an intermediate "moderate" category in the case of
the influence variable. "Clusters" of establishments were then developed,
each cluster including those whose patterns of "high," "moderate," and

[55] Derber, M., Chambers, W. E., & Stagner, R. *The local union-management relationship.* Urbana: Institute of Labor and Industrial Relations, University of Illinois,
1960.

"low" classifications were the same. An analysis of the differences among these clusters (based in part on other data) led to the following characterizations:

Cluster A. Aggression and resistance (a situation in which an aggressive union has the upper hand and management is unhappy about it).

Cluster B. Quiescence (a situation in which the union has little influence and, apparently, no desire for more).

Cluster C. Joint participation (a situation somewhat like B, but union influence is somewhat greater).

Cluster D. Repressed hostility (a situation in which union influence is moderate, pressure is largely absent, and attitudes are unfavorable on at least one side).

Cluster E. Extensive joint participation (a situation in which the union, with management approval, has developed a high degree of influence; characterized by low pressure as such).

These probing efforts to "describe" the nature of union-management relationships seem to offer some promise of bringing about greater understanding of this important aspect of our economic enterprise.

The Management of Conflict

In discussing conflict of various types—be it between individuals, groups, countries, or otherwise—Shepard[56] points out that the ways in which conflict between two parties can be resolved range across a gamut from suppression, through total and limited war, to bargaining and efforts at problem solving. This continuum is depicted in Figure 14.10. These methods, paraphrased from Shepard,[57] are:

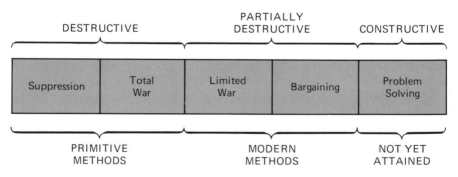

FIG. 14.10 Methods of conflict management, representing a range from destructive to constructive. (*Adapted from Shepard, 1962,* op. cit., *p. 33.*)

[56] Shepard, H. A. Responses to situations of competition and conflict. In *Conflict management in organizations, op. cit.,* pp. 33–41.
[57] *Ibid.;* and Shepard, H. A. The psychologist's role in union-management relations. *Personnel Psychology,* 1961, **14**, 270–279.

1. *Suppression*. This method is followed when the two parties are unequal in power, and the stronger uses this to his advantage for the satisfaction of his own interests, using his resources to keep the weaker suppressed.

2. *Total war*. This method normally is adopted only when each party believes that it has some chance of winning, but it may be used in rare cases when a "liberty-or-death" mentality may lead the weaker party to undertake a foolhardy battle with the strong. Total war is a very primitive form and a very irrational method of conflict resolution, as both sides usually suffer severe losses.

3. *Limited war*. "Limited war" is carried out between conflicting groups under conditions in which the weapons, arena, and methods are all predetermined (sometimes in legal terms), and in which the courtroom may be the arena. The "winner" is determined by some third party such as a judge, jury, or arbitrator. Even when a decision of some sort is made, however, the underlying conflict usually is not resolved.

4. *Bargaining*. Bargaining lies somewhere between the "limited war" and problem-solving methods. In poor bargaining, both parties feel deprived and each feels that it gave more than it received; the situation may deteriorate to a condition of limited war. In good bargaining, each party gives away something that matters little to him and gets something which means a great deal. This can lead to a problem-solving approach to conflict resolution.

5. *Problem solving*. Problem solving exists in those encounters in which the parties are able to treat the existence of a conflict as a problem they share in common and have a joint responsibility for solving. It involves a point of view in which the parties regard the advancing of the other's interests as having equal importance with the advancing of its own. In union-management relationships it represents a more advanced state of civilization than we have yet attained, but one toward which we can strive.

Strategies for dealing with industrial conflict. Although industrial conflict of some type is inevitable, its nature and intensity are to some degree the function of the situation. Because situational variables influence conflict, it is, of course, possible to modify the situation, thereby possibly contributing to the reduction of conflict. Despite the fact that there are no rules of thumb that lead to conflict reduction, an organization need not throw up its hands in despair, for certain positive programs and actions can be taken that might reasonably be expected to function in the direction of conflict reduction. Three basic strategies for dealing with conflict have been set forth by Katz.[58] These are: (1) making the system work; (2) setting up machinery for handling conflict; and (3) changing the organizational structure.

The strategy of trying to make the present system work places emphasis on human relations skills in the improvement of interpersonal relations. Some of the matters discussed earlier in this chapter (and in other chapters) are relevant to this effort, as, for example, the development of effective leadership, participation (where appropriate), and effective two-way com-

[58] Katz, D. Approaches to managing conflict. In *conflict management in organizations, op. cit.,* pp. 13–20.

munications (including feedback to employees). The use of sensitivity training and group dynamics techniques sometimes can bring about some modification of attitude (and attitudes are, of course, at the core of conflict). The potential effectiveness of all of these methods depends upon the sincerity and integrity of the actions taken by management in carrying them out.

The development of machinery for dealing with conflict places the emphasis on control of conflict rather than on its reduction as such. Such efforts move toward the containment of conflict, thereby reducing the likelihood of its spreading. Most typically, provisions are made for resolution of differences at the points where they arise; if they cannot be resolved at that point, they may be carried a step higher, as in grievance procedures.

In some circumstances, changes in the structure of the organization or some segment of it can contribute to conflict reduction by creating conditions in which conflict is less likely to develop. Although there are few clear guidelines toward the development of organizational structures that tend to minimize conflict, Katz[59] offers some suggestions such as: reducing process specialization (to give greater emphasis on the purpose of the organization); decentralization; restructuring to remove obvious differentials in "status" symbols between hierarchical interest groups; development of meaningful cycles of work, with opportunity for employees to "complete" tasks (to avoid tensions from interrupted tasks); and sharing in organizational rewards. Other reorganizational possibilities include job enlargement (to increase intrinsic job motivation), reorganization to facilitate communications (both vertical and horizontal), and providing the opportunity for informal groups to develop and exist without fear of counteraction.

It should be emphasized here that whatever strategies are adopted should be predicated upon an understanding of human behavior, including the role that motivation and perception play in conflict situations.

ADJUSTMENT TO CHANGE

Change is an inevitable feature of virtually every organization. Lawrence and Seiler[60] make the point that some changes are forced on an organization by pressures from without (such as competition, shifts in market patterns, and significant technological breakthroughs), whereas others are planned by the people in the organization, usually as a means of maintaining the health of the organization in a dynamic society. The forced changes are often regarded as challenges to be met, but it is the planned changes that

---

[59] *Ibid.*

[60] Lawrence, P. R., & Seiler, J. A. *Organizational behavior and administration.* Homewood, Illinois: Richard D. Irwin, Inc., and The Dorsey Press, 1965, p. 807.

are more often perceived as potentially disturbing to the equilibrium of individuals, groups, or the organization as a whole.

Resistance to Change

The prospect of some change in an individual's situation typically brings about some speculation—vague or definitive—as to the *nature* of various possible consequences (outcomes) to him; as to the *probabilities* of the various outcomes; and as to the *values* (plus or minus) of the various possible outcomes. If these tend to add up to the strong likelihood of probable gains to the individual, he usually adopts a favorable attitude regarding the change. If they add up to the strong likelihood of loss to the individual, he will be inclined toward resisting the change. And if he cannot really figure the odds very well—if he really doesn't have a very good basis for predicting the impact upon him, so that he is left in a state of considerable *uncertainty* about the possible outcomes—he might tend to take a dim view of the whole affair.

It is thus easy to see how an individual in a job, faced with the prospect of his job being changed, might focus on such possible outcomes as his having to learn a virtually new job or to work with new people and a new supervisor. Not knowing how well he might be able to make out under these new conditions, he readily could perceive the prospects unfavorably.

It has been suggested by Lawrence[61] that what employees resist is usually not technological change as such but social change—the change in human relationships that generally accompanies technological change. Although we cannot fully agree with the major emphasis he places upon the social aspects of change, we do feel that efforts should be made to ferret out the relative importance of these two facets in any given circumstance.

Some indication of the reactions toward possible technological change is shown in Figure 14.11, which is based on a survey by Scott *et al.*[62] carried out in a steel mill in Great Britain that was undergoing technological change in its processes. (The questions posed dealt with a "hypothetical" plant, but responses to such "oblique" questions generally are indicative of the respondent's own attitudes.) Although there were significant numbers of individuals who did *not* believe the new machinery should be installed, it should be noted that that there were marked differences by occupational groups in response to questions dealing with this matter. The crewmen and unskilled production workers—the ones who typically would be affected *most* by changes such as those postulated—were least favorably inclined toward the change.

[61] Lawrence P. R. How to deal with resistance to change. *Harvard Business Review*, 1954, **32**(2), 49–57.

[62] Scott, W. H., *et al. Technical change and industrial relations.* Liverpool: Liverpool University Press, 1956.

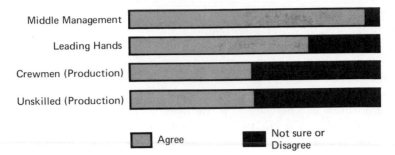

FIG. 14.11 Responses of personnel in a steel mill to the statement: "The firm should put in the new machinery." (*Adapted from Scott, et al.,* op. cit., *Table 29, p. 177.*)

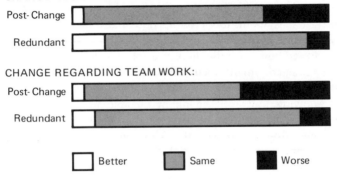

FIG. 14.12 Perceptions of melters in a steel mill regarding changes in their social relations after installation of new furnaces. The post-change melters remained on the new furnaces, although their jobs were somewhat modified. The redundant melters had been transferred to different jobs. (*Adapted from Banks,* op. cit., *Table 47, p. 81.*)

Some indication of the effect of change on social relationships in work comes from the results of a continuation of the above study, as reported by Banks.[63] This phase of the study covered a group of melters, whose work was affected by the installation of new furnaces. About sixty-five members of this occupational group became "redundant," which means that they were surplus on the furnaces, but most of them were transferred to other jobs in the plant. The jobs of those who remained on the new furnace were somewhat modified. The attitudes of both groups regarding the effects of the change on their social relationships with working companions and in team work are shown in Figure 14.12. In general, more of the post-change melters expressed the opinion that they were worse off than had been the case with the redundant melters; but perhaps the most surprising thing

[63] Banks, O. *The attitudes of steel workers to technical change.* Liverpool: Liverpool University Press, 1960.

about the results was the fairly high percentage in each group who reported "no change." Data such as these are, of course, after the fact of change and thus are not necessarily indicative of what the perceptions of the men would have been *before* the change took place.

In this connection, an interesting comparison can be made of the responses of employees from the study by Scott *et al.*[64] shown in Figure 14.11, with some follow-up data from Banks[65] on the perceptions of "overall" consequences of actual technological change. Figure 14.11 shows the following percentages (by occupational groups) of those who "agreed" with the statement that "The firm should put in the new machinery": leading hands, 72; crewmen, 49; and unskilled, 50. The follow-up data from Banks gives the following percentages who reported that they were "better off" as the overall consequence of certain changes: leading hands, 92; crewmen, 74; and unskilled, 64. Although some caution is necessary in leaning very heavily on such comparisons, they are at least suggestive of the hypothesis that the actual consequences of change may not be as unhappy as was anticipated before the change.

Banks concluded from her study of steel mill employees that there was no evidence of widespread hostility to technical change as such, although some cautions are in order in extrapolations from this one situation to others.

Dealing with Resistance to Change

Although resistance to change frequently bobs up in the operation of organizations, Lawrence[66] warns against the *expectation* that resistance will develop, for any implication of such expectation might operate in the direction of a self-fulfilling prophecy and actually trigger such resistance. Rather, he proposes that when resistance *does* appear, it should not be thought of as something to be *overcome*. Instead, it can best be thought of as a useful red flag—a signal that something is going wrong.

With change as with other management problems involving personnel there are no easy step-by-step "procedures" one can follow to reduce resistance. Many of the same matters discussed in earlier contexts are relevant to this topic as well—considerations of leadership, participation, communications, and so forth—for these aspects of an organization can serve to create an environment that is less threatening to employees, and in which resistance is therefore less likely to be strong.

Special note should be made of the usefulness of participation in this context, especially as related to the social aspects of resistance to change.

[64] Scott *et al.*, *op. cit.*
[65] Banks, *op. cit.*, Table 32, p. 59.
[66] Lawrence, *op. cit.*

Although participation can serve to minimize such resistance, it is by no means a panacea. In particular, if the personnel involved perceive the participation game as being a "manipulation" of them, it is almost certain to fail. "Participation" in the sense implied cannot be achieved simply by bringing people together and presenting them with "the problem"; rather, it can take place only where the basic climate is conducive to it.

Discussion

The success with which any organization is operated is very much a consequence of the way in which management provides for the effective application of human talent toward the objectives of the organization. Some of the actions that management can take that may contribute toward this end include the development of satisfactory organizations and the establishment of certain policies and programs such as those discussed earlier in this chapter and in other chapters. The mechanical adoption of "programs" and policies, the use of "gimmicks," and other efforts to "manipulate" people, however, are virtually doomed to failure. The critical ingredient is the climate within which such efforts are made. This climate must be generated by top management.

chapter fifteen

Financial Incentives
and Job Evaluation

Although the motivation for people to work is indeed complex, we find virtually unanimous agreement that money is a dominant factor in such motivation. In the labor market individuals have certain potentialities, skills, or other qualities that they seek to "sell" to prospective employers. In turn, the intent of employing organizations is to offer wages that will attract personnel who can perform the jobs that are available. Thus, the proffered wages are intended to serve as an incentive to accept employment. But there is more to it than that. Lawler,[1] for example, states that pay is typically thought of as performing a number of functions that contribute to organizational effectiveness; in particular, it serves as a reward to make employees satisfied with their jobs, motivate them, gain their commitment to the organization, and keep them in the organization.

To meet these ends, pay of course must serve as an incentive that is perceived as fulfilling certain needs of individuals. In this regard it is

---

[1] Lawler, E. E. *Pay and organizational effectiveness: A psychological view.* New York: McGraw-Hill, 1971, p. 1.

obvious that for most people money does provide the wherewithall to keep body and soul together—in effect to fulfill what Maslow describes as the individual's physiological needs. Its instrumentality for the satisfaction of other needs depends on the need in question. For example, Lawler[2] indicates that it generally is perceived primarily as satisfying the need for esteem, secondarily as being instrumental in satisfying the autonomy and security needs, and only marginally as satisfying the social and self-actualizing needs. In effect, he suggests that the importance of pay to any given individual is the combined effect of the importance of the various needs to the individual and the extent to which the individual perceives pay as being "instrumental" in satisfying those needs.

Granting that money is a very dominant facet of the employment relationship, it has been pointed out by Opsahl and Dunnette[3] that we knew amazingly little either about how money interacts with other factors or about how it acts individually to affect job performance of people—and, we might add, about how it causes people to accept or reject employment at given rates of pay.

THEORIES RELATING TO PAY

In probing for some understanding of the manner in which money in fact serves as an incentive to people in relation to their work behavior, various theories have been bandied about. A couple of these will be discussed here.

Equity Theory

One of the current theories relating to pay is the equity theory proposed by Adams.[4]

Outcome/input ratio. Adams' equity theory is rooted in the relationship between the perceived *outcomes* from the work involvement of the individual and the perceived *inputs* into his job.

The *outcomes* of a job situation include actual pay, fringe benefits, status, intrinsic interest in the job, or other factors that the individual perceives to have utility or value to him that result from his job relationship. In turn, the *inputs* include any and all of the factors that an indi-

[2] *Ibid*, pp. 33, 34.

[3] Opsahl, R. L., & Dunnette, M. D. The role of financial compensation in industrial motivation. *Psychological Bulletin*, 1966, **66**(2), 94–118.

[4] Adams, J. S. Wage inequities, productivity and work quality. *Industrial Relations*, October 1963, **3**(1), 9–16; Adams, J. S. Injustice in social exchange. In L. Berkowitz (Ed.), *Advances in experimental social psychology*, Vol. 2. New York: Academic Press, 1965; and Adams, J. S., & Jacobsen, P. R. Effects of wage inequities on work quality. *Journal of Abnormal and Social Psychology*, 1964, **69**(1), 19–25.

vidual perceives as being his "investment" in his job, or that he perceives as something of value that he brings or puts into this job relationship. Thus, the inputs could include a person's general qualifications for a job, his skill, his educational level, his effort, and other similar factors. The various specific outcomes and inputs as they are perceived by an individual are weighted according to his judgment of their relative importance to form a "total" outcome and a "total" input. These two totals combine to form an outcome/input ratio.

According to Adams' theory, a person is said to consciously or unconsciously compare his outcome/input ratio with that of other persons or other classes of persons whom he perceives as relevant for such comparative purposes. *Equity* is said to exist when an individual perceives the ratio of *his* outcome/input to be equal to that of other persons; and *inequity* is said to exist if the ratio is *not* the same as that of other persons. Inequity can be in either direction and of varying magnitudes. Let us use Pritchard's[5] H (High) and L (Low) notations to illustrate these ratios, and in particular to illustrate those combinations which, according to the theory, would result in equity and inequity (both under-reward and over-reward). The basic ratio is:

$$\text{Equity ratio} = \frac{\text{Outcome (H or L)}}{\text{Input (H or L)}}$$

In the following the first ratio is that of the individual himself, the second (following *v* for *versus*) that of the persons used for comparison.

Equity: $\frac{L}{L}v\frac{L}{L}\quad\frac{H}{H}v\frac{H}{H}\quad\frac{L}{L}v\frac{H}{H}\quad\frac{H}{H}v\frac{L}{L}\quad\frac{L}{L}v\frac{L}{L}\quad\frac{H}{L}v\frac{H}{L}$

Inequity (over-reward): $\frac{L}{L}v\frac{L}{H}\quad\frac{H}{L}v\frac{L}{L}\quad\frac{H}{L}v\frac{L}{H}\quad\frac{H}{L}v\frac{H}{H}\quad\frac{H}{H}v\frac{L}{H}$

Inequity (under-reward): $\frac{L}{L}v\frac{H}{L}\quad\frac{L}{H}v\frac{L}{L}\quad\frac{L}{L}v\frac{H}{L}\quad\frac{H}{L}v\frac{H}{H}\quad\frac{H}{H}v\frac{H}{L}$

Equity and inequity. The sense of inequity can be understood in the context of cognitive dissonance (discussed in Chapter 12). When dissonance exists, the individual seeks in some way to take steps to change the situation so as to reduce the dissonance. There are various ways in which the sense of inequity (i.e., dissonance) can be reduced, such as: (1) changing one's inputs or outcomes; (2) acting to have the comparison persons change their inputs or outcomes; (3) cognitively distorting either of the two ratios (one's own or those of the comparison persons); (4) changing the persons used for comparison; or (5) "leaving the field" (i.e., leaving the

[5] Pritchard, R. D. Equity theory: A review and critique. *Organizational Behavior and Human Performance,* 1969, 4, 176–211.

job). Because the predicted behaviors relative to one's own inputs and outcomes cover quite a gamut, we will touch here simply on certain illustrative predictions. In this regard, a distinction needs to be made between situations in which people are paid on a piece-rate basis and situations in which they are paid on an hourly basis. This difference arises from the fact that when a person on a piece-rate basis increases his input (i.e., productivity) he also increases his outcome (i.e., money), whereas this would not be the case with a person working on an hourly-paid basis. Certain predicted behaviors under the four resulting possible combinations of underpayment and overpayment and piece-rate and hourly basis are summarized below:

Condition	*Certain predicted behaviors*
1. Hourly pay, underpayment	Lower productivity and/or lower quality (thus reducing input)
2. Hourly pay, overpayment	Increase productivity and/or quality (thus raising input)
3. Piece-rate, underpayment	Increase productivity and reduce quality (thus raising outcome without increasing input)
4. Piece-rate overpayment	Lower productivity and/or increase quality (thus reducing outcome and keeping input constant)

Discussion. It should be noted that research relating to equity theory has been only partially confirming. For example, the "behaviors" predicted above have not always been found to occur when, according to the theory, they should occur. Questions about this and other facets of the theory have been raised by Lawler[6] and others. Indeed, Lawler argues that the concept of equity as set forth by Adams may be more applicable to piece-rate jobs than to those paid on the basis of time (hours, weeks, or months). In any event, it seems unwise at the present to cast equity theory entirely to the four winds. Rather, one should try to determine, through research, if it does have any substantial relevance in explaining the psychological aspects of pay, and if so in what specific respect.

Motivation Model

A second theory relating to pay is the motivation model proposed by Lawler.[7] This model is based essentially on expectancy theory, or what we referred to in Chapter 12 as valence-instrumentality-expectancy theories (VIE). Without going into the extensions of expectancy theory as related

[6] Lawler, *op. cit.*, Chapter 8.
[7] *Ibid.*, Chapter 6.

specifically to pay in Lawler's formulation, let us summarize the central features of this theory in this context. The model is predicated on the assumption that the motivation to perform at a given level is primarily determined by two variables: (1) the person's belief concerning the probability that if he puts effort into performing at that given level he in fact will be able to perform at that level; and (2) the combination of beliefs about what the outcomes of accomplishing the intended level of performance would be and the "valence" of those outcomes (i.e., their value to him). These outcomes and their valences to the person are based on the degree to which they are perceived as being able to satisfy his basic needs. (Further elaborations of his theory are presented by Lawler.[8])

EARNINGS AND RELATED VARIABLES

Both equity theory and the motivation model deal with the concept of "outcomes" that result from job relationships, and their perceived value to the individual. Although actual pay is indeed the dominant factor (at least to most of us mortals) there also can be other outcomes from the working relationship. Thus the absolute amount of the earnings associated with a job usually would not be considered in a vacuum by employees or prospective employees; rather, they would be considered in comparison with other features of the job situation. For example, a worker sometimes will forego higher earnings on piece-work jobs in order to avoid being an outcast from the work group. Or, in the case of people who view their jobs primarily as a means of self-actualization, pay will not constitute the foremost outcome of the job.

Preferences for Various Forms of Financial Benefit

People may juggle in their minds the relative pros and cons of various pay and financial benefit conditions, including so-called "fringe" benefits. A study of such preferences was carried out by Nealey[9] with three groups of employees. One group of employees was asked to indicate their relative preferences for the first eight job variables below, and another group was asked to express their preferences for all ten:

1. Pay raise of $190 a year
2. Pension increase of $45 a month
3. Eight days of additional paid vacation

[8] *Ibid.*
[9] Nealey, S. M. Pay and benefit preference. *Industrial Relations,* October 1963, 3(1), 17–28.

4. Family dental insurance ($50 deductible)
5. Medical care for retired employees
6. Twenty days' paid sick leave per year
7. $8,500 additional life insurance
8. Long-term disability pay
9. Short-term unemployment assistance
10. Long-term unemployment assistance

The preferences were obtained by two methods—the paired comparison method and a "game-board" method. In the latter method, the employee

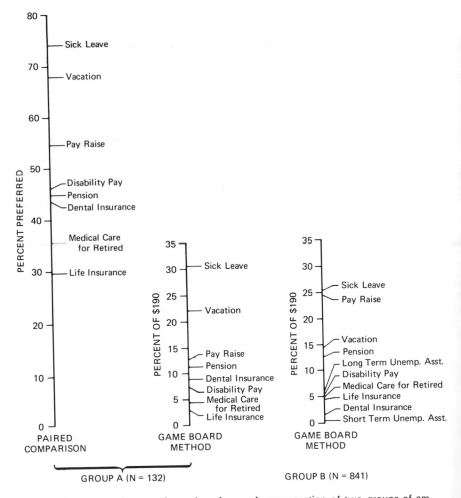

FIG. 15.1 Group preferences for various forms of compensation of two groups of employees. (*From Nealey,* op. cit.)

was given a hypothetical increase of $190 and was asked to indicate how he would spend it by "allocating" it across the several options. Some of the results of this study for two groups are given in Figure 15.1. It should be noted that the results from this particular study are not intended to imply that *other* groups of workers would have the same set of relative values. Rather, the results are given to illustrate the fact that there are indeed different types of "outcomes" associated with work that are relevant to people, and to suggest that the relative values associated with various such outcomes are by no means the same for all segments of the labor force. For example, older workers might place more emphasis on pensions, unskilled workers might be more interested in unemployment insurance, and so on. Further, such preferences can be related to individual attitudes and values. This was reflected in part by the results of another phase of Nealey's study in which certain attitude questions were asked, such as "What do you think of the company?" and "What do you think of your boss?" Defined by these questions, the low-attitude group tended to prefer pay to benefits, whereas the high-attitude group was more willing to let its "money" ride with the company in various forms of deferred payout (pension, hospital, vacation, and so forth). Aside from the specifics, these differences start to point up the interaction between management practices, wages, and morale, emphasizing the point that wages as such cannot be considered independent of other job variables, including other financial and nonfinancial benefits.

Cafeteria-Style Pay Plans

In the light of the fact that people vary in their expressed preferences for different forms of pay and/or related fringe benefits, the notion of cafeteria-style pay plans has been proposed by various people, including Lawler.[10] Such a plan provides that each individual be "assigned" a specified amount of money, based on his job, but allows each individual to select the combination of cash and fringe benefits (direct pay, insurance, retirement, vacations, and so forth) he wants. Granting some of the problems that such plans might generate, they would have the dominant advantage of relating the form of financial benefits to the value systems and psychological needs of the individuals themselves.

WAGES AND THE LABOR MARKET

An organization obtains its employees from one or more labor markets. A labor market comprises that general pool of people who are prospective

---

[10] Lawler, *op. cit.*, p. 198.

candidates for employment in some type of occupation. For example, the labor market for hourly-paid and office jobs usually consists of the local community, whereas that for certain types of professional and managerial jobs may be regional or national in scope, comprising those who have the particular qualifications required wherever they may be. Whatever the labor market in question, an organization that expects to obtain its employees from that market must be able to compete with other organizations in the market, and wage rates are one of the important bargaining ingredients.

The general wage level in any given labor market is a function of a number of different factors. (We will here use the terms *wage* and *wage level* in a general sense, to include not only hourly wages but also salaries and other forms of financial compensation.) These factors include: supply and demand; government wage controls; contract negotiations; general economic conditions (including the cost of living); general regional and industrial factors (wages are higher in certain regions or industries than in others); and productivity. In the long run, of course, "real" wages—that is, how much people can buy with their earnings—depend very much upon the productivity of industry. It is only by increasing general productivity that the general level of real wages can be raised.

CONFLICTING OBJECTIVES IN WAGE ADMINISTRATION

Let us now crystallize what appear to be the two dominant factors that an organization must take into consideration in establishing its wage administration policies. On the one hand, there is the company's economic situation. Most organizations have continuing pressures for economy in their operations toward the ends of economic survival and of profit, although these pressures differ in various companies and industries. And on the other hand, there is the competition of other companies in the same labor market. An organization needs to be in a reasonably competitive position, with regard not only to wages as such but also to the "package" of related incentives if it is to be able to employ people in its labor market.

The labor market is not a vague, ethereal concept. Rather, it is comprised of live people with motivations and sets of values which are reflected —in the labor market—by their behavior in offering their services and accepting or rejecting employment under specified conditions.

This inescapable fact recalls our earlier discussion of equity theory. Granting some question about certain aspects of this theory, we can nonetheless see how individual members of the labor market might, in a general way, think in terms of an outcome/input ratio applied to themselves,

based on their perceptions of the combination of the various types of outcomes and what they would put into the work situation. Further, we can
see that an individual might view this "ratio" as applied to himself in
relationship to his perceptions of the corresponding factors as related to
others in the labor market. Thus, an individual would be most likely to
consider proferred employment as "equitable" if the perceived outcomes and
inputs are reasonably in line with those of *others* in a similar line of work.
(Of course, people probably tend to be more perceptive of inequity of the
"under-reward" variety than of the "over-reward" variety.)

Thus, we probably can say that the "going rate" for a particular type
of work is in a sense a very rough-and-ready reflection of the notion of
"equity" in that it reflects the approximate level of (at least) the financial
"outcomes" for the typical "inputs" involved in the type of work in question. It thus provides an individual with a basis for his perceptions of the
outcome/input ratios of *other* people whose inputs into a job (i.e., their
job-related skills and other factors) might be comparable to his own.

EARNINGS AND JOB PERFORMANCE

The primary thrust of equity theory is that it provides a broad frame of
reference in which one may view the decisions of people to accept or reject
employment at given levels of compensation. But one would also wish to
have some more positive hints than are now available of the possible effects
of variations in financial compensation for inducing greater effort in the
job setting itself. In considering this question, one needs to differentiate
between those circumstances in which people are paid on a piece-rate or
incentive basis and those in which they are paid on an hourly-rate basis.

Incentive Pay

Workers on many jobs are paid in relation to their productivity. The
variations on this theme are numerous, ranging from simple piece-rate to
complex schemes in which increasing productivity is rewarded by differing
ratios. (We will here refer to all of these as incentive pay systems, although
technically this term should not be applied to straight piece-rate systems.[11])

Isolating the specific effects of wage incentives on job performance is
a fairly knotty process, in part because the installation of such a system
sometimes is accompanied by other changes. On the basis of indications
from various sources, Opsahl and Dunnette[12] conclude that there is consid-

---

[11] For a discussion of incentive systems the reader is referred to such souces as
Maynard, H. B. (Ed.) *Industrial engineering handbook.* (2nd ed.) New York: Mc-
Graw-Hill, 1963.

[12] Opsahl & Dunnette, *op. cit.*

erable evidence that the installation of wage incentive plans usually results in greater output per hour, lower unit costs, and higher wages, as contrasted with outcomes associated with straight time payment systems. But they echo the point made above that other accompanying changes make it difficult to filter out the exclusive effects of incentive systems as such.

Vroom[13] also concludes that the evidence generally supports the assumption that workers tend to perform more effectively if their wages are related to performance, as they are in incentive systems. (But at the same time he calls our attention to the occasional situations in which such plans have the boomerang effect of encouraging restriction of output.) In reflecting on the general pattern of the effects of wage incentive plans, Vroom[14] points out that these effects are consistent with—and hence support—his theory of work motivation discussed in Chapter 12. On the assumption that money is positively valent, we would predict that the "valence" of effective performance on a job would be directly related to the "instrumentality" of performance for its attainment.

In the case of group incentive plans, the wages of individuals are based on the total productivity of the group. One relevant aspect of group plans concerns the relationship between the size of the work group and its productivity. Among the few bits of data available on this point, Marriott[15] presents those given in Figure 15.2, which shows a modest decline in average piece-rate earnings with increasing sizes of work groups. Further,

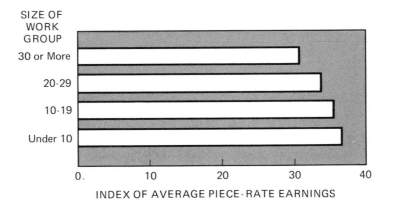

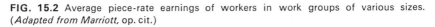

INDEX OF AVERAGE PIECE-RATE EARNINGS

FIG. 15.2 Average piece-rate earnings of workers in work groups of various sizes. (*Adapted from Marriott,* op. cit.)

13 Vroom, V. H. *Work and motivation.* New York: John Wiley, 1964, p. 258.
14 *Ibid.,* p. 260.
15 Marriott, R. Size of working group and output. *Occupational Psychology,* 1949, **23,** 47–57.

Marriott reports that workers in the same factory who were paid individually had higher average output than those in the smallest groups. The inklings from such data lead one to hypothesize that incentive systems tend to be most effective when the individuals perceive their own earnings to be most closely dependent upon their own efforts—which is most clearly the case with individual incentive systems. With group incentive plans, any one person's input has a diminishing impact on group productivity with increasing size of the group. In this regard, however, Vroom,[16] noting that group plans have been used most frequently for jobs that are highly interdependent in nature, points out that individual incentive plans are not more effective than group plans in all situations.

Although wage incentive plans generally tend to bring about increased productivity, they are not necessarily preferred by workers over time-based wages. In citing the results of four relevant surveys, for example, Opsahl and Dunnette[17] report that the majority of the personnel in only one of the four companies they studied favored incentive plans over time-based wages.

Time-Based Wages

Evidence about the relationship between time-based earnings and actual job performance is very sparse, and what bits and pieces of data are available tend to be peripheral rather than direct. For example, Schuster and Clark[18] report the results of a survey of 574 professional employees in one company who were asked to indicate their *perceptions* of their own annual salary growth rate compared to that of their peers. These comparisons were expressed on a scale ranging from "slow" raises to "fast." Because the respondents had been rated by their own supervisors in terms of their performance, it was possible to relate their responses to their rated performance levels. These results are summarized in Figure 15.3. This figure indicates rather clearly that in this company perception of financial reward was related to level of performance. This relationship might be a bit suspect on the grounds that supervisors may have had an influence in granting pay raises to those to whom they had given higher ratings, whether justified or not. Apart from this possibly contaminating influence, this relationship does, however, raise the chicken-and-egg conundrum about possible cause and effect. The investigators point out that they were unable to determine from their findings which was the causal variable: do individuals who are rated best by their supervisors reach higher salary levels *because* of their

---

[16] Vroom, *op. cit.,* p. 258.

[17] Opsahl & Dunnette, *op. cit.*

[18] Schuster, J. R., & Clark, B. Individual differences related to feelings toward pay. *Personnel Psychology,* 1970, 23, 591–604.

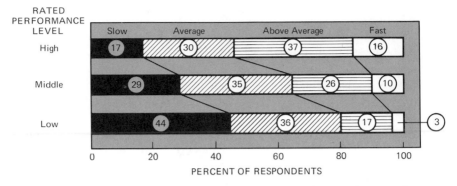

FIG. 15.3 Perceptions of 574 professional employees of their own salary growth rate as compared to their peers, as related to their performance level as rated by their supervisors. (*Adapted from Schuster and Clark, op. cit., p. 600.*)

performance? Or do supervisors rate the higher paid individuals higher to justify their current salary levels? One would hope that the first of these would be closest to the truth, inasmuch as it is consistent with the notion of reward for performance, but there is as yet no overwhelming evidence that this is the case.

If one is willing to assume—on the basis of faith or otherwise—that in the long run the rewarding of good performance serves to generate good performance, then wage policies should be geared toward this objective. The actual prevailing practices of organizations relating to pay increases, however, probably is not known. But one suspects that it comprises a mixed bag, as is implied by Haire[19] and by Haire, Ghiselli, and Gordon.[20] The study by Haire consisted of an analysis of pay and pay raises in two companies over five- and ten-year periods. He found no consistent pattern in the correlations between salaries and raises between adjacent years, implying that the companies had no consistent policies regarding the use of salary increases as incentives. Such analyses suggest that company policies regarding pay increases keep shifting from year to year, possibly without rationale, or possibly because of changes in policy—for example, from a policy of rewarding good performance to a "catch-up" policy of granting increases to those who had not had them, and then to a policy of rewarding long service, and so on.

On the other hand, Brenner and Lockwood[21] found, for a group of

19 Haire, M. The incentive character of pay. In R. Andrews (Ed.), *Managerial compensation.* Ann Arbor; Foundation for Research in Human Behavior, 1965, pp. 13–17.

20 Haire, M., Ghiselli, E. E., & Gordon, M. E. A psychological study of pay. *Journal of Applied Psychology Monograph,* 1967, 51(4), Whole No. 636.

21 Brenner, M. H., & Lockwood, H. C. Salary as a predictor of salary: A 20-year study. *Journal of Applied Psychology,* 1965, 49(4), 295–298.

fifty-two engineers in one company, a fairly consistent pattern of correlations of salaries for adjacent years, with the relationships decreasing as the time span between years increases. The results were interpreted as suggesting that the behaviors and/or personal characteristics that were being rewarded were being rewarded consistently. And in turn, Haire, Ghiselli, and Gordon,[22] who analyzed such relationships for three different industrial establishments, found certain parallels with the results reported by Brenner and Lockwood—but also some disparities.

The implications of the diverse results of such studies lend credence to the suspicion that policies regarding pay increases are far from consistent across organizations, and even in some instances within given organizations. If an organization changes the rules in the middle of the game, it can leave the employees in a quandary as to whether good performance is or is not to be reinforced by appropriate pay increases.

Haire, Ghiselli, and Gordon[23] express the lament that psychologists are seldom in a position to say how things *ought* to be in the real world, but they defend those psychologists who argue for consistency in pay policies in order, as they put it, to rescue individuals from the morass of insecurity engendered by situations in which the organization keeps shifting gears in its pay policies.

In connection with pay increases, incidentally, Hinrichs[24] surveyed about 1,500 white-collar workers to obtain their estimates of the sizes of the salary increases they had received, ranging from "just barely noticeable" to "small" to "average" to "large" to "extremely large." He found a pattern in which the magnitude of the judged increases of various sizes tended to be reflected as a ratio of the current salaries of people. This pattern was most consistent for the small and average increases, and was somewhat more erratic for the large and very large increases.

THE ESTABLISHMENT OF
WAGE SCALES

The point was made earlier that wage rates for various types of work presumably should be established in such a manner as to have some reasonable relationship to the going rates for corresponding activities in the labor market. In at least some organizations the establishment of rates of pay for various jobs is carried out on the basis of job evaluation systems. Job evaluation is the process of deriving indices of relative job

[22] Haire, Ghiselli, & Gordon, *op. cit.*
[23] *Ibid.*
[24] Hinrichs, J. R. Correlates of employee evaluations of pay increases. *Journal of Applied Psychology,* 1969, 53(6), 481–489.

values within an organization, usually on the basis of judgments about the jobs. In turn, these indices are used as the basis for determining wage rates for the jobs covered by the system. Usually this conversion to wage rates is made on the basis of a wage survey to determine "going rates" of a sample of jobs. In effect, then, a job evaluation program provides a systematic basis for an organization to establish compensation rates for its jobs so that they are in reasonable alignment with going rates for corresponding jobs in the labor market.

Installing a Job Evaluation Program

Although it is not appropriate here to go into the details of the development, installation, and operation of a job evaluation program, let us at least get an overview of these processes, which typically include the following steps:[25]

1. Establishing responsibility. Usually a job evaluation committee is set up to be responsible for a job evaluation program, although in some circumstances this responsibility will be assigned to one individual.
2. Development or selection of the job evaluation system to be used.
3. Preparing job descriptions.
4. Evaluation of jobs.
5. Converting evaluations to money values. This process frequently involves carrying out a wage or salary survey of going rates in the labor market.
6. Providing for evaluation of new jobs.

METHODS OF JOB EVALUATION

The four rather traditional job evaluation methods essentially are based on the judgments of individuals about job characteristics. In addition, a somewhat experimental approach to job evaluation, based on structured job-analysis data, seems to offer some promise of serving as the basis for establishing rates of pay. The first four of the methods listed are based on judgments of job characteristics; the fifth is based on structured job-analysis data.

1. Ranking method
2. Classification method
3. Point method
4. Factor comparison method
5. Job-component method

25 The reader interested in further discussion is referred to any of several texts on job evaluation such as: Belcher, D. W. *Wage and Salary administration.* (2nd ed.) Englewood Clliffs, N.J.: Prentice-Hall, Inc., 1962; Langsner, A., & Zollitsch, H. G. *Wage and salary administration.* Cincinnati: Southwestern Publishing Co., 1961;

Ranking Method

In the ranking method, jobs are compared with each other, usually on the basis of judged overall worth. Most typically, these judgments are obtained by a simple ranking of jobs—hence the name *ranking method*. However, because jobs can be judged relative to others by the use of other procedures, such as the paired comparison procedure, this method could more appropriately be called the *job comparison* method. The reliability of the evaluations usually is enhanced by having several individuals—preferably people who are already familiar with the jobs in question—serve as evaluators. When there are many jobs to be evaluated, however, it usually is impossible to find individuals who are familiar with all of them. Although there are ways of combining evaluations when each rater evaluates only some of the jobs, this method is usually most suitable in small organizations with limited numbers of jobs.

Classification Method

The classification method consists of the establishment of several categories of jobs along a hypothetical scale. Each such classification usually is defined and sometimes is illustrated. The Civil Service System of the federal government is essentially a classification system. In using this method, each job is assigned to a specific classification on the basis of its judged overall worth and its relation to the descriptions of the several classifications.

The classification method is a rather simple one to develop and use. However, unless special care is taken, it permits a tendency to perpetuate possible inequalities in existing rates of pay if it is used for evaluation of existing jobs that already have designated rates.

Point Method

The point method is without question the most commonly used procedure. It is characterized by the following features: (1) the use of several job evaluation factors; (2) the assignment of "points" to varying "degrees" or levels of each factor; (3) the evaluation of individual jobs in terms of their "degree" or level on each factor, and the assignment to each job of the number of points designated for the degree or level on the factor; and (4) the addition of the point values for the individual factors to derive

---

Lovejoy, *op. cit.;* Otis, J. L., & Leukart, R. H. *Job evaluation.* (2nd ed.) Englewood Cliffs, N.J.: Prentice-Hall, Inc., 1954; Patton, J. A. Littlefield, L. L., & Self, S. A. *Job evaluation: Text and cases.* (3rd ed.) Homewood, Ill.: R. D. Irwin, 1964; and Sibson, R. F. *Wages and salaries: A handbook for managers.* (Revised ed.) New York: American Management Association, 1967.

the total point value for each job. This total point value then serves as the basis for conversion to the corresponding wage or salary rate. The following illustration, taken from the system of the National Electric Manufacturers Association (NEMA), shows how one of the factors used in this system (experience) is converted into points for the various degrees of this factor.

Degree	Amount of Experience	Points
1	Up to three months	22
2	Over three months up to one year	44
3	Over one year up to three years	66
4	Over three years up to five years	88
5	Over five years	110

Similar "degree definitions" are included for the various degrees of the remaining factors, of which there are eleven in this particular system. The eleven factors and the point values assigned to the various degrees of those factors are given in Table 15.1. This particular system was designed for use with hourly-paid shop jobs. The system used by the National Metal Trades Association is essentially the same. Different systems usually are used for different major types of jobs, such as hourly-paid jobs, salaried jobs, and so forth.

TABLE 15.1 JOB CHARACTERISTICS AND POINT VALUES CORRESPONDING TO VARIOUS DEGREES OF EACH USED IN THE NATIONAL ELECTRICAL MANUFACTURERS ASSOCIATION JOB EVALUATION SYSTEM

Factors	First Degree	Second Degree	Third Degree	Fourth Degree	Fifth Degree
Skill					
1. Education	14	28	42	56	70
2. Experience	22	44	66	88	110
3. Initiative and ingenuity	14	28	42	56	70
Effort					
4. Physical demand	10	20	30	40	50
5. Mental or visual demand	5	10	15	20	25
Responsibility					
6. Equipment or process	5	10	15	20	25
7. Material or product	5	10	15	20	25
8. Safety of others	5	10	15	20	25
9. Work of others	5		15		25
Job Conditions					
10. Working conditions	10	20	30	40	50
11. Unavoidable hazards	5	10	15	20	25

Points Assigned to Factors and Key to Grades

Factor Comparison Method

The factor comparison method has been described in detail by Benge, Burk, and Hay.[26] In this method, fifteen or twenty tentative "key jobs" are first selected. These are jobs that have present rates not subject to controversy and that are considered by the job evaluation committee to be neither underpaid nor overpaid. These jobs then are compared to others in terms of factors common to all jobs. The factors used in the Benge, Burk, and Hay system are:

Mental requirements
Skill requirements
Physical requirements
Responsibility
Working conditions

The "key jobs" are first *ranked* on each of the factors mentioned, with all of the jobs appearing on each of the factor lists. The rankings usually are made independently by several people, and usually three times by each rater, with approximately one week intervening between each ranking. Next, these jobs are subjected to a *rating* process in which the going rate (salary or hourly rate) is divided for each of the tentative key jobs into the amount being "paid" for each of the factors. From these two independent procedures, two rank orders of the tentative key jobs on each factor are determined. The first ranking results from the direct ranking of the jobs on the factors. The second comes from the rank order of the monetary values that result from the rating process. Any of the tentative key jobs that do not come out with essentially the same rank orders in the two independent ranking procedures are eliminated from the list of key jobs. The jobs remaining constitute the framework of the factor comparison system for the company making the installation. All other jobs are compared with these key jobs, and each is located in its appropriate place on each of the factors included in the system. The amounts to be paid the job for the various factors are then added, which gives the evaluated rate for the job.

Job-Component Method

Behind what we will call the job-component method of job evaluation lies the implicit assumption that similarities in job content impose similar

[26] Benge, E. J., Burk, S. L. H., & Hay, E. N. *Manual of job evaluation.* (4th Ed.) New York: Harper & Row, 1941.

job demands upon the incumbents and should therefore warrant corresponding rates of pay. One could then agree that any given job component carries
its own "value," regardless of the combination of other job components
with which it might occur in any given job. The application of this
rationale in job evaluation leads to the use of structured job analysis
procedures that make it possible to identify and measure the level of each
of many job components as they occur in jobs.

One illustration of this approach is the use of the Job Analysis Check
List of Office Operations[27] as reported by Miles.[28] In the use of this checklist the analyst rates the importance to the job of each of many office
operations. In this study it was found that a weighted combination of the
five most important office operations resulted in total values that were
highly correlated with going rates for jobs.

In a more generalized application of the job-component method,
Jeanneret and McCormick[29] used the Position Analysis Questionnaire
(PAQ)[30] with a sample of 340 jobs of various kinds in various industries
in various parts of the country. As indicated in Chapter 3, the PAQ is a
structured job analysis questionnaire that provides for analyzing jobs in
terms of 194 "worker-oriented" job elements. In this particular study, job
dimension scores were derived statistically for the thirty-two factors that
resulted from a previous factor analysis of the PAQ. A statistically weighted
combination of scores on nine of these job dimensions produced correlations
with actual rates of pay for two subsamples consisting of 165 and 175 of
the jobs as well as for the total sample of 340. With a larger sample of
over eight hundred varied jobs, the correlation with actual rates of pay
was .85, as reported by Mecham.[31] And for a sample of seventy-nine jobs
in an insurance company, Taylor[32] reports a correlation of .93 between a
weighted combination of job dimension scores and actual rates of pay.
Although this approach to job evaluation is still in somewhat of an experimental stage, the results to date suggest that it may have substantial
potential.

[27] The Job Analysis Check List of Office Operations is available through the Village Book Cellar, 308 W. State Street, West Lafayette, Indiana 47906.

[28] Miles, M. C. Studies in job evaluation: a. Validity of a check list for evaluating office jobs. *Journal of Applied Psychology,* 1952, 36, 97–101.

[29] Jeanneret, P. R., & McCormick, E. J. *The use in job evaluation of job elements
and job dimensions based on the Position Analysis Questionnaire.* Lafayette, Indiana:
Occupational Research Center, Purdue University, June 1969. (Prepared for the Office of Naval Research under Contract Nonr–1100(28), Report No. 3.)

[30] The Position Analysis Questionnaire (PAQ) is available through the University
Bookstore, State Street, West Lafayette, Indiana 47906.

[31] Mecham, R. C. Personal communication, 1972.

[32] Taylor, L. R. Personal communication, 1971.

Discussion

It should be noted that, among the four traditional methods of job evaluation (i.e., ranking, classification, point, and factor comparison), there are differences both in the *techniques* of evaluation and in the *bases* of evaluation. These differences are illustrated below:

		Technique of Evaluation	
		By Comparison with Other Jobs	*By Evaluation Against a "Standard"*
Basis of evaluation	Whole job	Ranking method	Classification method
	Job factors	Factor comparison method	Point method

CONVERTING JOB EVALUATION RESULTS TO PAY SCALES

Most job evaluation systems result in jobs being placed at varying positions along a hypothetical scale of job values, as reflected by point values, rank orders, job classifications, or other measuring systems. In the case of some applications of the factor comparison and job component methods, the resulting evaluations actually are expressed in money terms, but most evaluations are expressed as point values which need to be converted to actual money values in order to establish the rates of pay for the jobs in question. This typically involves the establishment of a "going rate" curve and of an "organization rate" curve.

Developing a Going Rate Curve

At some stage of developing a wage or salary administration program it is necessary to determine the relationship between evaluations—usually of a sample of key jobs—and rates of pay for corresponding jobs in the labor market. In case data on the going rates of such jobs are not available, a wage or salary survey is carried out. For our present illustrative purposes, data on the median "going" rates of pay of a sample of jobs have been drawn from a survey by the Bureau of Labor Statistics.[33] (We could consider

---

[33] *National survey of professional, administrative, technical, and clerical pay.* Bulletin 1693, Bureau of Labor Statistics, 1971.

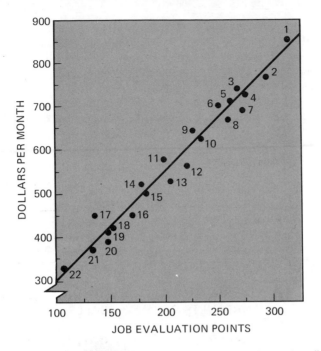

FIG. 15.4 Relationship between job evaluation points and median monthly pay rates for 22 jobs. The going rates are the median rates for a sample of jobs as reported by the Bureau of Labor Statistics. The line of best fit (in this case a straight line) is the going rate curve; it reflects the relationship of the job evaluation points to going rates.

these going rates as the median rates for a sample of companies in any given labor market.) These going rates along with illustrative evaluation points for the jobs are shown in Figure 15.4 to illustrate the establishment of a going wage curve. Although this particular relationship is linear, with some job evaluation systems the relationship is curvilinear.

Setting an Organization Rate Curve

The next stage is that of establishing a wage or salary curve for the specific organization. (In the case of private companies this is called the company wage or salary curve.) This curve, derived on the basis of the going wage curve, sets the general pattern of rates for the jobs covered by the job evaluation system. Although this curve is based on data for a sample of jobs that exist in other organizations in the labor market, it is of course used in establishing rates of pay for all of the jobs covered, including those that are

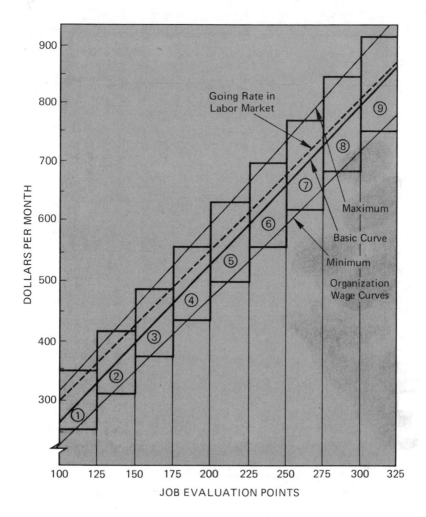

FIG. 15.5 Illustration of an "organization" wage curve, and of one pattern of conversion of job evaluation points into rates of pay. In this particular example, the point values are converted into nine pay grades, each of which has a range of rates.

unique to the organization. This assures that all the jobs covered will have their rates of pay established on the same basis.

Figure 15.5 shows an "organization" wage curve for the same jobs illustrated in Figure 15.4. In this case it is shown as slightly below the going rate curve of the labor market. Where this curve is actually set with respect to the going wage curve in any given case, however, is a function of various considerations, including economic conditions, contract negotiations, and fringe benefits. Thus, it can be at the *going* level of the going wage curve as such, or at various levels above or below.

In converting job evaluation points to actual rates of pay, different practices may be followed. It would be possible to take the evaluated points for a given job and derive the corresponding exact rate that would be applicable. Thus, every slight difference in points would result in some difference in hourly rate. In practice, most organizations (and unions) feel that the inherent lack of perfect accuracy in the judgments that underlie a set of job evaluations makes it desirable to bracket together jobs of approximately the same point value and to consider these jobs as equal in setting up the wage structure. This bracketing results in so-called *labor grades*. The number of labor grades found in specific wage structures varies from around eight or ten to twenty or twenty-five. The tendency of most current union demands in wage contract negotiations is to favor a relatively small number of labor grades.

When the jobs have been bracketed in labor grades, provision is usually made for wage increases within each labor grade, as illustrated in Figure 15.5. Various procedures have been used in granting wage increases within labor grades, as well as in upgrading employees to higher categories. Some organizations use an automatic acceleration schedule under which specified increases automatically become effective after a specified period of time on the job. This principle is employed most frequently in the lower labor grades and with new employees, but it is sometimes used at higher levels in the wage structure as well. A systematic merit-rating program is also used by some organizations as a means of identifying employees who are eligible for a pay increase under the prevailing pay structure.

As mentioned above, there are various policies followed in converting points to rates of pay. Although these will not be discussed here, two or three variations will be mentioned. Figure 15.5 shows an increasing range of rates with higher pay grades; in actual practice the range may be constant, or may be greater or less than that illustrated. In some systems the width of the pay grades (in terms of job evaluation points) increases with higher rates; these increases may be systematic or adapted in some way to the concentration of jobs along the evaluation scale.

RELIABILITY OF JOB EVALUATIONS

Inasmuch as most job evaluation systems are predicated on the use of human judgments, it is natural to be curious about the reliability of such

TABLE 15.2 RELIABILITY COEFFICIENTS OF THE NEMA JOB EVALUATION SYSTEM AND OF A SIMPLIFIED FOUR-FACTOR SYSTEM

	Evaluations of Factors		Total
	Range	Median	Points
NEMA System (11 factors)			
Pairs of raters	.34 to .82	.51	.77
Five raters	.72 to .96	.84	.94
Simplified System			
Pairs or raters	.51 to .86	.70	.89
Five raters	.84 to .97	.92	.98

Source: Lawshe and Wilson, *op. cit.* Copyright 1947 by the American Psychological Association, and reproduced by permission.

judgments. Most of the evidence about such reliability is based on the point system. In one of the several early basic studies of job evaluation carried out by Lawshe and his associates,[34] combinations of five raters were used in evaluating forty jobs using the eleven-factor NEMA system and a simplified four-factor system. Average reliability coefficients for pairs of raters were derived, as well as what are called "stepped-up" coefficients which reflect the pooled ratings of all five raters. The results are summarized in Table 15.2. These data probably illustrate the typical reliability of job evaluations with the point method. Incidentally, the data also illustrate the desirability of using several people in the evaluation of jobs, for the "pooled" reliability of the judgments of several people is substantially greater than the reliability of either individuals or pairs.

Some generally supporting reliability data are presented by Scott,[35] who arranged for the evaluation of fifteen jobs with a six-factor system. The evaluations were made individually by the members of several "committees," each of which consisted of five men. The members of some committees were experienced in job evaluation. Their average reliability coefficients ranged from .79 to .96 for the six factors and was .96 for total points. (Incidentally, the evaluations made by inexperienced men compared very favorably with these.) These and other studies indicate that the reliability of job evaluation judgments is quite respectable, especially when those of several raters are pooled.

[34] Lawshe, C. H., Jr., & Wilson, R. F. Studies in job evaluation: 6. The reliability of two-point rating systems. *Journal of Applied Psychology,* 1947, **31**, 355–365.

[35] Scott, W. E., Jr. The reliability and validity of a six-factor job evaluation system. Unpublished Ph.D. Thesis, Purdue University, January 1963.

FACTORS USED IN JOB EVALUATION SYSTEMS

The several different approaches to job evaluation tend to result in evaluations of various jobs that are relatively comparable. Years ago, for example, Chesler[36] reported intercorrelations among the systems of six different companies ranging from .89 to .93. These were based on the evaluation of thirty-five jobs using various systems, two of which were based on the factor comparison method, three on the point method, and one on a combination classification and ranking method. Such intercorrelations probably imply that the various systems measure substantially the same aspects of jobs, either directly or indirectly.

Combinations of Factors

This communality is reflected in the point systems by the fact that varying combinations of factors frequently produce substantially similar total point values for various jobs. The most exhaustive series of studies of this matter was carried out by Lawshe and his associates. In one of these studies, for example, Lawshe and Alessi[37] found that with a sample of salaried jobs in one company the total point values based on a weighted combination of three factors were highly correlated with total point values based on seven factors. Some of the results of this study are summarized below:

Factors	*Correlation with Total Points Based on 7 Factors*
Responsibility	.92
Responsibility plus manual skill	.97
Responsibility plus manual skill plus working conditions	.98

Other studies of the series demonstrated substantially the same fact—that a combination of a few factors (three or four, including particularly the responsibility factor) typically resulted in job values which were highly correlated with those based on more extensive systems, such as the eleven-factor NEMA system. These studies gave rise to the notion of simplified job

[36] Chesler, D. J. Reliability and comparability of different job evaluation systems. *Journal of Applied Psychology*, 1948, **32**, 465–475.
[37] Lawshe, C. H., Jr., & Alessi, S. L. Studies in job evaluation: 4. Analysis of another point rating scale for hourly-paid jobs and the adequacy of an abbreviated scale. *Journal of Applied Psychology*, 1946, **30**, 310–319.

evaluation systems. Subsequent analyses have tended to confirm the results of Lawshe's studies. For example, Scott[38] has developed a six-factor system that has been found to produce evaluations that are quite comparable to those of more extensive systems. The factors in his system are:

1. General Educational Development
2. Specific Job Preparation
3. Physical Demands
4. Working Conditions
5. Job Hazards
6. Supervision

It thus appears that, in general, abbreviated systems using only a few factors can produce evaluations of jobs that are substantially the same as those generated from more extensive systems. However, it can easily occur that the particular *combination* (and weighting) of factors that "works" in a specific setting may be somewhat different from the combinations that are more generally applicable. This can result from various situational aspects, such as the types of jobs or the nature of the working conditions in a particular organization.

Weighting of Factors

The weighting of factors in a job evaluation system is of course inextricably interwoven with the combination of factors used. In typical systems the various factors are assigned weights (the *intended* weights). These are usually determined by the job evaluation committee, frequently following the practice of other organizations. Such weights are reflected by the point values assigned to the various factors and the degrees of the factors, as shown for the NEMA system in Table 15.1. (The first column, which adds up to 100, reflects the intended weights for the individual factors.)

In discussing such weights, however, let us hark back to the discussion in Chapter 9 of the weighting of factors in performance evaluation systems. The point was made there that the *actual* or *effective* weights of factors (as opposed to the *intended* weights) are in part influenced by the variability (specifically the standard deviations) of the values assigned on the various factors to different cases in the sample. Thus, if the values on a given job evaluation factor that are assigned to different jobs show little variation, then that factor would have relatively nominal effective weight—*unless* appropriate statistical steps are taken to give it its intended weight.

---

[38] Scott, *op. cit.*

Optimum Combinations of Factors and Weights

As stated above, the usual practice in developing a job evaluation system is for the job evaluation committee to select the factors and to designate their intended weights. The optimum combination of factors and weights, however, can be determined by the use of statistical procedures. The use of such procedures, however, forces us to focus on this question: What is the *standard* (i.e., the criterion) by which we would determine that jobs have their own appropriate values? The criterion implicit in our previous discussions is that of going rates in the labor market, for the reasons previously expressed.

If one is willing to accept this criterion, it naturally follows that the combination of factors and weights used in a job evaluation system should be one that maximizes the correlation between total point values for jobs *within* the organization and for those *outside* the organization (i.e., in the labor market). The identification of such factors and of their optimum weights can be achieved with data on a sample of jobs within the organization that also exist in the labor market in question. The scheme to follow consists of the following steps: (1) the development of an "experimental" job evaluation system with several factors; (2) the evaluation of the sample of jobs using this system; (3) the determination of the going rates for the jobs in the labor market (by a wage or salary survey); (4) and the application of appropriate statistical procedures (specifically some form of regression analysis). The factors and their statistically determined weights could then be used in the organization with reasonable assurance that the rates of pay based on the system would have a reasonable relationship with rates in the labor market.

DISCUSSION

Wage and salary administrators must feel that they are continuously walking a tightrope because of the conflicting pressures that impinge upon them. A wage and salary program simultaneously must provide positive work incentives for the employees, must be generally acceptable to employees, must be reasonably competitive with conditions in the labor market, and must keep the organization solvent. Obviously, there are no pat and simplistic resolutions to meet these various objectives. The note on which we would like to close this discussion is that insight and knowledge relevant to the problem, derived through research such as illustrated in this chapter, can aid the process of developing a satisfactory program. Further, attention should be called to the fact that the field of job evaluation has not yet taken full advantage of certain scaling procedures that could be applied to the processes of making judgments about jobs and their characteristics.

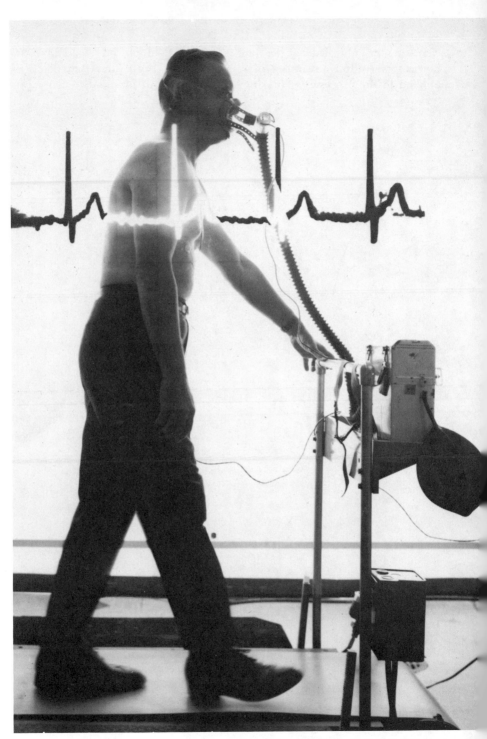

PART IV

The Job
and Work Situation

Part III dealt with the organizational and social context of human work. We will now turn our attention to the nature of the job activities involved in work, the equipment used, the physical working environment, and associated aspects of the work situation as these are related to human performance and general human welfare. During the last two or three decades increasing attention has been paid to the design of equipment and physical facilities with particular reference to considerations of human abilities and limitations. This area has become known as human factors engineering. In more recent years there has been growing concern about the effects of environmental variables upon the human race. This general interest in environmental factors has had the effect of further emphasizing the implications of such factors in working situations. It needs to be recognized that significant studies have been made over the years in improving the working environment for many people. At the same time, there remain some working conditions that still leave much to be desired in terms of human welfare. This section deals with various aspects of the job and the working situation.

chapter sixteen

Work and Equipment
Design

In large part this text is concerned with some of the factors that might have a bearing on job performance, job attendance, job satisfaction, and other criteria of human behavior in industry. In this context, we have discussed and illustrated the implications of individual differences and of certain social and organizational factors. Many pages ago (in pages 45 to 46, to be exact) we also made the point that the specific nature of a job and the working conditions related to it also can influence such criteria —for better or for worse as the case might be. To the extent that jobs and at least certain working and living conditions are created by man, they can—if one wishes—be created in such a way as to achieve certain possible advantages in terms of relevant criteria. But before touching further on these criteria, let us reflect for a moment about the processes or factors that influence the nature of jobs.

The nature of jobs—that is, their "content," methods, procedures, activities, and so forth—can be the consequence of any of several influences, some intentional and others unintentional. The specific characteristics of some jobs have come into being fortuitously, perhaps simply because someone "happened" to start doing a certain thing in a certain way; in other cases job characteristics have "evolved" over time as the result of the experience of individuals or a succession of individuals; and in yet other cases job characteristics are the natural outgrowth of cultural patterns. In connection with cultural effects, for example, the common squatting posture used in many jobs in India and other Asian countries and the common carrying of brick and other material in baskets beautifully balanced on the head are undoubtedly the consequences of physical postures and skills developed from childhood.

In the current century major efforts have been made in the direction of intentionally "designing" jobs in terms of certain principles or guidelines. Most of these efforts have been made by industrial engineers and their predecessors. Still another factor that influences the specific characteristics of at least some jobs is that of the design of the equipment and other physical facilities that people use in their jobs, for at least some design features of the things people use virtually predetermine what human activities will be required in their use.

CRITERIA IN EVALUATING
JOB-RELATED FACTORS

In Chapter 2 we referred to some of the types of criteria that may have relevance to some aspects of industrial psychology. These included (among others): performance, physiological measures, subjective reactions of people, and accidents. (Accidents will be discussed further in Chapter 19.) All of these can be useful as bases for comparing the appropriateness of one job design to another, of one design of equipment to another, of one aspect of the working conditions to another, and of other job-related variables. Because of the significance of criteria for such purposes, let us take a minute to discuss them further.

Performance Criteria

Probably the most common type of criterion used for such purposes is some measure of performance such as work output, time to complete some job activity, quality of performance, or performance decrement over time. In some circumstances, however, performance measures of more basic human processes, such as visual, motor, or mental performance, may be in the cards. Such criteria generally are most relevant in the research aspects of performance measurement.

Physiological Criteria

Human work is accomplished by certain physiological processes. As a person performs work, especially physical work, there typically are various changes in his physiological condition. If the work is severe enough or long enough, an individual's physical ability to perform the task deteriorates. The energy used in the execution of any muscular task comes from potential energy that is stored in chemical form in the muscles. As this energy is expended, the muscles become less and less able to perform their task. This reduction in potential energy available in the muscles is brought about by two processes; (1) the consumption, during muscle activity, of the contractile material or of the substances available for the supply of potential energy to this material; and (2) the accumulation of the waste products of muscle contraction, especially lactic acid; such waste products are the chemical result of muscle activity.

Muscle activity triggers, directly or indirectly, quite an assortment of physiological reactions, each of which, in a sense, can be thought of as an index of the muscle activity itself. These include changes in heart rate, blood pressure, oxygen consumption, breathing rate, blood composition, and electrical resistance of the skin. The heart rate recovery curve is a particularly good example of a physiological criterion. This measure, which has been used especially by Brouha[1] in some of his research, is obtained by counting the pulse rate at one-minute intervals during the first three minutes of the recovery period after the termination of work and while the subject is sitting quietly. The curve based on such readings indicates the actual value of the pulse and the rate of recovery toward resting level. Figure 16.1 shows the heart rate recovery curves resulting from one, two, and three repetitions of a strenuous physical operation. The differences in the levels of these curves are indicative of differences in the physiological stress of performing the operation once, twice, and three times.

Aside from physiological energy costs of work as such, there are other physiological effects that may occur as a consequence of some type of activity. These include what is sometimes called *physiological stress,* such as caused by heat, noise, or other environmental conditions, or by occasional heavy work demands.

The selection and use of physiological measurements should be undertaken only by those who are well versed in their use. Thus Burger[2] points out that there are certain pitfalls in the use of heart rate as a measure of work load. In skilled hands, however, it can be a useful measure for many situations, especially when used as a *comparative* measure of circulatory load under conditions of heavy dynamic muscular work, heat exposure, or emotional stress. Heart rate is less appropriate as a measure of static muscular load or of local dynamic muscular work, and is of little value as a measure of mental load. Other indices of circulatory load, such as oxygen consumption and blood pressure, also can be used in the measurement of

---

[1] Brouha, L. *Physiology in industry.* New York: Pergamon Press, 1960.
[2] Burger, G. C. E. Heart rate and the concept of circulatory load. *Ergonomics,* 1969, **12**(6), 857–864.

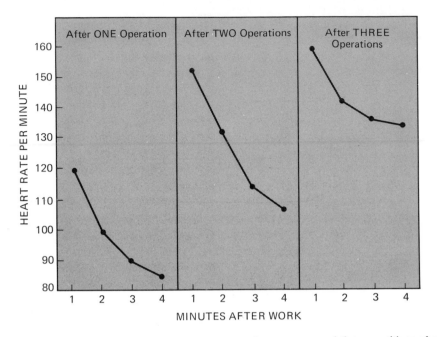

FIG. 16.1 Change in heart rate recovery curves after one, two, and three repetitions of a strenuous physical operation. (*From Brouha, op. cit., p. 91.*)

heavy physical work. In the analysis of mental activity other techniques are more appropriate, such as electroencephalography.

Subjective Criteria

It is a matter of common experience that work may be accompanied by some subjective (psychological) reactions to it. There are various dimensions of such reactions. Among the most common subjective reactions are those of *boredom* and *psychological stress*. What we commonly call boredom usually is associated with work that is intrinsically uninteresting to the individual performing it. Most frequently, boredom is associated with jobs that are repetitive or relatively simple. It should be pointed out, however, that it is the individual's *reaction* to the job that would cause him to describe a job as "boring." No job is, or can be, intrinsically boring, inasmuch as the term boredom refers to an attitudinal reaction of the individual. Psychological stress is most often viewed as the consequence of competition between two incompatible tendencies, one of which typically has a positive valence and the other a negative valence.[3] Thus, situations

3 Chiles, W. D. *Psychological stress as a theoretical concept.* USAF Wright Air Development Center, Technical Report 57–457, July 1957.

in which frustrations, conflict, fear, or anxiety can arise might give rise to psychological stress.

JOB DESIGN

Although the specific activities of some jobs are virtually predetermined by the objective to be achieved, perhaps most typically there is opportunity to "design" jobs, and thus to choose, from among various possible options, that option which seems best in terms of some appropriate criterion (such as time or physiological cost). To a substantial degree the specific features of jobs are the consequence of the design of the physical equipment and facilities used, of the methods for their use, and of the work space within which the individual works. These interrelated areas generally are subsumed under the heading of human factors engineering and are the subject of the industrial engineering practices of methods design. Collectively, these disciplines are concerned with the design of human work in terms of criteria relating to the effective use of human beings in performing work and the maintenance or enhancement of certain desirable human values (safety, health, satisfactions, and so forth). Although these areas cannot be treated in detail here, a brief review of each is in order because of their impact on the work activities of people.

HUMAN FACTORS ENGINEERING

What we refer to as *human factors engineering*[4] is also known in Europe and elsewhere as *ergonomics*. This field intermeshes with methods design, but is concerned more with the design of equipment and other physical facilities in terms of human considerations. Human factors engineering can be defined as designing for human use. Man has always striven toward designing the things he uses so that he can use them more effectively and with minimum effort on his part. Because the types of equipment and facilities used in the past were relatively uncomplicated, it was possible to try things out, and if they were not fully suitable for human use, the next version could be modified. Thus, many items of human use such as hand tools, went through an evolutionary process.

In more recent years, however, more systematic attention has been given

[4] Readers who are interested in a further treatment of this topic are referred to such sources as McCormick, E. J. *Human factors engineering.* New York: McGraw-Hill, 1970; Gagné, R. M., *et al. Psychological principles in system development.* New York: Holt, Rinehart & Winston, 1962; and Morgan, C. T., Cook, J. S., III, Chapanis, A., & Lund, M. W. *Human engineering guide to equipment design.* New York: McGraw-Hill, 1963.

to the design of equipment and other physical facilities from the human factors point of view. This recent concern was instigated primarily by the experience of the military services in the use of new types of weapon systems. It was found during World War II, for example, that some new systems could not be operated effectively because of design deficiencies related to their use by people. The subsequent development of space programs, and of more complicated industrial and other systems, has focused attention on the need to take human factors into account early in the design of such systems, in order to have greater assurance that the systems can be used effectively when they are produced. This shift has placed greater emphasis on the use of research as the basis for designing items for human use, for the slow, evolutionary process predicated on human trial and error is incompatible with today's fast-moving technology. Although the interest in human factors engineering has been most concentrated in the design of relatively sophisticated systems, it is proposed that we view this field as relevant to the creation of any facilities or items that people use. Thus the range of potential application includes the equipment, tools, machines, and other facilities people use in their jobs, and also the complete spectrum of things people use in their daily lives, including consumer products, automobiles, transportation systems, buildings, recreation facilities, and even complete communities. In a broad sense, the problem of pollution is essentially a human factors problem. The research that provides the base for human factors engineering comes from such fields as psychology, anthropology, physiology, and biology.

A helpful frame of reference for viewing human factors engineering can be achieved by considering human activity in terms of the following paradigm:

$$S \longrightarrow O \longrightarrow R$$

(Stimulus)   (Organism)   (Response)

In virtually every type of human activity an individual (the organism) receives certain stimuli that impinge upon him to bring about some response. Human work activities, of whatever type, basically conform to this pattern.

Using somewhat more operational terms, we can express this paradigm in terms of *information input, mediation* (i.e., mental) *processes,* and *action processes.* A generalized schematic diagram of these functions is given in Figure 16.2. Consider, for example, an electric power station operator. He receives information from the instruments of his control panel, and on the basis of this information (and of what he has learned), he decides what to do, and then takes corresponding action, such as opening one switch and closing another.

Many of the stimuli that impinge on an organism come from the ex-

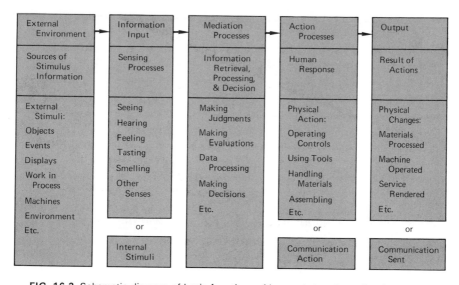

External Environment	Information Input	Mediation Processes	Action Processes	Output
Sources of Stimulus Information	Sensing Processes	Information Retrieval, Processing, & Decision	Human Response	Result of Actions
External Stimuli: Objects Events Displays Work in Process Machines Environment Etc.	Seeing Hearing Feeling Tasting Smelling Other Senses	Making Judgments Making Evaluations Data Processing Making Decisions Etc.	Physical Action: Operating Controls Using Tools Handling Materials Assembling Etc.	Physical Changes: Materials Processed Machine Operated Service Rendered Etc.
	or		or	or
	Internal Stimuli		Communication Action	Communication Sent

FIG. 16.2 Schematic diagram of basic functions of human beings in performing work and other activities. For each basic function a few examples are given in the lower part of the figure.

ternal environment and are sensed by the sense organs. On the other hand, many of the stimuli that trigger human activity are generated internally, as the result of mediation processes (such as recalling that a particular chore is to be done at a particular time) or of physiological processes (such as hunger pangs).

The stimulus-organism-response frame of reference is useful in designing physical equipment because it reminds us constantly of the three major factors that must be taken into consideration in designing the features that will influence, for better or for worse, the effectiveness with which people can perform these basic functions. Thus, well designed road signs can help drivers receive the information they need, and well designed control mechanisms (the accelerator, brake, and steering mechanisms) can help the driver to better control his vehicle. Because of the relevance of this basic frame of reference to the human factors area, we will deal with each of these aspects separately.

INFORMATION-INPUT PROCESSES

The sensory organs of the body are the avenues through which an individual receives information regarding the world about him, including the information that is available to him in performing his job. We commonly think that there are five senses—seeing, hearing, touch, taste, and smell. There are, however, certain other senses, such as sensations of heat and cold, of body movement, of body posture, of position of body members, and probably some others not yet identified. Seeing and hearing are the senses used most frequently in work or in our everyday lives, although some of the other senses are important in certain specific circumstances. We sense many things in our environment directly, but in some circumstances information is presented *indirectly* by the use of some man-made *display,* such as traffic lights, printed material, or warning bells.

Types and Uses of Displays

In general, displays can be described as either *static* (signs, printed material, labels, and so forth) or *dynamic* (speedometers, clocks, radios and so forth). These can be used for different purposes—that is, to present various "types" of information—of which the following are perhaps the most common:

Quantitative information, i.e., quantitative values such as weight, pressure, etc.

Qualitative information, i.e., the approximate value of some continuous variable, or an indication of its trend, rate of change, etc., such as approximate speed.

Check information, i.e., and indication as to whether a continuous changeable variable is or is not within a normal or acceptable range.

Alphanumeric or symbolic information.

Selection of Sensory Modality

In designing a display for presenting information to people, the designer *may* have a choice of the sensory modality to use, although in many circumstances the sensory modality is virtually predetermined for him by the nature of the case. When there is some option, there are two factors for him to consider—(1) the relative advantages of one sensory modality over another for the purpose at hand, and (2) the relative demands already made upon the different senses.

In connection with the latter, vision probably is used most extensively as a display input channel, followed by audition. The other senses are not now used very extensively for such purposes. However, the tactual sense is being used by some blind persons (e.g., with Braille print) and seems to offer reasonable promise for use in circumstances in which vision and audition are overloaded. When there is some option in choosing one channel over another, some consideration of the relative advantages of each can aid in making a selection. Such a comparison has been made for the auditory and visual channels by Singleton,[5] and is given in Table 16.1.

It should be noted that the auditory channel lends itself best to the transmission of messages that are simple and short, whereas the visual

5 Singleton, W. T. Display design: Principles and procedures. *Ergonomics,* 1969, **12**(4), 519–531.

TABLE 16.1   RELATIVE ADVANTAGES OF THE AUDITORY AND VISUAL SENSORY CHANNELS
IN INFORMATION INPUT

Basis of Comparison	Auditory (Hearing)	Visual (Seeing)
Reception	Requires no directional search	Requires attention and location
Speed	Fast	Slowest
Order	Most easily retained	Easily lost
Urgency	Most easily incorporated	Difficult to incorporate
Noise	Not affected by visual noise	Not affected by auditory noise
Accepted symbolism	Melodious Linguistic	Pictorial Linguistic
Mobility	Most flexible	Some flexibility
Suitability	Dominantly time information	Dominantly space information
	For rhythmical data For warning signals	For stored data For routine multichannel checking

Source: Singleton, *op. cit.,* p. 525.

channel can be used more effectively with messages that are complex and long.

Design Features of Displays

Once a determination has been made regarding the sensory modality to use in presenting information, a specific design of the display needs to be chosen or created. Considerable research has been carried out regarding the effectiveness of various design features in transmitting information to people. Although we will not summarize this research, a few examples can serve to illustrate the nature of such research.

Numerical visual scales. Among the more common visual displays are those that represent some numerical scale, for use either in quantitative reading tasks (to determine the actual numerical value) or qualitative reading (to determine an approximate value, direction, or other variable). Some examples of such scales are shown in Figure 16.3. These include instruments with *moving pointers* and fixed scales and instruments with *moving scales* and fixed pointers. Of the various studies relating to such instruments, let us review one by Elkin[6] in which he used circular (a), vertical (c), and open-window (f) designs for both quantitative and qualitative reading tasks.

[6] Elkin, E. H. *Effects of scale shape, exposure time, and display-response complexity on scale reading efficiency.* USAF, WADC Technical Report 58–472, February 1959.

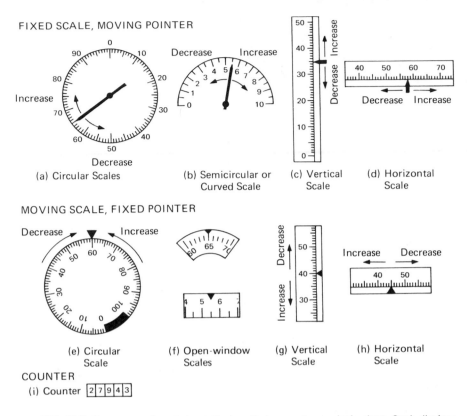

FIG. 16.3 Some examples of visual displays that present numerical values. Such displays are typically used for quantitative reading tasks, but in certain situations may also be used for qualitative reading tasks. (*Adapted from* Human factors engineering *by E. J. McCormick, p. 134. Copyright* © *1970 by McGraw-Hill, Inc. Used with permission of McGraw-Hill Book Company.*)

In different phases of the study, three different time limits were used, as well as a no-time-limit condition. In the quantitative reading task, the open window was read with shortest time and fewest errors, followed by the circular and vertical in that order. But the differences were greatest for the 0.12 second time limit; for longer time exposures (0.36 and 1.08 seconds) and no time limit, however, the differences were much less accentuated and generally not significant. In the qualitative reading phase of the study, the order of superiority of the three scales was different, the order being circular, vertical, and open window.

These findings, along with those from other studies, point clearly to the principle that visual displays should be designed for the specific purpose at hand. As another illustration of this principle we might cite the use of circular displays and counters, shown as (a) and (i) in Figure 16.3. There are bits and pieces of evidence indicating that if the purpose is one of obtaining a quantitative value (and if the values do not keep fluctuating), a counter (i.e., a digital display) frequently is superior. This was demonstrated by van Nes[7] in an experiment with a conventional clock and a counter (i.e., digital) time display. The task assigned to the subjects in this experiment was one of rating time differences between pairs of displays. Following are the average times taken by ten subjects in performing the task, along with their errors, when using circular and counter displays:

	Average Time	Average Errors
Circular (clock) display	118 sec.	15%
Counter (digital) display	51 sec.	5%

Although the absolute values given are not meaningful if the details of the task are not known, the relative differences clearly show the superiority of the counter display in this general type of task.

Visual displays for check reading. Sometimes several or many visual displays (such as circular scales) are used together for check reading purposes—that is, in determining whether each display is or is not at a "normal" condition. In various studies it has been found that any deviant display can be identified most readily if the pointers, when at the null or normal condition, are arranged in some systematic manner, such as at the nine or twelve o'clock positions; any deviant instrument then can be identified easily because it "breaks up" the otherwise consistent visual pattern.

In this connection, some interesting variations were tried out by Oatman.[8] He used the three patterns illustrated in Figure 16.4, presenting reproductions such as these for 1/25th of a second. Of the patterns shown

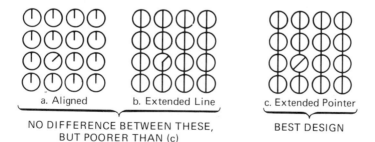

a. Aligned   b. Extended Line   c. Extended Pointer

NO DIFFERENCE BETWEEN THESE,   BEST DESIGN
BUT POORER THAN (c)

FIG. 16.4 Designs of check-reading displays used in study by Oatman. Design (c), the extended-pointer design, resulted in the most accurate detection and location of deviant pointers. (*Adapted from Oatman,* op. cit.)

[7] van Nes, F. L. Determining temporal differences with analogue and digital time displays. *Ergonomics,* 1972, **15**(1), 73–79.

[8] Oatman, C. L. Check-reading accuracy using an extended-pointer dial display. *Journal of Engineering Psychology,* 1964, **3**, 123–131.

here, the extended-pointer design resulted in most rapid *detection* of the deviant pointers and in the most accurate *location* of those that were so detected. In general, it appeared that the use of extended pointers (design c) tends to "break up" the visual field more than the use of aligned (but short) pointers (a and b), thus making the deviant instruments more detectable.

MEDIATION PROCESSES

As indicated earlier, virtually every human activity involves some mediation processes. The grist for these operations consists of input information and information retrieved from storage—that is, from memory. The nature of these mediation functions naturally varies with the situation, but can include the making of judgments and evaluations, reasoning, the making of computations, and other mental operations. Whatever their nature, however, the end result usually is some decision or choice of action. It should be noted, however, that these mediation operations cannot be neatly differentiated from the preceding information input and the succeeding output (i.e., response) functions. For example, the process of perception is inextricably intertwined with both sensation functions and mediation processes, for perception, as a psychological process, involves the attachment of meaning to that which is sensed.

The Nature of Decisions to be Made

Operationally, the nature or "quality" of the mediation processes that are required in at least some types of human work is influenced by the type or format of the input information presented, by the nature of the responses to be made, and by the interrelationship between these. The influence of the form of displayed information was studied by Silver, Jones, and Landis[9] in an experiment using a "gaming technique" that was a simulation of the management of a hypothetical trucking concern. The "traffic managers" used three different formats of "maps" in planning the utilization of trucks. Without going into details, it can be said that the efficiency of such utilization, as measured by mean "profit" per load, was significantly influenced by the format of the maps used.

Given certain informational input (stimuli), the mediation processes should lead to a decision which, when implemented by a human response, should bring about the most appropriate end result (output). In repetitive types of operations the decision as to what to do is virtually predetermined

[9] Silver, C. A., Jones, J. M., & Landis, D. Decision quality as a measure of visual display effectiveness. *Journal of Applied Psychology,* 1966, **50**(2), 109–113.

and the human response to a given stimulus is essentially a conditioned response. Such operations, of course, lend themselves most readily to mechanization or automation; however, economic factors, the state of the art, or other considerations may argue for the retention of human beings in some such operations. But it is in less structured, less predictable circumstances that the mental capacities of people are more effectively utilized. In fact, as pointed out by Singleton,[10] the basic reason for incorporating a human operator in a system is that certain required functions cannot be defined or predicted accurately. Thus, in a sense, the human being is needed most when there is an inherent uncertainty or vagueness about the problem at hand which requires indeterminate responses at indeterminate times. Although human beings certainly have their shortcomings (some more than others), they generally are more adaptable than machines, primarily because of their repertoire of mental abilities.

When for one reason or another a human being is used to perform a given function in a system, it may be desirable (and in some circumstances critical) to try to facilitate the mediation and decision processes for him by appropriate design of the system, including especially the information input and output (i.e., response) features of the system. In doing so, one should focus particularly on the decisions to be made, and then work backward to figure out what information should be presented to the individual to help him make such decisions. The displayed information then should be presented in such a manner as to facilitate the mediation and decision processes.

Facilitating Mediation Processes

We cannot here explore the various ways of facilitating the mediation functions in systems, but a couple of aspects will be discussed briefly as examples.

Decision time. In the first place, let us consider at least one factor that influences the time to make decisions in fairly well structured situations in which specific responses are to be made to specific stimuli. In such circumstances decision time (or response time) is clearly a function of the number of possible alternatives. This has been demonstrated frequently, such as in the study by Hilgendorf[11] in which he examined the relationship between information input (as measured by the number of equally probable alternative stimuli which could occur) and response time (RT) in a key-pressing task. The stimuli consisted of numerals, letters, and other typewriter symbols displayed in front of the subject. The subject responded by activating

---

10 Singleton, *op. cit.*, p. 520.
11 Hilgendorf, L. Information input and response time. *Ergonomics,* 1966, 9(1), 31–37.

corresponding keys on a specially prepared typewriter on which only the relevant keys were displayed (the others being covered). The number of possible stimuli in the six different "alphabets" and their symbols are shown below:

No. of Stimuli in "Alphabet"	Symbols Used in Alphabet
2	0, 1
4	$+, -, \times, +$
10	0, 1, 3 . . . 9
26	A, B, C . . . Z
100	00, 01, 02 . . . 99
1000	000, 001, 002 . . . 999

The results, summarized in Figure 16.5, indicate that response time varies directly with the logarithm of the number of alternatives for values up to 1,000. This generally confirms the results of previous studies except that it extends the range of application to the larger number of one thousand alternatives. It should be noted that the total response time is made up of two values—*recognition time* (the time the subject took to identify the stimulus and raise his hand from a resting position) and *movement time* (the actual time taken to make the response).

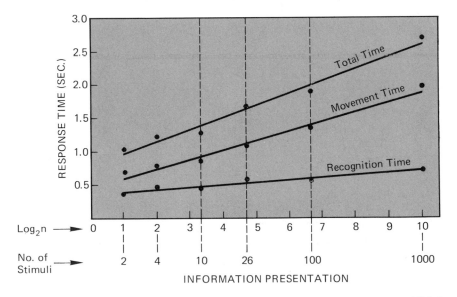

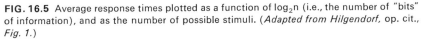

FIG. 16.5 Average response times plotted as a function of $\log_2 n$ (i.e., the number of "bits" of information), and as the number of possible stimuli. (*Adapted from Hilgendorf, op. cit., Fig. 1.*)

The implications of such findings probably are particularly pertinent to circumstances in which a premium is placed on the time to choose, from among various possible reactions, the one that is specifically indicated. In such circumstances, a reduction of the number of possible actions (if feasible) would tend to bring about a more rapid response.

Compatibility

The concept of compatibility in the human factors field refers to the spatial, movement, or conceptual features of stimuli and responses, individually or in combination, which are most consistent with human expectations. It has been demonstrated time and again that the use of compatible relationships definitely enhances human performance in terms of time, accuracy, and other criteria. Some examples will illustrate the concept.

Spatial compatibility. Spatial compatibility refers to the compatibility of the physical features, or arrangement, of items such as displays and controls. Figure 16.6, for example, shows two arrangements of a set of eight displays and their corresponding controls. Of these two, the first is the more compatible because of the closer one-to-one relationship of each control to its corresponding display, although the second arrangement also would be acceptable.

In one study of spatial compatibility, Chapanis and Mankin[12] tried out ten different linkages between four displays (arranged in a square) and four controls (arranged vertically). The subject's task was to push the appro-

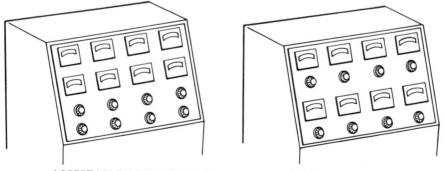

ACCEPTABLE ARRANGEMENT   PREFERRED ARRANGEMENT

FIG. 16.6 Illustration of spatial compatibility of a set of displays and their corresponding controls. The one at the left (a) is the more compatible because of the closer one-to-one relationship of each pair of displays and controls, although arrangement (b) also represents a reasonably compatible pattern.

[12] Chapanis, A., & Mankin, D. A. Tests of ten control-display linkages. *Human Factors,* 1967, 9(2), 119–126.

priate control button as soon as a light appeared in one of the displays. The ten linkages are shown in Figure 16.7, along with the mean response times. The first two or three arrangements are clearly the most compatible.

Movement compatibility. There are several variants of movement compatibility, but they all deal with the relationship between the direction of some physical movement (usually of a control device) and the direction of response of the system. Frequently the response of the system is shown by a display. It should be noted, however, that there is some parallel to the chicken-and-egg conundrum here inasmuch as in some circumstances the control action is to correspond with some indication such as a display, whereas in others the indication reflects the consequence of the control action. In general, those linkages that are most consistent with human expectations result in superior human performance. Some examples of compatible control-display relationships are shown in Figure 16.8.

Conceptual compatibility. Conceptual compatibility probably can be better illustrated than defined. Some examples are: the use of red for

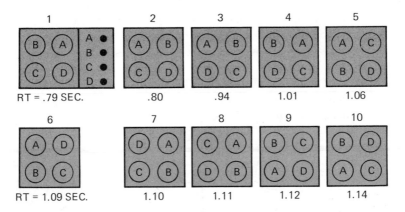

FIG. 16.7 Linkages of four displays and their corresponding controls used in study of spatial compatibility by Chapanis and Mankin. The mean reaction time (RT) for 8 subjects (96 trials for each) is shown for each linkage. The first shows the basic arrangement of the controls and displays (except that the displays were 4″ in size within a 30″ panel); the remaining nine figures show only the variations in the display arrangements, since the control arrangement was always the same. (*Adapted from Chapanis and Mankin, op. cit.*)

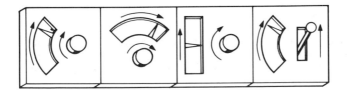

FIG. 16.8 Some examples of compatible movement relationships between controls and displays.

danger; the use of a curved line on a road sign to represent a curved road; and having the entrance to a supermarket on the right because—at least in most countries—people drive on the right-hand side of the road.

Reducing Short-term Memory Demands

Still another factor that can affect the mediation processes or quality of decisions is the need to depend upon short-term memory. This, in turn, can be influenced by the design features of the displays and the control devices, as was clearly demonstrated by the results of an investigation by Conrad.[13] Actually, this study dealt with only one facet of compatibility in that subjects performed a keyboard task (very much like using a push-button telephone) in which one keyboard had a "high-compatibility" layout (with the numbers arranged as on a push-button telephone) and the other had a "low-compatibility" layout (with the numbers jumbled around). Some of the results, based on twenty female subjects, are summarized below:

	Layout	
	High-compatibility	Low-compatibility
Mean number of wrong digits	1.18	1.45
Mean keying time, sec. (for 32 8-digit sequences)	6.28	7.14
Number of subjects faster	19	1

Conrad makes the point that the increased errors with the low-compatibility keyboard is essentially a function of short-term memory. In particular, he suggests that if the layout of a keyboard requires more time to locate each key, errors will increase because of the longer time involved in retaining the relevant information in short-term memory.

Discussion

Not all of the mediation and decision processes of mankind are contingent upon the design features of the physical things people use. But there are indeed some activities—including jobs—in which these processes are so contingent. Where this is the case, efforts should be made to create design features which facilitate these functions. Although some directions are discussed briefly above—such as taking advantage of compatibility relationships, reducing short-term memory demands, and so forth—there are also other avenues that will suggest themselves in specific circumstances.

[13] Conrad, R. Short-term memory factor in the design of data-entry keyboards. *Journal of Applied Psychology,* 1966, 50(5), 353–356.

ACTION PROCESSES

For a decision to be implemented, some action must be taken by the individual. This may be some physical action or a communication action. For our brief discussion here, we will concern ourselves with physical actions. In the design of equipment and the development of methods, it is of course desirable to provide for those human physical actions and responses that will result in the desired output. This can be done through the design, location, and arrangement of control devices, and through the methods that are established for doing the job.

Psychomotor Skills

The human being is capable of performing a wide variety of psycho-motor activities. Some of these were discussed in Chapter 6. The relevance of the psychomotor skills of people to work and equipment design perhaps can be viewed from two frames of reference—(1) performance on varia-tions of a given basic activity; and (2) individual differences in perfor-mance of a given activity.

Variations of a given activity. To optimize performance of some basic psychomotor activity, one can examine the efficiency of *variations* in that activity as related to *people in general*. Depending on the basic activity, variations may be related to parameters such as direction of movement or location of body member. A classic study by Fitts[14] will serve to illustrate this. This study dealt with making "blind-positioning" movements such as reaching for a control device while not looking. The subjects in the experi-ment were blindfolded and then seated in the enclosure shown in Figure 16.9. They were given a sharp-pointed marker and were asked to make blind-positioning movements to the various targets around the enclosure. There were three tiers of targets, the middle one being at approximately shoulder level and the others being about 45° above and below.

Accuracy was determined by "scoring" the position of the hits made with the marker; a bull's-eye was scored 0, a mark in the first circle around the bull's-eye was scored 1, and marks in the other rings were given higher scores up to the outside ring, which was scored 6. Thus, a low score indicates good accuracy. The results are shown in Figure 16.10. The size of each circle indicates the relative error-scores of the movements to the target at that particular location. The average error scores are given inside the circles. Figure 16.10 indicates that accuracy is greatest in the positions

---

14 Fitts, P. M. A study of location discrimination ability. In P. M. Fitts (Ed.), *Psychological Research on Equipment Design.* Superintendent of Documents, USAF, Aviation Psychology Program, Research Report No. 19, 1947.

FIG. 16.9 Experimental situation used in study of accuracy of blind-positioning movements carried out by Fitts, *op. cit.* (*Courtesy Psychology Branch, Aero-Medical Laboratory.*)

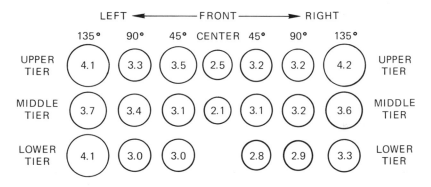

LEFT ◄————————FRONT————————► RIGHT

	135°	90°	45°	CENTER	45°	90°	135°	
UPPER TIER	4.1	3.3	3.5	2.5	3.2	3.2	4.2	UPPER TIER
MIDDLE TIER	3.7	3.4	3.1	2.1	3.1	3.2	3.6	MIDDLE TIER
LOWER TIER	4.1	3.0	3.0		2.8	2.9	3.3	LOWER TIER

FIG. 16.10 Accuracy of blind-positioning movements in different directions. Each circle represents the location of a target (left to right, and in upper, middle, and lower tiers). The average error-score for each target is given inside the circle, and the size of the circle is proportional to the error-score. (*Adapted from Fitts,* op. cit. *Courtesy Psychology Branch, Aero-Medical Laboratory.*)

straight ahead and is least in the extreme side positions. In terms of target level, the accuracy is greatest for the lowest tier and least for the highest tier.

The results of this and other studies dealing with human performance on variations of a basic psychomotor activity naturally can have implications in terms of equipment design and layout—in this particular instance in locating, say, control devices that might be used under blind-positioning conditions.

Individual differences in performance. The second frame of reference in considering the human factors implications of psychomotor activities relates to the range of individual differences in performance on any *given* activity. Let us consider a hypothetical example. Suppose, in line with the above discussion, a comparison has been made of the performance of people generally on the speed of activating a control mechanism in each of various locations, and that the optimum location has been identified as a result. We might now consider the individual differences in speed of activating the device in that specific location. As a general practice, one should consider the level of performance of the *poorest* individuals who would be likely to use the facility—in general, perhaps the fifth percentile. The resulting design should be such that the performance of such individuals would be satisfactory in terms of ultimate output. (If the system cannot be designed to be operable by such individuals, a program of careful personnel selection would be required to select those who would be superior in such performance.) One could apply this same general reasoning to situations involving other kinds of psychomotor activities and to other kinds of criteria, such as strength, endurance, or accuracy.

Control Devices

Three points should be discussed with respect to the many types of control devices that we use, each of which can affect their use. These are: (1) correct identification, which is essentially a coding problem; (2) specific design features; and (3) location.

Coding of control devices. Where a number of control devices of the same general class are to be used, mistakes may occur because of failure to distinguish one from another. Under such circumstances, some form of coding usually can reduce such errors. Different methods of coding can be used, such as shape, size, location, texture, and color. Examples of shape coding are shown in Figure 16.11. Shape-coded controls should be sufficiently different so that they can be identified by feel, which is the case with those illustrated. Those illustrated, however, also have another distinguishing characteristic—namely, the symbolic association of the shape of the control with the use in question. This has the effect of facilitating the

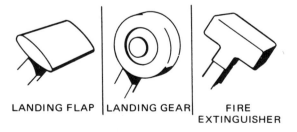

LANDING FLAP | LANDING GEAR | FIRE EXTINGUISHER

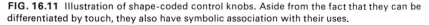

FIG. 16.11 Illustration of shape-coded control knobs. Aside from the fact that they can be differentiated by touch, they also have symbolic association with their uses.

learning of the shapes as related to their uses. Further, when control devices are common to different models of the same type of equipment (such as automobiles), a strong case can be made with respect to the standardization of their coding. Thus, when an individual changes from one model to another, his already learned associations can be transferred easily.

Design features of control devices. Control mechanisms can vary in many ways, such as in size, length, distance of movement, force required, or feedback to operator. As an example of such variations, let us review briefly the results of a study by Ziegler and Chernikoff[15] relating to three types of manual controls in a complex laboratory tracking task. The task was to operate the control device so as to cause a moving "dot" on a cathode ray tube to keep up with a changing target. The controls were: (1) a short lever *pressure* control, with which the amount of pressure applied controlled the amount of movement of the dot; (2) a twelve-inch lever *displacement* control, with which the distance of movement controlled the dot; and (3) an *on-off* control consisting of micro-switches on either side of the displacement control arranged in such a way that a one-eighth-inch movement of the control activated a micro-switch to cause a specified amount of change in the movement of the dot.

The learning curves of the subjects using these three types of control are shown in Figure 16.12. Aside from one crossover of the curves, we see

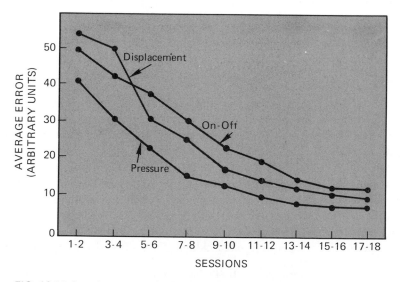

FIG. 16.12 Learning curves of subjects using three types of control devices in a complex ("third order") tracking task. (*From Ziegler and Chernikoff,* op. cit., *Fig. 2.*)

[15] Ziegler, P. N., & Chernikoff, R. A comparison of three types of manual controls on a "third-order" tracking task. *Ergonomics,* 1968, **11**(4), 369–374.

that, for *this* tracking task, the pressure control was superior, with the displacement control next, presumably in part because of the nature of the feedback provided to the operator. (It should be added that the dynamics involved in the control of some systems, such as some aircraft and ships, influence markedly the nature of the control demands placed upon the operator. Thus, the control system for any given tracking operation needs to be specifically appropriate to that system.)

Location of control devices. There are many examples of the effect of location on the operation of control devices, but for our purposes let us cite briefly the results of a study dealing with the juxtaposition of automobile brake and accelerator pedals.[16] In one experimental condition these two pedals were so positioned that they were "even" with each other, whereas in another condition the brake pedal was six inches above the accelerator pedal. The movement time for both locations was measured by a special device and the average movement times for ten subjects, ten trials each, are given below:

Condition	Average Movement Time (sec.)
A. Pedals even with each other	.149
B. Brake 6 inches above accelerator	.309

This difference means that, traveling at sixty miles per hour, the stopping distance could be reduced by about fourteen feet by placing the pedals even with each other.

METHODS DESIGN

As practiced by industrial engineers, *methods design* (also called motion study) is directed toward the development of preferred work methods. Methods design frequently is accompanied by work measurement (also called time study), which is used to determine the standard time to perform a specific task.[17]

From ordinary observations and the application of simple logic, it is apparent that different methods of doing a certain job may require different amounts of time and physical energy. The possibilities of improvement by such methods were dramatically demonstrated early in this century by Gilbreth[18] with the operation of bricklaying. He showed that the work of

[16] Davies, B. T., & Watts, J. M., Jr. Preliminary investigation of movement time between brake and accelerator pedals in automobiles. *Human Factors,* 1969, 11(4), 407–410.

[17] Barnes, R. M. *Motion and time study.* (6th ed). New York: John Wiley, 1968.

[18] Gilbreth, F. *Bricklaying system.* New York: M. C. Clark, 1909.

the average bricklayer can be increased from 120 bricks per hour to 350 per hour by following a more efficient pattern of movement.

Principles of Motion Economy

Early studies such as the one by Gilbreth pointed the way to the development of some of the techniques associated with methods design and work measurement, and also to the evolution of certain principles of motion economy. The principles of motion economy as presented by Barnes[19] are divided into three broad groups related to (1) the use of the human body; (2) the arrangement of the work place; and (3) the design of tools and equipment. Nine examples of the application of these principles to the use of the human body are listed below:[20]

1. The two hands should begin as well as complete their motions at the same time.
2. The two hands should not be idle at the same instant except during rest pauses.
3. Motions of the arms should be made in opposite and symmetrical directions and should be made simultaneously.
4. Hand and body motions should be confined to the lowest classification with which it is possible to perform the work satisfactorily. The five general classes of hand motions include, first, the fingers by themselves, with the others involving, progressively, other body members in this order: wrist, forearm, upper arm, and shoulder. Generally speaking, lower classifications require less time and physical effort than the higher classifications. There are, however, exceptions to this generalization.
5. Momentum should be employed to assist the worker whenever possible, and it should be reduced to a minimum if it must be overcome by muscular effort.
6. Smooth continuous curved motions of the hands are preferable to straight-line motions involving sudden and sharp changes in direction.
7. Ballistic movements are faster, easier, and more accurate than restricted (fixation) or "controlled" movements.
8. Work should be arranged to permit an easy and natural rhythm wherever possible.
9. Eye fixations should be as few and as close together as possible.

Measuring Effects of Methods

Principles of motion economy such as these generally have found considerable acceptance throughout industry as a basis for improving methods of work. Both experience and research have tended to support these principles when applied to work design. It should be noted, however, that the

[19] Barnes, *op. cit.,* p. 220.
[20] *Ibid.,* Chapter 17.

application of a set of methods-improvement principles does not in all cases ensure the development of an optimum method. A study reported by Lauru,[21] for example, raises some question about the general applicability of such principles. This report cites research on work activities with the Lauru platform, which is a device that measures the forces resulting from the activity of an individual when standing on a small work platform. The physical forces exerted are measured in three directions—vertical, frontal, and transverse. Using the Lauru platform, a comparison was made of the physical forces created by the movements of a bricklayer working by three different methods, as follows:

1. The conventional method.
2. The "improved" method developed by Gilbreth, mentioned earlier in this chapter; this method involves particularly the principle of bimanual *symmetry* of movements (moving the arms in opposite and symmetrical directions— principle No. 3).
3. A new method involving the use of only one hand at a time (thus departing from the principle of symmetry).

The forces resulting from these three methods are shown in Figure 16.13. In studying these, it should be kept in mind that the variability of the curves above and below the base line is indicative of the magnitude of the forces created by the worker during the task. It will be seen that there is noticeably less variation with the new method than with the others, including Gilbreth's, thereby suggesting that the new method requires less physical exertion than the others.

It also should be noted that the new method, aside from requiring less physical exertion, took less time; there was a saving of 18.4 percent in time over the original method, and of 6.4 percent over the Gilbreth method.

In particular, this study seems to cast some doubt about the general validity of the principle of bimanual symmetry. This should not be taken to suggest that this principle has no applicability in methods improvement,

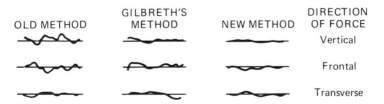

	GILBRETH'S		DIRECTION
OLD METHOD	METHOD	NEW METHOD	OF FORCE
			Vertical
			Frontal
			Transverse

FIG. 16.13 Physical forces exerted when laying brick by three different methods. Forces were measured by use of the Lauru platform in three directions, namely, vertical, frontal, and transverse. The third bricklaying method required the least exertion. (*Adapted from Lauru,* op. cit.)

[21] Lauru, L. The measurement of fatigue, part 2. *Manager,* 1954, **22**, 369–375.

but perhaps it does suggest that further research is needed to determine the work circumstances under which the principle is and is not applicable. Perhaps other principles of motion economy also could well be subjected to similar research.

WORK SPACE AND ARRANGEMENT

Fixed work stations should be so designed that the individuals can perform their tasks effectively, comfortably, and safely. There are two principal aspects of this design problem. One deals with the total work space, and the other with the arrangement of the facilities and features of that work space.

Workspace Envelope

The workspace envelope can be viewed as comprising the three-dimensional space around an individual that can be used for the physical activities he will be expected to perform. For a seated individual this typically consists of whatever space he can reach conveniently by hand. Of course, this gets us into the problem of individual differences, and although it is not appropriate here to present the masses of data that are available about body measurement of people,[22] we can at least illustrate the range of individual differences as these might influence the workspace envelope. In particular, let us present the differences in the "grasping reach," in a seated position, of a sample of Air Force personnel, as reported by Kennedy.[23] These values refer specifically to the grasping reach below (lower limit) and above (upper limit) a "seat reference point," and thus relate to the vertical dimension of the envelope.

Value in Distribution	Lower Limit	Upper Limit	Difference
Minimum (shortest reach measured)	2.5 in.	48.00	50.50
5th percentile	4.0	48.75	52.75
50th percentile	5.0	52.25	57.25
95th percentile	7.0	54.25	61.25

[22] For sources of data on body measurements of people, the reader is referred to such sources as: Damon, A., Stoudt, H. W., & McFarland, R. A. *The human body in equipment design.* Cambridge: Harvard University Press, 1966; and National Center for Health Statistics, *Weight, height, and selected body dimensions of adults.* Public Health Service, U.S. Department of Health, Education, and Welfare, Series 11, No. 8, 1965.

[23] Kennedy, K. W. *Reach capacity of the USAF population.* Technical Documentary Report AMRL–TDR–64–59, USAF, Behavioral Sciences Laboratory, Wright-Patterson Air Force Base, September 1964.

It is frequently the practice to design such envelopes for the fifth percentile in the distribution of values.

Arrangement of Facilities

Other aspects of the facilities within the work space also should be designed with due consideration given to the physical dimensions of people and the range and ease of movements of body members. These aspects include the design of seats, desks, benches, horizontal and vertical work surfaces, and consoles, and the physical location and arrangement of controls, devices, and materials. Figure 16.14 illustrates the implications of physical features of the body as related to at least one design problem.

FIG. 16.14 Generalized illustration of desirable and undesirable arrangements of wall control panels. (*From Morgan, C. T., Cook, J. S., III, Chapanis, A., & Lund, M. M.* Human engineering guide to equipment design. *New York: McGraw-Hill, 1963, p. 300.*)

HUMAN FACTORS IN JOB DESIGN

It has been suggested by Davis[24] that approaches to job design may be classified as: (1) process-centered (or equipment-centered); (2) worker-centered; and (3) the combination of these two. In the *process-centered approach,* jobs are designed by specializing activities or functions or by applying rational methods to determine minimum production time for different production methods. The *worker-centered approach* is represented

---

[24] Davis, L. E. The concept of job design and its status in industrial engineering. In *Symposium on human factors in job design.* (This symposium was held at the meetings of the American Psychological Association in New York, 1961; the papers are published by the Systems Development Corporation, Santa Monica, California, as Report SP–611, November 20, 1961.)

primarily by attempts at what is called job enlargement (which will be discussed shortly) ; approaches in which a team of workers participates in deciding how the work will be divided among them also fall into this category. In the worker-centered approaches to job design, motivation is a central consideration; in the process-centered approaches it is not.

Prevailing Considerations in Job Design

Historically, and at present, jobs are overwhelmingly designed in terms of process-centered considerations. Davis, Canter, and Hoffman[25] report a survey that was carried out to determine the precepts or principles used by the responding companies in designing jobs. This survey indicated very clearly that those in industry who create, design, or establish jobs are guided almost entirely by: economic considerations or hypotheses, process considerations, time or space considerations, skills available and numbers of people available, tools and equipment required, union-management agreements, custom or tradition, and precepts such as specialization, repetitiveness, and so forth. These considerations essentially are predicated upon a mechanistic philosophy, with the primary criterion being the immediate costs of production.

Motivational Considerations in Job Design

Chapter 12 included a discussion of the research of Herzberg et al.[26] relating to variables associated with job satisfaction. It will be recalled that the variables that were associated with positive job satisfaction generally were related to the *job activities* as such (achievement, recognition, the work itself, responsibility, and advancement) rather than with the work situation. The worker-centered approach to job design, as exemplified in the work of Davis,[27] is relevant in this context, for it is predicated on the principle of designing jobs with consideration of the workers' motivation in mind. The objective of this approach is to design jobs so that there is reasonable opportunity for employees to achieve positive job satisfaction from their work. But a worker-centered approach to job design cannot be justified exclusively on the grounds of satisfying the "human" requirements of jobs. It must also satisfy the technical organization requirements in an efficient, economical manner (which, incidentally, it usually does).

[25] Davis, L. E., Canter, R. R., & Hoffman, J. Current job design criteria. *Journal of Industrial Engineering,* 1955, 6(2), 5.

[26] Herzberg, F., Mausner, B., & Snyderman, B. B. *The motivation to work.* New York: John Wiley, 1959.

[27] Davis, *op. cit.*

Job Enlargement

Job enlargement is the obverse of job specialization. Based on the worker-centered principle of job design, it is an intentional modification of the content of jobs toward the end of providing the opportunity for the employee's psychological growth. The term *job enlargement* has been used for a number of years to refer to the expansion of the content of jobs. This can be done in various ways, such as by adding additional activities of the same general nature (for example, having individuals assemble complete parts rather than performing a single task), by adding activities of a more responsible nature (such as planning and scheduling), by job rotation, by making people responsible for the inspection of their own work, by having them repair their own work, or by allowing people to set their own work pace. In this regard, however, Herzberg[28] makes a distinction between job enlargement and job enrichment. He considers job enlargement to be the process of making jobs structurally "bigger" by the addition of more tasks of the same general nature, whereas job enrichment consists of modifications in jobs that provide opportunity for personal growth (including in particular the addition of job activities of a more responsible nature, with greater decision-making, and other similar additions). We will here use the term "job enlargement" to embrace the various aspects of expansion of jobs, including what Herzberg implies by "job enrichment."

The underlying assumption involved in enlarged jobs is that they will bring about various alterations in value to both the individual and the organization, such as increased motivation, decreased boredom and dissatisfaction, increased productivity, and improved job attendance. On the basis of the experience resulting from one job enlargement program, Sorcher and Meyer[29] express the following opinion:

> Simplification brought disadvantages along with its hoped-for advantages: it brought boredom, meaninglessness; it removed challenge and any sense of individual commitment. Not only does simplification carried to its limits do damage to the worker's self-esteem and motivation, but repetitiveness, when it entails boredom and lack of goals, also increases poor quality rather than decreasing it. So now, from every point of view, from considerations of humanity to those of profit, it now becomes the task of industry to engage the employee in a more meaningful role.

A few words of constraint probably should be added to these forthright pronouncements. In the first place, it should be noted that the desire of

[28] Herzberg, F. One more time: How do you motivate employees? *Harvard Business Review*, January-February, 1968, **46**(1), 53–63.

[29] Sorcher, M., & Meyer, H. H. Motivation and job performance. *Personnel Administration*, July-August 1968, **31**(4), 8–21.

employees for "enlarged" jobs probably is not universal; there are indications that at least some people prefer very simple, routine activities. And in the second place, it is probable that there are many types of necessary activity in this world of ours that probably *cannot* be organized in such a way as to be intrinsically meaningful and challenging to people generally.

But within these (and perhaps other) constraints, the objective set forth by Sorcher and Meyer—engaging the employee in a more meaningful role—is one that society needs to endorse and support. As Jasinski[30] points out, in recent years a number of social scientists have become concerned with this matter, and in fact with the entire spectrum of man's social-psychological relationship to the technological process with which he is associated. The current interest in job enlargement is a reflection of this concern.

To some extent, this recent interest in job enlargement was initiated by Walker.[31] Although the trend toward job enlargement has not taken on epidemic proportions during the years since Walker's study, there have been at least a handful of situations in which job enlargement efforts have been carried out.[32]

Results from job enlargement. The reported results of job enlargement programs have been rather spotty. We will here discuss briefly one program that did result in positive benefits. This program, reported by Biggane and Stewart,[33] dealt with the assembly of a water pump for an automatic washing machine. The original procedure consisted of having five men assemble the twenty-six parts on an assembly-line basis, each specializing in the assembly of a few parts. In the enlarged job each man performed all assembly operations. The investigators reported that the change brought about improved quality and housekeeping, cost reduction, and reduced turnover (presumably reflecting increased job satisfaction).

On the basis of this and two other case studies, Biggane and Stewart conclude that "job enlargement offers definite opportunities to enhance the meaning of work through greater involvement of the operator, to favorably affect quality and cost, and to provide an opportunity for greater job satisfaction for the man on the job, and his supervisor."

[30] Jasinski, F. J. Organization change and the job design process. In *Symposium on human factors, op. cit.*

[31] Walker, C. R. The problem of the repetitive job. *Harvard Business Review,* 1950, **28**(3), 54–58.

[32] Among the studies related to job enlargement programs are the following: Guest, R. H. Job enlargement—a revolution in job design. *Personnel Administration,* 1957, pp. 9–17; Davis, L. E., & Werling, R. Job design factors, *Occupational Psychology* (London), 1964, **34**(2), 109; and Biggane, J. F., & Stewart, P. A. *Job enlargement: A case study.* State University of Iowa, Bureau of Labor and Management, Research Series No. 25, July 1963.

[33] Biggane & Stewart, *op. cit.*

In reviewing various studies of job enlargement, however, Hulin and Blood[34] came to the conclusion that the case for job enlargement has been drastically overstated and overgeneralized. More specifically, they indicate that the assumed advantages of job enlargement tend to be realized when applied to only certain segments of the labor force, particularly to jobs of white-collar and supervisory workers and those of nonalienated blue-collar workers. Their findings imply that job enlargement should not be perceived as the panacea for all of the production problems or employee morale problems of an organization, but that it may be an appropriate program in certain types of job situations.

Guidelines in job enlargement. There probably are no simple, clear-cut procedures or rules to follow in the enlargement of jobs. As one possible set of general guidelines, however, Herzberg[35] offers a frame of reference and some general principles to go by. In the first place, he differentiates between "horizontal" job loading and "vertical" job loading. Horizontal loading, as he uses the term, consists of adding a number of tasks to a job, generally of the same nature and level as the initial activities, or rotating people from one activity to another. He is sharply critical of such "enlargement" on the grounds that this approach merely enlarges what he refers to as the "meaninglessness" of a job. On the other hand, vertical loading refers to various approaches to increase the job content in terms of authority, accountability, decision making, reduction of controls, and so forth. He argues that such an approach offers increased opportunity for job satisfaction on the grounds that the job content "motivators" (such as a sense of responsibility, achievement, or recognition) can then come into play. Toward this end he offers the set of principles shown in Table 16.2, in each instance listing what he considers to be the related "motivator" factors.

Following is a brief, modified summary of the steps toward the application of such principles, as suggested by Herzberg:

1. Select those jobs in which (a) the investment in industrial engineering does not make changes too costly, (b) attitudes are poor, (c) "hygiene" (i.e., job context) factors are becoming very costly, and (d) motivation will make a difference in performance.
2. Approach these jobs with the conviction that they can be changed.
3. Brainstorm a list of changes that may enrich the jobs.
4. Screen the list to eliminate those that involve "hygiene" rather than "motivation" factors.
5. Screen the list to eliminate any "generalities."
6. Screen the list to eliminate any "horizontal" loading suggestions.

34 Hulin, C. L., & Blood, M. R. Job enlargement, individual differences, and worker responses. *Psychological Bulletin,* 1968, **68**(1), 41–55.
35 Herzberg, *op. cit.*

TABLE 16.2 PRINCIPLES OF VERTICAL JOB LOADING AS PRESENTED BY HERZBERG

Principle	*Motivators Involved*
A. Removing some controls while retaining accountability	Responsibility and personal achievement
B. Increasing the accountability of individuals for own work	Responsibility and recognition
C. Giving a person a complete natural unit of work (module, division, area, and so on)	Responsibility, achievement, and recognition
D. Granting additional authority to an employee in his activity; job freedom	Responsibility, achievement, and recognition
E. Making periodic reports directly available to the worker himself rather than to the supervisor	Internal recognition
F. Introducing new and more difficult tasks not previously handled	Growth and learning
G. Assigning individuals specific or specialized tasks, enabling them to become experts	Responsibility, growth, and advancement

Source: F. Herzberg, One more time: How do you motivate employees? *Harvard Business Review,* 1968, **46**(1), Exhibit III, p. 59.

7. Avoid direct participation by the employees themselves (although any previous suggestions might well be considered). (This point is based on the assumption that such direct involvement contaminates the process with human relations "hygiene" and gives the employees only a *sense* of making a contribution.)

Step number seven, which in effect rejects employee participation in job enlargement, is of course 180° out of line with the position of the proponents of increased employee participation. This specific point reveals the cleavage between Herzberg's position and that of others and reflects a position with which we cannot concur. Despite Herzberg's missionary zeal for vertical loading (to the exclusion of horizontal loading), it is probably too early in the game to accept such a frame of reference lock, stock, and barrel. In the first place, one still must have qualms about the validity of his theory of job satisfaction based on the distinction between job content (motivation) factors, and job context (hygiene) factors, as discussed in Chapter 12. And in the second place, some "job enlargement" studies have been predicated on horizontal job loading and seem to have been reasonably successful—even in terms of employee attitudes. However, vertical job enlargement undoubtedly would be feasible and appropriate in at least some circumstances.

Discussion

The job enlargement concept in job design seems essentially incompatible with the traditional methods analysis approach of the industrial engineers, which has tended to be focused on a mechanistic, work-specialization approach to job design. To some degree human factors engineering also is guilty of concentrating on the mechanics of human activities from a "micro" point of view—of simplifying work for people and reducing it to fairly constrained, rather definitely programmed boundaries. The irrevocable shift in technology toward automation has contributed further to the proliferation of process-centered approaches to job design. And yet, to date, experience and research with job enlargement have not provided clear unequivocal evidence that job enlargement should be followed as a universal basis for job design—although it is indeed a very promising approach.

If one is interested in finding some rational basis for job design, where, then, does this leave us? Accepting some risks, we will offer some admittedly subjective observations. In the first place (as pointed out by Hulin and Blood[36]), job enlargement should not be expected to serve the motivational purposes attributed to it for all types of jobs and for all types of workers, but rather may serve such purposes in some circumstances. In the second place, it is doubtful if a job enlargement approach ever could be justified on practical grounds as "the" basis for job design; as Nadler[37] observes, it cannot and should not become a whole program. In the third place, it is probable that the very nature of some work processes precludes the practical possibility of job enlargement, thus imposing some limits on the possible range of *types* of work activities that would be susceptible to such an approach.

And, in the fourth place, it is suggested that the process-centered and worker-centered approaches to job design are perhaps not as incompatible as they might initially appear to be. In this connection, Davis[38] points out that operations planning takes place at two levels: namely, *task design* (to accomplish elements of operations), and *task combination,* in which tasks are combined into jobs. Davis expresses the opinion that, although industrial engineers generally cannot be criticized for the depth and intensity of their efforts in task design, they have not done well in task combination. It is primarily in the process of combining tasks into jobs that considerations of human motivation, job satisfaction, group behavior, and such variables come into play. Thus, at least in some job design situations, one can take a process-centered approach to task *design* and a worker-centered approach to task *combination.*

Because job enlargement involves change, we should reflect back to earlier discussions relating to organizational change in which it was noted that participation in the process of change contributes to the acceptance of

[36] Hulin & Blood, *op. cit.*
[37] Nadler, G. *Work Design.* Homewood, Ill.: Richard D. Irwin, Inc., 1963, p. 33.
[38] Davis, *op. cit.*

change. In this connection, Chaney[39] reports rather dramatic changes in both performance and attitudes resulting from employee participation in a job design program.

---

[39] Chaney, F. B. Employee participation in manufacturing job design. *Human Factors*, 1969, **11**(2), 101–106.

chapter seventeen

Working
Conditions

Although much of our weeping and wailing about the conditions in which we work and live is undoubtedly a manifestation of our all-too-human proclivities to gripe about something, the conditions in which people work and live can be such as to have adverse effects of various types that at times justify our lamentations. In addition to the social aspects of working conditions, which were discussed earlier, there are two other categories of working conditions that we will discuss here. One of these relates to the physical environment, including illumination, noise, and atmospheric conditions. Although we are particularly interested in the environmental aspects of working conditions, these environmental factors also are intimately related to other aspects of our lives. The deterioration of some aspects of our general environment is, of course, a matter of increasing concern in many countries. The second category of working conditions to be discussed relates to time, and specifically to hours of work, work schedules, rest periods, and other temporal factors.

It might be noted that the spectrum of working conditions can be viewed as related to Herzberg's concept of the hygiene factor discussed in Chapter 12, in the sense that these conditions characterize the job context—that is, the situation in which the individual works.

ILLUMINATION

We would all agree that reading the fine print in a contract requires more illumination than, say, dumping trash cans into a truck. The problem is one of determining how much illumination should be provided for any given task. As the basis for making such determinations, the Illuminating Engineering Society (IES)[1] has proposed that illumination levels for various tasks should be prescribed on the basis of two classes of criteria—visual performance and visual comfort. Of these, greater attention has been given to the former.

Factors that Influence Visual Performance

Of course, the visual performance of people in tasks that have significant visual components is in part the consequence of the visual abilities of the individuals, as discussed in Chapter 6. Our present interests, however, are more concerned with the task-related factors that may affect visual performance and thus should be considered in prescribing the levels of illumination for various tasks. The IES points out that there are two aspects of this question: the intrinsic characteristics of the task and the characteristics of the luminous environment. The intrinsic characteristics of the task that affect the ability to make visual discriminations include the brightness contrast of the "details" to be discriminated against their background, the size of the details to be discriminated, and the time available for seeing.

A couple of sets of data relating to task variables will be given to illustrate the effect of such variables on visual performance. One example, from a much broader study by Blackwell,[2] deals with the relationship between brightness contrast and visual performance. The details of this study will not be discussed here, but the results are shown in general terms in Figure 17.1. An example of low brightness contrast is gray printing on a slightly lighter gray paper; an example of high contrast is black printing on very white paper. Another example, also from Blackwell, shows the interaction between viewing time and brightness contrast, as related to illumination

[1] *IES lighting handbook.* (5th ed.) New York: Illuminating Engineering Society, 1972, pp. 3–14.
[2] Blackwell, H. R. Development and use of a quantitative method for specification of interior illumination levels. *Illumination Engineering,* June 1959, **54**(6), 317–353.

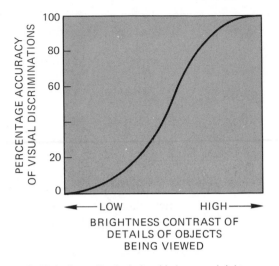

FIG. 17.1 Generalized relationship between brightness contrast of visual detail and accuracy of visual discriminations. (*Adapted from Blackwell, 1959,* op. cit., *Fig. 4.*)

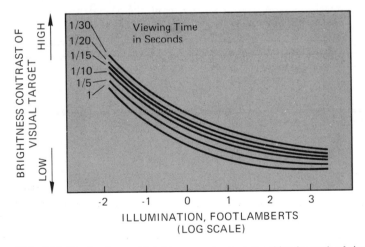

FIG 17.2 Illumination and brightness contrast relationships for each of six viewing times. The curve for any viewing time represents the combinations of illumination and brightness that are required for equal visual discriminability. (*Adapted from Blackwell, 1959,* op. cit., *Fig. 33.*)

level. The data, shown in Figure 17.2, indicate that for any given time curve (such as a one-second viewing time), the various combinations of illumination level and brightness contrast produce the *same level* of visual discriminability. (The level of discriminability depicted in this figure was 50 percent detection of the particular visual stimuli used.) For any given level of illumination, it can be seen that if viewing time is *decreased,* the brightness contrast must be increased in order to maintain the same level of visual discriminability.

Prescribing Illumination Standards

The specification of illumination standards—for kumquat inspectors, doughnut-hole punchers, pin-ball machine assemblers, or any other job— involves an intricate process that we cannot cover in detail here. But we will at least touch on one or two aspects of it. The basis for such prescriptions is the research of Blackwell,[3] which has been supported largely by the IES. His procedure in part is predicated on the concept of a visibility reference function, shown in Figure 17.3. The curve showing this function (the solid curve) represents the task contrast (C) required at different levels of task background luminance (in footlamberts) for equal threshold visibility of a specified visual task. (The reference task involves identifying a visual

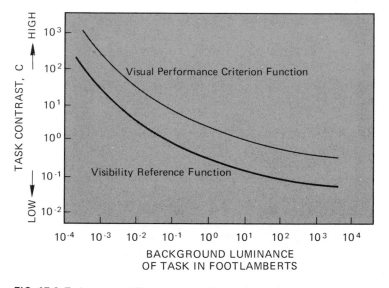

FIG. 17.3 Task contrast (C) required at different levels of background luminance in foot-lamberts for equal threshold visibility of a specified visual task. The solid line (the visibility reference function) relates to the identification (with 50 percent certainty) of a visual target that is 4-minutes of visual arc in diameter exposed for 1/2 second. The dotted curve (the visual performance criterion function) relates to the same task adjusted for other factors (such as movement, location, and 99 percent certainty of detection). (*From IES lighting handbook, op. cit., Fig. 3-24.*)

[3] *Ibid.;* and Blackwell, H. R. A human factors approach to lighting recommendations and standards. Proceedings of the Sixteenth Annual Meeting of the Human Factors Society, October 1972. Santa Monica, California: The Human Factors Society.

target four minutes of visual angle in diameter, exposed for one-half of a second.) The contrast is the ratio of the reflectance of the features of the visual target—that is, the ratio of the reflectances of the target to be discriminated and its background. We can see from the curve that with low contrast the background luminance needs to be much higher than with high contrast for equal visibility to be possible. The second curve in Figure 17.3, the visual performance criterion function, shows the same basic relationship except that it is adjusted to account for differences in contrast that would be required for equal visibility if the following factors are taken into account: the difference between a static (stationary) target and a dynamic (moving) target, which is more commonly found in practice; the difference between not knowing and knowing where and when the target will appear in the visual field; and the difference between being 99 percent sure of detecting the target and being 50 percent certain.

A second phase of the process requires the estimation of an *equivalent contrast* value for the actual work task as related to that of the reference task on which Figure 17.3 is based. The procedures for doing this will not be discussed. This step is followed by adjustments for other possible factors, such as glare and transient adaptation of the eye, with the end result that for any given task for which the equivalent contrast value has been derived it is possible to determine the background luminance (in footlamberts) that must be provided if visibility on the actual task is to equal that of the reference task as shown in Figure 17.3. But this is not the end of the line, for the prescribed level of footlamberts indicates the amount of light which must be reflected from the surface, but the amount of light to be provided needs to be expressed in terms of footcandles.

A footlambert can be thought of as the brightness of *reflected* light that is equivalent to a perfectly diffusing, perfectly white surface which is illuminated by one footcandle of light. The number of footcandles (fc) required to produce any specified level of footlamberts depends upon the reflectance of the surface. Let us take, as an example, a task that requires 100 footlamberts. If the surface reflected 80 percent of the light, the footcandles required would be 100 fc ÷ .80, or 125 fc. If the surface reflected only 25 percent, the footcandles required would be 100 fc ÷ .25 or 400 fc. Thus, for any level of footlamberts required for a given task, the actual footcandle requirements will depend very largely on the reflectance of the surfaces of visual attention. This argues for the use of fairly light work surfaces such as desks and work tables. On the basis of the procedures developed by Blackwell, illumination levels have been recommended for various types of tasks.[4] A few examples of these recommendations are given below:

4 *IES lighting handbook, op. cit.,* pp. 9–81 to 9–95.

Task	Recommended Illumination, Footcandles
Operating table (surgical)	2500
Very difficult inspection	500
Proofreading	150
General office work	70–150
Food preparation	70
Wrapping and labeling	50
Loading (materials handling)	20
Hotel lobby	10

There are other important aspects of illumination besides the level. One of these is the location of luminaries, which should be installed in such positions as to minimize glare. A major source of glare—what is called direct glare—comes from light sources or luminaries that are too bright or that are near the line of sight. Such glare may be a cause of visual discomfort and can even interfere with seeing.

A somewhat related aspect of illumination is the distribution of light throughout the work area. Not only should the immediate work area be illuminated at the level prescribed for the visual tasks in question, but there also should be a reasonably adequate level of general illumination.

ATMOSPHERIC CONDITIONS

Different kinds of variables can be thought of as aspects of our atmosphere. Besides temperature and humidity there are also factors of air flow, barometric pressure, composition of the atmosphere, and sometimes toxic conditions. There is also the factor of temperature of objects in the environment, which is not strictly an "atmospheric" condition but certainly relates to this subject. Our discussion will deal largely with the more common aspects of the atmosphere, especially temperature and humidity.

The Heat-Exchange Processes

The metabolic processes of the body result in the generation of heat, some of which the body normally has to dispose of. In disposing of such heat, the body is continually attempting to maintain a thermal equilibrium with its environment. The heat-exchange process is the method by which the body attempts to achieve this balance.

There are four ways in which this heat exchange takes place. Convection is the transmission of heat by a fluid that occurs when there is a temperature difference between an object and the fluid. In the case of people, the body typically transmits heat to the air (which is technically a fluid), although when the air temperature gets above body temperature the transmission is reversed. *Evaporation* is another method of heat exchange; this consists primarily of evaporation of perspiration, and to some degree of vapor that is exhaled from the lungs in breathing. *Radiation* is the process of transmission of thermal energy (either with or without an atmosphere) between objects such as the sun and the earth. When such transmission occurs, the warmer object loses heat to the cooler. Usually people transmit heat to *other* objects by this method, but occasionally a person may be in a situation where objects, such as boilers or heated metal, transmit heat to him. *Conduction* is the transmission of heat by direct contact, such as with chairs or the floor. Our clothing usually so insulates us that this is a very unimportant method of heat exchange.

Effects of Heat and Related Factors

Under conditions that we call "hot," the amount of surplus heat that the body can dissipate is affected by certain environmental conditions, in particular air temperature, humidity, air flow, and the temperature of objects in the environment (such as walls, ceilings, windows, furnaces, or the sun). The interaction of these conditions as they affect the heat exchange process, the subjective sensations of people, and job performance is quite complex and cannot be covered in detail here. But we can point out that under conditions of high air temperature and high wall temperature, heat loss by convection and radiation is minimized, so that heat *gain* to the body may result. Under such circumstances the only remaining means of heat loss is by evaporation. But if the humidity also is high, evaporative heat loss will be minimized, with the result that body temperature builds up. As Provins[5] points out, it is this rise in body temperature that is the real source of heat stress, rather than the climatic temperature itself, which merely contributes to the rise in body temperature.

Effects of heat on work performance. The metabolic processes involved in work result in the generation of heat, the amount varying with the nature of the work. Because of this, environmental heat has a more pronounced effect upon those doing heavy work than on those performing more sedentary activities.

Some evidence of the effects of high temperatures upon physical work comes from a study by Mackworth[6] in which a heavy pursuitmeter task was carried out by subjects under conditions of various combinations of effective temperatures. Effective temperature takes into account both

[5] Provins, K. A. Environmental heat, body temperature and behaviour: An hypothesis. *Australian Journal of Psychology,* 1966, **18**(2), 118–129.

[6] Mackworth, N. H. *Researches on the measurement of human performance.* Medical Research Council, Special Report Series 268. London: H. M. Stationery Office, 1950.

temperature and humidity; the numerical value is that of the temperature of still air in combination with 100 percent relative humidity, which would induce identical sensations. The task involved considerable physical effort in operating a weighted lever in a pursuit task. The results are shown in line *a* of Figure 17.4. The increasing error rate with increasing temperatures is quite clear.

In contrast, we can see that the effects of increasing temperature on a light telegraphy task (shown as line *b* in Figure 17.4) were relatively less marked. In connection with the effects of heat on mental activities, Wing[7] synthesized the results of fifteen different studies, presenting the generalized results shown in the lower line of Figure 17.5, which shows the upper tolerance limit (in terms of time) for carrying out mental activities without impairment of the work activity under different conditions of effective temperature. Work beyond the indicated limit typically suffered some degradation.

Limits of tolerance to heat. The upper line of Figure 17.5 shows, for comparative purposes, the approximate human tolerance limits to heat expressed in terms of the time that people generally can tolerate various effective temperatures. Looking at tolerance another way, Figure 17.6 shows the combinations of temperature and humidity that can be tolerated

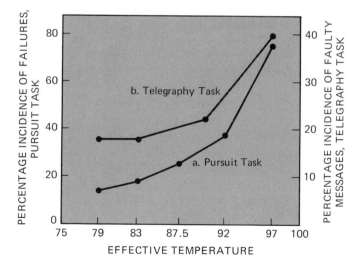

FIG. 17.4 Relationship between effective temperature and performance on a heavy pursuitmeter task and on a telegraphy task. (*Adapted from Mackworth, op. cit., Figures 51 and 52, permission H.M. Stationery Office, London.*)

[7] Wing, J. F. *A review of the effects of high ambient temperature on mental performance.* Technical Report AMRL–TR–65–102, USAF, Aerospace Medical Research Laboratories, Wright-Patterson Air Force Base, September 1965.

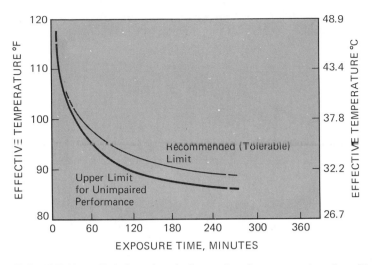

FIG. 17.5 Upper limit for unimpaired mental performance as based on 15 studies. For any given effective temperature, the point on the curve horizontally to its right represents the time limit (as read along the base) within which mental activity typically is not impaired; a longer period of work usually would result in work decrement. The upper curve, in turn, shows the upper limit of recommended exposure in terms of human tolerance to heat, as based on other research findings. (*Adapted from Wing*, op. cit., *Fig. 9.*)

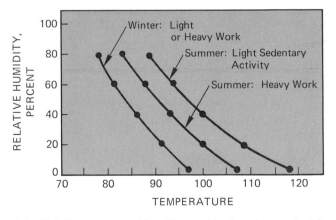

FIG. 17.6 Temperature and humidity combinations that can be tolerated daily for various types of work by healthy, acclimatized men wearing warm weather clothing. These data are for air movement of 15–25 ft/min. (Adapted from report of Committee on Industrial Ventilation, "Thermal Standards in Industry," *Year Book of the American Journal of Public Health* (May, 1950), p. 133.)

for various types of work. These data are based on tolerance limits for normal daily activity for healthy, acclimatized men; they do not show time limits as such. For persons who are not acclimatized or who are not in good physical condition, these limits should be lower. Indeed, it is preferable for all people to work in more "normal" temperatures than in those approximating "limits" of tolerance.

Effects of Cold

Exposure to cold is accompanied by a number of physiological changes, including the vasoconstriction of the peripheral blood vessels, which reduces the flow of blood to the surface of the skin and results in reduced skin temperature. This is a protective response of the body to minimize heat loss (although it numbs the fingers and toes). With reference to the performance of manual work under conditions of cold, Fox,[8] in summarizing many studies, makes the point that performance decrements appear to stem from this physical lowering of the hand skin temperature (HST) and the competing stimuli in a unique and sometimes stressful environment. Clark[9] found the critical skin temperature to be in the 55° to 60° range. Manual performance is not affected by skin temperatures above 60°, but decrements may be expected with skin temperatures below 55°.

Although there have been very few studies of the effects of cold on higher mental processes, available evidence suggests that such processes are not markedly affected by cold.

Comfort Zones

There are, of course, individual differences in relative comfort under different temperatures, but the maximum percentage of individuals feel comfortable in the summer at about 71° effective temperature, and in the winter at about 68°.[10] Variations of a degree or two either way from these norms still result in fairly high percentages of people feeling reasonably comfortable.

NOISE

There has been serious concern, over a period of years, regarding noise in industry and in communities, but in recent years this concern has taken on a more urgent note and has become more widespread. As we talk about various forms of environmental pollution, the term "noise pollution" has become a household word. It is, of course, man's technology that has created this problem, with the creation of machines, trains, airplanes, auto-

---

[8] Fox, W. F. Human performance in the cold. *Human Factors,* 1967, 9(3), 203–220.

[9] Clark, R. E. *The limiting hand skin temperature for unaffected manual performance in the cold.* Natick, Mass.: Quartermaster Research and Engineering Command, Technical Report EP–147, February 1961.

[10] American Society of Heating, Refrigerating and Air-Conditioning Engineers. *Handbook of fundamentals.* 1967, Chapter 7.

mobiles, motors, and the other mechanisms of our lives. And the problem is getting worse, rather than better. It has been reported by Jones and Cohen,[11] for example, that noise levels are increasing at the rate of 1 decibel per year; this means that over ten years the sound energy would increase tenfold!

Measurement of Sound

Before discussing the effects of sound, let us mention the primary physical characteristics of sound. These are *frequency* and *intensity*. The psychological counterparts of these are *pitch* and *loudness*. Vibrating objects (such as tuning forks and machines) cause fluctuating changes in air pressure to spread out away from them. This is something like the waves in a pond that are generated by a pebble thrown into it, except that sound waves travel in all directions. In the case of an object that has a *single* frequency, these waves, if shown graphically, form a sine (i.e., sinusoidal) wave, with the number of repetitions per second being the frequency. Frequency is expressed in terms of cycles per second (cps), or in terms of Hertz (Hz); the two terms are synonymous. Actually, most vibrating sources generate complex waves rather than pure waves; thus, although a middle C on the piano and on a trumpet have the same dominant frequency (256 Hz), their "qualities" are different because of the differences in the *other* frequencies that are also generated. Incidentally, one octave has twice the frequency of the one below it.

The intensity of sound is usually measured by decibels (dB). The decibel scale is actually a logarithmic scale, which accounts for the fact that a ten decibel difference in intensity actually reflects a tenfold difference in sound energy. Figure 17.7 shows a decibel scale with several sounds to illustrate it.[12]

Effects of Noise on Performance

The evidence from noise studies indicates that noise does not *generally* cause deterioration in work performance. In fact, Broadbent[13] states that a review of available reports shows no experiments in which there have been statistically significant effects of noise at noise levels less than 90 decibels, although there have been some studies of noise levels at about 90

11 Jones, H. H., & Cohen, A. Noise as a health hazard at work, in the community, and in the home. *Public Health Reports,* July 1968, **83**(7), 533–536.

12 Jones, H. Noise: An environmental health problem. *Journal of Environmental Health,* September-October 1968, **31**(2); 132–136; VanBergeijk, W. A., Pierce, J. R., & David, E. E., Jr. *Waves and the Ear.* Garden City, N.Y.: Doubleday, 1960.

13 Broadbent, D. S. Effect of noise on behavior. In C. M. Harris (Ed.), *Handbook of noise control.* New York: McGraw-Hill, 1957, Chapter 10.

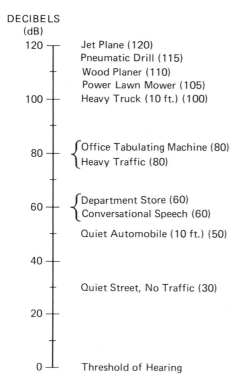

DECIBELS
(dB)

120	Jet Plane (120)
	Pneumatic Drill (115)
	Wood Planer (110)
	Power Lawn Mower (105)
100	Heavy Truck (10 ft.) (100)
80	{ Office Tabulating Machine (80) { Heavy Traffic (80)
60	{ Department Store (60) { Conversational Speech (60)
	Quiet Automobile (10 ft.) (50)
40	
	Quiet Street, No Traffic (30)
20	
0	Threshold of Hearing

FIG. 17.7 The decibel (dB) scale of sound intensity, with illustrative everyday sounds. The intensities of the various sounds are of course approximate. (*Adapted in part from Jones,* op. cit., *and from VanBergeijk, Pierce, and David,* op. cit.)

decibels that have shown significant decrements. (It should be noted, however, that there is no proof that lower levels will *not* impair performance.)

Broadbent points out further that there is no clear-cut and obvious distinction between tasks on which performance *is* affected and those on which performance is *not* affected. There are some inklings, however, discussed by Cohen,[14] that suggest that some simple, repetitive types of tasks are relatively insensitive to the effects of noise, but that performance on vigilance (i.e., monitoring) types of tasks may be adversely affected. Further, there are some hints (but not fully confirmed data) that noise may cause degradation on such tasks as complex mental tasks, tasks that call for skill and speed, and tasks that demand a high level of perceptual capacity.

In reflecting about the effects of noise on performance, however, it is probably safe to say that, in general, if noise levels are kept within reason-

[14] Cohen, A. Noise effects on health, production, and well-being. *Transactions of the New York Academy of Sciences,* May 1968, Series II, 30(7), 910–918.

able bounds in terms of *other* criteria (especially in terms of avoiding hearing loss), such levels typically would not have a serious effect on work performance as such.

Effects of Noise on Hearing

The effects of noise on hearing are much less controversial than are the effects of noise on work performance. Such effects have been demonstrated time and again in the case of people who are exposed to intense noise levels over a period of years. One such example is presented by LaBenz, Cohen, and Pearson.[15] Their survey dealt with the hearing loss of sixty-six earth-moving equipment operators, the noise levels of such equipment ranging from 90 to 120 dB.

Hearing tests were given to the men before their work shift, and the results were compared with estimates of the hearing losses that typically occur through age for individuals of comparable age. A comparison of these data is given in Figure 17.8, which shows, for each of three groups differing in years of exposure, the hearing loss, corrected for age. In other

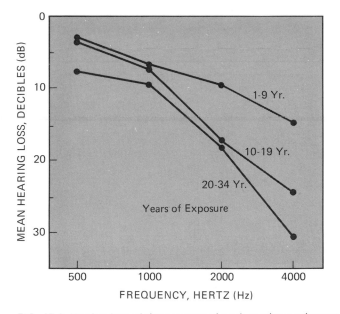

FIG. 17.8 Hearing loss of three groups of earth-moving equipment operators varying in length of exposure. These data are corrected for age, that is, the hearing loss shown is that over and above the normal hearing loss for men of corresponding age. (*Adapted from LaBenz, Cohen, and Pearson, op. cit., Table VI.*)

[15] LaBenz, P., Cohen, A., & Pearson, B. A noise and hearing survey of earth-moving equipment operators. *American Industrial Hygiene Association Journal,* March-April 1967, **28**, 117–128.

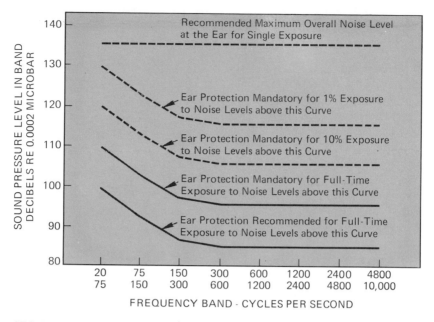

17.9 Broad-band noise level criteria for hearing protection. For each indicated duration of exposure, the noise spectrum should not exceed the intensities of the curve in question. (*From Williams, op. cit., Fig. 3.*)

words, the figure shows what could be considered as the hearing loss associated with the noise to which the subjects were exposed. The loss is especially pronounced at the higher frequencies (2,000 and 4,000 Hz).

Hearing loss is, of course, a function of several factors, such as the intensity and spectrum of the noise, its duration, and its continuity, as well as individual factors. Because of these several factors, it is not possible to establish definitive tolerance limits, but several noise-level criteria have been proposed for use as guidelines. One such set, proposed by Williams[16] is given in Figure 17.9. The United States Air Force[17] has set forth a very simple standard which provides that the sound pressure level shall not exceed 85 dB for *any* of four octave bands having the following center frequencies: 500, 1,000, 2,000, and 4,000 Hz. This standard applies to exposure during the conventional eight-hour day.

Discussion

We have discussed the possible effects of noise in terms of human performance and hearing loss. But noise can have other effects as well, such as serving as a source of annoyance (in communities and homes, as well

[16] Williams, L. J. Some industrial noise problems and their solution. *Noise Control*, 1959, 5(1), 36–43f.
[17] AF Regulation 160–3, USAF, October 1956.

as on the job) and interferring with communications. And there are some clues that there may be long-term physiological effects. For example, Cohen[18] reports that a five-year follow-up study of five hundred workers subjected to noise levels of 95 dB or above revealed higher incidence of somatic complaints of illness and diagnosed disorders than another group of workers who were not subjected to such noise levels. He also reported a higher absence rate for those working in high noise levels, which may indicate greater psychological stress.

The control of noise is, of course, very much an engineering problem. In general terms, it can include the following approaches: reduction of noise at the source (such as by proper machine design, lubrication, mounting) ; enclosing the noise; and the use of baffles and soundproofing materials. If these steps still do not bring the noise level within acceptable limits, the use of ear protection devices is in order.

MUSIC

During the 1940s and the early part of the 1950s there was quite a flurry of research interest relating to the effects of music during work. In more recent years there has been relatively little research in this area, but many organizations provide music for their employees. Such music is played for employees on the hypothesis that it is a "good thing" in one way or another—that there are benefits that accrue from such a program, such as improved performance and higher morale. It is, therefore, appropriate to raise the question as to whether music has the beneficial effects that have been postulated for it.

As an example of some of the surveys relating to music, Newman, Hunt, and Rhodes[19] varied the types of music played in a factory over a period of five weeks (including some periods of no music), and analyzed the effects in terms of employee attitudes. They found that music had no influence on either the units produced or the percentage of rejects. However, they found that almost all of the twenty-six workers tended to favor music during their work. On the basis of the employees' expressions of preference for various types of music, however, they make the observation that such preferences are quite variable and specific to the population, which suggests that, in planning a music program, the preferences of the employees be given full consideration.

18 Cohen, A. The role of psychology in improving worker safety and health under the Occupational Safety and Health Act. Paper given at the meetings of the American Psychological Association, Honolulu, Hawaii, September 1972.

19 Newman, R. I., Jr., Hunt, D. L., & Rhodes, F. Effect of music on employee attitude and productivity in a skateboard factory. *Journal of Applied Psychology*, 1966, 50(6), 493–496.

In reviewing the results of many such surveys, Uhrbrock[20] has found that the following points seem to be warranted on the basis of the evidence:

1. Unqualified claims that increased production results from the introduction of music into the work situation are not proven.
2. The social implications of music in industry as an incentive system ultimately should be faced. A question may be asked, "Is this a legitimate device that gives pleasure to workers and profit to employers?"
3. Feelings of euphoria during periods of music stimulation have a physiological basis which is evidenced by changes in blood pressure that occur in some subjects while listening to music.
4. Factory employees prefer working where music is played rather than where it is not played.
5. Not all workers like music while they work. From 1 to 10 percent are annoyed by it.
6. Quality of work can be adversely affected by the use of music in the work situation.
7. Instrumental, rather than vocal, music is preferred during working hours by the majority of workers.
8. There is a negative correlation between age and preference for work music.
9. At least three investigators have reported that young, inexperienced employees, engaged in doing *simple,* repetitive, monotonous tasks, increased their output when stimulated by music.
10. Evidence has been presented which demonstrates that experienced factory operators, whose work patterns were stabilized and who were performing *complex* tasks, did not increase their production when music was played while they worked.
11. At times music has had an adverse effect on the output of individual employees, even though they reported that music was "quite pleasant."

It is apparent from Uhrbrock's summary that music has not proved to be a universal boon to industry, and it should not be viewed as a panacea for all of the production ills of an organization. Perhaps the most relevant considerations in contemplating a music program should be the reactions of employees to it, and the type of work in question. In the latter connection, music probably can be of greater value as a morale booster with employees on simple, routine tasks than on more complex tasks.

WORK SCHEDULE

An important condition of any job is that of the work schedule, including the work shift and the hours of work. Although the human being has evolved in such a way that he typically is awake and active during the

20 Uhrbrock, R. S. Music on the job: Its influence on worker morale and productivity. *Personnel Psychology,* 1961, 14, 9–38.

day and sleeps at night, the nature of some types of work requires that some people need to work at night. This is mandatory in the case of certain continuous processes such as petroleum refining, and has become standard practice in the case of some services such as some transportation systems and restaurants. Furthermore, economic factors sometimes dictate multiple shifts to utilize plant facilities more fully.

There are, of course, many variations in the work schedules of those who work during nontypical day hours, but the most common schemes are regular shift work (such as 4 P.M. to midnight and midnight to 8 A.M.) and rotating shifts in which individuals change shifts every few days, every week, or every month.

Possible Effects of Shift Work

Because work at night is a bit at odds with man's typically diurnal pattern of living, it is reasonable to be curious about the possible effects of such schedules. It has been pointed out by Mott et al.[21] that the various studies of shift work generally fall into two groups: (1) those dealing with the possible effects of shift work on the worker (on physical health, family relations, social participation, family attitudes, affective states, and so forth); and (2) those dealing with the possible effects on the organization (on productivity, absences, turnover, and so forth).

With respect to the effects of shift work on health, Mott et al.[22] report that the results of several surveys suggest that shift work tends to affect the time-oriented body function such as sleep, digestion, and elimination. But these indications are not universal. In a survey of 275 workers reported by de la Mare and Walker,[23] for example, there were no worker-reported differences between the health of shift workers and that of regular day workers.

On the basis of their review of available studies, Mott et al.[24] conclude that shift work can and does have effects upon the worker's family relations, his social participation, and his opportunities for solitary leisure activities. But let us hasten to add that, although these effects may be commonly reported, they are by no means universal. And the same qualification applies to the most prevalent attitude of workers toward shift work, which is one of dislike. For example, in the survey by de la Mare and Walker,[25] the following expressions of preference were reported:

21 Mott, P. E., Mann, F. C., McLaughlin, Q., & Warwick, D. P. Shift Work. Ann Arbor: University of Michigan Press, 1965.

22 Ibid.

23 de la Mare, G., & Walker, J. Factors influencing the choice of shift rotation. Occupational Psychology, 1968, 42(1), 1–21.

24 Mott et al., op. cit.

25 de la Mare & Walker, op. cit.

TABLE 17.1 Rank Order of Reasons for Preference for Work Schedules of Men on Three Different Schedules

Permanent Days		Rotating Shifts		Permanent Nights	
Reasons for Preference in Combined Rank Order	No. Stating Personally Relevant (N = 17)	Reasons for Preference in Combined Rank Order	No. Stating Personally Relevant (N = 20)	Reasons for Preference in Combined Rank Order	No. Stating Personally Relevant (N = 20)
1. My wife doesn't like me to work nights	15	1. It is what I'm used to	15	1. Travelling is less of a problem	19
2. It is better for my health	13	2. I find night duty makes a pleasant change	14	2. It gives me more useful free time	20
3. It gives more useful free time	9	3. I can swap duties when I want to	11	3. I have more regular hours of work on nights	16
4. I just can't stand nights	9	4. Some night duties are useful to add up the overtime	5	4. Friendlier and pleasanter atmosphere at work on nights	16
5. I can see more of my family on days	8	5. It's better for promotion to do the full rota	1	5. Night duty is better for my health	7
6. I can't sleep during the day	7			6. I can get more overtime on nights	7
7. I'm kept busy all the time on days	6				
8. The day duties are shorter	3				

For married men only there were two further factors:

A 'I can see more of my family' ranked third after useful free time. Considered personally relevant by 10/14 married men.

B 'My wife is used to it and prefers it now' ranked seventh after health reasons. Considered personally relevant by 5/14 married men.

Source: de la Mare and Walker, *op. cit.*

Preferring permanent days	61%
Preferring rotating shifts	12%
Preferring permanent nights	27%

On the basis of interviews with samples of individuals on permanent day shift, rotating shift, and permanent night shift, some indication of the reasons for their preferences for their shifts were expressed, as shown in Table 17.1. A scanning of these expressions of preference gives one the impression that they are predicated on differences in personal value systems. This seems to imply that when shift work is necessary, individuals should be given their preference for shift, insofar as this is feasible. In some circumstances, such as in the company involved in the survey under discussion, those employees with greatest seniority are given their choices of shift.

Aside from trying to assign individuals to shifts of their choice, it is also reasonable to adapt the specific schedules of shifts to the expressed preferences of the group. In this connection, for example, Wedderburn[26] reports generally stronger preference for swiftly rotating shifts (with changes every two or three days, with breaks of twenty-four hours or more between changes) than for less frequent changes (such as on a weekly, fortnightly, or monthly basis). He further reports that the majority of such shift workers were not aware of any severe physiological discomfort or damage arising from the rather frequent changes in the diurnal patterns.

In connection with the possible effects of shift work on the organization, Mott et al.[27] report that there is some evidence indicating that errors tend to be a bit higher and output a bit lower on shift work, especially the night shift, but these effects are not consistent and may be attributable to certain characteristics of the workers. Therefore, we probably should be wary of any bland generalizations on this score.

Hours of Work

The sixty-, seventy-, and eighty-hour work weeks of bygone years are themselves virtually bygones, and for many kinds of work, schedules have settled down at somewhere around the conventional forty-hour week. In general, then, the total hours worked by people on their jobs is not now a major issue. For what interest it might be, however, a survey was carried out by Kossoris et al.[28] after World War II that dealt with the experiences of thirty-four plants in connection with various work schedules that they used during the war. The survey included seventy-eight "cases"

---

[26] Wedderburn, A. A. I. Social factors in satisfaction with swiftly rotating shifts. *Occupational Psychology,* 1967, **41**(2 and 3), 85–107.

[27] Mott et al., *op. cit.*

[28] Kossoris, M. D., Kohler, R. F., *et al. Hours of work and output.* U.S. Department of Labor, Bureau of Labor Statistics, Bulletin No. 917, 1947.

in these plants, covering 2,445 men and 1,060 women. Each "case" selected for the survey dealt with a particular organization unit (such as a department or section) for which there had been some change in hours of work from a prewar to war condition or from a war condition to a postwar condition, but for which there were no other major changes. For each case, data were obtained on "efficiency" (i.e., productivity per hour), injuries, and absenteeism.

The data from the survey indicated considerable variation in the effects of changes, depending on how heavy the work was, whether the work was machine paced or not, whether hours were being increased or reduced, method of pay (incentive or hourly), and other factors. Generally speaking, however, the results indicated that, everything else being equal, the eight-hour day and forty-hour week are best in terms of efficiency and absenteeism, and that higher levels of hours are less satisfactory. With few exceptions, the longer hours resulted in greater output than that produced during shorter schedules. As a rule, however, the increase fell considerably short of the increase in hours. For hours above eight per day and forty-eight per week, it usually took three hours of work to produce two additional hours of output when work was light. When the work was heavy, it took more than two more hours to produce one hour of additional output. Injuries also increased as hours increased, not only in absolute numbers, but also in the rate of increase.

REST PERIODS

Rest breaks during scheduled work sessions are becoming rather common practice, providing occasions for coffee, soft drinks, tea, and other refreshments. Although the use of such breaks tends to be predicated on the assumption that the breaks are "good" in terms of various criteria (such as productivity and employee reactions), it must be stated that there is actually not much hard data available to support such an assumption, although there has been a lot of fuzzy speculation about the accumulation of "fatigue" during the work period.

Employee Reactions Throughout Work Period

Among the few surveys relating to employee reactions to their work schedules, is one in which Nelson and Bartley[29] surveyed seventy-five female office workers, asking each to report, for the hours of each half of each work day, the hour during which she had become "most tired," "most

[29] Nelson, T. M., & Bartley, S. H. The pattern of personal response arising during the office work day. *Occupational Psychology*, 1968, *42*(1), 77–83.

bored," and "most rested." The average responses are shown graphically in Figure 17.10. On the basis of these results the investigators suggest that the "personal dimensions" of work are not the result of some simple and continuous "fatigue" variable, for if this were the case the "tired" curve would have built up continuously after some point, instead of actually dropping from the beginning of the work period. Rather, they maintain that the reactions of individuals depend upon the manner in which they "cognitively structure" the demands placed upon them.

In reviewing their results, it can be seen that the first hour is a period in which work demands are easily met by most workers (as shown by the high percentage who reported feeling most "rested"), but that some workers actually reported this as the period in which they were most "tired." The middle period is less likely to be accompanied by strong personal states of any quality, but the last hour seems to be one in which considerable adjustment to work frequently occurs.

It is interesting to note that Griffith, Kerr, Mayo, and Topal,[30] on the basis of a survey of 379 employees in one plant, report greatest feelings

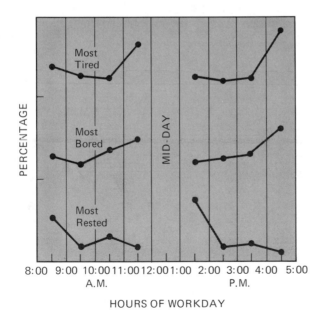

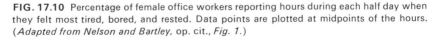

FIG. 17.10 Percentage of female office workers reporting hours during each half day when they felt most tired, bored, and rested. Data points are plotted at midpoints of the hours. (*Adapted from Nelson and Bartley, op. cit., Fig. 1.*)

[30] Griffith, J. W., Kerr, W. A., Mayo, T. B., Jr., & Topal J. R. Changes in subjective fatigue and readiness for work during the eight-hour shift. *Journal of Applied Psychology*, 1950, **34**, 163–166.

of "fatigue" during the fourth and eighth hours of the eight-hour shift, thus generally confirming the results shown in Figure 17.10 for the "most tired" and "most bored" responses. Their results, incidentally, were remarkably similar for manual, office, and supervisory personnel.

Rest Periods and Work Performance

Although, as indicated earlier, few hard facts are available about the effects of rest periods, the bits and pieces of evidence that are available suggest that rest periods typically do not reduce output even though there is less time worked, and in fact sometimes increase output. For example, the effects of rest pauses in a typical production job were analyzed in an early study in Great Britain by Farmer and Bevington.[31] Figure 17.11 shows the production of a group of employees before and after the introduction of scheduled rest periods. In another study, Miles and Skilbeck[32] found that two fifteen-minute change-of-work periods resulted in a 14.2 percent increase in performance.

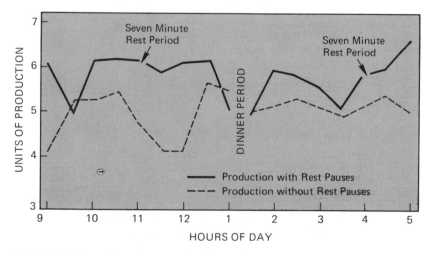

FIG. 17.11 Effect of rest pauses on production for a typical industrial job.

Scheduling of Rest Periods

Some work is so irregular that an individual has occasional or frequent periods of inactivity. When work activity does not provide such breaks, however, it is rather widely granted that people should have some breaks

[31] Farmer, E., & Bevington, S. M. An experiment in the introduction of rest pauses. *Journal of the National Institute of Industrial Psychology*, 1922, 1, 89–92.

[32] Miles, G. H., & Skilbeck, O. An experiment on change of work. Occupational Psychology, 1944, 18, 192–195.

during work periods; there is, then, a question as to whether they should be scheduled or taken at the discretion of the employee. There can be no single answer to this question, inasmuch as administrative considerations, the nature of the work, and other factors must be taken into account. In this connection, however, McGehee and Owen[33] found that in one office the introduction of two short rest pauses during the day reduced unauthorized rest periods and increased the speed of work.

As far as scheduling is concerned, it is reasonable to believe that there would be some optimum for any given type of work which—if circumstances permit, but they usually do not—could be ascertained experimentally. As an example of such an exercise, Bhatia and Murrell[34] experimented with two rest period schedules with an admittedly small group of twelve female operatives who had no previous rest schedule. A summary of some of the results is given below.

Condition	No. of Weeks	Mean Efficiency Index	Mean Earnings (£)
Control	9	100.2	14.60
Six 10-min. pauses	18	104.4	15.42
Four 15-min. pauses	7	102.5	14.40
Six 10-min. pauses	5	103.1	15.59

These results are not dramatic, but they do show that the introduction of rest pauses did not reduce productivity, even though the rest pauses reduced actual work from eight to seven hours. Further, there is a hint that six ten-minute pauses resulted in a slight increase in efficiency over four fifteen-minute pauses; what is more, there was overwhelming preference for the six ten-minute rest periods.

It is probable, as an unconfirmed hypothesis, that in the case of most sedentary and light physical activities, the possible gains from providing rest periods arise more from "psychological" factors such as boredom or some vague desire for change, than from any significant change in the physical or physiological condition of the individual. In the case of heavy or highly repetitive physical activity, however, physical wear and tear enters the picture. Especially in the case of heavy physical work, the schedule of work and rest should be such as to preclude the building up of physiological stress. Perhaps the most objective basis for doing so is to use physiological

    [33] McGehee, W., & Owen, F. B. Authorized and unauthorized rest pauses in clerical work. *Journal of Applied Psychology,* 1940, **24,** 605–614.
    [34] Bhatia, N., & Murrell, K. F. H. An industrial experiment in organized rest pauses. *Human Factors,* 1969, **11**(2), 167–174.

measures as guidelines, as proposed by Davis, Faulkner, and Miller.[35] They compared the effects on heart rate of two different rest breaks (one of two minutes, the other of seven minutes) interspersed between ten-minute work periods of a lifting task. The heart-rate patterns in the case of these two rest-break schedules are shown in Figure 17.12. It can be seen that the seven-minute rest breaks kept the heart rate at a fairly steady state, as contrasted with the two-minute schedule. If it is not feasible to obtain measures of physiological conditions such as heart rate to use as the basis for actual scheduling of rest breaks in the case of heavy physical work, it may well be that the workers should be encouraged to take rest breaks when they feel they need them.

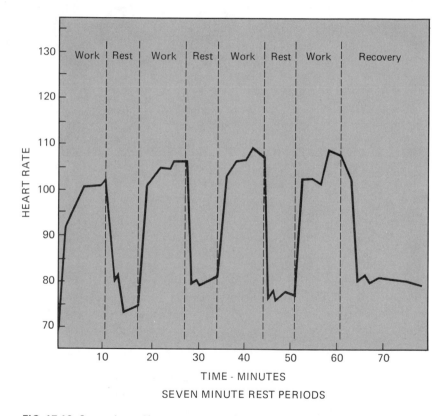

SEVEN MINUTE REST PERIODS

FIG. 17.12 Comparison of heart rate patterns for a lifting task carried out under two-minute and seven-minute rest-break schedules. The two-minute break is clearly inadequate in that it permits continued increase in the heart rate during successive work periods. (*From Davis, Faulkner, and Miller, op. cit., Fig. 2 and 3.*)

[35] Davis, H. L., Faulkner, T. W., & Miller, C. I. Work physiology. *Human Factors,* 1969, **11**(2), 157–166.

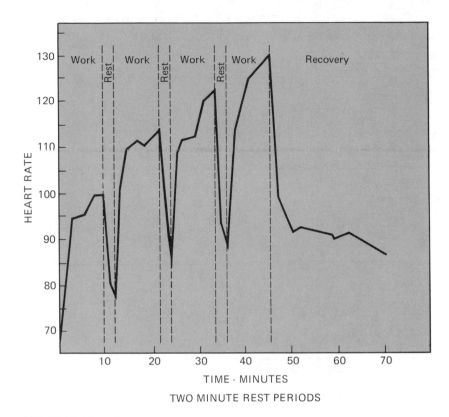

TIME - MINUTES

TWO MINUTE REST PERIODS

FIG. 17.12 (Cont.)

In discussing the scheduling of rest breaks, particular mention should be made of vigilance (or monitoring) types of tasks require continual attention to detect infrequent stimuli or signals. Such tasks will be discussed further in Chapter 18, but in the context of our present discussion it should be noted that performance on such tasks tends to deteriorate after twenty to thirty minutes. These findings suggest that in the case of monitoring activities rest periods, or changes in work, should be provided at twenty- or thirty-minute intervals.

In addition, special note should be made of the matter of rest breaks in certain types of activity for which there are special problems, because of the nature of the activity. A case in point is that of the operation of vehicles that demand continuous attention and control. It is of course difficult to study driver behavior in relation to driving time under everyday driving conditions, but in controlled experiments Herbert[36] and Herbert and Jaynes[37]

[36] Herbert, M. J. Analysis of a complex skill: Vehicle driving. *Human Factors,* August 1963, 5(5), 363–372.

[37] Herbert, M. J., & Jaynes, W. E. Performance decrement in vehicle driving. *Journal of Engineering Psychology,* 1964, 3, 1–8.

had 180 male drivers serve as subjects. Five different men served as subjects each of thirty-six days, one of the five being assigned to one of five experimental conditions—namely, driving for one, three, seven, or nine hours, or serving as a control (with no driving). Before and after completion of the specified number of driving hours, the men were given nine different driving tests, each test measuring some particular aspect of driving behavior, such as parking, "jockeying," or driving over specific courses. The control subjects were given the driving tests without any period of driving on the day in question.

It was found that all of the tests but one were significantly related to driving time. Figure 17.13 shows, for a combination of four of the tests, the decrement in test performance as a function of driving time. Although these findings are not necessarily indicative of deterioration in driving behavior or accident rates in actual driving, there is a strong implication of loss in performance over hours of driving.

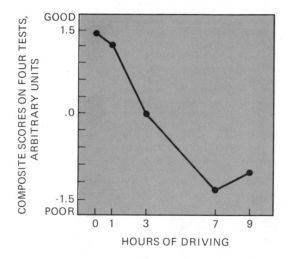

FIG. 17.13 Changes in performance on a combination of four driving tests as related to hours of vehicle driving. (The scores are z-scores.) (*From Herbert and Jaynes,* op. cit.)

PART V

Accidents
and
Human Errors

The tendency toward error is a pervading human trait. Errors of various kinds can, of course, affect the quality of work people do, and also can contribute to injuries and fatalities. The sources of errors and accidents, however, are not entirely to be found in the individuals in question; situational variables such as the nature of the work activities, the design of the equipment, the procedures, and the work environment can have a significant bearing upon the frequency and nature of errors and accidents. This section deals with some of the aspects of errors and accidents in industry.

chapter eighteen

Human Error

Human error is such a pervading fact of life that it has given rise to such literary expressions as "to err is human, to forgive divine." Although the consequences of some human errors are of minor importance, having little more than nuisance value, the consequences of others may be of major proportions in terms of human safety, effectiveness of operations, time, physical damage, economic loss, and other criteria. Although the notion of "error-free" performance and zero defects are probably will-o'-the-wisps, efforts to reduce errors usually can be justified, especially when the possible consequences of error are of major proportions.

THE NATURE OF HUMAN ERROR

Human error obviously takes many forms, but it has been generally characterized by Meister[1] and by Rook[2] in the framework of poor work-

[1] Meister, D. Applications of human reliability to the production process. In W. B. Askren (Ed.), *Symposium on reliability of human performance in work*. USAF, Aerospace Medical Research Laboratory, Report AMRL–TR–67–88, May 1967.

[2] Rook, L. W., Jr. *Reduction in human error in industrial production*. Albuquer-

manship. Some workmanship errors, of course, can be perceived readily either by direct observation or from subsequent consequences. But the quality of many types of workmanship (for example, inspection operations) varies along a continuum from good to poor; in such instances the line between acceptable and unacceptable workmanship needs to be delineated. An operational definition of human error has been proposed by Peters[3] as follows: "Any deviation from a previously established, required, or expected standard of human performance that results in an unwanted or undesirable time delay, difficulty, problem, incident, malfunction, or failure."

The Role of Human Behavior

We shall limit our discussion of error to those areas in which there is some element of human culpability or involvement. In such areas our all-too-human tendency toward error-producing behavior may not always produce errors but it has the effect of increasing the probabilities thereof. Payne and Altman[4] proposed that errors be characterized in terms of "behavior components" that reflect the basic type of human behavior that generates them. These components subsequently were incorporated as one phase of an error classification system developed by Rook,[5] as follows:

Input behaviors (errors of sensory or perceptual input)
Mediation errors (errors of some mediation or information processing type)
Output errors (errors in making physical responses)

Other systems for viewing the human behaviors involved in errors also have been formulated, such as Altman's[6] suggestion of relating error behaviors to what he refers to as "behavioral level." The behavioral level concept stems primarily from Gagné's[7] cumulative learning sequence discussed in Chapter 9 and illustrated in Figure 9.1. Altman's modification of Gagné's hierarchy, and examples of errors that correspond with the various levels of it, are as follows:

---

que, New Mexico: Sandia Corporation. Technical Memorandum SCTM 93–62(14), June 1962.

3 Peters, G. A. Human error and "goof proofing." Paper presented at Product Assurance Symposium, American Society for Quality Control, San Fernando Valley Section, Glendale, California, October 20, 1962.

4 Payne, D., & Altman, J. W. *An index of electronic equipment operability.* American Institutes for Research, Report AIR–C–43–1/62, 1962.

5 Rook, *op. cit.*

6 Altman, J. D. Classification of human error. In Askren, *op. cit.*

7 Gagné, R. M. *The conditions of learning.* New York: Holt, Rinehart & Winston, 1965.

Behavioral level	*Example of error behavior*
Problem solving	Failure to use available information to derive needed solution
Logical manipulation, rule using, and decision making	Failure to apply an available rule
Estimating with discrete or continuous responding	Inadequate magnitude of control action
Chaining or rate sequencing	Misordering procedural steps
Sensing, detecting, identifying, coding, and classifying	Failure to record or report a signal change

Variables that Contribute to Errors

It is frequently difficult to isolate the "real" causes of specific errors. However, it is reasonable to hypothesize that, theoretically, all errors could be attributed to either *situational* variables, *individual* variables, or a combination of both.

Situational variables. Of course, the situational variables that can contribute to errors are to a large extent specific to the situation, but Meister[8] indicates that in general they may be related to the following factors: workspace and equipment layout; environment; design of machinery, hand tools, and other equipment; methods of handling, transporting, storing, and inspecting equipment; job planning information and its transmission; and operating instructions. Ware[9] describes these categories in somewhat different terms, referring to them as task characteristics, system organization, test characteristics, and physical environment.

Individual variables. The relevant individual variables cover virtually the entire spectrum discussed in Chapter 2, including aptitudes, personality, physical skills, age, sex, education, and experience.

Discussion. In arguing for greater recognition of the distinction between these two types of error-producing factors, Ware[10] points out that both types of variables *mediate* human performance (i.e., they act as intervening variables), but they do not directly "control" performance. He suggests that the difference between them is the degree of *directness* with which they influence human performance. The situational variables "set the stage" or provide a framework within which the individual variables operate. In effect, they influence the probabilities of successful performance. In turn,

---

[8] Meister, *op. cit.*

[9] Ware, C. T., Jr. Individual and situational variables affecting human performance. *Human Factors,* 1964, 6(6), 673–674.

[10] *Ibid.*

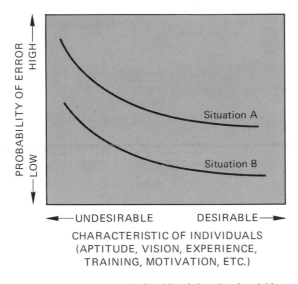

FIG. 18.1 Generalized relationship of situational variables and of individual characteristics as related to error rate (probability of error). Situations A and B might be differences in equipment design, methods, work periods, environments, etc. (*Adapted from Rook,* op. cit., *Fig. 1.*)

the individual variables can be viewed as the basis for predisposing individuals toward behaviors that, in turn, increase the odds of successful (error-free) performance or its obverse. An overly simplified and generalized representation of the relationship between situational and individual variables as related to error rate is shown in Figure 18.1. In particular, this illustrates how these two sets of variables might interact to affect the probability of errors.[11]

Classifications of Errors

Toward the end of providing data that can be used in figuring out what to do about errors, various schemes for classifying errors have been developed. In one such scheme, proposed by Altman,[12] errors are differentiated

[11] One method for quantitatively evaluating the contribution of human error to the degradation of product quality or performance has been developed by Rook, *op. cit.* The quantification of error (human and/or machine) in terms of probabilities is related to the concept of the *reliability* of man-machine systems as expressed in terms of probabilities of successful operation or performance. (In this sense, *reliability* has a different meaning than as used elsewhere in this text.)

[12] Altman, J. W. Improvements needed in a central store of human performance data. *Human Factors,* 1964, **6**(6), 681–686.

in relation to three general types of work activity, as follows (with some slight modifications) :

Work involving discrete acts
Omissions (failure to perform a required action)
Insertion (performance of a nonrequired action)
Sequence (performance of actions out of sequence, or at wrong time)
Unacceptable performance (usually unacceptable quality)
Continuous actions (as in continuous control of a process)
Failure to achieve end state in available time
Failure to maintain desirable degree of control over time
Monitoring (vigilance) function
Failure to detect relevant stimuli or signals
False detection of stimuli or signals

Altman proposes some other dimensions in his scheme, and other people have put forth other schemes, but the one given above serves to illustrate such systems in general.

ANALYSIS AND USE OF ERROR DATA

From the above discussion, it follows logically that corrective action should depend upon knowledge about the predominant sources of human error.

Methods of Identifying Sources of Human Error

It has been suggested by Peters[13] that there are four principal methods that can be used to identify sources of human error. These methods, in somewhat modified form, are described below.

Data collection and analysis. In the case of an ongoing operation, error data can be obtained through reported malfunctions, system failures, quality control and inspection reports, equipment logs, accident records, personal injury records, and other sources. Such data can be summarized in various ways, including the use of some type of classification scheme such as the one discussed above.

Direct observation. Observation of work in process either on a continuous or sampling basis sometimes can aid in identifying actual or potential error-producing factors. In this regard, Meister[14] has suggested a number of questions that can serve as cues in the observation process, such as questions relating to the design of equipment, work area, materials handling, and environmental factors.

[13] Peters, *op. cit.*
[14] Meister, *op. cit.*

Systems analysis. Where a new or modified system is being planned, an analysis of the job operations and operations sequence may serve to locate potential problems. Such analyses sometimes are made on the basis of design drawings or blueprints, with the view toward identifying potential sources of error before the system is developed.

Simulation. The experimental use of prototypes, mockups, or other forms of simulation may help to identify potential sources of error in the design and development of systems.

Discussion

Data collected by the four methods just mentioned as well as by other methods can start to focus attention on the variables that presumably are associated with error occurrence, thus leading toward possible corrective action. For example, if there is evidence that errors vary widely among *individuals* who are engaged in similar work, the possible appropriate actions lie in the direction of personnel selection, training, and motivation. If, on the other hand, there is evidence that error rates are associated with situational variables, the problem is one of determining if there are any features of the situation that are related to high error rates and that could be modified to reduce such rates. (Such features might include improperly designed or maintained equipment, unsafe procedures, improper arrangement of materials, or poor illumination.)

Because it is not feasible to discuss human error in all the various circumstances in which errors actually occur, we will discuss errors in the following contexts: monitoring tasks; inspection processes; and accidents (to be covered in the next chapter).

MONITORING TASKS

The trend toward greater and greater mechanization and automation is increasing the number of jobs in which a major function is that of monitoring an operation or process. In typical monitoring tasks (sometimes called vigilance tasks), the monitor's function is that of giving his attention to the operation in order to identify circumstances or events that require some action (response) on his part. In general, such tasks are characterized by prolonged periods of time during which there are infrequent stimulus events to be identified.

A primary requirement for a monitor is the correct identification of all, or most, of the events that should require his action. The input relating to these events may be presented to the monitor by various displays (such as cathode ray tubes, dials and gauges, instruments of various kinds, or auditory signals), or they may be observed or detected directly (such as by noticing a change in the sound of a machine, observing boxes moving off a conveyor after they have been labeled, or inspecting the parts made by an automatic machine). Although most monitoring tasks in industry are probably of the latter type, much of the monitoring research has involved the presentation of "signals" on displays of some sort, such as cathode ray tubes. In monitoring studies the performance of subjects is measured with such criteria as: (1) failure to detect relevant stimuli or signals; (2) false detection; and sometimes (3) response lag.

Although of course there are individual differences in the ability to monitor tasks, the primary concern with regard to errors in monitoring activities has been in connection with the effects of situational variables on monitoring performance. A couple of such variables will be discussed.

Duration of Monitoring Periods

The duration of monitoring periods is one of the primary factors that influences monitoring performance. McGrath et al.[15] called attention to this as a general phenomenon, pointing out that the probability of signal detection declines as time progresses. This decline generally reaches its maximum within the first hour, after which performance tends to become stabilized. However, the decline frequently (and perhaps most typically) occurs much earlier, sometimes within the first ten to thirty minutes.

This decline can be broken up by the introduction of almost any kind of interpolated rest, such as every twenty or thirty minutes. This effect was reflected by the results of an investigation by Bergum and Lehr[16] in which twenty male subjects sat in a booth watching a circular panel with twenty one-half-inch red lights which illuminated in sequence at a rate of twelve revolutions per minute. The "signal" to be detected consisted of the failure of a light to illuminate in its normal sequence (the signal rate was twenty-four per hour). Some subjects monitored this panel for ninety minutes continuously. Their performance (expressed as percentage of signals detected) is shown in Figure 18.2 as line A. This figure also shows, as line B, the performance of another group who were given ten-minute rest periods at the end of the first thirty minutes and after the next thirty minutes of monitoring.

[15] McGrath, J. J., Harabedian, A., & Buckner, D. N. *Review and critique of the literature on vigilance performance*. Santa Barbara Research Park, Goleta, California: Human Factors Research, Inc., Technical Report 206–1, December 1969.

[16] Bergum, B. O., & Lehr, D. J. Vigilance performance as a function of interpolated rest. *Journal of Applied Psychology*, 1962, **46**, 425–427.

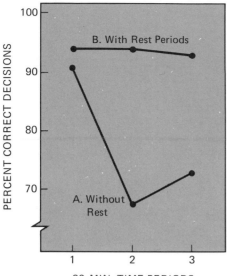

FIG. 18.2 Percentage of correct detections of visual signals for 90 minutes of continuous monitoring, and for 90 minutes with two 10-minute rest periods. (*Adapted from Bergum and Lehr, op. cit., Table 1. Copyright 1962 by the American Psychological Association, and adapted by permission.*)

Frequency Rate of Signals

Another factor that sometimes has been found to affect monitoring performance is the frequency of the signals (sometimes referred to as signal *density*). Detection of signals tends to *decrease* with *low* signal rates, as is illustrated by the results of a study by Deese[17] in which subjects were given ten, twenty, thirty, or forty signals per hour for various experimental periods. The results of this study are shown in Figure 18.3, which indicates quite clearly improved detection with higher signal rates. It should be noted that lower detection rates do not universally occur with low signal frequency, although this is a fairly common tendency. Although actual *detection* rates are not always affected by low frequencies, there is some indication that *response time* tends to be slower with the lower frequency rates. This was indicated by the results of a study by Smith *et al.*[18] in which there was a systematic increase in response time with reductions in signal density (i.e., frequency) from ninety-six to forty-eight to twenty-four to twelve to six.

[17] Deese, J. *Changes in visual performance after visual work.* USAF, Wright Air Development Center, Technical Report 57–285, 1957.

[18] Smith, R. P., Warm, J. S., & Alluisi, E. A. Effects of temporal uncertainty on watchkeeping performance. *Perception and Psychophysics,* 1966, **1,** 293–299.

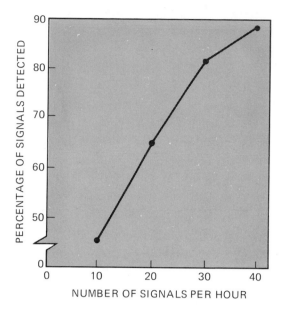

FIG. 18.3 Percentage of signals detected for varying signal frequencies. (*Adapted from Deese,* op. cit.)

Temporal Patterns of Signals

Related to the frequency of signals is the temporal distribution of their occurrence. A given number of signals per hour can be presented at regular, constant time intervals, or randomly, or with many different time patterns. Monitoring performance typically has been found to be related to such patterns, as summarized by O'Hanlon and McGrath.[19] Usually performance is better when the intersignal intervals are uniform than when they are random. In their own investigation, O'Hanlon and McGrath were curious about the ability of subjects to discern complex patterns of signals that change systematically during the watchkeeping period. They experimented with such a "patterned" schedule, along with a constant schedule and an irregular schedule, using response time as a criterion of subject performance. They found response time to be better (i.e., shorter) with the *constant* schedule than with either the *irregular* or *patterned* schedule. The generally better performance with a constant schedule usually is attributed to the "expectancies" of subjects, who learn to "expect" signals at the regular intervals.

[19] O'Hanlon, J. F., Jr., & McGrath, J. J. *Temporal patterns of signals and vigilance performance.* Santa Barbara Research Park, Goleta, California: Human Factors Research, Inc., Technical Report 719–3, February 1967.

Discussion

Aside from the variables discussed above, other factors also have been found to be related to monitoring performance, such as intensity of signals, the use of two or more sensory modalities in combination, feedback (i.e., knowledge of results), and supervision. Further, there apparently are some interactions among these. One needs to be aware of the word of caution expressed by Smith et al.[20] to the effect that the implications of monitoring investigations depend to some extent on the criterion used—whether signal detection or response time.

Various theories of vigilance have been postulated, generally relating to such concepts as conditioning and reinforcement, expectancy, sensory variation, arousal, and motivation. Although certain of these seem to account more adequately for monitoring behavior than do others, there is as yet no consensus regarding any single theory as completely adequate.[21]

Certain practical approaches to the achievement of reasonably adequate levels of performance in monitoring tasks have been given or implied above. Considering the results of available research, a number of principles have been suggested by Bergum and Klein[22] for the more effective design of man-monitored systems. These are given below (with minor adaptations):

1. Visual signals should be as large in magnitude as is reasonably possible. This includes size, intensity, and duration.
2. Visual signals should persist until they are seen (or otherwise detected), or as long as is reasonably possible.
3. In the case of visual signals, the area in which a signal can appear should be as restricted as possible.
4. Although "real" signal frequency often cannot be controlled, where possible it is desirable to maintain signal frequency at a minimum of twenty signals per hour. If necessary, this should be accomplished by introducing artificial (noncritical) signals to which the operator must respond.
5. Where possible, the operator should be provided with anticipatory information. For example, a buzzer might indicate the subsequent appearance of a critical signal.
6. Whenever possible and however possible, the monitor should be given knowledge of results.
7. Noise, temperature, humidity, illumination and other environmental factors should be maintained at optimal levels.

[20] Smith et al., op. cit.

[21] For discussions of various theoretical positions (and other aspects of vigilance), the reader is referred to the following sources: Bergum, B. O., & Klein, I. C. A survey and analysis of vigilance research. Human Resources Research Office, Research Report 8, November 1961; Buckner, D. N., & McGrath, J. J. (Eds.) Vigilance: A symposium. New York: McGraw-Hill, 1963; and Studies of human vigilance. Santa Barbara Research Park, Goleta, California: Human Factors Research, Inc., January 1968.

[22] Bergum & Klein, op. cit.

8. The system should be so designed that operators do not work in isolation from other individuals.

9. Whenever possible, individual watches should not exceed thirty minutes.

A couple of words of caution are in order in evaluating the potential practical implications of monitoring research. In the first place, the most common monitoring or watchkeeping chores in industry are somewhat different from those of typical "laboratory" studies. Further, there is as yet no substantial evidence relating to human performance on typical monitoring or watchkeeping jobs over weeks, months, and years, inasmuch as laboratory investigations usually are for periods of a few hours or at most a few days.

INSPECTION PROCESSES

Inspection processes represent another class of work activity in which human errors should be minimized as much as possible. Such errors may be of at least two types—failure to identify a defect that should be rejected, and rejecting an item that should be accepted. Because many inspection processes are somewhat akin to monitoring tasks, much of what was said above monitoring tasks is also applicable to inspection processes.

The Spectrum of Inspection Processes

Probably most inspection processes are visual, although some involve the auditory and tactual senses—and even the taste sense (as in tea tasting) and the olfactory sense (as was formerly the case with gas sniffers in the New York subways).

Basic elements in inspection tasks. It has been pointed out by Harris and Chaney[23] that inspection tasks consist of the following basic elements:

Interpretation (interpretation of some type of established standard which defines what is acceptable and what is not).

Comparison (comparison of the quality characteristic of the item being inspected with the specified standard).

Decision making (deciding whether the quality characteristic of the item conforms to the standard or not).

Action (disposing of the item, recording the results of the inspection, and so forth).

Types of inspection tasks. These basic elements occur in one form or another in virtually every inspection task. Most such tasks are of one of the

[23] Harris, D. H., & Chaney, F. B. *Human factors in quality assurance.* New York: John Wiley, 1969.

following types: (1) scanning tasks (searching for defects by scanning—usually visually, but sometimes by other senses such as by touch); (2) measurement tasks (use of some measuring device such as micrometers or calipers); and (3) monitoring tasks (monitoring some ongoing automatic or semiautomatic process for indications of out-of-tolerance conditions; sometimes this is done by monitoring instruments).

Quality Control

The equality control processes of many industrial organizations are carried out with the intent of providing assurance that items being inspected generally meet specified inspection standards—or at least that the percentage of "unacceptable" items that actually are "accepted" is within a specified limit.

Inspection Accuracy

Evidence about the performance of inspectors is sometimes hard to come by, but there are indications that the end results of some inspection operations leave much to be desired in that substantial percentages of "defects" sometimes are not identified as such. A few examples will illustrate this unhappy fact. These examples largely represent job samples which typically consist of a sample of items to be inspected in a simulation of the actual inspection job. The sample includes some acceptable items and some with known defects. Thus, after a subject "inspects" the lot it is possible to see how well he did in identifying the defective items. (Incidentally, obtaining data such as is given in these examples is a useful first step in taking remedial action to improve inspection accuracy.)

Machined parts. In one study, Chaney and Harris[24] had a group of twenty-six experimental inspectors inspect the same sample of machined parts; the results are given in Figure 18.4, which shows that the percentage of defects detected by the various inspectors ranged from around 20 to about 80, with a mean of about 40.

Bottle inspection. In the manufacture of bottles, inspectors (called selectors in the glass industry) examine the bottles before shipment to identify various types of defective items. One company arranged for an industrial psychologist to study the inspection operation in order to provide information that might be used in improving the accuracy of the process.[25] This study was carried out with a job sample of 288 bottles, 130 of which had

24 Chaney, F. B., & Harris, D. H. Validation of personnel tests for the selection of machined parts inspectors. Paper presented at Western Psychological Association Convention, Long Beach, April 1966. Cited in Harris and Chaney, *op. cit.*, pp. 167–169.
25 Coe, H. C. Studies in glass bottle selection. Unpublished Ph.D. thesis, Purdue University, 1956.

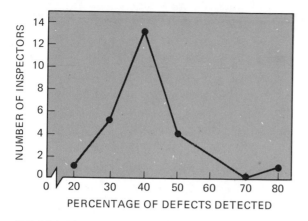

FIG. 18.4 Distribution of percents of defects in machined parts detected by 26 experienced inspectors. (*From Chaney and Harris, April 1966,* op. cit. *as presented by Harris and Chaney,* op. cit., *Fig. 11.2, p. 169.*)

no defects, with the remainder having any of five different defects. Forty-four of the experienced selectors were each asked to sort the 288-bottle sample and report how each bottle would be classified. The results obtained from each selector were then scored for each type of defect, and their accuracy was compared with that of four of the most accurate selectors. The analyses indicated that certain types of defects were most frequently missed by the selectors. This knowledge was used as the basis for setting up a program to train the selectors in identifying the "hard-to-identify" bottle defects; this was done largely by showing examples of those defects.

Tin-plate inspection. Still another study of the accuracy of inspection operations was carried out by Tiffin and Rogers[26] in relation to the inspection of tin-plate—an operation called assorting. The operation is essentially an inspection for appearance that is made while the inspector turns the sheets of tin-plate from one stack to another. As the sheet is turned, the inspector makes a decision from the appearance and feel of the sheet as to whether it is a prime or a second or contains one of a number of possible defects. In the plant studied, the work was done by women assorters. Supervisors generally have felt that inspectors on this job do not reach their maximum performance until they have had approximately six months of experience. The inspectors are paid on a straight hourly rate.

In the study of this inspection process (as in the others mentioned above), a job sample was used, consisting in this case of 150 sheets of tin-plate, with sixty-one prime sheets, twenty sheets with a "weight" defect, and thirty, twenty-six, and thirteen sheets with three different types of "appear-

[26] Tiffin, J., & Rogers, H. B. The selection and training of inspectors. *Personnel,* 1941, **18,** 14–31.

ance" defects that we will not describe. One hundred fifty inspectors were tested with the job sample, each being permitted to take her own time. The analysis of the data included the computation of the reliability coefficients (given below) for the various types of defects (based on the odd- and even-numbered items for each defect).

Type of Defect	Reliability
Weight defect	.74
Appearance defect no. 1	.86
Appearance defect no. 2	.87
Appearance defect no. 3	.68
Mixed sheets (all 150)	.90

In turn, frequency distributions were prepared for the various defects; these are shown in Figure 18.5. This figure also shows the time taken by the inspectors, which ranged from eight to forty-eight minutes, with an

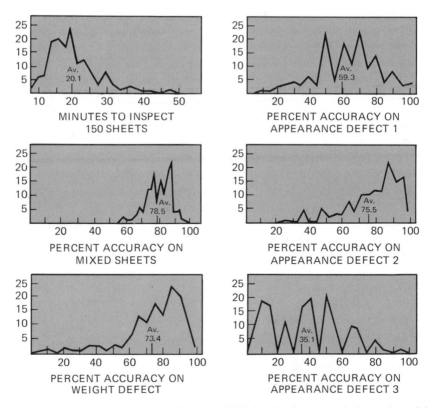

FIG. 18.5 Distribution of results of study of 150 tin-plate inspectors in inspecting a job sample of 150 sheets including some with each of various types of defects.

average of 20.1 minutes. We can see rather marked differences, ranging from 35.1 percent to 75.5 percent, in the inspection accuracy for the various types of defects. And the accuracy for the total sample is only 78.5 percent. Moreover, further analyses of time taken in relation to accuracy of inspection revealed certain interesting sidelights—in particular, that the accuracy of detecting the weight defects was not particularly related to time, but that the accuracy of detecting the other defects was related, in varying degrees, to the time taken.

Discussion. In these examples we have seen evidence of substantial variation in the accuracy of inspection processes. Further, it is obvious that some variation is a function of the nature of the inspection task, including the type of defect to be found. Such variation is, then, essentially that associated with the inspection situation. Some types of defects are obviously harder to detect than others. For example, Harris[27] found that the *percentage* of defects detected tends to be *lower* when the defect rates are very low—that is, when there are very few defects relative to all items being inspected—than when the defect rates are moderate.

On the other hand, some of the error analyses reported above also demonstrated marked *individual* differences in performance, as contrasted with situational differences. As indicated at the beginning of this chapter, the possible directions of corrective action relate both to the situational (i.e., task) factors and to the individual factors. The particular direction in any given circumstance would depend, of course, upon the indications from analysis of relevant data as to the major "sources" of errors (which, in the case of inspection tasks, are inaccuracies in inspection).

Methods of Inspection

The methods of inspection must be included among the various situational variables that can affect the accuracy of inspection operations. For any particular inspection task one should try to select the method that will optimally enhance the ability of inspectors to make the required discriminations, thus "increasing the odds" of achieving reasonable accuracy in the operation. Harris and Chaney[28] have developed several techniques that might be relevant in specific circumstances. These techniques deal with scanning methods, the use of overlay tools, comparison techniques, magnification, precision measurement aids, information transmittal forms, and inspection decision aids. A few of these will be illustrated to show how some modification of the situation (specifically the nature of the task) can help people perform more effectively.

[27] Harris, D. H. Effect of defect rate on inspection accuracy. *Journal of Applied Psychology*, 1968, **52**(5), 377–379.
[28] Harris & Chaney, *op. cit.*, Chapters IX and X.

Inspecting stationary and moving items. Scanning tasks are difficult to perform even under the best of conditions, but certain practices can improve efficiency in such tasks. For example, it is generally the case that people can make more accurate visual discriminations when the object of visual regard is stationary than when it is moving. The results of at least one study dealing with inspection operations—the study of tin-plate inspection mentioned above[29]—tend to confirm the application of this generalization to inspection processes. One objective of this study was the development of an improved method of inspection. For this purpose motion pictures were taken, at one thousand frames per minute, of twelve inspectors selected from those who had taken the job sample test.

An analysis of these films revealed that most inspectors followed the movement of the sheets with their eyes as they flopped them over from one side to another. In contrast, the most accurate inspectors tended to follow a different eye-movement pattern, in that they inspected the sheets during the time they lay on top of each stack. One sheet was inspected as it lay on the top of one stack before it was turned; the other side was inspected after the sheet was turned. Attention was then alternated between the two stacks of tin plate, ignoring the sheet being handled as it was being turned over. The results generally confirmed the ability of people to make better visual discriminations of stationary objects than of moving objects.

Number of characteristics being inspected. Another aspect of scanning inspection tasks is the number of characteristics for which the inspector is to search. Chaney and Harris,[30] in a study involving the inspection of a complex electronic chassis for more than twenty-five different types of quality characteristics, compared two methods of inspection. One of these was the previously common practice of scanning an area of an electronic chassis for all types of defects. The other consisted of scanning independently for each class of defects. The second method was found to be 90 percent more effective in the detection of critical defects, and also resulted in more complete detection of the various types of defects, including certain types which previously had tended to be overlooked. The explanation for this probably lies in the fact that, when scanning for many types of defects, the inspector is, in effect, required to apply several or many standards simultaneously. The inspection for one type of defect at a time requires, as Chaney and Harris put it, less "mental gear shifting."

Overlays in inspection. In certain inspection tasks the object being inspected includes so much visual detail that the specific features to be examined are sometimes "buried." This problem is so acute in the inspection of

29 Tiffin & Rogers, *op. cit.*

30 Chaney, F. B., & Harris, D. H. Human factors techniques for quality improvement. *Annals of the American Society of Quality Control Technical Conference,* 1966, **20,** 400–413.

electronic circuitry on circuit boards that Sadler[31] developed an overlay to facilitate the inspection. The circuit boards may consist of as many as three thousand small circular pads interconnected by lines, shown as (a) in Figure 18.6. The photographic overlay in this case consisted of a matrix of gray rings on transparent material; the rings corresponded to proper circuit pad positions. A section of such an overlay is shown as (b) in Figure 18.6. The effect of using this overlay was reflected in an overall increase of 42 percent inspection accuracy, an increase of 250 percent in detecting undersized and oversized pads, and an increase in the detection of misplaced pads from a miniscule percent to about 80 percent. The overlay obviously facilitated the making of visual discriminations of these types, although it did not contribute to the discrimination of oversized, undersized, or misplaced lines.

Overlays manifestly would not be useful in many inspection tasks, but for certain circumstances (as in the inspection of circuits) they can be of material assistance in the detection of certain types of defects.

Magnification. The visual and perceptual skills of some inspectors are sorely taxed because of the very small, detailed features of the items to be discriminated. Magnification offers possible relief for the bleary eyes of such inspectors by increasing the visual size of relevant features so that they are more within the range of the visual resolution capabilities of the eye.

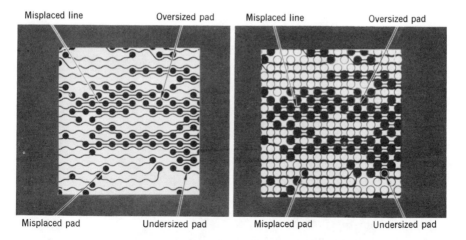

FIG. 18.6 Part of an electronic circuit board as seen with and without a photographic overlay that was used as an aid in the inspection of the board for defects. The overlay markedly assisted in detecting defects of the "pads," but did not assist in detecting defects of the "lines." (*From Sadler, op. cit., as presented by Harris and Chaney, 1969, op. cit., Fig. 9.6, p. 128.*)

[31] Sadler, E. E. The effect of an overlay field on visual inspection judgments. Paper presented to the Western Psychological Association, April 1966.

Examples of various magnification levels of a portion of a ceramic printed circuit are shown in Figure 18.7. The actual use of various levels of magnification by ten experienced inspectors led Harris and Chaney[32] to suggest that there may be some optimum level of magnification for any given type of item being inspected. (In this particular instance the optimum was about a tenfold magnification.) The increased size of the visual detail with "excessive" magnification presumably does not compensate for such factors as optical distortion and decrease in the contrast ratio of the relevant features.

Visual aids in inspection. In the inspection of certain types of items visual aids can be used to enhance the inspection process. For example, Chaney and Teel[33] developed visual aids for use in the inspection of machined parts for such defects as mislocated holes, improper dimensions, and lack of parallelism and concentricity. These aids consisted of a series of simple drawings of the sample parts. The dimensions and tolerances for each characteristic to be inspected were placed on the drawings to minimize the need for calculation or reference to other materials. The inspection aids were introduced as a part of the regular inspection operations in such a way that it was possible to compare the "before" and "after" accuracy over a six-month period, along with the effects of a specially designed training program. The results of this comparison, shown in Figure 18.8, clearly demonstrate the improvement in inspection accuracy associated with

FIG. 18.7 Examples of relative differences in magnification levels of part of a ceramic printed circuit. These examples show, for one feature of the circuit, magnification levels of 1-X (no magnification), 4-X, 10-X, and 20-X. (*From Harris and Chaney, 1969, Fig. 9.15, p. 139.*)

[32] Harris & Chaney, *op. cit.*
[33] Chaney, F. B., & Teel, K. S. Improving inspector performance through training and visual aids. *Journal of Applied Psychology,* 1967, **51**(4), 311–315.

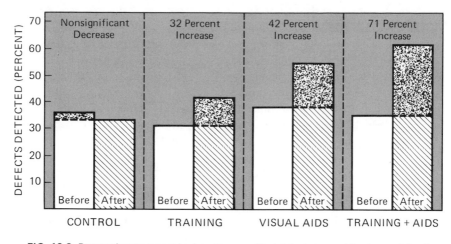

FIG. 18.8 Percent improvement in detecting specified defects in machined parts following introduction of visual inspection aids, special training, and their combination. (*From Chaney and Teel,* op. cit., *as presented by Harris and Chaney, 1969,* op. cit., *Fig. 9.20.*)

the visual aids as well as with the training. Of course, visual inspection aids are appropriate only in certain specific types of circumstances and in the detection of certain types of defects.

Inspection decision aids. The characteristics of some items being inspected vary along a "quality" continuum, with some point along the scale being declared to represent an "acceptable" level. Although this point is usually made clear to the inspector during an instructional period, the inspector thereafter is expected to "store" that image in his memory. In the inspection process the inspector then makes a judgment about the "degree" of that characteristic, and in turn decides if that degree represents a value above or below the "acceptable" dividing line. This decision has to be made for each characteristic being examined, a process that requires, in effect, an *absolute* decision regarding the degree of the characteristic in question. However, a number of psychological investigations have demonstrated rather clearly that people generally can make more accurate judgments about the amounts or degrees of qualities, traits, or characteristics of objects when *comparing* such objects with each other on a *relative* basis than when required to make an *absolute* judgment about the quality. This suggests that inspection decisions could be made more adequately if the inspector is provided with some representation of the minimum acceptable degree of the characteristic in question.

Limit samples. The use of so-called "limit samples" illustrates the recognition of the principle just described. A limit sample is a sample of a product that is just barely acceptable in terms of inspection standards; it represents the "limit" of acceptability. An inspector with a limit sample compares products with this sample, accepting them if they are equal to or better than the sample, and otherwise rejecting them. An example of this approach, as reported by Kelly,[34] involved the inspection of glass panels or face plates for the fronts of television picture tubes. The inspectors in the company in question originally accepted or rejected panels in terms of their memory of what constituted acceptable and unacceptable panels. The company then started using limit samples, one to represent each type of common defect. The company subsequently estimated that accuracy of inspection increased 76 percent after the inauguration of the new inspection procedure.

The procedures for the selection of limit samples in this instance consisted of first arranging a sample of several panels in order of "goodness." This was done by the paired-comparison method, which was discussed in Chapter 8. This method, which involves the judgment of each pair of objects, results in a scaling of the items. With a known "limit sample" panel in the lot to be scaled, one of the other panels was found to have nearly the same scale value as the true "limit sample" panel. This panel was then considered to be a "limit sample equivalent" and was given to an inspector to keep at her work place and to be used for comparison as additional panels were inspected.

When the use of actual limit samples is not feasible, it may be possible to represent such samples photographically. This procedure was used, for example, in representing minimum acceptable levels of solder connections, as reported by Teel and Harris.[35] In brief, they found that the use of photographic representations of acceptable solder connections resulted in about a 100 percent improvement in the differentiation of acceptable and unacceptable defects.

Discussion. Although the methods of inspection just described, as well as some others, have been very helpful in increasing inspection accuracy, it is of course manifest that the specific method used needs to be tailor-made for the specific inspection task. Properly developed methods can go a long way toward helping inspectors make the kinds of discriminations and decisions that are desired. At the same time, it must be recognized that some inspection tasks probably are of such a nature that perfection in inspection is an unrealistic goal.

In reflecting on inspection processes, we should refer back to the discussion of job enlargement in Chapter 16. One of the forms of job enlargement mentioned there involves making people responsible for the quality of their work—in effect, having them perform their own inspection.

[34] Kelly, M. L. A study of industrial inspection by the method of paired comparison. *Psychological Monographs,* 1955, **69**(9), No. 394.
[35] Teel, K. S., & Harris, D. H. New applications of engineering psychology. Paper presented at Western Psychological Association Convention, Honolulu, June 1965.

Selection of Inspectors

The development of a satisfactory method of inspection and the creation of satisfactory working conditions is, of course, only one side of the coin. The other side concerns individual variables as they relate to inspection performance. This is essentially a personnel selection matter, and inasmuch as this matter was discussed in earlier chapters we will not discuss it further here, except to say that in some circumstances tests developed specifically for use in the selection of inspectors have been found to be useful. One such test, for example, is the Harris Inspection Test,[36] which has been found to have substantial validity in the selection of inspectors for various inspection jobs.

[36] Harris, D. H. Development and validation of an aptitude test for inspectors of electronic equipment. *Journal of Industrial Psychology,* 1964, **2**, 29–35.

chapter nineteen

Accidents
and
Safety

We sometimes think of accidents as events that "just happen," but in our more rational moments we should of course realize that they really are brought about by some combination of present circumstances and preceding events.

DEFINITIONS

To reduce possible semantic confusion, let us first clarify certain terms as they will be used here. The term *accident* has been used with various shades of meanings, as pointed out by McGlade.[1] In part these variations are dictated by the specific focus of interest in mind, such as injuries, fatalities, property damage, responsibility, unsafe behavior, or some other focus. For our purposes, two variations on the theme are particularly relevant. One of these is the definition offered by Heinrich,[2] who views an

[1] McGlade, F. S. *Adjustive behavior and safe performance.* Springfield, Ill.: Charles C. Thomas, 1970, pp. 10–16.
[2] Heinrich, H. W. *Industrial accident prevention.* (4th ed.) New York: McGraw-Hill, 1959.

accident as an unplanned and uncontrolled event in which the action or reaction of an object, substance, person, or radiation results in personal injury or *the probability thereof*. The other, as expressed by Haddon *et al.*,[3] is restricted to the concept of an unexpected occurrence of *physical damage* to an animate or inanimate structure. There is, of course, a strong argument for Heinrich's broader definition (which embraces what are sometimes called "near accidents"), but operationally it is difficult to nail down because of the problem of identifying and recording those behaviors or circumstances which *could* have resulted in injury or damage. Thus, we will consider *accidents* as those occurrences in which physical damage (usually personal injuries) occurs. In turn, we will consider *accident behavior* (or unsafe behavior) in the sense proposed by Whitlock *et al.*,[4] as that behavior which might result in injury to the individual himself or to someone else; but we will stretch this concept to include possible physical damage (as in automobile driving) in addition to personal injury.

Accident behavior, of course, does not necessarily result in personal injury or physical damage, but can be considered as being a precipitating factor in by far the majority of accidents. The exceptions include acts of God and those circumstances in which strictly unexpected mechanical conditions or events are involved (although it can be argued that even extraordinary mechanical factors that precipitate accidents might be viewed as consequences of human accident behavior back in time, such as inspection failure to detect the relevant faults).

THE HUMAN AND ECONOMIC COSTS
OF ACCIDENTS

The number of fatalities from accidents is around 113,000 per year. Using data for 1970,[5] these may be broken down into classes as follows:

All accidents	113,000
Motor vehicle	55,300*
Public (excluding motor vehicle)	20,000
Home	27,000
Work	14,200

* Motor vehicle total includes about 3,500 fatalities that are also included in the home and work totals.

[3] Haddon, W., Jr., Suchman, E.A., & Klein, D. *Accident research: Methods and approaches.* New York: Harper & Row, 1964, p. 28.
[4] Whitlock, G. H., Clouse, R. J., & Spencer, W. F. Predicting accident proneness. *Personnel Psychology,* 1963, **16**(1), 35–44.
[5] *National Safety News,* March 1971, **103**(3), 116–117.

During that year there were about 2.2 million disabling injuries in industry, including about 90,000 cases of permanent impairment. On-the-job and off-the-job injuries totalled about 5.3 million. The National Safety Council estimates economic loss as follows:[6]

Wage loss, medical expense, overhead insurance costs	$4,000,000,000
Indirect costs (such as interference with schedules and property damage)	$4,000,000,000
Total	$8,000,000,000

Such human and economic costs add up to staggering totals and make it obvious that a major effort to lessen them is in order. Because of the magnitude of the situation, many companies have set up safety programs of various types to deal with the problem.

ACCIDENT RECORDS AND STATISTICS

Greater insight and understanding relating to accidents can be derived from the availability of relevant records and statistics.[7]

Injury Records

There are various systems for recording basic data relating to specific injuries, but that of the American National Standards Institute (ANSI)[8] has been the most widely accepted. It provides for recording data related to each of the following six categories:

1. The agency (the object or substance most closely related to the injury, and which, in general, could have been properly guarded or corrected)
2. The agency part (the particular part of the agency that is most closely associated with the injury, such as grease, chuck, drill, etc.)

6 *Ibid.*

7 For further discussion of accident records and statistics the reader is referred to such sources as: Gordon, J. B., Akman, A., & Brooks, M. L. *Industrial accident statistics: A re-examination.* New York: Praeger Publishers, 1971; *Accident prevention manual for industrial operations.* (6th ed.) Chicago: National Safety Council, 1969, Chapter 11, Accident records and injury rates; and *Proposed national system for uniform recording and reporting of occupational injuries and illnesses.* New York: American National Standards Institute, 1971.

8 ASI Standard Z1601–1967: *Method of recording and measuring work injury experience.* New York: American National Standards Institute, 1967. Note: The American National Standards Institute (ANSI) was formerly called the American Standards Institute (ASI) and the United States of America Standards Institute (USASI).

3. The unsafe mechanical or physical condition (the condition of the agency that could have been guarded or corrected)

4. The accident type (the manner of contact of the injured person with the object or substance, such as striking against, falling, slipping, etc.)

5. The unsafe act (such as making safety devices inoperative, failing to use protective goggles, etc.)

6. The unsafe personal factor (and mental or bodily characteristic which permits the unsafe act, such as lack of skill, bodily defects, etc.)

In 1971 a new procedure for recording and reporting occupational injuries and illnesses was promulgated under the provision of the Occupational Safety and Health Act of 1970.[9] This procedure, described in the Federal Register,[10] provides for recording injuries and illnesses that result in:

Fatalities

Lost workday cases (these sometimes are referred to as disabling injuries)

Nonfatal cases without lost workdays (cases without lost workdays which result in transfer to another job or termination of employment, or require medical treatment other than first aid.)

Injury Statistics

In the compilation of injury statistics for use within an organization and for reporting injuries to various government and private agencies, it is frequently the practice to derive certain indices, in particular the following:

$$\text{Frequency rate} = \frac{\text{No. of disabling injuries} \times 1{,}000{,}000}{\text{Employee-hours of exposures}}$$

$$\text{Severity rate} = \frac{\text{Total days charged} \times 1{,}000{,}000}{\text{Employee-hours of exposure}}$$

$$\frac{\text{Average days charged}}{\text{(Per disabling injury)}} = \frac{\text{Severity rate}}{\text{Frequency rate}}$$

In the case of death or permanent total disability, the "total days charged" is set at six thousand; other scheduled charges are used for certain permanent partial disabilities.[11]

In connection with severity of injuries, Heinrich[12] refers to a 300:29:1 ratio, as follows: for every three hundred no-injury accidents there are twenty-nine minor injuries and one major lost-time injury.

[9] The Occupational Safety and Health Act of 1970. *National Safety News,* February 1971, **103**(2), 36–37.

[10] *Federal Register,* Friday, July 2, 1971, **36**(128), 12612–12616.

[11] ASI Standard Z16.1, *op. cit.*

[12] Heinrich, *op. cit.,* p. 101.

THE "CAUSES" OF ACCIDENTS

The objective of accident research is to ferret out data that can be used as the basis for taking action which will reduce the possibilities of subsequent accidents. Thus, one would wish to determine the "causes" of accidents. As Haddon *et al.*[13] have pointed out, however, the "cause" of accidents frequently is used as a synonym for the mechanics of injury (e.g., "piercing instruments") without any recognition that this often contributes little to the understanding of the behaviors that lead up to the accident. Knowledge of the relationships of different variables to accidents—such as accident rates in different circumstances or for people of different ages—certainly can be useful, but one would hope ultimately to be able to "explain'" the accident behavior that contributes to accident occurrence—or, to accentuate the positive—to isolate and describe the patterns of behavior which, as McGlade[14] puts it, *consistently* produce *safe* performance.

Because such explanations continue to elude us, we still have to deal largely with empirical relationships. Recognizing that human behavior that contributes to accidents is the central focus, it is logical for us to discuss such behavior in terms of two classes of variables—namely, those of a *situational* nature and those of an *individual* nature. One could hypothesize that the occurrence of all accidents is associated, at least theoretically, with some combination of one or both of these factors.

SITUATIONAL FACTORS RELATED
TO ACCIDENTS

It is manifest that the incidence of accidents varies tremendously from situation to situation. If this were not so, the actuarial statisticians who deal with accidents would be out of a job. Variations in the actual frequency rates in different circumstances typically serve as the basis for estimating the *liability* to the various situations in question. Although there are many different types of situational factors that can be related to frequency rates, a few examples will illustrate the basic fact that such relationships exist.

Job Factors

The differences in accident rates as related to different jobs are illustrated in the following tabulation of the average number of hospital visits per year for employees on each of a few jobs in a steel mill:

13 Haddon *et al., op. cit.,* p. 17.
14 McGlade, *op. cit.,* p. 15.

Job	Average Number of Hospital Visits
Craneman	3.55
Reckoner	2.96
Sheet inspector	2.54
Potman	2.10
Foreman	1.16
Roll turner	.47

Closely associated with differences in rates for various jobs are the differences associated with various departments. In this regard, the average number of hospital visits of personnel in eleven departments of the steel mill mentioned above ranged from .55 to 1.26.

Work Schedules

There are indications that in some circumstances accident rates vary in relation to work schedules. Some years ago, for example, Vernon[15] noted that there is a tendency for accident rates to increase during the latter part of the working day. According to Vernon's findings, this tendency is so marked that during a twelve-hour working day women experienced two-and-one-half times as many accidents as during a ten-hour day. Although fatigue has often been considered the cause of this increase, the fact that the time of greatest accident rate as compared with hours worked is reversed on the night shift indicates that psychological rather than physiological factors are operating. Although Vernon's results attach somewhat more importance to the length of the working day than do other investigations of this subject, it is quite commonly agreed that as the working day is lengthened, the accident rate increases in greater proportion than the increase in number of hours worked.

In recent years some organizations have changed their schedules to a four-day work week with ten-hour work days. It will be useful in the course of time to see what effect, if any, such work schedules have upon accident rates.

Social-Situational Factors in Work

Kerr and his coworkers have published several interesting studies which reveal relationships between accident experience and a variety of what we might call social situational factors.[16] In one of the studies, injury *severity*

[15] Vernon, H. M. An experience of munitions factories during the great war. *Occupational Psychology,* 1940, **14,** 1–14.

[16] Slivnick, P., Kerr, W., & Kosinar, W. A study of accidents in 147 factories. *Personnel Psychology,* 1957, **10,** 43–51.

and *frequency* were separately correlated with seventy-five other variables. Data were obtained from 147 plants in the automotive and machine shop industry.

Injury frequency was found to be greatest in plants with a high seasonal layoff rate, where employees looked with disfavor on high-producing coworkers, where there were many other similar plants in the neighborhood, where employees frequently needed to lift heavy materials, where there were blighted living conditions, and there was a record of many garnisheed wages. Injury severity was found to be greatest where employees and management personnel did not use the same dining room, where national unions were very strong, where there was no stated penalty for tardiness, where there was no employee profit-sharing plan, where there were extreme work place temperatures, and where the work was "dirty-sweaty."

Many of these findings seem to show in common the operation of a persistent threat to, or undermining of, the status or comfort of the individual employee (seasonal layoffs, rival hostility among employees, social distance in eating practices, dominance of a national union in collective bargaining, no incentive in profit sharing, heavy and dirty work). Kerr feels that the loss of, or threat to, individuality may produce preoccupation which results in unsafe behavior.

Another group of correlates of high-injury plants relates to urban sociology (congestion, ugliness of other near-by plants, living conditions in blighted neighborhoods, and garnisheed wages). Kerr hesitates to attach any causal significance to these findings, but he emphasizes that they should be kept in mind as factors associated with both *frequency* and *severity* of injuries in industrial plants.

Other Work-Related Factors

One can enumerate other aspects of work situations that have been found to be related to accident frequency, such as the design of the work equipment, illumination and other working conditions, housekeeping practices, and work methods.

Types of Highways

In a study concerned with situational factors associated with driving rather than with industrial organizations, the Automotive Safety Foundation reports data on accident rates on various classes of highways, as given in Table 19.1. It can be seen that the accident rate per million vehicle miles is four times as high on four-lane undivided highways as on freeways.

TABLE 19.1 ACCIDENT RATES ON VARIOUS TYPES OF HIGHWAYS

Type of Highway	Accidents per Million Vehicle Miles
2-lane	2.38
3-lane	2.57
4-lane, undivided	4.09
4-lane, divided	2.91
Divided, controlled access	1.69
Freeway	1.00
Total	2.15

Source: Taken from American Safety Foundation, "Traffic Control and Roadway Elements: Their Relationship to Highway Safety," *Traffic Safety,* **7** (No. 3, September, 1963), 9–18, Table III.

Discussion

Figure 19.1 presents a general conceptualization of situational factors and the way in which they might influence the liability of any given circumstance. The liability of any situation is, in effect, the consequence of the *combination* of the probabilities of accident-inducing circumstances and the "normal" incidence of accident behavior, such as might be expected in the case of well-qualified, well-trained personnel. The attention of safety engineers is very largely directed toward modifying the characteristics of the situation that are potentially accident-producing and reducing the probabilities of the occurrence of circumstances that could contribute to accidents.

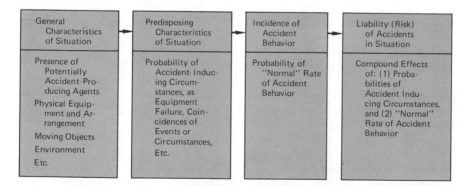

FIG. 19.1 Generalized illustration of the manner in which situational factors can influence the accident liability rate. This illustration is based on the incidence of some "normal" rate of accident behavior, such as might be expected on the part of well-qualified, well-trained personnel.

INDIVIDUAL FACTORS RELATED TO ACCIDENTS

Let us now look at the other side of the accident coin, the relationship of individual factors to accidents.

Accident Behavior and Accidents

There can be no question but that accidents are in large part the consequence of the "accident behaviors" of people—that is, the performance of unsafe acts. We are all guilty of such behaviors, which probably somehow have their origins in our general, and individualized, personnel characteristics. Figure 19.2 represents at least one formulation of the manner in which: (1) our personal characteristics can be viewed as serving (2) as the basis for certain behavior tendencies, which (3) in turn produce, in specific circumstances, types of behavior which (4) are of an "accident behavior" nature—that is, which can contribute to accidents. In addition to logical considerations and experience, the assumption that accident behavior is conducive to accidents is supported by some data, such as those presented by Whitlock et al.[17] They arranged for supervisors of 350 employees on similar production-type jobs to record the "unsafe behaviors" of the employees, using the critical incident technique over a period of about eight months. The number of unsafe behaviors served as an "accident-behavior" score for each individual. (The average score was 3.01). These scores, in turn, were correlated with injuries recorded during the eight-month period and for as long as five years after the study. The cor-

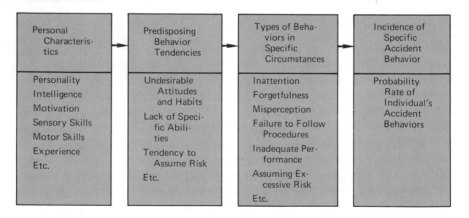

FIG. 19.2 Generalized formulation of the manner in which personal factors may influence the incidence of accident behaviors of individuals.

[17] Whitlock et al., op. cit.

relations, for 284 employees for whom injury records were available for various periods of time, are given below:

Time period (years):	1	2	3	4	5
Correlation:	.35	.49	.29	.51	.56

These correlations, along with data from other sources, strongly support the contention that accidents are in part the consequence of unsafe behaviors on the part of people, and that people tend somewhat to maintain over time a somewhat consistent pattern of such behaviors—a high, average, or low rate as the case may be.

Granting that we all perform unsafe acts and all experience accidents, the central questions for accident research as related to individuals are these:

1. Are there *significant differences* among people in the incidence of accident behaviors (and of accidents)—within specific situations and/or across different types of situations?
2. If so, what personal differences (if any) differentiate among individuals in terms of accident behavior or accidents?

Accident Behavior and Accidents within Specific Situations

One cannot say that there are significant individual differences in accident behaviors and accidents among personnel on each of the many types of jobs or in each of the many other situations in life, but one can say that on *some* jobs and in *some* situations of other types people do differ significantly in both of these respects.

Consistency of accident-related behavior. In the study by Whitlock *et al.*,[18] for example, the correlation between the numbers of unsafe behaviors between the odd-numbered weeks and the even-numbered weeks for the eight-month period was .74. (The corresponding correlation for a sample of workers in a chemical plant was .93.) In turn, correlations of numbers of injuries for odd-numbered months and even-numbered months also were derived; these were computed separately for personnel for whom data were available for the different periods of time. The resulting correlations were .63 for one year of data, .58 for two years, .75 for three years, .66 for four years, and .67 for five years. Data from this study thus reflect a distinct tendency for the personnel to maintain their own rates of accident behaviors and of injuries over time, regardless of whether these rates are high, average, or low.

Although people in any given situation might differ in the frequency of their accident behaviors and accidents, the mere fact of such differences should not *per se* delude us into concluding that those with high frequencies are "accident prone." The accident literature is strewn with instances

[18] Whitlock *et al., op. cit.*

in which individuals who having had above average numbers of accidents during *one* period of time have been erroneously labeled as "accident prone." Some years ago Mintz and Blum[19] called attention to the fact that if *only* chance factors were "causing" accidents, individuals would not be equally lucky or unlucky during given periods of work. If chance factors alone were operating, the situation would be quite analogous to tossing coins. If 1,000 men were each to toss ten coins, the average number of heads per man would be very close to five. But the individual men would vary in number of heads from very few (perhaps none) to many (perhaps ten). If we simply identify those men who tossed heads eight or more times, and call these men "heads-prone," we would be making the same error that is made when men who have more than the average number of accidents for one period of time are called "accident-prone." But if we find that those individuals with high accident rates in one period of time tend *also* to have high rates during *other* time periods, we have a more solid basis for concluding that there is some *consistency* in their higher-than-average accident rates. But such consistency needs to be established as being statistically significant to convince us that there are *real* individual differences in accident rates in the situation at hand. In this regard, Maritz[20] urges use of the technique of correlating accident records for consecutive periods of time as the basis for determining if there is such a pattern. Such correlations, of course, would have to be statistically significant to demonstrate this. Only when such patterns exist would we be justified in describing the individuals as showing accident repetitiveness.

Evidence of accident repetitiveness. Such statistically confirmed evidence has been presented for many different jobs and other siuations, indicating that—in such circumstances—there is a tendency for individuals to maintain their accident rates over time. Such evidence is presented by Mintz,[21] for example. And in a study by one of the authors, an injury index was derived for employees on three jobs. This index, based on the frequency of accidents per thousand hours worked, was derived separately for two six-month periods, and these were then correlated. The correlations are given below:

Job	Correlation
Drill press	.86
Assembler	.88
Machine operator	.74

[19] Mintz, A., & Blum, M. L. A re-examination of the accident proneness concept. *Journal of Applied Psychology,* 1949, **33,** 195–211.

[20] Maritz, J. S. On the validity of inference drawn from the fitting of Poisson and negative binomial distributions to observed accident data. *Psychological Bulletin,* 1950, **47,** 434–443.

[21] Mintz, A. The inference of accident liability from the accident record. *Journal of Applied Psychology,* 1954, **38,** 41–46.

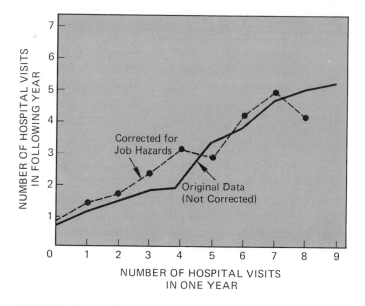

FIG. 19.3 Relationship between number of hospital visits for two successive years among about 9000 steelworkers. The solid line represents the original data, while the dotted line represents the same data "corrected" for differences in job hazards.

Such a pattern of accident repetitiveness is also evident from accident records for about nine thousand employees in a steel mill, as reflected by Figure 19.3. The solid line of this figure shows the relationship between number of hospital visits (which reflect injuries) for two successive years for the employees. These data cover eleven departments, and although the accident rates for the various departments varied (indicating varying liability), the relationship within each department was relatively the same as that shown in the figure.

Because of different accident liability for the various jobs included in these data, it is possible that that relationship might be accentuated or distorted to some extent. An adjustment was made to eliminate this possible distortion and the corrected curve in Figure 19.3 (the dotted line) turned out to be substantially the same, thus essentially confirming the implication that the employees tended to maintain their "individual" accident rates over time.

Accident Behavior and Accidents across Situations

As we shift to the discussion of accident behavior and accidents across situations, we can no longer stave off a discussion of the notion of accident proneness. The concept of accident proneness has been discussed since roughly the 1920s, with various implied meanings. Of these various meanings, Suchman and Scherzer[22] express what is perhaps the most common one as follows: "accident proneness . . . implies the existence of a particular personality type which is predisposed toward having repeated accidents. This predisposition is regarded as a psychological abnormality due to some underlying neurotic or psychopathic condition." They proceed to point out that the evidence in support of this concept of accident proneness is not conclusive and therefore argue against the use of the term in this sense.

Another possible interpretation of accident proneness sees it as a generalized pattern of accident repetitiveness which is reflected by a tendency on the part of some people to be accident repeaters in virtually any situation. In this sense, the concept of accident proneness is merely *descriptive* of such a tendency, not *explanatory* as to the basic nature of the personal factor(s) that induce the pattern. At present it is not possible to bring to bear any substantial body of data that unequivocally confirms this generalized repetitive pattern. This is not to say that such a pattern does *not* exist, but rather that it has not been demonstrably confirmed. Actually, there are some straws-in-the-wind that suggest there may be such a tendency, but even if it is confirmed, it probably will not "account" for a large portion of the many accidents that befall us.

Accident Proneness: An Operational Concept

As discussed above, there is no substantive evidence to support the contention that there is a "personality type" that can be characterized as accident prone. Unless such evidence later appears, the term should not be used in this frame of reference. If the term is used at all, we urge that it be used *strictly* in a statistical, descriptive sense, to refer to the *consistent* tendency of some individuals to have more accidents than reasonably can be attributed to chance. By and large, this implies that this tendency should be viewed as *situational,* for there is not yet convincing evidence that the accident repeaters in one situation are also accident repeaters in other circumstances (although this ultimately may prove to be the case).

Specific Personal Factors Related to Accidents

If, in any given situation with a given situation liability, there is confirmed evidence of accident repetitiveness, it is of course logical to wonder what personal qualities differentiate between those individuals with high accident rates and those with low rates. Analyses of such possible relationships are carried out in essentially the same manner as the validation of tests and other predictors as related to job performance criteria, except here

22 Suchman, E. E., & Scherzer, A. L. *Current research in childhood accidents.* New York: Association for the Aid of Crippled Children, 1960, pp. 7–8.

we would use a criterion of accidents or injuries. It appears from such analyses that quite a number of personal attributes have been found to be related to accidents in different situations. Such variations suggest that the personal factors associated with accident occurrence may be rather specific to the situation itself; these factors may be related to the specific types of behaviors that contribute to accidents (i.e., accident behaviors), or the converse (i.e., the "safe" behaviors). A few examples will illustrate the range of personal variables that have been found—in specific situations— to be related to accident frequency.

Vision. In many different types of jobs, it has been found that vision is related to accident frequency. This problem has been investigated by comparing the accident experience of employees whose visual skills meet certain statistically determined standards with the corresponding accident experience of employees whose vision does not meet these standards. Table 19.2 summarizes data from a study by Kephart and Tiffin[23] which attempted to determine the relationship between injuries and visual skills for twelve groups of people—passenger car drivers and employees on eleven different jobs. This table shows, for those who passed and those who failed the visual standards, the percentage who had no more than two injuries during a specified time period. In all but one of the groups those who passed the visual standards had better accident records than those who failed.

The results of another study dealing with vision and accidents are shown

TABLE 19.2   RESULTS OF VISUAL SKILL TESTS IN RELATION TO INJURIES

N	Group	Percent who had not over two injuries during the period of the investigation among those who:	
		Pass Visual Standards	Fail Visual Standards
59	Passenger car drivers	71	42
116	Mobile equipment operators	74	71
65	Machine operators	67	50
15	Machine operators	67	44
29	Sheet metal workers	58	41
105	Maintenance men	81	75
63	City bus drivers	44	33
66	Intercity bus drivers	54	30
68	Supervisors	65	57
125	Machine operators	56	32
102	Laborers	82	89
15	Skilled tradesmen	45	33
828	All groups combined	65	57

[23] Kephart, N. C., & Tiffin, J. Vision and accident experience. *National Safety News,* 1950, **62**, 90–91.

in Figure 19.4; this particular example concerned paper machine operators.

Age and length of service. A number of accident surveys have revealed relationships between age and accident data. As might be expected, these surveys do not reveal entirely consistent results, and one could hypothesize that different patterns might be found with different jobs or activities. Data from a steel mill on hospital visits for men of varying ages and lengths of service on their present jobs are shown in Figure 19.5. Both of these sets of data show a sharp rise and then a constant tapering off.

The age curve in this figure has the same general form as one based on three wage-injury surveys carried out by the California Division of Labor Statistics and Research,[24] covering 135,000, 153,000, and 169,000 men. The consolidated data are shown in Figure 19.6, as presented by Gordon

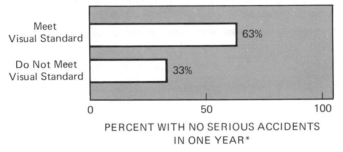

*A "serious" accident is one requiring the attention of the plant physician.

FIG. 19.4 Vision in relation to serious accidents among 104 paper machine operators.

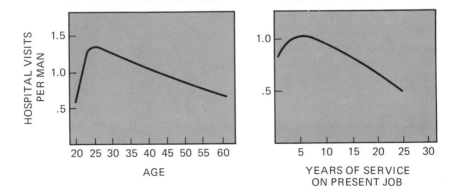

FIG. 19.5 Hospital visits per man per year in relation to age and years of service on present job among 9,000 steel workers.

24 *California work injuries, 1960, 1965, and 1968.* San Francisco: State of California, Department of Human Relations, Division of Labor Statistics and Research, November 1961, December 1966, and September 1969, Tables 16.

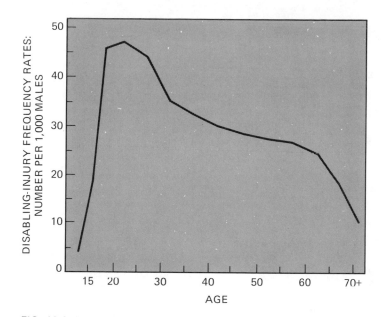

FIG. 19.6 Age-profile of disabling-injury frequency rates per 1000 males in the civilian labor force, as based on surveys of the California labor force in 1960, 1965, and 1968. (*Figure is from Gordon et al., op. cit., p. 211, as based on California work injury surveys, op. cit.*)

et al.[25] Granting the similarities of the age curves in Figures 19.5 and 19.6, both of which are based on large numbers of cases, one needs to interpret these with some caution, particularly because they do not control for accident liability. It is conceivable that, say, very young workers and older workers might be placed on jobs that are not as hazardous as those on which men in their twenties are placed. Despite this possible source of distortion, however, the impression still comes through that accident rates tend to be associated with age across a variety of jobs in the labor market, with the most susceptible ages being in the early twenties. Why this is so is not manifest, but the fact of such a relaionship is of course relevant in the management of a safety program.

Somewhat the same pattern is reflected in Figure 19.7, which shows data on age and reported accidents of male automobile drivers in Iowa, as summarized by Lauer.[26] One curve shows the average number of accidents for a two-year period, by age of the drivers; the other is adjusted for annual mileage driven, as reported by 1,004 men, thus correcting somewhat for liability associated with mileage. This curve shows a modest leveling of the curve by age, but the big bulge in the late teens and early twenties

[25] Gordon *et al.*, Figure 10.2, p. 211.
[26] Lauer, A. R. *Age and sex in relation to accidents.* Highway Research Board (Iowa), Bulletin 60, 1952, 25–35.

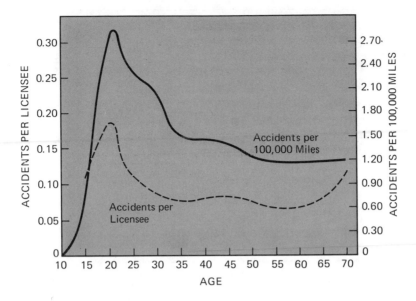

FIG. 19.7 Average number of automobile accidents in a two-year period of licensed male drivers in Iowa, by age, showing adjusted rates per 100,000 miles by age. (*Adapted from Lauer, op. cit.*)

still stands out. We also see an upswing for older drivers. Lauer makes the point that young male drivers drive about five years before improvement in their accident record appears.

Perceptual-motor relationships. As implied above, the specific behavior tendencies that predispose people to having high accident rates might well be different in different circumstances by reason of the unique activities involved in the various circumstances. Some years ago Drake[27] turned up some interesting data in a study of accidents in relation to perceptual speed and motor (i.e., muscular) speed in one industrial operation. He administered tests to measure these two variables to thirty-eight employees for whom an "accident index" was available. In the course of examining his data he noted that those with accident records tended to have motor speed scores that were relatively better than their scores on the perceptual speed tests. And conversely, the accident-free individuals tended to have scores on the perceptual speed tests that, relatively, were better than were their motor speed test scores. By a procedure that need not be described here, he derived a composite score that indicated the relative difference between each person's perceptual speed and his motor speed. The relationship of these scores to the accident indexes of the thirty-eight employees is shown

[27] Drake, C. A. Accident proneness: A hypothesis. *Character and Personality,* 1940, **8**, 335–341.

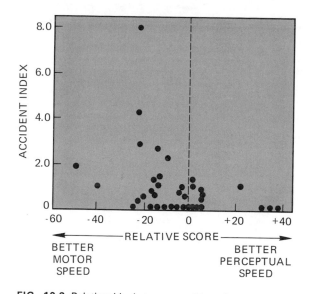

FIG. 19.8 Relationship between accident frequency of 38 industrial workers and the relative difference between their motor (i.e., muscular) speed and perceptual speed. (*From Drake* op. cit.)

in Figure 19.8. The general trend of the relationship is clear. Though it is not a straight line or linear relation, individuals with negative composite scores show a definite tendency to be among those with the high accident indexes, whereas those with the positive composite scores are relatively free from accidents. Drake's statement of the principle involved, as illustrated in Figure 19.8, is that "Individuals whose level of muscular action is above their level of perception are prone to more frequent and more severe accidents than those individuals whose muscular actions are below their perceptual level. In other words, the person who reacts quicker than he can perceive is more likely to have accidents than is the person who can perceive quicker than he can react."

More recently, investigation of perceptual-motor relationships has been revived by Babarik[28] in the context of automobile accidents. Suggesting the possibility that *specific* "refined" patterns of component perceptual-motor factors might be associated with *specific* driving acts, Babarik explored such a pattern in connection with rear-end or struck-from-behind accidents, which are quite common. Relative to emergency stopping in traffic, he argues that the driver who makes up for long "initiation" time with fast movements (that is, has short movement time and thus stops his vehicle more abruptly after applying the brake) would be expected to

[28] Babarik, P. Automobile accidents and driver reaction pattern. *Journal of Applied Psychology,* 1968, 52(1), 49–54.

have more rear-end accidents than a driver who—in the same time—initiates a movement more rapidly but makes a less abrupt stopping movement. A ratio of these was found to be significantly related to rear-end accidents with a sample of 104 taxi drivers. Those with the most markedly different such ratios were referred to as having "desynchronizing" reaction patterns, whereas the others were referred to as "normal." The results are summarized briefly below, in particular showing the percentage of drivers in these two groups who had two or more rear-end accidents.

Reaction-pattern Group	Drivers with Two or More Rear-end Accidents
Normal	10 percent
Desynchronizing	38 percent

Although certain other findings from this study left the water a bit murky, the fact that in both this study and Drake's[29] a combination of perceptual-motor factors was related to accidents in the specific situations under examination suggests that the way in which such factors are related to the *specific* activities of people may contribute to accident occurrence—and, conversely, to safety.

Perceptual style. Aside from the perceptual-motor relationships mentioned above as related to accidents, there are some clues that what is referred to as "perceptual style" is another personal factor that can contribute to the occurrence of at least one specific type of driving accident. Barrett and Thornton[30] were especially interested in Witkin's perceptual style concept of field-dependence versus field-independence.[31] This construct is viewed as a continuum along which individuals may be differentiated with respect to their perceptual abilities to discriminate figures in a complex background (or to "pull" a figure from an embedded context). Those who do not do this well are referred to as field-dependent (that is, the visual "field" somehow inhibits their perception of the "embedded figure" in the field) ; those who are better at "seeing" a figure in an embedded background are referred to as field-*in*dependent.

Using this distinction, Barrett and Thornton tested a group of fifty men in a driving simulator. They were particularly concerned with the response of the drivers to an "emergency" created by a "dummy" figure appearing in the simulated model. Various measures of subject response were obtained, including reaction time and deceleration rate. These, in turn, were related

[29] Drake, *op. cit.*
[30] *Barrett,* G. V., & Thornton, C. L. Relationship between perceptual style and driver reaction to an emergency situation. *Journal of Applied Psychology,* 1968, 52(2), 169–176.
[31] Witkin, H. A., Dyk, R. B., Faterson, H. F., Goodenough, D. R., & Karp, S. A. *Psychological differentiation: Studies of development.* New York: John Wiley, 1962.

to a measure of field-dependence and field-independence. The results as related to the deceleration rate criterion are shown in Figure 19.9. Although these results were obtained in a simulated situation, Harano[32] provides some data based on twenty-seven "no accident" subjects and twenty-eight "accident" subjects with records of accident which indicate that the relationship may hold up in actual driving, inasmuch as he found that field-independent individuals had better accident records for three years than did field-dependent individuals.

Vocational interest. Vocational interest is still another personal factor related to accidents in at least one circumstance. The study in question, carried out by Kunce,[33] dealt with sixty-two male employees of a food processing plant. The Strong Vocational Interest Blank (SVIB) was used as the measure of interest in order to test the hypothesis that a person's style of life, as reflected by his interests, is related to the incidence of accidents. Two of the SVIB scales were selected as indexes of "adventuresomeness" (Aviator scale) and "cautiousness" (Banker scale). An "accident proneness" index (AP) was derived by subtracting the second of these from the first. This AP index, in turn, was related to the accident rates of the employees. The results are shown in Figure 19.10 for personnel on what were rated as "hazardous" jobs (rated 4, 5, or 6 on a six-point scale) and "non-hazardous" jobs (rated 1, 2, or 3 on that scale). Those whose "accident

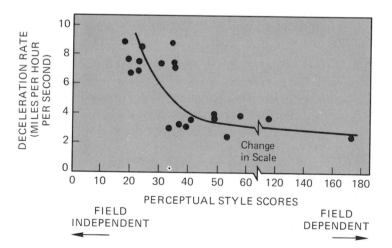

FIG. 19.9 Relationship between perceptual style and deceleration rate of 50 subjects in an "emergency" during a simulated drivering task. (*From Barrett and Thornton, Fig. 3.*)

[32] Harano, R. M. *The relationship between field dependence and motor vehicle accident involvement.* American Psychological Association, Experimental Publication System, October 1969, Issue No. 2, Ms. No. 065B.

[33] Kunce, J. T. Vocational interest and accident proneness. *Journal of Applied Psychology,* 1967, **51**(3), 223–225.

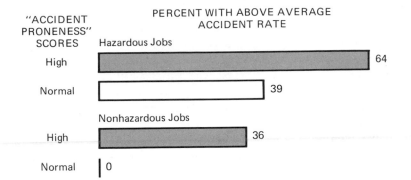

"ACCIDENT
PRONENESS"
SCORES

PERCENT WITH ABOVE AVERAGE
ACCIDENT RATE

Hazardous Jobs

High   64

Normal   39

Nonhazardous Jobs

High   36

Normal   0

FIG. 19.10 Relationship between an "accident proneness" index (based on the Strong Vocational Interest Blank) and accident rates of 62 male employees on jobs rated hazardous and nonhazardous in a food processing plant. (*Adapted from Kunce,* op. cit.)

proneness" indexes were high clearly had higher rates of accidents, thus supporting the initial contention of the investigator.

Other factors. One could mention other types of personal factors that have been found to be related to accident frequency in one situation or another—sometimes with opposing results in different circumstances. Years ago, for example, Hersey[34] pointed out that the emotional state of people— in particular the fluctuating emotional "ups and downs" of some people— are a factor in accident occurrence. He found, for example, that the average worker is emotionally "low" about 20 percent of the time, and reported that, in one plant, about half of the four hundred minor accidents occurred during these low periods. A study of fifty motormen of the Cleveland Railway Company by an insurance company also focused atten- tion on emotional factors associated with accidents and found four specific emotional "causes": faulty attitude, impulsiveness, nervousness and fear, and worry and depression—that accounted for 32 percent of the accidents.

Closely related to emotional factors are personality factors, which were shown to be related to accidents in a study by Spangenberg[35] in which scores on the Thematic Apperception Test (TAT)—a projective test—had a correlation of .53 with accident ratings for a sample of seventy-five bus drivers in South Africa. The results of this study, however, are in rather marked contrast with the analysis by Goldstein[36] of the results of several studies in which personal, emotional, and attitudinal factors were generally

34 Hersey, R. B. Emotional factors in accidents. *Personnel Journal,* 1936, **15**, 59– 65.
35 Spangenberg, H. H. The use of projective tests in the selection of bus drivers. *Traffic Safety Research Review* (National Safety Council), December 1968, **12**(4), 118–121.
36 Goldstein, L. G. Human variables in traffic accidents: A digest of research. *Traffic Safety Research Review* (National Safety Council), March 1964, **8**(1), 26–31.

found to be rather miserable predictors of traffic accidents. And Gumpper and Smith[37] found no significant relationship between scores on a couple of inventories of risk-taking propensity and accident records of 167 truck drivers. In fact, Goldstein's review indicated that measures of different kinds of personal factors typically have been found to have relatively nominal correlations with traffic accidents. As one exception to this pattern, Ruch[38] reported that a combination of two paper-and-pencil tests did a pretty good job of differentiating between "accident-free" and "accident prone" patrol car officers in a large metropolitan police department. The tests were the Space Visualization test of the Employee Aptitude Survey and the McGuire Safe Driver Scale. The results are recapped below:

	Number of Patrol Officers with:		
	No Accidents	*One Accident*	*Two or More Accidents*
Passed tests	40	15	8
Failed tests	6	8	13

Discussion. In taking something of an overview, we can see that quite a number of different types of personal variables have been found, in different circumstances, to be related to accident occurrence. Surry[39] summarized many other investigations of this type, including some dealing with personal factors other than the ones discussed above. But Surry's survey, and certain of the above studies, reveal that some factors that one might *expect* to be related to accident frequency have *not* been found to be so related. Such inconclusive findings may in part be a function of the limited reliability of criteria. As Goldstein[40] explains, accident records themselves do not measure a very stable human performance characteristic, and accident repeaters account for only a very small part of the total traffic accidents on record. This is so because the number of accidents per individual in the usual reporting periods is small, and because "chance" factors probably contribute to some of these, thus partially masking over whatever underlying "accident repeating" pattern there may be. Although Goldstein is referring specifically to automobile driving, the statement has some relevance also to industrial accidents.

[37] Gumpper, D. C., & Smith, K. R. The prediction of individual accident liability with an inventory measuring risk-taking tendency. *Traffic Safety Research Review* (National Safety Council), June 1968, **12**(2), 50–55.

[38] Ruch, W. W. Identification of accident proneness through paper and pencil tests. Paper presented at the meetings of the American Psychological Association, Chicago, September 4, 1965.

[39] Surry, J. *Industrial accident research: A human engineering approach.* Toronto: University of Toronto, Department of Industrial Engineering, June 1968, Chapter 4.

[40] Goldstein, *op. cit.*

ADJUSTIVE BEHAVIOR

In those situations in which relationships of personal factors and accidents are apparent, we have argued for viewing these relationships in the context of the specific situation at hand. Conversely, we also should argue for persistent efforts toward tracing down any patterns of relationships that may be more generally applicable between and among various accident situations or classes of such situations.

In this regard, McGlade[41] proposes use of the construct of *adjustive behavior* in relation to safe performance. He defines this construct as follows: *consistent* successful performance of an activity, in the face of possible unplanned interruptions, is *adjustive* behavior leading to safe performance. Expressed another way, such behavior is the capacity to "mesh" a person's "abilities, skills, and tasks into a meaningful whole which brings about successful performance of an activity in virtually all situations and under almost all conditions." McGlade[42] envisions the construct of adjustiveness as being more or less related to perceptual style or life style.

Of course, the specific "form" of adjustive behavior in any given situation would have to be appropriate to that situation, and could consist of varying combinations of both "unguided" behavior (automatic, habituated responses) and of "guided" behavior (intentionally performed responses). Such specific behaviors, however, are rooted in the individual's general abilities and skills. Thus, it seems that the effectiveness of one's adjustive behavior in achieving safe performance depends in part upon one's repertoire of relevant abilities and skills.

Although McGlade's construct of adjustive behavior probably needs to be seen at the present time as a hypothetical formulation rather than a confirmed fact, it does offer a potentially intriguing frame of reference for explaining at least some of the accidents which can be attributed to personal factors. Taking some licence in interpreting the construct, we may conclude that the "adjustive behavior" of those whose "life style" includes such adjustiveness tends to contribute to their more consistent *exercise* of those abilities and skills which—*in the specific situation*—are required for safe performance. In the absence of the required skills, individuals with such an adjustive "life style" might encounter accidents of course, but perhaps not to the extent experienced by others who also lacked the requisite skills but whose life styles did not incline them toward "adjustive behavior."

Adjustive behavior, then, can be viewed as a consistent predisposition toward safe behavior—essentially an attitude. Despite the generally meager

[41] McGlade, *op. cit.,* p. 18.
[42] *Ibid.,* p. 33.

implications of Goldstein's review,[43] he did discern a slight tendency to have higher accident rates on the part of drivers with poor attitudes (in terms of aggressiveness, social irresponsibility, and/or instability). One is thus led to speculate about the possibility that *if* there is in fact any general tendency for some people to perform more safely—wherever they may be—the underpinnings of that tendency might well be an attitudinal proclivity toward behaving in a safe manner. The actual *effectiveness* of such a tendency to engage in "adjustive behavior" would depend, of course, upon the possession of the requisite skills.

THE REDUCTION OF ACCIDENTS

From our previous discussion it follows that efforts to reduce accidents must be in the direction of (1) reducing the liability of the situation, or (2) minimizing the possible influence of any relevant personal factors. The wares of the safety engineers cover a spectrum of techniques, procedures, and guidelines that are directed toward the reduction of situational liability. These include the installation of protective guards on machines, changes of method, arrangement of materials and equipment, use of protective clothing and gear, and improvements in the environment.[44] As indicated in Chapters 16 and 17, the design of equipment and the nature of the physical environment can affect the accident liability of specific situations. In fact, a major thrust of the field of human factors engineering is directed toward the design of equipment and work environments for improved safety.[45]

In our present discussion we will touch on at least a few of the possible approaches toward the reduction of accidents from the human liability side of the coin, rather than the situational side.

Personnel Selection and Placement

When it has been demonstrated that some personal factor is *significantly related* to accident frequency on a given job or in some other circumstance, it is then possible to select those individuals who have characteristics associated with good accident records. In some circumstances items of biographical data might be relevant, such as age. In other circumstances certain tests might be appropriate, such as vision tests, psychomotor tests, and job sample tests. In connection with driver testing, for example, Greenshields

[43] Goldstein, *op. cit.*

[44] For specific practices of this type the reader is referred to the *Accident prevention manual for industrial operations* (6th ed.), *op. cit.*

[45] McCormick E. J. *Human factors engineering.* (3rd ed.) New York: McGraw-Hill, 1970; and Surry, *op. cit.*

and Platt[46] report their experience in testing drivers on a run of seventeen miles in an automobile with a "Drivometer," a device for automatically recording certain features of the driving behavior of the individuals, such as brake applications and steering wheel reversals. Driver scores on this device were significantly related to accident records of the subjects, thus suggesting the possibility that such a "job sample" test might be used in the selection of, say, taxi drivers or truck drivers—or conceivably as the basis for granting drivers' licences.

Safety Training[47]

Surry[48] has pointed out that past experience greatly reduces accidents and that training can provide certain aspects of this experience. Especially in the case of new employees, it may be appropriate to set up training programs before they begin their jobs, in order to familiarize them with possible hazards and with those practices and methods that will minimize the likelihood of their having accidents, and to develop proper attitudes toward safety practices. Training programs sometimes are also appropriate for present employees. In such training programs it is, of course, important to apply sound principles of learning, as discussed in Chapter 10.

An excellent example of a reduction in lost-time injuries which followed an intensive training program on safety teamwork has been reported by Ewell.[49] His report covers the experience of the Proctor and Gamble Company with its safety program—one aspect of which consisted of safety training—in twenty of its plants over a span of twenty-five years. Figure 19.11 shows the lost-time accident rates during that period, starting out at over 30 per million manhours and dropping to about 1.01. In the last year, incidentally, eleven of the twenty plants involved had perfect records. It should be added that this dramatic reduction was the consequence of a total safety program, including efforts to minimize hazards, publicity, training, and so forth, so that it cannot be entirely attributed to training as such. But the results do reflect what a comprehensive safety program can accomplish in an organization.

In connection with safety training, however, a note of caution is sounded by Surry,[50] who raises the question as to its long-term effects in accident reduction. Although there are suspicions that the effects may not be of

---

[46] Greenshields, B. D., & Platt, F. N. Development of a method of predicting high-accident and high-violation drivers. *Journal of Applied Psychology,* 1967, 51(3), 205–210.

[47] For a discussion of safety training the reader is referred to the *Accident prevention manual for industrial operations, op. cit.,* Chapter 7.

[48] Surry, *op. cit.,* p. 155.

[49] Ewell, J. M. *1955, a yardstick for '56.* Proctor and Gamble Safety Bulletin, January 1956.

[50] Surry, *op. cit.,* p. 156.

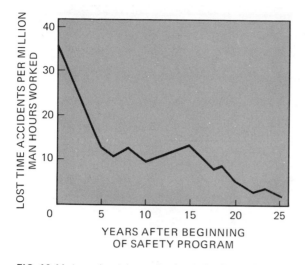

FIG. 19.11 Lost-time injury reduction following a safety program (including safety training) in 20 plants of the Proctor and Gamble Company. (*From Ewell*, op. cit.)

long duration, further evidence will be needed to confirm or contradict such suspicions.

Driver Improvement Interviews

In the automobile driving domain, Kaestner and Syring[51] report on the follow-up of an experimental accident-reduction program of interviewing drivers regarding problems in driving. The interviews ranged from thirty-five to fifty minutes, were structured, and were motivationally and educationally oriented. A total of 660 drivers in Oregon were interviewed in this way, and a follow-up analysis was made of their accident records and traffic violations over a two-year period. A matched control group (who were not interviewed) was also followed up. There was some attrition in both groups, as a result of people moving out of the state, not retaining their driver's licenses, or other reasons. Figure 19.12 summarizes the cumulative records of individuals with traffic incidents in the two groups, including both accidents and "moving violations," over the two-year period. The difference in recorded traffic incidents was statistically significant for the two years, although the difference became less marked over time. The differences in accidents alone—that is, excluding "moving violations"—was not statistically significant, in part because the total number of accidents was relatively moderate. But there was a significant difference in the

[51] Kaestner, N., & Syring, E. M. Follow-up of brief driver improvement interviews in Oregon. *Traffic Safety Research Review* (National Safety Council), December 1968, **12**(4), 111–117.

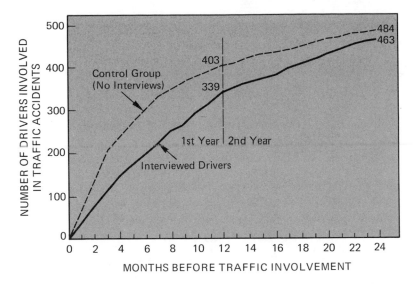

FIG. 19.12 Cumulative distributions of numbers of individuals with recorded traffic incidents over a two-year period, for drivers who had been interviewed about driving problems and for those in a control group. (*From Kaestner and Syring, op. cit., Fig. 2, and reproduced by permission of the National Safety Council.*)

median time (in months) before any traffic incident was recorded, which was 7.3 months for the interview group and 4.0 for the control group.

Although such an interview program presumably resulted in some reduction in traffic incidents, its effects appear to wear off with time, which is somewhat the same effect that is suspected in the case of safety training. Thus, as the investigators suggest, it might be appropriate to develop a program of "successive appearances" over time, especially in the case of problem drivers.

Persuasion and Propaganda

Various forms of persuasion and propaganda—posters and placards, for example—are used in most safety programs. The effect of such techniques, however, is sometimes difficult to assess. In one investigation, Laner and Sell[52] surveyed the effects of safety posters in thirteen steel plants in Great Britain during a six-week period, and reported that in seven of the plants "safe behavior" increased by more than 20 percent. In the use of posters and placards, however, both common sense and sound psychological principles argue for pinpointing their messages in terms of specific actions and

---

[52] Laner, S., & Sell, R. G. An experiment on the effect of specially designed safety posters. *Occupational Psychology*, 1960, **34**, 153–169.

practices that contribute to safe performance, or conversely to accidents, rather than simply using general platitudes such as "Be Careful."

Surry[53] offers certain suggestions for the development of propaganda campaigns, including the following: (1) use sound premises that are based on known cause-and-effect relationships; (2) use various media of information exposure; (3) use a direct (as opposed to a diffuse) approach in which the campaign is aimed at specific points rather than consisting of a more general appeal; and (4) make sure the appeal has relevance to the persons at whom it is directed.

Discussion

The occurrence of accidents is, of course, a matter of major concern to organizations and to their employees. The Occupational Safety and Health Act of 1970, one hopes, will serve as the impetus to improve working conditions in some industries toward the end of reducing accidents. But accidents pervade all areas of human life—driving, using consumer products, working around the home, mowing the yard, or mountain climbing. The point on which we will terminate this discussion is that in efforts to reduce accidents in any kind of situation one needs to be fortified with relevant research data to provide the basis for knowing what specific approaches and programs would most likely be appropriate for the specific situation at hand.

[53] Surry, *op. cit.*, pp. 158–162.

Courtesy The Kroger Company, Cincinnati

PART VI

Psychological

Aspects

of

Consumer Behavior

This text has been primarily concerned with some of the human problems involved in the production of goods and services—in other words, with the various aspects of the interface between organizations and those who are employed by them, including the individual-job interface and the individual-group interface. This is the arena in which most psychologists associated with industry are engaged.

But organizations also have an interface with the public at large. There are various dimensions of this interface, of which perhaps the most important is the organization-consumer interface inasmuch as the public are the "consumers" of the goods and services that organizations provide. The current interest in consumer affairs has tended to focus attention on this interface, primarily in terms of assuring the protection of consumers' interests. The behavior of people in their roles as consumers is a legitimate area of interest for those concerned with the study of human behavior, and one in which some psychologists are involved.

In our discussion of consumer behavior, we will define the consumer relationship as any relationship between an organization that provides goods and services and the individuals who are recipients thereof. Although consumer relationships usually are viewed in the context of consumer goods produced by private industry, it is equally reasonable to consider people as consumers of the services of many other types of organizations, such as educational institutions, governmental organizations, and the like. The operations of an economy are intended to serve the needs of people. It is suggested that consumer behavior be viewed in this broad framework— that of the utilization by people of the goods and services of our entire economy.

chapter twenty

Consumer
Psychology

Everyone is a consumer of at least some of the goods and resources of our economy. For our purposes, however, let us stretch the concept of "consumer" from its usual connotation relating to the consumption of the goods and services of private industry. Let us also think of people as consumers of the services of other types of organizations, such as educational institutions, government organizations (local, state, and federal), hospitals, religious organizations, and nonprofit organizations, as well as others. We, the public, are "users" of the services of the policeman, the mail carrier, the minister, the teacher, yes, even the tax collector, in a manner that is somewhat analogous to those services offered by the telephone company, the toothpaste manufacturer, the local retailer, the physician, or the loan company. The consumer relationship, then, can be considered as any relationship between an organization that provides goods or services and the individuals who are the recipients thereof.

Consumer research is concerned with the systematic study of the facets of this relationship. While there are, of course, many aspects of consumer research, a few of the more important ones are the following: studies of consumer preferences (taste, style, features of products, and so forth); product testing; consumer attitudes and motivation; buying habits and patterns; brand preferences; media research (such as composition of audiences reached through television, radio, newspapers, magazines, and other advertising media); effectiveness of advertisements and commercials; packaging; estimating demand for products or services; economic expectations of people; and studies of "images" of products. In this chapter we will be concerned with some of these aspects of consumer research.

A FRAME OF REFERENCE

In approaching the study of consumer behavior, the question of one's point of view or objectives might be raised. The study of consumer behavior in the past has been largely from the point of view of selling to the public certain goods and services that are proffered. In this connection, it is probable that these efforts generally have contributed to the development of our present economy and standard of living. In this process, unfortunately, there have been at least some circumstances in which the practices of purveyors of goods and services have raised questions of ethics and good taste. The reader undoubtedly can call to mind examples of, say, advertising or sales practices that are out of bounds by usually acceptable standards of ethics or good taste, or that might be considered unwarranted "manipulation" of consumers. Such practices, in turn, might cause one to wonder about the ethical aspects of research relating to consumer behavior. In this connection we would like to point out that knowledge as such has no positive or negative valence in terms of moral, ethical, or aesthetic considerations. It is the *application* of knowledge that takes on implications in terms of value systems. Knowledge about human behavior can be used to the advantage or disadvantage of mankind in many aspects of life, such as in politics, international relations, education and training, and personnel placement, as well as in the consumer domain.

With respect to the application of knowledge of consumer behavior, Perloff's[1] comments seem to offer a very appropriate frame of reference:

> Consumer benefits...would doubtlessly be multiplied if the psychologist should seek *directly and explicitly* to serve the consumer's needs, to study the consumer qua consumer, as it were, not as an individual whose attention and purchasing behavior are coveted to serve ends, the propriety and economic value of these ends notwithstanding, determined by advertising and the mass media. What I would like to propose, therefore, is that a relatively new frontier the industrial psychologist might scout would be that in which he seeks to study the consumer

[1] Perloff, R. Potential contribution of the consumer-oriented psychologist. *Business and Society*, Spring 1964, 4(2), 28–34.

for the sake of understanding consumer behavior because consumer behavior is scientifically important on the one hand, and is relevant to helping the consumer derive greater satisfaction and pleasure from the products he consumes, on the other.

THE BASIS OF CONSUMER BEHAVIOR

It has been pointed out by Katona[2] that five sets of variables are relevant to consumer behavior. In the first place, there are *enabling conditions* that set the limits to the consumer's discretion: his income, assets, and access to credit. Second, his economic behavior is influenced by *precipitating circumstances* such as increase or decrease in purchasing power, a change in family status, or a move to a new house. Third, *habit* plays an important role, especially in the purchase of such items as foods. Fourth, the *contractual obligations* of people (such as rent, life insurance premiums, taxes, and installment payments on automobiles) affect their economic behavior. The fifth factor is the consumer's *psychological state*.

The behavior of people in their roles as consumers is, of course, predicated upon essentially the same factors as is their behavior on their jobs or in other facets of their lives. Among the more important of these are motivation, perception, and learning. Because these have been discussed in earlier chapters, only brief mention will be made of them in our present context.

Human Motivation

As indicated in Chapter 12, people have *needs* which they seek to fulfill. *Incentives* are those things which are perceived as fulfilling *needs*. Human behavior consists of those actions that occur in the process of attempting to achieve the incentives that are sought. In the consumer context, the goods and services that people buy, or avail themselves of, are the incentives which they perceive as being capable of fulfilling their needs. In the earlier discussion of motivation, Maslow's[3] hierarchy of needs was presented. To the extent that this hierarchy has validity, it is reasonable to postulate that consumer behavior is dominated to a considerable extent by it, in the sense that the kinds of goods and services that people seek are related to the needs implied by this hierarchy. The starving individual would, of course, be primarily concerned with obtaining food. In turn—depending upon the general level of the needs that have been fulfilled—individuals will seek those goods and services which they perceive as being capable of fulfilling their next higher order of need, such as for personal safety.

[2] Katona, G. Economic psychology. *Scientific American,* October 1954, **191**(2), 31–35.

[3] Maslow, A. H. *Motivation and personality.* New York: Harper & Row, 1954.

Although all behavior can be viewed as the result of motivation, any single act typically involves several or many different motives, frequently operating in opposite directions. Because of the recognized importance of motivation in consumer behavior, some years ago there was considerable interest in what is called *motivation research*. Such research is directed toward deriving information about the motivational bases of consumer behavior.

Methods of study of motivation. The study of human motivation in the consumer context can be carried out in two somewhat different ways. One of these is essentially a clinical, individual approach, involving the use of depth interviews, projective devices, personality tests, and other techniques, in order to learn something about individuals and the motivational forces that presumably dominate their behavior. On the basis of data and inferences clinically obtained from samples of individuals, one might make some admittedly subjective assessments about the motivation of people as related to some product or service. This approach has been followed by such people as Dichter,[4] with particular emphasis on the use of depth interviews, for the purpose of identifying the major psychological variables and personality factors which may have a dynamic effect upon consumers' attitudes and behavior.

The other approach is essentially a statistical one, based on responses to survey questionnaires or fairly well-structured interviews, or on some type of behavior that can be observed. Although the statistical data consist of responses to the questions used or observations of actual behavior, inferences frequently can be made from such data about motivational variables.

Both approaches have their place in consumer research. Dichter[5] contends that such factors as insecurity, prejudice, and self-indulgence often are more dominant in their influence on consumer behavior than more "objective" factors about people, such as income or age. But the body of statistical research data about consumer attitudes and behavior is itself testimony to the relevance of the statistical approach.

Perception

How people view themselves and others, and the goods and services that are available to them, has significant effects on their behavior as consumers. Mention was made above, for example, of *incentives,* which are those things which are *perceived* as fulfilling needs. Whether a given incentive would seem to an outsider to be relevant to fulfill the "need" of another individual is beside the point. The individual's behavior will be influenced

---

[4] Dichter, E. *Handbook of consumer motivations.* New York: McGraw-Hill, 1964.
[5] *Ibid.*

by his *perception* of whether something will or will not fulfill his need. Thus, if an individual perceives a sports car as fulfilling his need for status, he will behave accordingly (perhaps buying such a car), even though, in the eyes of others, his status is not changed in the way he desires. In fact, others might perceive such an act as, say, an indication of "show-off" behavior. Many "perceptions" of people, then, stem from their own unique motivations and frames of reference.

In addition to such individualistic aspects of perception, however, there are certain patterns of perceptual processes that are more generalized. Some of these have considerable importance to various phases of consumer behavior. In advertising, for example, certain features of advertisements are more consistently perceived than others. Or in product design, certain features may generally be perceived as more adequately fulfilling certain "needs" than others.

Learning

Learning is another important factor that influences the behavior of people in their roles as consumers. Habits, for example, are manifestations of learning. Thus, to the extent that people buy products or avail themselves of services on an habitual basis, their behavior is "learned"—for better or for worse. Another aspect of the influence of learning on consumer behavior involves the remembering of experiences individuals have had with various products or services. If, for example, a farmer has had difficulty starting a particular tractor in the winter, this "learning" may influence his future tractor selection. Furthermore, people remember (recall) things to which they have been exposed by television, newspapers, magazines, and other media.

With respect to learning in the field of consumer psychology, Lucas and Britt[6] call particular attention to the distinction between *recognition* and *recall*. Many psychological investigations have demonstrated that people tend to forget rapidly, and that the speed of forgetting accelerates. In part because of this, the measure of learning (at various points in time) depends on whether one measures recognition or recall. In consumer research, recognition typically is measured by presenting subjects with advertisements, magazine articles, or other relevant material, and asking them if they can identify the material as having been seen (or "noted") previously. Sometimes a distinction is made between *noting* (seeing) and *reading most* (thorough reading).

Recall, on the other hand, usually is measured by asking people to reconstruct their impressions of, or to give information about, articles,

[6] Lucas, D. B., & Britt, S. H. *Measuring advertising effectiveness.* New York: McGraw-Hill, 1963.

advertisements, or whatever other material is being tested. Aside from the cues that are used to direct the attention of the respondent to the particular material in question, the method places a heavy burden upon memory of the content of the material. This usually is facilitated by trained interviewers who probe with such questions as: "Can you tell me about the article?" "What did the advertisement look like?" and "Can you be more specific?" The verbatim responses are recorded and subsequently analyzed.

Comparison of recognition and recall. A study of retention (or loss of memory) of information about advertisements is reported by Lucas.[7] In this study he distinguished between *recognition* (in terms of "noting" scores) and *aided recall.* In the study it was found that recall tended, relatively, to decline over a period of days, whereas recognition was maintained for at least a couple of weeks. This comparison is shown in Figure 20.1 for a period of seven days.

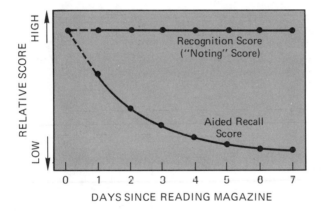

FIG. 20.1 Changes in recognition ("noting" scores) and aided recall of 96 advertisements in a national magazine (600 subjects). (*Reprinted from the ABC's of ARF's PARM by D. B. Lucas, Fig. 1,* Journal of Marketing, *July 1960,* **25**(*1*), *9–20, published by the American Marketing Association.*)

Recall of advertisements as related to interests. With respect to recall of advertisements, Buchanan[8] reports a carefully carried out study in which the interest of respondents in eight products was measured by a mail questionnaire. Ten days later the subjects were "exposed" to advertisements in the consumer laboratory—in the case of four products to ads in a "dummy" magazine, and in the case of the other four to television commercials. By an unexpected telephone call the next day the respondents

---

[7] Lucas, D. B. The ABC's of ARF's PARM. *Journal of Marketing,* July 1960, **25**(1), 9–20.

[8] Buchanan, D. I. How interest in the product affects recall: Print ads vs. commercials. *Journal of Advertising Research,* March 1964, **4**(1), 9–14.

were asked to recall these advertisements. The recall of the magazine advertisements was found to be significantly related to the previously measured "interests" in the various products. This was not the case with the television commercials, although there was no indication as to why the difference existed between the two media.

CONSUMER DECISION PROCESSES

Obviously, many factors impinge upon the consumer, including those of motivation, perception, and learning as discussed above. Ultimately, the influence of whatever factors are relevant is reflected in the decision making of the consumer. Taking something of an overview of consumer decision making, Katona[9] points out that a major finding of the consumer studies of the Survey Research Center may be summarized by simply saying that the consumer is sensible; although impulsive behavior does exist, it is much less frequent than is sometimes postulated.

In discussing the decision processes Katona differentiates between those consumer situations in which consumers make genuine decisions and those in which they act in a quasi-automatic, habitual manner. He points out that the consumer neither can nor should consider every action he takes as a problem which requires deliberation, weighing of alternatives, and solution. Rather, we typically act as we have before under similar circumstances; this goes back to the matter of learning discussed earlier. On the other hand, there are circumstances under which genuine decision making takes place, with consideration and weighing of various alternatives. Such decision making probably tends to occur in the case of expenditures which are subjectively thought to be major and which are fairly rare, where there have been unsatisfactory past experiences, sometimes in the first purchase of a product, or where other unusual conditions prevail. As Katona points out, when genuine decision making takes place, consumers are not marionettes that can be manipulated. Of course, the efforts of the federal government and certain consumer organizations in the consumer education area have the effect of furthering genuine decision making on the part of consumers.

A Model of the Decision-Making Process

In trying to conceive of the way in which the various elements of an individual's psychological field interact in affecting buying decisions, some model or organized structure would be handy. Such a model, as Engel *et*

[9] Katona, G. Consumer behavior surveys and marketing: A point of view. In *Psychological research on consumer behavior*. Ann Arbor. The Foundation for Research in Human Behavior, 1962.

al.[10] suggest, could serve as a testable "map" of reality—that is, of the way in which people do in fact behave. Various such models of consumer behavior have been set forth, including the one proposed by Engel *et al.*, which is shown in Figure 20.2. Although this appears to be a rather complex assortment of variables and processes, it is not really as complicated as it looks.

What Engel *et al.* refer to as the *central control unit* is the psychological command center, in that it includes both memory and basic facilities for thinking and behaving. The elements of an individual's psychological makeup, consisting of personality characteristics, stored information, past experience, and values and attitudes, interact to provide the composite base for one's *response set,* which is a predisposition toward behaving or reacting in some general manner. Various types of *inputs* from the environment (both physical and social) impinge upon one's *sensory receptors.* An individual must be "turned on" before behavior can occur, and the possible sources of such *arousal* include both the external stimuli that serve as inputs and one's internal sense of discomfort or unease.

Once the individual is so aroused, he perceives, or "sizes up," external inputs selectively as they are relevant to satisfying the aroused drive. This perceptual phase involves some *comparison* of the inputs with all that is stored in memory. The outcome of this comparison may be that the person *recognizes a problem,* which in turn can trigger a sequence of processes, specifically an *external search for alternatives*, the *evaluation of alternatives*, and the actual *purchase* of some item. At any of these stages the individual may engage in the process indicated (such as actually searching for alternatives), may proceed directly to the next stage (go), or may terminate the process (halt). In all of these cases the decisions are influenced by the *response set,* and the experiences of the individual become stored as a part of the past experience of the individual, thus possibly modifying his subsequent behavior. To this model one could add additional stages in the form of post-purchase evaluation and possibly other forms of behavior.

Discussion

Although we cannot go into the intricacies of these various components and processes, and the interrelationships among them, we can recall in our own experience some general parallel to this process, leading up to the decision to make (or not to make) a major purchase such as an automobile, a stereo set, or even a college education. Thus it may be possible to see how some of the aspects of consumer behavior discussed below can be "fitted in" to this framework.

10 Engel, J. F., Kollat, D. J., & Blackwell, R. D. *Consumer behavior.* Holt, Rinehart & Winston, 1968, Chapter 3.

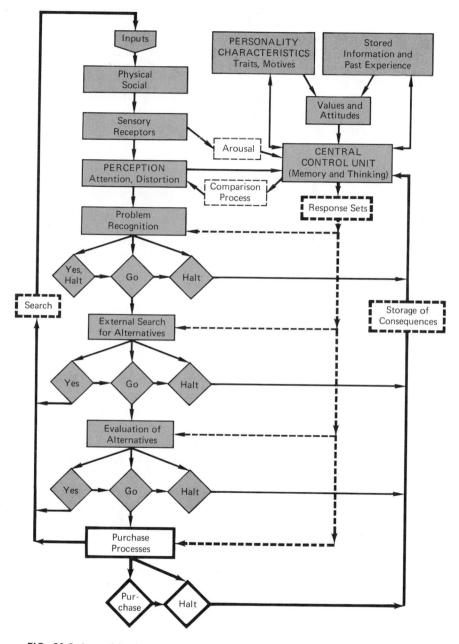

FIG. 20.2 A model of consumer purchase processes. (*From* Consumer behavior *by James F. Engel, David T. Kollat and Roger D. Blackwell, Fig. 21-2. Copyright © 1968 by Holt, Rinehart and Winston, Inc. Reprinted by permission of Holt, Rinehart and Winston, Inc.*)

DATA COLLECTION METHODS

In the various phases of consumer research, data are obtained regarding many aspects of consumers and their behavior and responses. One of the major aspects is the collection of data relating to consumer attitudes, opinions, motivation, values, preferences, buying habits, and other variables. Information about consumers and their opinions, motivations, values, preferences, and so forth can lead to the development or modification of products or services so that they meet more adequately the needs of consumers, and to the development of advertising programs that are more realistically related to such needs.

Some of the research methods used in these phases of consumer research are essentially the same as those used in other contexts that have been discussed earlier. These include interviewing procedures (discussed in Chapter 4), tests and measurements (Chapter 5), attitude and opinion measurement (Chapter 11), and various types of rating procedures, such as discussed previously in the context of performance evaluation (Chapter 9). Some of these methods as well as others will be further discussed or illustrated here, in some instances with the special or unique twists they have in the consumer field.

Requirements for Adequate Data Collection

Before discussing methods as such, it is important to mention two critical points that will influence the adequacy of the resulting data and the extent to which results can be extrapolated to populations generally.

Adequacy of method. One of these points relates to the adequacy of the method used, such as a questionnaire or an interview procedure. No fancy cover on a report is going to make up for inadequacies of the questionnaire or the interviewing procedures, or the lack of ability and training of interviewers, or the inadequacy of experimental or statistical methods.

Sampling. When one collects information from a sample of people for the purpose of extrapolating from that sample to a population, the nature of the sample can be a major factor in the validity of any such extrapolation. In consumer research, the investigator typically has some "population" in mind. Although this might comprise the population of the country in its entirety, it usually consists of some restricted segment, such as housewives, car owners, adult males, families with children, retired individuals, voters, or television viewers.

Given the population—however it may be defined—there are basically two methods of sampling that can be used. One of these is *random* sampling; the other is *stratified* sampling. In random sampling, the sample should be so selected that each individual within the population has an equal chance of being selected for the sample. In stratified sampling, the population is first categorized in terms of certain presumably relevant characteristics, such as age, sex, marital status, education, or income, in order to know what proportion of the population falls within each category. A random selection is then made within each such category so that there is proportional representation for each category.

If one departs from rigorous sampling procedures (as frequently is the case), one must face potential risks in extrapolating to the population in general. In such a circumstance one needs to recognize—and be willing to accept—such risks.

Consumer Panels

In the collection of data in consumer research, sometimes consumer panels or juries are used. Depending upon the purpose in mind, the members of the panel may be brought together as a group, dealt with individually, contacted by phone, contacted by mail, or used in some other manner. Such panels are used for various purposes, such as testing advertising copy, getting opinions about various products and packaging, and taste-testing food products. Certain of the television ratings are based on the use of samples of television viewers; such a sample might be thought of as a panel. In the case of one rating system, a device attached to the television set automatically records the programs to which the set is tuned. The way in which the panel is used will, of course, depend on the purpose of the survey. The panel, in effect, is then a sample of people. Frequently the same panel is used over a period of time.

Questionnaire Surveys

One of the most common methods used in consumer research is the consumer questionnaire survey method. This method consists of having questionnaires completed by a sample of people. The questionnaires may be distributed by mail, by hand, or by some other method.

Questionnaire development. As pointed out by Anastasi,[11] the responses to questions can be markedly influenced by the nature of the questionnaire and the questions, including such factors as the grammatical form of the questions, the number of possible responses provided, their order, and their other characteristics. For example, Weitz[12] obtained significant differences in preferences in a survey relating to cooking ranges when the alternatives

[11] Anastasi, A. *Fields of applied psychology.* New York: McGraw-Hill, 1964, p. 271.

[12] Weitz, J. Verbal and pictorial questionnaires in market research. *Journal of Applied Psychology,* 1950, **34**, 363–366.

were presented verbally than when they were presented pictorially. In addition, emotionally loaded words in questions usually will influence the responses of subjects. Anyone constructing a questionnaire should be familiar with these pitfalls, and should follow sound questionnaire-construction practices.

One important feature in questionnaire development is the form of the question used. This can have an influence on the responses obtained, and therefore can influence the interpretation of the results. The influence of the form of a question on responses was illustrated by a comparison made by Belson and Duncan[13] of the responses of over one thousand people to questions about the newspapers and magazines they had looked at and the television programs they had watched the preceding day. Half of the subjects were given a checklist questionnaire listing most newspapers, magazines, and television programs, with instruction to check off those that they had read or watched; there was also a checklist category for "all others" in each group. The other half received open-end questions and were asked to list the relevant items on the basis of their recall. The average checklist respondent claimed viewing half again as many programs as the average respondent using the open-end form. But on the other hand, the checklist form had a depressing effect on some free-recall items, especially for television programs with incidental viewing or hard-to-remember names; newscasts, for example, were mentioned by only 1 percent of the checklist respondents as opposed to 25 percent of the open-end respondents!

In the development of questionnaires, it is very strongly recommended that they be pretested on a small sample prior to their use on a wider basis. The pretest should be carried out with the same kinds of subjects as those who will complete the questionnaire later.

Biases in responses. An additional possible source of distortion in questionnaire responses is the subjects themselves. Their biases may be generalized tendencies, or they may be associated more with certain categories of subjects. In a study by the Federal Reserve Board as reported by Rikumo,[14] for example, about 1,800 people reported their monthly payments on loans and the amount of their loans. These reports were later compared with actual indebtedness. It was found that there was a significant tendency for people to report that they owed *less* money than they really did owe, by an average of about $83. Nearly half of the respondents reported lower values. There was, however, reasonable accuracy in reporting the amount of monthly payment. "Explaining" different behavior tendencies is frequently rather risky business, but it is possible that in this instance the

13 Belson, W., & Duncan, J. A. A comparison of the checklist and open response question systems. *Applied Statistics.* June 1962, **2**(2), 120–132.
14 Rikumo, I. An analysis of response errors: A case study. *Journal of Business,* October 1963, **36**(4), 440–447.

under-reporting bias may have been due to an inclination to "forget" some of the unpleasantness of life such as the amount of debt, or to engage in wishful thinking (hoping the debt would "go away").

Another aspect of bias arising from respondents is what Couch and Keniston[15] refer to as the tendency of some people to say "yes" consistently (yeasayers) and of others to say "no" consistently (naysayers) when responding to personality and attitude items. This pattern has been somewhat confirmed by various people, including Becher and Myers,[16] who found that the yeasayers tended to respond differently than the naysayers in a survey of attitudes toward three different grocery stores. In trying to trace down any personal factors that distinguished between these two groups, they found differences in their propensities on a couple of personality dimensions, as follows:

| | Personality Dimension | |
	Sensory-intuitive	Judgment-perception
Yeasayers	More intuitive	More perceptual
Naysayers	More sensing type	More judgmental

Rating and Scaling Methods

Closely related to questionnaires are various rating and scaling methods. Some such methods were discussed and illustrated in the earlier context of performance evaluation (Chapter 9). Essentially the same techniques are also applicable in the context of consumer research, with, of course, different content. For example, it would be possible to have respondents rank, in order of importance to them, the factors they consider in the selection of a house, such as type of neighborhood, convenience to schools, distance from public transportation, cost, and style of architecture.

Semantic differential. The semantic differential, as developed by Osgood et al.,[17] was discussed in Chapter 11 as a method of attitude measurement. As indicated there, it consists of pairs of opposite adjectives that might be relevant to the attitude object, with scale values representing varying positions between these. For each pair, a person marks the scale value that represents his own attitude toward the attitude object. In consumer research this technique is used especially to determine the "image" of products, media, people, and organizations. One example of this type of scale

[15] Couch, A., & Keniston, K. Yeasayers and naysayers: Agreeing response set as a personality variable. *Journal of Abnormal and Social Psychology*, 1960, **60**, 151–174.

[16] Becher, B. W., & Myers, J. G. Yeasaying response style. *Journal of Advertising Research*, December 1970, **10**(6), 31–37.

[17] Osgood, C. E., Suci, G. J., & Tannenbaum, P. H. *The measurement of meaning*. Urbana, Ill.: University of Illinois Press, 1957.

is part of a rather elaborate study conducted by Blackwell *et al.*[18] relating to the use of touch-tone telephones. The semantic differential technique was used to elicit the "image" of a housewife who might use such a phone. The questionnaire included the following as the pairs of opposite adjectives: young—old; shy—bold; poor—rich; old-fashioned—modern; smart—stupid; and interesting—boring.

An example of the types of results one can obtain with this technique comes from a comparison of the images of radio, television, and newspaper media in Richmond, Virginia.[19] All available adults and teenagers in a random sample of 447 households (drawn from newspaper route lists) were interviewed with a semantic differential type of questionnaire consisting of a number of pairs of potentially relevant adjectives. Two months later, one-half as many households next door to those of the original sample were interviewed in a similar way concerning radio and television. A comparison of the results is given in Figure 20.3, which shows the values of a rating index based on the responses. The results generally indicate that the public views television as having more warmth than newspapers, but newspapers as being more intelligent, credible, moral, courageous, and reliable than television.

Interview

The interview is another method of obtaining information from or about people.

Structured interview. In a structured interview such as might be carried out in a door-to-door marketing research survey, the interviewer follows a general predetermined interview procedure. This form of interview is somewhat akin to a questionnaire, except that the questions are asked orally. The questions used in such a situation should be framed with the same kinds of considerations in mind as in the case of questionnaires and, as with questionnaires, should be pretested.

Unstructured interview. A more flexible interview procedure has been proposed by Gallup[20] for the purpose of obtaining information from customers which will reflect something about the influence of specific advertisements on their purchases. Because many people tend to view their purchasing decisions as their own, uninfluenced by advertisements, it has been found to be fruitless to ask people if such-and-such an advertisement influenced their purchasing decision. Gallup's interview approach starts *from* the purchase

[18] Blackwell, R. D., Engel, J. F., & Kollat, D. T. *Cases in consumer behavior.* New York: Holt, Rinehart & Winston, 1969.

[19] *The climate of persuasion: A study of the public image of advertising media.* Richmond, Va.: The Richmond Newspapers, Inc., 1959.

[20] Gallup, G. *Activation: A major development in advertising research.* Princeton, N.J.: Gallup and Robinson, Inc., June, 1957.

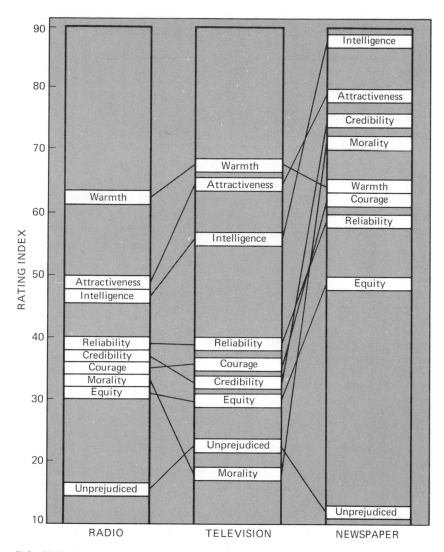

FIG. 20.3 Comparison of public images of three media as measured by the semantic differential technique. The position of each category indicates its average rating index. (*Courtesy of the Richmond Newspapers, Inc.*)

and then proceeds *to* the advertising. The interviewee is encouraged to recall the circumstances leading to a given purchase and, in particular, to give details about any advertisements that may have had some part in the choice.

Still another form of interview is what Lucas and Britt[21] refer to as an

[21] Lucas & Britt, *op. cit.*, pp. 140–142.

informal, unstructured interview, such as is used in testing advertisements. For example, the testing of a comic-strip character for possible use in a hairdressing advertisement was based almost entirely on impressions given by interviewees while they were looking at the display.

Depth interview. Still another form of interview is the depth interview, which is used occasionally for gaining insight into human motivation as related to the use of products. As indicated by Dichter,[22] the depth interview is used in order to elicit the freest possible associations on the part of the respondent. The role of the interviewer is that of establishing rapport with the respondent, of starting the interview in a very general way, and of encouraging the respondent to express himself. The respondent generally determines the direction and content that the interview takes, thus giving him the opportunity to talk about himself. Dichter proposes the use of depth interviewing (and also of projective techniques, which are discussed later) under the following circumstances: (1) whenever the data being sought may not be present at the rational or conscious level; (2) whenever we are dealing with psychological mechanisms and not with simple cause-and-effect relationships; and (3) whenever the respondent has a chance to produce interference consciously or unconsciously between the time he understands the question and the time he answers it.

Advantages and disadvantages of interviews. One of the advantages of the interview method is that it usually results in obtaining data from a higher percentage of those in the sample. Dudycha,[23] for example, indicates that in interviewing surveys, interviews usually are completed with 80 percent of the sample. With special efforts (including call-backs), it may be possible to contact successfully 90 to 95 percent of the sample. With mail questionnaire surveys the percentage of returns usually is much smaller. In addition, the interview may offer such advantages as being able to establish better rapport with subjects, thus maintaining subject interest for a longer period of time, which may be important when one is soliciting answers to many questions. This rapport, and the opportunity to clarify questions, can tend to elicit more accurate information. In the case of unstructured and depth interviews, it is possible to obtain data or impressions that could not be elicited by the use of more structured interviews or with questionnaires.

On the other hand, interviews are very time consuming and costly, which usually limits the number of individuals who can be surveyed. This constraint does not apply to anywhere near the same extent as to a questionnaire survey. In addition, there is the problem of selecting and training inter-

22 Dichter, E. Toward an understanding of human behavior. In Ferber, R. and Wales, H. G. (Eds.), *Motivation and market behavior.* Homewood, Ill.: Richard D. Irwin, Inc., 1958.
23 Dudycha, G. J. *Applied psychology.* New York: Ronald Press, 1963, p. 362.

viewers, and the very real risk that interviewer biases may influence the resulting data in some unknown manner and degree.

Projective Techniques

Projective techniques—whether used in personality measurement, in consumer research, or otherwise—are methods of eliciting responses from people to intentionally ambiguous, unstructured stimuli. Because the stimuli are vague, it is presumed that responses made by subjects are "projections" of themselves. Interpretation of the responses by a trained individual might, therefore, reveal information indirectly about the subject that it might not be possible to obtain directly. Projective techniques have been used primarily in the field of clinical psychology. They have been used in consumer psychology primarily to derive inferences about motivation, attitudes, and other variables that are relevant to consumer behavior. A few of the specific types of projective techniques that have been used in consumer psychology will be mentioned briefly.

Association techniques. In these procedures, the subject responds to some stimulus with some word or expression that the stimulus brings to mind—that is "associated" with the stimulus. An example of this procedure is a word-association test reported by Lucas and Britt.[24] This test was used to study people's associations with certain key words of advertisement copy that related to the promotion of butter. The five key copy words (buttery, snack, sizzling, bun, and aroma) were fitted into a larger group of words, as follows:

1. table _____	5. buttery _____	9. red _____
2. orange _____	6. cold _____	10. bun _____
3. snack _____	7. aroma _____	11. friend _____
4. white _____	8. owl _____	12. sizzling _____

Every word in the list, and especially the sequence of words, has an influence on each response. This cannot be avoided, although the sequence can be varied or other background words substituted. The pattern given here, used with hundreds of convenient subjects, produced such responses to the test as follows:

snack: tidbit, brunch, quick, hungry
buttery: smeary, fatty, greasy, yellow, heavy
aroma: smell, pleasant, odor, perfume
bun: roll, bread, gravy, oven
sizzling: hot, sputtering, spattering, meat

[24] Lucas & Britt, *op. cit.,* p. 143.

In the case of this particular example it was found that there were very few "taste" associations with *buttery,* possibly because of lack of relevant words in the English language. The results of association tests in advertisement copy writing can serve to guide the selection and avoidance of words for use in advertisement copy. Association techniques can also be used in other aspects of consumer research, such as in the more clinically oriented setting of depth interviewing, or in the measurement of personality variables. In this latter connection, for example, the Rorschach ink blot test is an example of an association type of test in which the subject is asked to indicate what he "sees" in (associates with) each ink blot.

Sentence completion tests. Sentence completion tests consist of parts of sentences, with certain words or phrases omitted. The omissions are of such a nature that the words or phrases filled in by the respondents have a significant influence on the meaning of the sentence, thereby making it possible to derive some inferences about the respondents.

An example of a sentence completion test is reported by MacLeod[25] in a study of the expressed choices relating to fictitious makes of automobiles. The test consisted of forty statements such as the following examples:

The best kind of car is one that _____ .
The most enjoyable thing when you go to buy a car is _____ .
Driving very fast in a car is _____ .

The responses of 368 men to the forty sentences were then subjected to a content analysis. (Content analysis was discussed earlier in the context of methods of measurement of attitudes and opinions, Chapter 11.) In this particular study, ninety-eight specific categories of "content" were set up, and these in turn were grouped into eighteen broader categories such as "desire for economy." By a special scoring scheme, each person was scored on each of these eighteen categories. (These scores, in turn, were used in further analyses that need not be discussed here.)

Construction techniques. In construction types of projective techniques, subjects are presented with a rather ambiguous type of stimulus such as a picture, and are asked to create or "construct" a story, description, expression, or other form of response. Here, also, the intent is one of getting the subject to "project" himself in such a way that his attitudes or feelings may be revealed indirectly.

An interesting example of this technique as applied to advertising is reported by Engel and Wales,[26] in which cartoons were used to elicit

[25] MacLeod, J. S. *Predicting the responses to advertising themes from sentence completions to direct attitude questions about an advertised product.* New York: Advertising Research Foundation, Inc., 1958.

[26] Engel, J. E., & Wales, H. G. Spoken *versus* pictured questions to taboo topics. *Journal of Advertising Research,* March 1962, 2, 11–17; and Engel, J. E. A. study of a selected projective technique in marketing research. Unpublished Ph.D. Dissertation, University of Illinois, 1960.

responses dealing with the testing of themes for advertising aspirin. In a cartoon picture a druggist says to a woman customer:

> This widely known brand of aspirin gives you 100 tablets for 67 cents, and that brand gives you 100 tablets for 27 cents. Which would you like?

The respondent is asked to "fill in" the answer of the customer. In the survey 150 housewives completed the responses, which were then categorized by content analysis. Their responses were compared with responses of another sample who were asked a direct question about their preference but not shown the cartoon. A comparison of some of the responses from these two methods is given below:

Response	Cartoon Respondents	Respondents to Questions
Choice: 67-cent aspirin	48%	74%
Choice: 27-cent aspirin	30%	18%
No choice	22%	8%

This comparison points up the possible influence of the method of data collection on the results one obtains, and serves as a warning that methods have to be chosen with care and results interpreted accordingly. In this instance Engel expresses the opinion that cartoon responses may be more accurate because the respondents are under less implied pressure to show that they are concerned with aspirin "quality."

Other Methods

Although the methods mentioned above are the more common ones in consumer research, there are other procedures that are used for some purposes. Perloff,[27] for example, refers to the use of various types of apparatus such as eye cameras (used in recording eye movements of subjects when scanning advertisements, printed pages, television screens, or other visual stimuli); mechanical devices for individuals to use in recording quickly their preferences of products or brands and of their opinions regarding packaging styles; and one-way mirrors. In addition there are observational techniques for observing consumer behavior in natural settings, either by having observers on hand (such as recording traffic patterns in a supermarket), or by use of photographic techniques.

In connection with taste-testing, two rather common procedures are the use of triangle taste tests and paired preference tests. Triangle tests are

[27] Perloff, R. Determining opinions and attitudes through survey research. In *Studies in Organization Management*. Washington, D.C.: Institute Department for Organization Management, Chamber of Commerce of the United States, 1962.

used to determine if a particular food product can be differentiated by taste from another. For this purpose, two samples of one product and one sample of the other are given to the subject, with instructions to identify the one that is different from the others. The paired preference test involves samples of two related food products, with instructions to the subject to indicate which one he prefers.[28] (As an aside, it might be noted that people's expressed preferences for something are sometimes influenced by factors completely unrelated to the one in question; for example, something may "taste" better if it has a familiar label, a fancy package, or a pleasing odor.)

The various methods of data collection mentioned above can be used in different facets of consumer research. Most of the remainder of this chapter will consist of illustrations of a few aspects of consumer research in which one or another of the various methods of data collection have been used.

MARKETING RESEARCH

One of the important areas of consumer psychology is that of market research, which deals with the many facets of behavior of consumers in the marketplace and the variables related to such behavior.

Consumer Expectations

The response set of individuals is the consequence of their personality, experience, and values, as modified by the influence of the family, reference groups, and social class. Response set obviously comprises a major basis for wide individual differences in the attitudes and behavior of consumers. But such attitudes and behavior are also in part influenced by time-changing factors, such as economic conditions and unemployment. The inclination of people to buy or not to buy various products and services can be a function of their current optimism or pessimism about such affairs. The Survey Research Center of the University of Michigan has for some years been measuring consumer attitudes and inclinations to buy (especially durable goods), using an Index of Consumer Sentiment developed by Katona et al.[29] The shifting values on this index over the years for samples of consumers are shown in Figure 20.4. These shifts presumably reflect the extent to which people are attuned to changing economic and related factors in their environment.

[28] Some of the statistical aspects of triangle and paired tests are discussed by Radkins, A. P. Some statistical considerations in organoleptic research: Triangle, paired, duo-trio tests. *Food Research*, 1957, **22**(3), 259–265.

[29] Katona, G., Mueller, E., Schmiedeskamp, J., & Sonquist, J. A. *1966 Survey of consumer finances.* Ann Arbor, Michigan: Survey Research Center, Monograph No. 44, 1967.

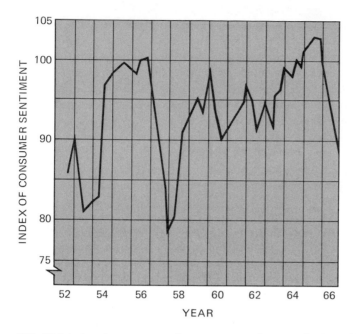

FIG. 20.4 Index of consumer sentiment over several years, reflecting shifts in attitudes of pessimism and optimism that might influence their inclinations to buy. (*Adapted from Katona, et. al., 1967,* op. cit., *Table II-I, p. 243-244.*)

One might wonder about the extent to which such expressed attitudes are related to subsequent buying behavior—or, more broadly, how accurately buying behavior can be predicted from various variables, including expressed attitudes. A study of this matter is reported by Mueller[30] in which she was interested in determining the extent to which discretionary spending by consumers is a function both of financial variables (consumer incomes, assets, debts, prices) and of attitudes and expectations. "Discretionary" expenditures generally refer to outlays for durable goods (cars, appliances, and so forth), travel, recreation, and, to some extent, what one might think of as luxury foods and clothing. On the whole, consumer expenditures for "necessities" (food, shelter, and so forth) are less influenced by financial variables or attitudes. In her study, Mueller analyzed both financial and attitudinal variables as related to expenditures for durable goods, as reflected by twenty-one surveys over nine years. The specific predictor variables used were: (1) disposable personal income during the half-year preceding survey (a Department of Commerce index); (2) current disposable income as a ratio to income two quarters earlier; (3) consumer attitude index (a predecessor to the index of consumer sentiment); (4) same as (3) but

[30] Mueller, E. Survey methods as a forecasting tool. In *Psychological research on consumer behavior.* Ann Arbor, Michigan: The Foundation for Research on Human Behavior, 1962.

including two questions on attitudes toward the automobile market; and (5) an index of stated buying intentions. These variables, for which data were available as of the times of all twenty-one surveys, were correlated with three measures of durable goods expenditures. Multiple correlations of weighted combinations of certain of these were then computed, for three criteria, as follows (in each instance the numbers of the variables that entered into the multiple correlation are listed) :

Criterion	Multiple Correlation
Durable goods expenditures (1, 3, 5)	.88
Installment credit (1, 3)	.87
New cars sold (2, 4)	.80

These three multiple correlations indicate that, to a very substantial degree, actual consumer expenditures for durable goods can be predicted on the basis of a combination of economic variables (1 and 2 above), attitudinal variables (3 and 4), and buying intentions (5), with the attitude variables (3 and 4) being dominant.

Product Testing

It is becoming a very common practice to pretest new products before they are placed on the market in order to determine the extent to which the product will be acceptable to potential consumers. An example of this type of product testing has been published by Harris,[31] who discusses an approach to pretesting product designs and describes a study involving the validity of a method for predicting sales of dinnerware patterns. In one part of the study, ten fine china patterns were investigated. Ten dinner plates from each pattern being investigated were placed on a table and identified by a letter of the alphabet. Each of 140 women was brought individually to the table, instructed to assume that she was in the market for a set of fine china, and that the patterns before her were all available at the same price. She then ranked the patterns in order of her preference and indicated the degree of her preference for each pattern using a twenty-one-point rating scale.

A Preference Index was then computed for each pattern, which was the percentage of respondents rating the pattern in the top three positions on the rating scale. The correlation between Prefence Indices obtained in this manner and actual sales of the patterns obtained from company records was .91. This relationship is shown graphically in Figure 20.5. It is obvious from this figure that patterns with high Preference Indices also are high in sales. Following this investigation, seventy new patterns were pretested

[31] Harris, D. H. Predicting consumer reaction to product designs. *Journal of Advertising Research,* June 1964, 4(2), 34–37.

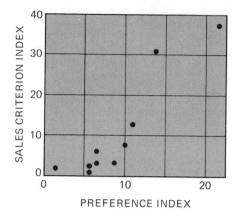

FIG. 20.5 Relationship between Preference Index for ten fine china patterns (as based on ranking by 140 women) and actual sales of patterns. The correlation between the two is .91. (*Adapted from Harris,* op. cit., *from the* Journal of Advertising Research. *Copyright* © *1964 by the Advertising Research Foundation.*)

on a national scale and fourteen were marketed on the basis of the results. Several patterns marketed on the basis of these pretest results have become top selling patterns in their grades.

Packaging

Another aspect of marketing research relates to packaging of products. The producers of some products carry out research relating to package design in order to determine the opinions and preferences of people about various possible designs. Such opinions and preferences usually are obtained by the use of interviews with samples of customers. A rather ingenious method of obtaining responses is by the use of a push-button voting machine[32] that is installed in stores such as supermarkets. In one particular situation, two designs of packages of Vicks Vapo-Rub were tested, one of which was the old design, the other a new design which shows a color reproduction of the familiar Vicks jar.[33] Three thousand machine votes were obtained in three days in selected supermarkets. The responses indicated quite clearly that the new design was the more popular.

Family Participation in Purchasing Behavior

Still another facet of marketing research is focused on the study of the roles of different family members in purchasing behavior. As an illustration of this aspect of research, Blackwell *et al.*[34] summarize the results of a study

[32] The mechanical testing machines are owned, installed, and serviced by the Automated Preference Testing Division of the A.C. Nielsen Co.

[33] A robot redesigns Vicks. *Modern Packaging,* March 1961, **34**(7), 90–91.

[34] Study conducted for Life Magazine by Jaffee and Associates, Inc., as reported by Blackwell *et al., op. cit.,* pp. 156–163.

in which the roles of the husband and wife in the several stages of the decision-making process were dissected. These stages are listed in Table 20.1, along with the percentages of self-reported roles of husbands and wives in a sample of 301 households as related to purchasing decisions about refrigerators and automobiles. These roles obviously would be very different for other products.

As an aside—and as a word of slight caution—it should be noted that the roles of husbands and wives in these various stages were somewhat different as reported by the individual (the husband or wife) and as reported for the individual by the spouse (the wife or husband). Generally, these differences were not of major proportions, but in a few instances they differed by rather marked degree.

ADVERTISING EFFECTIVENESS

Another important aspect of consumer research relates to advertising effectiveness. It has been suggested by Lucas and Britt[35] that the measurement of advertisement effectiveness involves two different problems—namely, measuring advertisements and advertising effectiveness as such, and measuring the media which expose the advertising messages to consumers. These, however, are inseparably intertwined. Examples of both aspects will be given for illustrative purposes.

TABLE 20.1 PERCENTS OF 301 HUSBANDS (H) AND WIVES (W) REPORTING INVOLVEMENT IN VARIOUS STAGES OF DECISIONMAKING IN PURCHASING REFRIGERATORS AND AUTOMOBILES.

	Percent Reporting Involvement			
Stage of Decision-making	*Refrigerators*		*Automobiles*	
Planning-prepurchase				
The initiator	71	89	93	39
Suggestor of type or style	33	70	80	29
Suggestor of brand	33	45	73	21
Budgeter	35	45	73	17
Information seeking				
Information gatherer: people	92	85	80	81
Information gatherer: media	59	55	57	43
Buying				
Shopper	88	86	96	73
Purchaser	71	79	94	52

Source: Adapted from a study for *Life Magazine* by Jaffee and Associates, Inc. on human behavior, copyright © 1965 Time Inc.; as presented in *Case in consumer psychology* by Roger P. Blackwell, James F. Engel, and David T. Kollat, Table 9–1, copyright © 1969 by Holt, Rinehart and Winston, Inc.

[35] Lucas & Britt, *op. cit.,* p. 3.

Advertising Research

Advertising research deals with the various aspects of printed advertisements, television and radio commercials, and other media.

Printed characteristics of advertisements. The printed features of advertisements can be characterized in many different ways. In an analysis of 1,379 advertisements, Assael *et al.*[36] coded the messages in terms of 208 different characteristics grouped into ninety broader categories. For our illustrative purposes, the results of an analysis of certain "print ad" characteristics of these advertisements will be reported.[37] The analysis consisted of deriving an IARI index (the index of the Industrial Advertising Research Institute), which is essentially based on the percentage of advertisements "noticed" by readers. The averages of these indexes for various categories of the 1,379 advertisements are given in Figure 20.6, which shows the indexes for the following subgroups: (1) black and white and two-color; and (2) three- or four-color. These were also broken down into advertisements with "spread" (two pages) and without spread (one page). This figure reflects the fact that there are differences in the percentage of people "noting" ads that differ in color (black and white and two-color versus three- or four-color), and also in terms of "spread" versus "no spread."

Copy testing of advertisements. It is frequently the practice in developing advertisements (especially for use in magazines with large circulations)

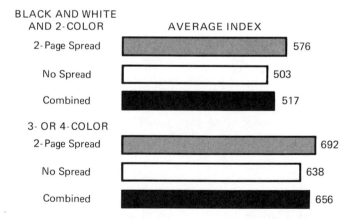

FIG. 20.6 Average indexes based on the percent of readers who "noticed" ads with different characteristics. (*Adapted from Assael* et al., op. cit., *Table 2, p. 25, from* Journal of Advertising Research. *Copyright* © *1967, by the Advertising Research Foundation.*)

[36] Assael, H., Kofran, J. H., & Burgi, W. Advertising performance as a function of print ad characteristics. *Journal of Advertising Research,* June 1967, **7**(2), 20–26.
[37] *The IARI letter grade ad scoring system.* Princeton, N.J.: Industrial Advertising Research Institute (now the Marketing Communications Research Center), 1964.

to "test" the copy of alternative advertising designs. Usually this is done with samples of subjects before running the advertisements in any copies of the magazine. In some cases, however, different versions of advertisements may be run in limited editions of the magazine (such as the copies prepared for different cities), and then tested by interview follow-up. In still other circumstances, each version of an advertisement may be included in all copies of a different issue of the magazine, and then tested. In such a case the purpose of the testing is to provide guidance for the development of future advertisements.

An instance of this latter type is one in which two different advertisements for the Renault automobile were run in two separate issues of *Life* magazine, one in September, the other in November. These two versions were rated by both men and women, with their ratings being converted into Starch scores. Starch scores, developed by Daniel Starch & Staff, Mamaroneck, New York, provide the basis for a relative comparison of advertisements in terms of three types of criteria—namely, "noted," "seen associated," and "read most," as based on the responses of subjects to interviewers' questions. In the case of these two advertisements, the results of these comparisons are given below:

		Starch Scores	
	Noted	Seen Associated	Read Most
Advertisement A			
Men	49	49	25
Women	19	15	7
Advertisement B			
Men	35	32	24
Women	12	7	4

It can be seen that there were generally higher ratings for advertisement A than for B, especially in the case of the "noted" and "seen associated" scores.

Media Research

Advertisements can be presented by different media, such as newspapers, magazines, direct mail, outdoor billboards and car-cards, and television and radio. In comparing various media for communicating with potential consumers, one needs some measure of effectiveness. With respect to magazines, for example, a very gross index is, of course, the number of copies sold. Such a measure, however, does not necessarily reflect readership. As indicated earlier, measures of recognition (also referred to as "noting") and of recall reflect different aspects of learning as the consequence of exposure (usually to particular articles or advertisements). Such measures have some relevance to the measurement of magazine audience. For example, the "audience" of magazines as characterized in one study were those who had seen at least one major editorial feature of the previous issue. Sometimes people are asked outright what magazines they read or prefer. There is, however, a potential pitfall to data obtained in such surveys. As pointed out by Lucas and Britt,[38] the act of reading, including that of reading most popular magazines, carries with it a degree of prestige. This can lead to inflation of the number of people who say they read particular magazines. In one survey, for example, the number of people claiming to be readers of a given magazine was fifteen times the number of copies printed! To avoid such inflation, the questions that are posed to the respondents (either by interviews or in questionnaires) should lead to no loss of status for admitting to the reading, or the failing to read, certain magazines. In this connection, Lucas and Britt[39] point out that one technique that is used is that of having interviewers go through a magazine issue with a respondent, first noting the major editorial features, and afterward asking such questions as: Just for the record, now that we have been through the issue, would you say you definitely happened to read it, or aren't you sure?

Comparison of different media. The source of the "exposure" of people to information about any given commodity naturally depends upon the media of advertisements and other types of information. Aside from the amount of exposure to a given medium, however, media can differ in their relative effectiveness in the decision-making process. Both of these aspects are illustrated by a survey reported by Blackwell et al.[40] of a sample of five thousand households that had purchased carpeting within the previous six months. The intent was to find out how people had heard about a specific brand of carpet and, in the case of those who had purchased that brand, the "effectiveness" of each different source as it may have influenced their decision. Effectiveness was categorized as follows: *effective exposure* (the most important information source); *contributory exposure* (the source played a role but not the most important); and *ineffective exposure* (the source did not play a role in their decision). Figure 20.7 shows both the extent of exposure to each of six sources and the effectiveness of each. There are very marked differences in both of these, with personal contact with other purchasers, magazines, and salesmen all playing dominant roles.

IMAGES

We hear much these days about images—of products, services, corporations, and even politicians. Images do not necessarily correspond with reality, although one hopes that they do. Be that as it may, it is undoubtedly

---

[38] Lucas & Britt, *op. cit.,* p. 223.
[39] *Ibid.,* pp. 228–229.
[40] Blackwell *et al., op. cit.,* pp. 198–205.

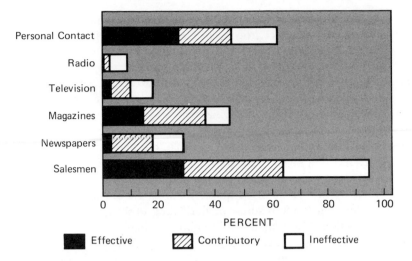

FIG. 20.7 Amount and effectiveness of exposure to various sources of information about a particular brand of carpet in the case of purchasers of that brand. The length of the bar represents the percent reporting exposure to the source, and the shadings indicate the relative effectiveness. (*Data from* Cases in consumer behavior *by Roger D. Blackwell, James F. Engel and David T. Kollat, Table 11-16. Copyright* © *1969 by Holt, Rinehart and Winston, Inc.*)

the case that the image people have of some attitude object (i.e., their perceptions of the object) influences their behavior for better or worse. The process of getting some impressions of people's images of some attitude object typically involves the use of a questionnaire. Various formats can be used. For example, the results of a survey sponsored by one airline are given by Blackwell *et al.*[41] In a very summary way these results are expressed below in qualitative terms.

Comparison of Airline A with Other Airlines

Relatively Higher	*Relatively Lower*
Flight availability	Safety record
Extensive routing	On-time performance
Baggage, reservations	Efficient hostesses
Help with children	Good food on flight
Comfortable terminal facilities	In-flight information

Such data, of course, should be of interest to management, especially in attempts to improve those aspects of the operations of the organization that in fact leave something to be desired.

In another study of "images," Cohen[42] experimented with a new twist

[41] *Ibid.,* pp. 94–102.
[42] Cohen, L. The differentiation ratio in corporate image research. *Journal of Advertising Research,* September 1967, **7**(3), 32–36.

in the procedures for deriving some indication of the basic corporate images. The technique is one of using a "differentiation ratio" based on the frequency with which respondents refer to a particular characteristic of the organization when the organization is ranked "No. 1" in its field and when it is not so ranked (i.e., when it is ranked 2, 3, or in some other position). In the case in point, which dealt with companies in the control instrument industry, five most differentiating characteristics in order were: (1) diversified line; (2) leader; (3) power; (4) dependable; and (5) accurate. Using the more conventional approach to determining the "most important" characteristics, the first three characteristics would have been ranked much lower. Cohen gives some evidence to suggest that the method is a somewhat more sensitive one for deriving a basis for differentiating companies in terms of their images.

CONCLUSION

The burgeoning interest in the consumer is an encouraging development in the affairs of man, for it marks a shift from what one hopes are the bygone days of the *caveat emptor* philosophy. In promoting the interests of the consumer, it is hoped that consumer research can provide the basis for understanding the consumer and his legitimate needs. It is in this vein that one looks forward to an increased sense, on the part of the "providers" of the goods and services of the economy, of their responsibility for actually providing those goods and services that optimally fulfill such needs.

appendix A

Elementary Descriptive Statistics

DESCRIPTIVE *VS.* SAMPLING STATISTICS

Two basic purposes are served by statistical methods. One of these is to describe a body of data. This is done by means of *descriptive statistics,* which deals with the reduction of a body of data by means of graphic methods, computational methods yielding numerical measures, and tabular methods. The sole aim of *descriptive statistics* is to reduce the original data to charts, graphs, averages, and the like so that the salient facts concerning the data will be more apparent.

The second purpose of statistical methods is to enable the experimenter to learn how safely he can generalize from *descriptive statistics* obtained on a sample. This approach is known as *sampling statistics.* It involves applications of the mathematics of probability and is a very important part of the field of industrial psychology.

This appendix will deal only with certain concepts of *descriptive statistics,* but the importance of *sampling statistics* should not be underestimated and every serious student of industrial psychology should become familiar with these methods.

Descriptive statistics in industrial psychology are used for summarizing the various types of raw data typically dealt with, such as test scores, attitude measures, and criterion values.

GRAPHIC REPRESENTATION OF DATA

In discussing various types of descriptive statistics, let us use as an example a set of data such as that shown in Table 21.1. These data represent the number of defects identified by each of sixty inspectors during a week.

TABLE 21.1 NUMBER OF DEFECTS DETECTED BY EACH OF 60 INSPECTORS DURING ONE WEEK OF WORK

15	36	40	37	32	13	35	20	33	36	33	16	38	19	33	34	24
36	25	29	27	39	42	31	21	26	28	53	23	51	21	26	39	28
30	31	32	30	29	49	39	30	44	34	37	35	38	35	41	37	43
42	38	45	22	46	41	47	48	34							

Frequency Distribution

A frequency distribution consists of the number of cases in each of various *class intervals* of the value in question; in this case it would be the number of inspectors for each of the various class intervals of numbers of defects detected. The steps involved in constructing a frequency distribution are as follows:

1. Determine the range of the values in the raw data. Quickly glance through the data to determine the *highest* and the *lowest* values. The range is the difference between these values. In the case of the sixty inspector records, the highest figure is 53 and the lowest is 13. The range is therefore $53 - 13 = 40$.

2. If we find that the range of the data is large (that they are widely spread), it will usually be more convenient to group them by class intervals (abbreviated c.i.) with a range in each c.i. of more than 1 unit. A simple rule of thumb that is helpful in deciding upon the correct size of the c.i. is to divide the range by 15 (because, on the average, this is the most desirable number of c.i.'s) and take as the c.i. the whole number nearest to the quotient. In our problem, the range divided by 15 would be $40 \div 15 = 2.66$. As 3 is the whole number nearest to 2.66, 3 would be the size of the c.i. to be used.

3. Arrange the adjacent c.i.'s in a column, leaving a blank space immediately to the right of this column. The arrangements of the c.i.'s pre-

TABLE 21.2 Illustration of Data Relating to a Frequency Distribution, and of Data Used for Computing the Arithmetic Mean and Median

1	2	3	4	5	6	7	8
Class Interval (c.i.)	Tally Marks	Frequency (f)	Calculation of Percentage	Percentage	d	fd	Cumulative f
51–53	//	2	2/60 = .033	3	6	12	60
48–50	//	2	2/60 = .033	3	5	10	58
45–47	///	3	3/60 = .050	5	4	12	56
42–44	////	4	4/60 = .066	7	3	12	53
39–41	＋＋＋ /	6	6/60 = .100	10	2	12	49
36–38	＋＋＋ ////	9	9/60 = .150	15	1	9	43
33–35	＋＋＋ ////	9	9/60 = .150	15	0	0	34
30–32	＋＋＋ //	7	7/60 = .117	12	−1	−7	25
27–29	＋＋＋	5	5/60 = .083	8	−2	−10	18
24–26	////	4	4/60 = .066	7	−3	−12	13
21–23	////	4	4/60 = .066	7	−4	−16	9
18–20	//	2	2/60 = .033	3	−5	−10	5
15–17	//	2	2/60 = .033	3	−6	−12	3
12–14	/	1	1/60 = .017	2	−7	−7	1
		Total = 60		100		$\sum fd = -7$	

paratory to the construction of a frequency distribution are illustrated in the first column of Table 21.2.

4. Place a tally mark for each value in the original list of raw data opposite the appropriate class interval. As the first value among the sixty listed in Table 21.1 is 15, the first tally mark should be in the 15–17 c.i. The second value, 36, is represented by a tally mark in the 36–38 c.i. Usually it is advisable to tally the fifth entry in each c.i. with a line across the preceding four tally marks. When all the tallies have been made, they will appear as in column 2 of Table 21.2. Column 3 simply reflects the count of the tally marks for each.

In some circumstances it may be desirable to show the percentage of cases in each class interval instead of (or in addition to) the frequency. This may be done by dividing each f value (in the third column) by the total number of cases in the distribution. Each quotient thus obtained indicates the percentage of the total number of cases that fall in the respective c.i.'s. These computations are shown in column 4 of Table 21.2 and the computed percentages in column 5.

Frequency Polygon

A frequency polygon is a graphic representation of the frequency data—in this case, the data in column 3 of Table 21.2. In making a frequency polygon, first lay off appropriate units on cross-section or graph paper in such a manner that the midpoints of the c.i.'s can be plotted on the base line as shown in Figure 21.1 and the frequencies plotted on the vertical axis as shown by the left-hand vertical scale of that figure. Then actually place a dot representing each frequency and connect these dots in the

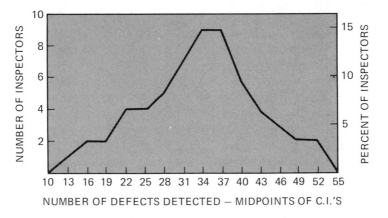

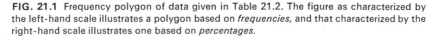

FIG. 21.1 Frequency polygon of data given in Table 21.2. The figure as characterized by the left-hand scale illustrates a polygon based on *frequencies,* and that characterized by the right-hand scale illustrates one based on *percentages.*

manner shown in the figure. When it is desirable to compare a frequency polygon with other polygons, it usually is desirable to plot the *percentages* (as given in column 5 of Table 21.2) rather than the actual *frequencies* (as shown in column 3). Such a polygon would have the same form as that based on frequencies, but the vertical scale would be shown as percentages, as illustrated by the right-hand vertical scale of that figure. In either form (whether based on frequencies or percentages), a frequency polygon gives a graphic impression of the data represented.

The Normal Distribution

The shape of the frequency polygon shown in Figure 21.1 is typical of the kind of distribution usually found when data obtained from a group of people are plotted. It will be noted that the curve is approximately "bell-shaped," that is, it is high in the center and tapers off toward the base line at both ends. If we were to divide the area under such a curve by drawing a perpendicular line from the central high point to the base line, the two parts would be approximately equal in area and would be bilaterally symmetrical in shape. It is well recognized that all, or nearly all, measurements of human traits and abilities result in distributions of approximately this form. Such distributions are called *normal distributions.* A strictly normal distribution conforms to a symmetrical bell-shaped curve that is defined by a mathematical equation, the basis of which is beyond the scope of the present discussion. It will suffice for the beginning student to know that:

1. A normal distribution is bell-shaped—that is, it is high in the center and low at both ends. Its two halves are symmetrical.
2. Measurements obtained from a group of persons usually approximate this type of distribution.

MEASURES OF CENTRAL TENDENCY

For some purposes it is desirable to have a single numerical value that "represents" a set of data. For such purposes a measure of central tendency is used. A measure of central tendency may be defined as a single figure or value that is representative of the entire set of data. Three such measures in common use are the *arithmetic mean,* the *median,* and the *mode.*

The Arithmetic Mean

The arithmetic mean, sometimes simply called the mean, may be defined as the sum of the measures divided by the number of measures. In the case of the sixty values previously discussed from which a frequency polygon was constructed, the mean is obtained by finding the total of the sixty measures and dividing this total by 60, thus:

$$\text{Arithmetic Mean } (A.M.) = \frac{\text{Sum of measures}}{N} = \frac{2016}{60} = 33.6$$

This is the procedure followed in computing the exact value of the arithmetic mean of any set of values. In practice, a shorter method of computation utilizing data as tabulated in a frequency distribution and yielding an approximation (rather than the exact value) of the mean is often used. This shorter method assumes that each score as tabulated in a frequency distribution has the same value as the midpoint of the c.i. in which it falls. For further convenience in calculation, the mean is first computed in c.i. units from an arbitrary base selected near the center of the distribution at the midpoint of one of the c.i.'s. The base selected is entirely arbitrary—it may be taken as any point in the distribution. We have chosen one near the center of the distribution to simplify computation.

If this method is used, columns such as 6 and 7 in Table 21.2 should be prepared. Column 6(d) represents the number of c.i. units that each c.i. is located above or below the c.i. that has been arbitrarily chosen as the base for the calculations. (For example, the c.i. 51–53, which has two scores, is 6 c.i. units above the arbitrary base.) The values in column 7(fd) are derived by multiplying for each class interval the f value by the d value. (For the 51–53 c.i. this value is 12, which is the product of the f of 2 multiplied by the d of 6.) The scores tabulated in c.i.'s below the arbitrary base are represented by negative values in the fd column. The arithmetic mean (A.M.) is computed with the following formula:

Formula for Computing A.M.

$A.M. = M° + c.i.(c)$

$M° =$ assumed mean

$c.i. =$ size of c.i.

$c = \dfrac{\Sigma fd}{N} =$ summation of deviations from assumed mean divided by N

$A.M. = 34 + 3 \left(\dfrac{-7}{60}\right) = 34 - .35 = 33.65$

In this formula the fd value is the algebraic sum of the values in the fd column (column 6). This sum divided by the number of cases indicates how far the computed mean will deviate from the assumed mean (base) in terms of c.i. units. From the tabulation, this deviation in c.i. units from the arbitrary base (assumed mean) is defined as:

$$\text{Deviation in c.i. units from base} = \frac{\Sigma fd}{N}$$

Carrying through this computation for the data under consideration shows that:

$$\text{Deviation in c.i. units from base} = \frac{\Sigma fd}{N} = \frac{-7}{60} = -.117$$

This is interpreted to mean that the *A.M.* is .117 of a class interval below the midpoint of the arbitrary base (see formula in illustrative problem). In order to transmute this deviation ($-.117$) into raw score units, we would multiply it by 3 (the size of the class interval). Thus, in terms of raw score units, the deviation is $-.35$. The mean, as computed by this method, is therefore .35 raw score units below the midpoint of the 33–35 c.i. As the midpoint of this is 34, the mean is $34 - .35 = 33.65$. This approximation does not agree exactly with the exact method in which all raw data are added and the sum is divided by the number of cases; but the approximation is sufficiently close to justify its use in many cases.

The Median

The median is a measure of central tendency defined as that score (or value) that exceeds, and is exceeded by, half the measures; that is, it is that point in the distribution above and below which 50 percent of the values lie. A logical (though laborious) method to determine the median consists in arranging all the raw data in rank order from lowest to highest and counting off the bottom half of the measures. The value at this point is the median. If this method is followed for the data in Table 21.1, the following arrangement of the scores is obtained:

53	45	41	38	36	34	32	29	26	21
51	44	40	38	36	34	31	29	25	20
49	43	39	37	35	33	31	28	24	19
48	42	39	37	35	33	30	28	23	16
47	42	39	37	35	33	30	27	22	15
46	41	38	36	34	32	30	26	21	13

Counting from the lowest score up, we find that the thirtieth from the low end is 34, and the thirty-first from the low end is also 34. The median score would therefore be 34. If there had been a difference between the thirtieth and the thirty-first scores, the median would be the value halfway between these scores. If an odd number of cases were included in the original set of scores (sixty-one instead of sixty), the median would be the value of the middle score.

In practice, the median as well as the mean may be conveniently approximated from a tabulated frequency distribution. This requires the preparation of a *cumulative f* column, shown as column 8 of Table 21.2. This column shows the cumulative frequencies by c.i., starting with the lowest c.i. The median value in this distribution is that value which separates the lower thirty from the upper thirty, which is within the c.i. of 33–35. There is a procedure for determining the specific value within this c.i. that characterizes the median, but that procedure will not be discussed here.

The Mode

A third measure of central tendency is the mode, which is defined as the measure appearing most frequently. This value, as well as the mean and the median, may be determined directly from the raw data (if one value appears more often than any other) or may be approximated from a frequency distribution of the data.

In computing the mode directly from the raw data, the values are inspected to determine which one appears most frequently. Sometimes, as in the case of the values shown in Table 21.1, several of the measures appear an equal number of times. In this case, each of the values 30, 33, 34, 35, 36, 37, 38, 39 appears three times. In such an instance an approximation of this value may be obtained from a frequency distribution by means of the following empirical formula:

$$\text{Mode} = 3(\text{Median}) - 2(\text{Mean})$$

In the case of the data we have been discussing, this formula gives the following value for the mode:

$$\text{Mode} = 3(34.2) - 2(33.65) = 35.30.$$

When to Use the Mean, Median, and Mode

Why is it necessary to have three different measures to indicate the central tendency of a set of data? The answer is that each is best adapted to certain uses; that is, in some cases one may be most representative of a set of data, while in other cases another measure may be most suitable. The mean is ordinarily used if the distribution is approximately normal. (If the distribution is perfectly normal, the three measures of central tendency have the same value.) If, on the other hand, there is a preponderance of extreme cases at either end of the distribution, the mean may give an incorrect impression of the central tendency of the data. Under these circumstances, the median or mode is more suitable. Consider, for example, the following monthly incomes of five persons:

$800 $900 $850 $750 $5,000

The mean for these five incomes is

$$\frac{\$800 + \$900 + \$850 + \$750 + \$5,000}{5} = \$1,660.$$

This figure, though an accurate statement of the mean, is not typical of the group as a whole because it is so markedly affected by the one income of $5,000. The median income is $850, and this value is more typical for the group as a whole than is the mean income of $1,660. We may generalize in the above illustration by saying that if a distribution is very much *skewed* (that is, contains more cases at one extreme than at the other), the median or mode is more likely to give a representative picture of the typical score than is the mean.

MEASURES OF VARIABILITY

In addition to a measure or value to represent the central tendency of a set of data, there is also quite frequently a need for some measure of the spread, or variability, of the data. The need for a measurement of this type may be seen by comparing the data shown in Table 21.1 (the mean of which, computed from the frequency distribution, was found to be 33.65) with another set of data that, for purposes of illustration, we might assume to consist of twenty-one scores of 33, and thirty-nine scores of 34, making sixty scores in all. The mean of sixty such scores may readily be found to be 33.65.

$$\frac{(21)(33) + (39)(34)}{60} = 33.65$$

While both distributions have the same mean, they differ markedly in variability or spread. The former distribution is made up of scores varying from 13 to 53, while the latter consists entirely of scores of 33 and 34. A quantitative measure of variability is therefore of considerable value. Statistical procedures have been designed that yield a single value descriptive of this variability; as in the cases of means and medians, these measures tell us something about the group as a whole.

The Standard Deviation

The standard deviation is the most widely used measure of variability. It is defined as the square root of the mean square deviation. Defined by formula:

$$\text{Standard Deviation} = S.D. = \sigma = \sqrt{\frac{\Sigma D^2}{N}}$$

where ΣD^2 is read "the sum of the squared deviation of the scores from their mean" and N is the number of cases. S.D. and σ are abbreviations for the standard deviation. They are used interchangeably.

Although the standard deviation may be computed directly from a set of raw data by means of the formula

$$S.D. = \sqrt{\frac{\Sigma D^2}{N}},$$

this process is laborious. For example, in the case of the set of data we have been using for illustrative purposes (tabulated in Table 21.1), we would proceed by determining the difference between each raw score and the mean of the sixty scores, squaring these differences, summing the sixty squared differences, dividing by 60, and extracting the square root of the quotient. The first score tabulated is 15. The difference between this value and the mean of the sixty scores (as computed directly from the raw data) is $D = 33.6 - 15.0 = 18.6$. D^2 would therefore be $(18.6)^2 = 345.96$. This process must be repeated for every one of the sixty scores before the sum of the squared deviations can be obtained.

Because of the excessive labor in computing the S.D. directly from the raw data, a simple process that approximates the true value of the S.D. has been developed. This is used in the computations shown in Table 21.3, in which is computed the standard deviation of the data shown previously in Table 21.2.

TABLE 21.3 COMPUTATION OF THE STANDARD DEVIATION FROM A FREQUENCY DISTRIBUTION*

c.i.	f	d	fd	fd²	
51–53	2	6	12	72	
48–50	2	5	10	50	
45–47	3	4	12	48	
42–44	4	3	12	36	
39–41	6	2	12	24	
36–38	9	1	9	9	$\text{Mean} = M° + c.i.\left(\frac{\Sigma fd}{N}\right)$
33–35	9	0	0	0	
30–32	7	−1	−7	7	$\text{Mean} = 34 + 3\left(\frac{-7}{60}\right) = 33.65$
27–29	5	−2	−10	20	
24–26	4	−3	−12	36	$S.D. = \sqrt{\frac{\Sigma D^2}{N}} = c.i.\sqrt{\frac{\Sigma fd^2}{N} - \left(\frac{\Sigma fd}{N}\right)^2}$
21–23	4	−4	−16	64	
18–20	2	−5	−10	50	$= 3\sqrt{537/60 - (.117)^2}$
15–17	2	−6	−12	72	$= 3\sqrt{8.950 - .014}$
12–14	1	−7	−7	49	$= 3\sqrt{8.936}$
					$= 3(2.99)$
Total = 60			$\Sigma fd = -7$	$\Sigma fd^2 = 537$	S.D. = 8.97

* The data used in this table are from Table 21.2.

The standard deviation is the most commonly used measure of variability. Usually when the mean value of a set of data is given, the S.D. is also given to indicate the variability of the data.

COMPARABLE SCORES

The S.D. performs another useful function—it can be used in comparing individual scores from different distributions. For example, suppose that two inspectors from departments A and B, who are working at different inspection jobs, detect respectively 45 and 89 defects during a week of work. How can we compare the efficiency of these two employees? It will be seen immediately that a direct comparison of the figures 45 and 89 is not valid, because the two inspection jobs may be very different. It will also be seen that we can say little concerning the position of these inspectors in their respective groups without knowing their relation to the mean of their group in inspection work. To make a comparison, then, we must first compute the mean number of defects spotted by all inspectors in Department A, and the mean number spotted by all inspectors in Department B. Suppose that those means are respectively 38 and 95. We thus see that the inspector from Department A is $45 - 38 = 7$ pieces *above* the mean for that department, and that the inspector from Department B is $89 - 95 = -6$, or 6 pieces *below* the mean of inspectors from that department. We can thus say, at this point, that the inspector from Department A is above average in ability on the job and that the inspector from Department B is below average. But how about their relative distance from the average? To answer this question we must compute the S.D.'s of the two distributions and determine how many S.D.'s each inspector is above or below average.

Suppose we find the S.D. of the operators in Department A to be 5.5 pieces. Our first inspector is therefore

$$\frac{45 - 38}{5.5} = 1.27 \text{ S.D.'s}$$

above average. If the S.D. of the inspectors in Department B is 9.5, the inspector from the group who detected 89 pieces is

$$\frac{89 - 95}{9.5} = -.63 \text{ or .63 S.D.'s}$$

below average. *The deviation of a score from the mean of the distribution expressed in S.D. units results in a measurement that is comparable with similarly determined measurements from other distributions.* Thus, we may say that our first inspector is about *twice* as far above average, in terms of comparable scale units, as the second operator is below average. Scores computed in this manner are known as *z*-scores. The formula for a *z*-score is as follows:

$$z\text{-score} = \frac{\text{Raw Score} - \text{Mean of Raw Scores}}{S.D. \text{ of Raw Scores}}$$

The *z*-score is helpful not only when comparing scores from one distribution to another but also when, for any reason, it is desired to combine scores with the same or differential weighting. A typical example of an industrial situation that requires this technique is in the combination of factors in a personnel evaluation system such as those illustrated in Chapter 8. Let us suppose, for purposes of illustration, that it is desired to combine the evaluations of each person on these two factors into an overall rating. (If more than two factors are included in the system, as is usually the case, the procedure is identical.) Suppose that an employee, Mr. A, has received 40 points on industriousness and 30 points on knowledge of job, making a total of 70 points if the ratings are added directly. Suppose that another employee, Mr. B, has received 30 points on industriousness and 40 points on knowledge of job, which also results in a total of 70 points if the ratings are added directly. It is clear that such direct and immediate combination of ratings would result in identical overall ratings for these two employees. The question we may raise is whether such a statement of equal ratings is justified. The answer is that it is not. If the mean rating of all employees on industriousness was 33 with a S.D. of 3, then A's rating would be

$$\frac{40 - 33}{3} = 2.33, \text{ or } 2.33 \text{ S.D.'s}$$

above the mean, and B's would be

$$\frac{30 - 33}{3} = -1.00, \text{ or } 1.00 \text{ S.D.}$$

below the mean on this trait. If the mean rating for all employees on knowledge of job were 25, with a S.D. of 6, A would be

$$\frac{30 - 25}{6} = +.83, \text{ or } .83 \text{ S.D.'s}$$

above average in knowledge of job while B would be

$$\frac{40 - 25}{6} = 2.50 \text{ or } 2.50 \text{ S.D.'s}$$

above average in this respect. Now, the proper combination of the two factors, if we wish to weight them equally, would be:

Employee	Rating in Industrious- ness	Rating in Knowledge of Job	z-Score in Indus- triousness	z-Score in Knowledge of Job	Sum of Scores for Both Units
A	40	30	+2.33	+.83	+3.16
B	30	40	−1.00	+2.50	+1.50

This transfer of ratings into z-scores and the adding of the z-scores show that the two employees A and B are not equal in rating (as we would infer if the raw ratings were added), but rather that A is definitely higher than B. The procedure described is based on the assumption that the two factors should receive equal weights, and shows how they can be combined with equal weight into a composite score. One might think that conversion of raw scores to z-scores is not necessary if the raw scores are to be given equal weight in the combination score. Actually, if we do not give the raw scores equal weight by converting them into z-scores, the scores will weight themselves according to the size of their respective standard deviations. In other words, if combined directly, the raw scores will be weighted too much or too little, depending upon their position relative to the means of their respective distributions and upon the variability of the distribution of which they are a part. When scores are combined, they are *always* weighted in some manner, whether we deliberately weight them or not. It is highly important, therefore, to weight them deliberately (either with equal weight or otherwise) by converting them into z-scores and then combining them.

It does not follow from the above discussion that combined scores should always be weighted equally. Indeed, it is often desirable to weight various scores according to some plan that has been decided upon before the scores are combined. When this is desired, such weighting can be accomplished very easily by multiplying each z-score by the appropriate weight before they are combined. In our illustrative case, suppose that we have decided that *industriousness* should be given twice as much weight as *knowledge of job* in determining the total rating. This would be accomplished as follows:

Employee	z-Score in Indus- triousness	z-Score in Knowledge of Job	Weighted z-Score in Indus- triousness	Weighted z-Score in Knowledge of Job	Combined Weighted z-Scores
A	+2.33	+.83	+4.66	+.83	+5.49
B	−1.00	+2.50	−2.00	+2.50	+.50

The combined ratings so obtained show a still greater difference between employees A and B than was obtained when the scores were equally weighted. If, on the other hand, it is desired to give the rating on *knowledge of job* twice as much weight as the rating on *industriousness,* the following computations would be made:

Employee	z-Score in Industriousness	z-Score in Knowledge of Job	Weighted z-Score in Industriousness	Weighted z-Score in Knowledge of Job	Combined Weighted z-Scores
A	+2.333	+.833	+2.333	+1.666	+4.0
B	−1.000	+2.500	−1.000	+5.000	+4.0

Essentially the same procedures can be followed when it is desired to combine other sets of data with specified weights, such as in combining various subcriteria, job evaluation factors, or test scores. As an example, in the selection of candidates for electrical apprentice training in one company it was desired to assign differential weights to four factors on the basis of the judged importance of these factors for apprentice training. These weights were as follows:

General intelligence	40%
Knowledge of electricity	30%
Merit rating	20%
Seniority or service with the company	10%

To score the candidates according to this plan, each was given a general intelligence test and a test covering technical phases of electricity. Merit ratings and seniority were obtained from the company records. Each of the four scores for each candidate was converted into a z-score and the four resulting z-scores were respectively multiplied by 40, 30, 20, and 10. For each candidate the sum of the weighted z-scores was used in indicating whether or not he was selected for apprenticeship training.

PERCENTILES

The discussion of comparable scores should have made clear the fact that a raw score on any test is relatively meaningless unless it is interpreted in terms of its location in a distribution of other scores made by other people. If a test consists of seventy-five very easy questions, a score of 65 might be near the bottom of the distribution and hence should be interpreted as a very low score. On the other hand, if a test consists of seventy-five very difficult questions, a score of 65 might be at or near the top of the distribution and should therefore be considered a very high score. In other words, a raw score of 65 might be a low score or a high score, depending upon the distribution of scores from which it is drawn.

One convenient and widely used method of interpreting a raw score is by using *percentile ranks*. A percentile rank may be defined as the number showing the percentage of the total group equal to or below the score in question. Thus, on a certain test, if 65 percent of the total group scored 129 or below, the score of 129 would be at the 65th percentile, or would have a percentile rank of 65. The 50th percentile, it will be noted, is the same as the median as previously defined.

A convenient, practical method of determining by close approximation the percentile equivalents of a set of raw scores makes use of a cumulative frequency distribution such as the one tabulated in Table 21.4. This tabulation is based on the same distribution previously used in Table 21.2.

The percent values in column 4 of Table 21.4, are obtained by dividing each of the values in the cumulative f column (column 3), by the total of column 2, in this instance 60. The percent values in column 4 are then plotted against the upper limits of the class intervals, as shown in Figure 21.2. From Figure 21.2 the percentile ranks of the raw scores may be read directly, with sufficient accuracy for most purposes.

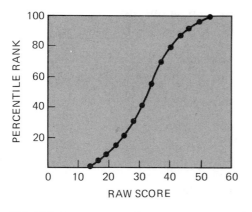

FIG. 21.2 Chart for converting raw scores into percentile ranks for illustrative data in Table 21.4.

The manual published with standardized tests usually includes percentile tables making possible the conversion of raw scores into percentile ranks. Because the percentile rank of a given raw score is dependent upon the nature of the group used in constructing the conversion table, several raw-score-to-percentile-rank conversion tables, based on different groups, are often published with standardized tests.

TABLE 21.4 CUMULATIVE FREQUENCY DISTRIBUTION USED IN DETERMINING PERCENTILE RANKS OF RAW SCORES

(1) Class Intervals	(2) f	(3) Cumulative f	(4) Percent
51–53	2	60	100
48–50	2	58	96
45–47	3	56	93
42–44	4	53	88
39–41	6	49	81
36–38	9	43	71
33–35	9	34	56
30–32	7	25	42
27–29	5	18	30
24–26	4	13	22
21–23	4	9	15
18–20	2	5	8
15–17	2	3	5
12–14	1	1	2
	Total = 60		

CORRELATION

In dealing with quantitative data about a sample from a population (such as a sample of people), there may be two items of data for each of the several cases that are so related that they vary, or tend to vary, with each other. An obvious example would be the height and weight of people —two variables that are somewhat related. A correlation is a statistical index of the degree of relationship between two such variables. A correlation can range from $+1.00$ (a perfect positive relationship) through to -1.00 (a perfect negative relationship). Graphic examples of correlations are shown in Figure 21.3.

For illustrative purposes in discussing correlations, let us use data for eight punch-press operators for whom we have two items of data, as follows: (1) production for a given period of time; and (2) pounds of waste (material that has been wasted by mispunching or otherwise). Following are these data for the eight operators:

Operator	Production	Waste
1	95	3.0
2	103	4.5
3	88	3.5
4	98	4.0
5	93	3.0
6	107	4.5
7	114	4.0
8	106	5.0

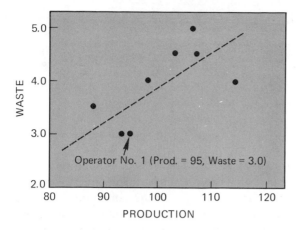

FIG. 21.3 A plot of the production and waste records for the eight punch-press operators shown above.

A graphic representation of these data can be presented as in Figure 21.3. This is done by plotting the values on coordinate axes, with one variable (production) being represented on the x or horizontal axis, and the other (waste) on the y or vertical axis. Such a representation gives a better indication of the relationship between the two variables than the data in the columns above, and it is even possible to draw in by inspection a line or curve that represents this relationship in an approximate form.

Although this simple method of studying the relationship between two variables is sometimes adequate for very simple problems or for those that involve only a small amount of data, it is not adequate for an exact study because it does not result in a quantitative statement of the degree of relationship. The slope of the dotted line cannot be considered such a quantitative statement because: (1) this line is drawn in by inspection, and (2) its slope depends upon the units of measurement on both the x and y axes. Two commonly used quantitative methods for measuring the degree of relationship between two paired sets of data are rank-order correlation and product-moment correlation.

Rank-Order Correlation

The use of this method may be described by applying it to the data for the eight punch-press operators.

In Table 21.5 the two columns headed *Rank* give, respectively, the rank of the operators on the two measures (production and waste). The highest producing operator (in this case the seventh in the list) is given a rank of 1, the second highest a rank of 2, and so on. In like manner, the rank of each operator in wastage is placed in the waste-rank column. In case two or more operators are tied for a given rank (as in the case of the second and sixth operators, who are tied at 4.5 pounds of waste each), the tied scores are all given the same rank, which is the average of the ranks that would have been assigned to the tied scores if they had not been tied. The values in the D^2 column are obtained by squaring each D value. The sum of the D^2 column is determined and the correlation computed by means of the formula:

$$\text{Rho} = 1 - \frac{6\Sigma D^2}{N(N^2 - 1)}$$

where N is the number of cases entering into the computation.

This formula for the rank-order correlation is an empirical formula. It yields a value of $+1.00$ if the data are in exactly the same rank order. (The reason for this may be seen from the fact that if all ranks are the same, all D's are zero, all D^2 values are zero, ΣD^2 is zero, and the formula becomes $1 - 0 = 1$.) If the data are in exactly reverse order (that is, if the individual who ranks highest on one series is lowest on the other, and so on), the formula will yield a value of -1.00, but if no relationship exists between the two sets of data, a correlation of zero will be found.

If an appreciable number of cases are involved, however, the rank-order method of computing the degree of relationship is extremely laborious. For this reason—and for other reasons of a mathematical nature—it ordinarily is used only when the data are limited to a very few cases (less than thirty).

The Product-Moment Coefficient

This is the most widely used measure of relationship. Like the rank-order correlation, it may vary from $+1.00$ (indicating perfect positive relationship) through zero (indicating no relationship) to -1.00 (indi-

TABLE 21.5 COMPUTATION OF RANK-ORDER CORRELATION

Operator	Production	Waste	Rank in Production	Rank in Waste	Difference in Rank (D)	(D)²
1	95	3.0	6	7.5	1.5	2.25
2	103	4.5	4	2.5	1.5	2.25
3	88	3.5	8	6.0	2.0	4.00
4	98	4.0	5	4.5	.5	.25
5	93	3.0	7	7.5	.5	.25
6	107	4.5	2	2.5	.5	.25
7	114	4.0	1	2.5	3.5	12.25
8	106	5.0	3	1.0	2.0	4.00
						25.50

$$\text{Rho} = 1 - \frac{6\Sigma D^2}{N(N^2 - 1)} = 1 - \frac{153}{504} = .70$$

cating perfect negative relationship). The product-moment correlation, represented by the symbol r, may be defined in several ways. One of the simplest definitions is that r *is the slope of the straight line that best fits the data after the data have been plotted as z-scores on co-ordinate axes;* that is, it is the tangent of the angle made by this line with the base line.

Several terms in this definition require further definition. By *slope* is meant steepness with which the line rises. The slope of a straight line drawn in any manner across co-ordinate paper is defined as the distance, y, from any given point on the line to the x intercept, minus the distance, a, from the origin to the y intercept, divided by the distance, x, from the point on the line to y intercept. Thus the slope, which we will call b, is defined in Figure 21.4 as follows:

$$b = \frac{y - a}{x}$$

It should be remembered that, on co-ordinate axes, distances above and to the right of the origin are positive, while distances measured below and/or to the left of the origin are negative. The slope of any line that *rises* as it goes from left to right will therefore be positive (the greater the rise in a given distance to the right, the larger the positive value of the slope), and the slope of any line that *falls* as it goes from left to right will be negative (the greater the fall in a given distance to the right, the greater the negative value of the slope).

By line of *best fit* in the definition is meant a line so drawn that the sum of the squared deviations in a vertical direction from the original points to the line is less than the sum would be for any other straight line that might be drawn.

A rough approximation of the value of r may be obtained by plotting the z-scores of the two variables, fitting a straight line to these points by inspection, and graphically measuring the slope of this straight line. Although this method is never used in practical computation (because it is both inaccurate and laborious), the application of it to a set of represen-

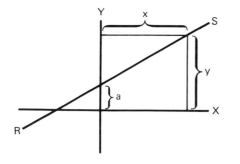

FIG. 21.4 The slope of the line RS is defined as $b = \frac{y - a}{x}$.

tative data may serve to clarify the meaning of the correlation coefficient, r. Returning to the data for which we have previously computed the rank-order correlation (see Table 21.5), we first compute the z-scores for each measure as shown in Table 21.6.

These pairs of z-scores are used as the x and y values for eight points that are plotted on co-ordinate axes as in Figure 21.5. The straight line that seems best to fit these points is then determined (as with a stretched string that is moved about until the desired location is obtained) and drawn on the graph. The correlation, r, as determined by this crude method, is obtained by measuring the slope of this line. The procedure applied to Figure 21.5 gives a value of $r = .61$, but it should be emphasized that this value is affected by:

1. The accuracy with which the straight line has been located, and
2. The accuracy with which the slope of the line has been measured after it has been drawn.

TABLE 21.6 PRODUCTION AND WASTE FOR EIGHT PUNCH-PRESS OPERATORS WITH CORRESPONDING z-SCORES OF THE PRODUCTION AND WASTE FIGURES

Operator	Production	Waste	z-Score in Production	z-Score in Waste
1	95	3.0	−.69	−1.38
2	103	4.5	+.31	+.82
3	88	3.5	−1.56	−.65
4	98	4.0	−.31	+.09
5	93	3.0	−.94	−1.38
6	107	4.5	+.81	+.82
7	114	4.0	+1.69	+.09
8	106	5.0	+.69	+1.56
Mean	100.5	3.94		
S.D.	8.0	.68		

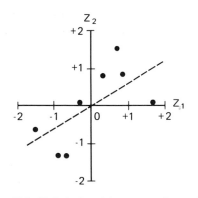

FIG. 21.5 A plot of the z-scores for production and waste records of the eight punch-press operators shown above.

Points 1 and 2 both operate to eliminate the possibility of complete accuracy in this method of determining a correlation coefficient. Therefore, a mathematical method has been devised to make the computation, so that no plotting of points or graphic measurements are required. This method involves determining the equation of the straight line that, if plotted, would best fit the points, and computing the slope of this straight line of best fit from the equation.

It may be proved mathematically that the slope of the straight line of best fit is given by the following equation:

$$\text{Slope} = r = \frac{\Sigma Z_x Z_y}{N},$$

where $\Sigma Z_x Z_y$ is read "the sum of the products of the z-scores for the pairs of points or values."

Applying the formula to the data in Table 21.6, we may compute the correlation as in Table 21.7. The value of r thus obtained by computation, .67, differs from the value of .61 obtained by plotting and inspection. The plotting and inspection method yielded a value that was somewhat in error for the data in question.

While the z-score method of computing a correlation coefficient illustrated in Table 21.7 may be used with any number of cases and will yield the correct mathematical value of r, the use of this method when many pairs of data are to be correlated is very laborious. It is therefore recommended, under such circumstances, that a modification of the fundamental formula

$$r = \frac{\Sigma Z_x Z_y}{N},$$

which makes it possible to compute r from raw score values rather than z-score values, be used. One convenient formula for determining the coefficient of correlation directly from the raw data is:

$$r = \frac{N\Sigma XY - \Sigma X\Sigma Y}{\sqrt{N\Sigma X^2 - (\Sigma X)^2}\sqrt{N\Sigma Y^2 - (\Sigma Y^2)}}$$

When we apply this formula, for illustrative purposes, to the data tabulated in Table 21.7, the computations shown in Table 21.8 result.

When a considerable number of pairs of data are to be correlated, the use of a chart will still further simplify the computations. Several forms of such a chart have been prepared. One convenient form is shown in Figure 21.6. This chart shows the computation of the correlation between time used in inspecting three hundred pieces of material and the number

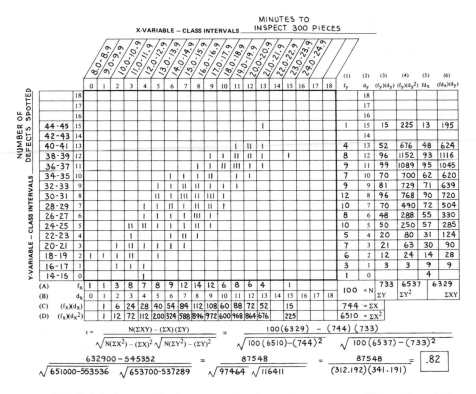

FIG. 21.6 A chart used in the computation of a product moment coefficient of correlation.

of defective pieces detected. In using this chart the following steps should be followed:

1. Decide upon appropriate class intervals for one of the variables (using the rules given on p. 572) and write these in on either the x or the y axis.

2. Decide upon appropriate class intervals for the other variable and write these in on the axis not used in (1) above.

3. Place 1 tally mark on the scattergram for each pair of values being correlated. For example, if an inspector spotted 33 defects in 16.5 minutes, the tally mark would go in the cell that is found at the intersection of the *row* containing 33 defects and the *column* containing 16.5 minutes.

4. After all tally marks have been placed on the chart, the rows should be added horizontally and the sum of the tally marks in each row written opposite this row in the f_y column (Column *1*).

5. The tally marks in each column should be added and the sum written at the bottom of each column in the row (A), the f_x row.

6. The f_y column should be added and the sum written opposite N at the bottom of this column. *The value of N thus obtained may be checked by adding the values in the f_x row. The sum of these values should also give the value of N.*

TABLE 21.7   COMPUTATION OF r BY z-SCORE METHOD BETWEEN PRODUCTION AND WASTE FIGURES

Operator	Production	Waste	z-Score in Production	z-Score in Waste	$(z_1 z_2)$
1	95	3.0	−.69	−1.38	+.95
2	103	4.5	+.31	+.82	+.25
3	88	3.5	−1.56	−.65	+1.01
4	98	4.0	−.31	+.09	−.03
5	93	3.0	−.94	−1.38	+1.30
6	107	4.5	+.81	+.82	+.66
7	114	4.0	+1.69	+.09	+.15
8	106	5.0	+.69	+1.56	+1.08
					+5.38

$$r = \frac{Z_x Z_y}{N} = \frac{+5.38}{8} = .67$$

TABLE 21.8   COMPUTATION OF r DIRECTLY FROM RAW DATA

Operator	Production (X)	Waste (Y)	X^2	Y^2	XY
1	95	3.0	9,025	9.00	285.0
2	103	4.5	10,609	20.25	463.5
3	88	3.5	7,744	12.25	308.0
4	98	4.0	9,604	16.00	392.0
5	93	3.0	8,649	9.00	279.0
6	107	4.5	11,449	20.25	481.5
7	114	4.0	12,996	16.00	456.0
8	106	5.0	11,236	25.00	530.0
	$\Sigma X = 804$	$\Sigma Y = 31.5$	$\Sigma X^2 = 81,312$	$\Sigma Y^2 = 127.75$	$\Sigma XY = 3,195.0$

$$r = \frac{N\Sigma XY - \Sigma X \Sigma Y}{\sqrt{N\Sigma X^2 - (\Sigma X)^2}\ \sqrt{N\Sigma Y^2 - (\Sigma Y)^2}}$$

$$r = \frac{8(3,195) - (804)(31.5)}{\sqrt{8(81,312) - (804)^2}\ \sqrt{8(127.75) - (31.5)^2}}$$

$$r = .67$$

7. Each value of f_y in the column so headed should be multiplied by the value of d_y opposite it, and the resultant product written in Column 3, headed $f_y d_y$. *The sum of Column 3 is the value of ΣY which is used in the formula.*

8. Each value in Column 3, the $f_y d_y$ column, should be multiplied by the corresponding value in Column 2, the d_y column, resulting in the values for Column 4, or the $f_y d_y^2$ column. *The sum of Column 4 is the value of ΣY^2 which is used in the formula.*

9. The values going into Column 5, the fd_x column, are determined by finding, for each row, the sum of the products of the number of cases in each cell times the x value of that cell. For example, in the first row in which a tally mark appears, there is only a single case, which appears in the cell under an x value of 13. The value to go into the blank in Column 5 is therefore

$(1)(13) = 13$. In the next row no tally marks appear; therefore, this row is blank. In the next row, 1 tally mark appears in the cell under an x value of 11, 2 in the cell with an x value of 12, and 1 in the cell with an x value of 13. The value to go into the blank cell in Column 5 is therefore $(1)(11) + (2)(12) + (1)(13) = 48$. The remaining cells in Column 5 are filled in a similar manner.

10. The cells in Column 6, the $fd_x d_y$ column, are filled with values obtained by multiplying each value in Column 2, the d_y column, by the value in that same row appearing in Column 5, the fd_x column. The value in the first cell in Column 6 is therefore $(15)(13) = 195$. *The sum of Column 6 is the value of ΣXY which is used in the formula.*

11. The values in row C are obtained by multiplying each value in row A, the f_x row, by the value directly below it in row B, the d_x row. The values appearing in row A have already been obtained (see Step 5 above). The resultant values are entered in row C, the $f_x d_x$ row. *The sum of the values appearing in row C is the value of ΣX which is used in the formula.*

12. Each value in row B, the d_x row, should be multiplied by the value directly below in row C, the $f_x d_x$ row. The resultant values should be entered in row D, the $f_x d_x^2$ row. *The sum of the values in row D is the value of ΣX^2 which is used in the formula.*

13. The value for N (see Step 6), ΣY (see Step 7), ΣY^2 (see Step 8), ΣXY (see Step 10), ΣX (see Step 11), and ΣX^2 (se Step 12) are now entered in the formula. The indicated arithmetic computations are then performed, yielding the value of r.

The use of this method assumes that each measure has the value of the midpoint of the class interval in which it falls. The computations indicated on the chart result in obtaining not only the value for r but also the mean and the standard deviations of both the X and Y arrays.

appendix B

Taylor-Russell Tables[1]
(For Institutional Prediction)

Tables of the Proportion who will be Satisfactory
among those Selected for Given Values of the
Proportion of Present Employees Considered
Satisfactory, the Selection Ratio, and r

PROPORTION OF EMPLOYEES CONSIDERED SATISFACTORY = .05

SELECTION RATIO

r	.05	.10	.20	.30	.40	.50	.60	.70	.80	.90	.95
.00	.05	.05	.05	.05	.05	.05	.05	.05	.05	.05	.05
.05	.06	.06	.06	.06	.06	.05	.05	.05	.05	.05	.05
.10	.07	.07	.07	.06	.06	.06	.06	.05	.05	.05	.05
.15	.09	.08	.07	.07	.07	.06	.06	.06	.05	.05	.05
.20	.11	.09	.08	.08	.07	.07	.06	.06	.06	.05	.05
.25	.12	.11	.09	.08	.08	.07	.07	.06	.06	.05	.05
.30	.14	.12	.10	.09	.08	.07	.07	.06	.06	.05	.05
.35	.17	.14	.11	.10	.09	.08	.07	.06	.06	.05	.05
.40	.19	.16	.12	.10	.09	.08	.07	.07	.06	.05	.05
.45	.22	.17	.13	.11	.10	.08	.08	.07	.06	.06	.05
.50	.24	.19	.15	.12	.10	.09	.08	.07	.06	.06	.05
.55	.28	.22	.16	.13	.11	.09	.08	.07	.06	.06	.05
.60	.31	.24	.17	.13	.11	.09	.08	.07	.06	.06	.05
.65	.35	.26	.18	.14	.11	.10	.08	.07	.06	.06	.05
.70	.39	.29	.20	.15	.12	.10	.08	.07	.06	.06	.05
.75	.44	.32	.21	.15	.12	.10	.08	.07	.06	.06	.05
.80	.50	.35	.22	.16	.12	.10	.08	.07	.06	.06	.05
.85	.56	.39	.23	.16	.12	.10	.08	.07	.06	.06	.05
.90	.64	.43	.24	.17	.13	.10	.08	.07	.06	.06	.05
.95	.73	.47	.25	.17	.13	.10	.08	.07	.06	.06	.05
1.00	1.00	.50	.25	.17	.13	.10	.08	.07	.06	.06	.05

[1] SOURCE: Taylor, H. C. & Russell, J. T., The relationship of validity coefficients to the practical effectiveness of tests in selection: Discussion and tables. *Journal of Applied Psychology*, 1939, **23**, 565–578.

PROPORTION OF EMPLOYEES CONSIDERED SATISFACTORY = .10
SELECTION RATIO

r	.05	.10	.20	.30	.40	.50	.60	.70	.80	.90	.95
.00	.10	.10	.10	.10	.10	.10	.10	.10	.10	.10	.10
.05	.12	.12	.11	.11	.11	.11	.11	.10	.10	.10	.10
.10	.14	.13	.13	.12	.12	.11	.11	.11	.11	.10	.10
.15	.16	.15	.14	.13	.13	.12	.12	.11	.11	.10	.10
.20	.19	.17	.15	.14	.14	.13	.12	.12	.11	.11	.10
.25	.22	.19	.17	.16	.14	.13	.12	.11	.11	.11	.10
.30	.25	.22	.19	.17	.15	.14	.13	.12	.12	.11	.10
.35	.28	.24	.20	.18	.16	.15	.14	.13	.12	.11	.10
.40	.31	.27	.22	.19	.17	.16	.14	.13	.12	.11	.10
.45	.35	.29	.24	.20	.18	.16	.15	.13	.12	.11	.10
.50	.39	.32	.26	.22	.19	.17	.15	.13	.12	.11	.11
.55	.43	.36	.28	.23	.20	.17	.15	.14	.12	.11	.11
.60	.48	.39	.30	.25	.21	.18	.16	.14	.12	.11	.11
.65	.53	.43	.32	.26	.22	.18	.16	.14	.12	.11	.11
.70	.58	47	.35	.27	.22	.19	.16	.14	.12	.11	.11
.75	.64	.51	.37	.29	.23	.19	.16	.14	.12	.11	.11
.80	.71	.56	.40	.30	.24	.20	.17	.14	.12	.11	.11
.85	.78	.62	.43	.31	.25	.20	.17	.14	.12	.11	.11
.90	.86	.69	.46	.33	.25	.20	.17	.14	.12	.11	.11
.95	.95	.78	.49	.33	.25	.20	.17	14	.12	.11	.11
1.00	1.00	1.00	.50	.33	.25	.20	.17	.14	.13	.11	.11

PROPORTION OF EMPLOYEES CONSIDERED SATISFACTORY = .20
SELECTION RATIO

r	.05	.10	.20	.30	.40	.50	.60	.70	.80	.90	.95
.00	.20	.20	.20	.20	.20	.20	.20	.20	.20	.20	.20
.05	.23	.23	.22	.22	.21	.21	.21	.21	.20	.20	.20
.10	.26	.25	.24	.23	.23	.22	.22	.21	.21	.21	.20
.15	.30	.28	.26	.25	.24	.23	.23	.22	.21	.21	.20
.20	.33	.31	.28	.27	.26	.25	.24	.23	.22	.21	.21
.25	.37	.34	.31	.29	.27	.26	.24	.23	.22	.21	.21
.30	.41	.37	.33	.30	.28	.27	.25	.24	.23	.21	.21
.35	.45	.41	.36	.32	.30	.28	.26	.24	.23	.22	.21
.40	.49	.44	.38	.34	.31	.29	.27	.25	.23	.22	.21
.45	.54	.48	.41	.36	.33	.30	.28	.26	.24	.22	.21
.50	.59	.52	.44	.38	.35	.31	.29	.26	.24	.22	.21
.55	.63	.56	.47	.41	.36	.32	.29	.27	.24	.22	.21
.60	.68	.60	.50	.43	.38	.34	.30	.27	.24	.22	.21
.65	.73	.64	.53	.45	.39	.35	.31	.27	.25	.22	.21
.70	.79	.69	.56	.48	.41	.36	.31	.28	.25	.22	.21
.75	.84	.74	.60	.50	.43	.37	.32	.28	.25	.22	.21
.80	.89	.79	.64	.53	.45	.38	.33	.28	.25	.22	.21
.85	.94	.85	.69	.56	.47	.39	.33	.28	.25	.22	.21
.90	.98	.91	.75	.60	.48	.40	.33	.29	.25	.22	.21
.95	1.00	.97	.82	.64	.50	.40	.33	.29	.25	.22	.21
1.00	1.00	1.00	1.00	.67	.50	.40	.33	.29	.25	.22	.21

PROPORTION OF EMPLOYEES CONSIDERED SATISFACTORY = .30
SELECTION RATIO

r	.05	.10	.20	.30	.40	.50	.60	.70	.80	.90	.95
.00	.30	.30	.30	.30	.30	.30	.30	.30	.30	.30	.30
.05	.34	.33	.33	.32	.32	.31	.31	.31	.31	.30	.30
.10	.38	.36	.35	.34	.33	.33	.32	.32	.31	.31	.30
.15	.42	.40	.38	.36	.35	.34	.33	.33	.32	.31	.31
.20	.46	.43	.40	.38	.37	.36	.34	.33	.32	.31	.31
.25	.50	.47	.43	.41	.39	.37	.36	.34	.33	.32	.31
.30	.54	.50	.46	.43	.40	.38	.37	.35	.33	.32	.31
.35	.58	.54	.49	.45	.42	.40	.38	.36	.34	.32	.31
.40	.63	.58	.51	.47	.44	.41	.39	.37	.34	.32	.31
.45	.67	.61	.55	.50	.46	.43	.40	.37	.35	.32	.31
.50	.72	.65	.58	.52	.48	.44	.41	.38	.35	.33	.31
.55	.76	.69	.61	.55	.50	.46	.42	.39	.36	.33	.31
.60	.81	.74	.64	.58	.52	.47	.43	.40	.36	.33	.31
.65	.85	.78	.68	.60	.54	.49	.44	.40	.37	.33	.32
.70	.89	.82	.72	.63	.57	.51	.46	.41	.37	.33	.32
.75	.93	.86	.76	.67	.59	.52	.47	.42	.37	.33	.32
.80	.96	.90	.80	.70	.62	.54	.48	.42	.37	.33	.32
.85	.99	.94	.85	.74	.65	.56	.49	.43	.37	.33	.32
.90	1.00	.98	90	.79	.68	.58	.49	.43	.37	.33	.32
.95	1.00	1.00	.96	.85	.72	.60	.50	.43	.37	.33	.32
1.00	1.00	1.00	1.00	1.00	.75	.60	.50	.43	.38	.33	.32

PROPORTION OF EMPLOYEES CONSIDERED SATISFACTORY = .40
SELECTION RATIO

r	.05	.10	.20	.30	.40	.50	.60	.70	.80	.90	.95
.00	.40	.40	.40	.40	.40	.40	.40	.40	.40	.40	.40
.05	.44	.43	.43	.42	.42	.42	.41	.41	.41	.40	.40
.10	.48	.47	.46	.45	.44	.43	.42	.42	.41	.41	.40
.15	.52	.50	.48	.47	.46	.45	.44	.43	.42	.41	.41
.20	.57	.54	.51	.49	.48	.46	.45	.44	.43	.41	.41
.25	.61	.58	.54	.51	.49	.48	.46	.45	.43	.42	.41
.30	.65	.61	.57	.54	.51	.49	.47	.46	.44	.42	.41
.35	.69	.65	.60	.56	.53	.51	.49	.47	.45	.42	.41
.40	.73	.69	.63	.59	.56	.53	.50	.48	.45	.43	.41
.45	.77	.72	.66	.61	.58	.54	.51	.49	.46	.43	.42
.50	.81	.76	.69	.64	.60	.56	.53	.49	.46	.43	.42
.55	.85	.79	.72	.67	.62	.58	.54	.50	.47	.44	.42
.60	.89	.83	.75	.69	.64	.60	.55	.51	.48	.44	.42
.65	.92	.87	.79	.72	.67	.62	.57	.52	.48	.44	.42
.70	.95	.90	.82	.76	.69	.64	.58	.53	.49	.44	.42
.75	.97	.93	.86	.79	.72	.66	.60	.54	.49	.44	.42
.80	.99	.96	.89	.82	.75	.68	.61	.55	.49	.44	.42
.85	1.00	.98	.93	.86	.79	.71	.63	.56	.50	.44	.42
.90	1.00	1.00	.97	.91	.82	.74	.65	.57	.50	.44	.42
.95	1.00	1.00	.99	.96	.87	.77	.66	.57	.50	.44	.42
1.00	1.00	1.00	1.00	1.00	1.00	.80	.67	.57	.50	.44	.42

PROPORTION OF EMPLOYEES CONSIDERED SATISFACTORY = .50
SELECTION RATIO

r	.05	.10	.20	.30	.40	.50	.60	.70	.80	.90	.95
.00	.50	.50	.50	.50	.50	.50	.50	.50	.50	.50	.50
.05	.54	.54	.53	.52	.52	.52	.51	.51	.51	.50	.50
.10	.58	.57	.56	.55	.54	.53	.53	.52	.51	.51	.50
.15	.63	.61	.58	.57	.56	.55	.54	.53	.52	.51	.51
.20	.67	.64	.61	.59	.58	.56	.55	.54	.53	.52	.51
.25	.70	.67	.64	.62	.60	.58	.56	.55	.54	.52	.51
.30	.74	.71	.67	.64	.62	.60	.58	.56	.54	.52	.51
.35	.78	.74	.70	.66	.64	.61	.59	.57	.55	.53	.51
.40	.82	.78	.73	.69	.66	.63	.61	.58	.56	.53	.52
.45	.85	.81	.75	.71	.68	.65	.62	.59	.56	.53	.52
.50	.88	.84	.78	.74	.70	.67	.63	.60	.57	.54	.52
.55	.91	.87	.81	.76	.72	.69	.65	.61	.58	.54	.52
.60	.94	.90	.84	.79	.75	.70	.66	.62	.59	.54	.52
.65	.96	.92	.87	.82	.77	.73	.68	.64	.59	.55	.52
.70	.98	.95	.90	.85	.80	.75	.70	.65	.60	.55	.53
.75	.99	.97	.92	.87	.82	.77	.72	.66	.61	.55	.53
.80	1.00	.99	.95	.90	.85	.80	.73	.67	.61	.55	.53
.85	1.00	.99	.97	.94	.88	.82	.76	.69	.62	.55	.53
.90	1.00	1.00	.99	.97	.92	.86	.78	.70	.62	.56	.53
.95	1.00	1.00	1.00	.99	.96	.90	.81	.71	.63	.56	.53
1.00	1.00	1.00	1.00	1.00	1.00	1.00	.83	.71	.63	.56	.53

PROPORTION OF EMPLOYEES CONSIDERED SATISFACTORY = .60
SELECTION RATIO

r	.05	.10	.20	.30	.40	.50	.60	.70	.80	.90	.95
.00	.60	.60	.60	.60	.60	.60	.60	.60	.60	.60	.60
.05	.64	.63	.63	.62	.62	.62	.61	.61	.61	.60	.60
.10	.68	.67	.65	.64	.64	.63	.63	.62	.61	.61	.60
.15	.71	.70	.68	.67	.66	.65	.64	.63	.62	.61	.61
.20	.75	.73	.71	.69	.67	.66	.65	.64	.63	.62	.61
.25	.78	.76	.73	.71	.69	.68	.66	.65	.63	.62	.61
.30	.82	.79	.76	.73	.71	.69	.68	.66	.64	.62	.61
.35	.85	.82	.78	.75	.73	.71	.69	.67	.65	.63	.62
.40	.88	.85	.81	.78	.75	.73	.70	.68	.66	.63	.62
.45	.90	.87	.83	.80	.77	.74	.72	.69	.66	.64	.62
.50	.93	.90	.86	.82	.79	.76	.73	.70	.67	.64	.62
.55	.95	.92	.88	.84	.81	.78	.75	.71	.68	.64	.62
.60	.96	.94	.90	.87	.83	.80	.76	.73	.69	.65	.63
.65	.98	.96	.92	.89	.85	.82	.78	.74	.70	.65	.63
.70	.99	.97	.94	.91	.87	.84	.80	.75	.71	.66	.63
.75	.99	.99	.96	.93	.90	.86	.81	.77	.71	.66	.63
.80	1.00	.99	.98	.95	.92	.88	.83	.78	.72	.66	.63
.85	1.00	1.00	.99	.97	.95	.91	.86	.80	.73	.66	.63
.90	1.00	1.00	1.00	.99	.97	.94	.88	.82	.74	.67	.63
.95	1.00	1.00	1.00	1.00	.99	.97	.92	.84	.75	.67	.63
1.00	1.00	1.00	1.00	1.00	1.00	1.00	1.00	.86	.75	.67	.63

PROPORTION OF EMPLOYEES CONSIDERED SATISFACTORY = .70
SELECTION RATIO

r	.05	.10	.20	.30	.40	.50	.60	.70	.80	.90	.95
.00	.70	.70	.70	.70	.70	.70	.70	.70	.70	.70	.70
.05	.73	.73	.72	.72	.72	.71	.71	.71	.71	.70	.70
.10	.77	.76	.75	.74	.73	.73	.72	.72	.71	.71	.70
.15	.80	.79	.77	.76	.75	.74	.73	.73	.72	.71	.71
.20	.83	.81	.79	.78	.77	.76	.75	.74	.73	.71	.71
.25	.86	.84	.81	.80	.78	.77	.76	.75	.73	.72	.71
.30	.88	.86	.84	.82	.80	.78	.77	.75	.74	.72	.71
.35	.91	.89	.86	.83	.82	.80	.78	.76	.75	.73	.71
.40	.93	.91	.88	.85	.83	.81	.79	.77	.75	.73	.72
.45	.94	.93	.90	.87	.85	.83	.81	.78	.76	.73	.72
.50	.96	.94	.91	.89	.87	.84	.82	.80	.77	.74	.72
.55	.97	.96	.93	.91	.88	.86	.83	.81	.78	.74	.72
.60	.98	.97	.95	.92	.90	.87	.85	.82	.79	.75	.73
.65	.99	.98	.96	.94	.92	.89	.86	.83	.80	.75	.73
.70	1.00	.99	.97	.96	.93	.91	.88	.84	.80	.76	.73
.75	1.00	1.00	.98	.97	.95	.92	.89	.86	.81	.76	.73
.80	1.00	1.00	.99	.98	.97	.94	.91	.87	.82	.77	.73
.85	1.00	1.00	1.00	.99	.98	.96	.93	.89	.84	.77	.74
.90	1.00	1.00	1.00	1.00	.99	.98	.95	.91	.85	.78	.74
.95	1.00	1.00	1.00	1.00	1.00	.99	.98	.94	.86	.78	.74
1.00	1.00	1.00	1.00	1.00	1.00	1.00	1.00	1.00	.88	.78	.74

PROPORTION OF EMPLOYEES CONSIDERED SATISFACTORY = .80
SELECTION RATIO

r	.05	.10	.20	.30	.40	.50	.60	.70	.80	.90	.95
.00	.80	.80	.80	.80	.80	.80	.80	.80	.80	.80	.80
.05	.83	.82	.82	.82	.81	.81	.81	.81	.81	.80	.80
.10	.85	.85	.84	.83	.83	.82	.82	.81	.81	.81	.80
.15	.88	.87	.86	.85	.84	.83	.83	.82	.82	.81	.81
.20	.90	.89	.87	.86	.85	.84	.84	.83	.82	.81	.81
.25	.92	.91	.89	.88	.87	.86	.85	.84	.83	.82	.81
.30	.94	.92	.90	.89	.88	.87	.86	.84	.83	.82	.81
.35	.95	.94	.92	.90	.89	.89	.87	.85	.84	.82	.81
.40	.96	.95	.93	.92	.90	.89	.88	.86	.85	.83	.82
.45	.97	.96	.95	.93	.92	.90	.89	.87	.85	.83	.82
.50	.98	.97	.96	.94	.93	.91	.90	.88	.86	.84	.82
.55	.99	.98	.97	.95	.94	.92	.91	.89	.87	.84	.82
.60	.99	.99	.98	.96	.95	.94	.92	.90	.87	.84	.83
.65	1.00	.99	.98	.97	.96	.95	.93	.91	.88	.85	.83
.70	1.00	1.00	.99	.98	.97	.96	.94	.92	.89	.85	.83
.75	1.00	1.00	1.00	.99	.98	.97	.95	.93	.90	.86	.83
.80	1.00	1.00	1.00	1.00	.99	.98	.96	.94	.91	.87	.84
.85	1.00	1.00	1.00	1.00	1.00	.99	.98	.96	.92	.87	.84
.90	1.00	1.00	1.00	1.00	1.00	1.00	.99	.97	.94	.88	.84
.95	1.00	1.00	1.00	1.00	1.00	1.00	1.00	.99	.96	.89	.84
1.00	1.00	1.00	1.00	1.00	1.00	1.00	1.00	1.00	.89	.84

PROPORTION OF EMPLOYEES CONSIDERED SATISFACTORY = .90
SELECTION RATIO

r	.05	.10	.20	.30	.40	.50	.60	.70	.80	.90	.95
.00	.90	.90	.90	.90	.90	.90	.90	.90	.90	.90	.90
.05	.92	.91	.91	.91	.91	.91	.91	.90	.90	.90	.90
.10	.93	.93	.92	.92	.92	.91	.91	.91	.91	.90	.90
.15	.95	.94	.93	.93	.92	.92	.92	.91	.91	91	.90
.20	.96	.95	.94	.94	93	.93	.92	.02	.91	91	.90
.25	.97	.96	.95	.95	.94	.93	.93	.92	.92	.91	.01
.30	.98	.97	.96	.95	.95	.94	.94	.93	.92	.91	.91
.35	.98	.98	.97	.96	.95	.95	.94	.93	.93	.92	.91
.40	.99	.98	.98	.97	.96	.95	.95	.94	.93	.92	.91
.45	.99	.99	.98	.98	.97	.96	.95	.94	.93	92	.91
.50	1.00	.99	.99	.98	.97	.97	.96	.95	.94	.92	.92
.55	1.00	1.00	.99	.99	.98	.97	.97	.96	.94	.93	.92
.60	1.00	1.00	.99	.99	.99	.98	.97	.96	.95	.93	.92
.65	1.00	1.00	1.00	.99	.99	.93	.98	.97	.96	.94	.92
.70	1.00	1.00	1.00	1.00	.99	.99	.98	.97	.96	.94	.93
.75	1.00	1.00	1.00	1.00	1.00	.99	.99	.98	.97	.95	.93
.80	1.00	1.00	1.00	1.00	1.00	1.00	.99	.99	.97	.95	.93
.85	1.00	1.00	1.00	1.00	1.00	1.00	1.00	.99	.98	.96	.94
.90	1.00	1.00	1.00	1.00	1.00	1.00	1.00	1.00	.99	.97	.94
.95	1.00	1.00	1.00	1 00	1.00	1.00	1.00	1.00	1 00	.98	.94
1 00	1.00	1.00	1.00	1 00	1.00	1.00	1.00	1.00	1.00	1.00	.95

Lawshe Expectancy Tables[1]
(For Individual Prediction)

	INDIVIDUAL PREDICTOR CATEGORIES				
r	Hi 1/5	Next 1/5	Middle 1/5	Next 1/5	Lo 1/5
.15	38	32	30	28	22
.20	40	34	29	26	21
.25	43	35	29	24	19
.30	46	35	29	24	16
.35	49	36	29	22	14
.40	51	37	28	21	12
.45	55	38	28	20	10
.50	58	38	27	18	09
.55	61	39	27	17	07
.60	64	40	26	15	05
.65	68	41	25	13	04
.70	72	42	23	11	03
.75	76	43	22	09	02
.80	80	44	20	06	01
.85	85	45	17	04	00
.90	90	46	12	02	00
.95	96	48	07	00	00

[1] SOURCE: Lawshe, C. H., Bolda, R. L., & Auclair, G. Expectancy charts, III: Their theoretical development. *Personnel Psychology,* 1958, **11**, 545–599.

PERCENT OF EMPLOYEES CONSIDERED SATISFACTORY = 40%

	INDIVIDUAL PREDICTOR CATEGORIES				
r	Hi 1/5	Next 1/5	Middle 1/5	Next 1/5	Lo 1/5
.15	48	44	40	36	32
.20	51	45	40	35	30
.25	54	44	40	34	28
.30	57	46	40	33	24
.35	60	47	39	32	22
.40	63	48	39	31	19
.45	66	49	39	29	17
.50	69	50	39	28	14
.55	72	53	38	26	12
.60	75	53	38	24	10
.65	79	55	37	22	08
.70	82	58	36	19	06
.75	86	59	35	17	04
.80	89	61	34	14	02
.85	93	64	32	10	01
.90	97	69	29	06	00
.95	100	76	23	02	00

PERCENT OF EMPLOYEES CONSIDERED SATISFACTORY = 50%

	INDIVIDUAL PREDICTOR CATEGORIES				
r	Hi 1/5	Next 1/3	Middle 1/5	Next 1/5	Lo 1/5
.15	58	54	50	46	42
.20	61	55	50	45	39
.25	64	56	50	44	36
.30	67	57	50	43	33
.35	70	58	50	42	30
.40	73	59	50	41	28
.45	75	60	50	40	25
.50	78	62	50	38	22
.55	81	64	50	36	19
.60	84	65	50	35	16
.65	87	67	50	33	13
.70	90	70	50	30	10
.75	92	72	50	28	08
.80	95	75	50	25	05
.85	97	80	50	20	03
.90	99	85	50	15	01
.95	100	93	50	08	00

PERCENT OF EMPLOYEES CONSIDERED SATISFACTORY $= 60\%$

	INDIVIDUAL PREDICTOR CATEGORIES				
r	Hi 1/5	Next 1/5	Middle 1/5	Next 1/5	Lo 1/5
.15	68	64	60	57	52
.20	71	63	60	56	48
.25	73	65	60	55	48
.30	76	66	61	54	44
.35	78	68	61	53	40
.40	81	69	61	52	37
.45	83	71	61	51	34
.50	86	72	62	50	31
.55	88	74	62	48	28
.60	90	76	62	47	25
.65	92	78	63	45	21
.70	94	80	64	43	18
.75	96	83	65	42	14
.80	98	86	66	39	11
.85	99	90	68	36	07
.90	100	94	71	31	03
.95	100	98	77	24	00

PERCENT OF EMPLOYEES CONSIDERED SATISFACTORY $= 70\%$

	INDIVIDUAL PREDICTOR CATEGORIES				
r	Hi 1/5	Next 1/5	Middle 1/5	Next 1/5	Lo 1/5
.15	77	73	69	69	62
.20	79	75	70	67	59
.25	81	75	71	65	58
.30	84	76	71	65	54
.35	86	78	71	64	52
.40	88	79	72	63	49
.45	90	80	72	63	46
.50	91	82	73	62	42
.55	93	83	73	61	39
.60	95	85	74	60	36
.65	96	87	75	59	32
.70	97	89	77	58	29
.75	98	91	78	57	25
.80	99	94	80	56	20
.85	100	96	83	55	16
.90	100	98	88	54	10
.95	100	100	93	52	04

Representative
Personnel Tests

This appendix consists of a listing of some of the more commonly used personnel tests. This list includes most of the tests that are referred to in this text, but it also includes some not mentioned there. The most comprehensive source of information about commercially available tests is *The Seventh Mental Measurements Yearbook,* Vols. I and II, edited by O. K. Buros (Highland Park, N.J.: The Gryphon Press, 1972). This book, and its earlier editions, gives information about publishers of tests and usually reviews of individual tests by one or more competent authorities.

The listing of tests below is divided into various classes of tests. For each test listed there is a code that refers to the publisher.

Name of test	*Code to publisher* *(see p. 608)*
Mental Ability Tests	
Adaptability Test	13
Alpha Examination, Modified Form 9	11
Army General Classification Test (AGCT)	13
California Test of Mental Maturity	5

D.A.T. Abstract Reasoning	11
D.A.T. Numerical Ability	11
D.A.T. Verbal Reasoning	11
Otis Self-Administering Tests of Mental Ability	19
Primary Mental Abilities	13
PTI-Oral Directions Test	11
Purdue Non-Language Personnel Test	17
Revised Beta Examination (nonverbal)	11
SRA Nonverbal Form	13
SRA Verbal Form	13
Thurstone Test of Mental Alertness (TMA)	13
Wonderlic Personnel Test	18

Clerical, Stenographic, and Typing Tests

Bennett Stenographic Aptitude Test	11
D.A.T. Clerical Speed and Accuracy	11
General Clerical Test	11
Minnesota Clerical Test	11
Purdue Clerical Adaptability Test, Form A	17
Seashore-Bennett Stenographic Proficiency Test	11
SRA Clerical Aptitudes	13
SRA Typing Skills Test	13
Thurstone Typing Test	6

Industrial Vision Tests

Keystone Telebinocular	9
Ortho-Rater	2
Sight-Screener	1
Vision Tester	16

Psychomotor and Manipulative Tests

MacQuarrie Test for Mechanical Ability	5
Minnesota Rate of Manipulation Test	15
O'Connor Finger Dexterity Test	10
O'Connor Tweezer Dexterity Test	10
Purdue Grooved Pegboard	10
Purdue Hand Precision Test	10
Purdue Pegboard	10, 13

Mechanical Tests

Bennett Mechanical Comprehension Test	11
D.A.T. Mechanical Reasoning	11
D.A.T. Space Relations	11
Minnesota Paper Form Board, Revised	11

Industrial Test Batteries

TEST PUBLISHERS

1. American Optical Company
   Safety Products Division
   Southbridge, Massachusetts 01550

2. Bausch & Lomb Optical Company
   635 Saint Paul Street
   Rochester, New York 14602

3. Brown & Associates
   252 Pleasantburg Building
   Box 5092 Station B
   Greenville, South Carolina 29606

4. Consulting Psychologists Press, Inc.
   577 College Avenue
   Palo Alto, California 94306

5. CTB/McGraw-Hill
   Del Monte Research Park
   Monterey, California 93940

6. Harcourt Brace Jovanovich, Inc.
   757 Third Avenue
   New York, New York 10017

7. Human Engineering Laboratory, Inc.
   347 Beacon Street
   Boston, Massachusetts 02186

8. Humm Personnel Service
   1219 West 12th Street
   Los Angeles, California 90015

9. Keystone View Company
   Meadville, Pennsylvania 16335

10. Lafayette Instrument Co.
    Sagamore Parkway
    P.O. Box 1279
    Lafayette, Indiana 47902

11. Psychological Corporation
    304 East 45th Street
    New York, New York 10017

12. Psychological Services, Inc.
    4311 Wilshire Boulevard
    Suite 600
    Los Angeles, California 90005

13. Science Research Associates
    259 East Erie Street
    Chicago, Illinois 60611

14. Sheridan Psychological Services, Inc.
    P.O. Box 837
    Beverly Hills, California 90213

15. C. H. Stoelting Company
    424 North Homan Avenue
    Chicago, Illinois 60624

16. Titmus Optical Company
    Petersburg, Virginia 23804

17. University Book Store
    360 State Street
    West Lafayette, Indiana 47906

18. Wonderlic Personnel Test Co.
    P.O. Box 7
    Northfield, Illinois 60093

19. World Book Co.
    Cross Country Medical Hospital
    Yonkers, New York 10704

Index